C000126917

1 MONTH OF
FREE
READING

at

www.ForgottenBooks.com

By purchasing this book you are eligible for one month membership to ForgottenBooks.com, giving you unlimited access to our entire collection of over 1,000,000 titles via our web site and mobile apps.

To claim your free month visit: www.forgottenbooks.com/free131430

ISBN 978-0-265-63509-4
PIBN 10131430

This book is a reproduction of an important historical work. Forgotten Books uses
state-of-the-art technology to digitally reconstruct the work, preserving the original format
whilst repairing imperfections present in the aged copy. In rare cases, an imperfection in
the original, such as a blemish or missing page, may be replicated in our edition. We do,
however, repair the vast majority of imperfections successfully; any imperfections that
remain are intentionally left to preserve the state of such historical works.

THE

WETMORE FAMILY

OF AMERICA,

AND

OF THE

ITS COLLATERAL BRANCHES.

WITH

GENEALOGICAL, BIOGRAPHICAL, AND

HISTORICAL NOTICES.

BY

JAMES CARNAHAN WETMORE.

ALBANY:

MUNSELL & ROWLAND 78 STATE STREET.

1861.

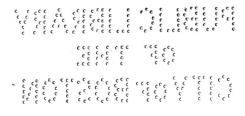

Arms—He beareth argent, on a chief azure; three martlets or.
Crest—A Falcon, ppr.

"Children's children *are* the crown of old men; and the glory of children *are* their fathers."—*Prov.*, xvii, 6.

"Though not perfect and infallible, in all respects, were a religious, brave and virtuous set of men, whose love of liberty, civil and religious, brought them from their native land into the American deserts."—*Rev. Dr. Mayhew's Election Sermon*, 1774.

"To let the memory of these men die, is injurious to posterity; by depriving them of what might contribute to promote their steadiness to their principles, under hardships and severities."—*Rev. Dr. E. Calamy's Preface to his Account of Ejected Ministers.*

TO

THE MEMORY

OF

REV. OLIVER WETMORE,

THIS VOLUME

IS AFFECTIONATELY INSCRIBED

BY HIS SON,

THE AUTHOR.

*   *   *   *   "A MAN BENEATH WHOSE STERN EXTERIOR
INNOCENT HUMOUR PLAYED AND WARM AFFECTIONS GLOWED; OF THE
MOST UNBENDING INTEGRITY AND ABOVE ALL MEANNESS; WHILE
UPRIGHT AND HONORABLE IN HIMSELF, INDIGNANT AT OUGHT ELSE
IN OTHERS; AN ARDENT FRIEND OF HUMANITY, OF PUBLIC SPIRIT
AS A CITIZEN, FAITHFUL AND TENDER AS A HUSBAND AND PARENT,
UNDAUNTED IN COURAGE, AND PERFECTLY UNYIELDING IN HIS DE-
LIBERATE AND INTELLIGENT CONVICTIONS OF RIGHTEOUSNESS AND
TRUTH."—*Rev. Dr. Fowler.*

PREFACE.

This work was commenced with a view only to arrange a brief genealogy and biography in manuscript, of the author's branch of the family of Wetmore for his own satisfaction; as he progressed he discovered many things that would interest other branches, and being urgently solicited by influential members of the family to advance his researches, he consented, supposing a few months would enable him to compile a work that would be acceptable to those directly interested, and at the same time in some measure, perpetuate the MEMORY of The FOUNDER of the Family, as well as many of his worthy descendants. Proceeding in his labors, material increased upon his hands, until nearly two years and a half had been devoted *exclusively* to collecting and arranging what the reader finds before him.

If the object he had in view, which was to place in an enduring form the memory and virtues of his kindred shall have been accomplished, he will consider the time and labor well expended.

Should any find their names omitted or not properly recorded, he trusts they will make due allowance for the difficulties attending the compiling of such a work. Every possible effort has been made to give publicity to his undertaking. Many families might have been

1*

more fully noticed had the members taken the pains to furnish information.

To those whom he has particularly noticed, now living, he may owe an apology for the freedom he has taken. It has always been considered an extremely difficult thing to write biographies, particularly of the gentler sex. He would deprecate their criticism, reminding them that a work of this kind is intended only for private circulation, among those of the same kith and kin; hence what might be deemed improper in the pages of a public journal, would be perfectly proper and in good taste in a Family Genealogy.

The arrangement of the book differs somewhat from kindred works; in place of numbering the persons named, the pedigree of every individual, as *son*, or *dau.* of, &c., is given, so that the heading of each particular family, together with the heading of the page above, gives the entire genealogy back to Thomas, the founder of the family. For instance, see page 281. " Maud Douglass, child of Oscar Davison, son of James Merritt, son of James, son of John, son of James," which, together with the head line, " Rev. James, son of Izrahiah, son of Thomas," makes the pedigree through nine generations complete.

The history, dates of birth, marriage, &c., of the different ancestors, the reader will find by referring, *ante*, under head of the several generations.

The several branches have been placed by themselves, in chronological order. By branches he means the descendants of the children of THOMAS. JOHN, the oldest son and child of Thomas and his descendants by themselves. Those of this branch living, reside chiefly in Central New York, and in Ashtabula county, Ohio, Iowa and Minnesota. The descendants of SAMUEL, the third son of

Thomas, are commonly known as the Winchester and Torringford (Ct.) branch.

The descendants of IZRAHIAH, the fourth son of Thomas, the compiler has divided, for the reason that his (Izrahiah's) sons have formed distinct branches: the descendants of his son, Rev. IZRAHIAH, being generally known as the Stratford branch, while those of his son, the Rev. JAMES, of Rye, as the Rye or New Brunswick and Nova Scotia branch, and of his son, Judge SETH, as the Middletown branch, and his son Jeremiah, as more particularly the North Carolina branch, while the descendants of his son, Dea. Caleb, reside in the Western Reserve, Ohio, Litchfield, Ct., &c.; his son JOSIAH, left no male descendants, his branch is represented by the families of Phillips and Magill. The descendants of Beriah, the 5th son of Thomas, the author has not been able to trace down as fully as could be desired. The descendants of NATHANIEL, the 6th son of Thomas, reside chiefly in Schoharie, St. Lawrence and Lewis counties, N. Y., and in Illinois; and the descendants of JOSEPH, 7th and youngest son of Thomas that had issue, reside in Western New York and Pennsylvania.

The record of descendants of daughters of Wetmore, it will be perceived, immediately follow their mother's name, while the record of descendants of sons are carried forward (after recording their christian names) under head of their proper generation.

The motto used in connection with the Coat of Arms in this work—*Tentanda via est* (the way remains to be tried, or the way is to be tried)—is used by a part of the family only, while a portion use the motto: *Virtus, Libertas et Patria*, both of which, it is believed, have been long in use by the different branches.

A list of the works to which the compiler has had occasion to refer, and in some instances to make liberal quotations from, may be found under head of Index of Titles of Works.

Before closing, the writer would here acknowledge his gratitude to his many attentive correspondents, and would express his regret that the closing of his labors will be, he fears, the closing of a correspondence which has been to him of a most pleasant and agreeable nature. To the following he would in particular return his thanks: Samuel Wetmore, Esq., of N. Y. City, and Dr. D. Williams Patterson, an accomplished genealogist, residing at West Winsted, Ct., for copies of early genealogical records; Wm. H. Whitmore, Esq., of Boston, for valued suggestions respecting the probable ancestry of Thomas Whitmore; Judge A. K. Smedes Wetmore, of Woodstock, N. B.; Judge Justus S. Wetmore, Co. Kings, N. B.; and Dr. Thos. Saunders Wetmore, of St. John's, N. B., for valuable genealogical records, &c., of the family residing in the British Provinces; William T. Coggeshall, Ohio State Librarian, and his assistant, Mr. Francis A. Marble, for many acts of politeness and attention; Mr. Joel Munsell, his publisher, for carrying out so satisfactorily his plans respecting the typography and arrangement of the work.

And to the subscribers, for confidence reposed in their friend and obedient servant, THE AUTHOR.

Columbus, Ohio, Aug., 1861.

CONTENTS.

ERRATA AND ADDITIONS.

Page 9, line 3, for Whyttemore read Whyttemere.
" 18, " 2, for *T.* H. Trumbull read *J.* H. Trumbull.
" 22, " 22, for *Robinson* read *Bradford.*
" 32, " 6, insert comma after Izrahiah.
" 65, " 27, *dele* Sarah M. Whitman, and see page 89.
" 98, " 4, *dele* comma after Sarah Jane.
" 99, " 15, for 1837 read April 13, 1842; had Sophia, b. Aug. 17, 1844;
     " 26, for *Honesdale* read *Hornellsville.*
" 100, " 3, for Burnel read Burrel.
     " 20, for *Nancy* read *Mary.*
" 108, " 13, for Regulus read Regulus *L.*   See 6th, errata.
" 206, " 26, for David read David *Brown.*
" 208, " 12, for Greffeth read Griffeth.
" 224, " 37, *dele* comma after Sarah.
" 225, " 27, for Debros *Steward* read Deborah *Sherwood.*
" 251, " 13, *dele* comma after David.
" 265, " 13, insert comma after Charles.
" 267, " 28, *dele* comma after Frances Sophia.
" 277, " 8, for Joshua read Josiah.
" 303, " 35, after m. insert Dea. Chauncey Whittlesey.
" 326, " 20, for Robert read Roger.
" 342, " 37, for *Long*street read *Stone*street.
" 343, " 8, for *Aug.* 15 read *March* 23.
     " 15, for *Richard* read *Roland.*
" 415, " 24, for 1848 read 1838.
" 452, " 9, after Capt. John (Andrew?) insert Mather.
" 454, " 24, for *Geo.* read *Gov.*
" 477, " 2, before Jeremiah insert Charles.
" 488, " 15, for son read *grand*son.
" 489, " 30, for A*b*ijah read A*h*ijah.
" 490, " 4, for Erelina read Evelina.
" 508, " 4, for Balsom read Balsora.
     " 5, *dele* comma after Almira.
" 509, " 2, insert comma after Isaac.
     " 23, *dele* comma after Barron.
" 513, " 18, "   "   " Timothy.
" 531, " 17, for Dunton read Denton.
" 538, " 31, for *relation* read *writing.*
" 539, " 13, for *Whitmore read *Wetmore.*

THOMAS WHITMORE (WETMORE)=1st, SARAH, dau. of John Hall. 2d, MARY, dau. of Richard Platt. 3d, KATHERINE LEET, wid. of Mr. Robards.

——HANNAH 2d=NATHANIEL BACON. For her record, see pp. 12 and 36.

——ABIGAIL=SAMUEL BISHOP. For her record, see pp. 12 and 36.

——BENJAMIN. For his record, see pp. 12 and 36.

——MAHITABLE=ANDREW BACON. For her record, see pp. 11 and 35.

—·JOSIAH. For his record, see pp. 11 and 35.

—·SARAH 2d=JOHN BACON. For her record, see pp. 11 and 35.

—·JOSEPH=LYDIA, dau. of Nathaniel Bacon. For his record and descendants, see pp. 11, 35, and 512–530.

——NATHANIEL=DORCAS, wid. of Obadiah Allen. For his record and descendants, see pp. 11, 35, and 505–511.

——BERIAH=MARGERET, dau. of Rev. Samuel Stow. For his record, see pp. 11, 34, and 502–504.

——IZRAHIAH=RACHEL, dau. of Rev. S. Stow. For his record, see pp. 11, 32, 33, and 34.

——SAMUEL=MARY, dau. of Nathaniel Bacon, Sr. For his record and descendants, see pp. 11, 30–32, and 50–111.

——HANNAH=NATHANIEL STOW, SR. For her record, see pp. 11 and 30.

——THOMAS=ELIZABETH, dau. of Geo. Hubbard, Sr. For his record and descend'ts, see pp. 11, 30, and 49.

——SARAH. For her record, see pp. 11 and 30.

——MARY=JOHN STOW. For her record, see pp. 11, 28, and 29.

——ELIZABETH=JOSIAH ADKINS. For her record, see pp. 11 and 28.

——JOHN=ABIGAIL, dau. of And. Warner. For her record, see pp. 11, ·27, 28, and 37–48.

——Rev. IZRAHIAH (of Stratf RAH BOOTH. For his r descendants, see pp. 32, 144.

——STOW. For his record, se

——Rev. JAMES (of Rye)=A his record and descen pp. 32, and 145–281.

——ICHABOD. For his record,

—·Judge SETH (of Middleto MARGERET, wid. of S. 2d, HANNAH, dau. of J more; 3d, HANNAH, da Timo. Edwards. For l and descendants, see pp 282–439.

—·JEREMIAH=ABIGAIL BUTI his record and descen pp. 32, and 440–483.

——CALEB=MARY ——. For and descendants, see p 484–497.

—·JOSIAH= ——. For his I descendants, see pp. 32, 501.

ABBREVIATIONS.

b., born ; m., married ; bap., baptised ; chil., children ; dau., daughter ; s p., *sine prole*, without issue ; unm., unmarried ; *ante*, before ; *dele*, omit ; *post*, after ; etc.

Arms.—Or, gold or yellow ; ar., argent, silver ; gu., gules, red ; vert, green ; sa., sable, black ; purp., purple ; chev., cheveron ; loz., lozenge ; ppr., proper, etc.

N. B. A complete Chart of the Family, showing at a glance the relationship of one member to another, measuring 70 by 72 inches, containing 2250 names, has been executed by the Author, to be issued, on cloth, and folded in cases, *as soon* as a sufficient number of subscribers are received to warrant its engraving. Price of Book and Chart, $9 ; Book or Chart separately, $5 each.

INTRODUCTION.

The WETMORE FAMILY, of America, is descended from Thomas Whitmore, who came from the west of England to Boston, Mass., in 1635, being the eleventh year of the reign of Charles the First; and was among the early settlers in the Connecticut colony.

There were other settlers in New England of the same surname, and it is therefore worth while to attempt to discover what relationship, if any, existed between them.

John Whitmore[1] was of Wethersfield, Connecticut, in 1640, and in the town records of deeds, vol. I, p. 121, is the following entry:

"The 2d month and 5 daie 1641, The lands of John Whitmore lying in Wethersfield on Connecticut river. One piece whereon his house and barne standeth containing twelve acres and half more or less. The ends abut against the Common or landing place, and part against the house lot of Robert Batte, west, and ye meadow Francis Norton east. The side against ye lands of Ro. and Tho. Curtice north, and ye lands

[1] See Appendix A.

2

of Tho. Whitmore, Francis Norton, Mr. Denton, John
Gossope and Tho. Coleman south."

John Whitmore removed to Stamford in 1641, with
Rev. Richard Denton and many others who had been
settlers at Watertown, Mass.   He was a man of considerable importance.   Of his family we have only a
few traces.   In the Stamford records we find " March
7nth 1649.   The testimony of John Whitmore, his wife
being no . . . .   Goodwife Whitmore affirmeth that
her husband sold to her son John . . . . . five acres
land on ye plane." . . . . . . Another deposition says,
"That Brother Whetmore told him he had sold his
son John five acres in ye East Field on ye Playne,
and if it did not come to so much, he would make it
up in ye other plain, and so make it good; it lay in
yt plain, and this land was Ro. Fisher's by gift from
ye Corte."

From the records of New Haven Colony, vol. xi, p.
134, 1657, 25th 3d mo.   Edward Jessup brough⁴
Joseph Mead of Stamford, as his witness, who did now
affirm upon oath, that Edward Jessup and his mother,
widdow Whitmore, went from Stamford to live elsewhere; they left two mares at Stamford and desired
him to take care of them."   We conclude then, that
John Whitmore had a son John of age before 1648,
and a daughter who had married Edward Jessup.[2]   We
may also presume that it was this son John, who had
a daughter Sarah, born at Hartford, Dec. 16, 1647.

[2] Edward Jessup was of Stamford 1641-9.   Sascoe-Neck, Fairfield
county, Ct., 1653; Newton, L. I., 1653; Westchester, N. Y., 1662.
His will, dated Augt 16, 1666, mentions, wife Eliz Bridges and
daus Hannah and Elizabeth; the latter of whom md Thomas Hunt.

Our Thomas Whitmore was living at Hartford at that time, and had children baptized there in 1646, and 1648. Wm. S. Porter in his *Historical Notices of Connecticut*, p. 41, says, that a John and Thomas Whitmore owned land in Hartford in 1646.

There was a Francis Whitmore of Cambridge, Mass., who married previous to 1649, and became the progenitor of a family which has always preserved this spelling, and whose record has been published in a pamphlet form, by William H. Whitmore, Esq., of Boston. There is no evidence to show any connection between him and Thomas, except that his eldest son Francis Jun. moved to Middletown, Ct., where Thomas had settled, and their descendants intermarried. As several other families moved at the same time from Cambridge farms (now Lexington) to Middletown, where Thomas was living, we must not lay too much stress upon this circumstance.[3] At that time there were two persons named Whitmore, residing in Essex county, Mass., namely, *Ann*, who married George Farrow, or Farrar, February 16, 1643-4, and had issue; also *Mary*, who married John Brewer, Oct. 23, 1647. It is probable they were relatives, but highly improbable that they were in any near degree of relationship

---

[3] Among the descendants of the family at Middletown, there has always been a tradition that our ancestor, Thomas Whitmore, was accompanied to this country by two brothers, Francis and John. While we are *not* disposed to reject this tradition wholly, from the fact that it was a received truth among those of the 4th generation, we are nevertheless not disposed to offer it as evidence, for the *reason* that genealogists, generally, attach but little importance to such testimony.

with Thomas or John Whitmore. It is possible these
two girls were related to Francis Whitmore of Laxton,
county of Notts, England, whose will, dated January
26, 1644-5, mentions sister Anne Farrar, nephew
Robert Farrar (if he be alive and in England), nephews
John, William, Francis, Thomas and George Farrar.

We may think it possible that these Whitmore girls,
and possibly Francis W. of Cambridge, were nieces and
nephew of the testator, and one of them married her
cousin, a Farrar here; but this is all a conjecture and
offered only to call future inquiries to the point as
worthy of attention.

Now a John and Thomas Whitmore were at Wethersfield together in 1640-1, and John Jun. and Thomas
were together in Hartford in 1646. We are justified
in assuming that they were near relatives, and the
dates make it probable that John Sen. was the father.
As it respects Francis of Cambridge, it is possible he
may have been a brother of Thomas and John Jun., *but
this is only conjecture.*

We have been unable to find any trace of the
English ancestry of Thomas Whitmore. There were
families of the name among the gentry of Cheshire,
Stafford and Salop, but we cannot trace any connection to them, nearer than that our ancestor came from
the west of England, where those counties are
situated.

It may be well to note in this connection, that there
has been a generally received tradition that our ancestor came from Wales. That his father's family may
have resided for a time in Wales, previous to his

embarking for America is very possible; but that he was not a Welshman, his name itself would prove.

Our family coat of arms is different from that used by the English families[4] (save one branch, given by Joseph Emerson's edition of Heraldry, London, 1780, which coincides with ours), and very probably was first brought here in 1723, by the Rev. James Wetmore of Rye. It is like that used by the Cheshire family, but with the addition of three martletts, which in the estimation of Mr. A. S. Somerby, a high authority, is proof that the person who obtained the arms, could not prove his relationship to that family, and hence this difference was made; however, these arms were assumed in colonial times, though members of the family are fully justified in using them as any English family would under similar circumstances.[5]

In regard to the surname of our ancestor, being Whitmore, it is so written wherever we have found it recorded in the Colonial records. The Wethersfield Town records of 1639-40, has his name registered as *To. Whitmore*, in connection with certain lands; his name is spelt *Whitmore* on the records of the General

---

[4] For notices of Coats of Arms of Whitmores in England, see Appendix B.

[5] It is remarkable however that the descendants of branches of the family other than the Rye, have always used this coat, and tradition carries the use back prior to the time of the Rev. James Wetmore's return, and this gives an additional strength to our assertion that the family have a right to use it.

The Stratford branch have a copy which was obtained in England for the Rev. Izrahiah (4th gen.), by William Samuel Johnson, LL. D., while agent there for the colony of Connecticut in 1766, which agrees with the one used by the various branches in this country.

court of Connecticut, May 20, 1652, when made a freeman; again when he was a member of the said court in 1654 and 1655. In the copy of his will on file in the Recorder's office at Hartford, dated July 20, 1681, his name is written distinctly, *Thomas Whitmore*, senior; and wherever the surname of his children are entered in the body of the will, they are written *Whitmore*.

A petition from his son Izrahiah, to the General court, is preserved in the Secretary of state's office at Hartford, which is signed in a bold, clear hand, *Izrahiah Whitmore*, and wherever we have seen the names of other sons of his given, they have been invariably Whitmore.

If the family name had been Wetmore in England, it is fair to presume that some one of that name (other than those who have descended from the American Wetmores) could be found there. We have, with other members of the family, been unable to discover, in traveling in various parts of England, any native Briton who spelt his name Wetmore. Mr. A. S. Somerby, an accomplished English genealogist, heretofore referred to, has made (by request of parties interested) diligent search among parish records, and in offices of registry of wills, in many counties of England, and has forwarded abstracts of wills[6] made by persons of names similar to Wetmore, and has reported, at the same time, his inability to find any record of a family spelling their surname *Wet*more.

At what particular time the family changed the spelling of their name, we have been unable to dis-

[6] See Appendix C.

cover; are led, however, to think that the children of
the third (possibly some few of the second) in part, and
the descendants of the fourth generation very generally
adopted the name of Wetmore. What induced them
to make the change we have no means of determining,
unless it was, as says a correspondent, "probably a
matter of convenience to them, growing out of the
greater number of families in Middletown of the same
name,[7] that a part of them should vary the spelling
to avoid confusion, and without sufficient consideration
of the greater evils which follow such a change."

The first record we find of the name being Wetmore,
is in a joint affidavit made by the widows of Andrew
Warner Sen. and Thomas Whitmore, as follows:

Rebecca, widow of Andrew Warner Sen., testified that
at her husband's request, some time before his decease,
she had written a deed of gift of a parcel of meadow and
swamp, to his son in law John Wetmore, but that he died
before executing it. Catherine, widow of Thomas *Wetmore*, testified that her husband intended to perfect a
deed of gift, written, but not signed, to his son John Wetmore, of certain lands.—*Priv. Controv.* ii, 49.

Upon these affidavits the General court made the
following order:

October 12, 1682. This Court orders that the executors of Thomas Whitmore's will, and the administrators of
Andrew Warner's estate, doe signe the respective deeds of
land that were given to John Whitmore by Thomas Whitmore, and that land was given by Andrew Warner to John

---

[7] Francis, son of Francis Whitmore, of Cambridge, removed to
Middletown, and md Hannah Harris, Feby 8, 1674, and had eight
children, four sons and four dau^s; two of his sons md in M— and
they each had 10 children born to them.

Whitmore; they both deceasing before the deeds were
made by their order for the settlement of those lands were
signed.—*Trumbull's Pub. Rec. of Conn.*

We here give all we have had the means to discover
respecting the origin of the name Whitmore.

Robert Ferguson, in his work entitled *English Surnames, and their Place in the Teutonic Family*, London
and New York, 1858, says:

Lastly, I take the names derived from seabirds. I
doubt whether GULL, is derived from the bird. It might

Gull,
Mawe,
Mew,
More,
Whitmore,
Beardmore,
} be from the old Norse *gulr*, golden, elsewhere referred to as probably a term of affection. The Anglo-Saxon words *meaw, mœw*,
whence probably the names *Mawe* and *Mew*.
The old Norse was *már*, which is a common
baptismal name in the Landnamabok. Hence may be our
name *More*, while WHITMORE and BEARDMORE may be from
hvitmar and beartmár signifying a white gull. But as an
Anglo-Saxon name *More* is probably derived from *már*,
renowned, famous, and both Whitmore and Beardmore
may be compounds of this, *wight*, a man, and *beart*, bright,
entering into a great many Anglo-Saxon names.

Burke in his *Encyclopædia of Heraldry* (London,
1847), also in his *Landed Gentry*, in noticing the
family of Whitmore of Apley, county Salop, says:
"Was originally seated in the northwest side of the
Parish of Bobbington,[8] in the manor of Claverly;

---

[8] The parish of Bobbington is situated partly in the hun[d] of
Brinstrey, co. of Salop, and partly in the southern division of the
hun[d] of Seisdon, 152 miles from London, 9 from Wolverhampton,
18 from Birmingham. * * * The living (St. Mary or Holy Cross)
a perpetual curacy, in archdy of Salop and diocese of Litchfield and
Coventry; present income £97. Patron, T. Whitmore, Esq.—
British Gazetteer.

subsequently they removed to Claverly and acquired considerable possessions there; derived from John, Lord of Whyttemore (temp. Henry III and Edward I, the tenth from whom, Sir William Whitmore of London, *Knt.*, purchased the estate); his son was Phillip *de* Whytemere.. Subsequently the *de* was dropped, and the name continued for several generations as Whytemere, when it was changed to Whitmere, and then Whitmore. That the *seat* or manor of Whytemere, now known as Whitmore Hall, thus derived its name (as the author of *English Surnames* concludes) is possible; but the family of Whitmore, we are fully persuaded, derived their surname from the name of their ancestral home. By a marriage connection between the family of Mainwarings and Whitmore, the manor of Whitmore passed into the succession of the Mainwarings, who are the present proprietors. Whitmore Hall is situated in the parish of Whitmore, county Stafford, "a parish in the northern division of the hundred of Pierhill, union of New Castle under Lyne, within the honor of Stutbury, in the duchy of Lancaster, 146 miles from London, 5 from New Castle under Lyne, 8 from Stone. * * * The charities produce about £8 per year. The living is a rectory in the diocese of Litchfield; present net income £470. Patron, Capt. Mainwaring; present incumbent C. H. Mainwaring. Contains 3350 acres; 46 houses; population in 1841, 367; assessed property £2,433; poor rates in 1848, £168. Tithes commuted in 1839."—*British Gazetteer*, London, 1852.

3

WETMORE MEMORIAL.

THOMAS WHITMORE,

Was born in England in 1615, the 13th year of the reign of James I; came to America, as before stated, in 1635;[1] tradition says that he embarked from Bristol. The first mention that we find of his name in the Colonial records, is in the Wethersfield Town records, in 1639-40, as owner of certain lands; where it appears he first settled on coming on to the Connecticut river.

He subsequently removed to Hartford, at what time we have no data for determining, unless it was, at, or about, the time the difficulty arose among the colonists at Wethersfield in 1640-41, which caused many of them to disperse; a large number of whom removed with their pastor, Richard Denton, to Stamford.

He first married *Sarah*, daughter of John and Ann (Willocke) Hall, of Hartford, Dec. 11, 1645; had issue, John, Elizabeth, Mary, Sarah, Thomas, Hannah, Samuel, Izrahiah, Beriah, Nathaniel, Joseph, Sarah 2d, and Josiah: he married 2d, Mary, daughter of Richard Platt, of Milford, and widow of Luke Atconson (Atkinson?) Jan. 3, 1667;[2] had Mahitable: he married, 3d,

---

1 A genealogical record before us of the Wetmore family, made by Judge William Wetmore of Boston, in 1792, for the use of the Rev. Robert Griffeth Wetmore, says: "He (Thomas Wetmore) came to Hartford from the west of England, as his grandson Beriah told my father, who informed me (*sed qu.*, from what town?) in 1635, when he was twenty years old."

2 Luke (Atkinson, Adkinson, or Atkeson), New Haven, of the earliest sett. sign. the compact 1639, bef. 1643 is count. with fam. of four, md 1 May, 1651, prob. a sec. w. Mary dau. Richd Platt of Milford, had Mary b. 1652; Hannah b. 1653; and Sarah, b. 1655; rem. next year, whither is unkn. perhaps to Middletown, for there his wid. md 3 Jany, 1667, Thomas Whitmore;

Katharine Leet, widow of Mr. Robards, Oct. 8, 1673 ; had Benjamin, Abigail and Hannah 2d.

He, with his father-in-law John Hall, William Smith, Samuel Stocking, and Robert Webster, were the first to settle the plantation of Mattabesek ; the exact time it is difficult to determine, for the reason that a few of the first pages in the Town records of Middletown are lost, and others illegible. The General court in 1646 appointed a Mr. Phelps to join a committee for the planting of Mattabeseck, but they appear not to have accomplished much towards that object; for on the 20th March, 1649-50, the General court made the following order: " And Samuel Smith senior of Wethersfield to ye comittee about ye lands at Mattebebeseck in ye roome of Jeames Boosey." Most of the authorities agree, that a settlement was commenced the same year, namely, in 1649, old style.

The following year the General court "Ordered, sentenced and decreed, that Mattabeseck shall be a Towne, and they shall make choice of one of theire inhabitants, according to order in that case, that so hee may take ye oath of a Constable ye next convenient season."

The proprietors of the place changed its name to Middletown, which was confirmed by the General court as follows : " Nov. 23, 1653. This Courte approues that ye name of ye Plantatyon commonly called Mattabesick shall for time to come bee Middletowne."

The most of the very early inhabitants of Middletown lived in, or near, the town ; the largest collection being about the Meeting house yard. At the north end of Main street there were Thomas Allen, William Markham, Nathaniel Brown, Rev. Samuel Stow, George Hubbard, John Hall, and Thomas Whitmore. The homestead of the latter was situated upon the north end of Main street, east side, being the square, now bounded north by Green street, east a river, south on Ferry street, west on Main street; one of the most

or Wetmore, and bore him *two* chil. nam. in his will by their gr. f. Platt in 1683.—*Savage's Genealogical Dictionary.*

desirable locations upon the town plot, part of which is still known by the name of *The Wetmore Property*.

May 20th, 1652, Thomas Whitmore was made a *freeman* by the General court. The qualifications necessary to be a freeman at that time were, namely: the citizen had to be orthodox, twenty years of age, and worth £200, and was obliged to take the following oath:

I, A B, being by the Pruidence of God an Inhabitant wᵗʰin the Jurifdiction of Coneⅇtecott, doe acknowledge myfelfe to be fubjeⅇte to the Gouerment thereof, and doe fweare by the great and fearefull name of the euerliving God, to be true and faythfull vnto the fame, and doe fubmitt boath my pʳfon and eftate thereunto, aecording to all the holfome lawes and orders that there are, or hereafter fhall be there made, and eftablifhed by lawfull athority, and that I will neither plott nor praⅇtice any euell agᵗ the fame, nor confent to any that fhall fo doe, but will tymely difcouer the fame to lawfull authority there eftablifhed; and that I will, as I am in duty bownd, mayntayne the honner of the fame and of the lawfull mageftratts thereof, pʳmoting the publike good of yᵗ, whilft I fhall foe continue an Inhabitant there; and whenfoeuʳ I fhall giue my voate or fuffrage touching any matter wᶜʰ concerns this comon welth be cauled thereunto, will giue yᵗ as in my concience I fhall judge, may conduce to the beft good of the fame, wᵗʰout refpeⅇt of pʳfons oꝝ favor of any man, Soe helpe me God in oʳ Lord Jefus Chrifte.

He, together with Robert Webster, represented Middletown in the General court in 1654, and 1655. We here give the proceedings of the court while he was a member.

[57] A SESSION OF THE GENERALL COURTE AT HARTFORD.
September 14ⁿᵗʰ 1654.

Mʳ Wells, Deputy Govenʳ.

Magiftrates: Capt Cullick, Mʳ Woolcott, Mʳ Clarke, Mꝝ Willis, Mʳ Talcott.

Deputyes: Mʳ Steele, Mʳ Trott, Mʳ Phelps, Mʳ Gaylor, Mʳ Allen, Mʳ Fitch, Mʳ Weftwood, Edw: Stebbin, And: Bacon, Mʳ Hollifter, John Biffell, Natha: Dickerfon, Mʳ Ward, Will: Hill, *Abfent;* Tho Coleman, Steph Hart, Tho: Fairechild, Richᵈ Olmfted, Rob Webfter, *Tho: Whitmore,* Will Cheefbroock. Hugh Calkin, John Clarke, Rob. Chapman.

The lift of the Perfons & Eftates in the feverall Townes within this Jurifdiⅇtyon.

	Perfons.	£		*Perfons.*	£
Hartford,	177.	19,609	Norwaake,	24.	2,309
Windfor,	165.	15,833	Stratford,	74.	7,958
Wetherffield,	113.	12,602	Fairefield,	94.	8,634
Middletowne,	31.	2,173	Pequott,		
Farmington,	46.	5,519	Seabrook,	53.	4,437

The lifts of Perfons & Eftates of Pequott is to bee perfected & returne thereof bee made to the Magiftrates when they keepe the perticuler courte there, as is after ordered.

This Courte orders that the eftate of Capt. Baxter, attached by the Cônftable of Fairefield for the forfeiture of his recognizance, fhall bee remitted.

This Courte orders that when execytyon is don ypon the goods of Tho. Staples of Fairefield, ypon a verdict graunted to Capt Baxter, forthwith attachm^t bee graunted upon thofe goods for the ufe of the country, untill this courte fees what is to be done in reference to this fine.

Whereas, notwithftanding former provifion made for the conveyance of the knowledge of God to the natives amongft us, little hath hitheto beene attended through want of an able Interpreter, this Courte being earneftly defirous to promoate & further what lyes in them a worke of that nature, wherein the glory of God & the euerlafting welfare of thofe poore loft, naked fonnes of Adam is fo deeply concerned, doe order that Thomas Mynor, of Pequott fhall bee wrott unto from this Courte & defired that hee would forthwith fend his fonne John Mynor to Hartford, where this Courte will provide for his meintenance & fchooling, to ye end hee may bee for ye prefent affiftant to fuch elder, elders or others as this Courte fhall appoint, to interprett ye things of Gôd to y^m as hee fhall bee directed & in ye meane time fitt himfelfe to bee inftrumentall that way as God fhall fitt & incline him thereunto for the future.[3]

[58]   It is ordered by this Courte, that Capt. Cullick, Mr Steele, Mr Allen, as a Comittee by this Courte appointed, are to confider of Mr Whiting's will, & a right interpretatyon thereof, togeather with the Sur Pre . . rs of the faid will & make report thereof to this Courte.

It is ordered by this Courte that Mr Talcoat, Mr Allen, Mr Hollifter, fhall joyne with Capt. Cullick in receiving accounts for the forte rate, for the yeare paft, of the Conftables for the feverall Plantatyons uppon the River.

Maior Mafon & Capt. Cullick, (if his occafions permit him, if not) Mr Clarke, are defired to go to Pequott & with Mr Winthrop to keepe a p^{r}ticuler courte, before winter, to execute juftice there as caufe fhall require.

This Courte graunts power to Maior Mafon to call the Traine bands togeather once in 2 years, to exercife in a Generall training on the firft or fecond week in September.

It is ordered y^t warrants fhall goe forth from the Treafurer for a whole

---

3 Vppon a motion made to ye Commiffioners by Capt. Cullick, from the Generall Courte of Connecticott, to take into ye confideration ye inftruction of ye Indians in theire Jurifdiction, in ye knowledge of God, and theire defire y^t John Minor might bee enterteined as an interpreter to communicate to ye faid Indians thofe inftructions wch fhall bee deliuered by Mr Stone, Mr Newton or any other allowed by the Courte and allfo y^t ye faid Minor may bee further inftructed and fitted by Mr Stone to bee a meet inftrumente to carry on the works of propagating ye Gofpell to ye Indians, ye Commiffioners conceiving ye faid propofitions to bee much conducing to ye propagating of y^t hopefull work, doe defire ye Magiftrates of Connecticott to take care y^t ye faid Minor bee enterteined at Mr Stones or fome other meete place, as they fhall order y^t due allowance bee made for his dyet and education out of the Corporation ftock.—*Rec. U. Colonies, Sept.* 23, 1654.

rate for the Country, according to the order of rating, to be payd ¾ in wheate, ⅛ in peas, ¼ in Indyan: Wheatt at 4s. Peas at 3s. pʳ bush: Indyan at 2s 6d.

It is ordered by this Courte, that yᵉ next Wednefday come three weekes, bee kept a day of Publique Thankfgiuing in yᵉ feuerall Plantatyons wᵗʰin this Jurifdictyon.

This Courte is adiorned to the firft Wednefday in March next ecept the Deputy Govornor fee caufe to call it fooner.

A Sᴇssɪᴏɴ ᴏꜰ ᴛʜᴇ Gᴇɴᴇʀᴀʟʟ Cᴏᴜʀᴛᴇ ɪɴ Hᴀʀᴛꜰᴏʀᴅ
the 3ᵈ of October 1654.

Mʳ Wells, *Deputy Goᵘʳ*
Magiftrates: Mʳ Webfter, Mʳ Woolcut, Mʳ Cullick, Mʳ Clarke, Mʳ Willis, Mʳ Tailecoat.
Deputyes: Mʳ Steele, Mʳ Gaylerd, Mʳ Trott, Mʳ Allen, Mʳ Fitch, Mʳ Weftwood, Edward Stebbing, Nath: Dickerfon, John Biffell, Andrew Bacon, John Hollifter, Tho: Coleman, John Clarke, Rob: Webfter, Tho Chapman, Tho: Sherwood, Tho: Fairechild, *Tho: Whitmore.*

The diftribution or divifion of men to bee preffed out of each Towne, to attend the expedition to Narrarganfett, according to the conclufion of the Commiffioners,[4] is as followeth:

Windfor, 8 perfons, Wetherffield, 6 perfons, Pequott, 4 perfons.
Norwacke, o " Farmington, 2 " Fairefield, 6 "
Hartford, 9 " Stratford, 5.———45.

The perfons that are to goe firft wᶜʰ are 24, are to bee out of the Townes following: Windfor, 4; Pequott 4, Mattabeefeck, 1; Hartford, 6; Wetherffield, 4; Farmington, 1; Sea broock, 4—24. The remainder of the firft number being 21, wᶜʰ are to attend and bee in reddinefs as a referue, are to goe out of the townes following: Windfor, 4; Hartford, 3; Wetherffield, 2; Farmington, 1; Fairefield, 6. Stratford, 5—21.

Mr. Webfter, Mʳ Stone, Mʳ Fitch, Mʳ Will. Whiting & Mʳ John Whiting, prefenting to this Courte a diftributyon of Mʳ Whitings eftate, agreed upon by them, and under all their hands, & bearing date the 30ᵗʰ September, 1654, the Courte allowes the faid diftributyon and orders it to bee recorded.

The Courte allfo allowes and approues of yᵉ judgement and apprehenfions of yᵉ Comittee, (viz: Mʳ Cullick, Mʳ Steele & Mʳ Allyn) about Mʳ Whitings will fo farr as they all agree & order it to bee recorded.

This Courte giues Mʳ Will: Goodwin libberty to make vfe of wᵗᵗ

4 The Commiffioners, at their meeting in September, had refolved upon war with Niniget, and had ordered 40 horfemen and 250 foot foldiers to be forthwith levied from the feveral colonies. Of thefe Maffachufetts were to furnifh 40 horfe and 153 foot; Conn. 45 foot; Plymouth 41; and N. Haven 31. A part of this force was to be difpatched with all expedition to the Niantic country, and the remainder to hold themfelves in readinefs to march upon notice from the Commander in chief, the felection of whom was conceded by the Commiffioners to Maffachufetts.—*Rec. of U. Colonies; Hutchinfon's Hift.*, vol. 1, pp. 186, 187, *and Collections*, 261; *Trumbull's Hift. of Conn.*, vol. 1, pp. 223, 224.

Timber from the wafte land belonging to the Country, hee fhall have occafion for to keepe his fawe mill in employement.

This Courte graunts to Mr Cullick libberty to draw and fell one hogfhead of Clarrett & a quater cafck of red wine to his friends and neighbors, free from the countryes excife. And this Court doth allfo further graunt unto the faid Mr Cullick, free licenfe & libberty for the futur to draw out or fell to his friends and neighbors w^{tt} wine and liquors hee fhall fee caufe, free from the Countryes excife.

[55] It is ordered by this Courte, that it fhall not be lawfull for any p^rfons whatfoeuer to draw any Wine, Strong waters of any forte or Kind, Stronge Beare or Syder & Sell it out by retaile to any p^rfons whatfoeur, except fuch p^rfon or p^rfons in each Towne as are licenfed fo to doe from the Courte.

Whereas, Notwithftanding, a former order reftraining the felling of all wine & liquors to the Indyans, that greate and crying finn of Drunkenes reignes amongft them, to the greate difhonor of God & hazard of the liues and peace boath of the Englifh & Indyans wch as this Courte is informed is by frequent felling of Syder or ftrong Beare to them, It is now ordered by this Courte, that it fhall not bee lawful for any p^rfon or p^rfons whatfoeur within thefe libbertes directly or indirectly, to fell, lend, barter, or giue to any Indyan or Indyans whatfoeur, fmall or greate, one or other, any wine, liquor, beare, Syder[6] or metheglin, or any forte or kinde whatfoeur except it bee their ordinary houfehold beare, for wch they fhall haue noe recompenfe, Vppon the former penality of fiue pounds for euery pinte & 40*ss*. for the leaft quainty, one third part to bee to the partyes informing, and the other to the publique Treafury.

This Courte orders, that the 5th day of the next weeke bee kept a publique Faft & day of humiliation throughout all the Plantatyons in this Jurifdiction, to feeke the p^rence and blefling of the Lord vppon the p^refent expedition to the Narraganfetts, according to the conclufioner of ye Commiffioners, wherein o^r future peace & comforts are much concerned.

This Courte defires and appoints ye Magiftrates to take the moft feafonable time to giue order for a publique day of Thankfgiving throughout this Jurifdictyon.

This Courte frees Thom : Allen, the fonne of Mr Mathu Allyn, from his fine of 2ol.

The Comittee chofen by this Courte to prefs men and neceffaryes in each Towne, for this expedition, in each Towne till it bee ended, is as followeth :

For Windfor Mr Phelps, & Mr Allyn, to joyne with ye Magiftrates there :

For Hartford, Mr Webfter & Andrew Bacon, to joyne with the Magiftrates there :

For Farmington, Mr Steele and the Conftable :

For Wetherfield, Mr Hollifter, Thomas Coleman & Nath Dickerfon, to joyne with the Deputy Govornor :

For Middletown, Rob : Webfter : *Tho : Whitmore*, with the Conftable.

---

6 [In Margin.] "The p^rticular refpecting Sider in this law is repealed Mch 11th '58 '59."

[56] For Seabrooke, John Clarke & Rob Chapman, with the Maior.

For Stratford, Tho : Sherwood & Tho : Fairechild, with the Affiftant Conftable :

For Fairefield, Mr Ward & Alexander Knowles, with the Conftable.

For Pequott, Capt. Denifon & Hugh Calkin, with the Constable. One drum & 1 p^r Cullers, fro Pequett :

From Hartford, a Lievetenant, & Surgeon & 4 hogfhead of Bifkett :

From Windfor, a Seriant, and 2 bar : of meale, 1 bar : of Peas & a boate.

The men are to bee on there march next Tuefday morning ; and are to meete in Hartford from Windfor & Farmingtone.

It is ordered that the fize for all Cafck for Beefe and Porke, after the 1 of March next fhall bee 31 Gall & ½.

The Courte is adiorned to ye 1 Wednefday in March next.—*Trumbull's Colonial Records.*

[64] A *Seffion* of the GENERALL COURTE in HARTFORD the 7^{nth} day of March 1654–55.

Mr Wells Deputy.

Magiftrates : Mr Webfter, Mr Woolcutt, Mr Cullick, Mr Clarke, Mr Willis, Mr Tailecoate.

Deputies : Mr Steele, Mr Phelps, Mr Trott, Mr Gaylerd, Mr Allyn, Mr Weftwood, Mr Hollifter, Edw : Stebbing, John Biffill, Andrew : Bacon, Nath : Dickerson, Steph : Harte, Tho : Coleman, Tho : Whittmore.

Riehard Church is freed from watching, warding and training.

This Courte allowes the fouldiers y^t went uppon the laft expedition to ye Narraganfetts, by vertue of the determination of ye Comiffion^{rs} as followeth : To the comon fouldiers 16d a day ; To the Drumers 20d a day ; To the Serieants, 2s a day ; To the Enfigne, 2s 6d a day ; To the Lieftenant 3s. a day ; To the Stewart, 2s a day ; ·

This Courte defires Mr Wells & Nath : Dickerfon, for Wetherffield ; Mr Webfter and Mr Cullick for Hartford ; Mr Clarke & Mr Allyn for Windfor ; Mr Steele & Mr Harte for Farmingtone ; Tho : Allyn & Robt Webfter for Middletowne ; to receiue, allowe and figne to the Treafurer, fuch bills of debts from ye Country to any p^rticular perfon as fhall bee brought in to them in theire feuerall Townes. And Mr Webfter & Mr Cullick are defired to audite the Treafurers acco^t for the yeare paft.

This Courte hath ·confidered ye acknowledged tranfgreffion of lawe, about cafting Ballaft in an inconvenient place, at Wetherffield, by William King, Mariner ; uppon feverall grounds they doe mitigate ye penality of ye faid order, and doe adiudge ye faid King to pay for his tranfgreffion aforefaid 10fs.

This Courte advifes that it bee p^rfented to the Gen : Courte in may next, that it may be ordered, that notwithftanding ye former order wch req : that fuch goods as are diftreined uppon execution fhould be apprized by 3 men, as ye lawe directs, wch now proues to bee inconvenient & fometimes iniurious to ye creditors, it fhall hereafter bee lawfull for ye Marfhall to make fale of fuch goods diftreined wthout the apprizm^t before fpecified, as well as hee may, for the good of the debtor, for the fame pay that the debtor was to make.—*Colonial Rec. of Conn:* T. H. Trumbull, Hartford, vol. i.

The amount of property assessed in the town of Middletown, March 22, 1670, was £4322.10s. The list of Freeholders and Proprietors, and the amounts assessed to each were as follows :

	£ s.		£ s.
Thomas Allen,	103.10	Anthony Martin,	60.10
Obadiah Allen,	30.00	Tho⁵ Miller,	50.10
Nathˡ Bacon,	119.00	Tho⁵ Ranney,	105.00
Wᵐ Briggs,	42.00	David Sage,	68.10
Alex. Bow,	45.00	John Savage,	129.00
William Cheney,	101.00	Samˡ Stocking,	113.10
Jasper Clements,	98.10	Samˡ Stow,	194.00
Henry Cole,	115.00	Tho⁵ Stow,	54.00
Nathanˡ Collins, stock and person, with 150£ given him in land by the town,	225.00	John Stow,	24.00
		James Tappin,	50.00
		Edward Turner,	44.00
		William Ward,	110.00
		John Ward,	44.00
Samuel Collins,	58.00	Rich Hall,	75.00
Wᵐ Cornwall,	160.00	Samˡ Hall,	130.00
John Cornwall,	41.00	John Hall jr,	26.00
Samˡ Cornwall,	45.00	Giles Hamlin,	134.00
Wᵐ Cornwall jr,	45.00	Wᵐ Harris,	200.00
George Durant,	34.00	Daniel Harris,	132.00
Samˡ Eggleston,	55.00	George Hubbard,	90.10
Edwᵈ Foster,	26.00	Andrew Warner,	84.00
John Hall,	99.00	Robᵗ Warner,	87.10
Joseph Hubbard,	38.00	John Warner,	96.10
Daniel Hubbard,	24.00	*Thomas Whitmore,*	125.10
Thomas Hubbard,	61.00	Nathaniel White,	169.10
John Hurlburt,	26.00	John Wilcox,	140.00
Isaac Johnson,	24.00		
John Kirby,	88.00		£4322.10
Isaac Lane,	40.00		*Hist. Sketches of M.*
Wᵐ Lucas,	42.00		

The foregoing list composed all the householders of the town, at that date, and it will be perceived that

there are but thirty-five surnames and from them
have many of the present inhabitants of Middletown
descended. That our readers may have some idea
what constituted the material wealth of the colonies
at the time this assessment was made, as well as to
preserve in these pages a curious historical sketch of
things as they were in New England at the time our
common ancestor was living, we give the following
interesting paper, which was furnished to the *Boston
Traveller*, from a magazine published in the last century, entitled, *Observations made by the Curious on
New England about the year* 1673.

There are about
$\begin{cases} 120,000 \text{ Souls,} \\ 13,000 \text{ families,} \\ 16,000 \text{ that can bear arms.} \end{cases}$

12 Ships of between 100 and 200 Tons;
190 " " 20 and 100 Tons;
500 Fifher boats about 6 Tons;
There are 5 Iron Works, which cast no Guns;
There are 15 Merchants worth about £50,000, or about 500 one with
another.
500 p^{r}fons worth £3,000.
No houfes in New England has more than 20 rooms.
Not 20 houfes in Bofton which have 10 rooms each.
About 1500 families in Bofton.
The worft houfes in New England are lofted.
No beggars.
Not three perfons put to death for theft (annually).
About 35 Rivers & harbers.
About 23 Ifland and fifhing places.
The provinces of Bofton, Maine & New Hampfhire make about three
fourths of the whole ftrength. The other three of Connecticott, Rhode
Ifland & Kennebeck being one fourth of the whole effect. Not above
three of their military men have been actual fouldiers as y^e artillery men
in London.

Among y^e Magiftratts
y^e moft popular are
$\begin{cases} \text{Leverett, y}^e \text{ Govorno}^r \\ \text{Maj Dennifon} \\ \text{Maj Clarke} \\ \text{Mr Bradftreet} \end{cases}$

Among y^e Minifters
$\begin{cases} \text{Mr Thacher} \\ \text{M}^r \text{ Oxenbridge} \\ \text{M}^r \text{ Higginfon} \end{cases}$

There are no muficians by trade.
A dancing fchool was fet up, but put down.
A fencing fchool is allowede.
All Cordage, Sail Cloth, & Nets come from England.

No Cloth made there worth 4*s* a yarde.
No linen above 2*s* 6*d*.
No allum, nor copperas, nor falt made by their fun.
They take an oath of fidelity to ye Govorno^r but none to ye King.
Ye Govorno^r is chofen by evry freeman.

From the Rev. Dr. David D. Field's *Centennial Address*, delivered at Middletown, Nov. 13, 1850,[1] we take the following respecting Thomas Whitmore and other original settlers of that town.

As for early settlers, John Hall, William Cornwall, William Smith, Samuel Webster, and Thomas Wetmore, were settlers in 1652, and settlers probably, some or all of them, from the beginning. Thomas Allen, Andrew Warner, Nathaniel Bacon, William Markham, Nathaniel Brown, George Hubbard, Henry Cole, Giles Hamlin, George Graves, William and Daniel Harris, Thomas Miller, and a man by the name of Martin, supposed to be John Martin, were settlers in 1654, and probably earlier; they may have been here as early as the settlers first named.

John Savage, Samuel Stow, Robert Warner, John Wilcox, William Bloomfield, Mathias Treat, and Nathaniel White, were early settlers; and so were persons by the name of Cheney, Clement, Bow, Eggleston, Lucas, Tappin or Tapping, Turner, and some others.

The character of the early settlers of Middletown may be given in a few words. It is not pretended that they were a perfect community. They had their faults as other settlers of New England. But their faults were not peculiar to themselves; they pertained to the age in which they lived, and are susceptible of much palliation from the circumstances in which they were placed. This admitted, they were as a body, a very religious people, possessed of much practical knowledge, not derived altogether from experience and observation, but also from reading and intercourse with literary and well-informed men: friends of liberty, constitutional liberty, regulated by righteous laws.

They were a very religious people. All attended public worship. Before they had a meeting-house, they worshiped God under the boughs of a tree, and in less than two years they built them a sanctuary, and eighteen years after, ano-

[9] *Centennial Address*, by David D. Field, D.D., with Historical Sketches of Cromwell, Portland, Chatham, Middle Haddam, Middletown and its Parishes. Middletown, Ct., W. B. Casey, 1853.

ther. These were humble structures, it is true, but they were grateful for the accommodations they afforded. They secured regularly the services of a minister of the gospel. Not long after the settlement commenced, the people employed Mr. Samuel Stow, a native of Concord, Mass.[10] * * * *The settlers possessed much practical knowledge*, the result of observation and reading, and intercourse with the wise and the good. The early clergy were superior men, men of talents and learning, and the magistrates and public men were well-informed. The people themselves were able to read; the most of the males at least to write and keep accounts, and they united their efforts with those of their superiors for the right training of their young. Family worship and government were maintained with strictness. Attending public religious instruction with their children, they welcomed their minister to their dwellings, and ordered their families so as to have these visits the most profitable to their entire household. The Bible, that inexhaustible source of knowledge, and what other books they had, were more read, more studied at home by old and young, and their contents made the subjects of more reflection and conversation, than are found now in the abodes of their descendants. Nor let us think too meanly of the common schools which were established by law, and the people were required to maintain. All deemed them indispensible to the diffusion of knowledge through the entire community. Hence we find the town in March, 1676, when their means were small, agreeing to pay a Mr. Webb twenty-five pounds for keeping school a year. * * * Parents were glad to send their children to school; ministers visited the schools and encouraged the children to learn: yea, they often took youths into their houses and instructed them themselves.

·*The settlers were the friends of constitutional liberty, and of righteous laws, well administered.* They came here under the wing of the constitution which went into operation in 1639, allowing them to elect their own officers, and to unite with others in the election of officers of the commonwealth. That constitution was superceded by the charter of Charles the Second; a charter liberal for a monarch to grant, and which showed the adroitness of Gov. Winthrop, in obtaining it. Thus the people had what they wished, the privilege of managing legally their own concerns, whether of town

---

[10] In an appendix Dr. Field corrects the error that he has fallen into here. The Rev. Mr. Stow was born in England, and came from Roxbury, Mass., to Middletown.

or society, school district, or any other corporation with which they were connected, while they took part with others in elevating men to higher stations, and more extensive trusts. They knew their rights, though for more than twenty years the public laws were in manuscript, copies of them were sent to the towns, publicly read, and left for examination by the inhabitants; and when they were printed and bound in volumes with blank leaves, every family was required to purchase a copy. * * * Thus the people had the laws continually before them, and were probably more conversant, than the people now are, with the existing statutes.

One trait of the early settlers was, that when they found public men very faithful, they elected them repeatedly to office, sometimes for long periods, and to old age.

That we may the more fully fix in our minds the age in which our ancestor lived, let us note some of the leading English characters and personages of his time.

First, he was a subject of James I, Charles I, and Charles II. Shakespeare was living, and died when he was a year old (1616) : Sir Walter Raleigh was beheaded two years later; Brewster, Robinson and Miles Standish, with their fellow voyagers of the Mayflower, landed at Plymouth four years afterwards; George Fox founded the society of Quakers two years later(1624); Bacon died in 1626; John Bunyan was born two years subsequently (1628); Dryden three years later, and Sir Christopher Wren the year following; Ben Jonson, the friend and contemporary of Shakespeare, died 1637-8. Newton was born four years later, and William Penn two years afterwards; Cromwell, Lord Protector from 1653 to 1658, and Milton, who died in 1674.

Rubens and Vandyke, though not English born, were famous in England at that time as well as in the rest of Europe, as painters.

He died, December 11, 1681, aged 66 years, and the subjoined is a copy of his will taken from a record in the Probate court's office in the city of Hartford :

The *Last Will* and *Testament* of *Thomas Whitmore* Senior, aged about sixty and six years, being at present under some considerable weakness of body, yet having through ye mercy of God, ye comfortable use of my understanding as formerly, is as followeth :

After committing my soul to God as to a faithful creator, and my body to a decent burial, I doe here leave this as my last *Will* and testament for the disposal of that portion of worldly estate Which God hath given me, amongst these my children and relations which I shall leave behind me, as followeth :

Imprimis. I give to my son John Whitmore a part of my lot in ye boggy meadow quarter. That is twenty rods wide of y^t part of ye land Within the fence that now is to lie on ye south west side that lot, and to go from y^t fence as far east as my land goeth, Moreover I give to my said son three quarters of my great lott that lyeth westward from the town, to take the whole breadth, half ye length, beginning at ye farther end and likewise the half ye breadth of ye other half next ye town and to take it on ye North Side. And my Will is y^t my son BERRIAH shall have the other half of that part next the town. Moreover it is my will y^t my said son John shall have all my proportion and interest in the three mile lott on the east side of ye great river, that is the farther three miles on y^t side eastward, Moreover I give to my said son a part of my meadow at Wauggunk being that piece which lying athwart east and west and from the north side of y^t on the east of my meadow to Deacon Allyn^s meadow.

It. I give to my son Thos Whitmore my long meadow lott lying on the north side, Moreover I give to my said son Thomas half my lott at Longer chunk and the other half to my daughter Hanna Stow to be equally divided between them as they shall agree or if they agree not, as indifferent men which they shall choose shall judge equal.

It. I give my son Samuel Whitmore a parcell of land on ye North Side of ye three Mile River which I bought from Goodman Savage by exchange of land being about ten acres lying at ye west End Goodman Savage's lott, only Reserving fourteen acres of y^t land for my Daughter —— if she survive me, Moreover I give my said Son two acres of meadow lying in ye farther neck ; and a piece of swamp in the Round meadow swamp being one acre and sixteen rods lying between Capt Harris's swamp and swamp which was Thos Hubbards. Moreover I give my said son Round Meadow lott being near six acres only Reserving and Willing a third part of it for my daughter Abigaill if she survive me or else to Remain to Samuel.

It. I give to my son JZRAHIAH WHITMORE my upland lott, on the east side of the Great River being about twenty and two acres lying in ye half mile lott, as also a piece of meadow at Wauggunk adjoining to his Brother John's line from John's North to a piece of meadow we call Flee Meadow, as also four acres in ye pond on the east side ye great River between Ensign Cheeny and Mr Nathaniel Collins's meadow. I give my said son one parcell of land in ye last half mile division on ye east side the Great River, that is all I have in y^t division on y^t side.

It. I give my son BERRIAH Whitmore that piece of meadow at Waugunk called ye Flee Meadow, and it is my will herein that my sons y^t have meadows there, shall all of them allow each other a lane highway, as shall be needful to come to their land there. Moreover I give to my said son y^t parcell of upland in my westermost lott by his brother John's as above specified. Moreover I give to my said son one acre of my home lott next the Great River, on this condition that he come settle upon it but if not he shall not have it, but it shall remain to the lott for them I shall appoint that lott to, On further consideration, I see not cause to give my said son that acre of my house lott.

It. I give to my son NATHANIEL WHITMORE half my land in the boggy meadow quarter of that which lyeth without the fence as it now standeth, and the other half to my son Joseph Whitmore Northward to be on the north Side that land and Joseph on the south side, and the other part within ye fence which is not disposed of to John Whitmore, I give to Nathaniel and Joseph to be delivered equally between them. Nathaniel on the north side, and Joseph next John, and it is my will herein to reserve a piece of land in Nathaniels part of the two acres which lieth within the compass of ye swamp, to be for my wife, as long as she liveth, and in order hereunto I do appoint & it is my will herein, that John and Nathaniel and Joseph, shall clear and break up that to fit it for improvement, Moreover I give to my said Sons Nathaniel and Joseph part of my boggy meadows, That is all the Westermost end coming down to the head of John Stow's answering the Crook of the River, and I do herein engage on y^t I doe interest in y^t meadow not to hinder each other for water courses through ye land, where shall be for ye good of ye whole.

It. I give to my Daughter Sarah Whitmore & my son Josia Whitmore & my Daughter Mehetable, my great lott at the Straits Hills to be equally divided among them three, Sarah first, and Josia next, and Mehetable last from ye homeward side.

It. I give Katheren my loving wife the rest of my home lott, with all the housing thereon, during her natural life as also, the one half of my long meadow on the south side of y^t lott and a parcell of land which I have at Paschoug on the east side the Great River, and the remainder of my boggy meadow to be devided between my wife and my son Thomas, and after my wife's decease, my will is that my son Thomas shall possess as his own. My home lott, that is all but that disposed of and the other half of my long meadow & also my land at Pascouchoug. Moreover I give to my loving wife my field lott during her natural life or until Benjamin fulfill the age of twenty-one years and then it shall be settled on him as his, Moreover as I received of my wife Katheren twenty pounds of her estate, six pounds whereof I have already paid her, yet I appoint and my will is that twenty be paid her out of my estate in household stuff and stock, so as may be most convenient to her and not hurtful to ye estate. Moreover I give to my loving wife two Cows, the two Cows to be a part of the twenty pounds above specified.

It. I give to my Daughters Sarah, Mehetable, Abigaill and Hanna junior, six pounds apiece out of my estate & to this my youngest daughter Hanna one piece of land of twenty acres lying near the straits on the west side of the Great River. To my other three daughters I give ten shillings a piece as a Remembrance of me, they being already disposed of and provided for.

Futher I give Thomas and Joseph my Carpentering tools between them. Moreover it is my will to leave my loving wife and my son John my sole Executors of this my last will and testament, appointing y^t when my just debts are paid out ye estate and ye legacies likewise paid also, if then, the Estate arise to leave anything more my will is that my Executors shall have the one half of that as theirs, and the other to be devided equally, to my children which are yet unmarried to be paid to them at their mothers death, or at her marriage if she marry again.

Further it is my will that my son Thomas at my decease shall enjoy one acre of my home lott next the great river for his present use with the housings that are there upon it, and I intend herein and it is my will that my son Thomas, shall take care of the orchard to look after it, and that his mother and he shall part the fruit as they shall agree, as also Thomas shall have the liberty to make use of a part of the barne for his own use and this is my full intent in this My last Will and Testament, I testify by setting to my hand and fixing my seal July 20th 1681.

THOMAS WHITMORE Senior.

Signed sealed and delivered Seal^d.
   in presence of us
      Deacon Samuel Stocking
      John Hall, Senior.

             I also request my loving and trusty Friends, Deacon Samuel Stocking and my brother John Hall to answer to this my last will, to lend their help and advise to the performance thereof as need shall be.

The names of his children are recorded in the Probate office at Hartford, immediately after the will, and their ages annexed.

Sons.		Daughters.	
John	36 years old	Elizabeth	32 years old
Thomas	29	Mary	31
Samuel	26	Hannah.	28
Izrahiah	25	Sarah	17
Beriah	23	Mahitable	13
Nathaniel	20	Abigail	3
Joseph	18	Hannah	1
Josiah	13		
Benjamin	7		

Thomas Whitmore's first wife, Sarah, died Dec. 7, 1664–5. Her father, John Hall, was one of the original grantees of Middletown, and was the third appointed Town clerk of M., 1665. He (says Note B, in *Historical Sketches of Middletown*) had been in a family estate many years before he left England, and was an early settler both in Hartford and Middletown.

John Hall Senr lands recorded June 10th 1654 vol I, p. 5. He died May 26, 1673 in the 89th year of his age and the 40th of his being in New England. July 20th 1673, Ann, wife of John Hall, and dau. of John Willcocke ended this life about the 57th year of her age. He was accompanied to Middletown by his three sons, Rich^d, Samuel, and John Hall jr. Richd Hall lands recorded June 10th, 1654, p. 5, vol. I. He died Mar 24, 1740, in the 82^d year of his age. *Chil.* of Rich^d and Mary Hall. John b. May 1654; Richard b. June 1655; Samuel b. Sept. 1658; Anna b. Nov. 20, 1661; Rich Hall Senr d. Mar 30, 1691. Mary his wife d. Mar 30, 1691.—*M. Rec.*

One of the first elected ordained Deacons was John Hall, son of the first John Hall; he died Jany 22, 1694, aged 75 and his Epitaph declares his virtues:

Here lyes our Deacon Hall
Who studied peace with all,
Was upright in his life,
Void of malignant strife;
Gone to his rest, left us in sorrow
Doubtless his good works will him follow.

These rhymes are as quaint as Cotton Mather's and not a whit quainter than some epitaphs found on grave stones in old England.—*Dr. Field.*

Samuel Hall (son of John Sen.) lands recorded June 10, 1654, vol. I, p. 5, d. Mar 24, 1740, in his 82^d year, had Saml b. Feby 3, 1663, John b. Aug 7, 1668, Thomas b. Augt 29, 1691.—*M. Rec.*

Thomas Whitmore's second wife, Mary Attconson, died June 1, 1669, after giving birth to her daughter Mahitable.

Mrs. Catharine Leet, third wife of Thomas Whitmore, died Oct. 13, 1693; her will was made Aug. 14, 1688, by which she bequeathed her property to her first children, William, Samuel and John Robards, and her last children, Benjamin, Abigail and Hannah Whitmore.

IMMEDIATE DESCENDANTS

OF

THOMAS WHITMORE.

JOHN, b. —; bap. at Hartford, Sept. 6, 1646; m. Dec. 30, 1680, Abigail dau. of Andrew and Rebecca Warner, of Middletown, Ct.; she d. May 5, 1685; had Thomas, and Abigail; m. (2d) April 1, 1686, Mary, dau. of John Savage Sen., of Middletown; had Elizabeth, Mary, John, and Ebenezer.

He had land recorded in Middletown in 1668. He was made a freeman Oct. 8, 1685.

General Court held at Hartford.
[171]   Maj. Robt Treat Esqr. Govr
         James Bishop Esq Dept Govr
    *   *   *   *   *   *   *

Propounded for Freeman, Thomas Hall, David Hall, Josh: Culver, Samuel Merriam, of Wallingford; Jno Leonard, Saml Bristol, Edwd Lee, Tho Dowd, John Parmele of Guilford; John Stow S^r. *John Whitmore*, Natha^l Stow, Isaac Wilcox, Richd Hubbard, John Clarke, William Cornelle of Middletown; Samuel Hubbard of Hartford.

He d. Aug. 31, 1696. Will dated Aug, 6, 1689. Inventory of his property taken by his brother Izrahiah, Nathaniel Stow, and Edward Shepard, Dec. 1696.

His widow, Mary Savage, m. Obadiah Allen; she d. Oct. 20, 1723.

Andrew Warner, the father of Mary (Warner) Whitmore, was one of the fifty-two householders who were registered as proprietors of Middletown in 1670. He was a settler there as early as 1654. See under head of Thomas Whitmore Sen.

Andrew, Robert, and John Warner were sons of Andrew Warner, who emigrated from Hatfield, England, about 1630, who was at Cambridge in 1632, and at Hartford among the early settlers. He was a deacon in the Rev. Mr. Hooker's church, and an influential man in that town. He removed to Hadley in 1659, where he died at an advanced age in 1684. The three sons in Middletown were farmers. Robert repeatedly represented the town in the General court; he d. April 10, 1690. John d. in 1700. The Warners in Lyme and Chester are descendants of Daniel Warner, one of their brothers.—*Hist. Sketches of Middletown, note B.*

For descendants of John and Rebecca (Warner) and Mary (Savage) Whitmore, see under head of Descendants of John, son of Thomas.

ELIZABETH, b. —, 1648; m. Oct. 8, 1673, Josiah son of William Adkins, of East Hartford; removed to Middletown; had I *Sarah*, July 16, 1674, d. Feb. 25, 1719; II *Abigail*, b. Sept. 11, 1676, m. Robert Hubbard 1703; III *Solomon*, b. July 25, 1678; IV *Josiah*, b. March 9, 1680; V *Benjamin*, b. Nov. 19, 1682; VI *Ephraim*, b. March 9, 1685; VII *Elizabeth*, b. Aug. 11, 1687, m. Samuel Ward, 1711.

Josiah Adkins[1] Sen. d. Sept. 12, 1690; will dated March 1, 1690; inventory, by John Hall Sen., Nathaniel Stow, and Samuel Stow, Jan. 1, 1691. Their son Solomon was elected deacon of the First congregational society of M., Jan. 8, 1735; d. Oct. 5, 1748, aged 70. William Adkins came from Wales.

MARY, b. 1649; m. Nov. 13, 1668, John, son of Thos. Stow Sen., of Middletown; had I *John*, b. Oct. 10, 1669, drowned in a well April 10, 1679; II *John 2d*, b. March 3, 1672; III *Thomas*, b. April 10, 1674; IV *Nathaniel*, b. Feb. 22, 1675; V *Mary*, b. June 7, 1678; VI *Hannah*, b. Aug. 25, 1680; VII *Sarah*,

---

[1] Josiah, Middletown d. Sept. 12, 1690, leaving 7 chil. minors. Sarah aged 16; Abigail 14; Solomon 12; Josiah 10; Benjamin 8; Ephraim 6; and Eliz. 3; but by a former w. thot to be an Andrews, others had rec. their portions, name Thomas, Samuel, and Eliz. Gilman, who perhaps was dec. bef. the m. "8 Oct. 1673, with Eliz. Whitmore, mo. of the young ones for wh. and her chil. he made provision in his will a few days before his death."—*Dr. Savage*, II, 19.

b. March 25, 1683, d. April 12, 1683; VIII *Samuel*, b. April
30, 1684, d. April 12, 1690; IX *Thankful*, b. July 15, 1686,
d. Jan. 15, 1689; X *Experience*, b. Sept. 30, 1688, d. same
month.

Thomas, the father of John, came with his brothers
John and Rev. Samuel Stow, from Roxbury, Mass., with
their families.   Samuel, John and Thomas Stow Srs.,
were among the fifty-two householders and proprietors
of M. in 1670; for further notice of them see forward
under head of Izrahiah Whitmore.   John Stow, the
husband of Mary Whitmore, d. Oct. 18, 1688, aged 48.
It would appear from the following that he was for a
time a soldier during the wars with the Indians:

A MEETING OF THE COUNCIL IN HARTFORD, May 31, 1696.
Robt Treat. Efq^r. Dep^t Govr; Mr Sam^ll Willys, Capt John : Allen,
Capt Dan^ll Clarke.

  *   *   *   *   *   *   *

RIGHT WORSHIPF^LL
        Sir, by poft from Hatfield we recieued intellegence even now that
ye Indians have donne much fpoile; many howfes burnt, without the
fortification; feueral men from Hadly went over for y^r relíefe, of which
y^t is fiue Kild and three wounded; two of our men kild, Jobama Smith
& Ric^d Hall; John Stoe wounded in ·ye foott, and Roger Alvis is alfo
wounded in ye foott; John Smith of Hadly kild, and two of ye garrifon
fouldiers; y^t was about a hundred & fifty Indians y^t fought; y^y vp y^e
meadow all like to be kild & taken, but y^t men iffued out from towne for
ye relief; none flayne till almoft come vp to ye towne; many more Indians y^t were at ye towne doeing fpoyle, at y^t time, y^t o^r men were fought
w^th, they drew off and ambufh^t ye way twixt Hampton and Hatfield to lay
waiett for o^r fources; but fearing it beforehand, went not that way, but
drew over to Hadly; could not gett to Hatfield by reafon they lay fo
thick about ye landing place; many cattle and horfes flayne and taken
away: y^s is ye fubftance of w^t intellígence we have to impart.   The
Lord' fanctify his hand to vs for our good and be p'fent wth you in all
yor waighty concernes vnder hands.   Intellegence from Bofton you have
already.   Not elfe but cordiall refpects to yo'felfe and all relations w^th
you; take leave remaining, yo'^r humble ferv^t,

                                        BENJAMIN NEWBERY.

Northampton ·
   ye 30th 1676.
        Oct 1682 John Stow by reafon of fome weaknefs of body that doth
attend him, doe free his perfon from publiqué fervice and rates dureing
the Courte's pleafure.—*Colonial Rec.*

SARAH, b. — 1650, bap. April 20, 1651, d. July 14, 1655, aged 5 years.

THOMAS, b. Oc-. 19, 1652; m. Feb. 20, 1684-5, Elizabeth, dau. of George Hubbard Sen.; had Elizabeth and Thomas.

He died Feb. 11, 1689; she died Dec. 6, 1725.

George Hubbard Sen.[2] was one of the early settlers and proprietors of Middletown (see under head of Thomas Whitmore). Dr. Field in speaking of him says: "he had six sons, Joseph, David, Samuel, George, Nathaniel and Richard. The two oldest settled in Middletown. This George Hubbard was a distinct person from the George Hubbard who resided in Wethersfield, Milford and Guilford. The genealogies of their families show this. He was made a freeman by the General court May 18, 1654.

For the descendants of Thomas and Elizabeth (Hubbard) Whitmore, see under head of Descendants of Thomas, son of Thomas.

HANNAH, b. Feb. 13, 1653; m. Nathaniel Stow Sen.,[3] son of Thomas Stow Sen., April 4, 1677.

We have been unable to find any record of her descendants, if she had any. His father it will be perceived, by reference under head of Thomas Whitmore Sen., was also one of the fifty-two householders and proprietors in 1670. He was made freeman by the General court, Oct. 8, 1682.

SAMUEL, b. in Middletown, Sept. 10, 1655; m. Dec. 13, 1687, Mary dau. of Nathaniel (Sen.) and Ann Bacon b. April 7, 1664; had Mahitable, Samuel, Mary, Benjamin, Thomas, Daniel, Bethiah, and Jabez.

He removed to the Middlefield Society in 1700. He d. April 12, 1746; his wife d. May 24, 1709.

---

[2] George Hubbard of Hartford perhaps as early as 1639; removed to M. betw. 1650-1652; d. March 18, 1685. In May foll. div. his estate. Seven chidren are named.—*Dr. Savage, Gena. Dict.*

[3] A brother of John Stow, the husband of his wife's sister Mary.

The settlement in this society (Middlefield) was begun about 1700. The earliest settlers were Samuel Allen, Benjamin Miller, and Samuel Wetmore, from the First society. With these, others united from the same society, by the name of Bacon, Hubbard, Stow, Turner and Ward; from Dunham by the name of Camp, Coe, and Lyman; from Stratford by the name of Birdseye; from Guilford by the name of Bartlett; persons were there also by the name of Chilson and Hale. When the society was incorporated in Oct. 1744, there were more than fifty families living within its limits. The names of the heads of these families were, Samuel Allen Sen., Samuel Allen Jun., Ephraim and Obadiah Allyn, Thomas Alvord, Nathaniel and Joseph Bacon, John Bartlett, John Birdsey, John Brown, Abraham and Edward Camp, John Chilson, and John Chilson Jun., Joseph, David and Robert Coe, Gideon and Thomas Cooke, John and Isaac Dowd, Daniel Driggs, Jeremiah Guild, Ebenezer and Joseph Hale, Eliakim Hall, Samuel Stow, Hawley and Ebenezer Hubbard, Jeremiah Leaming, Benjamin Miller, Benjamin Miller Jun., Joseph Miller Sen., Ichabod, Amos and David Miller, Moses Parsons, John Rockwell, Daniel Stow, David Strickland, David Strickland Jun., Stephen Turner Sen., and Samuel Warner, Samuel Wetmore Sen., Benjamin Wetmore Sen., Benjamin Wetmore Jun., Beriah, Joseph, Thomas, Daniel, Caleb, Prosper, and Josiah Wetmore Jun., and Titus John Whitmore, the aggregate list of all these persons exceeded £3000. Almost all these persons were farmers, and soon after the incorporation of the society, the population reached a point from which it did not vary for many years.—*Hist. Sketches of Middletown*, 1853.

Nathaniel Bacon probably came direct from England. He was a nephew of Andrew Bacon of Hartford; his family were from Stratton, England, co. Rutland.[4]—*Id.*

---

[4] Nathaniel Bacon Sen. had lands recorded June 9, 1654, vol. i, p. 111.— *N. E. Reg.*

Children of Nathaniel and Ann Bacon: Hannah, b. April 14, 1635; Andrew, b. February 4, 1656, d. July 5, 1662; Nathaniel, b. July 20, 1659, d. April 18, 1663; John, b. March 14, 1661-2. he d. Nov. 4, 172–; Mary, b. April 7, 1664; Andrew 2d b. June 4, 166–; Abigail, b. July 13, 1670; Lydia, b. Feb. 18, 1672.

Nathaniel Bacon Sen. m. 2d, Elizabeth Perpont, April 17, 1682; had Beriah, b. Aug. 17, 1683, who m. Ann Odell of Stratfield, and d. May 15, 1730. Nathaniel Bacon Sen. d. Jan. 27, 1705-6.—*N. E. Hist. Reg.*

For descendants of Samuel and Mary (Bacon) Whitmore, see under head of descendants of Samuel, son of Thomas.

IZRAHIAH, b. in Middletown, March 8, 1656-7 (March 9, 1656?); m. May 13, 1692, Rachel,[5] dau. of the Rev. Samuel and Hope (Fletcher) Stow, of M.; had Izrahiah Stow, b. Jan. 31, 1694, d. young; James, Ichabod, b. April 18, 1698, d. Jan. 7, 1715; Seth, Jeremiah, Caleb and Josiah.

He was a magistrate of the town, and a deputy to the General court, from 1721 to 1728 inclusive; he was a man of fine abilities, says tradition, and enjoyed the confidence and esteem of the colonists. His father in law made him his executor, and speaks of him in his will in terms of the highest praise. He died at the age of 86 years.

The Rev. Samuel Stow, the father of Mrs. Rachel Stow Whitmore, born in 1622, was son of John and Elizabeth (Biggs) Stow, who came from Kent, England, to Roxbury, Mass., in 1634 (*Roxbury Rec*). He married Hope, the daughter of William Fletcher (*Mid'n Rec.*), and had "John, b. at Charlestown, Mass., June 16, 1650; Ichabod, b. Feb. 20, 1652; Hope, b. Feb. 1656; Dorothy, b. Aug. 1, 1659; Elizabeth, b. Aug. 1, 1662; Thankful, b. May 1664; Rachel, b. March 13, 1666-7. —*N. E. Reg.*

He graduated at Harvard college, 1645. Studied for the ministry, and soon after became the first pastor of the First orthodox congregational society of Middletown. As it was the custom to have clergymen some time on trial, he was not regularly settled till 1657, where he continued his ministrations for three years, when it appears that a difficulty arose between him and his people, and was succeeded by the Rev. Nathaniel

[5] Sister of Margaret, wife of Dea. Beriah Whitmore, and cousin to John and Nathaniel Stow, husbands of her sisters in law Mary and Hannah Whitmore.

Collins.[6] It would seem from the following record that he, some twenty odd years later, established a church at Simsbury :.

Vpon yᵉ prefentation of an addrefs by Mʳ Stowe and Michael Humphries, on behalfe of the inhabitants of Simſbury,[7] for liberty to gather a church and fettlement of a paſtor there, with the approbation of this Genˡˡ Court, according to Goſpell order, after yᵉ uſuall maner in this colony, we fee no caufe to difcourage, but to alow them fo to. doe, it being done with the obfervation and approbation of three or foure of the elders and meffengers of the neighbouring churches, advifeing that theire inhabitants. doe choofe a competent number of the moft fober and godly perfons to begin that church and call the officer, as is defired. by them.—*Trumbull's Col. Rec. of Conn.*, vol. III, p. 101.

The Rev. Samuel Stow in connection with Nathaniel White and Jasper Clements, made bequests for the support of common schools in Middletown, thereby laying the foundation probably of the first free schools in Connecticut. He died May, 1704, leaving considerable landed property to his heirs.

John Stow, the father of the Rev. Samuel, was made freeman at Roxbury, Mass., in 1634, and member of the Ancient and Honorable artillery company, 1638; and representative to the General court of Mass. in 1639. "Elizabeth wife of John Stow died and was buried 21 (6) 1638."—*Boston Rec.*

[6] Mar. 14, 1660. This Courte haueing heard and confidered yᵉ difference twixt ye Towne of Middle Towne and Mr. Stow, and theire allegations [138] and anfwers, doe judg and determine, that yᵉ people of Middle Town are free from Mʳ Stow as their engaged minifter. 2ly. That yᵉ people of Middle Town fhall giue to Mr Stow Lʳˢ Teftimonial, according as drawn vp by the Worfhipfull Gouernoʳ in yᵉ Courte. . And Mʳ Stow is not infringed of his liberty to preach, in Middle Town, to. fuch as will attend him, vntill there be a fettled miniftrey there. * * * * * * * It is ordered by this court, that yᵉ people Middle Town fhall pay vnto Mʳ Stow, for his labbur in yᵉ miniftrey the year paft, £40, wᶜʰ is to be paid vnto by the 10ᵗʰ of April next.—*Trumbull's Col. Rec.*, vol. I, p. 361–362.. ·

[7] Ecclefiaftical, I, 80; fignede by, Jofhua Houlcombe, Michell Humphrey, John, Terrey, John Cafe Sen. and eighteen others. The petioners, " hauing knowledge and tryall of Mr. Samuell Stow in yᵉ labours of yᵉ Word & doctrine of yᵉ Gofpell " manifift their defire for his continuance " to be a paftor and Watchman over our Soules and yᵉ Soules of ours," and ask ye countenance of the Generall Courte to their fettlement and order. Mʳ Stow and Mʳ Humphrey were chofen by the town to. prefent the petion to yᵉ Courte.—*Colonial Rec.*

For descendants of Izrahiah and Rachel (Stow) Whitmore, see under head of Descendants of

Rev. Izrahiah, son of Izrahiah, son of Thomas.
Rev. James,   "   "   "   "
Judge Seth,   "   "   "   "
Jeremiah,   ··   "
Caleb,   "   "   "
Josiah,

BERIAH, b. in Middletown, Nov. 2, 1658; m. Margaret dau. of Rev. Samuel and Hope Stow, April 1, 1691 (Sept. 2?); had Sarah, Hope, Thomas (d. March 2, 1798), Margaret, Hannah, Bethiah (d. Jan. 5, 1706), Beriah; she d. Feb. 21, 1710: he m. 2d, Mary dau. of Dea. Obadiah Allen, of Middletown, Nov. 11, 1714; had Mary b. Oct. 6, 1715; d. Dec. 11, 1715.

He was elected a deacon of the First church of M., May 5, 1713. He died April 11, 1756, aged 97. His wife Mary d. July 24, 1737, aged 62.

Dea. Obadiah Allen was one of the fifty-two house-holders and proprietors of Middletown in 1670. He was recommended by the elders of the church in Windsor, which renders it probable that he resided in that town for a time. The name of Allen was not always spelt with an *e;* we find it written in Town records Allyn, and on the old Church record All*i*n. He was made freeman by the General court, Oct. 11, 1672, and elected deacon of the First congregational society May 31, 1704. May 16, 1685, had confirmed to him by the General court, certain land as follows :

Upon requeſt of Mrs. Mary Collins, this Court doth impower her to confirm to Obadiah Allyn by deed of ſale, two acres of land that he bought and payd for to Mr Collins, and deed of ſale was by Mr Collins' order made in his life time, though not perfected according to law; her confirmation of the ſayd ſale by a deed, to be of full value to hold the ſayd land firme to him the ſayd Allyn, his heirs and aſſigns forever.— *Colonial Rec.*

For descendants of Dea. Beriah and Margaret (Stow) Wetmore, see Descts Dea. Beriah, son of Thomas.

NATHANIEL, b. in Middletown, April 21, 1661; m. Dorcas, wid. of
Obadiah Allen, Dec. 29, 1703; had Thomas, Moses, Esther.

He died November 7 (March 7?), 1708-9. For his
descendants see Descdts Nathaniel, son of Thomas.

JOSEPH, b. in M. March 5, 1662-3; m. June 26, 1706, Lydia,[8] dau.
of Nathaniel and Ann Bacon, of Middletown, b. Feb. 18, 1672;
had Joseph, Lydia, Ann, b. Feb. 11, 1711, d. same year; Ann
2d, Nathaniel.

He removed to Middlefield society; see under head
of Samuel, son of Thomas. He d. March 25, 1717.
Letters of administration granted 1718; his wife d.
Jan. 24, 1750 (1759-60?). For their descendants see
under head of Descendants of Joseph, son of Thomas.

SARAH 2d, b. in M. Nov. 27, 1664; m. Nov. 26, 1689, John,[9] son
of Nathaniel and Ann Bacon Sen., b. March 14, 1661-2; had
I *John*, b. Jan. 30, 1694; II *Sarah*, b. Sept. 14, 1696; she
d. Feb. 14, 1698 : m. 2d, Mary Cornwall, wid. of Jacob Cornwall, April 13, 1710.

John Bacon Sen. d. Nov. 4, 1732; his wife Mary d.
Nov. 15, 1732.

JOSIAH, b. in M., March 29, 1667-8.

We have been unable to find any further record of
this son of Thomas, except finding his name attached
to a copy of his father's will, as aged 16 years at the
date of the will, 1681.

MAHITABLE, b. in M., June 10 (17?), 1669; m. Feb. 12, 1691-2,
Andrew, son of Nathaniel and Ann Bacon of Middletown, b.
June 4, 1666; had, I *Andrew*, b. Nov. 21, 1692; II *Ann*, b.
Jan. 30, 1694; III *Nathaniel*, b. July 10, 1697; IV *Josiah*,
b. Sept. 27, 1699; V *Daniel*, b. March 5, 1702; VI *Mehitable*,
b. Feb. 28, 1704; VII *Joseph*, b. April 20, 1706; VIII *John*,
b. Oct. 30, 1708; IX *Esther*, b. Oct. 9, 1711; X *Abigail*, b.
Feb. 5, 1713.

[8] Sister to Mary, wife of Samuel, son of Thomas.
[9] Brother to Mary, wife of Samuel, son of Thomas, also to Lydia, wife of
Joseph, and Andrew, husband his wife's sister Mahitable.

Andrew Bacon Sen. d. Jan. 1 (June 1 ?), 1723 ; his wid. d. Jan. 19, 1732.

BENJAMIN, b. in M., Nov. 27, 1674.   His mother left him a legacy Oct. 13, 1693.   He died 1699.

ABIGAIL, b. in M., Nov. 6, 1678 ; m. Samuel Bishop of Guilford, Conn., April 2, 1697 ; had I *Samuel,* b. March 14, 1698-9 ; II *Abigail,* b. April 17, 1701, m. Gideon Chittenden,.March 21, 1721 ; III *Susannah,* b. Jan. 12, 1703-4, m. Samuel Chittenden, Nov. 7, 1726 ; IV *Catherine,* b. July 23, 1710, m. Daniel Field, May 17, 1731 ; V *Sarah,* b. Aug. 28, 1716, m. James Landon, Jan. 14, 1732 ; VI *Mary,* b. Aug. 4, 1717, m. Joel Bissell of Litchfield.

HANNAH, b. in M. Jan. 4, 1680 ; m. Feb. 5, 1701-2 Nathaniel Bacon 3d ; had I *Catharine,* b. Feb. 1, 1703-4, d. April 20, 1741 ; II *Nathaniel,* b. Feb. 16, 1706-7 ; III *Benjamin,* b. Nov. 28, 1708 ; IV *Hannah,* b. April 19, 1712 ; V *Jeremiah,* b. Nov. 28, 1715-16 ; VI *Mary,* VII *Sarah,* b. Dec. 24, 1719, d. same day.

She d. Sept. 7, 1722.

Sargt. Nathaniel Bacon 3d m. 2d, Anna wid. of John Lane, Jan. 31, 1723 ; she d. Dec. 26, 1751.   Lieut. Nathaniel Bacon 3d m. 3d Rebecca Doolittle, Nov. 28, 1752.   He d. Jan. 6, 1759.

Descendants of John, Son of Thomas.

THIRD GENERATION.

Children of John,

First child of Thomas and Sarah (Hall) Whitmore.

THOMAS, born in Middletown, April, 1682.

We find no record of his marriage, nor have we been able to trace any of the name back to him. We presume he had a family from the fact that we see his name given among some fifty heads of families as belonging to the Middlefield society in 1744.

ABIGAIL, b. in M., May 2, 1685; m. June 21, 1733, Ebenezer Clark; had I *Abigail*, b. April 1, 1734; II *Jedediah*, b. Jan. 16, 1738; she d. April 2 (9?) 1738, æ. 53: he m. 2d, Ann Warner; had 7 children.

ELIZABETH, b. in M., March 20, 1686-7; m. Richard Elton, son of John and Jane Elton, July 6, 1708; had I *Recompense*, b. Apl 2, 1709, d. Apl 8, 1732; II *Mary*, b. Jan. 9, 1740.

MARY, b. in M. Jan. 18, 1691-2,-

JOHN, b. in M. May 21, 1694; d, Feb. 2, 1724 probably unmarried.

EBENEZER, b. in M. Sept. 17, 1696; m. Elizabeth Cornwall, Mar. 26, 1724; had Mary, John, Elizabeth, Sarah, John 2d, Christian, Lois, Ebenezer and a dau. (twins); the dau. died the day of her birth. Ebenezer Sen. d. Jan. 11, 1742-3.

FOURTH GENERATION.

Children of EBENEZER WETMORE.[1]

MARY, b. in M. April 29, 1725-6; m. Jacob Dowd, Dec. 11, 1745;
had I *Mary*, b, July 27, 1746; II *Dinah*, b. June 14, 1748;
III *Eunice*, b. May 30, 1750; IV *Jacob*, b. July 5, 1752;
V *Jesse*, b. June 20, 1754; VI *Elizabeth*, b. Sept. 25, 1756;
VII *John*, b. Dec. 17, 1758.

JOHN, b. in M. Feb. 22, 1726-7, d. Dec. 29, 1731.

ELIZABETH, b. in M. Sept. 22, 1730.

SARAH, b. in M. May 3, 1732.

JOHN 2d, b. in M. Mar. 27, 1734; m. Marcy Bacon, May 4, 1757;
had Ebenezer, John, Ebenezer 2d, Ebenezer 3d, Elizabeth,
Elisha, Mary, Benjamin.

He held a commission of ensign under the crown;
at the commencement of the Revolution he gave up
his post in his majesty's army, and joined the volunteers, then being organized by Col. Ebenezer Sage of
Middletown, and was appointed captain, and served
his country during the entire war. On peace being
established, he settled in the south part of the town
of M. and was one of eighty that formed the South
congregational church there, as will be seen by the
following agreement:

" We the subscribers of the Second strict congregational church and society in this town, believing it to
be our duty to attend public worship of God, and support the Gospel Minister, do agree according to our
several abilities, to raise such supplies as shall be
necessary to render the life of a Gospel Minister comfortable, in order for his usefulness among us, and that
we will attend a society meeting, annually, on the last
Monday in September, in order for raising such sup-

---

[1] From and including the fourth generation of all the different branches,
we record the name Wetmore, instead of Whitmore.

plies as shall be necessary for the comfortable support
of a Gospel Minister.   And we further agree that we
will be accountable to this church and society for any
neglect of fulfilling this our agreement, provided always
that no force of civil law is to be used in collecting
support for the Gospel ministry among us."[2]—*Hist.
Sketch of M.*

Dated Oct. 13, 1788, and signed by

JOHN WETMORE,

and 79 other male citizens.

CHRISTIAN, b. in M. Nov. 30, 1735; d. Dec. 24, 1742.

LOIS, b. in M. Jan. 27, 1737; d. Feb. 15, 1737-8.

EBENEZER, b. in M, ⎫ Jan. 7, 1738-9; d. 18th same month.
  A dau. b.   "   ⎭   "   "   "   ; d. same day.

FIFTH GENERATION.

Children of Capt. JOHN,

Son of Ebenezer.

EBENEZER, b. in Middletown Feb. 4, 1759; d. Nov. 25, 1761.

JOHN, b. in Middletown Sept. 19, 1760; m. Mahitable ———; had
  John, Thomas, Ebenezer, Abigail, Mercy, Mitty, Mahitable.

He enlisted in the Continental army at 15 years of
age.   Serving out the time for which he had enlisted,
and his father drafting a second company, he reënlisted.
Was taken a prisoner and placed in one of the old
Jersey prison ships, where he suffered greatly from
sickness consequent upon close confinement and an
over-crowded hulk.   Through the kindness of a Mr.
Sholer, or Shaler, a gentleman attached to the British

---

[2] Their first pastor was Stephen Parsons, a native of the town; he remained
their minister till Aug. 1795, when he was dismissed on account of his views
upon the subject of baptism, and was succeeded by the Rev. David Huntington of Lebanon.

service, he was released and returned to his friends at Middletown.

After the close of the war, he followed the sea some years as captain of a merchant vessel. In 1792, he, with his brother Elisha and his brother-in-law George Paddock, removed to Paris, Oneida county, N. Y., where he bought lands, and turned his attention to farming. At that time there were but *three* buildings where the city of Utica now stands.

EBENEZER 2D, b. in Middletown, Jan. 10, 1762; d. Jan. 27, 1762.

EBENEZER 3D, b. in M., May 2, 1763; d. Dec. 6, 1766.

ELIZABETH, b. in M., June 4, 1766; m. Mr. Wynchop; resided in Middletown.

ELISHA, b, in M., Dec. 6, 1768; m. Feb. 2, 1792, Cynthia Guild, b. Nov. 3, 1768,. and removed to Herk. co., N. Y., same year; had Polly, Elisha, Rhoda, Samuel, Cynthia, William, Nancy, Clarinda, Louisa, Patty Marilla, John, and Emily.

He died in Paris, N. Y., Aug. 3, 1846, aged 77. He was one of the early settlers in that part of the country. An obituary notice of him says that he left a good name, and was universally loved and respected. "An aged widow, eleven children, seventy-two grandchildren and ten or more great grand children, mourn the loss of a valuable counsellor, and the community in which he resided that of an esteemed friend. His funeral was attended in the Presbyterian church in the neighborhood, and the consolations of the gospel tendered to the mourners by the Rev. T. I. Whitcomb." His wid. d. May 13, 1848.

MARY, b. in M., May 12, 1771; m. George Paddock; removed to Herk. co., N. Y. in 1792; subsequently removed to Wyoming county, Pa.; had ten or twelve children.

BENJAMIN, b. in M., April 4, 1774; m. Mar. 2, 1797, Thankful G. Lucas b. Dec. 13, 1776 (m. by the Rev. Enoch Huntington of M.); had Elnathan, Benjamin, Ebenezer, Eliza, Sally, Mary, Margerett, Abigail, John, Lucretia, and Hannah.

He removed with his family to Ashtabula county,
Ohio, Aug., 1819; subsequently removed to Monroe,
Ohio. He d. July 13, 1846.

SIXTH GENERATION.

Children of JOHN,

Son of Capt. John, Son of Ebenezer.

JOHN; d. aged about 21 years.

ABIGAIL.

MITTY.

THOMAS; d. young.

MERCY.

MEHITABLE.

EBENEZER; d. s. p.

Children of ELISHA,

Son of Capt. John, Son of Ebenezer.

POLLY, b. Nov. 16, 1792; m. Sept. 11, 1811, William Hatfield, of
Paris, N. Y., b. Sept. 5, 1791; he d. at Brookfield, Clinton co.,
Iowa, Sept. 6, 1854; had, I *Clark*, b. at Paris, Jan. 16, 1812,
m. Sophia Stimson, of Freedom, Cattaraugus co., N. Y., Jan. 21,
1834, resides at Osage, Mitchell co., Iowa; II *Malissa*, b. in
Gainesville, March 21, 1814, m. George Cadwell of Freedom,
Dec. 23, 1837, resides at Centerville, Allegany co., N. Y.;
III *Nathan*, b. in Wethersfield, Wyoming co., N. Y., Feb. 11,
1816, m. Julia Ann Gillett, of W., May 1, 1840, resides at
Bloomfield, Clinton co., Iowa; IV *Eli*, b. in Wethersfield,
Dec. 13, 1817, m. Ann Thayer, or Thuja, of Yorkshire, June
1, 1843, resides in Bloomfield, Iowa; V *Sophronia*, b. in W.
Feb. 15, 1820, m. Levi Jones, of Freedom, Cattaraugus co.,
N. Y., Feb. 2, 1840; VI *Louisa*, b. in W. Nov. 17, 1821, m.
Alfred Briggs, of Freedom, June 1, 1845, resides at Wethers-
field Sp., Wyoming co., N. Y.; VII *Perkins*, b. in Freedom,
Nov. 18, 1825, m. Ann Eliza Janes, Feb. 16, 1853, resides at
Brookfield, Clinton co., Iowa; VIII *Polly M.*, b. in Freedom,
Dec. 15, 1827, m. Philo E. Powell, Aug. 27, 1846, resides at
Eagle Village, Allegany co., N. Y.; IX *William H.*; b. in

Freedom, Feb. 24, 1830, m. Martha Thompson, of Sharon, Sept. 11, 1855, resides at Quincy, Olmstead co., Minn; X *Mary, C.*, b. in Freedom, May 14, 1832, m. Amicy W. Sleeper, of Bloomfield, Iowa, Sept. 9, 1853, she d. May 24, 1860; XI *Mason*, b. in Freedom, May 14, 1832, m. Caroline Gregory of Brookfield, Iowa, Sept. 20, 1855, resides at Quincy, Olmstead co,, Minn.; XII *Cynthia W.*, b. in Freedom, Aug. 1, 1837, m. Alvah B. Libby, Oct. 11, 1857, resides at Quincy, O. co., Minn.

Mrs· Hatfield Sen. resides at Maquoketa, Jackson co., Iowa; her sons and sons in law, are highly respectable farmers in Iowa and Minnesota.

ELISHA, b. January 29, 1794; m. Polly Hatfield, Oct. 22, 1815; had Mason Hatfield, William Henry, Harriet Maria, Henry Elisha, William Hatfield, and Nathan Irvin; she d. April 18, 1833, æ. 39 years: m. 2d, Mary Howard, July 31, 1833; had Mary Louisa, Ann Elizabeth, Charles Whitman, James Howard, John Wallace, and Sarah Jane.

He is a much respected citizen of Grafenberg, Herkimer county, N. Y.

RHODA, b. Jan. 5, 1796; m. Perkins Hatfield, Jan. 9. 1817; had, I *Orlow Hatfield*, b. Oct. 24, 1818, m. Amanda Gillet, July 28, 1836, he d. ——, his wid. resides at Maquoketa, Jackson co., Iowa; II *Cynthia Marilla*, b. Oct. 24, 1819, m. William Wolcott, Aug. 7, 1835, resides Hermitage, Wyoming co., N. Y.; III *Oscar Fitzland*, b. May 30, 1821, m. Elizabeth S. Enos, Sept. 14, 1843, resides Hermitage, Wyoming co., N. Y.; IV *Mason*, b. Feb. 3, 1823; m. Harriet Briggs, Dec. 24, 1844, resides Hermitage, Wyoming co., N. Y.; V *Marshall*, b. Dec. 5, 1824, m. Marion Hibbard, Dec. 11, 1849, resides Hermitage, Wy. co., N, Y.; VI *William*, b. April 15, 1826, m. Caroline McReynolds, Dec. 18, 1852, resides at Ellicottville, Cattaraugus co., N. Y.; VII *Alvira*, b. Feb. 5, 1829, m. John Boddy, Sept. 1, 1848, resides at Hermitage, Wy. co., N. Y.; VIII *John*, b. Dec. 24, 1832, m. Sylpha Newkirk, March 7; 1858, resides at Portage, Kalamazo co., Mich.; IX *Hannah Abigail*, b. Feb. 8, 1836, m. William Boddy, May 1, 1856, lives at Hermitage, Wy. co., N. Y.

Resides at Hermitage, Wyoming co., N. Y.

SAMUEL, b. July 28, 1797; m. Jerusha Donaghy, Feb. 26, 1817; had Lovice and William Donaghy.

Resides at Spring, Crawford co., Pa. Mrs. Wetmore's mother, Mrs. Olive Donaghy, is still living at the advanced age of 102 years, retaining her mental and physical faculties to a remarkable degree.

CYNTHIA, b. Sept. 19, 1799; m. Daniel Driggs, Nov. 12, 1825: m. 2d, Nathan Hatfield, Nov. 12, 1829; had, I *Hannah Louisa*, b. Feb. 24, 1830, m. James H. Howe, May 9, 1850, resides Mayville, Huron co., O.; II *William Henry*, b. April 9, 1832, m. Margaret Evans, Jan. 7, 1857; III *Harriet Emily*, b. Dec. 1833, m. George Rowcliff, March 25, 1853, resides at Peru, Huron co., O.; IV *Charles Nathan*, b. May 29, 1836, d. Feb. 11, 1849.

Mr. Hatfield Sen. d. Feb. 2, 1847; his wid. d. Nov. 6, 1855.

WILLIAM, b. Feb. 2, 1801; m. Sally Cossitt, Feb. 22, 1823, had William Chauncy, Sarah Amelia, Henry Augustus, Harriet Euphrania, Emily Jane, Caroline Marion, Frances Cordelia.

He d. Sept. 10, 1858, in his 58th year.

NANCY, b. July 20, 1802; m. Ebenezer Lockwood Selleck, April 3, 1822; had, I *Morris*, b. June 9, 1824; m. Olive Shaw, Nov. 14, 1849, resides at Adrian, Mich.; II *Nancy Matilda*, b. Sept. 12, 1826, m. John Lewis Knapp, April 2, 1851, resides Adrian, Mich.; III *James*, b. June 22, 1828: m. Kate Yakely, Feb. 5, 1857, resides at Adrian, Mich.; IV *Ruth*, b. July 15, 1831, d. June 18, 1850; V *Mary Lousia*, b. Dec. 18, 1833; VI *Cynthia Elizabeth,* b. Dec. 27, 1835, d. Feb. 19, 1845; VII *Charlotte*, b. May 3, 1838, m. Hiram Knapp, March 26, 1854, resides Adrian, Mich.; VIII *Harriet Irene*, b. Oct. 28, 1840; IX *Charles Wetmore*, b. March 9, 1843; X *Homer Elisha*, b. Oct. 17, 1846.

Mr. Selleck Sen. resides at Adrian, Mich.

CLARINDA, b. at Paris, Oneida co., N. Y., April 2, 1804; m. Jan. 29, 1824, Oren Green of P., b. in Litchfield, N. Y., April 16, 1802; had, I *Horace*, b. in Wethersfield, Wyoming co., N. Y., March 4, 1825, d. April 25, 1827: II *Elisha W.*, b. Jan. 21, 1827, m. Laura Wells, Oct. 11, 1852; had 1st, Frank V., b. Nov. 13, 1853, 2d, Clarinda W., b. Nov. 31, 1858, res. Spring, Pa.: III *Charles H.*, b. April, 11, 1828, m. Colisla Casler, Sept. 6, 1849; had 1st, John C., b. May 27, 1850, 2d, Mary, b. Nov. 20, 1854, d. Dec. 10, 1855; resides Spring, Pa.: IV *Helen C.*, b. Sept. 22, 1829: V *Mary M.*, b. in Spring, Pa.,

July 18, 1831, m. Charles C. Kindall, May 1, 1852; had 1st, Adelaide, b. Feb. 26, 1853, 2d, Frank O., b. Dec. 17, 1857, 3d, William W., b. April 27, 1860, res. Spring, Pa.: VI *Henry I.*, b. in Spring, Pa., Jan. 7, 1833, m. Nancy Thompson, April 1, 1857, had Florence M., b. Feb. 26, 1858, res. Maquoketa, Iowa: VII *Hannah Louisa*, b. in Spring, Pa., May 14, 1834, m. Ira Williams, Aug. 14, 1851, had 1st, Eathon Elisha, b. March 18, 1854, 2d, James Homer, b. Feb. 26, 1856, 3d, Abby, b. July 4, 1858, resides Laure, Marion co., Ohio: VIII *George W.*, b. in Spring, Pa., Feb. 6, 1836; IX *Emily M.*, b. in Spring, Pa., June 14, 1838; X *Emory O.*, b. in Spring, Pa., June 14, 1838.

Mr. Oren Green d. April 17, 1838; she resides in Spring, Pa.

LOUISA, b. Dec. 15, 1806; m. Dec. 30, 1822; d. Aug. 5, 1833.

PATTY MARILLA, b. Feb. 15, 1809; m. April 15, 1829, Andrew Mills, b. May 9, 1805; had I *Charles*, b. Jan. 18, 1830, d. April 3, 1857; II *Charlotte Louisa*, b. May 19, 1833, m. June 2, 1852, Kendrick G. Fairchild, b. Nov. 10, 1827; had Adelbert Mills, b. March 13, 1855: III *Andrew Wetmore*, b. Nov. 30, 1836; IV *Harriet Maria*, b. July 25, 1839; V *Edgar Delos*, b. July 8, 1844.

Andrew Mills resides in Clinton, Oneida co., N. Y.

JOHN, b. May 7, 1811; m. Hearty Parkhurst, March 23, 1831, d. s. p. Nov. 17, 1845; m. 2d, Nov. 24, 1846, Mary Jerusha Risley, b. June 27, 1828, had George Sanford, Charles Morris, Ruth Maretta, John E.

Resides at Maquoketa, Iowa.

EMILY, b. July 19, 1813; m. James Thurstin, April 3, 1839; had I *Wayne Wetmore*, b. Oct. 26, 1840; II *Albert Marion*, b. Feb. 22, 1843; III *Harrison Eugene*, b. Dec. 21, 1849.

Resides in Paris (Sauquoit P. O.), Oneida co, N. Y.

Children of BENJAMIN,

Son of Capt. John, Son of Ebenezer.

ELNATHAN, b. in M., Dec. 6, 1797; m. April 25, 1843, Elizabeth Bovee, b. Oct. 25, 1797.

Resided in Monroe, Ashtabula co., Ohio.

BENJAMIN, b. Sept. 7, 1799; unmarried.

Resides in Kelloggsville, Ashtabula co., O., where he has been postmaster for many years.

EBENEZER, b. Sept. 2, 1801; m. Dec. 22, 1847, Lovinia Bovee, of Coneaut, Ashtabula co., O., b. Oct. 18, 1809.

ELIZA, b. Nov. 2, 1803; m. in Monroe, O., Dec. 1822, Daniel Bennet, b. in Woodstock, Mass., June 5, 1797; had, I *Edwin*, b. Dec. 16, 1823, m. Judith Masterson, May 10, 1855, at Stevens Point, Wis., had Eliza, b. Aug. 1858, d. July 1, 1859: II *Orville*, b. May 15, 1827, m. Feb. 23, 1858, Ellen Dunn, b. June 3, 1832; had *Charles Henry*, b. June 6, 1859; IV *Emeline*, b. Nov. 6, 1829, unmarried; V *John*, b. Sept. 28, 1836, m. April 9, 1859, Clarissa Thains, of Beloit, Wis., b. in Frederickton, N. B., had Daniel James, b. Dec. 9, 1859.

Resides at Beloit, Wisconsin.

SALLY, b. Feb. 28, 1806.

MARY, b. Feb. 22, 1808; d. March 11, 1844.

MARGARET, b. April 10, 1810; m. Sept. 18, 1833, Peter Bovee, b. March 13, 1806; had I *Hannah Wetmore*, b. Dec. 10, 1834, d. May 21, 1859; II *John Emory*, b. May 24, 1836; III *Margaret Amelia*, b. Oct. 26, 1838; IV *Abigail Maria*, b. Jan. 7, 1841, d. April 13, 1844.

He resides at Kingsville, Ashtabula co., O.   She d. July 13, 1843.

ABIGAIL, b. March 1, 1812; d. Oct. 27, 1841.

JOHN, b. July 18, 1814; m. Sept. 8, 1850, Juliet Sands, b. July 26, 1826; had Henry Elnathan, Thomas Ebenezer, Ida Thankful.

LUCRETIA, b. Sept. 9, 1816.

HANNAH, b. Oct. 13, 1818; d. Oct. 13, 1832.

SEVENTH GENERATION.

Children of ELISHA.

Son of Elisha, Son of Capt. John, Son of Ebenezer.

MASON HATFIELD, b. Oct. 10, 1816; m. Lucy Ann Risley, April 16, 1839. Res. St. Charles, Wiona co., Minn.

WILLIAM HENRY, b. Dec. 22, 1818.

HARRIET MARIA, b. May 17, 1821; m. George Goodale, Dec. 27, 1842; had I *Mary Jane,* b. Oct. 8, 1843; II *Elizabeth Livona,* b. July 13, 1848; III *George Henry Irvin,* b. Dec. 23, 1851.

She resides at Litchfield, Herkimer co., N. Y. He d. July 20, 1854.

HENRY ELISHA, b. Nov. 25, 1822; m. Margeretta Bouck; he d. Oct. 25, 1852.

WILLIAM HATFIELD, b. Nov. 8, 1828; d. Oct. 2, 1830.

NATHAN IRVIN, b. Aug. 26, 18—; m. Cynthia Root, Jan. 1, 1856.

MARY LOUISA, b. July 23, 1834; m. Robert Clarke Cook, Dec. 27, 1858; res. Frankfort, Herk. co., N. Y.

ANN ELIZABETH, b. June 13, 1836; res. New Grafenberg, N. Y.

CHARLES WHITMAN, b. Aug. 29, 1837; res. Frankfort, N. Y.

JAMES HOWARD, b. Jan, 17, 1840; res. Frankfort, N. Y.

JOHN WALLACE, b. June 19, 1842; res. Frankfort, N. Y.

SARAH JANE, b. April 18, 1844; res. New Grafenberg.

Children of SAMUEL,

Son of Elisha, Son of Capt. John, Son of Ebenezer.

LOVICE, b. May 31, 1821; m. Lyman Hall, April 12, 1838; had I *Scott W.,* b. Jan. 11, 1839; II *Harriet L.,* b. Feb. 22, 1843, d. June 7, 1851; III *Julia J.,* b. Oct. 14, 1845; IV *Louisa L.,* b. July, 16, 1854, d. June 24, 1855; V *Catherine D.,* b. Nov. 30, 1857; res. Spring, Pa.

WILLIAM DONAGHY, b. July 21, 1827; m. Harriet E. Ward, Feb. 2, 1848; res. Spring, Pa.

Children of WILLIAM,

Son of Elisha, Son of Capt. John, Son of Ebenezer.

WILLIAM CHAUNCEY, b. Feb. 11, 1824; m. Cornelia A. Bailey, Aug. 26, 1857; res. Concord, Jackson co., Ohio.

SARAH ARMIDA, b. Aug. 22, 1825; m. William Ferguson, Jan. 31, 1854; res. Oriskany Fall, Oneida co., N. Y.

HENRY AUGUSTUS, b. Nov. 12; 1827; res. Concord, Jackson co., Michigan.

HARRIET EUPHRONIA, b. Dec. 15, 1829; m. Alex. E. Mason, Dec. 24, 1849; res. Washington Mills P. O., Oneida co., N. Y.

EMILY JANE, b. Oct. 18, 1831; m. Nathan E. Millington, Sept. 28, 1859; res. Russia, Herk: co., N. Y.

CAROLINE MARION, b. Jan. 15, 1834; res. Paris, N. Y.

FRANCES CORDELIA, b. April 13, 1836. "   "

Children of John,

Son of Elisha, Son of Capt. John, Son of Ebenezer.

GEORGE SANFORD, b. Sept. 4, 1847.

CHARLES MORRIS, b. April 24, 1850.

RUTH MARETTA, b. Aug. 24, 1851.

JOHN E., b. May 17, 1857.

JAMES A., b. May 15, 1859.

Children of JOHN,

Son of Benjamin, Son of Capt. John, Son of Ebenezer.

HENRY ELNATHAN, b. in Ohio, Dec: 23, 1851.

THOMAS EBENEZER. b. in Ohio, March 14, 1854.

IDA THANKKFUL, b. in Ohio, Feb. 14, 1858.

EIGHTH GENERATION.

Daughter of NATHAN IRVIN,

Son of Elisha, Son of Elisha, Son of Capt. John, Son of Ebenezer.

IDA JANE, b. Jan. 18, 1858.

DESCENDANTS OF THOMAS, SON OF THOMAS.

THIRD GENERATION.

Children of THOMAS,

Second Son and Fifth Child of Thomas and Sarah (Hall) Whitmore.

ELIZABETH, b. in Middletown Sept. 2, 1686-7 ; m. June 16, 1709,
her cousin Ephraim son of Josiah and Elizabeth (Wetmore)
Adkins, b. Mar. 9, 1685; had I *Thomas*, b. April 5, 1710 ; II
Ephraim, b. July 18, 1712, d. June 27, 1713 ; III *Elizabeth*,
b. Dec. 6, 1714, d. May 30, 1730 (1750 ?) ; IV *Ephraim* 2d,
b. Mar. 22, 1717, d. Feb. 26, 1735 ; V *Naome*, b. June 6, 1719 ;
VI *Ebenezer*, b. Oct. 1, 1721; VII *James*, b. April 9, 1724 ;
VIII *George*, b. Dec. 26, 1726.

She d. May 20, 1752 ; her husband d. Dec. 26,
1760.

THOMAS, b. in Middletown Jan. 8, 1689 ; d. Nov. 24, 1711.

We presume he died unmarried, as we find no record
to the contrary; consequently the name ended in his
line with him.

DESCENDANTS OF SAMUEL, SON OF THOMAS.

THIRD GENERATION.

Children of SAMUEL,

Third Son and Seventh Child of Thomas and Sarah (Hall) Whitmore.

MAHITABLE, b. in Middletown Nov. 14, 1689.

SAMUEL, b. in Middletown March 13, 1692; m. June 21, 1722 Hannah Hubbard b. July 21, 1700; had Samuel, Hannah, John, Noah, Mehitable, Sarah, Lois, Joel, Millicent, Mary.

He was a member of the Middlefield society[1] (Middletown); removed with his family to Winchester, Ct., on election day, 1771, where he purchased land. The farm that he then settled still remains in possession of his descendants, as will be seen in the pages following. He died Dec. 30, 1773, and was the first person interred in the old Winchester burying-ground. His wife died in W. June 4, 1794.

MARY, b. in Middletown June 29, 1694.

BENJAMIN, b. in M. May 17, 1696; m. Sept. 24, 1719, Marcy dau. of Samuel and Mary Roberts; had Benjamin, Josiah, Marcy, Mary, Anna, Abigail, Berthia (dau.), Abner.

We find the following in relation to him in *Mid. Hist. Sketches*, under head of Middlefield Society.

[1] May ye 2 A D 1773. Furthermore, Samuel Wetmore 1st and his wife Hannah, together with Mahitable their daughter, were admitted into this church by A letter from ye ch h at Middlefield. Attest, Joshua Knapp, Pastor.—*Winchester First Ch. Rec.*

* * * * When the society was first incorporated in Oct. 1744, there were more than fifty families living within its limits. The names of the heads of these families were, Samuel Allen Sen., Samuel Allen Jun., Ephraim and Obadiah Allen, Thomas Alvord, Nathaniel and Joseph Bacon, John Bartlett, John Birdsey, John Brown; Abraham and Edward Camp, John Gibson Sen. and John Gibson Jun., Joseph, David and Robert Coe, Gideon and Thomas Cooke, John and Isaac Dowd, Daniel Driggs, Jeremiah Guild, Ebenezer and Joseph Hale, Eliakim Hall, Samuel Stow, Hawley and Ebenezer Hubbard, Jeremiah Leaming, Benjamin Miller and Benj. Miller Jun., Joseph Miller Sen., Ichabod, Amos and David Miller, Moses Parsons, John Rockwell, Daniel Stow, David Strickland and David Strickland Jun., Stephen Turner Sen., Samuel Warner, Samuel Wetmore Sen., Benjamin Wetmore Sen., and Benj. Wetmore Jun., Beriah, Joseph, Thomas, Daniel, Caleb, Prosper, and Josiah Wetmore Jun., and John Titus Whitmore, the aggregate list of all these persons exceeded £3000.

Almost all these persons were farmers, and soon after the incorporation of the society, the population reached a point from which it did not vary greatly for many years. * * *

THOMAS, b. in M. Aug. 26, 1698; m. Dec. 11, 1751, Ann Wall (Hale?); had Thomas, Rebecca; m. 2d Rebecca Lewis of Simsbury, May 22, 1754-5; had Ann, Jobe, Phebe, Mindwell, Experience.

Mrs. Ann Hale Wetmore died Sept. 28, 1753.

DANIEL, b. May 9, 1703, in Middletown; m. Aug. 26, 1725, Dorothy Hale; had Increase, Ruth, David, Daniel, Gideon and Elias (twins), Ruth 2d, Jabez.

It appears from record, under head of Benjamin, that he belonged to the Middlefield society.

BETHIAH, b. in M. Jan. 22, 1706-7; m. Joseph Bacon April 20, 1732; had I *Bethiah*, b. June 29, 1733; II *Joseph*, b. May 11, 1735; III *Mahitable*, b. Aug. 24, 1737; IV *Daniel*, b. Dec. 1, 1739; V *Mary*, b. Nov. 24, 1742; VI *Abigail*, b. April 17, 1745; VII *Moses*, b. Oct. 16, 1747.

JABEZ, b. in M. May 14, 1709; m. —; had Oliver.

Descendants of Samuel, son of Thomas.

FOURTH GENERATION.

Children of SAMUEL WETMORE.

Dea. SAMUEL, b. in Middletown, Dec. 24, 1723; m. Feb. 6, 1752 Anna Roberts, of Durham, Ct., b. March 16, 1723; had Abel.

He came, with his father, from the Middlefield society, to Winchester, in 1771. He was one of the first appointed Deacons of the First congregational church of Winchester, and held the office until an advanced age. It is reputed of him that he was a Christian of the old Puritan stamp, possessing a strong mind, a thorough knowledge of the Bible, a firm reverence for the sabbath, and the institutions of the gospel, and was well anchored on the Rock of Ages, which he esteemed the only sure security. The Winchester First church register contains the following record respecting him: "July 26, A. D. 1772. Samuel Wetmore and Anna his wife were admitted members of this chh by a letter from ye chh at Middlefield." He died Sept. 22, 1804, in his 82d year; his wife died March 2, 1809, in her 86th year.

HANNAH, b. in M. Dec. 18, 1725; m. —— Graves; had Maj. Timothy, of Hoosic, and Leves.

JOHN, b. in M., Oct. 27, 1727; m. 1758, Elizabeth Leming;[2] had Elizabeth, Seth, Samuel.

He lived in Torrington. In a book of records, kept by the Rev. Nathaniel Roberts, first pastor of Torrington church, the following entry appears: "John Wetmore and Elizabeth his wife owned Covenant, June 18, 1758." He was killed Aug. 27, 1795, while

[2] Collateral branches of Lemings, were Rev. Jeremiah, an Episcopal clergyman; Mathias m. a Gould; Aaron m. a Grant; Lucy a spinster; Abigail m. a Coe, and Jane m. Marshall.

riding on horseback, on the highway, by the falling of a tree during a heavy thunder storm.

Rev. NOAH, b. in M., April 16, 1730; m. Submit, dau. of Ithiel Russel, of Branford, Ct., b. April 16, 1735; had Irena, Hannah, Ann, Noah, Appolos, Samuel Ithiel.

He graduated at Yale College, 1757; studied for the ministry; was ordained in Nov. 1760. The Church records of Torrington contain the registry of children of Noah Wetmore, being baptized there in 1761 and 1768, which leads us to think that he resided there for a time after his ordination. On the 25th of Nov., 1770, he was settled as the first pastor of the Congregational church at Bethel, Fairfield co., Ct., where he ministered till 1784. In April, 1786, he was called to the First presbyterian church at Brook Haven, Long Island, to succeed the Rev. Benjamin Tallmadge, who had deceased the fifth of February previous; here he faithfully labored in the cause of his Lord and Master, till his death, March 9, 1796. His funeral sermon was preached at Huntington, L. I., by the Rev. William Schenck,[3] from the text: "That ye be not slothful, but followers of them, who through faith and patience inherit the promises." *Heb.* vi, 12. In commenting upon his life and character, Mr. Schenck said:

And here, though I am not over fond of funeral encomiums, yet upon this occasion it is proper to observe a few things; not so much to celebrate our departed friend's virtues, as to excite in us his survivors a laudable imitation of them. I know little of Mr. Wetmore's ancestry; only that he descended from worthy, pious parents, and a family remarkable for promoting the interest of religion.

As a preacher of the gospel his sermons were well composed, and animated with a sacred regard to the honor of

[3]*An Attempt to Delineate the Character and Reward of Faithful Servants of Christ*, in a SERMON, preached at the Funeral of the Rev. Noah Wetmore, A. M., late Minister at Brook Haven, L. I., March 10, 1796, by William Schenck, A. B. and M. V. D.—*David Frothingham, Sag Harbor.*

his divine Master, and the salvation of immortal souls. In the pulpit, you well know my brethren, he spoke the word in all plainness and godly simplicity, and labored hard to win souls for Christ.

In private social life, he excelled as an agreeable, instructive companion. Upon religious subjects he appeared judicious, and distinguished well between true and false marks of religion : the doctrines he taught, and duties he pressed upon others, were happily exemplified in his own life and conversation, agreeably to the apostle's charge to Timothy, "He was an example to believers, in word, in charity, in conversation, in faith, in purity." In domestic life his character shone with peculiar lustre, as a tender and affectionate husband, a prudent, cautious, indulgent father, a compassionate master, and faithful friend. And shall we lament his departure? Nay! rather let us be earnest to live, and die the death of the righteous, that our latter end may be peace.

Thompson, in his *History of Long Island*, says of him, that :

He was a gentleman of respectable talents, and experienced a powerful influence among his clerical brethren. His social disposition made his company the delight of every circle, and it may safely be said, that few clergymen were ever more beloved.

His wife survived him till Aug. 17, 1798 (9 ?).

MAHITABLE, b, in M., Aug. 5, 1732; m. Capt. Asa Upson, of New Cambridge (Farmington), Ct., Aug. 14, 1776 (*Winchester Ch. Rec.*); died s. p. 1816, aged 84.

SARAH, b. in M., March 31, 1734; m. Nov. 16, 1758, James, son of Nathaniel and Jane Bacon; had *Sarah*, b. June 16, 1760.

Mrs. Bacon d. at Torrington, —, 1803, æ. 69.

LOIS, b, in M., March 6, 1736; m. Jan. 7, 1762, John, son of Caleb Wetmore.

For her issue see forward, under head of John, son of Caleb, son of Izrahiah Sen.

Descendants of Samuel, son of Thomas.

JOEL, b. in M., March 9 (7?), 1738; m. Sarah Lyman, Nov. 23, 1765; had Olive, Ebenezer Lyman, Milicent, John Pomeroy.

He resided in Torrington, Ct. In a registry kept by the Rev. Nathaniel Roberts, of T., the following entry stands: "Joel Wetmore and wife owned Covenant, March 10, 1765." His wife Sarah (says a correspondent well informed in the genealogy of this branch of the family) was probably the daughter of Deacon Ebenezer Lyman, of Torrington.

He d. in T. Feb. 1814, æ. 75; his wife d. 1832, æ. 92.

MILICENT, b. in M., Sept. 15, 1739.

MARY, b. in M., July 23, 1741; m. according to the following in First church Winchester records: "1775 October ye 8, Abraham Loomis of Torrington and Mary Wetmore of Winchester were married." She m. 2d, a Baldwin.

Note. —— —— Wetmore, of Torringford, m. Abigail, dau. of Samuel Hayden, of Windsor, Ct., b. Dec. 21, 1745.—*Dr. Stiles's Hist. of Windsor, Ct.*

Children of BENJAMIN.

BENJAMIN, b. in Middletown, March 22, 1719-20; m. Jemima Hurlburt, June 24, 1744.

JOSIAH, b. in M., Aug. 21, 1721; m. Esther Caldwell, of Hartford, Ct., Nov. (May?) 11, 1745.

MARCY, b. in M., Feb. 14, 1725-6.

MARY, b. in M., Aug. 24, 1727; m. Akimaz Spencer, Sept. 15, 1743; had I *Elizabeth*, b. May 21, 1744; II *Moses*, b. Jan. 5, 1746; III *Mary*, b. April 1, 1753.

ANNA, b. in M., June 23, 1730.

ABIGAIL, b. in M., June 30, 1732; m. Jonas Burt, of Worcester, Mass., July 25, 1752.

BETHIAH (dau.), b. in M., Oct. 2, 1734.

ABNER, b. in M., May 2, 1736.

We have been unable to find any further record of the descendants of the above Benjamin Sen.

9

Children of THOMAS.

THOMAS, b. 1752.

REBECCA, b. 1753.

ANN, b. June 5, 1755.

JOBE, b. Sept. 10, 1756; d. young.

PHEOBE, b. March 16, 1758.

MINDWELL, b. Oct. 9, 1760.

EXPERIENCE, b. March 11, 1765.

We have no further record of the descendants of Thomas, son of Samuel, son of Thomas.

Children of DANIEL.

INCREASE, born June 2, 1726; m. March 24, 1746, Sarah, dau. of Daniel Chilson, of Middletown, Ct. ; had Ruth, Sarah, Hope, Dorothy, Elias and Ezra (twins), John, Chloe, Eunice.

RUTH, b. Sept. 12, 1727; d. same day.

DAVID, b. in M., March 17, 1728-9; m. Sarah Stanton, of Wallingford, Ct., Sept. 16, 1756; had Elihu, Hannah, David, Eunice.

DANIEL, b. Nov. 15, 1730; m. Hannah Center, March 20, 1755; had Jesse, Martha, Elizabeth, Thankful, Hannah, Milicent, Dorathy.

GIDEON, } b. Aug. 21, 1734; d. young.
ELIAS, } b.   "   "   "

RUTH 2d, b. Aug. 11, 1737; m. Joseph Washburn, Sept. 21, 1763.

JABEZ, b. ——; m. Esther Whitmore, Oct. 24, 1763; had Jabez, Clarissa, Gideon, Jacob, Esther, Nicholas, Howell, Issac, Daniel, Parmelia, Rhoda.

Son of JABEZ.

OLIVER, b. Feb, 4, 1737-8.

FIFTH GENERATION.

Son of Deacon SAMUEL,

Son of Samuel.

ABEL, b. in Middletown, Ct., April 6, 1753; m. May 12, 1774, Jerusha, dau. of John and Jerusha Hills, b. in Winchester, Nov. 26, 1755; had Truman Spencer, Anna Jerusha, John, Samuel; she d. in W., April 30, 1780; he m. 2d, Mary (Smith) Allen (wid.), April 13, 1783, had Abel and Elisha.

He was reputed in his time a good scholar, though he had never had the advantages of a collegiate course, owing to his father having lost a large portion of his property in the depreciation of the old continental money. He was considered one of the best informed persons and "the greatest head piece" living in Winchester at his time. He died of epilepsy, May 20, 1796, æ. 43; his widow m. a Mr. Loveland.

Children of JOHN,

Son of Samuel.

ELIZABETH, b. —; bap. in Torrington Oct. 15, 1758; m. David Alvord of Winchester, Sept. 8, 1774; had I *Persis*, b. in W. Dec. 18, 1775; II *Ursula*, b. in W. Feb. 13, 1778.

SETH, b. in Torrington March 20, 1761; bap. March 30, 1761; m. Dec. 9, 1779, Lois, dau. of Col. Ozias Bronson of W.; had John, Seth, Abigail, Artemisia, Alphonzo, Salmon B., Pythagoras, Lois Malinda; m. 2d, Lucy Doolittle; had Lucy Elizabeth, and George Clinton.

He resided in Winchester till 1805, when he removed to central New York, and died at Corners Village, Canajoharie, April 16, 1836. An obituary notice of him contains the following :

Died at his residence, Canajoharie, N. Y., the Hon. Seth
Wetmore, aged 75. He was one of the first and leading
Democrats of Litchfield county, Ct. ; was fined for sedition
under the Alien and Sedition laws, for urging the right of
universal suffrage; he lived to see the universal prevalence
of the principle he early advocated; he filled many offices
of trust and profit under the government; was three times
a member of the legislature of Connecticut. After his removal to the state of New York, he held the office of magistrate, sheriff, and judge of Montgomery county; was
one of the most active and leading men of the Democratic
party who brought about the extension of elective fran-
chise; died as he lived, a Democratic Republican of the
old school, plain and unassuming in his manners, firm and
consistent in his principles.

SAMUEL, b. Dec. 31, 1764 (1763?); m. May 15, 1788, Hannah
Griswold, b. in Wethersfield April 8, 1767; had Selima, Leaming, Ruby, Almeda, Candace, Calvary, Samuel, Hannah, Harriet, Hubert, Griswold, Clarrissa.

He was a captain in the Connecticut state militia;
removed to Vernon, Oneida county, N. Y., in 1800;
held the office of justice of the peace about twenty
years; was county supervisor for many years, and
served one or more sessions in the legislature of his
adopted state; was one of the early appointed deacons
of the first Baptist church formed in Vernon. He died
Nov. 8, 1824; his wife died July 17, 1839.

Children of Rev. NOAH,

Son of Samuel.

JUNIA, b. —; bap. in Torrington March 30, 1761.[4]

IRENA, b. Sept. 11, 1762; m. Dr. David Woodhul, of Setauket,
L. I. Dr. Woodhull was g. g. grandson of Richard Woodhull,[5]

---

[4] Junia, bap. Mar. 30, 1761, child of Noah Wetmore.—*Torrington Church
Record*, Rev. Nath. Roberts pastor.

[5] The family from whom this gentleman was descended is said to be very
ancient, and may be traced to an individual who came from Normandy

who settled on Long Island in 1656. He died without issue at Newton, L. I. She died Aug. 11, 1848, in her 86th year, with the full assurance of meeting in a brighter world friends loved and lost.

HANNAH, b. Jan. 22, 1765; d. Nov. 29, 1795.

NOAH, b. May 4, 1767; m. Winfred Smith Feb. 14, 1792; had Appolos Russel, William Henry, Appolos Russel 2d, David Woodhull, Irena Winfred; m. 2d, Magdalen Brower Dec. 11, 1816.

He removed to the city of New York, when about 45 years of age, where he became widely known, and where he enjoyed the confidence and esteem of his

with William the Conquerer, in 1066. The name was originally written Wodhull, and continued to be so spelled for many years after the removal of the family in this country.

Richard, the common ancestor in America, was born at Thenford, North-hamptonshire, England, Sept. 13, 1620. The precise time of his arrival in this country is not known, but it must have been as early as 1648. The name of his wife was Deborah. His zeal in the cause of English liberty during the protectorate, and the danger to be reasonably apprehended upon the restoration of the monarchy, probably induced him to leave Europe, and seek an asylum in a distant country.

He is first known in the town of Jamaca, L. I., where his name appears associated with the early settlers of that place. But disliking the policy and measures of the Dutch government, he left the western part of the Island and seated himself permanently, at Setauket, then called Cromwell Bay, or Ashford, and became one of the most useful and valuable citizen of that place. His particular knowledge in surveying and drawing conveyances, rendered his services invaluable at that early period of the settlement, and his name is found associated with most of the transactions of the town during his life. His death occured Oct. 1690, leaving issue, Richard, Nathaniel, Deborah. The second son d. unm. in 1680. Deborah m. Capt. John Lawrence of Newton, and d. Jan. 6, 1742. Richard was born Oct. 9, 1649, and like his father was an intelligent and useful man. He was chosen a magistrate, and retained the office till near his death, Oct. 18, 1699, having survived his father only about nine years. His knowledge and integrity endeared him to the people, and he died much lamented. His wife was Temperance, dau. of Rev. Jonah Fordham of Southampton, and sister of the Rev. Josiah Fordham, who preached awhile at Setauket, after the death of the Rev. Mr. Brewster, in 1690. His will is dated Oct. 13, 1699, and was proved before Chief Justice William Smith, May 28, 1700. His children (named in said will) are Richard, Nathaniel, John, Josiah, Dorothy, and Temperance.

By an original letter now in the possession of his descendants, it appears that a relationship existed with Lord Crewe, the Bishop of Durham, and other respectable families in England. This letter is as follows:

"Sr. I was heartly glad to find by yr letter, that it has pleased God to blesse and prosper your family, and that you received the small present [crest and arms of the family] I sent you some time since wh I thought

fellow citizens to a great degree. He died July 18,
1848, in his 82d year. An obituary notice of him before us says :

He came to this city about the year 1808, to take the
superintendence of the New York hospital, in which charge
he remained thirty years, or more, discharging it to great
acceptance as the general kind respect of the medical profession uniformly testified. His Christian spirit and character, combined with those of his excellent consort, rendered his intercourse and influence with the children of
disease and affliction most salutary.

had been lost. For our country news, take this account. My father departed this life, Dec. 12, 1679, and as he lived well, soe he had great joy at
his death, with a Longing to leave this world. I have six children, but
noe sonne, it having pleased God to take him in ye 15th yeare of his age a
man growne and very hopefull, God's will be done. My brother Walgrave
hath left one sonne, who stands heire both to ye Bishop of Duresme [Dur-
ham] and myself for Thenford. Yr cozen Wodhull lives very well, is a
justice of peace and very well beloved ; the three brothers live all together
with the greatest kindnesse that can bee. My uncle Sol died last yeare and
is buried at Hinton ; my uncle Thomas a yeare before ; my uncle Nathaniel
is still living. I have enclosed the papers you desire. My service to all
my cozens. I rest your loving friend and kinsman."
　"Steane, Sept. 5, 1687."　　　　　　　　　　　　　　　　CREWE.
　(Superscribed) "ffor my Loving kinsmans Richard Wodhull Esq."
　To his eldest son, Richard, who was born Nov. 2, 1691, the testator de-
vised his paternal estate in Setauket, now in possession of his descendant
of the sixth generation. He, like his father, was a magistrate for many
years, and was in all respects a useful and highly exemplary man. He
married Mary, daughter of John Homan of the same town, by whom he
had issue Richard, Mary, John, Nathan, Stephen, Henry and Pheobe.
His death took place Nov. 24, 1767, aged 76, and his widow died in 1768.
His will bears date April 16, 1760. His eldest daughter Mary was born
April 11, 1711 ; m. Sept. 30, 1734, Jonathan Thompson, and was the grandmother of the compiler of this work (Hist. Long Isl.). She died Jan. 30,
1800, aged 88. Her sister died unm. in 1734. Henry became a lunatic, so
continued till his death in 1770. Richard 3d, the eldest son, commonly
called Justice Woodhull, took the paternal estate at Setauket. He was born
Oct. 11, 1712, and m. Margaret, dau. of Edmund Smith of Smithtown. He
was among the most useful men, and filled the office of magistrate for a
large portion of his life. His death occurred Oct. 13, 1788, but his widow
survived till Oct. 11, 1803, when she died at the age of 80 years (leaving
issue) * * * *
　Nathan Woodhul 3d, son of Richard 3d, was born July 5, 1720; married
Joanna Mills, and died at Setauket, where he spent his life as a merchant,
Oct. 27, 1804 ; his wife having died Oct. 5, 1783 : issue, Nathan, Nathaniel,
David (the subject of the above notice), Sarah, and Pheobe (Thomp. Hist. L.
I., pp. 397-9, 401). Gen. Nathaniel Woodhull, the patriot of the Revolu-
tion, was grandson of the second Richard.—Compiler.

He consistently displayed a simplicity and integrity of character commending itself to the whole circle of his acquaintance, which was evidently founded on firm religious principle.

He was born near Danbury, Ct., where his father was settled as a minister of the Congregational church, whence he removed and became the pastor of a church in Suffolk county, Long Island, where he died. On removing to New York; Mr. Wetmore united with the Presbyterian church in Cedar street, under the pastoral care of the Rev. Dr. Romeyn, then first formed. He subsequently, on account of the nearness of his residence, joined the Presby-. terian church in Pearl street, of which he was for a number of years a prominent elder in the session.

For sixteen or seventeen years he has been a member of the Collegiate reformed Dutch church, and has been for a number of years a ruling elder. Under the religious influences which guided his early education, his character became formed and developed in a consistency and symmetry through the whole course of his life. He was strongly attached to the doctrines of grace, as presented in the standards of the Presbyterian and Dutch reformed churches, and he embraced and adhered to them, not in mere speculative regard to them as orthodox truths, but embodied them in the constant culture of Christian experience and in the exercise of his Christian hope and service. He was a man of prayer, a lover of the house and people of God, and was ready in the measure of his opportunity and ability for every good work in the Master's cause. His venerable personal appearance, combined with the weight of his acknowledged Christian character, marked him to the view of all around, *as an old disciple*, a *father in Israel*.

During the brief illness which ended in his death, he firmly rested on those precious truths which were so dear to him in life, and calmly and peaceably died in the exercise of that "hope which is cast as an anchor within the veil, both sure and steadfast." "Mark the perfect man, and behold the upright; for the end of that man is peace."

APPOLOS, b. Dec. 14, 1771 ; m. Dec. 29, 1797, Mary, dau. of Isaac Ketchum, b. Oct. 18, 1773 ; had Appolos Edwards, Hannah, Oliver, Harry, Maria, Augustus, William Walter, Walter 2d.

He d. May 6, 1833 ; she d. May 3, 1857.

SAMUEL ITHIEL, b. Dec. 30, 1774; m. Liberty (Lybia?), dau. of Dr. Benjamin Youngs Prime; had Ebenezer Walter, Julia Ann, Maria, Erastus, Egbert, Cornelia L.

He d. Dec. 31, 1823; his widow d. May 20, 1855. Dr. Prime, the father of Mrs. Lybia Wetmore, was a patriot of the Revolution, and did much by his counsels and writings to bring about an independent and confident spirit among the people, which finally led to the throwing off the yoke of the mother country. Thompson in his *History of Long Island*, vol. I, p. 479, says:

Dr. Benjamin Youngs Prime, son of the Rev. Ebenezer Prime, was born here,[6] 1733, graduated at Princeton, 1751, and in '56 and '57, was employed a tutor in the college. He subsequently entered upon a course of medical studies with Dr. *Jacob Ogden*, of Jamaica, L. I. After finishing his preparatory studies, and spending several years in the practice of physic, he relinquished his extensive business, and with a view of qualifying himself still more, sailed for Europe. In the course of the voyage the vessel was attacked by a French privateer, and the Doctor was slightly wounded in the encounter.

He attended some of the most celebrated schools in London, Edinburgh and Paris, making an excursion to Moscow. He was honored with a degree at most of the institutions which he visited, and was much noticed for his many accomplishments. On his return to America, he established himself in the city of New York, where he acquired a high reputation: but on the entry of the British troops, in Sept. 1776, he was compelled to abandon his business and prospects, taking refuge with his family in Connecticut. He was a diligent student, and made himself master of several languages, in all which he could converse or write with equal ease. Although driven from his home, he indulged his pen with caustic severity upon the enemies of his country, and did much to raise the hope and stimulate the exertions of his fellow citizens. Soon after his return from Europe, he married Mary, widow of the Rev. Mr. Greaton, a woman of superior mind and acquirements, and peace being restored, he settled as a

[6] Huntington, L. I.

physician in his native place, where he enjoyed a lucrative practice, and the highest esteem of all who knew him, until his death, Oct. 31, 1791. His widow survived more than 40 years, and died at the extreme age of 91 years, in March, 1835. By her Dr. Prime had sons Ebenezer and Nathaniel, and daughters Libia, Nancy and Mary.

The mother of Dr. Prime was Mary, daughter of John and grand daughter of the celebrated Rev. John Wheelright, who came to Boston in 1636, who in 1637, with his sister-in-law Ann Hutchinson, was expelled from the colony for preaching *Antinomian* errors.[7] She went to Rhode Island, from thence removed to the Dutch settlements in New York, where she, with her son Francis, and her son-in-law, Mr. Collins, with the rest of the family, were killed by the Indians in 1643; he, together with a number of emigrants from Braintree, then a part of Boston, purchased from the aborigines a large tract of land on the then frontier, now constituting a part of Rockingham and Strafford, and established the town of Exeter, N. H., where the first church was organized in 1638, and he became the pastor; subsequently he removed to Wells, where some of his descendants still live. Soon after removing to the latter place, he wrote a letter to the governor of the colony of Massachusetts, acknowledging his errors, and desiring pardon for the offensive language used towards the authorities in his sermon delivered Nov. 1637 (which was the exciting cause of his banishment); he was permitted, by order of the General court, to return to Boston. He was a man of learning; from his family proceeded all the Wheelrights in Massachusetts and New Hampshire.[8]

[7] Antinomians denied civil government to be proved of Christ.
[8] *Mass. Hist. Soc. Coll.*, iii, 138; iv, 87, 89; viii, 6; ix, 22, 27, 48.

10

*Children of JOEL,

Son of Samuel.

OLIVE, b. in Torringford, Ct., March 10, 1765; m. Ezra Hayden, of Windsor, Ct., July 13, 1786; had I *Malinda*, b. July 25, 1787, who m. Levi Joy, of Amherst, Mass.; II *Amanda*, b. May 10, 1792, m. Elijah Mills, of Bloomfield; III *Altumia*, b. April 7, 1794, m. Norman Griswold, of Otsego co., N. Y.

She d. Nov. 1848, æ. 83; he d. July 3, 1819.

EBENEZER LYMAN, b. 1766; bap. in Torrington, Dec. 28, 1766; m. 1795 (Sept.?), Elizabeth Miller, of T.; had Nancy, Lauren, Maria, Amanda, and Louisa.

He spent a long and virtuous life at the town of Torrington, and d. March 3, 1848, æ. 81; his widow d. Sept. 18, 1850, æ. about 80.

MELICENT, b. in Torrington, Ct., Jan. 10, 1772; m. Jan. 1, 1797, Capt. Thomas Watson, b. in New Hartford, Ct., Oct. 15, 1763, son of Levi and Abigail (Ensign) Watson; she d. Sept. 19, 1848; he d. Jan. 23, 1850; had I *Roman*, b. in New Hartford, Sept. 27, 1797, d. unm. at Roseville Ill., Feb. 12, 1848. II *Thomas*, b. in N. H. Feb. 5, 1800; m. Nov. 10, 1829, Emeline Curtiss, b. in N. H. Aug. 3, 1807, dau. of Elizur and Amanda (Steele) Curtiss; res. in West Winstead, Ct., and have 1, Caroline Amanda, b. in N. H., Oct. 7, 1831, m. Dec. 13, 1853, Dr. Gaylord Brown Miller, b. in Torrington July 25, 1831, son of Dea. Thomas A. and Mary (Hudson) Miller, res. in Harwinton, Ct., and have child. Mary Emma, b. in Harw. July 25, 1855, Thomas Watson, b. in Harw. May 3, 1859 : 2, Charlotte Emeline, b. in N. H. Jan. 8, 1835; m. May 20, 1857, Henry Gay, cashier Winsted bank, b. in Salisbury, Ct. April 5, 1834, son of Henry Sanford and Mary (Reed) Gay; have 1 child, Mary Watson, b. June 19, 1860 : 3, Emma Adelaide, b. in N. H. June 30, 1840. III *Hiram*, b. in N. H. Jan. 21, 1802; m. Nov. 10, 1829, Elizabeth Stoughton Ellsworth, b. May —, 1806, dau. of Timothy and Ann Ellsworth; he is a physician, res. at Detroit, Mich.; has 1, Mary Ann Mather, b. Aug. 27, 1830, d. June 16, 1831; 2, Mary Ann Mather 2d, b. May 6, 1832, m. May 15, 1855 Henry B. Chandler of Detroit, one of the proprietors of the *Detroit Free Press ;* 3, Roman, b. March 21,

Descendants of Samuel, son of Thomas.

1834, d. Feb. 7, 1838 ; 4, Ellen Frances, b. March 25, 1836, m. April 29, 1856 Henry W. Nall, she d. April 16, 1857; 5, Roman, b. Jan. 8, 1838, d. Aug. 6, 1841 ; 6, Frederick Roman, b. May 14, 1839, d. Nov. 28, 1857; 7, Elizabeth Caroline, b. Nov. 27, 1841 ; 8, Oliver, b. Sept. 26, 1842, d. Feb. 7, 1844 ; 9, Henry Ellsworth, b. June 30, 1845, d. April 3, 1849.   IV *Melicent Wetmore*, b. in N. H. Dec. 29, 1808; m. Feb. 29, 1836, Augustus E. Bissel, b. Feb. 13, 1805 ; res. in Detroit, a forwarding merchant; has 1, Augustus, b. Jan. 10, 1837, d. Nov. 3, 1838; 2, Henrietta Augusta, b. Oct. 16, 1839; 3, Adam, b. April 5, 1842, d. same day; 4, Edward Watson, b. Sept. 16, 1843 ; 5, George Henry, b. Nov. 4, 1845, d. Aug. 9, 1854 ; 6, Roman Augustus, b. March 16, 1848; 7, Thomas Watson, b. May 25, 1850.   V - *George*, b. in N. H. March 12, 1812 ; m. Sept. 10, 1833 Jane Belden; had 1, Henry Belden, b. Feb. 5, 1837 ; 2, Emorett Victoria, b. May 1, 1838 ; 3, a son, b. Nov. 11, 1839, d. young; 4, Irene Jane, b. Nov. 3, 1840 : m. 2d, July 1, 1847, Sophia White; had 5, Hiram, b. May 2, 1849 ; 6, Sarah Allen, b. April 4, 1851 ; 7, Augustus Edward, b. Aug. 3, 1852; 8, Emeline, b. Dec. 31, 1855 ; Mr. George Watson resides at Roseville, Ill., farmer.

JOHN POMEROY, b. in Norfolk, Litchfield county, Ct., June 15, 1770 ; m. Nov. 1795 Miriom Dibble of Torrington, b. March 28, 1776, d. July 26, 1806, æ. 32 years; had Delia, Fanny, Julia Emeline, Adeline : m. 2d Mirah Atwater, of Burlington, Vt., b. in Cheshire, Ct., April 17, 1782 ; had Mariana, Sally Ann, Frederick P., Sarah M. Whitman, Henry A., Harriet M., William L., Clarissa A., and Russel C.

He removed to Burlington, Vt., where he resided many years, when he changed his residence to Norfolk, St. Lawrence county, N. Y., where he died Aug. 22, 1853, in his 84th year.

SARAH, b. in Torrington; m. Giles Whiting, of T.; had 2 sons.

Children of INCREASE,

Son of Daniel.

RUTH, b. Aug. 11, 1747.

SARAH, b. April 12, 1749.

HOPE.

DOROTHY.

ELIAS, d. young. } twins.
EZRA.

CHLOE.

EUNICE.

Children of DAVID,

Son of Daniel.

ELIHU, b. July 23, 1757: m. ——; had Norman, Bertha, David, Elihu, Lydia, Noble.

HANNAH, b. Dec. 25, 1758.

DAVID, b. Sept. 16, 1760.

EUNICE.

Children of DANIEL,

Son of Daniel.

JESSE, b. Dec. 1, 1755; m. Temperance Hall, of Middletown, June 24, 1784; had Nancy, Collins, Polly, William, Comfort, Horace.

He removed to Ashtabula, Ohio, in 1818, where he died in 1826; his wife died the same year.

MARTHA, b. Dec. 29, 1757.

ELIZABETH, Jan. 15, 1760.

THANKFUL, b. Sept. 30, 1761; m. Jonathan Gilbert, Dec. 5, 1785; had I *Lucy*, b. Nov. 3, 1786; II *Prudence*, b. Oct. 28, 1788; III *Hannah*, b. Aug. 2, 1790; and 5 others.

HANNAH, b. May 15, 1763.

MILICENT, b. Oct. 17, 1766.

DOROTHY.

Children of JABEZ,

Son of Daniel.

JABEZ, b. Aug. 7, 1766.

CLARISSA, b. May 30, 1768.

GIDEON, b. March 26, 1770.

JACOB, b. Jan. 19, 1772.

ESTHER, b. Nov. 16, 1773.

NICHOLAS HOWELL, b. Jan. 29, 1775.

ISAAC.

DANIEL.

PARMELIA.

RHODA.

Note. For the following, from East Haddam, Ct., To. Rec. we are indebted to Dr. D. W. Patterson :
John Wetmore m. Sept. 15, 1763, Martha Stancliff.
Children of Ira and Hannah Wetmore.
Sarah, b. Dec. 4, 1762 ; Bela, b. June 1, 1764 ; Jabez, b. Nov. 2, 1766 ; Welles, b. Nov. 26, 1768 ; Minnie, b. April 1, 1771 ; Anne, b. Sept. 8, 1773. We have no connecting link with the above.

SIXTH GENERATION.

Children of ABEL,

Son of Samuel, Son of Samuel.

Dr. TRUMAN SPENCER, b. in Winchester Centre, Ct., Aug. 12, 1774; m. Oct. 18 (10 ?), 1799, Sylvia, dau. of Thomas and Pheobé (Griswold) Spencer, b. in W., April 12, 1778 ; d. March 27, 1800 ; m. 2d, at Burlington, Vt., Dec. 25, 1804, Elizabeth, dau. of John Jarvis, Esq., of Norwalk, Ct. ; had Sylvia Elizabeth, Darwin Woodward, William Jarvis, George Whitfield, and Charles Fitch.

He resides in his native town, where he is much respected. Losing his first wife the following year after their marriage, by way of more intimately associating her maiden surname with his own, he had, by lawful authority, *Spencer* added to his Christian name;[9] and becoming as he did during her short but painful illness, deeply interested in the subject of materia medica, caused him after her death, to turn his attention to the study of the medical profession, and subsequently became a successful practitioner. He was for many years a magistrate of Winchester. Through the kindness of one of our correspondents, we are enabled to give the following biographical sketch of him :

He chose as his profession medicine, and studied under the celebrated Doctors Samuel Woodward of Torringford, Ct., and McLaren of Albany, N. Y., and received his diploma in 1802.

In the practice of his profession, he was eminently successful, and a very thorough student, and so continued until the great number of years removed him from professional life.

When in the year 1807, the spotted fever appeared in Litchfield county, he was prosecuting a very extensive practice and applied the strength of his intellect to investigating the scourge, its cause and treatment, and was the first physician that treated it successfully, and triumphed over its fearful ravages.

He continued in practice until he was about 75, when he gave it up altogether, and retired to his old homestead in the pursuit of comfort and the fullfilment of his days. His life has been one full of incident and trial, and his sensitive mind has occasionally broke forth in song and poesy, in both of which departments of literature, he has shown much taste and ability.

Upon the occasion of the death of his wife Sylvia, he wrote the following lines, and composed a sweet and flowing melody as an accompaniment.

---

[9] Dec. 27, 1800. The above Truman, son of Abel and Jerusha Wetmore, now makes the addition of Spencer after Truman, to his Christian name.— *Winchester T. Rec.*

Let music roll in mournful strains,
While death his pris'ner, binds in chains;
Each harper drest in grief's attire,
While sorrow tunes her mournful lyre.

Awake, awake, each silent string,
With melting notes, new sorrows bring,
Till in the dirge, my spirit flies
To the dark shade where Sylvia lies.

Huge troubles rise on every side,
Like the fierce ocean's rapid tide;
The raging billows' ceaseless roar,
Proclaim my Sylvia is no more.

O! cruel tyrant! monster death,
To stop so soon my Sylvia's breath;
To deck in mourning garbs of woe,
The face of nature where I go.

What mighty sorrows veil the land,
The lofty hills in mourning stand,
The crystal streams in sorrow glide,
And roll to meet the swelling tide.

Ye silent groves and meadows wail,
While anguish moves in ev'ry gale;
On swifter wings let nature fly,
To bear my troubled soul on high.

He has composed many popular sacred pieces.

While sick with small pox, and pronounced by his physicians past recovery, his young friends, who were confined with him in what was termed the *pest house*, informed him he could not live, and desired him to compose a piece of music to be sung at his funeral. He consented, if they would furnish him with the *staves*, and turn him on his face. They did so, and the result was the piece called *Florida*, which is sung to this day, in all the places of Methodist worship, and also his entire recovery.

Kind and generous in all his relations in life, mirth, song and sociality occupied his leisure hours, and the strict and urgent duties of a business life, were often put aside for the pleasure of friends and early friendships.

At this late period of life, being in his 86th year, his epistolary correspondence is unexceptional, and shows a wonderful preservation of all his mental faculties, and his beautiful penmanship gives evidence also of his physical abilities.

Mrs. Elizabeth Jarvis Wetmore, died May 7, 1844, aged 58. Mr. Jarvis, the father of Mrs. W., was a commissary in the British army, during the Revolutionary war, and a nephew of the late Right Rev. Bishop Jarvis of Connecticut; the father of the late Rev. Samuel Farmar Jarvis, D. D. LL. D., and was near of kin to Earl St. Vincent Admiral Jervis.[10]

[10] The family of Jervis appears to have been seated at Chatkill and Meaford, Co. Stafford, as early as the reign of Henry VIII. John Jervis was living 1664; I *William* of Meaford; II Sir Humfry, who was lord mayor of Dublin; III John, who was father of John Jervis of Durlaston, Co. Stafford, m. 14 July, 1692, Mary only child of John Swynfen, Co. Stafford, and d. 3 Jan., 1746, leaving issue I John, ancester of the Jervises of Durlasten; II William, rector of Steine; III Thomas, m. and left issue; IV Benjamin; V Swynfen Jervis, who was a bencher of Middle Temple, consul to the admiralty, and auditor to the Greenwich hospital, m. Elizabeth, dau. of George Parker of Park Hall, Co. Stafford, Esqr., d. 19 Nov., 1771, leaving issue, I William of Meaford, b. 1728, m. Jane, only surviving sister of Thomas Hatzell of Newcastle-under-Lyne, gent., and d. 1813, without issue, his wid. d. 1817; II John, earl of St. Vincent (Admiral Jervis), b. at Meaford, 9 Jan., 1734, entered the navy at the early age of ten years and obtained the rank of post captain 13 Oct. 1760. In 1782, on account of the well known action between his ship and the Pegase, French 74, he received the order of the Bath. In 1797, with a fleet of 15 sail of the line only, he engaged and totally defeated the Spanish fleet, consisting of 27 sail, 7 of which carried from 112 to 130 guns each, and was immediately elevated to the peerage, by the titles of Baron Jervis, of Meaford, and earl of St. Vincent, by patent, 23 June, 1797, taking his title from the cape of that name, near which he had achieved his glorious victory. In 1801, he was appointed lord of the admiralty, and 27th April in that year was created viscount *St. Vincent*, with remainder to his two nephews, William Henry Ricketts and Edward Jervis Ricketts, and the heirs male of their bodies successively, and failing such, to his niece, Mary countess of Northesk, and the heirs male of her body. His lordship at the time of his death was admiral of the fleet, and general of the marines. He m. 5 June, 1783, Martha, dau. of Sir Thomas Parker, lord chief baron, but by her (who d. 8 Feb. 1816), he had no issue. His lordship d. 13 March, 1833, aged 89, when the titles of earl of St. Vincent and Baron Jervis became extinct and his elder nephew having d. without male issue before him, the viscounty devolved on his 2d nephew *Edward Jervis*, present and 2d viscount. (*Collen Genealogical Peerage of England and Ireland.*) William Henry and Edward Jervis Ricketts, were sons of Admiral Jervis sister Mary, who m. 19 April, 1757, William Henry Ricketts of Canaan, in Jamaica, and of Longwood, Co. Hants, and d. 12 March, 1828, æ 90. *Arms of the Jervis family.* Sable, a chevron ermine between three martlets or. CREST—out of a naval coronet or, encircled around the rim by a wreath of oak vert, a demi-pegasus argent, wings elevated azure, and charged on the wing with a fleur-de-lis gold. SUPPORTERS.—Dexter, an eagle wings elevated, grasping in the left claw a thunderbolt, all proper. *Sinister*, a pegasus argent, wings elevated azure, thereon a fleur-de-lis or. MOTTO, Thus.—*Collen Peerage.*

Descendants of Samuel, son of Thomas.

ANNA JÉRUSHA, b. in Winchester, March, 1776 ; m. Elijah Stark-
weather, of East Windsor, Ct., Jan. 21, 1802 ; had I *Jerusha
Ann*, b. in W. Nov. 12, 1802, who m. Oct. 31, 1822, Sheldon
Miller b. in W. Nov. 1799, had 1, Lewis Allen, b. in W Nov.
3, 1823, m. in Lee, Mass., April 8, 1846, Pheobe Ann Sheffield,
b. in Stonington, Ct., Jan. 21, 1822 ; they have Frances Amelia, b. in Lee, Aug. 11, 1847, Edward Lewis and Emma Louisa,
twins, b. in Lee April 2, 1851 : 2, George Hudson, b. in W.
June 24, 1825 ; m. Oct. 16, 1848, Eusebia Naville Herrick, of
Canaan, N. Y., b. in Lebanon, N. Y. Sept. 10, 1826 ; had Emma
Jane, b. in West Stockbridge, Mass., Nov. 9, 1849, d. in Collins,
N. Y., July 13, 1850 ; Eva Maria, b. in W. S. June 6, 1857 :
3, Henry Elijah, b. in Tyringham, Mass., April 18, 1830 ; m.
in Lee, Mass., Nov. 29, 1853, Caroline Moore, b. in Valatie,
N. Y., May 1, 1834, s. p. : 4, Laura Ann, b. in Lenox, Mass.,
Aug. 29, 1832 ; m. in Lebanon, N. Y., May 7, 1851, Henry
McCullock, b. in Dalton, Mass., Oct. 21, 1830 ; had Agnes Ma-
rilla, b. in Lee, Mass. April 9, 1852 ; Albert Henry, b. in Lee,
April 5, 1853, d. Aug. 28, 1853 ; Lilla Ann, b. in Lenox May
1, 1855, d. in L. March 8, 1857 ; Charles Sheldon, b. in Lee
April 8, 1857 : 5, Mary Maria, b. in Lenox Dec. 6, 1841, d. Mar.
23, 1842 : 6, Mary Jerusha, b. in Lee Jan. 13, 1844. II *Laura*,
b. in W. Oct. 26, 1804. III *Huldah Andrews*, b. in W. Aug.
28, 1806 ; m. Oct. 9, 1828, Sydney Hoyt, b. in W. April 2,
1804, son of Micajah and Esther (Trowbridge) Hoyt ; res. in
Barton, Tioga co., N. Y. ; chil., 1, Harriet, b. in Veteran, N. Y.,
March 27, 1830 ; m. Shubal Cotton Brown, (b. in Lansing, N.
Y., Nov. 12, 1826), Dec. 25, 1848 ; have Sidney Deville, b. in
Barton, Aug. 17, 1851 : 2, Julia, b. in V. Oct. 13, 1832 ; m.
John Wesley Skilling, of Barton, Nov. 23, 1851, s. p. : 3, Lou-
isa, b. V. Jan. 16, 1836, m. Eli Davis Manning, of Barton, N.
Y., Feb. 17, 1856 ; have Judge Hoyt, b. Sept. 29, 1856 : 4,
Delia Andrus, b. in B., Aug. 10, 1847 : 5, Frederick Durrells,
b. in B., May 21, 1852. IV *Julia Maria*, b. in Winchester,
Jan. 6, 1809 ; m. May 10, 1841, Samuel Ward Coe, merchant
of West Winstead, Ct., b. in W. June 10, 1805, son of Davis
and Prudence (Ward) Coe (she is the 2d wife ; his 1st, Abigail
Baldwin Sanford d. in W. Dec. 23, 1838, leaving issue Charles
Betts, b. in W. Jan. 15, 1832 ; David Ward, b. May 11, 1836) ;
have 1, Frances Abby, b. in W., June 26, 1842 ; 2, Wilbur
Fisk, b. Nov. 23, 1844. V *Samuel Wetmore*, b. in W. Aug.
31, 1812 ; m. May 8, 1839, Flora Murry, b. Sept. 4, 1814, dau.
of David and Roxana (North) Murry ; res. in W. ; chil., 1,
Jane Flora, b. in W. March 18, 1840 : 2, Darwin Samuel, b.
in W. Aug. 24, 1843 : 3, Huldah Annie, b. in W. Dec. 11,
1846 : 4, Hattie Murray, b. in W. March 30, 1856. VI *Sybil*

11

Anderson, b. in W. May 14, 1815; m. in W. May 14, 1845, Amos Lorenzo Hull, b. in Tolland, Mass., Nov. 6, 1814; res. in Tolland; chil., 1, Anna Rebecca, b. in T. Feb. 8, 1846: 2, Helen Sybil, b. in T. Sept. 18, 1847: 3, Clarissa Virginia, b. in W. Oct. 8, 1841; 4, Abbie Frances, b. Oct. 8, 1854: 5, Jennie Starks, b. in W. Sept. 10, 1859. VII *Frederick Elijah*, b. in W. Nov. 21, 1819; unm.

JOHN, b. in Winchester, Feb. 6, 1778; m. Nov. 19, 1801, Lucy dau. of John and Elizabeth (Whiting) Nash Jun., of W., b. in Torrington May 8, 1783; had Abel Samuel, Lucy Esther, Hannah Jerusha, Clarissa Whiting, and Rebecca Nash.

A farmer, lived and died on the homestead of his father, grandfather and great grandfather, at Winchester, May 24, 1832.

SAMUEL, b. in W. March 24, 1780; m. Sally dau. of Adna Beach; had Mary Sophronia, and Harriet Eliza.

He added the initial *H* to his Christian name, after attaining his majority. He studied law, and removed to Vernon, N. Y., where he died at the age of 33 years.

ABEL, b. in W. Sept. 23, 1783; d. unm.

He followed the sea, and while in the port of Surinam of South America, died of fever, aged about 25 years.

ELISHA, b. in W. April 11, 1785; m. Anna Rood, of Torrington, Ct.; had Lucretius Allen, Lavinia Ann, Flora R., and Sophronia; his wife d. June 12, 1831; m. 2, Achsa Richardson, wid. of Mr. Beatty, of Freedom, Portage co., Ohio, April 22, 1832; had Emily and Lucia.

He removed to Charleston, Portage co., O., in 1815, with an ox team for locomotion, and was 49 days in making the journey. A farmer, and a highly respected citizen.

Children of SETH,

Son of John, son of Samuel.

JOHN, b. in Winchester, Oct. 1780; m. Dec. 30, 1802, Huldah, dau. of Thomas and Pheobe (Grennell) Spencer, b. Oct. 1, 1780; had Horatio, Lucius, Celestia, Sarepta, Louisa Matilda, Willard Spencer, John Grennell, Huldah Ann; he d. in 1823; she m. 2d, Jonathan Coe Esq. of W.; she d. July 10, 1845.

SETH, b. in Winchester, Oct. 1784; m. Lucina Cook, of Canajoharie or Sharon, N. Y.; had Lois L., Flint, Mary Eleanor Mitchell, Seth Franklin, Titus C., Silonia Caroline, Adelia A., Lucy L., Matilda D., Julia L., Elizabeth Leaming, Emily R.

He died at Mount Pleasant, N. Y., Nov. 1831.

ABIGAIL, b. in W. Jan. 1787; m. Daniel Beach of Hebron, Ct., 1804; had I *Narcissa A.;* II *Abigail;* III *Hiram Wetmore;* IV *Eunice Louisa;* V *Verlot Daniel;* VI, *Emmet Adis;* VII *Sorena Desire;* VIII *Philo Plato.*

Mr. Beach was one of the early pioneers of western N. Y., he died at Eagle Village, Wyoming co., N. Y., 1836.; she m. 2d Jacob Wart, former husband to her sister Artemisia; she d. Sept. 17, 1858.

ARTEMISIA, b. in W. Nov. 1789; m. Jacob Wart, of Canajoharie, N. Y.; had I *Caroline;* II *Narcissa;* she d. at the birth of the latter, about 1813; he m. 2d, as next above.

ALPHONZO, Maj., b. in W. Feb. 17, 1793; m. Sept. 5, 1813, Mary Smith, of Ames, N. Y., b. June 26, 1793: had Diogenes, Leonidas, Thaddeus Kosciusko, Calphina, Lintz, Roxana Bacon, Sarah, Thomas J. Smith, Alphonzo.

He entered the army in April, 1812, as ensign in the 23d Infantry, and experienced much actual service.

Lost an arm in action, in an expedition under Col. Winder, to the Canada shore, below Fort Erie, Nov. 28, 1812; promoted to second lieutenant, June 13, and first lieuten-

ant, July, 1814; retained in the peace establishment in the
6th Infantry, May, 1815, made regimental pay master 14
Oct., 1815; captain, Dec., 1819; relinquished rank in the
line, Feb. 21, resigned, May 1, 1833.—*Mo. State Gazeteer,*
1837.

He marched with the army (taking his family with
him), to Missouri in 1816-17, and settled in Franklinton. After resigning his commission, he removed to
St. Louis, where he was engaged in the practice of the
law. Died from the effects of his wounds, June 13,
1849.

SALMON B., b. in W. Sept. 5, 1795; m. Hannah Waffule, of Canajoharie, Sept. 15, 1816; had Regulus, Eliza Jane, Harriet
Mary, Vernon B., Henry Oscar, Mary A.

He died at Canajoharie Aug. 2, 1854; she d. Sept.
19, 1854.

PYTHAGORAS, b. in W. April 20, 1798; m. Nancy dau. of Joseph
Jessup, of Greenwich, Ct., Dec. 27, 1819; had Burnel J., Alphonzo, Justus F., Catherine E., Nancy Louisa, Byron L.

He served as a volunteer in the war of 1812, and
subsequently held the rank of major in the Veteran
corps of the state of New York. Is an attorney and
counsellor at law, Canajoharie, N. Y.

LOIS MALINDA, b. in W. 1800; m. Henry Thorp; removed to
Northampton, N. Y., subsequently to Pennsylvania; had Henry
and two daughters.

LUCY ELIZABETH, b. —; m. Simon D. Kittle, of Canajoharie, sub-
sequently merchant in the city of New York; had I *Marietta
Snell;* II *Charlotte Berry;* III *George Wetmore,* mercht. N.
Y. city, IV *Edward;* V *Newell;* VI *Downer;* VII *Herbert
C.;* VIII *Charles A.*

Resides at Fonda, N. Y.

GEORGE CLINTON, b. Oct. 18, 1809; m. Nov. 23, 1831, Jane Ann,

---

[11] Collateral branches of the Whites, were Sally White, Mary Hibbard,
Nancy Durham, Abijah L., Lucinda Geortner, Amos H., Laura Wheeler,
and Jane A. Wetmore.

dau. of Abijah and Hannah White,[11] of Ames, N. Y., b. April,
1810; had George, Florence; m. 2d, Nov. 22, 1855, Catherine,
dau. of Col. Herman I. Ehle (of the Veteran corps of the state of
New York) and Christiana Vrooman Van Slyke; had Herman.

He settled in the state of Missouri, in 1837. He is
a planter, and resides upon the banks of the Missouri
river; his place is known as Glenrose, situated in the
town of Dover, where he says he " thinks he has settled
down, having fallen in love with the muddy Missouri
in youth, I was never content away from her banks,
and here I am where her waters greet me in the
morning, and are the last thing to gaze on at night."
His first wife died in Salina co., Mo., May 2, 1844, his
second and present wife is the grand daughter of Harmanus and Mary (Vrooman) Van Slycke, and great
grand dau. of the late Judge Isaac Vrooman of Albany
co., his family residence was a few miles south of Schenectady. Her father, Herman J. Ehle, was born in
Canajoharie, March 29, 1790, and was married by the
Rev. Abraham Van Horne of Caughnawaga, Jan. 29,
1809, had Eliza Maria (dead), James R. (dead), Charles,
Catherine, Caroline, Henry (dead), and Herman (dead)
James K., married Catherine daughter of Henry
Loucks of Palatine, N. Y., Jan. 1833. He is the son
of John Ehle, whose father and mother (maiden name
Miller) came from Prussia about 1752. His grand-
father, on the maternal side, was John Failing, and his
grandmother, Madalen Waggoner; both his grand-
mothers lived to be over 100 years of age. His wife
Christiana Vrooman, was born Dec. 17, 1789, died
May 5, 1854. Her paternal grandfather, Adam Van
Slycke, came from Holland, received a large grant of
land from the crown called *Van Slyck's patent*, north
of the Mohawk river, in the county of Montgomery.
Harmanus Van Slycke had one sister who married
John Thorn of the British army, and had a large
family; two sons were killed by the Indians at Asto-

ria, while exploring the Pacific coast, in connection with the late John Jacob Astor; one was killed by the bursting of a cannon; one, the Rev. John Thorn, is a Lutheran clergyman; and the late Col. Herman Thorn of New York city (who married a daughter of Col. Jauncey of N. Y., and had several children); daughters: Catherine, married Moncrieffe Livingston; Jane, married Judge Peter R. Livingston; Eliza, married Ellis; and Cornelia.[12] Christiana Vrooman Van Slycke had sisters, Dorathy Van Buskirk, married Samuel Lock; Catherine Van Epps, married Joseph Cook, had William Henry, Aaron (died), Eli, attorney at law and ex-mayor of Buffalo, N. Y., Elisha, lawyer, Buffalo, Mary Catherine (dead), Susan and Christiana.

John Jacob Ehle, named in the following biographical sketch, was half brother of Herman J. Ehle's father. The interesting historical items that the notice contains will be a sufficient apology for our occupying so much space with it.

John Jacob Ehle.

One of the early settlers of the town of Palatine N. Y., was the Rev. John Jacob Ehle, or Oel, as he himself sometimes spelled it. He took up a small patent of land of 600 acres, extending from the river back on to the hills, but eventually sold off the east end, reserving the west, which still remains a homestead in the hands of his descendant of the fourth generation, Mr. Peter Ehle. This Mr. Peter Elhe is the third in succession who has borne the name *Peter*.

The first *Peter* assisted his father in building the old stone house which now stands on the rail road track, not far from the river; before which time they probably dwelt, something like Abraham of old, in tents, or such temporary

---

[12] We give this record as we received it, we are, however, inclined to believe that these several Thorns, are children of Thomas Thorn, and Catherine, dau. of Gilbert and Cornelia (Beekman) Livingston, and *grand children*, not children, of John Thorn as above.

tenements as the facilities of the region in those early days afforded. There was an old road running along by the river side, where the rail road track now is, sometimes called the Indian road, and sometimes the old French road, which explains the otherwise apparently secluded locality of the old stone house. The date on the house, together with the initials P. E., are in iron figures.

The precise date of the death of Domine Ehle, seems to be lost to the family, as the family records, many years since, went into the hands of a female branch, that removed hence, and are not known now to be in existence. But he must have died about the time of the breaking out of the Revolution. He was interred in what is known as the Frey's burying ground, but no stone or memorial designates precisely where.

By two antique certificates in the possession of Mr. Peter Ehle, and which should be forever preserved and kept at the old homestead, it seems that he was an Episcopal clergyman. His parish extended all abroad, east, west, north, and south, among the Indians, whose missionary and pastor he was. His chief preaching place, according to the tradition of his family, was at the Castle, now in the town of Danube.

The testimonials of his priesthood are on parchment, in the Latin language, and run as follows :

" By these presents, We John, by Divine Permission Bishop of London, make known to all persons, that on this 12 day of August, A. D. 1722, at the Chapel within our Palace at Fulham, in the county of Middlesex, we, the aforesaid John, Bishop as aforesaid, representing, by the help of Almighty God, the Holy Orders, have admitted and promoted John Jacob Ehle, beloved by us in Christ Jesus, a scholar, abundantly commended to us as laudable in life, unblemished in morals and virtue, skilled in the knowledge and study of good letters, and sufficiently entitled, and moreover examined, and approved by our own examiner, to the sacred order of Presbyter, according to the custom and rite wisely appointed and provided for in this part of the English Church ; and him we did, then and there ritually and canonically, ordain Presbyter.

In testimony whereof, we have caused to be affixed to these presents the seal of our Episcopate, according to the

day and year aforesaid, and in the ninth of our translation.   JOHN, London."

The other certificate of his deaconship, corresponds precisely with this, excepting the substitution of *deacon* for
presbyter. The signature is the autograph of the bishop himself.

The early date of these papers, suggests that he may
have been educated partly in England; at least, have
stopped there on his way to this continent.

According to tradition, he was a great favorite with the
Indians, so that they greatly lamented his death. In
his stone house, he had a large cellar-kitchen, which always furnished a free lodging to travelling Indians, and
others, and not unfrequently his house presented the appearance of an inn.

A curious letter of his is extant, addressed to Sir William Johnson, printed in the 4th vol. of the *Documentary
History of New York,* in reference to an eastern enterprise
for the education of Indian youth. A Boston society, together with the Rev. Dr. Wheelock, strengthened and encouraged by a legacy of Sir Peter Warren, an uncle of Sir
William Johnson, were desirous of getting some Indian
boys to educate, and also of setting up one or more English
schools among the Mohawk Indians; and corresponded
with Sir William respecting it.

Sir William seemed to have favored the design, though
the establishment of schools here was never carried out.
It was in reference to this that Mr. Oel wrote the following
letter:

At mine House, Feb. 8, 1762.
THE HON. SIR WILLIAM JOHNSON:

That I write these letters and trouble you with them, is
because I am forced to it. The reason is because I heard
yesterday, at the Castle, that the Bostoniers were designing
to erect schools in every Castle, by choosing out two young
boys for to be sent into New England to be instructed
there, that they might instruct the others in proper learning. Now learning is good, and is most necessary among the
Indians: that cannot be contradicted. But I want to know
to what design as it is to introduce their own Presbyterian
Church, then it cannot be. For if it prejudice our church

---

and church ceremonies, and is not agreeable nor conforms to them, then it must not be allowed, because it is against them. But should their design be with that purpose, then I have nothing to say, but must be content with it.

Now, Sir, I let it to your Sir's wise consideration, as one likely to know better than myself of what is in these matters. But I think it shall not be taken in a wrong sense, that I write these things to your honor, whom I name freely my best friend whom I have here and can trust. I want your presence, and to talk freely to you, though I have not the opportunity, for to hear your meaning in that matter. If it is for the prejudice and wrong of the church, I can not consent to it. For I must maintain, and will maintain the church of our denomination, so long as I can. And what is my little power I shall do, and will do. Always, I remain, in haste, your friend and well wisher.

With all respect, and humble servant,

JOHN JACOB OEL.

P. S.—I hope and think Sir William, and your honour, shall be for our churches. If I can have an answer, though of but a few lines, I shall take it for a great honor.

(Addressed.) This letter, is directed to the honorable Sir Baronet William Johnson, overseer over the Indian officers, and now present at Cunad, Schoharie.

The editor of the *Documentary History of the State,* says in a note, after the letter, that Mr. Oel was appointed assistant missionary to the Indians in 1750. What his means of information are, we are not informed; but, from the far prior date of his ordination to the ministry, and there being no Episcopalians in this particular region, at that time, but Indians, it seems more probable that he had been their missionary long before 1750.—*Mohawk Valley Register.*

Children of SAMUEL,

Son of John, son of Samuel.

SELIMA, b. in Winchester, March 13, 1789; m. E. Cheever; had 2 sons and 1 daughter.

12

LEAMING, b. in W. Feb. 14, 1791; m. Charity Davis; had Solomon, Samuel M., and 4 daughters.

RUBY, b. in W. June 27, 1793; m. Festus L. Thompson; had 1 son and 1 dau.; m. 2d, Stephen Brigham Esq.; had 1 dau., who m. Isaac Adams, res. in Illinois; she d. in Vernon, N. Y., June 16, 1828, æ. 35.

ALMEDA, b. in W. March 28, 1795.

CANDACE, b. in W. Aug. 31, 1797.

CALVARY, b. in W. March 24, 1799; m. Althea eldest dau. of Levi Skinner Esq., Jan. 10, 1827; had Calvary Levi; m. 2d, Elizabeth dau. of Isaac Bronson of W., Jan. 7, 1834; had son, d. young, Ann Elizabeth Althea; res. in Vernon, Oneida county, New York.

SAMUEL, b. Feb. 17, 1801; m. Lovina, dau. of Levi Skinner Esq., of Vernon, N. Y., Sept. 26, 1827; had Samuel Levi, Maria Hungerford, and 3 others; 3 of his children d. in infancy; res. in Adams, Jeff. co., N. Y.

HANNAH, b. in Vernon, N. Y., June 6, 1804; m. Dr. George Foote, of V., Jan. 11, 1827; had I *Emergene*, b. Oct. 24, 1828; II *George Newton*, b. Jan. 22, 1833; III *Charles Henry*, b. May 4, 1835; and a dau.; res. at Beaverdam, Wis.

HARRIET, b. in V. May 3, 1806; m. Rev. Conant Sawyer; had 3 daus.; she d. in Randolph, Mass., Feb. 7, 1837.

HURLBURT (Herbert?) GRISWOLD, b. in V. Nov. 10, 1808; m. Jane Tyler, of Florence, Oneida County, N. Y.; had James, Henry, and 2 daughters.

CLARISSA, b. in V. June 22, 1810; d. Aug. 2, 1828.

Children of NOAH,

Son of Rev. Noah, son of Samuel.

APPOLOS RUSSEL, b. Nov. 17, 1792; d. Jan. 10, 1796.

WILLIAM HENRY, b. Aug. 6, 1794; m. Oct. 24, 1821, Sarah Brinckerhoff; had Catherine, David, Abraham, Brinckerhoff, William Henry; she d. Jan. 18, 1829.

APPOLOS RUSSEL 2D, b. in Danbury, Ct., Nov. 11, 1796; m. Mary
    Carmer, April 30, 1822; had Henry Carmer, George Carmer,
    Theodore Russel, William, Elizabeth Carmer, and Mary Carmer.

Resides in the city of New York, where he has long
been distinguished as an honest, upright and opulent
merchant, and a philanthropic, and public spirited
citizen. For the following notice of him, we are indebted to *The Chronicle*, a periodical published in the
city of New York, and we regret that we have not at
our command, a more full account of Mr. W.'s life and
character, than this furnishes, especially of his Christian
and benevolent enterprises, and of his many acts of
generosity and love.

In every trade, business, and profession, there are men,
whose bright example may well be regarded by those who
are to come after them, and who will in the future, fill the
places made honorable by their predecessors. It is not
necessary that men should die, in order that their names,
deeds, and talents, may find a record. There is much
practical benefit to be derived by those whom noble lives
should stimulate, in sketches of the living, as in obituaries
that are forgotten almost as soon as read. There is a vast
difference between the facts when stated "he *has* done"
and "he still *does!*" There is a vitality in the latter that
is derived from the knowledge that the benevolent mind
is still active, that its mission is not yet ended, that its
eulogy is being daily engraved upon a myriad of hearts,
instead of being sculptured upon a lifeless tombstone.
    When we thrill with the sacred thoughts of charity, when
we regard those who have happily been brought under its
ministrations, and see the changes that its harmonizing
power has brought, we can realize the benefit conferred
upon society and ourselves more fully, if we can point to
an individual and say: "There is the agent of all this
good."
    In this, the great Metropolis of the Western World,
where a greater necessity exists for philanthropic effort
and charitable institutions, than in almost any other part
of our flourishing country, there are thousands who have
given their hearts to objects that benefit and assist the

needy. Charity, with them, is not a theory about which
they can only speculate, it has become the broad basis upon
which all practical reform is established. And amid all
the cares of a prosperous business, they pursue their self-
imposed tasks, through difficulties, depression, and sometimes partial defeat, up to a commensurate success.

As all professions are proud of their prominent men, so
may the hardware trade congratulate itself upon numbering among its merchants many of those who deserve all
the praise that our above general remarks can convey.
From among the oldest of them we have chosen an individual. to whom all will cheerfully accord the title of
" a man and gentleman." * * * * He had attained
the age of about ten years, when his father, Noah Wetmore,
was called to the superintendence of the New York Hospital. * * * *

" The subject of our sketch, about 1812, entered Columbia College, with the intention of fitting himself for the
medical profession, but two years close application, so impaired his health, that he was compelled to seek some
more active employment. Whatever regret he might
have felt at thus abandoning a favorite study, was overcome by the solicitations of his friends. He accordingly
left college, and entered the hardware store of Messrs.
Kip & Ingraham, located in Greenwich street, in which
his future partner, William Green, Jr., was then employed.
After they had served this firm about three years, Mr.
Green opened a hardware and iron store on the corner of
Greenwich and Vesey streets, and Mr. Wetmore, in connection with his brother, Mr. D. W. Wetmore, entered
the business upon his own account at the corner of Canal
and Hudson streets. Shortly after, Mr. Green was afflicted
with a severe illness, rendering it impossible for him to
attend to his business. At this juncture, the friendship
of Mr. Wetmore, led him to offer his services, in superintending the interests of his former fellow-clerk. This act,
and its satisfactory nature, led, after Mr. Green's recovery,
to a consolidation of the two firms under the business
style of Green & Wetmore.

In 1824, Messrs. Green & Wetmore purchased the lots
corner of Washington and Vesey streets, and erected the
stores which have been so long occupied by them and the
present firm—a period of *thirty-five* years. The business

was conducted under the name of Green & Wetmore, until 1835, when the former retired, leaving the establishment to be continued by the two brothers, under the style of Wetmore & Co., which has been retained until the present time. In 1843, Mr. D. W. Wetmore withdrew from the business, since then Mr. A. R. W. has continued it with a son, George C. Wetmore, and a nephew, David Wetmore.

Of the probity and honor with which Mr. W. has conducted his business, it is unneccessary for us to speak; these things are patent to all who know him, and could derive no lustre from our utmost laudations.

We come now to speak of "the better part," which he has chosen, and which has so eminently marked his career. And in doing this, we know that we are almost perpetrating a violence upon the unambitious spirit that has prompted every act. We are aware that he has never sought a blazon for his deeds, but that he rather shrinks from giving them publicity. We *may* meet his frown, and how shall we excuse the liberty we have taken with his name unless we claim that "the lives of all good men belong to the public?"

About thirty years ago, he united with the Presbyterian church in Laight street, under the pastoral care of Dr. Cox. This was, perhaps, the most important movement in identifying him with the various efforts that have from time to time been made to advance Christianity, ameliorate the condition of the poor, provide refuges for the homeless, and subserve the interests of all classes of the community, in a moral aspect.

Thirty-two years ago, Mr. W., with one or two others, commenced what is known as The New York City Tract Society. It would be difficult to find a Christain effort that has been marked with a greater degree of success than this. From a feeble beginning it has increased and grown strong, until in 1858, as we learn from its report, the society had the services of *twenty-eight* missionaries, and an average of 1,134 visitors. They distribute over *one million* tracts yearly, and on behalf of the New York Bible Society, some *seventeen hundred* Bibles and Testaments. Our limits will not, however, allow us to go into the statistics of this society, or we might make extracts which would astonish as well as please. The City Tract Society purchases of the American Tract Society, the tracts that it distributes monthly throughout the city of New York, and thus aids that society by relieving it of an onerous duty. But the operations, the officers, the management, and the funds of the two societies, are altogether distinct and independent of each other. During the last twenty years, Mr. W., now the corresponding secretary, has regularly met the board of managers, weekly, to confer and advise.

Mr. W. is also one of the vice-presidents of The New York Association for Improving the Condition of the Poor. To him is due much of the credit of its inception and organization, as well as its widely extended benefits. Much of his time and attention have been bestowed upon it, both as an officer, and a visitor of those needing its support. The operations of this society, have been extended and beneficial. During some of our recent winters, thousands have received assistance from it, in articles of food, clothing and fuel. Many a heart has been lightened of its sorrow, many a lonesome attic and miserable cellar, has been made. to glow with the cheerful rays of comfort. One of the best features of this charity is, that it encourages labor. It is not a part of their economy to support, for a length of time, those who are able to work, but by a careful interest in the affairs of the poor, they not only relieve temporarily, but assist the worthy to employment, and a final independence of all charitable institutions.

Another association for the poor has been fostered and encouraged by the subject of our sketch. We can only give its title : The Washing and Bathing Association, and state that its practical working is designed to benefit largely those who use its advantages.

The New York Juvenile Asylum is one of the last but not the least of his efforts. As president of this new institution he has been able, with those who have nobly assisted him, to extend a protecting hand to the homeless and destitute youth of our city. Unlike the penal establishments of our land, no associations can here be formed that will endanger the young mind. The refugees of this kind have generally grown up under the supervision of the state and city. The lax discipline or promiscuous mingling of criminal and pauper, has had there a most disastrous result. How the children received into this

---

asylum, are finally disposed of, may be learned from the report of Mr. A. C. Pearcy, the superintendent of the House of Reception.

" Three companies of children have been sent to Illinois during the year, and indentured under the personal supervision of Mr. A. C. Pearcy.

" The first company left Feb. 8, and consisted of 16 girls and 23 boys, total 39; and were settled at Atalanta, Logan co., Ill.

" The second left May 17, and consisted of 11 girls and 26 boys, total 37 ; and were settled at Havana, Mason co., Ill.

" The third left Oct. 11, and consisted of 17 girls and 28 boys, total 45 ; and were settled at Pana, Christian co., Ill."

We have above, only referred to such works as have gone abroad with the name of Mr. W. attached to them. They are local, it is true, but their effects may be felt throughout the world. We might go on to enumerate others in which he has borne a part, but it will be enough, finally, to refer to his connection with Dr. Adams's church for the last fifteen years, during which time he has been constantly consulted upon the various projects started by the benevolent and philanthropic. His sympathy is ready for all, and his ears never closed to the appeals of the worthy. * * * *

We acknowledge the imperfections of our hasty sketch, for we have not said a half what is due the man. We therefore plead in extenuation, our own inability, and the delicate matter of obtaining such data.

> " Not to the past, but the future looks
> True nobility, and finds its blazon
> In posterity."

DAVID WOODHUL, b. June 26, 1798; m. Harriet Sharpe, Aug. 30, 1827; had Harriet Cooper, Jacob Sharpe, Cornelia Brower, Peter Sharpe, Christiana Sharpe, Irene, James Scott, Fanny.

He was for many years actively engaged in company with his brother, Appolos Russell, in mercantile pursuits in the city of New York, importing and jobbing of iron and hardware, but more recently, the manufacturing of iron has occupied his business hours. In whatever branch of trade he has associated himself, there he has left the impress of prudence, liberality and uprightness of dealing. As an evidence of his unselfishness and patriotic feeling, we will here note, that nothwithstanding his direct interests as an importer favored free trade, he has always been an ardent supporter of the principle of a tariff looking to the protection of American industry.

IRENA WINIFRED, b. Oct. 2, 1800; m. March 23, 1820, Anthony Post Halsey Esq., of N. Y.; had I *James Wetmore*, b. July 19, 1821, who m. Agnes McClure, had Anthony Post Jun.: II *Cornelia Brower*, b. Oct. 29, 1823: III *Seaton*, b. Feb. 19, 1826, m. and had Noah Wetmore: IV *Mary Wetmore*, b. Aug. 23, 1827, m. James Dwight, had Irene Wetmore: V *Henry Martin*, b. April 10, 1829, d. Sept. 11, 1829: VI *Noah Wetmore*, b. Aug. 23, 1830, d. March 30, 1834: VII *Euphemia*, b. June 6, 1833, m. Joseph Wales, had Mary Wetmore, Frederick: VIII *Anna*, b. Oct. 14, 1838: IX *Elizabeth*, b. May 26, 1836, d. Dec. 30, 1836.

Mr. Halsey occupied, for many years, the responsible position of cashier of the Bank of New York, in the city of New York, and more recently that of president of the same institution. In all the commercial and banking crises that have visited Wall street, since he has been connected with *the street*, he has kept that institution from reproach, and his own name unsullied, and enjoys the confidence and esteem of the citizens of the metropolis, in a marked degree.

Children of APPOLOS,

Son of Rev. Noah, Son of Samuel.

APPOLOS EDWARDS, b. Nov. 23, 1797; m. Feb. 10, 1827, Charlotte dau. of Lewis Prall, of New Jersey, b. Oct. 12, 1810; had Henry Augustus, Oliver, Lewis Prall, William Walter.

Merchant in the city of New York; since his majority he has changed his name to Edward Appolos.

HANNAH, b. Aug. 8, 1799; unm.

OLIVER, b. Aug. 13, 1801; m. June 27, 1850, Harriet Woolworth; had Florence.

Merchant in the city of New York.

HENRY, b. Oct. 12, 1803; d. March 21, 1827.

MARIA, b. Dec. 17, 1806; unm.

AUGUSTUS, b. Nov. 11, 1808; m. March 1, 1831, Jane Eliza Furman; had Augustus, Emily, Edward Leslie.

He died June 23, 1857.

WILLIAM WALTER, b. June 13, 1811; d. Aug. 24, 1812.

WILLIAM WALTER 2D, b. March 29, 1813; m. Nov. 26, 1839, Caroline Shipman; had Stephen Shipman.

Children of SAMUEL ITHIEL,

Son of Rev, Noah, Son of Samuel.

Dr. EBENEZER WALTER, b. —; m. ——; had Lybia; d. March 31, 1854.

JULIA ANN.

CORNELIA S.

MARIA, b. —; m. Capt. William S. Hoyt; had I *Samuel Ithiel;* II *Amelia K.;* III *Stanley.*

She d. Nov. 20, 1846.

ERASTUS, b. —; m. Louisa Hill; had Samuel Ithiel, Timothy Burger.

He died Feb. 7, 1842.

EGBERT, b. —; m. Eliza H. Mantam; had Egbert, Charles J., Coggill, and George.

13

Children of EBENEZER LYMAN,

Son of Joel, Son of Samuel.

NANCY, b. July 19, 1796; m. Israel Coe; had 4 sons and 3 daus.
She d. Aug. 30, 1838.

LAUREN, b. in Torrington, Ct., July 9, 1801; m. Fanny C. Austin, of T., s. p.

He has ever been an active business man, and enterprising citizen. Save eighteen years spent in mercantile life, in the city of New York, has resided in his native town, Wolcottville being his post office address.

MARIA, b. May 14, 1805; m. Asahel Coe; had 6 sons and 2 daus.

AMANDA, b. Jan. 25, 1808; m. Elisha Baldwin, of Goshen, Ct.; has 1 son and 1 dau.

LOUISA, b. 1810; m. Phineas North, of Torrington; has 1 son and 1 dau.

Children of JOHN POMEROY,

Son of Joel, Son of Samuel.

DELIA, b. in Burlington, Vt., July 29, 1797; m. William Atwater, Feb. 1820; had I *Frances M.*, b. Nov. 1820; m. Judge Lawrence, of Moira, N. Y.: II *William H.*, (dead): III *George E.*, res. in New York city: IV Dr. *Hiram H.*, res. in Lawrence, N. Y.: V *Edward*, gov't surveyor in Minnesota: VI *Frederick A.*, merchant in Illinois: VII *John P.* (dead): VIII *Lyman*, photographist in New York city.

Resides at Moira, Franklin county, N. Y.

FRANCES, b. in Burlington, Nov. 28, 1799; m. William W. Moulton, Feb. 1827; had I *Norman S.*, Norwalk, Ohio, rail road contractor, Wis.: II *Mariam A.*, m. L. Baldwin, La Salle, Ill.; III *Horace S.*, machine manufacturer, Galveston, Texas; IV

Harriet F.: V *Julia* (dead): VI *Ogden W.* (dead): VII *Julia*.

Mrs. Frances Moulton died in 1844.

JULIA, b. in B. March 6, 1802; m. —— Knapp, 1842; res. North Stockholm, St. Lawrence county, N. Y.

EMELINE, b. in B., Feb. 28, 1804; d. April 19, 1805.

ADELINE, b. in B. Dec. 4, 1805; m. Milo Lafflin Feb. 16, 1832; had I *Pomeroy W.*, b. Jan. 1835; II *Henry* (dead); III *William*, b. 1844; IV *Frederick*, b. 1846.

Resides at Hinckley, Ohio.

MARIANA, b. in B. April 22, 1808; d. Sept. 3, 1809.

SALLY ANN, b. in B. March 15, 1810; d. Sept. 17, 1810.

FREDERICK P., b. in B. Aug. 3, 1811; d. Feb. 13, 1813.

FREDERICK P. 2D, b. Oct. 30, 1813; m. Nov. 28, 1844; Sarah M. Whitman, b. at East Haddam, Ct., March 4, 1820; had Russel C., Charles W.

Merchant at Hinckley, Ohio.

HENRY A., b. in B. Feb. 18, 1816; m. Maria Bradley, 1845.

Resides Norfolk, N. Y.

HARRIET M., b. in B. Oct. 25, 1818; m. Philander Robbins, 1838; had I *Byron*, b. 1840; II, *Jane*, b. 1844; III *Harriet*, b. 1846.

He d. ——.   She resides at Ogdensburgh, N. Y.

WILLIAM L., b. in B. Jan. 3, 1821; m. Louisa A., dau. of Nicholas Le Pelly of St. Peters, Port Gurnsey; had William, Edwin, Atwater, Carrie Louise, Ernst Le Pelly.

He is of the firm of Wetmore & Co., shipping merchants at Marqueta, Lake Superior.

CLARISSA A., b. in Norfolk, N. Y., March 4, 1823; d. Feb. 4, 1826.

RUSSEL C., b. in N. Oct. 4, 1826; d. July 10, 1845.

Children of ELIHU,

Son of David, Son of Daniel.

NORMAN.

BERTHA.

DAVID.

ELIHU.

LYDIA.

NOBLE.

Children of JESSE,

Son of Daniel, Son of Daniel.

NANCY, b. in Middletown, Ct., April 19, 1785; m. Adna Benham, 1811; m. 2d, —— Viets.

She died May 2, 1860, in her 76th year. Removed to Ashtabula, Ohio, 1816. One of the last acts of her life, was to write to the compiler of this work, detailing some interesting historical items, concerning the early Wetmores. She was warmly imbued with a spirit of regard for her kindred.

COMFORT, b. in Middletown, Jan. 1, 1786; m. in New Hampshire, Anna Tuttle; had Josiah, Amsden, Samuel William, Barnet Woodbury.

He removed with his father to Ashtabula co., Ohio, in 1816, where he has ever since lived a quiet unpretending farmer's life. He had the misfortune, in the fall of 1859, to have his dwelling consumed by fire with nearly all its contents. One of his grand children was sleeping in the house at the time, and being unable to escape, was burned to death. Resides at Ashtabula, Ashtabula co., Ohio.

COLLINS, b. Sept. 16, 1786.

He died Aug. 1859, in Ashtabula co., O., where he had resided for some forty or more years; much respected.

POLLY, b. in Middletown, April 13, 1788; d. unm.

WILLIAM, b. in M., Oct. 7, 1789; d. about 1835.

Resided in Ashtabula co., O.

HORACE, b. in M. March 27, 1798; m. —— ; had ——.

He died while journeying from California, when within about 20 miles of his home in Illinois.

SEVENTH GENERATION.

Children of Dr. TRUMAN SPENCER,

Son of Abel, Son of Samuel, Son of Samuel.

SYLVIA ELIZABETH, b. in Winchester, Oct. 20, 1805; m. Oct. 21, 1835, Leonard Beach, son of Leonard and Huldah (Cone) Hurlburt, b. July 23, 1811; had I *Sylvia Elizabeth,* b. in W. Sept. 29, 1840; II *Charlotte Jarvis,* b. in W. Sept. 13, 1845.

DARWIN WOODWARD, b. in W. Sept. 2, 1807; m. Ellen Diehl of New York; had Elizabeth.

He was the oldest son of Dr. Truman S., and at an early age and against the wishes of his parents, declined a profession; in other respects was a dutiful son, kind to those about him, of a cheerful and humorous disposition, one who seemed never to let care and trouble hang heavily upon his mind, until his only child fell a victim to disease. She was the idol of his heart.

On the evening of August 20, 1853, he was found on the Harlem road, with his throat cut and life quite extinct.

Suspicion of murder was fastened upon two persons who were known to have been with him during the day, and up to the time he left Harlem, for his home in New York that evening.

When discovered, two dollars and sixty-two cents only were found upon him of five hundred dollars that he was known to have had when he left his residence in the morning. His watch was broken in pieces, while his spectacles were left in his waistcoat pocket uninjured. The only wound upon him that could cause death, was the long deep gash in his throat. Kind and affectionate in all the relations in life, generous and frank in all his impulses, full of life and activity, he is greatly missed from the family circle; his widow lives in sadness over his and their daughter's decease.

Dr. WILLIAM JARVIS, b. in W. June 30, 1809; m. Eliza Jane
  Campbell of New York, Jan., 1844; had Emma Jarvis.

Resides in Brooklyn, N. Y. He is somewhat celebrated as a composer of sweet song, in the style of the *Irish Melodies;* this passion he inherited in some degree from his father. He, like his older brother, refused to follow the profession his father provided for him, to till the unfruitful (?) fields of music and poetry and cultivate aromatic peans and unsightly crotchets.

One of our correspondents in writing of him says that he

Commenced the study of the classics with the Rev. Mr. Marsh of his native town, and after the completion of his academic career, gave his attention to the study of medicine, under the direction of his father, and his uncle Doct. George O. Jarvis.

He graduated at the Medical College of New Haven, at 21 years of age, but having, while at his studies, listened to the flattering tales of poesey and song, he refused, after graduating an M. D., to undertake its labors and responsibilities, and devoted his time and attention to the more congenial, but less reliable, pursuits of music and her sister art.

In the prosecution of his musical career, he has been associated with some of the most eminent musicians. Signor De Begnis, the great buffo and accomplished Italian composer, was his daily companion for the last ten years of Signor De Begnis's life.

Many beautiful compositions of Donizetti, the pupil of De Begnis, written for Madame Ronzi, and sung by her, were subsequently published under the supervision of De Begnis and himself, with English translations, furnished by Dr. W.

He has composed a number of popular songs, of which ·Hinda's Lament was one, and was his earliest production, Sweet Annie of the Vale, The Lilac at the Door, and many others followed in rapid succession. A musical annual, entitled, L'Isola Incantata, or The Fairy Isle, founded upon the beautiful superstition, that there is an island in one of the eastern seas, where perpetual summer reigns, which when approached, gradually disappears. For this annual he wrote the words, as well as for nearly all the songs he published.

For Anthony Philip Heinrich, the old Bohemian musician, a most celebrated composer, he wrote many ballads, to which Von Heinrich adapted music, and they were finally translated into German.

At the time he was associated with Signor De Begnis, he also engaged the friendship and musical abilities of the lamented Charles E. Horn, one of the most distinguished composers of his time, and one of the finest singers of his day.

It was by such associations and facilities, that he cultivated his natural tastes for music and poetry, and is it wonderful that he should turn a deaf ear to the cold salutations of Esculapius, to listen to the sweet murmurings of Apollo, and the gushing melodies of Helecine.

Dr. GEORGE WHITFIELD, b. in W., Oct. 11, 1812; m. Sarah Ann, dau. of Dea. Seth and Anne (Burton) Thompson, Nov. 29, 1843; had George Thompson, Elizabeth Jarvis, Mary Fitch.

He graduated at the New Haven Medical College, removed to Amenia, Dutchess county, N. Y., in 1839, and returned to his native town in 1849, and settled in the village of Winsted, where he has since been engaged in the practice of his profession.

CHARLES FITCH, b. in W., Aug. 21, 1815; m. Sarah Astor Bryden, April 11, 1850; she d. June 5, 1855, leaving Mary Jarvis.

Resides in the city of New York, and is a lawyer by profession. He finished his preparatory course of study to enter college, under the instruction of the late Rev. Doctor Morgan, of Cheshire, Ct., and entered Trinity College, Hartford, 1837; graduated A. B. 1841, and immediately thereafter commenced the study of the law with the Hon. L. Livingston of New York, and was admitted as an attorney, solicitor and counsellor to the courts of that state in 1845.

While in college he delivered two poems, by appointment, before the Athenæum Literary Society, one entitled Venice, the other Scio. When he graduated he was selected by the faculty to deliver an oration upon Saracen Literature, and in 1844 received the degree of M. A. from the same institution.

Children of JOHN,

Son of Abel, Son of Samuel, Son of Samuel.

Dea. ABEL SAMUEL, b. in Winchester, Nov. 16, 1802; m. Nov. 24, 1829, Lucy Almira, dau. of Miles and Anna (Butterick) Hills, b. in Goshen, Ct., March 18, 1810; had Julia Ann, John Nash, Ellen Eliza, Leroy Whiting, Miles Hills, Samuel Abel, Hubert Porter.

Resides in his native place at the homestead of his great-great-grandfather, Deacon Samuel. His paternal ancestors, for four generations, lived and died on the same place that he has inherited. It is to be hoped that his descendants will never permit the place to go out of their possession.

He was made a deacon of the First Congregational (orthodox) Church in 1835, which office he held for nearly 20 years. He represented the town of Winchester in the state Legislature in 1848 and 1849.

LUCY ESTHER, b. in W., Dec. 12, 1806; m. Sept. 11, 1833, Frederick Porter, son of Miles and Anna (Butterick) Hills; had I *Lucy Ann*, b. in W., Sept. 7th, 1841.

HANNAH JERUSHA, b. in W., June 11, 1809; m. Oct. 13, 1840, Lewis Whiting of Torrington, s. p.

CLARISSA WHITING, b. in W., May 14, 1816; m. March 30, 1836, George Leroy Whiting, s. p.

REBECCA NASH, b. in W., Dec. 8, 1828; m. Nov. 11, 1846, Alonzo Whiting of Torrington, s. p.

Children of SAMUEL H.,

Son of Abel, Son of Samuel, Son of Samuel.

MARY SOPHRONIA, b. in W., May 10, 1803; m. Jan. 11, 1842, Silas Hurlburt, eldest child of John and Margeret (Hurlburt) McAlpin, b. in W., Sept. 2, 1794; he d., s. p.: she m. 2d, May 15, 1845, Samuel Avery, b. in W., Nov. 15, 1802, 3d child of John and Margeret (Hurlburt) McAlpin, s. p.

She resides in Winchester.

HARRIET ELIZA, b. in W., Nov. 8, 1806; m. Aug. 6, 1845, John, 4th child of John and Margeret (Hurlburt) McAlpin, b. Nov. 1, 1805, s. p.

Resides in W.

Children of ELISHA,

Son of Abel, Son of Samuel, Son of Samuel.

LUCRETIUS ALLEN, b. in Torringford, June 21, 1814; m. Catherine Catlin, of Charleston, Ohio, Jan. 3, 1844: had Willis L.

He died March 13, 1848.

14

LAVINIA ANN, b. Feb. 28, 1818; m. John Worden, Nov. 7, 1849.

FLORA R., b. Nov. 21, 1820.

SOPHRONIA, b. Sept. 4, 1824; d. Sept. 25, 1849.

EMILY, b. March 5, 1833.

LUCIA, b. Sept. 25, 1834.

Children of JOHN,

Son of Seth, Son of John, Son of Samuel.

HORATIO LUCIUS, b. in Winchester, Sept. 24, 1803; m. May 20, 1829, Hannah, dau. of Horace and Hannah (Bull) Catlin, b. in Harwinton, June 24, 1802; had Sarah Louisa.

He died in Winchester, Sept. 20, 1856.

CELESTIA, b. in W., May 30, 1805; m. Jan. 20, 1831, Luman, son of Luman and Chloe (Kellogg) Catlin; had I *Exene*, b. in Harwinton, May 16, 1835; II *Mary Lucretia*, b. in H., Nov. 19, 1839.

SAREPTA, b. in W., Aug. 2, 1807.

Resides in W.

LOUISA MATILDA, b. May 24, 1810; m. Oct. 19, 1830, Jabez Gillet of New Hartford, Ct., b. Nov. 24, 1804, son of Uri and Esther (Gillet) Curtiss; had I *George Wetmore*, b. Feb. 23, 1834; m. in Springfield, Mass., Oct. 18, 1835, Caroline Lee, dau. of Dr. John and Betsey Maria (Lee) Bridgman, and g. dau. of Col. Roswell and Pheobe (Potter) Lee, who reside in N. H.; had Harriet Jane, b. in N. H., Aug. 10, 1840, d. in Torrington, Sept. 6, 1843; Jabez Gillet Curtis, d. in T., Dec. 13, 1848.

She resides in Winchester.

WILLARD SPENCER, b. in W., May 18, 1813; m. Oct. 24, 1839, Julia Ann Woodford, b. Feb. 14, 1811, dau. of Erastus and Ruth (Barber) Woodford; had Willis, b. —, d. infant; Julia b. May —, 1849, d. infant.

Resides in Winchester.

JOHN GRENELL, b. in W., April 27, 1817; m. Oct. 3, 1841, Eliza
Frisbe Rosseter, b. in Harwinton, Ct., Jan. 24, 1821, dau. of
Jonathan and Anna (Barber) Rosseter; she d. in W., March
9, 1847, of lung fever; he m. 2d, Nov. 1, 1848, Eliza Pheobe,
dau. of Col. Roswell and Pheobe (Potter) Lee, b. in Springfield, Mass., April 17, 1820; had Eliza Rosseter.

Resides in Winchester.

HULDAH ANN, b. in W., July 1, 1821; m. April 17, 1844, Jonathan Addison, b. in Harwinton, Dec. 13, 1818, son of Jonathan
and Anna (Barber) Rosseter; children I *Jonathan Spencer*, b.
in Harwinton, Aug. 17, 1846; II *Charles Wetmore*, b. in H.,
Sept. 7, 1848; III *Frank Warner*, b. in H., Jan. 26, 1851;
IV *Cora Jane*, b. in H., Sept. 25, 1853; V *Effie Louisa*, b. in
H., April 1, 1856; VI *Hattie Bentley*, b. in H., June 5, 1857.

Resides in Winchester.

Children of SETH,

Son of Seth, Son of John, Son of Samuel.

TITUS C., b. —; m. ——; had 1 son and 2 daughters.

Resides at DeKalb Center, Ill.

LOIS L.

FLINT.

MARIA ELANOR MITCHELL.

SETH FRANKLIN.

SILOMA CAROLINE.

ADELIA A.

LUCY L.

MATILDA D., d. young.

JULIA L., d. young.

ELIZABETH LEAMING.

EMILY R.

Children of Maj. ALPHONZO,

Son of Seth, Son of John, Son of Samuel.

DIOGENES, b. in Ames, N. Y., June 17, 1814; m. May 8, 1836, Sarah Jane, David Hume; had Octavia; m. 2d, June 30, 1846, Deborah L. Conger; had Mary Eliza and Hugh Alphonzo.

Resides Oneida, Knox co., Ill.

Capt. LEONIDAS, b. on Governor's Island, N. Y. Harbor, May 4, 1816; m. Amelia K. S. de Bovis, March 14, 1849.

Was an officer in the U. S. army. We regret that we have not at our command a more full account of his services to his country than the following, which we take from Charles K. Gardner's *Dict. of the Army,* 1853, and *Am. Almanack,* 1851:

Second lieut. 6th infantry Dec. 31, 1839; asst. com. of subs's April 1840; first lieut. May 1846; reg. qr. master Dec. 1847 to June 1848; brevet captain for gallant and meritorious conduct in battle of El Molino del Rey Sept. 8, 1847 (July 1848).

He was in several engagements with the Indians in the Florida war, and participated in the battles in Mexico; was at the storming of Vera Cruz, at Cerro Gordo, at Churubusco, at Molino del Rey, and in the battles before the city of Mexico.

He died near Hannibal, Mo., while on board the steamer Highland Mary, on her trip from Fort Snelling to St. Louis, Nov. 18, 1849.

THADDEUS KOSCIUSKO, b. at Plattsburgh, N. Y., July 15, 1818; m. April 11, 1850, Caroline V. Conger; had Frank and Carlos.

Resides St. Louis, Mo.

CALPHINIA, b. in St. Louis, 1822; m. 29 Oct., 1844, Montgomery Pike Leintz; she d. June 12, 1849; issue, I *Mary Wetmore,* b. Aug. 1, 1845; II *William Alphonso,* b. March 28, 1848.

ROXANA, b. St. Louis, Sept. 15, 1824; m. March 15, 1849, George T. Bacon.

Resides Marine Mills, Minnesota.

SARAH, b. St. Louis, May 27, 1828; m. Oct. 12, 1852, Charles G. Weber; had I *Henry Edward*, b. April 4, 1857.

Resides St. Louis.

THOMAS A. SMITH, b. Franklinton, Mo., Oct. 21, 1830; m. May 3, 1849, Elizabeth A. Spencer; had *Thomarine A.*

He died Oct. 25, 1850, æ. 20 years.

Dr. ALPHONZO, b. St. Louis, Oct. 22, 1836; unm.

Is a practicing physician, Monroe city, Ill.

Children of SALMON B.,

Son of Seth, Son of John, Son of Samuel.

REGULUS L., b. Dec, 29, 1817; m. Elizabeth Wooster, of Esperance, 1837; had Eliza Jane (d. æ. 3 years), Sarah, George W.

Resides in Albany, N. Y.

ELIZA JANE, b. Dec. 20, 1819; m. Edwin Williams, of Canajoharie, N. Y.; had I *Thomas;* II *Hetty O.;* III *Edwin Emerson;* IV *Eliza Jane;* V *Henrietta* and VI *Mary Edgar* (twins); VII *Jemima;* VIII *Olive.*

HARRIET ANN, b. Sept. 11, 1822; m. John W. Conover of Canajoharie, Oct., 1846; had I *Helen Louisa;* II *Henry Oscar.*

She died Feb. 11, 1856, in her 33d year.

VERNON B., b. April 6, 1824; m: Mary Olendorff of Lawrence, Otsego co., N. Y.; had a son.

Resides at Honesdale, N. Y.

HENRY OSCAR, b. Nov. 19, 1832; d. July 4, 1846.

MARY ARTEMESIA, b. March 11, 1836; m. John Q. Adams of Canajoharie, Feb. 9, 1853; had Edwin, b. Nov. 23, 1855.

Children of PYTHAGORAS,

Son of Seth, Son of John, Son of Samuel.

BURNEL J., b. June 5, 1820; d. Aug. 18, 1843.

ALPHONZO, b. Dec. 3, 1821; m. Mary, dau. of Rev. John Pegg; had John P., Ida.

JUSTUS F., b. Feb. 1, 1824; m. Rhoda Bailey of Canajoharie; had Charles; m. 2d, Aug. 13, 1860, Cornelia, dau. of Martin Brownell, Esq., of Hornelsville, N. Y.

Resides at Hornelsville.   Attorney at Law.

ELIZA CATHERINE, b. July 8, 1829; m. David Zeilly of Palatine, N. Y., May 21, 1851; had I *Anna*, b. Feb. 22, 1852; II *Mary Louisa*, b. July 26, 1854; III *Isabella*, b. April 17, 1859.

NANCY LOUISA, b. May 7, 1834; m. George A. Gilderslive of Palatine Bridge, N. Y., April 20, 1853; had I *Harriet*, b. April 26, 1854; II *Catherine*, b. June, 1857; III *Louisa*, b. Sept. 3, 1858.

BYRON LOISA, b. June 15, 1838; d. May 21, 1844.

Children of GEORGE CLINTON,

Son of Seth, Son of John, Son of Samuel.

NANCY, b. Oct. 2, 1832; d. Nov. 14, 1833.

GEORGE, b. in Ames, N. Y., July 18, 1834; d. in Saline co., Mo., Feb. 28, 1845.

FLORENCE, b. in Franklinton, Mo., July 10, 1845.

HERMAN, b. in Carroll co., Mo., Dec. 21, 1858; d. March 22, 1859.

Sons of LEAMING,

Son of Samuel, Son of John, Son of Samuel.

SOLOMON.

Descendants of Samuel, son of Thomas.

SAMUEL M.

4 daughters.

Resides in Illinois.

Children of CALVARY,

Son of Samuel, Son of John, Son of Samuel.

CALVARY LEVI, b. in Vernon, N. Y., July 13, 1828 ; m. Kate dau. of William Maxwell Esq., of Elmira, N. Y.

Merchant ; res. in Chicago, Ill.

ANN ELIZABETH ALTHEA, b. in Vernon, Aug. 9, 1841.

Children of SAMUEL,

Son of Samuel, Son of John, Son of Samuel.

SAMUEL LEVI, b. in Adams, Jeff. co., N. Y., Aug. 8, 1834.

MARIA HUNGERFORD, b. in A., April 10, 1843.

Children of HERBERT GRISWOLD,

Son of Samuel, Son of John, Son of Samuel.

JAMES.

HENRY.

2 daughters.

Children of WILLIAM HENRY,

Son of Noah, Son of Rev. Noah, Son of Samuel.

CATHERINE, b. Aug. 15, 1822 ; m. John H. Whiteside ; had I *Sarah ;* II *Thomas Whiteside ;* III *William Henry ;* IV *Frank ;* V *Mary ;* VI *Infant.*

DAVID, b. Oct. 31, 1823 ; m. Caroline Bixby ; had Calvin Mather, Catherine Hoffman.

ABRAHAM BRINCKERHOFF, b. Sept. 17, 1825 ; m. Martha Emma Fobos, Dec. 6, 1859.

WILLIAM HENRY, b. June 23, 1827 ; d. Dec. 5, 1859 ; unm.

Children of APPOLOS RUSSEL 2D.

Son of Noah, Son of Rev. Noah, Son of Samuel.

HENRY CARMER, b. in New York city, Aug. 6, 1823 ; m. Mary Jane Bird ; had Thomas Bird, Mary Carmer, Henry, Alethea, Edith.

Resides in Dutchess co., N. Y., which county he represented in the state senate, 1859-60.

GEORGE CARMER, b. in New York city, Jan. 9, 1829 ; m. Elizabeth Graham Williams, June 1, 1852 ; had Charles Williams, Howard Graham, George Carmer.

He is one of the house of Wetmore & Co., importing merchants, corner of Greenwich and Vesey sts., New York.

THEODORE RUSSEL, b. in city of New York, Jan. 28, 1826 ; m. Elizabeth Russel Pitcher, Dec. 12, 1849 ; had Russel, Marie Bleecker, Alice Josephine, Theodore ; she d. Oct. 13, 1857 ; he m. 2d, Ellen N. D'Arcy, Sept. 20, 1859.

Resides in the city of New York ; one of the firm of Churchill Rogers and Wetmore, wholesale merchants.

WILLIAM, b. in New York, Oct. 4, 1829 ; m. Annie Dougherty, March 4, 1856 ; had Florence, Theodore, Anderson.

Wholesale merchant, New York city.

ELIZABETH CARMER, b. in New York, March 29, 1831.

MARY CARMER, b. in N. Y., July 31, 1846.

Children of DAVID WOODHULL,

Son of Noah, Son of Rev. Noah, Son of Samuel.

HARRIET COOPER, b. July 10, 1828.

JACOB SHARPE, b. Aug. 26, 1830; m. Mary Leonard Lovejoy; had Elizabeth Courtney.

CORNELIA BROWER, b. Sept. 11, 1832; m. Richard H. Chappell; had I *Harriet W.;* II *Henry Haven.*

PETER SHARPE, b. Aug. 11, 1834. } twins.
CHRISTIANA SHARPE, "   "   } twins.

IRENE, b. July 12, 1836; m. Andrew Herman DeWitt; had Anna.

JAMES SCOTT, b. July 12, 1836.

FANNY, b. Oct., 1840.

Children of APPOLOS EDWARDS,

Son of Appolos, Son of Rev. Noah, Son of Samuel.

HENRY AUGUSTUS, b. Dec. 15, 1827; m. Oct. 14, 1849, Louisa J., dau. of James W. Pinckney; had Frank Ward, Maria Louise, Ida, Emily Ann.

OLIVER, b. July 12, 1829; m. Oct. 25, 1853, Elizabeth, dau. of Amos F. Hatfield, late sheriff of Westchester co., N. Y.; had Estelle, Stanley Hatfield.

Merchant in the city of New York.

LEWIS PRALL, b. Jan. 13, 1837.

WILLIAM WALTER, b. May 19, 1844.

Daughter of OLIVER.

Son of Appolos, Son of Rev. Noah, Son of Samuel

FLORENCE, b. Aug. 8, 1851.

15

Children of AUGUSTUS,

Son of Appolos, Son of Rev. Noah, Son of Samuel.

AUGUSTUS, b. Jan. 24, 1832.

EMILY, b. March 25, 1843 ; d. Jan. 29, 1846.

EDWARD LESLIE, b. Feb. 4, 1847.

Son of WILLIAM WALTER, 2D,

Son of Appolos, Son of Rev. Noah, Son of Samuel.

STEPHEN SHIPMAN, b. May 1, 1846.

Daughter of Dr. EBENEZER WALTER,

Son of Samuel Ithiel, Son of Rev. Noah, Son of Samuel.

LYBIA, b. Feb. 22, 1832; m. H. Quackenboss of New York; d. July
10, 1860.

Children of ERASTUS,

Son of Samuel Ithiel, Son of Rev. Noah, Son of Samuel.

SAMUEL ITHIEL, b. — ; d. July 16, 1838.

TIMOTHY BURGER.

Children of EGBERT,

Son of Samuel Ithiel, Son of Rev. Noah, Son of Samuel.

EGBERT.

CHARLES J. COGGILL, b. — ; d. Dec., 1844.

GEORGE MANTAN.

Children of FREDERICK P.,

Son of John Pomeroy, Son of Joel, Son of Samuel

RUSSELL C., b. May 6, 1847.

CHARLES W., b. Oct. 6, 1854.

Children of HENRY A.,

Son of John Pomeroy, Son of Joel, Son of Samuel.

HARRIET, b. about 1849.

FREDERICK, b. about 1851.

EVA.

CLARA.

Children of WILLIAM L.,

Son of John Pomeroy, Son of Joel, Son of Samuel.

WILLIAM G., b. Aug. 10, 1852; d. Oct. 10, 1853.

EDWIN ATWATER, b. Aug. 12, 1854.

CARRIE LOUISA, b. Sept. 10, 1856; d. Sept. 6, 1860.

ERNEST LE PELLY, b. Oct. 13, 1860.

Children of COMFORT,

Son of Jesse, Son of Daniel, Son of Daniel.

JOSIAH AMSDEN, b —; m. 1st, ——; had Horace; m. 2d, ——; had dau.

Resides at Madison, Lake co., Ohio.

BARNET WOODBURY, b. —; m. ——; had 3 sons and 1 dau. Ophelia.

Resides at Austinsburg, Ashtabula co., Ohio.

DR. SAMUEL WILLIAM, b. in Ashtabula co., O.; April 30, 1832; m. Oct. 26, 1855, Mary E. Barbour of Coneaut, O.; had Willis Ashton.

He graduated at Michigan University. Resides at Kingsville, Ashtabula co., O.

EIGHTH GENERATION.

Daughter of DARWIN WOODWARD,

Son of Dr. Truman Spencer, Son of Abel, Son of Samuel, Son of Samuel.

ELIZABETH, b. in New York, Oct. 4, 1851; d. March 26, 1853.

Daughter of Dr. WILLIAM JARVIS,

Son of Dr. Truman Spencer, Son of Abel, Son of Samuel, Son of Samuel.

EMMA JARVIS.

Children of Dr. GEORGE WHITFIELD,

Son of Dr. Truman Spencer, Son of Abel, Son of Samuel, Son of Samuel.

GEORGE THOMPSON.

ELIZABETH JARVIS.

MARY FITCH.

Daughter of CHARLES FITCH,

Son of Dr. Truman Spencer, Son of Abel, Son of Samuel, Son of Samuel.

MARY JARVIS, b. Sept. 14, 1852.

Children of Dea. ABEL SAMUEL,

Son of John, Son of Abel, Son of Samuel, Son of Samuel.

JULIA ANN, b. in New Hartford, Ct., Aug. 18, 1830 ; d. June 5, 1831.

JOHN NASH, b. in Winchester, Ct., March 8, 1833.

ELLEN ELIZA, b. in W. Oct. 29, 1834 ; m. Aug. 14, 1856, Stephen Grenville, son of Stephen and Antha (Stone) Beecher, b. Dec. 9, 1832 ; had I *Henry Ward*, b. in New Milford, Ct., July 22, 1857 ; II *Mary*, b. in N. M., Jan. 14, 1859.

LEROY WHITING, b. in W. Sept. 23, 1836.

MILES HILLS, b, in W. Sept. 6, 1840.

SAMUEL ABEL, b. in W. Sept. 25, 1842.

HUBERT PORTER, b. in W. Feb. 21, 1847.

Son of LUCRETIUS ALLEN,

Son of Elisha, Son of Seth, Son of Samuel, Son of Samuel.

WILLIS L.

Daughter of HORATIO LUCIUS,

Son of John, Son of Seth, Son of John, Son of Samuel.

SARAH LOUISA, b. in Winchester, Ct., April 12, 1833.

Children of DIOGENES,

Son of Maj. Alphonzo, Son of Seth, Son of John, Son of Samuel.

OCTAVIA, b. Sept. 11, 1837.

Resides St. Louis.

MARY ELIZA, b. Oct. 6, 1848.

HUGH ALPHONZO, b. March 5, 1851.

Children of THADDEUS KOSCIUSZKO,

Son of Maj. Alphonzo, Son of Seth, Son of John, Son of Samuel.

FRANK.

CARLOS, b. 1855.

Children of THOMAS A. SMITH,

Son of Maj. Alphonzo, Son of Seth, Son of John, Son of Samuel.

THOMERINE A., b. Oct. 10, 1850.

Daughter of JOHN GRENELL,

Son of John, Son of Seth, Son of John, Son of Samuel.

ELIZA ROSSETER, b. in Winchester, Feb. 20, 1847.

Children of REGULUS,

Son of Salmon B., Son of Seth, Son of John, Son of Samuel.

SARAH.

GEORGE W.

Children of ALPHONZO,

Son of Pythagoras, Son of Seth, Son of John, Son of Samuel.

JOHN P.

IDA.

Son of JUSTUS F.,

Son of Pythagoras, Son of Seth, Son of John, Son of Samuel.

CHARLES.

Children of DAVID,

Son of William Henry, Son of Noah, Son of Rev. Noah, Son of Samuel.

CALVIN MATHER.

CATHERINE HOFFMAN.

Children of HENRY CARMER,

Son of Appolos Russel 2d, Son of Noah, Son of Rev. Noah, Son of Samuel.

THOMAS BIRD.

MARY CARMAN.

HENRY.

ALETHEA.

EDITH.

Children of GEORGE CARMER,

Son of Appolos Russel 2d, Son of Noah, Son of Rev. Noah, Son of Samuel.

CHARLES WILLIAMS.

HOWARD GRAHAM,

GEORGE CARMER.

Children of THEODORE RUSSEL,

Son of Appolos Russel 2d, Son of Noah, Son of Rev. Noah, Son of Samuel.

RUSSEL.

MARIE BLEECKER.

ALICE JOSEPHINE.

THEODORE.

Children of WILLIAM,

Son of Appolos Russel 2d, Son of Noah, Son of Rev. Noah, Son of Samuel.

THEODORE.

FLORENCE, d. young.

Daughter of JACOB SHARPE,

Son of David Woodhull, Son of Noah, Son of Rev, Noah, Son of Samuel.

ELIZA COURTENAY,

Children of HENRY AUGUSTUS,

Son of Appolos Edwards, Son of Appolos, Son of Rev. Noah, Son of Samuel.

FRANK WARD,

MARIE LOUISE,

IDA.

EMILY ANN.

Children of OLIVER,

Son of Appolos Edwards, Son of Appolos, Son of Rev. Noah, Son of Samuel.

ESTELLE, b. Oct. 23, 1854,

STANLEY HATFIELD, b. Nov. 10, 1856.

Son of JOSIAH AMSDEN,

Son of Comfort, Son of Jesse, Son of Daniel, Son of Daniel.

HORACE.

Son of BARNET WOODBURY,

Son of Comfort, Son of Jesse, Son of Daniel, Son of Daniel.

OPHELIA, b. —. She was burned to death at the time the house of her grandfather, Comfort Wetmore, was destroyed by fire, Sept. 1859, aged about 12 years.

Son of Dr. SAMUEL WILLIAM,

Son of Comfort, Son of Jesse, Son of Daniel, Son of Daniel.

WILLIS ASHTON, b. Dec, 18, 1859.

DESCENDANTS OF IZRAHIAH, SON OF IZRAHIAH, SON OF THOMAS.

THIRD GENERATION.

Rev. IZRAHIAH WETMORE,

Was the eldest of eight sons of Izrahiah and Rachel (Stow) Whitmore, son of Thomas and Sarah (Hall) Whitmore, b. in Middletown, Ct., June 28 (Jan. 29 ?), 1693 ; m. Sarah Booth[1] of Stratford ; had Prosper, Rachel, Mary, John Booth and Izrahiah.

He studied for the ministry, probably under the Rev. William Russell, the pastor of the church at Middletown. He removed to, and was settled over the Presbyterian church at Stratford, about or soon after his majority, where he labored, doing missionary work there in the surrounding country till he was called to his heavenly home, Sept. 14, 1728, in his 36th year.

[1] BOOTH, EBENEZER, Stratford s. of Richard ; m. Elizabeth, dau. of Richard Jones of Haddam ; had 3 sons, Benjamin, Edward, Ebenezer, besides daus. Deborah, Elizabeth, and Abigail, all liv. at his d., and he gave Nathaniel s., of his s. Ebenezer, and d. 1732. EPHRAIM, Stratford, eldest son of Richard, in his will of Feb. 1683, short. bef. his d., names w. Mary, and minor chil. Richard, Mary, Joanna, Bethia, and cous. Samuel Hawley.
RICHARD, Stratford 1640, m. a sis. of the first Joseph Hawley ; had Elizabeth, b. 12 Sept., 1641 ; Ann Feb. 14, 1644 ; Ephraim, Aug., 1648 ; Ebenezer, Nov. 19, 1651 ; John, b. Nov., 1653 ; Joseph, Feb., or 8 March, 1656 ; Bethia, 18 May, 1658 ; and Joana, 21 March, 1661 ; was a selectman in 1669, and on Freeman's list the same yr., and after 1673, prob. liv. many years. He testif. that he was 80 years old in 1687. His dau. Eliz. m. 19 Oct. 1658, John Minor. JOSEPH, Stratford, youngest s. of Richard, in his will of 14 Aug., 1703, pro. Jan. following, names, W. Eliz., d. ; Hannah, s., James, Joseph, Robert, David, and Nathan, but another s., Zachariah, is omit. His est. was good. JOHN Southhold, L. I., 1659, refused obedience to Conn. jurisdiction.—*Savage Gen. Dict.*, vol. i., p. 212.

His remains lie interred in the old East burying
ground of Middletown ; a stone, with a record of his
name, dates of birth and death, mark the spot, says a
record before us, dated 1792, made by Judge William
Wetmore of Boston.

FOURTH GENERATION.

Children of Rev. IZRAHIAH.

PROSPER, b. May 14, 1722; m. Nov. 18, 1756, Keturah (Katurah?)
Cheesborough,[2] b. 1734; had Nathan, Anna, Izrahiah, Mary,
Sarah (Polly?), James, Eunice.

He early removed to Norwich, Ct. In Miss F. M.

[2] WILLIAM (Cheesbrough or borough), Boston, came from Boston, co.
Lincoln (in or near wh. prob. he was born about 1594), with w. Ann,
1630, arr. in the fleet with Winth. He had m. 15 Dec., 1620, Ann Steven-
son, and they had in Eng., Mary, bapt. 2 May, 1622; Martha, 18 Sept.,
1623 ; David and Jonathan, twins, 9 Sept. 1624; all d. soon; Samuel, 1
April, 1627; Andronicus, 6 Feb. 1629 (wh. d. in two days, as did Junia, a
tw. ch. the day bef.) and Nathaniel, 25 Jan., 1630. On this side of the
water they were among the earliest mem. of the first ch. of B. Nos. 44 and
5 on the list, he was adm. freem. 18 May 1631, and the same day his house
was burn. Ch. in Boston bapt. were John, 2 Sept. or 11 Nov. 1632, as the
numerals for mo. and day are various ; read, wh. d. at Stonington, prob.
unm. ; Jabez, 3 May 1635, d. young; Elisha, 4 June 1637 ; and at Braintree b. Joseph, 18 July, 1640; and this year he was rep. Soon after he
rem. to Rehoboth, where he was active 1643, and in less than seven years,
to Pawcatuck, where he was the earliest perm. sett. in that part of New
London called Stonington. This brought the Conn. govt. to vindicate their
territorial right, and very curious matter may be read about the jurisdiction
in Trumbull's *Col. Rec.*, I, 216-17; to the result however the judicious
mildness of C. led soon, and he was a rep. 1653, 5, 7, and 64, for N. London
or Stonington. He d. June 9, 1667, leav. wid. Ann, wh. d. 29 Aug. 1673.
His son Joseph, under 12 yrs. old, cut his leg with a scythe, and bled to
death. A mother or sister I think may be found for him in the Boston list
of mem. of the ch. Sarah C. No. 78, and upon the margin, is mark. early d.
SAMUEL, Stonington, youngest son of the first Nathaniel of same, m. 4 Jan.
1699, Priscilla Alden, call g. dau. of Mayflower John, but wh. was her f.
I see not; had Mary b. 21 Sept. 1702; Priscilla, 6 Nov. 1704 ; Nathaniel,
19 Aug. 1706, d. young; Amos, 2 Feb. 1709; Hannah, 6 July 1712; Sarah,
14 Aug. 1714, and Prudence, b. 28 Feb. 1722. Six of his chil. lived to
be married. WILLIAM, Stonington, son of Samuel of the same, m. Dec. 13,
1698, for sec. w. Mary dau. of Fergus McDowell, had William, David, Thomas, Abigail and Mary.—*Savage's Gen. Dict.*, I, 374.

Caulkins's *Hist. of Norwich,* we find his name recorded as one of the officers of the sixth Ecclesiastical (Chelsea) Society, organized Nov. 29, 1751, and at a later date renting pew No. 17, in the same church, in company with Ebenezer Fitch, and in 1765 preferring charges before the council (along with Ephraim Bill, Peter Lanman, and the two Backuses) against their clergyman, the Rev. Mr. Whitaker; "he on his part charging them of violent language and unchristian conduct." The council appears not to have decided the matter.

He was for many years, sheriff of New London co., and as sheriff took a conspicuous part in the stirring events pertaining to those troublesome times.

Dr. Church, a prisoner of the Continental Congress, having been delivered by Gen. Washington into the hands of Gov. Trumbull for safe keeping, the latter directed him to be confined in the gaol at Norwich. He was accordingly conveyed thither and given into custody of Prosper Wetmore Esq., sheriff of New London county. The orders respecting him were strict and minute. Other prisoners of war, occasionally in large bands, were brought hither for confinement.

Respecting Dr. Church and others, the Council of safety made the following orders:

At a meeting July 30, 1776.

Present: His Honor the Governor: Eliphalet Dyer Jr, Titus Hosmer, Richd Law, Jed Elderkin. Wm Hillhouse, Nathl Wales, Benjamin Huntington Esquires. * * *

Voted and allowed Prosper Wetmore Esq., sheriff of New London, of the county of New London, the sum of £12, 2s, 10d, for his expense and trouble in supporting and guarding twenty-two Continental prisoners, taken by Commodore Hopkins, and transporting them with their baggage to Windham jail, as pr bill.

Also voted and allowed to said Wetmore the sum of £11, 4s, for transporting Dr. Church, by order of congress, from Norwich to Boston, and from thence to Watertown, as per bill.

Also voted and allowed to said Wetmore the sum of £9, 5s, for his trouble and expense with Dr. Church while a prisoner in his care, from Nov., 1775, until the 27th of May, 1776, and for his trouble in waiting on Dr. Church, abroad for his health, at sundry times during his imprisonment, as was ordered by Congress, amounting in the whole, to £32, 11s, 10d, lawful money, order drawn and delivered, Mr. Wetmore.—5 *American Archives*, I, 683.

This Dr. Church, was Dr. Benjamin Church, director general of the hospital (Gen. Sullivan's division in camp at Cambridge, Mass.). He was also a member of the General Court from Boston. He had been complained of, for neglect of duty, and suspected of want of fidelity to the cause of independence, when he was detected in secret communication with the enemy. He was expelled from the General Court of Mass., Nov. 4, 1775, and the Continential Congress passed the following resolution: (See *Am. Archives.*)

Philadelphia, Nov. 6, 1775.

Resolved, That Dr. Church be closely confined in some secure jail in the colony of Connecticut, without the use of pen, ink or paper, and that no person be allowed to converse with him except in the presence or hearing of a magistrate of the town, or the sheriff of the county, where he shall be confined, and in the English language, until further order from this, or a future Congress.

By order of Congress.   JOHN HANCOCK, Pres't.
Attest.   CHARLES THOMPSON, Sect'y.

And underwritten:

Sir:—In consequence of the above resolves, I now transmit to your care, Dr. Church, under the guard of Captain *Israel Putnam*, a sergent, and seven men. You will please comply in every pariicular, with the above resolution of Congress.   I am, with great respect, Sir, your
most humble and obedient servant,
GEORGE WASHINGTON.

The above was addressed to the governor and council of safety, then, (Nov. 22, 1775,) sitting at Lebanon, Ct. They "*Voted* and *resolved* that the said Dr. Church be committed to, and confined, and kept in the same manner as ordered by said Congress, in the jail in Norwich, in the county of New London, until further orders from said Congress and this board."—4 *Am. Archives*, III.

Connecticut Council of Safety, Dec. 10, 1776.

At a meeting of the Govenor; Eliphalet Dyer, John Huntington, William Williams, William Hillhouse, Nath¹ Wales Jr, Benj. Huntington and Thoˢ Seymours Esquires.

Voted; To give Prosper Wetmore Esq., Sheriff on Capt. Harding's producing and lodging with him his power of Attorney from the Officers and men on board the Brig Defence, in the capture of the Prize ship *John*, taken by them and brought into New London and condemned, that first deducting the charges and condemnation and all other expenses, then one-twentieth part of net proceeds of the avails of the ship and cargo, being the Admirals part settled by congress; then the one-third of the remainder to be by him paid to Captain Harding for his and Brigs Crew their share in said prize, taking his receipts therefor, and to call upon Capt. Bell for the bill of expenses, and they are all properly collected in order to make settlement. (Order given Dec. 13, 1776.)   *   *   *   Directed Prosper Wetmore Esqr., to pay Capt. Harding £716, 12*s*, 10*d*, of the States money in his hands, which together with £683, 7*s*, 2*d*, makes the sum of £1400, contained in the order given above as on this page to Capt. Harding.—*Am. Archives*.

He and his wife were buried at Norwich; the following is a copy of the inscription on their joint tombstone, in the old burying ground of that place.

Katurah Consort of Prosper Wetmore Esqr.,
died 13 Feby 1789; aged 53
Mʳ James, Son of Prosper and Katurah
died at Sea Oct 17, 1787, aged 17.
Prosper Wetmore Esqr, who for many years
was Sheriff of New London County
died Oct 15, 1787 in his 65ᵗʰ year

RACHEL, b. Oct. 2, 1723; d. young.

MARY, b. July 15, 1725; m. Nathaniel Wales, Esq., of Norwich, ·Ct.

JOHN BOOTH, b. in Stratford, March 30, 1727; d. young.

IZRAHIAH, Rev., b. in Stratford Aug. 30, 1729; m. Dec. 30, 1756, Pheobe, dau. of Hon. Robert Walker of Stratford; had Sarah Salima, Victory, Prosper, Rebecca, Robert William, Victory 2d, William Walker, Charles Henry, Tryphenia, Richard Montgomery, Charles Joseph and Charles Henry 2d; m. 2d, Annie Ward of Middletown, who d. July 5, 1812, s. p.

He graduated at Yale college, 1748. Took the degree of M. A., at the same institution, 1751. Studied theology and entered the ministry; was pastor of the Presbyterian church of Stratford and Trumbull 45 years. He preached the election sermon before the Legislature of Connecticut in 1773. A sermon in pamphlet form entitled :

" The Important Duties and Qualifications of Gospel Ministers, considered in a Sermon preached at the Ordination of the Reverend DAVID LEWIS BEEBEE to the Pastoral office over the first Church of Christ, in Woodbridge, February 23, 1791. By Izrahiah Wetmore, A. M., Pastor of a Church in Stratford. 'And I will give you pastors according to mine heart; which shall feed you with knowledge and understanding.'— *Jeremiah,* 3 xv. New Haven, Printed by A. Morse. MDCCXCI."

Together with two autograph sermons, by the same, have been kindly placed in our hands for inspection, by Gen. H. B. Carrington of Columbus. We regret that we have not the space to give one or more of them in extenso. The manuscript sermons are written in a a very small clear hand, and seem to be marked with much vigor of thought and terseness of language. They are headed as follows :

Descendants of Rev. Izrahiah, son of Izrahiah, son of Thomas.

No. 69, The Sin of Tempting God, from

1 Corinthians x Chapter the ix Verse.	Neither Let us Tempt Christ as some of them also tempted and were destroyed of Serpents.	Textus . . . .

At the end of the manuscript the following appears :

Composed at Abbington, May 8th [1752]
by Izrahiah Wetmore, M. A.,
In the 23d Year of His Age.

No. 55.

Text.	So I gave them up unto their own Hearts' Lust: & they walked in their own Counsels.	Psm 85	12 verse.

and has-inscribed at the end :

Composed at Reading Nov. 25,
1755, by I. Wetmore, A. M.
Anno Ætatis ** — . 24c

He was, as were most of the Dissenting ministers of his day, warmly attached to the cause of Independence. This anecdote is related of him : When the news of the surrender of Lord Cornwallis to Gen. Washington reached Stratford, it was on Sunday, and during the hours of worship. Word was immediately taken to the pulpit, where Parson Wetmore was engaged in delivering his discourse. Drawing himself up to his fullest height, and making known the intelligence, he said : " My friends, the house of God is no place for boisterous demonstrations ; we will therefore, in giving *three cheers*, only go through the motions." That the *motions* were given with an *emphasis*, the reader will readily imagine.

He died at Trumbull, Aug. 3, 1798, and was buried at Stratford. His wife Pheobe Walker died Sept. 12, 1784. She was of a highly honorable family; her father, the

Hon. ROBERT WALKER,

Held many important civil and military posts. For many years before, and at the time of his death, he was one of his majesty's council for the Colony of Connecticut; was one of the judges of the superior court; colonel of the colonial militia; all of which duties he discharged with fidelity and honor.. . He firmly believed and consistently practised the precepts of the gospel. He died July 13, 1772, aged 68 years:... His wife, Mrs. Rebecca Walker, died Feb. 28, 1805, æ. 89.

ROBERT WALKER Jun., brother of Mrs. Pheobe Walker Wetmore, was a man of influence. A record of him says :

In private life his deportment was in the highest degree exemplary. The urbanity of his manners, the amiability of his disposition, and the benevolence of his character, were peculiarly conspicuous. He was kind, courteous and charitable, ardent in his friendship, and forgiving in his · resentments. To his strong intellectual powers was added a quick, discerning judgment. He was honored with many important civil offices, the duties of which he discharged with unswerving fidelity. He was a firm believer in Christianity, and a powerful advocate of good morals.

Gen. JOSEPH WALKER, also a brother of Mrs. Wetmore, was an officer in the army of the Revolution; was elected captain by the Connecticut assembly in Oct. 1776. Of his subsequent rise to that of general, we are unadvised. He died Aug. 12, 1810, æ. 55.

Note. Samuel Beers m. Feb. 19, 1758, Sarah Wetmore. She d. Dec. 4, 1784; issue Lucy, b. Sept. 10, 1760; Sarah Anna, b. June 20, 1762; William Peet, b. April 12, 1766. (*Stratford Town Rec.*) . We have no connecting link for the above Sarah (Wetmore) Beers.

17

FIFTH GENERATION.

Children of PROSPER.

NATHAN, b. at Norwich, Ct., Aug. 25, 1757; m. 1783, Elizabeth
Bushnell of Lebanon, b. Feb. 5, 1761; had Prosper, Augustus,
and Ebenezer.

He was a man of respectability and influence, holding the office of deputy sheriff of the county of New
London, Ct., at that time a position of trust and importance, which he retained till his death, Nov. 5,
1791; his widow survived him till July 17, 1849.

ANNA, b. Jan. 20, 1759; d. —.

IZRAHIAH, b. Oct. 21, 1766; m. ——; had James, George Washington, Ruben Schuyler, Sarah Ann, Ann, Lucy and Izrahiah.

Removed to Albany, N. Y., where he died.

MARY, b. March 16, 1761.

SARAH, b. Sept. 27, 1763.

EUNICE,

JAMES, b. 1770-1; d. at sea, Oct. 17, 1787; æ. 17 years.

Children of Rev. IZRAHIAH Jun.

SARAH SELINA, (Selene, *Town Rec.*) b. in Stratford, Oct. 3, 1757;
m. Abijah Brooks of S.; had I *Burr;* II *Sarah;* III *Major.*

She d. June 11, 1813; æ. 56; he d. April 4, 1829;
æ. 77.

VICTORY, b. in S.; d. Nov. 1762, æ. 3 years.

His death was caused by falling upon the point of a
stick.

PROSPER, b. in S.; m. Catherine McEwen; had Robert Walker, Mary Ann, and Malcom McEwen.

He was an aid-de-camp to General Joseph Walker during the Revolutionary war. At the time of his first engaging in the service of his country, he was but 14 years of age. After the close of the war, and the country was once more undisturbed, he turned his attention to mercantile pursuits in the city of New York, and became extensively engaged in the China and West India trade, under the firm of Prosper Wetmore & Brothers, his younger brothers Victory 2d and Robert William, being partners.

In 1817, he took passage on board of one of his own vessels for France. The vessel after leaving the port of New York, was never heard of again. It was supposed that the ship with all on board were lost in a gale. He died aged 50 years. His wife was of Scotch descent. She died ——.

REBECCA, b. in S., March, 1760; d. Dec. 1, 1760; aged 10 mos.

ROBERT WILLIAM, b. in S.; m. Amelia, dau. of Richard Hubbell, Esq., of Bridgeport, Ct.; had Cornelia Roxanna, Frances Caroline, Prosper Montgomery, and Robert Charles.

He was engaged in the China and West India trade with his brothers, Prosper and Victory, in the city of New York, residing himself at Bridgeport, Ct. Died ——.

VICTORY 2D, b. in S.; m. April 3, 1791, Katherine Maria McEwen; had Sidney, George McEwen, and William Courtney.

He resided in Stratford where he was engaged in the mercantile business for many years. Represented the town in the Connecticut Legislature. He d. March 10, 1817.

WILLIAM WALKER, b. in S. March 29, 1769; m. Sarah Bogardus, Jan. 10, 1793, who was b. March 28, 1773; had Anna Maria Patience, William Chauncey, Emeline Augusta, William

Henry, William Whiting,, Maria Louisa, Gustavus George Washington.

He died Dec. 2, 1837.

CHARLES HENRY, b. in S.; d. young.

TRYPHENIA, b. in S.; m. John Strong of Poquonak (Fairfield co.), Ct.

She died about 1828, s. p.; was buried at Bridgeport.

RICHARD MONTGOMERY, b. in S.; d. young.

CHARLES JOSEPH, b. in S. 1780; d. July 17, 1816; aged 36 years.

CHARLES HENRY 2D, Dr., b. in S. May 12, 1784; m. June 1, 1814, Eliza, dau. of John Rathbone of New York city, b. in Stonington, Ct., Sept. 13, 1791; had John Rathbone, Charles Joseph, Ann Eliza, Prosper Montgomery, Juliet Tryphenia, James Manning, Eunice Mary, Eunice Mary 2d, infant dau., Cornelia Roxana, and Emma Maria.

He entered Yale College in 1800, and graduated in 1804. In 1805 he commenced the study of medicine with Doct. Henry of Lansingburgh, N. Y.; at the same time teaching in the academy at that place, under the charge of the Rev. Samuel Blatchford; continued his medical studies during the years 1806, 7 and 8 with Dr. Eli Burritt of Troy. Having attended medical lectures at the College of Physicians and Surgeons of the University of New York, he obtained from the censors of the Rensselaer County Medical Society, a license to practice physic and surgery. After practicing his profession some months in Troy, he removed to Waterford (1810) where he was early admitted to the confidence of leading families, and received the warm support of many friends.

During the war of 1812 he was commissioned by Gov. Tompkins surgeon of the 144th regiment of New York infantry. He was however only a short time in active service, peace having been declared soon after the regiment had been ordered into the field.

In 1816 he removed to the city of New York, where he at once formed new acquaintances and friends, and was soon established in a lucrative practice.

His father-in-law having extensive landed interests in central Ohio, he was induced to remove there in November, 1819. He settled on a military tract, near the town of Worthington, where he immediately commenced the practice of his profession, combining with it agricultural pursuits, and soon became widely known as a skilful and successful physician; and was often called to distant parts of the country, to hold consultation with his professional brethren. After an arduous and laborious practice of more than a quarter of a century in that vicinity, his infirm health compelled him to withdraw from the active discharge of professional duties.

Dr. Wetmore's genial, humorous, and hospitable nature, always made his residence at Locust Grove, a favorite resort of the educated and refined. He has the family characteristic of love of kindred, particularly for those of his own name, in a marked degree. To him are the Wetmores much indebted for genealogical records of an early date : in 1818 to 1820 he had extensive correspondence with members of the family of that day; which enabled him to compile a chart, which has since been often referred to by those desiring to be informed of the genealogy of the family. We have had recourse to the same since we have been engaged in our present undertaking. He resides at Columbus, O.

Mrs. Eliza, wife of Dr. Wetmore, died at Columbus, Feb. 24, 1853. She was loved and revered by all who knew her. She animated her family circle by her cheerful and affectionate disposition, which she adorned by an unaffected piety. Her conversation was intelligent and instructive, and her life was governed by strict religious principle. She was the idols of her household, and the sweet remembrance of her many virtues will be fondly cherished when she has long slept with her ancestors.

Her father, the late John Rathbone, of New York, was a man of indefatigable energy and perseverance. The distinguishing traits of his character were sound judgment, prudence, firmness, and unswerving integrity. He died in the city of New York, March 14, 1843; at the advanced age of 91 years; having amassed an ample fortune. His son John Rathbone Jun. inherited his father's distinguishing qualities, and also became widely known as a successful merchant and financier. He was deeply interested in the inauguration of the canal movement in Ohio, and in connection with Eleazer Lord Esq., of New York, took the entire amount of the first Ohio canal loan, in 1825, of $400,000, and subsequently made a loan in connection with John Jacob Astor Sen., to the same state. He died at New York in 1842.

SIXTH GENERATION.

Children of NATHAN.

Son of Prosper.

PROSPER, b. in Norwich, Ct., Nov. 15, 1784; m. Apame Hinckley, Dec. 17, 1817; had Martha Elliot and Harriet Hinckley.

He resided at Lebanon, Ct., where he was extensively engaged in farming, manufacturing of leather, &c., and was a much respected citizen. He died April 24, 1826. She died ——.

AUGUSTUS, b. in Norwich, Ct., Nov. 6, 1786; m. Feb. 26, 1816, Emily T. Hinckley; had William Augustus, Charles Hinckley, Edwin Dutton, Edwin Dutton 2d; she d. April 3, 1825; and he m. her sister Sarah Hinckley, Nov. 27, 1825; had Emily Cornelia, Catherine, Sarah Jane, and William Augustus 2d.

He resides at Lebanon. During his early life he was engaged in business with his brother Prosper, and step-father Capt. Amasa Dutton, who had served honorably in the Revolution. A correspondent speaks thus of him:

Mr. Wetmore removed with his father to Lebanon in 1791, where he has ever since resided, save a few years spent at Millington, during his youth. By reason of age and its incident infirmities, though comparatively few have fallen upon him, he no longer confines himself to business. His three score years and ten, with their abundant cares and toils, are more than past, and it surely is befitting that the remainder be spent at ease in the bosom of his family.

He united with Congregational (orthodox) Church at 22 years of age. In public life he has been little seen, all his tastes leading another way. But in private he is well known as a man of umimpeachable integrity, strict honesty, warm friendship, unwavering fidelity, the purest life and sincerest piety. His tastes are simple and manners unaffected, and without ostentation. Though his efforts have not been crowned with affluence, at the call of the poor and needy his benevolence finds no excuse in that for witholding from his means. In person, Mr. Wetmore is about five feet six inches, in height, his frame well knit and muscular, inclining of late years somewhat to corpulence.

Of his father's children, he only remains a connecting link between the past and present.   D. H.

EBENEZER, b. Dec. 23, 1789; d. at Lebanon, June, 1790.

Children of IZRAHIAH,

Son of Prosper.

JAMES.

RUBEN SCHUYLER.

ANN, d. young.

IZRAHIAH.

GEORGE WASHINGTON.

SARAH ANN, d. young.

LUCY, d. young.

Children of PROSPER.
Son of Rev. Izrahiah 2d, Son of

ROBERT WALKER, d. young.

MALCOM McEWEN, d. unm.

MARY ANN, b. in New York, July 18, 1794; m. March 23, 1831, Alden Spooner[1] Esq., of Brooklyn, N. Y., b. Jan. 23, 1783; had Catherine McEwen Douglass, b. July 15, 1835.

Mr. Spooner was a native of New London, Ct.; was editor of the *Suffolk Gazette,* published at Sag Harbor, L. I., from 1804 to 1811; and of the *Long Island Star,* Brooklyn, which he conducted from 1811 till his death. He was for many years alderman of the city of Brooklyn. Mr. Spooner was an ardent admirer and personal friend of De Witt Clinton. It is said that Gov. C. once

---

[1] SPOONER GENEALOGY.

1. *William Spooner,* in Plymouth, 1637, rem. to Dartmouth, d. 1684. 1st, w. Elizabeth Partridge. She d. 28 April, 1648. Their only child, it is believed

2. *John.* 2 — ? d. — ? Dartmouth, was one of the proprietors of D., whom he m. not known. His first child was

11. *John,* b. 2 July, 1668; d., will probated 1728. Is mentioned in the confirmatory deed of Bradford, as one of the proprietors of Dartmouth. He m. 20 June, 1705, Rose Hammond of Rochester, who d. 1727. Their fifth child was

49. *Thomas,* b. July 16, 1718. He m. 10 June, 1742, Rebecca, dau. of Judah and Alice (Alden) Paddock, b. May 12, 1718, d. Jan. 1812. Children,

198. *Judah P.,* b. 5 Nov. 1748; d. Feb., 1807. He m. 10 Sept. 1770, Deborah Douglass of New London, Ct., b. Oct. 18, 1753. Their sixth child was

896. *Alden,* b. 23 Jan. 1783; d. 24 Nov. 1848. He m. 1st, 24 Feb. 1807, Sag Harbor, N. Y., Rebecca, dau. of John and Margeret Jermain. She b. 2 Oct., 1786; d. 15 March, 1824. They had eleven children. He m. 2d, 23 March, 1831, Mary Ann, dau. of Prosper and Catharine (McEwen) Wetmore; had

4012. Catherine McEwen Douglass, b. 15 July, 1835.—*From Thomas Spooner's (Reading, Ohio,) Manuscripts.*

remarked of him : " Mr. Spooner has been my most devoted and disinterested friend; he has never asked an office for himself or friends, and would not accept one." He died March 24, 1848.

Children of ROBERT WILLIAM,

Son of Rev. Izrahiah 2d.

CORNELIA ROXANA. b. —; m. Tredwell; had I *George; II Benja-min; III Alfred.*

FRANCES CAROLINE, b. —; d. unm.

PROSPER MONTGOMERY, Gen., b. on that part of the town of Strat-ford, on which now stands the city of Bridgeport, Feb. 14, 1798; m. Lucy Ann, dau. of Francis Ogsbury, Esq., of New York city; had 12 child.: 9 daus. and 3 sons, of whom 3 daus. are married and living, and 3 daus, and 1 son deceased,

He resides in the city of New York, where he has been distinguished for many years, in political, lite-rary, benevolent and commercial circles.

In 1834 and 5, he represented the city in the state Legislature. Having a great partiality for the military service, entered the state artillery, a volunteer corps, and was commissioned in 1819. In 1825, he organized and established, the 7th regiment of National Guards, was its first colonel commandant, which regiment has become famous in military circles;[2] was subsequently appointed pay master general of the state militia, which office he held till 1841. In 1834, was elected by the Legislature one of the Regents of the University of the State of New York, a body having charge of the higher interests of education. This office he still holds, giving it his active attention. Has filled for several

---

[2] This is the same 7th New York Regiment, now (April 26, 1861), at our national capital, under command of Col. Marshall Lefferets, standing ready to defend it, by their strong and well disciplined arm, from the ruth-less hands of *rebels* and *traitors*. ALL HONOR TO THE SEVENTH REGIMENT OF NEW YORK.

years the office of vice-president and secretary to the
Chamber of Commerce of New York, and several other
offices connected with the objects of commerce, literature and social organization in the city of New York.
Mr. Wetmore was one of the founders of the American
Art Union, and for three years its president. Under
his management the largest amount of subscriptions,
in the aid of the cause of art, was obtained and applied
to that object, which has ever been accomplished, by
any similar institution, either in this country or in
Europe.

For fifteen years, he devoted his best energies to
the management of the New York Institution for the
Deaf and Dumb, of which he was for many years, the
senior vice-president.

For the following notice of Gen. Wetmore, we are
indebted to the *Cyclopedia of American Literature*,
Scribner, N. Y., 1856, ii, 279.

At an early age he removed with his parents to New
York. His father dying soon after, he was placed, when
scarcely nine years of age, in a counting room, where he
continued a clerk till he reached his majority. He has
since that period been engaged in mercantile business in
the city of New York.

With scant early opportunity for literary culture, Mr.
Wetmore was not long in improving a natural tendency to
the pursuits of authorship.

He made his first appearance in print in 1816, at the age
of seventeen, and soon became an important aid to struggling literature, and it may be added, writers of the times.
He wrote for the magazines, the annuals, and the old
Mirror, and as literature at that period was kept up rather
as a social affair than from any reward promised by the
trade, it became naturally associated with a taste for the
green-room and the patronage of the theatricals of the day.
Mr. Wetmore was the companion of Price, Simpson,
Brooks, Morris, and other members of a society which
supported the wit and gaiety of the town.

In 1830, Mr. Wetmore published, in an elegant octavo volume, *Lexington, with other ·Fugitive Poems.* This is the only collection of his writings which has been made. Lexington, a picture, in an ode, of the early revolutionary battle, is a spirited poem. It has fire, and ease of versification. The Banner of Murat, The Russian Retreat, Greece, Painting, and several theatrical addresses possessing similar qualities, are among the contents of the volume.

In 1832, Mr. Wetmore delivered a poem, in Spenserian stanza, on Ambition, before one of the literary societies of Hamilton College, New York, which has not been printed.

In 1838, he edited a volume of the poems of James Nack, prefaced with a brief notice of the life of that remarkable person.

Mr. Wetmore, however, has been more generally known as a man of literary influence in society than as an author. He has been prominently connected with most of the liberal interests of the city, both utilitarian and refined; as a member of the Regents of the University, to which body he was appointed in 1833, promoting the public school system; as chairman of the committee on colleges and academies in the state Legislature, to which he was selected in 1834 and 1835; as a member of the city Chamber of Commerce; as an efficient director of the Institution for the Deaf and Dumb; as president of the American Art Union, which rapidly extended under his management to a national institution; and as a most active member and supporter of the New York Historical Society. These varied pursuits, the public indexes to more numerous private acts of liberality, have been sustained by a graceful personal manner, a sanguine temperament which preserves the freshness of youth, and a wide versatility of talent.

The military title of General Wetmore, by which he is widely known, is derived from his long and honorable service in the militia organization of the state, of which he was for many years paymaster general.

PAINTING.

Peopling with art's creative power, ·
The lonely home, the silent hour.

'Tis to the pencil's magic skill,
Life owes the power, almost divine,

To call back vanished forms at will,
  And bid the grave its prey resign :
Affection's eye again may trace
  The lineaments beloved so well ;
The speaking look, the form of grace,
  All on the living canvas dwell :
'Tis there the childless mother pays
  Her sorrowing soul's idolatry ;
Their love can find in after days,
  A talisman to memory !
'Tis thine, o'er history's storied page,
  To shed the halo light of truth ;
And bid the scenes of by-gone age
  Still flourish in immortal youth—
The long forgotten battle-field,
  With mailed men to people forth ;
In bannered pride, with spear and shield,
  To show the mighty ones of earth—
To shadow, from the holy book,
  The images of sacred lore ;
On Calvary, the dying look
  That told that life's agony was o'er—
The joyous hearts and glistening eyes,
  When little ones were suffered near,
The lips that bade the dead arise,
  To dry the widowed mother's tear :
These are the triumphs of the art,
  Conceptions of the master mind ;
Time-shrouded forms to being start,
  And wondering rapture fills mankind !

Led by the light of Genius on,
  What visions open to the gaze !
'Tis nature all, and art is gone,
  We breathe with them of other days :
Italia's victor leads the war,
  And triumphs o'er the ensanguined plain :
Behold ! the Peasant Conquerer
  Piling Marengo with his slain :
That sun of glory beats once more,
  But clouds have dimmed its radiant hue.
The splendor of its race is o'er,
  It sets in blood on Waterloo !

What scene of thrilling awe is here !
  No look of joy, no eye of mirth ;

With steeled hearts and brows austere,
　　Their deeds proclaim a nation's birth;
Fame here inscribes for future age,
　　A proud memorial of the free;
And stamps upon the deathless page,
　　The noblest theme of history!

We take the following beautiful stanzas, written by
Mr. Wetmore, from a work recently edited by the
Rev. Charles W. Everest, entitled *The Poets of Con-
necticut*, S. A. Rollo, New York.

Twelve Years Have Flown.

Twelve years have flown, since last I saw
　　My birth-place, and my home of youth,
How oft its scenes would memory draw
　　Her tints, the pencilings of truth!
Unto that spot I come once more,
　　The dearest life hath ever known,
And still it wears the look it wore,
　　Although twelve weary years have flown.

Twelve years have flown! those words are brief,
　　Yet in their sound what fancies dwell!
The hours of bliss, the days of grief,
　　The joys and woes remembered well;
The hopes that filled the youthful breast,
　　Alas, how many a one o'erthrown!
Deep thoughts, that long have been at rest,
　　Wake at the words, twelve years have gone.

The past, the past! a saddening thought,
　　A withering spell is in the sound!
It comes with memories deeply fraught
　　Of youthful pleasure's giddy round!
Of forms that roved life's sunniest bowers,
　　The cherished few forever gone,
Of dreams that filled life's morning hours;
　　Where are they now? twelve years have flown!

A brief but eloquent reply!
　　Where are youth's hopes, life's morning dream?
Seek for the flowers that floated by
　　Upon the rushing mountain-stream!

> Yet gems beneath that wave may sleep,
> Till after years shall make them known ;
> Thus golden thoughts the heart will keep,
> That perish not, though years have flown.

ROBERT CHARLES, Col., b. in the town of Fairfield, village of Pe-
quonnock, near Bridgeport, Ct.; m. June 1830, Adaline dau.
of Seth Geer Esq., of the city of New York; had Charles
Frederick, Florence Adele, and Victorine Upsher.

At an early age he was taken by his parents to the
city of New York, where he was prepared for a mercantile life, and when quite a youth was placed in the
house of the late Robert Christie, with whom he continued, save a short interval, till he established himself
in 1830, in the wholesale and importing business. The
house, of which he was the founder, became extensively
as well as favorably known throughout the country.

At an early period of his life he attached himself to
the military of New York; passing through the various grades of a commissioned officer, to that of colonel
in the staff of Gen. Sanford, where he still remains in
active duty.

He has always taken a lively interest in the political
questions of the day. He was conspicuous among the
opposition in the city of New York to President Jackson's administration, and in forming the old Whig
party out of the then opposition elements; and for
many years occupied the honorable as well as responsible position of chairman of the Young Men's Whig
Central Committee of that city. On Gen. Harrison
taking the presidential chair in 1841, he was appointed
navy agent for the port of New York, which office he
held for some years with credit to himself and service
to the navy department.

During Mr. Wetmore's public life in New York, he
has been esteemed liberal in his principles; popular in
his manners, and affable in his address; estimable for
his private worth, and respected for his virtues, his
public spirit, and unimpeachable integrity. He has

now retired from an active business life, and has sought quiet in his native town.

The late Mr. Geer, the father of Mrs. W., was for many years a prominent architect, and public spirited man in the city of New York. It was he who built, at his own risk, those famous marble palaces in Lafayette place, opposite the Astor Library. At the time they were constructed, we remember they were considered the wonder of New York.

Children of VICTORY,

Son of Rev. Izrahiah.

SIDNEY, b. in Stratford, July 5, 1792; m. ——; had Mary, Catherine, Virginia.

GEORGE McEWEN, b. in S. July 14, 1794; m. ——; had Mary, Robert Henry, and Grace Noble.

WILLIAM COURTNEY, b. in S. Oct. 12, 1796; m. Elizabeth Lovejoy; had Sarah, Elizabeth, Benjamin Clark, John McEwen, George William, Victory Ezekiel.

He graduated at Yale College 1815. Is an attorney and counsellor at law in the city of New York.

Children of WILLIAM WALKER,

Son of Rev. Izrahiah.

ANNA MARIA PATIENCE, b. Oct. 26, 1795; m. Richard Dunn of New York, 1828; he died 1840; leaving I *Mary Wetmore,* b. Dec. 3, 1830; m. David W. Miller of Greenville, N. Y., 1850; had Edward, b. Oct. 30, 1852: II *Anna Wetmore,* b. June 3, 1832; m. Franklin Curtiss of N. Y., 1852: III *John Wetmore,* b. March 24, 1833; m. Mary Morris of Brooklyn, N. Y., Sept. 4, 1858: IV *Rose Wetmore,* b. Sept. 14, 1838; m. Thomas J. Jones, U. S. navy, of Greenville, N. Y., 1858; had Anna Maria, b. Sept. 19, 1859.

WILLIAM CHAUNCEY, Commander, b. Dec. 20, (21 ?) 1798 ; m. Susan
Matilda, dau. of James Orem, of New York ; had William and
Francis Gregory.

He entered the navy as acting midshipman when in
his fourteenth year, June 1, 1812, receiving his first
order from Com. William Chauncey (after whom he was
named), to repair on board the frigate Essex ; and was
appointed a midshipman on the 14th of the same
month. He sailed on the 3d of July on a cruise from
New York harbor in the Essex, Capt. Porter commanding. The Essex meeting the British sloop of war
Alert, Capt. Langhorne, an action ensued, and in a few
minutes the Alert surrendered. She was the first ship
of war taken by the Americans, and her flag the first
British flag sent to the seat of government in the late
war. Mid. Wetmore was put on board the prize, Aug.
10, 1812.[3] Sept. 10, 1812, he received from Com.
Chauncey, a midshipman's commission, and went on
board the U. S. schooner Hamilton at Sackets Harbor,
first of the following month. Nov. 8, Commodore C.
with his squadron, consisting of 7 small vessels, sailed
out of Sackets Harbor. In a few hours after sailing,
the British man of war, the Royal George, was discovered, and chase was given. The next morning,
the Royal George ran into Kingston harbor, Chauncey's
flotilla pursuing her, an engagement took place between the ship, 5 shore batteries, and the American
squadron. As the British proved much stronger than
was anticipated, Chauncey had to haul off. From this
time to the close of the season, the sqadron was mostly
employed in cruising in the vicinity of Kingston. The
winter of 1812-13, Com. C. and those under his command were busily engaged in building and fitting out
armed vessels, to be ready on the opening of navigation. April 13, 1813, the lakes were considered safe,

[3] For dates of orders, transfers together with names of vessels, we are indebted to the navy department, for a tabular record furnished us.

and the squadron, now consisting of 13 sail, went out with a detachment of 1700 soldiers under Gen. Pike. Chauncey's broad pennant was borne by the Madison, a sloop of war of 24 guns. Upon this vessel young Wetmore had been ordered 12th Feb. previous. The squadron arrived off York (now Toronto), the capital of Upper Canada, on the same day of sailing; in two hours the troops were landed without material loss, and immediately advanced to the assault, while the squadron engaged the batteries. The place was soon taken, not, however, without a considerable loss to the Americans. Gen. Pike was killed by an explosion. The squadron also suffered. The place remained in the possession of the Americans, till the first of the next month. The squadron again coöperated with the land forces, in the capture of Fort George, May 27. This caused the British to evacuate the whole Niagara frontier. During the entire summer, the squadron was engaged in watching the enemy; Sept. 7, they were discovered some six miles distant, and chase was given, and on the 11th, a partial engagement took place. The superior sailing qualities of the British vessels, enabled them to escape. Commodore C. removing his broad pennant from the Madison to the Gen. Pike, young Wetmore was transferred to the latter vessel. On the 27th of Sept., Com. C. brought on an action. The Pike was manœuvred on that occasion with much skill, and his officers and men fought with great courage and perseverance, so much so, that it has ever since been a theme of admiration in the navy. The combat was closed by the English taking refuge in Burlington bay, under cover of guns on shore. On the 5th of October, the squadron captured five of the enemy's transports, which had on board a foreign regiment, consisting of 264 officers and men; soon after, the navigation closed.

On the 9th of May, 1814, Midshipman Wetmore

19

was detached from the lake service, where he had served some twenty months, with credit and honor to himself, and benefit to his country.

On the 16th of May, 1815, he sailed from New York in the U. S. brig Fire Fly, on a cruise to the Mediterranean. The vessel returned on the 6th of the following month, in distress, to the port from whence she sailed.

On the 1st of December, the same year, he sailed from Portsmouth, N. H., in the U. S. ship Washington 86 guns, on a cruise to the Mediterranean. On the 5th of Jan., 1817, he was at Port Mahon, where he was transferred to the U. S. ship Erie, 20 guns, returning to New York in the Washington July 17, 1818, having been absent, and in constant service, near upon 32 months. In 1820, he was passed for promotion. Jan. 18, 1821, he sailed in the Ontario, 20 guns, on a cruise to the West Indies, and Mediterranean, returning to Boston in the Columbus, 90 guns, the 22d of July, same year. Jan. 13, 1825, he was made lieutenant, and the 1st of May following, he sailed from Norfolk, Va.; in the John Adams, 24 guns, on a cruise to the West Indies, where he continued (serving on board the brigs Leader and Shark,) till March 26, 1826, when he returned to New York, in command of the brig Leader. Feb. 1st, 1829, he sailed from Norfolk on the frigate Guerriere, 44 guns, for the Pacific ocean, where he remained, cruising on that vessel and the schooner Dolphin, two years and eleven months. Oct. 1st, 1833, he sailed from New York for the West Indies, in the U. S. sloop of war St. Louis, where he remained seven months. From 1836 to 1841, he served at the New York station. Was commissioned a commander, Sept. 8, 1841; from that time to the date of his death, he was attached to the North Carolina (74), at the New York navy yard.

Commander Wetmore died at his residence on Bergeri Hill, New Jersey, Aug. 8, 1846. "The services of this gentleman," writes one noticing his demise, "have been very strongly marked by personal bravery. He was a strict disciplinarian; one of the best navigators of his grade in the service; he was the possessor of all that constitutes an accomplished officer."

The following, detailing an account of Mr. W's funeral, is from one of the New York daily papers:

The funeral of Commander Wetmore, who died on Saturday morning last, at Bergen Hill, New Jersey, was attended on Sunday afternoon by a large concourse of citizens, and by the officers attached to the navy yard and receiving ship, and a party of sailors, Capt. English and Lieut. Dougherty of the marine corps, were also present. The ceremonies at the house were performed by the Rev. Mr. Taylor of the Reformed Dutch Church, after which the procession moved off with solemn music of the band from the North Carolina. The officers of the navy present in uniform, acted as pall bearers. Among them were Capt. Stringham, Commanders Sands and Hudson, Lieuts. Gordon and Moore, and Dr. Bates, and the marine officers mentioned. The services at the grave were performed by the Rev. Mr. Stockbridge, amid a slight sprinkling of rain, and occasional peals of heavy thunder, more solemn and impressive than earth's artillery. The large concourse of people was dispersed, immediately after the conclusion of the funeral solemnities, by a heavy rain, which set in and continued for an hour or two.

It is a remarkable fact, that the day Capt. W. was taken ill, his favorite dog fell sick, and was found the next day in a ditch, dead. When informed that the dog was missing, he remarked, he was only gone a little before his master; a presentiment which helped to render his disease more unmanageable.

EMELINE AUGUSTA, b. June 20, 1800; unm.

WILLIAM HENRY, b. Dec. 7, 1803; d. Aug., 1805.

WILLIAM WHITING, b. Oct. 7, 1806; m. Eleanor Beebee, Nov., 1827; had Sarah Bogardus, Ellen, Rebecca, William Walker.

MARY LOUISA, b. April 21, 1809; m. Josiah H. Reave, July, 1838, s. p.

GUSTAVUS GEORGE WASHINGTON, b. Oct. 9, 1811; d. Oct. 16, 1838.

Children of Dr. CHARLES HENRY,

Son of Rev. Izrahiah.

JOHN RATHBONE, Dr., b. in Waterford, N. Y., April 29, 1815; m. Samantha R. Hesket.

He removed with his parents to Ohio, in 1819; commenced the study of medicine with his father, in 1834; graduated at Jefferson Medical College, Philadelphia, 1843; he died ———; a sincere believer in the Christian faith.

CHARLES JOSEPH, b. in Waterford, N. Y.; m. Pheobe Ann Weaver of Worthington, Ohio, July 16, 1844; had Clara Cornelia, Charles Henry, Mary Florence, Eliza Rathbone.

Resides in Columbus, Ohio.

ANN ELIZA, b. at Locust Grove, Worthington, O., June 12, 1819; m. Dr. J. Robinson, March 15, 1854.

Immediately after her marriage, she removed with her husband to Oregon, Missouri, where she died the 27th of May following. An obituary notice in the *Ohio State Journal,* says:

She was always ready to minister to others in sickness and sorrow, and who had so many dear friends should be called to die and make her grave among strangers. * * Mild, gentle, prudent, generous, and just, the mantle of Christian loveliness so meekly worn by her sainted mother, whose life was also a beautiful example of Christian faith and love, fell gently on her shoulders, and meekly and lovingly did she wear it. The loss of that mother was a sad blow to her sensitive heart. It was the means, through grace, of turning her attention more decidedly to things beyond this life. Like her mother, trusting not in uncer-

tain riches, but in the living God, she was rich in faith and
good works, "ready to distribute, willing to communicate,
laying up in store for herself a good foundation against the
time to come." Within a few months the church of her
love has administered to her the offices of baptism, con-.
firmation, communion, marriage, and burial; and in the
fellowship of that church she has gone, we trust, to para-
dise, to wait "her perfect consummation and bliss, when
the bodies of those who sleep in Christ shall be raised, and
made like unto his own glorious body, according to his
mighty working, whereby he is able to subdue all things
unto himself.".

PROSPER MONTGOMERY, b. at Locust Grove, W., April 25, 1821.

Resides Columbus, O., unm.

JULIET TRYPHENIA, b. at Locust Grove, W., Jan. 19, 1823; m.
George B. Smith of Deleware, O., May 13, 1845; had I *Emma
Mary*, b. July 28, 1846; II *Dudley Wetmore*, b. Dec. 10, 1849;
III *Juliet Eliza*, b. —; d. in infancy.

Mrs. Smith died Aug. 31, 1854.

JAMES MANNING, b. at Locust Grove, W., May 13, 1825; m. Lor-
inda Harris of Worthington; had Frank Herbert, Albert Prosper, Everett Maurice.

Resides upon a part of the Locust Grove farm near
Worthington.

EUNICE MARY, b. at Locust Grove, W., June 11, 1827; d. Aug.
12, 1827.

EUNICE MARY 2D, b. at Locust Grove, W., July 21, 1828.

INFANT SON, b. at Locust Grove, W., Sept. 27, 1830; d. same day.

CORNELIA ROXANA, b. at Locust Grove, W., Dec. 1, 1831; m. Dr.
James Rigby Lotspeich, March 14, 1860; had Charles Henry,
b. Jan. 25, 1861.

Resides at West Jefferson, Ohio.

EMMA MARIA, b. at Locust Grove, W., June 19, 1834; m. Dr. Nel-
son S. Darling of Columbus, O., June 5, 1855; had I *Howard
Wetmore*, b. Feb. 28, 1856; II *Eliza*, b. Dec. 1, 1857; III
Grace, b. Aug. 19, 1860.

Dr. D. removed to London, Madison co., O., where he practiced medicine till the fall of 1860, when he removed to La Porte, Ind., to establish himself in $_{\circ}$agr$_1$cu$_{lt}$ura$_l$ pursuits in connection with his profession.

SEVENTH GENERATION.

Children of PROSPER,

Son of Nathan, Son of Prosper.

MARTHA ELLIOT, b. Feb. 20, 1822; m. March, 1853, Henry Palmer; had I *Lydia Louisa*, b. Sept. 16, 1854; d. Oct. 27, 1857; II *Willard Henry*, b. Feb. 12, 1859.

HARRIET HINCKLEY, b. Feb. 21, 1824; m. Nov. 28, 1844, Thomas F. Rodgers; had I *Ellen Lathrop*, b. Sept. 8, 1845; d. April 16, 1847; II *Daniel Huntington*, b. Nov. 30, 1847; III *Ella Augstine*, b. June 4, 1852; IV *Katie Eliot*, b. Nov. 1, 1854.

Resides in Lebanon, Ct.

Children of AUGUSTUS,

Son of Nathan, Son of Prosper.

WILLIAM AUGUSTUS, b. April 5, 1818; d. July 7, 1831.

CHARLES HINCKLEY, Dr., b. Feb. 8, 1820; m. Sept. 25, 1848, Lucy S. Taylor; had Charles, Fannie, Kate Willis, Lucy Taylor.

He studied medicine and graduated at Pittsfield, Mass. Medical College, and became a practitioner at Lebanon, Ct. Soon after his marriage (Oct. 14, 1848), he, with his wife, sailed for Hilo, Sandwich Islands, as missionaries, where they now reside:

EDWIN DUTTON, b. Dec. 6, 1821; d. Sept. 19, 1823.

EDWIN DUTTON 2D, b. Sept. 19, 1823.

EMILY CORNELIA, b. Jan. 4, 1827.

CATHERINE, b. April 14, 1831; m. May 24, 1853, William R. Gay; had I *Emma Francis*, b. March 7, 1857; II *Mary Reed*, b. Nov. 15, 1858.

Resides Lebanon, Ct.

SARAH JANE, b. in Hebron, Dec. 25, 1834.

She just on "entering upon a womanhood of promise faded and passed away, sincerely lamented and affectionately remembered." She died Jan. 1, 1860.

WILLIAM AUGUSTUS 2D, b. in Hebron, May 6, 1838; m. June 27, 1858, Abbie F. Peckham; had George Perry.

Children of Gen. PROSPER MONTGOMERY,

Son of Robert William, Son of Rev. Izrahiah.

A DAU., b. —; d. unm.

A DAU., b. —; m. ——.

A DAU., b. —; m. ——.

A SON, b. —; d. unm.

A DAU.

A DAU.

A DAU.

A DAU.

A DAU.

A SON.

A SON.

A DAU.

Children of Col. ROBERT CHARLES,

Son of Robert William, Son of Rev. Izrahiah Jun.

CHARLES FREDERICK, b. —; m. ——, dau. of Daniel Holsman, of New York; had Kitty Holsman. He res. in New York.

FLORENCE ADELE.

VICTORINE UPSHUR.

Children of SIDNEY,

Son of Victory, Son of Rev. Izrahiah Jun.

MARY.

CATHERINE.

VIRGINIA.

Children of GEORGE McEWEN,

Son of Victory, Son of Rev. Izrahiah Jun.

MARY.

ROBERT HENRY.

GRACE NOBLE.

Children of WILLIAM COURTNAY.

SARAH.

ELIZABETH.

BENJAMIN CLARK.

JOHN McEWEN.

GEORGE WILLIAM.

VICTORY EZEKIEL.

Children of Commander WILLIAM CHAUNCEY,

Son of William Walker, Son of Rev. Izrahiah.

WILLIAM, b. March 21, 1823; m. Sarah McCool of New York; had Susan.

He died July 2, 1855.

FRANCIS GREGORY, b. Dec. 23, 1824; m. Julia Emily, dau. of John Tonnele of New Jersey; had Francis Sales, Fanny.

Resides Jersey City, office 117 Wall street., N. Y.

Children of WILLIAM WHITING,

Son of William Walker, Son of Rev. Izrahiah.

SARAH BOGARDUS, b. Aug. 16, 1828; m. Sylvester Symonds of Connecticut; had I *Blanche*, b. July 19, 1852; II *Ellen*, b. April 2, 1854; III *Sylvester R.*, b. Oct. 8, 1857; IV *Wellington*, b. May 5, 1860.

ELLEN, b. July 19, 1834; m. John I. Riddell; had Lucia, b. Dec., 1859.

REBECCA, b. June 16, 1836; m. W. Riddell; had I *Julie*, b. Feb. 13, 1854; II *Isadore*, b. Nov. 25, 1856.

WILLIAM WALKER, b. Feb, 9, 1839.

Children of CHARLES JOSEPH,

Son of Dr. Charles Henry, Son of Rev. Izrahiah.

CLARA CORNELIA,

CHARLES HENRY.

MARY FLORENCE.

ELIZA RATHBONE.

Children of JAMES MANNING,

Son of Dr. Charles Henry, Son of Rev. Izrahiah.

FRANK HERBERT, b. at Locust Grove, Worthington, June 23, 1857.

ALBERT PROSPER, b. at Locust Grove, W., Nov. 20, 1858,

EVERETT MAURICE, b, at Locust Grove, W., Sept. 27, 1859.

20

EIGHTH GENERATION.

Children of Dr. CHARLES HINCKLEY,

Son of Augustus, Son of Nathan, Son of Prosper.

CHARLES, b. in the Sandwich Islands, March 3, 1853.

FANNIE, b. in the S. I., July 24, 1855.

KATE WILLIS, b. in the S. I., Jan. 24, 1859.

LUCY TAYLOR, b. in the S. I., Nov. 9, 1860.

Son of WILLIAM AUGUSTUS,

Son of Augustus, Son of Nathan, Son of Prosper.

GEORGE PERRY, b. March 30, 1860.

Daughter of CHARLES FREDERICK,

Son of Col. Robert Charles, Son of Robert William, Son of Rev. Izrahiah.

KITTY HOLSMAN.

Son of ROBERT HENRY,

Son of George McEwen, Son of Victory, Son of Rev. Izrahiah.

VICTORY, b. 1850.

Daughter of WILLIAM,

Son of Com. William Chauncey, Son of William Walker, Son of Izrahiah.

SUSAN, b. May, 1847.

Children of FRANCIS GREGORY,

Son of Com. William Chauncey, Son of William Walker, Son of Rev. Izrahiah.

FRANCIS SALLS, b. March 7, 1858.

FANNY, b. in Jersey city, Aug. 7, 1859.

REV. JAMES, SON OF IZRAHIAH, SON OF THOMAS,
AND HIS DESCENDANTS.

THIRD GENERATION.

THE REV. JAMES WETMORE, A. M.

Was the third son of Izrahiah and Rachel (Stow)
Whitmore, son of Thomas and Sarah (Hall) Whitmore, born in Middletown, December 31, 1695 (o. s).
He was a man of talents and of very marked religious
principles; what he esteemed to be his duty *that* he
did.

From him has sprung the most numerous branch of
the Wetmore family, and one that has furnished many
members of intellectual ability, elevated character and
high toned morality, and we feel assured that we shall
be excused by our readers, if we give him and his
descendants more than usual space in these pages.
Mr. Wetmore received his first academical instruction
at the Saybrook Academy,[1] from which he entered
Yale College, where he took the degree of A. B. in
Sept., 1714, and that of Master of Arts in Sept., 1717.
After graduating, his attention was turned towards
the ministry; from whom he received his ministerial
instruction, we are unable to say. As there were no
theological institutions at that early day, students of
divinity had to pursue their studies with the various
clergymen of the country. At the time he graduated
and for some time subsequently, the Rev. William,

---

[1] At the commencement of the Saybrook Gymnasium, in Sept., 1716, a
majority of its trustees resolved to unite the institution with that of Yale,
at New Haven.

son of Rev. Noadiah Russell, was the pastor at Middletown, and with him, we conjecture, he prepared himself for the ministry. In 1718, he was called to North Haven, Ct., and in the fall of that year he was ordained the first Congregational minister of that place; "Here (says Bolton, in his *History of the Epsicopal Church*, in Westchester co., N. Y.), Mr. Wetmore was generally esteemed and beloved by his people, as might be reasonably expected from the suavity of his temper and the regularity of his conduct." He continued his labors at that place for some four years, when he became convinced that the ordination under which he was ministering was not valid, whereupon, he, with the rector of Yale College, Dr. Cutler, the Rev. Samuel Johnson (subsequently Dr. Johnson, president of Kings College, N. Y.), wrote the following paper, which we extract from the *Mass. His. Soc. Collections*, ii, 129, 2d Series, 1814.

Some Original Papers respecting the Episcopal Controversy in Connecticut, 1722.

From the very Choice and Valuable Collection of the late Rev. John Elliott, D. D.

To the Rev. Mr. Andrew and Mr. Woodbridge, and others, our reverend Fathers and Brethren, present in the Library of Yale College, this 13th of Sept., 1722.

Reverend Gentlemen:
Having represented to you the difficulties which we labor under, in relation to our continuance out of the visible communion of an Episcopal Church, and a state of seeming opposition thereto, either as private Christians or as officers, and so being insisted on by some of you (after our repeated declinings of it), that we should sum up our case in writing; we do (though with great reluctance, fearing the consequences of it), submit to and comply with it:
And signify to you that some of us doubt of the validity, and the rest are more fully persuaded of the invalidity of the Presbyterian ordination, in opposition to Episcopal, and should be heartily thankful to God and men, if we may receive from them satisfaction herein, and shall be willing to embrace your good counsels and instruction

in relation to this important affair, as far as God shall direct and dispose us to it.

TIMOTHY CUTLER,

A true Copy of   JOHN HART,
  the original.   SAMUEL WHITTLESEY,
Testify   JARED ELLIOTT,
  Daniel Brown.   JAMES WETMORE,

SAMUEL JOHNSON,

DANIEL BROWN.

The publishing of the above created a great sensation throughout all New England, and the controversy became very bitter, as the reader will perceive by a perusal of the following letters, which we also take from the *Mass. His. Soc. Collections;* IV, 297, 2d Ser. :

ORIGINAL PAPER RESPECTING THE EPISCOPAL CONTRO-
VERSY IN CONNECTICUT, 1722.

Very Reverend Sirs :

We have taken it that yourselves were consulted upon the first erecting a collegiate school in our colony, nor can we account it improper, that yourselves and our reverend fraternity in the principal town of our country, be apprized of the dark cloud drawn over our collegiate affairs, a representation whereof may already have been made by some of our reverend brethren trustees. But if not, and the case being of general concern, we are willing to make our mournful report, how it hath been matter of surprise to us (as we conclude it hath been or surely will be to you), to find how great a change a few years have made appear among us, and how our fountain, hoped to have been and continued the repository of truth, and the reserve of pure and sound principles, doctrine and education, in case of a change in our mother Harvard, shews itself in so little time, so corrupt. How is the gold becoming dim! and the silver become dross! and the wine mixed with water! Our school gloried and flourished under its first rector, the Rev. Mr. Pierson, a pattern of piety, a man of modest behavior, of solid learning, and sound principles, free from the least Arminian or Episcopal taint. But it suffered a decay for some years, because of the want of a resident rector. But who could have conjectured, that its name being raised to Collegium Yalense from a Gymnasium Saybrookense, it should groan out Ichabod in about three years and a half under its second rector, so unlike the first, by an unhappy election set over it, into whose election or confirmation, or any act relative to him, the senior

Rev. James, son of Izrahiah, son of Thomas.

subscriber hereof (though not for some reason, through malice or mistake, bruited) never came. Upon the management of our college three years and a half, how strangely altered is the aspect thereof! that its regents, &c., rector and tutor, are become such capable masters of Episcopal leaven, and in such a time so able to cause how many to partake of it!

It appears surprisingly strange, that it should so diffuse itself into our ministry, and many of them, not of the least note, now appear in the company, viz: Mr. Hart of East Guilford, Mr. Whittlesey of Wallingford, and Mr. Eliot of Killingworth; these, perhaps, not much short of the rector's years, and two societies, branches of the famous New Haven, one on the north, and the other on the west, are mourning because of their first ministers, in so little a time after their ordination, declaring themselves Episcopal, and their ordination, lately received, of no value, because á non habentibus potestatem.

Upon our commencement, Sept. 12, the rector distinguished this performance by the closing words of his prayer, which were these, viz: *and let all the people say, amen.*

On the evening of said day, it was rumored there, that on the next day the gentlemen become Episcopal, designed to propound to the trustees three questions. 1 Q. Whether ordination from such ministers, whose ordination was from the leather jacket, be valid? 2 Q. Whether ordinations from ministers, only presbyters, be valid? 3 Q. Whether an uninterrupted succession from the apostles' days, be not absolutely necessary to the validity of a minister's ordination? But these were not so propounded.

But the day following the commencement, after dinner, these gentlemen appeared in the library before the trustees, where many other ministers were present, and first declared themselves viva voce, but after that, on the direction of the trustees, declared themselves in writing, a copy whereof is not with us, but the substance thereof, is this. Sc.

Some of us, doubting the validity of Presbyterial ordination, in opposition to Episcopal ordination, and others of us fully persuaded of the invalidity of said ordination, shall be thankful to God or man helping us, if, in an errour. Signed, Timothy Cutler, John Hart, Samuel Whittlesey, Jared Eliot, James Wetmore, Samuel Johnson, Daniel Brown. The persons doubting were Mr. Hart and Mr. Whittlesey.

Consequent to this declaration, the trustees advised that doubters continue in the administration of the ministry of the word and sacraments, but that the fully persuaded forbear sacramental ministration, until the meeting of the trustees, which was appointed on the Tuesday evening at New Haven, following the opening of our General Assembly there, the said Tuesday being the 16th of the next month.

The trustees also advised, that the said ministers would freely declare themselves to their respective congregations.

It may be added, that Mr. C. then declared to the trustees, that he had for many years been of this persuasion (his wife is reported to have said that to her knowledge he had for eleven or twelve years been so persuaded), and that therefore he was the more uneasy in performing the acts of his ministry at Stratford, and the more readily accepted the call to a college improvement at New Haven.

But then if he knew the college was erected for the education of such as dissented from the Church of England (and how could he not know it), and knew himself not one; with what good faith could he accept said call, and the considerable encouragement he had, and the rather if he disseminated his persuasion so contrary to the very design of its erection, and the confidence of those that called him. Indeed he hath said, that he hath labored only with one to be of his persuasion; were it so, there would, in one instance, be a foul frustration of the confidence reposed in him, but what a member above one of the students have been leavened by him, who can be assured, but coming time may discover the unhappy instances of it.

Further, Mr. C. then also declared it his firm persuasion, that out of the Church of England, ordinarily, there was no salvation.

To the last we only say, Mγ γενοιτο for we dare not so offend the generation of the righteous, nor disturb the ashes of the myraids that have slept in Jesus, of the Catholick professors of the orthodox faith in these kingdoms, yea, and in all reformed Christendom, and in New England particularly, who have not been of the communion of the Church of England.

It must be acknowledge to the divine goodness, that all the trustees then present (and of the whole number wanted, only three, Sc. of Lime, N. London, Stamford), shewed themselves constraint to your principles, and effected to the trusts committed to them; yet desirous that the meeting of the trustees might (if possible), be fuller, and also their doings might be in the face of the colony represented in General Assembly; they took care that Mr. C. might have the use of the house they had hired for him until the Wednesday next after the opening of the General Court, viz: October 17.

No wonder that it is said in all our towns on the seaside, and probably in our inland likewise, the talk in every one's mouth is the surprising conjuncture, wherein such a number, who are now said, at least for a year past, to have distinguished themselves by their frequent meetings together, the design whereof the late declaration is accounted to open, appear fond of that way, an unembarrassment from which moved our predecessors to so voluntary an exile into a then rude wilderness. And in the vagrant surmises of the people, others of our principal men are by way of question or affirmation talked of, to belong to this set of deserters; of whom, till time shew otherwise, better things are hoped.

Rev. James, son of Izrahiah, son of Thomas.

One of us subscribing, who was then present, could have the above account only by report, when the other being present, bore a part with the trustees at N. H.

Reverend Sirs, having thus bemoaned the dark providence over us, we may not doubt your Christian sympathy, nor of your prayers, which we yet earnestly ask, unto Him, that holdeth the stars in his right hand, and walketh in the midst of the golden candlesticks. We ask also your assistance, what you may think proper, in a conjoined testimony in the cause of Christ to our government and people, and the encouragement of the trustees, and the recovery, if possible, of those that are gone from us. And with sincere prayers, that how grievous soever our sins may have been, and how much his anger hath been kindled against us, it may please the Lord, who is God and not man, yea the God of pardon, not to give us up, cast us off, forsake us, nor to call our name לא רחמה but that his gracious-blessing-presence, may be and continue in you and our churches,

We subscribe ourselves,
Reverend sirs,
Your unworthy fellow-partners
In the ministry of the gospel,
JOHN DAVENPORT,
S. BUCKINGHAM,

To Very Reverend,
   Increase Mather, D. D.,
   Cotton Mather, D. D.
Stamford, Sept. 25, 1722.

LETTER FROM REV. JOSEPH MOSS[2] TO REV. C. MATHER,

DERBY, OCT. 2, 1722.

Reverend Sir :

I presume, though unacquainted, to humbly ask your advice and help in a matter of great weight and moment, at which we are all amazed and filled with darkness, in our parts of the country, viz: no less than five ordained ministers (all but one of our association of New Haven), have declared before the trustees of the college, in the library, when many others also were present, that they were fully persuaded that only an Episcopal ordination was valid, and according to divine institution, and therefore inasmuch as their own ordination was by presbyters only, they esteemed it invalid; three of them said notwithstanding, they should go on to administer sacraments, &c., as before, for a while, waiting for further light; but if they could get no better light than they now had, thought

---

[2] Rev. Joseph Moss was minister of Derby.

Rev. James, son of Izrahiah, son of Thomas.

that in time it would come to pass with them, that they should proceed no further to minister at the altar without a reordination by a bishop; two of them pretended to be conscience-bound at present to cease all sacred administrations until they had further light, or an Episcopal ordination. The aforementioned three are Mr. John Hart, Mr. Samuel Whittlesey, Mr. James Wetmore. The two aforesaid are Mr. Jared Eliot, Mr. Samuel Johnson. And after these, both the rector and tutor of our college declared themselves for Episcopacy; and they scrupled communion in sacerd things with any other but the Church of England, because of the invalidity of a Presbyterian ordination. I can not pretend to have set down the very words in which these gentlemen declared themselves, but to this purpose (though in many more words), they did declare themselves, in the audience of a large assembly of ministers and scholars.

Now, reverend and learned sir, two things I crave your advice and help in: 1st, Your advice in what we shall say to the people over whom these gentlemen are ordained pastors; (the people are uneasy and come to us neighboring ministers for advice, they would choose to have their ministers desist their ministry, and have their pulpits free for others that may be ordained, but the ministers, I perceive, are willing to hold their posts still), what advice shall we give these poor people in their darkness and distress? 2d, I have not read much upon this controversy, should be very glad to have some books that do nervously handle this point, concerning ordination by presbyters, whether good or not. I have according to my mean ability studied the scriptures upon this point many years past, and have been and now am, most fully satisfied in my own mind, that the truth is on our side, and that there is no difference between a bishop and a presbyter, jure divino, and that there is no such superior order of church officers, as the diocesan bishops are, by divine institution. But it is now a time with us, that we must put on our armour and fight, or else let the good old cause, for which our fathers came into this land, sink and be deserted. I pray, sir, that you would furnish me with some such books, as with most strength of reason and argument, plead our cause, especially in this point of the validity of Presbyterian ordination, and I shall be very much obliged; and if the books that may be sent come as lent, I will safely and seasonably return them, but if they come as sold (which I rather choose), I will quickly send the money for them.

There is at Boston, I suppose, Mr. Jeremiah Atwaters of New Haven, who is my brother-in-law, and by whom there may be a conveniency of sending to me, or by any of our coasting vessels that come to any of the towns neighboring to New Haven.

I humbly ask your pardon, sir, that I have been so prolix in my writing, and for my presumption in requesting from you such favors, as above desired, which I dare not have done to so great a superior, if it had not a reference to the advancement of the kingdom of our great Redeemer, for which I know you are evermore greatly concerned, and are always ready to spend and be spent, and in endeavors for its growth and flourishing estate, you have been in labours more abundant than any of us.

I subscribe sir, your very humble servant, and unworthy fellow-laborer in the gospel, JOSEPH MOSS.

LETTER FROM THE REV. JOSEPH WEBB[1] TO REV. DR. C. MATHER.

Fairfield, Oct. 2, 1722.

Reverend and honored Sir:

The occasion of my now giving you the trouble of these few lines is to me, and I presume to many others, melancholy enough. You have perhaps heard before now, or will hear before these come to hand (I suppose), of the revolt of several persons of figure among us unto the Church of England. There's the Rev. Mr. Cutler, rector of our college, and Mr. Daniel Brown tutor thereof. There are also of ordained ministers, pastors of several churches among us, the Rev. Messieurs following, viz: John Hart of East Gilford, Samuel Whittlesey of Wallingford, Jared Elliott of Kennelworth [Killingworth], Samuel Johnson of West Haven, and James Wetmore of North Haven. They are most of them reputed men of considerable learning, and all of them of a virtuous and a blameless conversation. I apprehend the axe is hereby laid to the root of our civil and sacred enjoyments, and a doleful gap opened for trouble and confusion in our churches.

The Churchmen among us are wonderfully encouraged and lifted up by the appearance of these gentlemen on their side. And how many more will, by their example, be encouraged to go off from us, God only knows. It is a very dark day with us, and we need pity, prayers and counsel. And I am humbly of the opinion that the churches and pastors in your colony are concerned (though something more remotely), as well as we, in the present threatenings of Divine Providence; and I cannot but hope some measures will be concerted by yourselves in this juncture for the preservation of the good old cause, so signally owned by God, and witnessed unto by the practice and sufferings of so many eminent ministers and Christians. There is with you the advantage of age, learning, experience, books, &c., and therefore we cannot but earnestly desire your assistance in all that is proper on the sorrowful occasion. As for the gentlemen who have declared themselves in favor of the Church,

[1] Rev. Joseph Webb was minister of Fairfield.

some of them declared themselves much in doubt, about the validity of Presbyterian ordination, others of them (if I remember right) declared their satisfaction as to the invalidity thereof. As to this we value them not, so much, as long as Acts xx, 17–28; Phil. i, 1; 1 Pet. v. 1, 2, 3, and other texts are a part of holy scripture, though I should be glad of the help of some good arguments used by those skilled in the controversy, and have acted well therein. But if our antagonists should not be able to answer what may be alleged from scripture, &c., concerning the power of presbyters to ordain, they will, I conclude, allege that the ordinations among us were not Presbyterian, because several pastors in our colony in the more ancient days of it, were ordained by laymen, and those pastors so ordained, have acted in the late ordinations among us. This, the Churchmen among us improve, and fling every now and then about the leather mitten that was laid on the head of the Rev. Mr. Israel Chauncey of Stratford, many years since deceased, by one of the brethren acting in his ordination. It is also suggested, that the Rev. Mr. Andrew of Milford, was ordained by laymen, in part at least. What there is of truth in it I cannot tell. I heard nothing of this latter instance till within about the compass of a week ago. And as to what is alleged relating to the Rev. Mr. Chauncey of Stratford, deceased, I heard nothing thereof (that I remember) till many years after my ordination. I know the Rev. Messieurs Chauncey and Andrew abovesaid were actors in my ordination, together with the Rev. Mr. Walker of Woodbury, deceased. What led those eminent men, who first settled the country, to allow laymen to act in such an affair, is not for me to say.. But what I would know in this case is, how we shall be able to justify ourselves if this article be insisted on by our antagonists. The notion of these ordinations by laymen will, I fear, do us more damage than all the arguments that can be brought for the necessity of Episcopal ordination. Our condition I look upon, as very deplorable and sad. Please to communicate the contents of my letter to your venerable and honored father, and to as many of the ministers of Boston, &c., as you judge meet. And let me (though unworthy) have, as soon as may be, what comfort, light and strength is needful in our sad circumstances, from as many of you as will please to engage in the cause. Thus desiring an interest in your prayers for us,

I subscribe,

Reverend sir,

Your humble servant,

JOSEPH WEBB.

FROM A MS. IN THE HAND WRITING OF REV. COTTON MATHER, D. D., AND SUPPOSED TO HAVE BEEN SENT TO THE BRETHREN IN CONNECTICUT.

The sentiments of several ministers in Boston, concerning the duty of the distressed churches, with relation to their pastors, who, in an instrument under their hands have publickly declared. that they, some of them, *doubt the validity*, others of them *are fully persuaded of the invalidity*, of the Presbyterian ordination.

It plainly appears,

I. These new Episcopalians have declared their desire to introduce an usurpation and a superstition into the church of God, clearly condemned in the sacred scriptures, which our loyalty and chastity to our Saviour, obliges us to keep close unto; and a tyranny from which the whole church, which desires to be reformed, has groaned that it may be delivered.

II. They have had the temerity and presumption to deny the ministry and renounce the communion of all Protestant Churches in the whole world; except that little party that submits to the English Episcopacy. Such a schism do they run into.

III. The scandalous conjunction of these unhappy men with the Papists, is, more than what they have themselves duly considered. For first, the great and almost last clamour with which the Papists try to perplex and weaken the reformed churches. is. that their ministry is invalid for want of Episcopal ordination. These men strengthen the common enemy in the boundless mischief attempted by this foolish cavil. Secondly, even England and Ireland found it necessary to decry the necessity of Episcopal ordinations at their coming out of Babylon. They did generally. notoriously. authentically. or they could not have shaken off the mother of harlots. God forbid, that we should be such grievous revolters, as to go back from what the very dawn of the reformation arrived unto! Thirdly, to maintain their Episcopal ordination they set up that vile, senseless, wretched whimsey of an interrupted succession. which our glorious Lord has confuted with such matters of fact. that it is amazing the builders of Babel are not ashamed of it; and they will have none owned for ministers of Christ in the world, but such as antichrist has ordained for him; such as the paw of the beast hath been laid upon, them that they pretend a succession from. Do not those men worship the beast, who allow no worship in the church but by them who have their consecration legitimated by a derivation through the hands of the beast unto them? Finally, it is well known that at this day. the men who are well-willers to the claims of a Popish pretender, are the main assertors of the Episcopal ordination being essential to their Christian priesthood. and the most violent and signalized assertors of this paradox are such as deny the

Rev. James, son of Izrahiah, son of Thomas.

happy revolution, which every sincere Protestant, and honest and sober Englishman must be a friend unto. Will these men unite with such adversaries, to their assembly, O my soul, be not thou united!

IV. They have cast a vile indignity upon those burning and shining lights, the excellent servants of God, who were leaders of the flocks that followed our Lord Jesus into this wilderness, and upon the ministry of them and their successors, in which there has been seen the power and blessing of God for the salvation of many thousands in the successive generations, with a success beyond what any of them, who set such an high value upon their Episcopal ordination, could ever boast of. A degenerate offspring have declared these men of God, than whom the world has rarely been illuminated with brighter stars, to be no true ministers of Christ, but usurpers of the ministry and invaders of a sacred office; robbers, that have not entered in by the door. They have also treated with the utmost contempt the glorious cause and work of God, by which the churches of the Lord in this country have been so remarkably distinguished, and encouraged the posterity of our faithful predecessors to shake off the faith and order of the gospel, which was the main end that the country was planted for.

V. They have done what is likely to throw the churches of the country into disturbance and confusion, beyond anything they have ever met withal, and animate an ungodly generation to set up a lifeless religion and an irreligious life, in the room of that which has hitherto been our glory.

VI. They have rashly done all this before they used the proper means to obtain the light which they pretend they are looking for. They have not read many of the most enlightened treatises, and they have not once addressed, so much as by writing to them, those persons for their satisfaction, who are, of all, the most capable of enlightening them.

VII. It may be that some of the churches are not satisfied, what these gentlemen intend by waiting for further light.

VIII. In the mean time it is to be doubted, how they can lawfully and honestly go on with pastoral administrations and keep on good terms with the last words in the fourteenth chapter of Romans. Inasmuch as it is affirmed, that those of them whose doubts had made the least impression on them, yet professed that if the doubts which they now have should continue unremoved, they could not go on with the exercise of their ministry.

IX. The offence which these backsliders have given to all the churches has been such, that the particular churches to which they belong may, and should make them sensible, that they are greatly offended at them; and we see not why the flocks may not as much decline the owning of them as ministers, as they themselves question the validity of their ministry. The churches, by continuing

Rev. James, son of Izrahiah, son of Thomas.

to acknowledge the pastoral relation and oversight of these men, may give them greater opportunities to produce and increase [insidious] parties among them,. than they may be at first well aware of.

X. Nevertheless, and after all, we have not heard all that these gentlemen have to say for themselves. And we ought to do nothing rashly; the peace of God, also, in the utmost expressions of reasonable charity, should rule on such occasions, which will not work the righteousness of God. It is likewise to be remembered, that none of these men were ordained without a council of churches, to countenance their introduction into the ministry. It seems therefore necessary that the churches that withdrew from the ministry of the men, that have so disappointed them, and disobliged them, should have some countenance and assistance and instruction from a council of churches for what they have to do in this lamentable affair. But the councils ought to be so chosen, that the churches may reasonably expect impartial proceedings in them; and therefore the choice had not best be limited by such prudential rules of vicinity, as might be agreed when there were no such extraordinary occasions to be imagined. Perhaps, the General Court may see cause, these awful and grievous and threatning occurences, to nominate a very large council of churches, to consider what may be the duty of the day, especially for those churches more immediately now encumbered.

May the glorious Head of the Church, whose name is the Counsellor, graciously grant his counsel to his people, that they may let no men take away their crown; but may faithfully preserve his institutions."—*Mass. Hist. Soc. Coll.* ii, 129, x, 136, *2d series.*

A FAITHFUL RELATION OF A LATE OCCURENCE IN THE CHURCHES OF NEW ENGLAND.

[Not very candid or temperate, if faithful.—*Editor Mass. Hist. Soc. Coll.*, ii, 137, 2d Ser.]

New England has lately had in it an occurence, that has been a matter of some surprise, and much discourse unto the country.

The colony of Connecticut being willing to have their churches well supplied, from an education in the principles which moved their predecessors to settle in those parts of the world, erected not long ago a college at New Haven. This little college or collegiate school which wears the name of Yale College, was lately so unhappy as to borrow a pastor of a church at Stratford, whose name is Mr. Timothy Cutler, for a rector.[4]

This man was a secret Episcopalian, of such high flights that he looks upon his Presbyterian ordination as a nullity; and the acts of

[4] Used here in the sense of ruler-governor, or what is more familiar to us of the present day, president.—*Compiler.*

Rev. James, son of Izrahiah, son of Thomas.

his ministry as invalid, and his invitation to the rectorate of the college of that collegiate school, was the more agreeable to him for its delivering him from a ministry which he took to be a cheat; it also gave an opportunity privately to destroy the principal intention of the academy, and blow up the churches which he appeared a friend unto. He privately, for some time, carried on a conversation with several young ministers of the neighboring churches, whose frequent meetings at his house, were what the people knew not what interpretation to put upon. At last, by a strange coincidence of several circumstances, the plot broke out sooner than it is thought they would have had it; for on September 13th, the day after their commencement, these men appeared in the publick library before the trustees of the college, and many other ministers; and there exhibited a short instrument, wherein they declared that some of them doubted the validity, and others of them were fully persuaded of the invalidity of their Presbyterian ordination. Signed by Cutler, the rector, and Brown, a tutor of the school, and five more that were young ordained pastors of churches in the neighborhood. The trustees were very much distressed on an occasion so unexpected, and so likely to be attended with a train of unhappy circumstances, but they treated the men with all the charity, and lenity, and forbearance that the case would possibly admit of. Nevertheless, the action and apostacy of these men, has caused a considerable commotion in the minds of the people, not only in the churches more immediately betrayed, but also through all the country.

It has appeared marvelous unto them, that a little knot of young men that had read a very little of controversy, but only a few Episcopalians' things which their library at New Haven had been unhappily stocked with, all with little or nothing of the antidote (and indeed, the most of that the poor children have to subsist upon, is the pretended epistles of Ignatius, which yet, if they were not imposters, we would be of no service to them!), that these young men should have the temerity and presumption to declare for an usurpation in the church of God, so clearly condemned in the holy scriptures; which it is the profession and endeavor of those churches to keep close unto, yea, and thereupon to deny the ministry, and renounce the communion of all the Protestant churches in the world, except that little party that submits to the English Episcopacy! It has amazed them to see the sons of New England strengthen and assist the common enemy, by coming in to the great, and almost last clamorer with which the Papists are trying to weaken and perplex the Reformed churches, and that when it is notorious, that the whole body of our first reformers at their coming out of Babylon, denied the necessity of an Episcopal ordination, and found that they could not shake off the mother of harlots, without their doing so: they should in such a country go back from what the very dawn of the Reformation arrived unto!

Rev. James, son of Izrahiah, son of Thomas.

It has caused some indignation in them, to see the vile indignity cast by these *cudweeds* upon those excellent servants of God, who were the leaders of the flock that followed our Saviour into this wilderness; and upon the ministry of them, and their successors, in which there has been seen for more than fourscore years together, the power and blessing of God for the salvation of many thousands in the successive generations; with a success beyond what any of them which set such an high value on the Episcopal ordination could ever boast of! To vilify this as an invalid ministry; for a degenerate offspring to declare those men of God, and those burning and shining lights, to be no true ministers of Christ; but invaders and intruders upon a sacred office; and robbers that have not entered in by the door; they cry out upon it, Good God, unto what times hast thou reserved us!

That which adds very much to the concern on the minds of the good people, is, that such highflyers as these, who derive their ordination from Rome, do generally discover themselves too well affected unto a Popish pretender, and enemies to the happy Revolution: and though of late several conversions to high church have been made among their children, wherein to their honour, the great converter has been a foolish and sorry toy-man, who is a professed Jacobite, and printed a pamphlet to maintain that God whom King William and the churches there prayed unto, is the devil! (horresco referens!) yet they commonly lament it, that the church rarely gains a proselyte, but King George loses a subject.

It is a sensible addition, unto their horrour, to see the horrid character of more than one or two, who have got themselves qualified with Episcopal ordination, to fortify little and wretched parties, in disturbing the churches of New England, and come over as missionaries, perhaps to serve scarce twenty families of such people, in a town of several hundred families of Christians, better instructed than the very missionaries; to think that they must have no other ministers, but such as are ordained, and ordered by them, who have sent over such tippling sots unto them, instead of those pious and painful and faithful instructers which they are now blessed withal. The churches treat their new invalids with much civility, and such as can go on in their ministry, they allow to do so. But the spirit of the country, and their zeal for the pure and undefiled religion and profession of their fathers, has been so conspicious on this occasion; and the folly of the deserters has been so mainfest unto all men (and unto some of themselves), that they will proceed no further. The apostacy will stop here; and what has happened, will strongly serve to the establishment of the churches, and the abbetors of these disorders may spare any further pains for the furnishing of the country with any such missionaries. Nor will they be received there by any, but a few people of such a character, as will be no great honor, either to Christianity, or the Church of England.

Since the writing of this faithful relation, a letter from a very eminent person in the government of Connecticut, dated Nov. 9, 1722, has these passages.

The endeavors of the trustees of the college have been so far succeeded, as to remove the scruples of those ministers, who had entertained some doubt about their ordinations, so that we have a prospect of peace in the churches they were set over, and that they may go on in the work of the ministry with hope of success. We are not without hopes that what had so fearful a tendency to the prejudice of that gospel-order, which the churches here have from the beginning observed, may rather tend to their confirmation therein.— *Mass. Hist. So. Col.*, II, 137.

We regret that we have not at our command Rev. Dr. Chandler's life of Dr. Samuel Johnson, in which he gives, we are informed, an interesting history of the *Episcopal Controversy in Connecticut in* 1722. As a part of that history we extract the following, from a work published in London, 1781, entitled, *A General History of Connecticut, by a Gentleman of the Province*.

The Episcopal church in Stratford is the oldest of that denomination in the state. Of the origin of this, an account was given in the first volume of this history.[4] But Episcopacy made very little progress in Connecticut, until after the declaration of Rector Cutler, Mr. Johnson, Mr. Wetmore and Mr. Brown, for Episcopacy, in 1722. Numbers of Mr. Johnson's and Mr. Wetmore's hearers professed Episcopacy with them, and set up the worship of God, according to the manner of the Church of England, in West and North Haven. Mr., afterwards Dr. Johnson, was a gentleman distinguished for literature, of popular talents and engaging manners. In 1724, after receiving Episcopal ordination in England, he returned.

The trustees, wishing to remove all inconveniences, and to put the college under the best advantages, convened the next year in March, and made choice of the Rev. Timothy Cutler of Stratford, to be the resident rector until their next meeting. He came almost directly to New Haven, and entered on the instruction and government of the college. When the trustees met at the next commencement, they voted that Mr. Cutler's services hitherto, in the place of a rector was to their satisfaction, and therefore they desired him to continue in it.

While the trustees were attempting to put the college upon the best establishment, the Legislature had enacted for their encouragement, that three hundred pounds worth of new lands should be sold,

[4] For the account alluded to by the author, see forward.

and that forty pounds annually should be paid to the instructors for the term of seven years.

To make compensation to the people of Stratford for the removal of their minister, the trustees agreed to give them Mr. Cutler's house and home lot, which they purchased for forty-four pounds sterling. To accommodate Mr. Cutler and his family at New Haven, they built the rector's house, which, with the lands on which it was erected, cost them two hundred and sixty pounds sterling.

Rector Cutler was popular, acceptable to the Legislature and the clergy, and the students were quiet under his instructions and government. The college appeared now to be firmly established, and in a flourishing and happy state. But, from a quarter entirely unexpected, it suffered a sudden and great change.

At the commencement, it was discovered, that the rector and Mr. Brown, one of the tutors, had embraced Episcopacy, and that they and two of the neighboring ministers, Mr. Johnson of West Haven, and Mr. Wetmore of North Haven, had agreed to renounce the communion of the churches in Connecticut, and take a voyage to England and receive Episcopal ordination. Scarcely anything could have been more surprising to the trustees, or the people in general, as they had no suspicions that the rector was inclining to Episcopacy, as there was no Episcopalian minister fixed in the colony, and as very few of the laity were inclined to that persuasion.

Governor Salstonstall was a great man, well versed in the Episcopal controversy, and the tradition has been, that he judged it of general importance, in the then circumstances of the colony, that the point should be well understood, that he publicly disputed with Mr. Cutler, at the commencement, and he was judged by the clergy and spectators in general to have been superior to him as to argument, and gave them much satisfaction relative to the subject. It was supposed that several other gentlemen of considerable character among the clergy, were in the scheme of declaring for Episcopacy, and of carrying over the people of Connecticut in general, to that persuasion.

But as they had been more private in their measures, and had made no open profession of Episcopacy, when they saw the consequences with respect to the rector, and the other ministers, that the people would not hear them, but dismissed them from their service, they were glad to conceal their former purposes, and to continue in their respective places.

The trustees at the commencement, passed no resolve relative to the rector, but gave themselves time to know the general opinion of the people, and to consult the Legislature on the subject. But, meeting in October, while the Assembly were in session at New Haven, they came to the following resolutions: That the trustees, in faithfulness to the trust reposed in them, do excuse the Rev. Mr.

Rev. James, son of Izrahiah, son of Thomas.

Cutler from all further services as rector of Yale College. That the trustees accept the resignation of Mr. Brown as tutor. Voted, That all such persons as shall hereafter be elected to the office of rector or tutor in this college, shall, before they are accepted therein, before the trustees, declare their assent to the confession of faith, owned and assented to by the elders and messengers of the churches in this colony of Connecticut, assembled by delegation at Saybrook, Sept. 9th, 1708, and confirmed by the act of the General Assembly, and shall particularly give satisfaction to them, of the soundness of their faith, in opposition to Arminian and prelatical corruptions, or of any other of dangerous consequence to the purity and peace of our churches. But if it cannot be before the trustees, it shall be in the power of any two trustees, with the rector, to examine a tutor, with respect to the confession and soundness of his faith, in opposition to such corruptions.

They also voted; "That upon just ground of suspicion of the rector's or tutor's inclination to Arminian or prelatic principles, a meeting of the trustees shall be called as soon as may be, to examine into the case.

Mr. Cutler and Mr. Brown, having been thus dismissed from their services at the college, and Mr. Johnson about the same time, having been dismissed from his pastoral relation, soon after went to England, with a view to receive Episcopal ordination. They all received holy orders.

While they were in England they visited the universities, and were received by the vice-chancellor of each and the heads of houses with peculiar marks of esteem. Mr. Cutler had the degree of doctor of divinity conferred upon him, and Mr. Johnson master of arts, in both universities.[5] Dr. Cutler returned in the character of a missionary from the Society,[6] to the Episcopal Church in Boston.

Mr. Johnson, upon his return about the year 1724, became the fixed missionary of the church at Stratford. Mr. Brown died soon after he had received orders. Mr. Wetmore, about this time, made a voyage to England, received Episcopal ordination, and was fixed as a missionary at Rye, in the province of New York. He enjoyed a long ministry, and died at Rye, 1760. These were the first of the clergy who declared for Episcopacy in Connecticut, and were very much the fathers of the Episcopal Church in Connecticut and New England. *Note (a.) and (b.)*, p. 395-6-7-8, and 9.

The work from which the foregoing has been taken, was supposed to have been written by the Rev. Samuel

[5] Oxford and Cambridge Universities.—*Compiler*.

[6] The Society for the Propagation of the Gospel in Foreign Parts.—*Compiler*.

Peters. A person answering to the description of Mr.
Peters flourished at Hebron, Ct., and by reason of his
attachment to the Church of England, and his open
and undisguised loyalty, was obliged, during the Revolution, to take refuge in the mother country. From
the same volume, we glean the subjoined, which
throws some further light upon the circumstances
attending Mr. Wetmore's becoming a clergyman of the
Established Church, which we think will not only be
interesting to the Wetmore family, but the casual
reader. We transfer it to our pages, as an offset to
some of the preceding epistles, especially to the one
entitled, *A Faithful Relation of a Late Occurrence in
the Churches of New England:*

Stratford lies on the west bank of Osootonoc river, having the sea
or sound on the south. There are three streets running north and
south, and ten east and west. The best is one mile long. On the
center square stands a meeting house with a steeple and a bell, and
a church with a steeple, bell, clock and organ. It is a beautiful
place, and from the water has an appearance not inferior to that of
Canterbury. Of six parishes contained in it, three are Episcopal.
The people are said to be the most polite of any in the colony, owing to the singular moderation of the town in admitting, latterly,
Europeans to settle among them. Many persons came also from the
islands and southern provinces for the benefit of their health.

Here was erected the first Episcopal Church in Connecticut. A
very extraordinary story is told concerning the occasion of it, which
I shall give the reader the particulars of, the people being as sanguine in their belief of it as they are of the ship's sailing over New
Haven.

An ancient religious rite called the *pawwaw*, was annually celebrated by the Indians, and commonly lasted several hours every
night for two or three weeks. About 1690 they convened to perform it on Stratford point, near the town. During the nocturnal
ceremony, the English saw, or imagined they saw, devils rise out of
the sea, wrapped up in sheets of flame, and flying round the Indian
camp, while the Indians were screaming, cutting and prostrating
themselves before their fiery gods. In the midst of the tumult, the
devils darted in among them, seized several, and mounted into the
air. The cries and groans issuing from them quieted the rest. In
the morning, the limbs of Indians, all shrivelled, and covered with
sulphur, were found in different parts of the town. Astonished and

Rev. James, son of Izrahiah, son of Thomas.

terrified at these spectacles, the people of Stratford began to think
the devils would take up their abode among them, and called together
all the ministers in the neighborhood, to exorcise and lay them.
The ministers began, and carried on their warfare with prayers,
hymns and objuration ; but the pawwaws continued, and the devils
would not obey. The inhabitants were about to quit the town,
when Mr. Nell spoke and said, "I would to God that Mr. Visey[7]
the Episcopal minister at New York, was here, for he would expel
these evil spirits." They laughed at his advice ; but on his reminding them of the little maid who directed Naaman to a cure for his
leprosy, they voted him their permission to bring Mr. Visey at the
next pawwaw. Mr. Visey attended accordingly, and as the pawwaws commenced with howlings and whoops, Mr. Visey read portions of the Holy Scriptures, Litany, &c. The sea was put into
great motion. The pawwaws stopped. The Indians dispersed, and
never more held pawwaws in Stratford. The inhabitants were
struck with wonder at this event, and held a conference to discover
the reason why the devils and pawwawers had obeyed the prayers of
one minister, and had paid no regard to those of fifty. Some
thought that the reading the Holy Scripture, others that the Litany
and the Lord's Prayer, some again that the Episcopal power of the
minister, and others that all united were the means of obtaining the
heavenly blessing they received. Those who believed that the Holy
Scriptures and Litany were effectual against the devil and his le-
gions, declared for the Church of England ; while a majority ascribed their deliverance to a complot between the devil and the
Episcopal minister, with a view to overthrow Christ's vine, planted
in New England. Each party acted with more zeal than prudence.
The church however increased, though oppressed by more persecu-
tions and calamities, than ever experienced by Puritans from bishops
and pawwawers. Even the use of the Bible, the Lord's prayer, the
Litany, or any part of the Prayer Book was forbidden. Nay, ministers taught from their pulpits, according to the Blue Laws, That
the lovers of Zion had better put their ears to the mouth of hell,
and learn from the whispers of the devils, than read the bishop's
books, while the Churchmen, like Michael the Archangel contend-
ing with the devil about the body of Moses, dared not bring against
them a railing accusation. But this was not all. When the Episcopalians had collected timber for a church, they found the devils
had not left the town, but only changed their habitations—had left
the savages and entered into fanatics and wood.' In the night before
the church was to be begun, the timber set up a country dance,
skipping about, and flying in the air, with as much agility and sul-
phurous stench, as ever the devils had exhibited around the camp
of the Indian pawwawers. This alarming circumstance would have

[7] Rev. Mr. Visey was rector of Trinity Church, New York.

Rev. James, son of Izrahiah, son of Thomas.

ruined the credit of the church, had not the Episcopalians ventured to look into the phenomenon, and found the timber to have been bored with augers, charged with gunpowder, and fired off by matches—a discovery of bad consequence in one respect, it has prevented annalists of New England from publishing this among the rest of their miracles.

About 1720, the patience and sufferings of the Episcopalians, who were then but a handful, procured them some friends, even among their persecutors, and those friends condemned the cruelty exercised over the Churchmen, Quakers and Anabaptists, in consequence of which, they first felt the effects of those gentle weapons in New England, whisperings and backbitings, and were at length openly stigmatised, as Arminians and enemies of the American vine. This conduct of the *Sober Dissenters*, increased the grievous sin of moderation; and near twenty ministers, at the head of whom was Dr. Cutler, president of Yale College, declared on a public commencement, for the Church of England. Hereupon the General Assembly and Consociation, finding their comminations likely to blast the American vine, had recourse to flattery, larded over with tears and promises, by which means they recovered all the secessors, but four, viz: Dr. Cutler, Dr. Johnson, Mr. Whitmore and Mr. Brown, who repaired to England for orders. Dr. Cutler had the misfortune to spend his life and great abilities in the fanatical, ungrateful, and factious town of Boston, where he went through fiery trials, shining brighter and brighter, till he was delivered from New England persecution, and landed where *the wicked cease from troubling*. Dr. Johnson, from his natural disposition, and not for the sake of gain, took pity on the neglected church of Stratford, where he fought the beast of Ephesus, with great success. The doctor was under the bountiful protection of the Society for the Propagation of the Gospel in Foreign Parts, incorporated by William the third, to save from the rage of republicanism, heathenism, and fanaticism all such members of the Church of England, as were settled in our American colonies, factories and plantations beyond the sea. To the foresight of that monarch, to the generous care and protection of that society under God, are owing all the loyalty, decency, Christianity, undefiled with blood, which glimmer in New England. Dr. Johnson having settled at Stratford among a nest of zealots, and not being assassinated, other dissenting ministers were induced to join themselves to the Church of England, among whom were Mr. Beach and Mr. Punderson. Those gentlemen could not be wheedled off by the Assembly and Consociation; they persevered, and obtained names among the literati that will never be forgotton.

The sentiments of this enthusiastic churchman and royalist, which we have so extensively quoted, should

Rev. James, son of Izrahiah, son of Thomas.

be read by the *younger* members of the family, with several degrees of allowance.

As we have given what was probably the extremes of both sides of the controversy, we trust that none of our readers will take exceptions; they will not, we are persuaded, if they bear in mind that a compiler is in duty bound to take history as he finds it.

The students of Yale were compelled to submit to a fine, as often as they attended the worship of the Church of England.

The church wardens and vestrymen of Newport, R. I., in a letter to the secretary, dated 26th of October, 1722, say: This example will be followed by many, if not by most considerable men amonst them ; wherefore we have an instance in one Mr. Wetmore, a man of learning and piety, who has now become zealous for the service and interest of the church, but whose circumstances won't at present allow him to apply for Episcopal ordination.—*Conn. Mss. from Archives at Fulham,* p. 79, *Dr. Hawks.*[8]

The Rev. A. B. Chapin, D. D., in a sermon preached in Christ Church, Hartford, Ct., January, 1851, gives the following account of the movement of 1722, and of those who did at the time, and subsequently, participate in it.

But though neither civil nor ecclesiatical power could plant the church in a Puritan soil, God had determined its existence, free from all the entanglements of state, to be the defender of the faith, and the conservator of the peace of the country. In the town of Guilford, there was a pious layman, still clinging to the church of his affections, and to his Prayer Book. That book became known to a promising youth among his neighbors, and was thenceforth his inseparable companion through life. He goes to college, graduates with the honors of the university, enters the Congregational ministry, and is settled over one

[8] Bolton, Hist. of the Church in Westchester.

of the Congregational societies in New Haven. That
Prayer Book went with him, and became the pattern of
his public devotions that attracted the attention, and commanded the admiration of all who witnessed his labors.
Slowly and insensibly, that book was doing an effectual
work, and in 1721, Johnson, the minister of the Congregational Church, on the west side of New Haven, now West
Haven, and with him, Cutler, president of the College,
Brown, a tutor in the same, and Wetmore, the Congregational minister of North Haven, publicly declared their
belief in the divine origin and perpetual obligation of
Episcopacy. These were all able, prominent men, the
pride of the people, and were not to be given up without
an effort. A disputation was held before the governor,
the students became interested, the flame spread, controversy increased, and thirty graduates of Yale, entered the
ministry of the church in that generation, many of them
having been previously in the ministry of the Congrega-
tionalists, all more or less, directly through the influence
of Dr. Johnson.

Johnson, after receiving orders in England, in 1722,
became a missionary of the Society for Propagating the
Gospel in Foreign Parts, and was stationed at Stratford,
and the adjacent towns. Cutler was sent to Boston, Wetmore to Rye, in New York, and Brown died in England.
The labors of Johnson were not confined to Stratford, but
were extended to West Haven, Fairfield and Newton,
where he established other parishes, within a few years.
The elder Seabury, who was a student at Yale, left at the
time of the Episcopal discussions, and went to Cambridge,
where he was graduated in 1724. After having been a
Congregational minister at Groton, now Poquetanock, for
several years, he declared for Episcopacy in 1728, and becoming a missionary of the society already named, was
stationed in New London. In the same year, 1732, Johnson had the pleasure of seeing his old friend and companion, John Beach, the Congregational minister of Newton,
who had graduated at the ever memorable discussion of
1722, declare for the church. He also became a missionary of the same society, and was stationed at Newton and
Reading. Two years later, 1734, Jonathan Arnold, Johnson's successor in the Congregational parish at West Haven,
came into the church, and having received orders, was

Rev. James, son of Izrahiah, son of Thomas.

stationed by the same society, as a missionary at West Haven and vicinity. Richard Miner graduated at Yale, 1726, for many years Johnson's neighbor as Congregational minister at Ripton, declared for Episcopacy in 1742, but died in England, whither he had gone for orders. Ebenezer Punderson, a native of New Haven, who was graduated at Yale in 1726, and succeeded the elder Seabury as Congregational minister at Groton, also followed his example in declaring for Episcopacy, which he did about 1732, and became a missionary of the same society at Groton and Hebron, and subsequently at West Haven and vicinity. He was instrumental in founding Trinity parish, New Haven, more than twenty years after the beginning of the parish of West Haven, and organized ten other parishes in this diocese. Solomon Palmer, a native of Branford, graduated at Yale in 1729, after having been the Congregational minister of Cornwall, for many years, declared for Episcopacy in 1754, was enrolled among the missionaries of the same venerable society, and was also stationed in Connecticut. Henry Caner of New Haven, graduated at Yale in 1724, and his brother Richard, graduated at the same place in 1734, though born of Congregational parents, entered the ministry of the Church, and became missionaries of the same society, one in Massachusetts, the other in Connecticut. Isaac Browne graduated at Yale in 1729, the brother of Daniel Browne, who died in England in 1723, came into the church at West Haven, with his parents, along with Johnson in 1722, and was for many years a missionary of the same society in New York and New Jersey. The same may be said of Ebenezer Thompson, graduated in 1733, for many years a missionary in Massachusetts. Henry Barclay graduated at Yale in 1734, first a missionary of the Propagation Society to the Indians, and then rector of Trinity Church, New York, is also to be reckoned among the number of those whose services in the church, resulted from the influence of Johnson. So also, Ebenezer Dibble, graduated in 1734; Christopher Newton, graduated 1740; Richard Mansfield and Joseph Lamson, graduated in 1741; Ichabod Camp, graduated in 1743; Thomas Bradbury Chandler,[9] and

[9] Rev. THOMAS BRADBURY CHANDLER, D. D., born at Woodstock, Mass., April 26, 1726, grad. at Yale Coll. 1745, was called to be catechist to St. John's Church, Elizabethtown, N. J., Dec. 26, 1747, where he officiated till

Rev. James, son of Izrahiah, son of Thomas.

Jeremiah Leaming, graduated in 1746; were all the sons of Congregational parents, and missionaries of the venerable Society for the Propagating the Gospel in Foreign Parts. Within the same period, Daniel Dwight, graduated in 1721, came into the church, and went to South Carolina; John Pierson, graduated in 1729, went to New Jersey; Ephraim Bostwick graduated the same year, and Jonathan Copp, graduated in 1745, and went to Georgia; William Sturgeon, graduated in 1745, went to Pennsylvania; Walter Wilmot, graduated in 1735, and Hezekiah Watkins, graduated 1737, went to New York. Besides these, Barzillai Dean, graduated in 1737; Jonathan Cotton, graduated in 1745, and James Usher graduated in 1753, all died abroad, having successively gone to England for orders for Hebron. It may be proper to mention here, as showing the great obstacles which the church had to encounter at that early period, that of fifty-two candidates that had gone to England for orders, from the northern colonies, previous to 1777, ten of them died abroad, or were lost at sea.

1751, when he went to England for ordination. On his return he was made rector of same church at E. He received £50 sterling annually from the Society for the Propagation of the Gospel, which was his chief support. His loyalty and zeal for the home government during the Revolution making him many enemies among the colonists, caused him to retire to England in 1776, where he remained till 1786; when he returned to America. While in England his influence was largely felt for the strengthening of the church of his adoption in his native land. In addition to his salary of £50 from the society, which was continued to him, he received from the government £200 annually. The degree of Doctor of Divinity was conferred upon him by the university at Oxford, Eng. He was appointed bishop of Nova Scotia, which he was obliged to decline owing to physical disabilities. The bishoprick was subsequently conferred, by his recommendation, upon the Rev. Charles Inglis, D. D., rector of Trinity Church, New York, from 1765 to 1783. He was a forcible and prolific writer. By the ill-judged advice of a friend of the family, a large collection of his writings and correspondence with distinguished persons of his time, was destroyed soon after his decease. He died in 1790, and was buried under the chancel of the church at Elizabethtown, where he had so long labored. He had issue four daughters; Mary R. d. June 28, 1784, æ. 22 years; Elizabeth C., wife of Gen. E. B. Dayton of New Jersey, d. Nov. 6, 1806, aged 41 years; Jane, wife of William Dayton, Esq., (died,) she survived till ab. 1859, æ. ab. 90; and Mary G., the wife of The Rt. Rev. John Henry Hobart, D. D., late Bishop of New York. Dr. Chandler was a descendant of Col. John Chandler of Andover, and his wife ——, second daughter of William Peters, brother to the Rev. Hugh Peters, chaplain to Oliver Cromwell —*Early Life and Professional Years of Bp. Hobart*, by John McVicar, D. D.; *Memoir of the Life of Bishop Hobart*, by the Rev. Dr. Berrian; *His. of Trinity Church*, by Dr. Berrian; *History of St. John's Church, Elizabethtown*, by Rev. Samuel A. Clark, Rector of the same. J. B. Lippincott, Phila., 1857.

Rev. James, son of Izrahiah, son of Thomas.

All the persons mentioned, born and educated Congre-
gationalists, are known to have come into the church,
more or less directly through the influence of Johnson,
and all were missionaries of the Society for Propagating
the Gospel. To these must be added, William, the son of
Samuel Johnson; Samuel, the son of Samuel Seabury, and
John Ogilvie, the successor of Barclay, as missionary to
the Indians, all graduated in 1748; Jacob Greaten, graduated in 1754; Lucas Babcock, graduated in 1755; and
Abraham Beach, graduated in 1757; all missionaries in
New York; James Scoville and Samuel A. Peters, graduated the same year; Roger Viets, Bela Hubbard, and
Thomas Davies, graduated the year following, 1758,
missionaries in Connecticut; also Samuel Andrews, graduated in 1759; Abraham Jarvis and Ebenezer Kneeland,
graduated in 1764; Gideon Bostwick and Richard Clarke,
graduated in 1762; who were among the missionaries of
the same society in Connecticut.

These are the principal of the clergy of Connecticut, for
half a century after the conversion of Johnson, sustained
every one of them, in whole or in part, by the funds of an
English missionary society.

As soon after the declaration as arrangements could
be perfected, Mr. Wetmore sailed for England, where
he was ordained a priest in the Protestant Episcopal
Church, by the Right Reverend Edmund Gibson, D.
D., Lord Bishop of London.

We have before us the original certificate (in manuscript) of ordination, given by Bishop Gibson to Mr.
Wetmore, the following being a copy:

EDMUNDUS [   ] Londinenfis Epifcopus Dilecto Nobis in
⎡Epifcopal⎤ Chrifto Jacobo Wetmore Clerico, Salutem et Gratiam; Ad.
⎣ Seal. ⎦ peragendum Officium Minifteriale in provincia Nov. Ebor
in America, in precibus communibus aliifque Ministerii.
Edm^s. London^s. Ecclefiafticis ad officium Curati pertinentibus juxta
formam descriptam in libro publicarum precum, Au-
thoritate parliamenti hujus inclyti Regni Magnæ
Britanniæ in ea parte Edit. et provis; et Canones et
Conftitutiones in ea parte legitime ftabilitas et publica-
tas et non aliter negue alio modo; Tibi cujus Fidelitati

Rev. James, son of Izrahiah, son of Thomas.

numen, integritati Literarum Scientiæ Sanæ Doctrinæ et Diligentiæ plurimum Confidimus (præftito primitus per Te coram Nobis Juramento tum, de agnofcendo Regiam Supremam Majeftatem juxta vim formam et effectum ftatuti parliamenti dicti Regni Magnæ Britanniæ in ea parte Edit. et provis, quum De Canonica Obedientia Nobis et fuccefforibus noftris in omnibus licitis et honeftis per te præftanda et exhibenda fubfcriptifque per Te tribus illis articulis exemplis in triceffimo fexto Capitulo Libri Conftitutionum Sive Canonum Ecclefiafticorum Anno Domini 1603 Regia Authoritate Editorum et promulgatorum) Licentiam et Facultatem Noftras concedimus et impartimus per præfentes ad noftrum Beneplacitum duntaxat duratoras. In cujus rei testimonio Sigillum (quo in hac parte utimer) præfentibus apponi facimus Dat. triceffimo die Menfis July, Aº Domi. 1723 Noftræque Translationis Anno primo.

5 Shilling Stamps.

Three Government.

While in London, he received from the Society for Propagating the Gospel, &c., the appointment of catechist, to Trinity Church, New York, in the place of the Rev. Mr. Neau. He embarked for America soon after receiving his ordination, and arrived in New York, Sept. 24, 1723. The circumstance attending his appointment and his labors as assistant to the Rev. Mr. Vesey, together with his call to Rye, we give from the Rev. Dr. Wm. Berrian's *Historical Sketch of Trinity Church, New York,* 1847. On the application of the vestry of Trinity Church to the London society, for an assistant, the following reply was returned:

LONDON, March 2, 1723.

Gentlemen: The Society for the propagation of the Gospell in Foreign parts, have some time since taken into consideration your letter, dated the 18th December, 1722, wherein you desire the Society would send a person in Priest's orders to be an assistant to the Reverend Mr. Vesey, and Lecturer, when they send a Catechist to succeed Mr. Neau. I do therefore acquaint you that the Society have appointed the Rev. Mr. Wetmore to be Catechist at New York in the place of Mr. Elias Neau, and to be assistant to Mr. Vesey in his parochial dutys. The Society do expect that you will make

Rev. James, son of Izrahiah, son of Thomas.

him a sufficient allowance for his decent and commodious support, agreeable to your engagement to the Society by your aforementioned Letter.

I am, Gentlemen, yr. most humble Servt.,
DAVID HUMPHREYS, Secretary.
To the Church Wardens and Vestry
of Trinity Church, New York. }

Another letter was (says Dr. Berrian) written to the Rev. Mr. Vesey, of the same tenor, but with the following addition:

I have wrote to the Rev. Mr. Wetmore by this Conveyance, and suppose he will soon wait upon you. I desire to hear from you, as soon as it is convenient, what proceedings have been made in this affair, and hope it will succeed as the Society intend, towards your relief in the better performing your Parochial duties, and the supplying Mr. Neau's place as Catechist.

I am, Reverend Sir, Your most humble servant,
DAVID HUMPHREYS, Secretary.
P. S. The Society, upon your recommendation, and that of the Mayor of New York, have appointed Mr. Thos. Huddlestone to be schoolmaster in the Room of his father, dec'd, with the same salary that was allowed him.

After which another letter of the same date, to the Reverend Mr. Wetmore, was read in the words following, viz :

LONDON, March 2, 1723.

Rev'd Sir.: The Society for the propagation of the Gospell in foreign Parts, have taken into consideration your letter to them, dated New York, Nov. 11th, 1722, wherein you acquaint them that the Reverend Mr. Harrison is fixed at Staten Island, by His Excellency the Governor. The Society do therefore appoint you to be their Catechist at New York, in the place of the late Mr. Neau, and do expect you would forthwith repair to the charge assigned you. The Society doe allow you for that service a salary of fifty pounds a year, to continue from your first admission here in London. And they have also appointed you to be the assistant to the Reverend Mr. Vesey, Rector of Trinity Church in New York, in his parochial dutys, and have wrote to the Church Wardens and Vestry of that Church, to make you a further handsome allowance as Assistant, towards your more decent and commodious support, which the Society expect they will, according to their promise made to them by the letter, readily doe.

It will be proper for you to let me know what steps you shall
take in this matter, and what encouragement you meet with from
the Parish.

I am, Reverend Sir, your most humble Servant,

DAVID HUMPHREYS, Secretary.

For the Reverend Mr. Wetmore }
in New York.   }

Whereupon it is ordered that the subscription paper
now before this Board, and subscribed by most of them,
be carried round to the Inhabitants of this City, to receive
their subscription towards supporting the said Mr. Wetmore.

The Rev. Mr. Wetmore entered upon his duties in 1723,
as catechist at New York, in the room of Mr. Neau, and
assistant to the Rev. Mr. Vesey. It appears from the proceedings of the society, that he attended to the catechiz-
ing of the blacks every Wednesday, Friday and Sunday
evening, at his own house, besides in the church every
Sunday before evening service; and that he had sometimes nearly 200 children and servants to instruct, whom
he taught the Church Catechism, and that he commonly
added some practical discourse suitable to their capacities,
joined with some appropriate devotions.

In 1726, a communication was received by the vestry
from the Rev. Mr. Wetmore, in which he acquainted this
Board that he had lately been called by the church wardens and vestry of the parish of Rye, to be their minister,
in the room of the Reverend Mr. Jenny, whom the Society
had appointed for the parish of Hempstead; and that he
had been inducted in the said parish of Rye, by virtue of
letters of induction from His Excellency Governour
Burnet. And also, that if the society should be pleased
to approve thereof, he intended to accept of the said parish
and remove thither, and he thanked the vestry for their
subscriptions and favors to him, and assured them that his
intentions for removing did not proceed from any dislike,
but purely because he conceived that it would be for the
better and more certain support and maintainance of himself and family.

Measures were immediately taken, as it appears from
the minutes, for supplying his place.

Mr. Vesey, and the rest of the committee, appointed by

the order of the last vestry, to prepare an address to the Honorable Society for appointing a person to officiate in the place of the Rev. Mr. Wetmore, and also another address to the bishop of London, desiring his favour and assistance therein, acquainted this board, that in pursuance of the said order, they had prepared the following letters, which were accordingly read:

NEW YORK, July 5, 1726.

Reverend Sir:

Wee, the Rector, Church Trustees, and Vestry of Trinity Church, in the City of New York, in America, being informed by the Reverend Mr. Wetmore, of his call and Induction to Rye, and his resolution, with the Society's leave, to settle in that Parish, Doe most humbly address that Honorable Body to appoint another Catechist, with the usual salary, to officiate in that place, there being about one thousand and four hundred Indian and Negro slaves, and the number daily increasing by Births and Importations from Guinea and other parts. A considerable number of those Negroes, by the Society's charity, have already been instructed in the principles of Christianity, have received Holy Baptism, are communicants of our Church, and frequently approach the Altar. We doubt not but the Society has received from Mr. Neau, their former Catechist, repeated accounts of the great success of his Mission; and since Mr. Wetmore's appointment, we have with great pleasure observed on Sunday, upwards of an hundred English children, and Negro servants attending him in the church; and their catechetical instructions being ended, singing Psalms and praising God with great devotion. The Honorable Society at all times, and more especially of late, has most zealously patronized the cause of those poor Infidells, who otherwise might still have remained ignorant of the true God, and the only way to happiness; and their great charity dispenced among them here having already produced such blessed effects, must raise in them an extraordinary Joy at present, will be a vast occasion to their future happiness, and encrease their rewards of Glory in another world. We could say much more on this occasion, but this we hope will be sufficient to guard them against any attempts to persuade them to turn their Bounty another way, and Induce them to believe that the Office of a Catechist here is of as great an importance as ever, and that his salary is as well and charitably bestowed as any Missionary's in all those parts. If the Society, on these considerations, should be pleased to appoint a Catechist, we humbly pray that he may be one in orders, and directed to assist in our Church; who in many respects will be more capable than a layman to discharge that office, and answer their pious designs, by inculcating on the Catechumens the principles of Religion, both in public and private, with greater authority; visiting them in their sickness, and as occasion requires can Baptize them, and administer the Holy Communion to them in their dying hours. Besides, this will be an act of charity to us, who being deeply involved in debt, enlarging our Church, and at present having small hopes of discharging it, are unable of ourselves to raise a sufficient maintenance for one to assist our Rector in his declining age, and to preach an afternoon sermon; tho^{h.} it. is of absolute necessity and great importance in this populous city, a place of considerable trade and resort, and the centre of America. A good English preacher, of such a clear and audible voice as may reach our large church, and the eares of the numerous hearers, will, by the Divine Influence, very much advance the Glory of God, the Interest of our Holy Church, and Religion, at this time; and we shall be the more Capable of raising, by annual subscriptions, soe much, as with the Society's salary, will be a comfortable subsistence for him, and a suitable encouragement for a man of piety & learning to come among us; and if he has an inclination to teach a Latin school, he will also find a very good account in the discharge of that Office. Were it possible for the Society to have a perfect view of this Infant Church, planted among many different nations, and severall Meeting Houses, wee persuade ourselves that her Interest would lye as near their hearts, as it does want their assistance. All which is nevertheless most humbly submitted to their consideration by us, who Heartily pray for their Health and Happiness, and shall endeavor on all occasions to approve ourselves their and your most obedient humble servts.

To the Revd. Mr. David Humphreys, Secretary to the
Honorable Society for Propagating the Gospell in
Foreign Parts.

Another letter on the same subject was addressed to the Bishop of London:

NEW YORK, July 5, 1726.

My Lord:

Wee, the Rector, Church Wardens, and Vestry of Trinity Church, being assured of Mr. Wetmore's resolution to remove to Rye, with the leave of his superiors, have most humbly addressed ourselves to your Lordship and the Honorable Society, to appoint another Catechist in Orders to officiate in this city. Inclosed is a copy of our Address, which we humbly conceive will convince your Lordship, and all the worthy patrons of our Church, that the office is still as absolutely necessary and of as great Importance as ever, and the Society's charity as well bestowed this way as on any Missionary on the Continent. To whom shall we goe, under God, but to our right

Rev. James, son of Izrahiah, son of Thomas.

Reverend Father, who, by Divine providence is appointed the Great Shepard and Bishop of these American Churches; and as you have authority and Interest, see we are well assured of your good inclinations to recommend our petition to that venerable Body, and by your powerful intercession render it successfull.

My Lord, among the Infinite Blessings of Almighty God vouchsafed this country, wherein we live, none is or can be more dear to us than the free exercise of our true Religion, and it is from hence, with Your Lordship's great goodness and piety, that we take this encouragement to address you in this manner, and the more from the consideration of our aiming at that which your Lordship has very wisely made the supreme end of all your actions, the promoting of God's glory and of being instrumentall in establishing and propagating the Gospell in foreign parts, and it is a vast advantage to our poor endeavors for this pious end, that they are sure of being countenanced by your Lordship's approbation of them, and by your zealous application in favour of our Christian Church, which God has purchased with his own Blood.

May Almighty God long preserve you, and may his Blessings be upon all your endeavors for this and other good purposes, and for all your acts of piety and charity may you be in some measure rewarded in this world, and finally receive the crown of rightousness laid up for you in Heaven. These are the hearty and most earnest wishes of, may it please your Lordship, your Lordship's most obedient humble servants.

To the Right Honorable and right Reverend Father in God Edmund, Lord Bishop of London, and one of his Majesty's most honorable privy Councill:

The Rev. Mr. Wetmore acquainted this board that the society had been pleased to appoint and send over, the Rev. Mr. Colgan, for the parish of Rye, unto which the said Mr. Wetmore had already been called and Inducted; and inasmuch as he was willing and desirous to officiate in the said parish, until the society's further pleasure should be known therein, he and Mr. Colgan had agreed that Mr. Colgan should officiate here in his stead, until such time as they should receive further orders from the society. And the said Mr. Colgan also appearing before this board, and declaring his assent thereto, it was consented to and approved of accordingly, and it was thereupon ordered that a letter be writt to the venerable society, desiring them to appoint the said Mr. Colgan to officiate here in the stead of Mr. Wetmore, if they had not already been pleased to appoint some other person; and that Mr. Vesey, the two church wardens, or either of them, and Mr.

Livingston, be a committee to prepare the same. And it is further ordered, that a subscription paper be prepared and carried about for Mr. Colgan, to commence from the first of November next.

The committee appointed by the last vestry to prepare a letter to the venerable Society for Propagating the Gospell in foreign parts, to appoint the Rev. Mr. Colgan to officiate here in the stead of the Reverend Mr. Wetmore, presented to this board, a letter for that purpose, which was read in these words following, viz:

NEW YORK, October 17th, 1726.

Rev'd. Sir:

We, the Rector, Church Wardens, and Vestry of Trinity Church, in the City of New York, in America, did some time agoe, in a most humble manner pray the Honorable Society to send a Catechist in Priest's Orders to officiate here, if they should be pleased to order the Reverend Mr. Wetmore to settle in Rye, where he had been legally called and Inducted, pursuant to an act of Assembly of this Province. But since that Address the Reverend Mr. Colgan is arrived, with orders to officiate as the Society's Missionary at Rye, but finding that Mr. Wetmore had a great desire to live there, and the Vestry of that town very much inclined that he should settle among them, he being called by them, born in the country, and best acquainted with their tempers, has agreed to an exchange if the Society should be pleased to approve of it.

Wee therefore heartily concur with them and the Vestry of Rye, in addressing that Honorable Body, humbly to desire that they would be pleased to confirm that agreement, and to order the Reverend Mr. Colgan to officiate here if they have not already appointed another Catechist, for such an exchange, as we humbly conceive will, in the present posture of affairs, prevent some trouble and confusion, and most effectually promote the great end of the Society's pious and charitable endeavors, the peace and prosperity of the Church, and the interest of Religion in those parts.

And tho' we have a great regard for the Reverend Mr. Wetmore, whose life and conversation is unexceptionable, and have hitherto expressed it by our subscriptions according to our abilitys, yet inasmuch as he can't be so well heard and understood in our large church, and since his call and Induction to Rye, we are not sure of raising a sufficient support for his family, by voluntary subscriptions; whereas Mr. Colgan's clear, distinct and loud voice, can reach the remotest hearers in the church, where he has read divine service, and preached with great applause, and this with his recommendations from England, gives him a prospect of doing more good

Rev. James, son of Izrahiah, son of Thomas.

doubt of raising so much by subscription as, with the Society's
annual allowance, may be a suitable encouragement to him to continue among us.   All which is nevertheless most humbly submitted
to the consideration of the Honble. Society by us, who sincerely pray
for their Temporall and Eternall Happiness, and subscribe ourselves
their and your much obliged and most humble servants.

To the Reverend Mr. David Humphreys, Secretary
   to the Honorable Society for propagating the
   Gospell in foreign parts.

The church wardens and vestry men desired the favour
of Rev^{d.} Mr. Vesey, that when the Reverend Mr. Colgan
comes to town from his parish of Rye, he may have the
liberty of reading prayers and preaching in the afternoon,
which request Mr. Vesey readily granted and consented to.

Mr. Vesey presented to this board a letter from the
Rev^{d.} Mr. David Humphreys, Secretary to the Society,
which was read in the words following, viz:

LONDON, Septr. 19, 1726.

Rev'd Sir:

I have communicated to the Society the letter from yourself, and
the Church Wardens and Vestry of your parish, and upon considering the state of your parish, as represented there, they have agreed
to send a Catechist to succeed Mr. Wetmore, to continue to instruct
the Negroes and other Slaves in the principles of the Christian
Religion.   The Society have also agreed that such Catechist shall
assist you in your parochial cure, but with this consideration, that
the people who have subscribed to Mr. Wetmore doe continue to
pay the same subscriptions to the Catechist the Society sends, above
the salary which the Society shall allow him.   I am Reverend S^{r.}
your most humble Servant,

DAVID HUMPHREYS, Sec'y.

P. S. :

The Society have agreed to send a Missionary to Albany.

To the Rev. Mr. Vesey, New York.

In answer to which the following letter was wrote, viz:

NEW YORK, December 27, 1726.

Reverend Sir:

This day Mr. Vesey communicated to us, in Vestry, your's of the
nineteenth of September last, wherein you inform us that the
Honble. Society has been pleased to agree to send a Catechist to succeed Mr. Wetmore, and to assist our minister in his parochial cure.
We are very sensible of their great goodness and charity, in con-

Rev. James, son of Izrahiah, son of Thomas.

tinuing the office of a Catechist, to instruct the great numbers of Negro Slaves in this city in the principles of Religion, do most gratefully acknowledge the favour thereby intended to our Infant Church, and shall cheerfully contribute to his support according to our several ability.

Wee observe that the Catechist is to assist our minister, on consideration that the subscriptions shall amount to the same given Mr. Wetmore. We make no doubt of raising as much for a good preacher, who can be clearly understood, and distinctly heard; and if the Society would be so favourable to us, as to appoint the Reverend Mr. Colgan Catechist, we believe the people would more generously subscribe, for the Congregation is very much pleased with his preaching, and reading divine service; his voice is clear and distinct, and reaches to the remotest parts of our large Church. However, by this we would not be understood to prescribe to our Superiors, but humbly beg it as a favour of great importance to the Interest of our Church and Religion in this place, and shall, nevertheless, readily submit to their most prudent choice and determination, and on all occasions endeavor to approve ourselves the Society's and your much obliged and most obedient and humble Servants.

Which letter was approved of, and signed, by all the members present, and ordered that the church wardens do send down the same by some safe hand to Capt. Downing, who went away this afternoon.—*His. Trinity Ch.*, p. 40–49.

Mr. Wetmore was installed into his parish duties, June the 19th, 1726, agreeable to the letters of induction of His Excellency Gov. Burnett.

Mr. Wetmore was called to Rye, to fill the vacancy caused by the removal of the Rev. Mr. Jenny from that parish, the following being copies of the correspondence upon the subject of his call.

To the Rev. Mr. David Humphreys, Secretary to the Hon. Society for propagating the Gospel, &c., At the Archbishop's Library, At St. Martins in the Fields, London.

Rev^d· Sir,

We, the church wardens and vestry of the Parish of Rye, humbly present our thanks to the Hon. Society for their pious and charitable assistance, thus long continued to our parish; and whereas the Hon. Society have thought fit to remove from us to Hemstead, our minister, the Rev. Mr. Jenney, whose removal lays us under the necessity to

Rev. James, son of Izrahiah, son of Thomas.

obtain another as soon as possible, to be actually resident among us; so we, in pursuance of ye Act of the Assembly, impowering us thereto, have already proceeded to elect and call the Rev. Mr. James Wetmore, who has declared his acceptance of our call upon condition the Hon. Society will give leave for his removal. Until their pleasure be known, he has promised to supply this parish once in three weeks, according to their directions to Mr. Jenny.

We therefore humbly request the Hon. Society would consent to his removal, and that he may as speedily as may be, appointed to reside constantly among us.

We conclude with our hearty prayers that the blessing of God Almighty may attend the pious and charitable designs and endeavors of that Venerable Body.

We are Rev. Sir,

Yours, and the Hon. Society's

most dutyfull and humble servants,

[Signed by order,]   JOHN CARHARTT, Clerk.

Rye Vestry Records.

CALL OF THE VESTRY TO MR. WETMORE.

Whereas, by the removal of our late incumbent, the Rev. Mr. Robert Jenny (to the parish of Hemstead), this parish is become vacant:

We therefore, the church wardens and vestrymen of the parish of Rye, whose names and seals are hereunto affixed, pursuant to the tenor and interest of an Act of General Assembly of this Province, entitled an Act for settling a ministry and raising a maintenance for them, in the City of New York, county of Richmond, Westchester and Queens county, do call the Rev. Mr. James Wetmore, to officiate and have the care of souls within this parish of Rye aforesaid. And the said Mr. James Wetmore, having told them he was ready to execute the function he was called unto, when he should be inducted into the same:

Whereupon, it is ordered, that this Board do forthwith present the said Mr. James Wetmore, and pray his Excellency for his induction into the Church of the said parish,

with all and singular, the rights, privileges and appurte-
nances to the same belonging, or in any ways appertaining.
Given under our hands and seals, this seventh day of
June, Anno Dom., 1726.

SAMUEL PURDY,   [Seal.] ⎫ Church
BENJAMIN BROWN.   [Seal.] ⎭ Wardens.

JOHN BRUNDIGE,   [Seal.] ⎫
JOSEPH SHERWOOD,   [Seal.] ⎪
DANIEL PURDY,   [Seal.] ⎬ Vestrymen.
JONATHAN HAIGHT,   [Seal.] ⎪
WILLIAM WILLETT.   [Seal.] ⎭

Parish Records.

The following order was issued by the Governor,
the original of which, we have before us :

MANDATE FROM GOVERNOR BURNET TO INDUCT MR. JAMES
WETMORE TO THE RECTORY OF THE PARISH CHURCH OF
RYE.

GULIELMUS BURNET armiger, Provinciæ Novi Eboraci,
nec non Novæ Cæsariæ in America strategus et Imperator
Ejusdemque Vice Admiralis, &c. Universis et singulis
Clericis et Ministris Ecclesiæ Anglicanæ quibuscumque in
et per totam Provinciam Novi Eboraci ubilibet constitutis
ædelibus Ecclesiæ Parochialis de Rye in comitatu cestriæ
occidentalis intra Provinciam Novi Eboraci prædict pro hoc
tempore salutem. Cum dilectum in Christo Jacobum Wetmore, Clericum et Rectoriam sive Ecclesiam Parochialem
prædict Parochiæ de Rye in dict. comitatu dicta tam Provinciæ Novi Eboraci in America jam vacantem ipsumque
præsentatum Rectorem ejusdem Rectoriæ sive Ecclesiæ
parochialis in et de Eadem admiserim, vobis Conjunctim et
divisim Committo et firmiter injungendo mando, Qua-
tenus eundem Jacobum Wetmore, Clericum, ceu Procura-
torem Suum Legitimum Ejus Nomine et pro eo in Realem
actualem et Corporalem possessionem ipsius Rectoriæ et
Ecclesiæ parochialis de Rye prædict Glebarum, Juriumque:
et pertinentium suorum universorum, Conferatis Induca-
tis, Inducive faciatis; et defendatis Inductum. Et quid in
præmissis feceritis me aut alium Judicem in hac parte
competentem quemcumque debite (cum ad id congrue

Rev. James, son of Izrahiah, son of Thomas.

fueritiis requisiti) certificetis seu sic certificet ille vestrum qui præsens hoc meum mandatum fuerit Executus.

Datum sub sigillo prærogativo dictæ Provinciæ Novi Eboraci, xvii die Junii anno salutis MDCCXXVI.

W. BURNET.

By his Excellency's command,
JAS. BOBIN, Dep. Secretary.

On the back of the above order is endorsed the certificate of induction of the tenor and date below.

RYE, June 19, 1726.

These are to certify that on the day and year above written, by Vertue of the within mandate from his Excellency the Governour, I, Robert Jenney, Rector of the Parochial Church of Hempsted, on Long Island, in Queens County in yᵉ province of New York, have inducted the Revᵈ. Mr. James Wetmore, into the real actual and corporal possession of the Parocial Church of Rye in the county of West Chester and province of New York, together with Parsonage Glebe and all the appurtenances thereof, as witness my hand.   (Signed.)   ROBT. JENNEY.

In presence of
Samᵉˡ Purdy,
Jonaᵗʰ Haight,
John Horton,
Jnᵒ Carhartt,
Anthony Miller.

At an ajourned meeting of the Vestry, held January 24, 1726-7, present Rev. James Wetmore, &c., it was agreed to raise this year as follows:

For the Minister, - - -	£50. 0. 0.
For the Poor, - - - - -	10, 0. 0.
For the Clerk of the Vestry, -	1, 10. 0.
For the Clerk of the Church, - -	1, 0. 0.
For the Drummer, - - - -	1, 0. 0.
For Expenses and incidental charges,	3, 10. 0.
For Mʳˢ Budd, for her Negroe's work, Seven day's at the Parish house, at 2s. 6d., per day, - - - -	17. 6.

£67, 17. 6.

Collecting money, -	-	-	3, 11. 6.

£71, 9. 0.

Quoted as follows:

Rye, - - - - - -		£35, 10. 0.
Bedford, - - - - - - -		17, 0. 0.
Mamaroneck, - - - -		10, 12. 0.
Scarsdale, - - - - - - -		5, 0. 0.
North Castle, - - - - - -		3, 7. 0.

£71, 9. 0.

Bolton's Hist. Ch. in Westchester.

It will be perceived by the following, that the Society for the Propagation of the Gospel, on removing Mr. Jenny to Hempstead, appointed the Rev. Mr. Clogan to supply his place at Rye, before receiving the petition of that parish for the appointment of Mr. Wetmore.

Rev. Sir:

We, the church wardens and vestry of the parish of Rye, return our humble thanks to yᵉ honorable Society for their pious and charitable efforts in providing so speedily to fill vacancy by appointing yᵉ Rev. Mr. Colgan for us. We conclude they have before this time been acquainted by our letters, how far we have proceeded to obtain a minister, fearing the ill consequences of being left destitute, and we hope yᵉ honorable Society will put a favorable construction upon our proceedings, though we have given our call to the Rev. *Mr. Wetmore*, and he received induction immediately upon it yet he always declared that he should submit to yᵉ resolution of the honorable Society, and not in any way interfere in their determination, and though we find yᵉ inclinations of yᵉ people very much to have *Mr. Wetmore* appointed for us, on which account we can't but desire yᵉ honorable Society would be pleased to favor it, yet we shall always yᵉ greatest difference to their pleasure, and if they finally determine that Mr. Colgan shall be for us, against whom we have no exceptions, as being a stranger to us, we shall give him the best welcome we are capable of, but inasmuch as yᵉ Rev. Mr. Colgan is willing by exchange with Mr. *Wetmore*, to continue at New York, and that Vestry has signified their approbation, we heartily join with them in requesting of yᵉ honorable society that would confirm that agreement, and give liberty to Mr. Wetmore to come to this parish, who being born in the country, and acquainted with the dispositions and customs of yᵉ people here, will be acceptable to us, and we hope do much service for religion. But all this with sub-mission to that venerable body, whose pleasure we shall most cheer-fully submit to; and we pray ye continuance of their favor and charity, and that God would prosper their pious designs.

We are reverend Sir,
the Honorable Society's,
and your most humble and
Obt. Servants,

Signed by order.   JOHN CARHART, Clerke.

To the
   Rev. Mr. David Humphreys, Secretary
   to ye Hon'ble Society for Propagation
   ye Gospel, &c., Archbishop's Library,
   at St. Martins in ye Fields, London.

Church Rec.

The request of the parish was immediately granted, and the vestry, by their clerk, forwarded the following to the Society, April 25, 1727.

Rev. Sir

The church wardens and veftry men of ye parifh of Rye have ordered me to return their humble thanks to you and the Honourable Society for ye favour of yours of September 30th, in which you acquaint us that the Honourable Society have confented to ye exchange for which we had humbly addreffed, and accordingly have appointed ye Rev. Mr. Wet-more, to be our Minifter, which is very much to ye fatiffaction of ye whole parifh, even thofe who are diffenters from our church.

And now we are once more peaceably fettled, we hope by the bleffing of God, to fee religion revive among us, which by contentions and di-vifions is funk to a very low ebb. As the Rev. Mr. Wetmore has been born in this country, and long known among us, who has had his con-verfation becoming his facred character and profeffion, we doubt not but ye people of this parifh will continue their affection to him, and hope to fee this good fruit of it, viz: that they be brought to a proper fence of religion, and more general and conftant attendance in ye public worfhip and facraments, which for a long time have been very much neglected among us; we earneftly pray for the bleffing of Almighty God upon that venerable fociety, whofe extenfive charity (under God), finds for fo many fouls famifhing in ignorance and error, and fhall always look upon our-felves strictly bound to pay it, the greateft honor and moft cheerful obedi-ence to all their commands and directions, and beg leave to fubfcribe with all dutiful refpects,   Rev. Sir, Your and ye Honorable Society,

Moft humble and obedient fervants,
Signed by order of the Veftry,
JOHN CARHART, Clerke.

25

LETTER FROM MR. WETMORE IN REPLY TO ONE FROM THE
SECRETARY OF THE SOCIETY, IN LONDON.

RYE, May 11th, 1727.

Rev. Sir:

I received yours of December 30th, wherein you acquaint me
that the Honourable Society have appointed the Rev. Mr. Colgan,
to New York, and me to Rye, according to our request, for which I
return my humble thanks, and inasmuch as the people of Rye, appear to me to be much gratified by this exchange, I shall endeavor
to make the best use I can of the good affection they profess to me,
to promote the interest of piety and religion among them, which
seems to be sunk to a very low ebb. My labours have been divided
the winter past, between Westchester and Rye, but so that when I
preached for Mr. Colgan at Rye, he preached for me at Westchester, and our labors have not been without success. Besides those
baptized by him in both parishes, I have baptized about 40 infants,
and 1 adult person, and have had 7 adult persons apply to me for
baptism, whom I have deferred for further preparations, two of
which are negroes. I have admitted to the communion, three new
communicants, all converts from Dissenters, and several others, with
whom I have taken particular pains, have promised to come to the
communion when they shall have gained some further knowledge
of the virtue and necessity of the institution. The town of Rye,
tho' by much the greater part Dissenters, have upon my request,
chosen trustees, who are empowered to raise a tax upon the town,
to repair and finish the church, which is now in a very poor condition, and I have promised to give them a bell if they will build a
steeple to hang it in, which I believe they will comply with. I shall
be able to give more particular accounts of the state of the parish,
when I have been some longer time with them. Mr. Henry Caner,
being as he tells me, about to undertake a voyage to England, to
offer himself to the service of the Honorable Society, I beg leave
to recommend him as a person of a good character among us, and
qualified to serve the church; sober, grave, and exemplary in his
conversation, and of good report, even among those that are without,
of whom I speak with the greater assurance both as to his piety and
loyalty to his majesty, because I have been personally and intimately
acquainted with him for more than three years. It is a matter of
joy to me, to see so many new churches going forward in this country,
and the good position of so many people in all parts of it, notwithstanding the violence and bitterness of its numerous adversaries. I
pray God to bless and reward the charity of that venerable body,

which gives life and motion to the church in these parts, and beg leave to subscribe with all dutiful regard,

Rev. Sir, Yours, and the
Honorable Society's most humble
and obedient servant,
JAMES WETMORE.

Mss. from Archives, at Fulham, i, 676-7.—*Dr. Hawks.*

Again Mr. Wetmore writes to the secretary, under date of

RYÈ, February 20, 1727–8.

Rev. Sir :

Yours of June 16, came not to hand, till the 14th of November. I have since used my utmost diligence to prepare myself to answer the queries contained therein, which is something difficult, consider-ing the extent of my Parish, in which is but one Church, viz : the town of Rye, built by a license from Lord Cornbury, Governor of New York, in the year 1706, the materials of which are rough stone, from the foundation to the roof, and the east end was first built with stone to the top, but the weather beating through to the preju-dice of the ceiling, it has since been pulled down and built with wood and shingled, and the ceiling repaired, which cost £30, which £30 was part of a year's salary, after Mr. Bridge's death, applied to that use by order of the General Assembly. The chief promoter of the church, and its greatest benefactor, was Col. Caleb Heathcote, who gave the nails and all the iron work; Mr. Murison paid the masons, whose work amounted to about £40, whether he procured the money by donations in York, or otherways, I can't certainly find; the remainder was paid by tax upon the Town, but nothing of the inside was then done, but the ceiling. In the Rev. Mr. Bridge's time, a subscription was promoted for finishing the church, but nothing more was done, than building the pulpit and altar, and laying part of the place afterwards. When Mr. Jenny was minister of the parish £8 was raised by the parish to make shutters for the windows, and six pieces were built by particular men. Upon the first town meeting after I was appointed to this parish, I prayed the town to take into consideration the neglected and ruinous state of the Church, being gone very much to decay, and to think of some method that would be more acceptable to the people, to put it into a better condition, upon which they chose trustees, to repair it according to an act of Assembly of the Province, empowering trus-tees so chosen to repair public buildings. These trustees made a tax of £100, and immediately provided for repairing and finishing the Church, and have put a new cover of cedar shingles upon it, the

Rev. James, son of Izrahiah, son of Thomas.

old one which was of oak, being worn out; they have also finished
the floor and all the pews, and would have proceeded to repair the
doors and glass which are gone much to decay, and to paint the
walls and clean the church, but are obliged to cease for the
present, by reason of some opposition they meet with from some of
the Presbyterian party, instigated by a very troublesome fellow, one
John Walton, who set up for a Teacher among them, before my
being appointed here, from whom I have met with a great deal of
opposition.   These Presbyterians have commenced a law suit against
the collector of the tax, and tho' we hope they will finally get no
advantage, yet it caused the work to cease; but I hope we shall
find some method to revive it again and to build a steeple, to encourage which, I have promised to give them a bell when the steeple
is finished.   The church is 49 feet in length from west to east, and
34 in width; there are two large aisles in the church, one from the
west door up to the altar, the other from the south door up to the
reading pew, which stands before the pulpit; the rest is now filled
in with handsome pews, the altar is raised two steps and railed in,
but a poor altar piece.   We have a silk carpet for the communion
table, and a pulpit cloth, given by Queen Anne, of blessed memory,
with a Chalice and Paten; we have a folio Bible and Common
Prayer Book, worn old, given by the Honourable Society, or by the
Queen, as also the library as usual, to every minister.

There is a salary of £50 per annum, New York money, which is
equivalent to about £31 sterling, settled by an Act of Assembly
upon an orthodox minister, called by the vestry and inducted by
the Governour.   This vestry consists of ten men and two Church
wardens to be chosen annually, the second Friday in January, by
the votes of the whole parish.   The glebe is a small old house, and
three acres of land lying near the church, one acre of which was
given by Justice Denham, and about eight acres, a mile distant,
lying in such a form as to be of very little use, but at present rented
for three bushels of wheat per annum, for seven years.   The house
was built by the town for a Presbyterian minister, before there was
a church in town, but never any particular settlement of it upon
any; when a minister of the Church came, and they had no Presbyterian minister, the house was put into his possession and enjoyed
successively with the glebe, by the minister of the church, but the
Presbyterian party threatening to give trouble about it in Mr. Jenney's time, he procured a survey of it for the Church, and got it
entered upon the public records of the Province; he also repaired
the house, which was almost fallen down, being neglected by Mr.
Bridge, who thought it not worth repairing.

When the Church was first built, the town was but small and the
people poor.   I find by an old list, that the number of people taxed
for building the Church were about ninety-three, some of which

Rev. James, son of Izrahiah, son of Thomas.

were widows, and some young men without families, and though they were generally Presbyterians, by Col. Heathcote's influence, and Mr. Muirson's industry and good behavior, and the Governour of the Province being zealous to encourage the Church, they all united in building the Church, and frequented the worship in it, as long as Mr. Murison lived, and so they did in Mr. Bridge's time, but after his death they fell into division, and invited a Presbyterian minister among them, and tho' they have never had one ordained in the Presbyterian or Independent way, yet they kept up their party, and whenever there has been a vacancy, the Independent ministers from the Colony of Connecticut have then especially been very busy to strengthen that party and increase their prejudices against the church. This Walton I before mentioned, took an opportunity to get into the parish at a time when there was a contest between the Rev. Mr. Jenny and the people, concerning the salary, during the vacancy after Mr. Bridge's death, which the vestry raised, rather than stand a trial at law, and Mr. Jenny laid it out in repairing the house and glebe, but many that before came to the Church, and some who had been communicants in Mr. Bridge's time (yet always lovers of Independency), being now disaffected, readily fell in with this Walton, and being a bold, noisy fellow, of a volible tongue, drew the greatest part of the town after him, and he had taken all imaginable pains to give them ill impressions of the Church; he spurred them forward to build one meeting house at the White Plains, about six miles from the Church, and has set them on to build another in town, within one hundred rods of the Church, to defray the expenses of which, they have obtained briefs from the General Assembly of Connecticut Colony, to beg in all the towns and villages of that Colony, who being great enemies of the Church, have contributed largely out of mere opposition to the Church. I have used my utmost diligence and prudence since my coming among them, to dispose them to reconciliation, and to establish and strengthen the wavering, and my endeavors have in some degree, been successful. I have brought some over to the Church, several to the Communion, and inspired others with a greater love and zeal for the worship and constitution of the Church, tho' it must be confessed to their shame, there is still a very great indifference and slackness in attending the public worship of God, among those that profess themselves churchmen, as well as among the sectaries.

As to the general condition, employ, and business of those who frequented the Church at first, their estates lay much in unimproved lands, and I can't learn that they raised much, if anything for the market, but what they trafficked with, was chiefly wood and cattle. As to their sentiments in the matters of religion, I have already intimated they were by profession, Presbyterians, and always loved the Independent principles, but the act of Assembly providing for the support of a ministry, being so worded as to give the benefit

Rev. James, son of Izrahiah, son of Thomas.

only to ministers of the Church of England, tho' many of the Assembly, perhaps, might design other ways, and the Governour's being zealous to encourage the Church, and Colonel Heathcote, being in the parish, a man of great influence over the people, and especially the better sort; and Mr. Muirson being acceptable to the people, by his sober and grave conversation, and very industrious to remove the scruples that they had conceived, and their prejudices against the Church, they generally fell in, to encourage and promote the Church, and frequented the worship of it, but those of them now living, who have left the Church, say they were always Presbyterians, but while they were in no condition to get a minister according to their own mind, they thought it was better to go to church, than to have no religion (tho' we have some now that are hardly of that opinion). Their manner of living was at first somewhat more compact than it is now, for as they increase, they move out into the woods and settle where they can get good farms.

The parish consists of three towns: Rye and Mamaroneck, about four or five miles south, and Bedford, about twenty miles north. The nearest English church is Westchester, about fifteen miles north from Rye, and very bad travelling in the winter and spring, but in the summer pretty good, but from Bedford to Westchester is thirty-five miles and always bad travelling.

The parish is very much improved since the first settling of the Church here, especially as to their numbers, and tho' there are many that live very meanly, and counting the value of unimproved lands (all which belonged to a few men, and now sold or divided among their children), we may look upon the former inhabitants as possessing better estates than most of their children now; yet, 'tis certain in general, that the manufacture of the country is very much increased, and there are more hundreds of bushels of wheat sent to market in a year now, than single bushels twenty years past. There are now in the whole parish, as I find by the several lists for the year past, three hundred and forty persons upon whom tax is levied, heads of families, and young men in the township of Rye two hundred, in Mamaroneck twenty, in the manor of Scarsdale thirty, in Bedford sixty, and thirty in North Castle, a new settlement between Rye and Bedford, about six miles from Bedford; this place was chiefly settled by people of no religion at all, very ignorant and barbarous, being descendants of the Long Island Quakers, and having more knowledge of Quakerism, than of any other religion, are more receptive of that, but there being a few people of the Church among them, Mr. Jenny first began to take pains with them, preached among them, and baptised several, tho' they are since all returned to Quakerism or nothing; and 'tis certain they have left the Church, partly by the instigation of the Quakers (who have been very busy among them while they were long neglected), from Mr. Jenney being called to Hemstead, at my being fixed here, and partly upon disgust, being disappointed of some preferments they expected Mr. Jenny would procure for them, and being reproved for bringing a scandal upon religion by their loose and irregular living; however there are a few sober people that live there, and to accommodate them and Bedford, or at least some from Bedford that are willing to come to church, I preach about once in five weeks at North Castle. There are three meeting houses in the parish, one at Bedford, built for and used by the Presbyterians, one in the township of Rye, about seven miles from the Church towards North Castle, built last year by the Quakers, and one at White Plains in the township of Rye, about six miles from the Church, built last year by the followers of Walton, who are the only Independent party, and they are about building another near the church. The haughty, insolent behaviour of Walton, drew upon him the displeasure of the Dissenting teachers, on which account he removed from the parish a few days ago, but introduced a young man to be his successor, who holds forth one Sunday at White Plains, and another in the town of Rye, alternately, for which they give him £50 per annum, which they raise by subscriptions; they have besides given him money to purchase house and land, but how much I can't tell. The Quakers have no constant holder forth among them, but keep silent meetings, unless when some travelling speaker chances to straggle among them, and then they follow it every day in the week, from one place to another, taking all imaginable pains to seduce the ignorant and unstable. At Bedford they have had a Presbyterian minister, they gave him a house and farm to work upon, and £40 per annum, but finding it not sufficient to support him with a numerous family, he has left them, and they are now settled with another young man, to whom they give the same allowance. As to the number of people dissenting from the Church, of all sorts through the parish, they are much the greater part at Mamaroneck. They are chiefly Quakers in the town of Rye; the number of Church people and Independents are near equal, about sixty families each — about fifteen families, Quakers, and the rest are a sort of people that frequent no manner of public worship, and by all I can learn have no private worship, neither. There are some of this sort at North Castle, about ten families of the Church, and the rest Quakers; at Bedford there are about eight or ten families of the Church, and the rest Presbyterians or Independents; at the Manor of Scarsdale, about eight families of the Church, and the rest Dissenters of one denomination or another. There are no more Dissenting teachers in the Parish than I have mentioned, these officiate without any sort of ordination, and without qualifying themselves according to the act of toleration; in that people are suffered to do and say what they please about religion under a notion that the laws

Rev. James, son of Izrahiah, son of Thomas.

of England relating to religion don't extend to the plantations. As to schools for teaching children, there are several poor ones in different parts of the Parish; while Mr. Cleator had his sight, they tell me he kept a constant and good school, but now, where a number of families live near together, they hire a man and woman at a cheap rate, subscribing every one what they will allow; some masters get £20 per annum and their diet, some £12, but there is no public provision at all for a school in this parish, except what the Honourable Society allow Mr. Cleator, nor is there any donations or benefactions to the minister or school master, besides what I have mentioned, nor is there any library besides the Honourable Society's.

The number of negroes in the parish is about one hundred; since Mr. Cleator has been blind and unable to teach school, he has taken pains with the negroes, so many as their masters would allow to come, but of late, they have left coming altogether; those that belong to Quaker masters, they will allow them no instruction; some Presbyterians will allow their servants to be taught, but are unwilling that they should be baptised, and those of the church are not much better, so there is but one negro in the parish, baptized. I had two of my own, which I baptized, but I have lately sold them out of the parish, and I have another, which I have instructed and design to baptize very speedily.

Since I received my Lord of London's letters to the Masters and Mistresses, I have taken particular pains with them, and they give me encouragement that they will send them to be instructed, if the masters can agree upon some regulations to prevent the common inconveniences of their meeting together, and I hope I shall prevail upon many of them to send their servants upon Sunday afternoons, and if Mr. Cleator can do anything towards the instruction it will be a pleasure to the good old man, and I shall assist him in it myself, and endeavor that many of them may be brought to receive christian baptism.

This is the most true and exact account I can anyways give in answer to the queries contained in your letter.

Rev. Sir, Your and the Honourable

Society's most obedient humble Servant,

JAMES WETMORE.

New York Mss. from Archives at Fulham, I, 683, 694.—*Dr. Hawks.*

Letters from Mr. Wetmore to the secretary of various dates, from the date of the above written, to 1732, contain accounts of his ministrations, and the progress of the church in his and the neighboring parishes.

Rev. James, son of Izrahiah, son of Thomas.

The following to the bishop of London, refers to his printed dialogues with the Quakers, which ended the controversy with them, and also to the urgent want of a suffragan bishop :

RYE, PROVINCE NEW YORK, April 3, 1732.

My Lord,

I take this opportunity, by Mr. Beach, who waits upon your Lordship for your benediction and orders, to return my humble thanks for the favour of your letter, in approbation of what I had undertaken in respect of the Quakers. I now send by Mr. Beach, the dialogue I printed in reply to the Quaker's answer to my letter, in which I should have spared some expressions, if I had received your Lordship's directions before they were printed, but the greatest asperity being only the relating of such facts as are open and notorious, they can make little advantage of it. They are a sort of people that take greatest advantage from being used with smoothness, which they fancy their own merit extorts. They did not expect I would have treated them with so much freedom and plainness, but I am well assured it has done good; it has opened the eyes and awakened the consideration of some that were almost drawn over to them upon account of their being thought a sober, virtuous, good people, though they have as many vitiary people in their herd as among any sort of professors, but their trick is to call such only *hangers-on*, though they are as zealous for their principles as the best of 'em.

It is now 9 months since the dialogues were printed, and though at first they gave out they had an answer ready, yet it does not appear, and of late not a syllable is heard about it, they are mighty still now, and rather afraid of losing their own people than intent upon prostituting ours.

Mr. Beach will be able to acquaint your Lordship how fast the principles of the Church gain ground in New England, chiefly among the teachers in Connecticut, on which account we might hope to have this country reclaimed from this schism, so dishonourable and prejudicial to religion, and destructive to the souls of men, if some method could be projected for perfecting an establishment of religion here, and removing the difficulty which is indeed great and burthensome, of going 1000 leagues over sea, through many perils, for ordination; if only one suffragan was allowed under your Lordship (tho' two or three would do better to ordain and confirm), in other things Commissaries might answer, it would give a new tone to the Church among us, and I believe the country would generally submit to an Episcopal government, in a little time, if there was provision, that laws or canons might be made here for

Rev. James, son of Izrahiah, son of Thomas.

regulating some circumstantial things, according to the peculiar circumstances of this country, I mean in reference to the calling of ministers and their maintenance, which the people will be fond of having their voice in, and in respect of which they are afraid of imposition, and perhaps it may be thought not necessary to insist upon a perfect uniformity, in things indifferent, as a term of communion, where unity in government, and all essentials can be gained for which a discretionary power in your Lordship, or your suffragan, to prescribe for this country, the form and method of worship at Croft, wherein it may be thought proper to bar in any respect, from the established English Liturgy would be sufficient.

I have not the vanity to think of projecting a scheme or prescribing to your Lordship, but only to breathe out my own and others wishes and desires into the bosom of your Lordship, as the Father and head of the Church, in the Plantations, who have expressed a zealous and fraternal care of us, and whose wisdom and goodness we confide in with pleasure, to project for us, and still further bring about that what is wanting, may be perfected and set in order, I am with all dutiful submission,

My Lord, &c.,

JAMES WETMORE.[10]

N. Y. Mss. from Arch. at Fulham, II, 54, 56.—*Dr. Hawks.*

[10] Mr. Wetmore did not live to see his desires for a bishop for the American colonies appointed, for it was not till 1784 accomplished, when Samuel Seabury was consecrated in Scotland, November 14th, of that year, by Bishops Petrie, Skinner and Kilgour, of the Scotch branch of the established church.

The following, relative to Bishop Seabury's consecration, is from a communication of the Rev. T. B. Chandler, D. D., to Isaac Wilkins, dated London, February 25, 1785.. The bearer of which (says Bolton in his *History of the Church of Westchester*), was the Rev. Dr. Seabury.

My Dear Sir:

I hope that you may happen to be in Halifax when this arrives there, both for your own sake and that of the bearer, who is no less a person than the *Bishop of Connecticut.* He goes by the way of Nova Scotia, for several reasons, of which the principal is, that he may see the situation of that part of his family, which is in that quarter, and be able to form a judgment of the prospects before them. He will try hard to *see you*, but, as he will not have much time to spare, he fears he shall not be able to go to Shelburne in quest of you.

You were acquainted with this bishop, and his adventures from the time of his leaving New York, in 1783. He came home with strong recommendations to the two archbishops, and the bishop of London, from the clergy of Connecticut, and with their most earnest request that he might have Episcopal consecration for the church in that state. Though no objections could arise from his character, the bishops here thought such a measure would be considered as rash and premature, since no fund had been established for his support, and no consent to his admission had been made by the states; besides, no bishop could be consecrated here for a *foreign* country, without an act of Parliament to dispense with the oaths

Rev. James, son of Izrahiah, son of Thomas.

Mr. Wetmore closes his semi-annual report to the secretary under date of June 6, 1732, as follows:

Our trustees are repairing the windows of the Church, for which they raised £20 last year by a public rate, and we are contriving to build a steeple to the Church, for which we have begun subscriptions. I have bought a bell to make a present of, weighing 93 lb., that, for the bigness, sounds well, and I have subscribed thirty shillings besides to the steeple; Mr. Cleator has also, upon his death bed, given half his last year's salary to this use, so that I hope we shall accomplish it, tho' I do not find the people so ready to subscribe as I expected; a zeal for the honour and decency of God's house, and worship, is a temper very much wanting in this country. I pray God to increase it, and to give abundant success to the pains and charitable designs and endeavours of the Honourable Society, &c.

JAMES WETMORE.

N. Y. Mss., from Archives at Fulham, I, 67-8.—*Dr. Hawks.*

required by the established office. These difficulties and objections continued to operate through the winter, and several candidates for priests' orders, who had been waiting near a twelve month, were about going over to the continent, to see for ordination in some foreign Protestant Episcopal Church. At length a short act was obtained, authorizing the bishop of London and his substitutes to dispense with the aforesaid oaths in the ordination of priests and deacons for the American states; but nothing was said in it about the consecration of bishops. The minister, it seems, was fearful that opening the door for the consecration of bishops, would give umbrage to the Americans, and, therefore, every prospect of success here was at an end. Dr. Seabury, with his wonted spirit and resolution, then thought it his duty to apply elsewhere, and by the intervention of a friend, consulted the Bishops in Scotland, who were equally without the protection and the restraint of government. They cordially met the proposal, and our friend was consecrated Bishop for Connecticut, at Aberdeen, on the 14th of November last. I have been thus particular, on the supposition that you may not have been acquainted with so much of this history.—From the original letter in the possession of Gouverneur M. Wilkins Esq.—*Bolton Hist. of W.,* pp. 102, 103.

Rev. Isaac Wilkins, D. D., to whom the above was addressed, was a son of a wealthy planter of Jamaica, W. I., who in youth was sent to New York, to be educated. After concluding his studies, he settled in Westchester co., and married Isabella Morris, a sister of Lewis Morris, one of the signers of the declaration of independence; he was returned to the General Assembly, where he delivered a warm loyalist speech, which made him obnoxious to the whigs, and for peace's sake, he removed to England in 1775, returning to Long Island the following year, where he remained till the peace; when he retired to Shelburne, Nova Scotia. He returned to Westchester again about 1800. Studied divinity and became a minister of the gospel, and was settled over an Episcopal parish in that county some thirty years.—*Compiler.*

Rev. James, son of Izrahiah, son of Thomas.

Agreeable to Mr. Wetmore's recommendation, the secretary appointed Samuel Purdy school teacher at Rye, with a salary of £15 per annum.

The following to the secretary, gives some account of Mr. Wetmore's missionary labors in Connecticut, in addition to his laborious duties in Westchester:

RYE, June 24, 1734.

Rev. Sir:

My parish continues in a flourishing state, tho' we have many yet that show too little reverence for religion. The church is commonly more filled this summer than heretofore, and since my last, I have baptised in my own Parish, twenty-seven children and two adults, in Greenwich in Connecticut, three children; and Norfolk in Connecticut, two children and one adult, an Indian slave, and I have admitted eight new communicants, all of very sober conversation, and good lives. The people of Connecticut begin to show a friendly disposition towards the constitution of the Church of England, which disposition seems to increase apace, which makes more and more want of a Bishop in the country, that some places might be supplied with ministers, that now cannot, without burthening the Honourable Society. Some zealous bigots among the Independent teachers are awakened to make fresh attempts to amuse and enslave the people by their scurrillous pamphlets, which they spread industriously, full of bold audacious calumnies, but little argument, yet would be of mischievous consequence, if we did not antidote their poison by printing and dispersing such books as appear serviceable to this end, in which I was urged last summer to give some assistance by printing an answer to a pamphlet that undertook to prove the necessity of separating from the Church of England, and the divine right of Presbyterian ordination and government. There is now dispersing in this country a defence of that pamphlet, stuffed with vile aspersions and unmannerly reflections upon the civil and ecclesiastical government of the nation, done by two or three hands, one of which I conclude Mr. Browne of Providence, will reply to, and the other Mr. Johnson and I must prepare the antidote for, which I hope will prove to as good acceptance in the country as what we printed last year, and have the same good effect, which has been very visible in promoting the interest of the church.

My prayers and endeavors shall always be zealous to promote the great and charitable designs of the Honourable Society for propagating the Gospel of Christ.

I am, Rev. Sir, your most
Obedient, humble Servant,
JAMES WETMORE.

N. Y. Mss. from Arch. at Fulham, II, 74, 75.—Dr. Hawks.

Rev. James, son of Izrahiah, son of Thomas.

In letters to the secretary at London, during the
years 1735, 1736, 1738, and 1739, Mr. Wetmore reports his doing duty, in addition to his own charge at
Rye, at North Castle, White Plains, Bedford, in Westchester county, and Stamford, Greenwich, and Horse-
neck, in Connecticut, making mention of baptizing one
hundred and eleven children, of whom five were negroes,
and seven adults, of whom one was a negro, between
the 3d of May, 1739, to the 5th of August of the same
year.   In 1741 he reports having baptized within
twelve months, sixty-nine children, four of whom were
negroes; and four adults, one of whom was a negro.

His letters to the secretary in 1743, 1744, and 1745,
besides reporting the state of his several charges, alludes
to his controversy with the Dissenters, especially with
Mr. Dickerson a Presbyterian, who published a work
on the *Nature and Necessity of Regeneration;* to which
Mr. W. published a reply, entitled, *A Defence of Water-
land's Discourse on Regeneration.*[11]

The following letter to the secretary gives us some
insight into Mr. Wetmore's visits to his native place:

PROVINCE OF NEW YORK, Rye, Oct. 3, 1745.
Rev. Sir :
   I was three weeks ago at Middletown, in Connecticut, the place of
my nativity, which I have been used to visit annually while my
father lived there, and have not only frequently preached among
them and baptized many children and some adults, but taken pains
in conversation with my relations and acquaintances to give them
just notions of religion and beget in them a liking to the Church of
England, and I am rejoiced to see very hopeful prospect of a good
church gathering in that place chiefly promoted by some brethren
of mine ;[12] and it was a pleasure to me to observe at the *Commence-*

[11] For interesting epistles from the Rev. James Wetmore, to the Bishop of
London, and the Secretary of the Propagation Society, we would refer the
reader to the *History of the Protestant Episcopal Church of Westchester co.,*
by Robert Bolton, A. M. ; Stanford & Swords, New York : 1855, 8vo.
   [12] SKETCH OF THE EPISCOPAL CHURCH IN MIDDLETOWN.—That there was
occasionally Episcopal worship before 1750, is altogether probable, aside
from tradition.   Rev. James Wetmore, a native of the town, the first Congregational minister of North Haven, became an Episcopal minister about

ment, in New Haven, (at which I was present in my way to. Middletown, with Dr. Johnson and several *others* of our clergy), no less than five of the *Batchelors* graduated this year, openly professing the Church of England, and was told some others of them had a good disposition towards it, by whom we were treated very respectfully; and if we may imagine the questions defended in public disputation as the prevailing sentiments of the country, we may see a great change in that colony for the better in a very few years, by the following questions, which indeed I was surprised to hear defended by those whose fathers have held, and acted upon their reverse, in their separation from the Church of England. The questions publicly disputed were :·

· 1st. The Protestus legislativa sit unicumque societati Essentialis affirmat respondens.

2d. Aures in se indiffiantes sunt proprie humonie potestatis objectum respondens affirmat.

3d. An conscientia dictermina, conferent jen agendi vel cogitandi contra veritatem nuget respondens.

Reverend Sir,

Yours, &c.;

JAMES WETMORE.

N. Y. Mss. from Arch. at Fulham, II, 155.—*Dr. Hawks.*

1724, and it is very likely performed service sometimes in the dwellings of his friends. Jeremiah Leaming, a native of the town at a late period, an Episcopal clergyman, may have done the same before 1750. Before that time, some of the inhabitants had become so much attached to Episcopal forms, that they took some steps to secure a site on which to erect a house of ·worship, to the building of which Mr. Wetmore most earnestly advised them. Hence the town voted, April 29th 1749, that professors of the Church of England, have liberty to erect their church in the highway, between Jeffries corner (so called), John Fosters corner and the dwelling house of Mr. Ephraim Doane, and the select men, or any three of them, are hereby empowered to stake out the place for the said building.

Many years since the writer was assured that at the close of 1749, there were sixteen Episcopal families in the town, though measures in due form do not appear to have been taken to organize a parish till Easter Monday, April 16th, 1750. A church was erected on the site, designated in the vote of the town in· 1752, fifty feet long, and thirty-six wide, with a towering steeple, though not finished for two or three years. This was. used as a sanctuary for more than eighty years; when the ·proffer of a thousand dollars from the ladies of the Assistant Society prompted the gentlemen to the work of erecting their present edifice. This was completed in 1834. It is of Portland stone, seventy-eight feet by sixty, twelve feet porch, and cost $14,000.

A bell for the first Episcopal Church was procured in 1759, and a second was given by Mr. John Alsop, a-wealthy merchant of New York, a brother of Richard Alsop of this place, in 1785. This is now in use in the present church.

For many years, the people were aided in the support of their ministers by the society in England, for the Propagation of the Gospel in Foreign Parts. Rev. Dr. Leaming, already spoken of, and Dr. Richard Mansfield, performed at least occasional services for them.—*Historical Sketches ·of Middletown, &c., W. B. Casey*, 1853.

The following letter to the Rev. Dr. Barclay, we give from the original manuscript copy, made by Mr. Wetmore :

RYE, Oct. 28, 1747.

Revd. Sir :

I thank you heartily for your care in transmitting our letters from the society, and your congratulations thereupon.

The Secretary acquaints me that the address of our clergy which I had the care of transmitting, was presented to his Majesty by his Grace the Lord Arch Bishop of Canterbury, and was very graciously received. He tells me also the society have appointed Mr. Lamson to Fairfield, and at the same time granted my request in appointing Mr. Chandler Catechist at North Castle & Bedford with a salary of £10 pr. annum; whether Mr. Chandler will accept of that with the care of a school so as to be able to attend the service expected from him, I am uncertain.; because he has declined it since he gave me leave to write for it and thinks his prospects at Westchester are better. I have not yet received my Books from Boston, as soon as they come to hand will send you a dozen, and am well pleased that the performance has your approbation, and Bro. Seabury's, as it had Dr. Johnson's, before it went to the Press, who added the appendix. As you have not yet advised upon the affair of the Petition, I conclude it has not been offered, and am at a loss what retards it thus long, unless there has been some proposals to amend the same.

My service to Mrs. Barclay and all Friends concludes this from
Rev. Sir,
Your Bro. & humble Servant,
J. W.

Rev. Mr. Barclay.

The Rev. Henry Barclay, D. D., to whom the above was addressed, was in early life a missionary to Albany and the Mohawk Indians. On the 17th of Oct. 1746, he was called by the vestry of Trinity Church, New York city, to succeed the Rev. Mr. Vesey (who had deceased the 11th of July previous), as their rector; where he labored till his death, the 28th of Aug. 1764. He was the father of the late Thomas Barclay, consul general of Great Britain in the United States, residing at New York, where he was highly esteemed. Mr. Anthony Barclay, for many years British consul at New York, was a grandson of the Rev. Dr. Barclay.

Rev. James, son of Izrahiah, son of Thomas.

Mr. Wetmore, under date of March 26, 1748, details to the secretary the state of religion in his parish; the troubles that he experienced from enemies in their endeavors to promote divisions among his people, and in the lukewarmness of professors in his church, &c.

To the Secretary :

RYE, Sept. 29, 1748.

Rev. Sir:

In compliance with the commands of the Honourable Society, to which I would always pay dutiful and strict obedience, I give you this trouble, with my Notitia Parochialis enclosed, and acquaint you that I have drawn upon the treasurer a sett of bills, bearing date this day, for £25 sterling, payable at thirty days sight in favour of Mr. Samuel Farmer, merchant. Since Mr. Lamson has removed from this Parish, and Mr. Chandler declined accepting the catechetical mission at North Castle and Bedford, I do the duty at these places as formerly; and although I find large congregations when I preach among them, yet I don't find that forwardness I could wish, to exert themselves in building churches and providing for the support of a minister or catechist; and it is a trouble to me that the same negligent temper prevails in other parts of my Parish.

Our church, the only one in the Parish, is much out of repair, which, after several year's endeavoring to bring my people to a scheme to make descent and ornamental, I am yet unable to effect, obstructed by the difficult humours of some professing themselves of the Church, chiefs of the Parish for estates, from whom I have had my greatest troubles since I have had the care of this Parish. To whom also, I esteem it owing that the dissenters are now endeavoring to get into their possession the small glebe belonging to our church, which is scarcely worth the charge of a law suit; yet I have commenced a suit to defend it, which I believe, the wealthiest of my parishoners will not assist me with a farthing to support.

I have enlarged and repaired the parsonage house some years ago, at my own charge, solely, and it is now grown so old and decayed, that it is scarce worth repairing. As I find it agreeable to the sentiments of the Honourable Society, that the people to whom they send missionaries, should provide a house and glebe for their minister, I believe a line or two from you on the subject, directed to the church wardens, would be of more effect than many words of mine, which I therefore request the favour of; and as I have not been troublesome by begging books from the Society for many years, and Prayer Books and Catechisms are grown very scarce in my Parish, and poor people frequently applying to me to be supplied, a small present of that kind would be thankfully received by me, and the

poor people that are destitute. I only add further, my humble
duty to the Venerable Board, and hearty prayers to Almighty God
to bless all their pious and charitable designs, and am, with much
submission,

Rev. Sir,

Your most obedient,

and most humble servant,

JAMES WETMORE.

N. Y. Mss. from Arch. at Fulham, II, 202, *Dr. Hawks*.

Agreeable to Mr. Wetmore's suggestion, the Society
forwarded to the wardens and vestry the following letter, which was laid before them at a meeting held Jan.
16, 1749.

LONDON, Charter House, June 27, 1749.

Gentlemen:

It is with much concern that the Society for the Propagation of
the Gospel in Foreign Parts are informed, that your *church* and *parsonage house* are very much out of repair, and that even the possession of the glebe is disputed against your very worth pastor, Mr.
Wetmore, whose great pains and abilities in the cause of God's
Church, cannot but reccommend him to every worthy member of
it ; therefore, the society hope and expect, that upon due consideration, you will give orders for the full repair of the church and the
parsonage house, and defend Mr. Wetmore in the maintainance of
all his just rights, as you desire his longer continuance among you.

I am, Gentlemen, Your

Very humble servant,

PHILIP BEARCROFT, Secretary.

To the Church Wardens and Vestry of the Church of Rye, New
York.　　　　　　　　　　　　　　　*Rye Parish Records.*

It appears that the letter from the Society had the
desired effect. In a report from Mr. Wetmore to the
secretary, written in 1751, in speaking of the church
edifice, he says : " It had been lately improved, and is
made neat and beautiful, and not only things but persons are amended ; several who were formerly very
negligent in their attendance on the church, and very
remiss in religion, being reformed in those particulars."

He writes the secretary, April 2, 1752, that "the
party disputes which have run high among us for

27

several years, to my great grief, obstruct the success which I might otherwise hope for, in my endeavors to promote a becoming zeal for piety and reformation of manners among the looser sort of my parishioners, which are too numerous.

I am glad to hear of more visible success among my bretheren, especially in Stamford parish, which I am told flourishes happily, and increases by the diligent endeavour of good brother Dibblee, who, nevertheless, finds himself hard put to it, to support a family with so small a salary as he has, and I am afraid the zeal of some young men in New England, to undertake the ministry with such slender supports, and in expectation of more assistance from the poor people, than they will find, may in the end, prove of bad consequence in bringing contempt upon our order."—*Arch. of Fulham*, II, 242, *Dr. Hawks.*

In his report to the secretary for 1753, he informs the Society of the death of Mr. Purdy, the church's school teacher. "His corpse was attended to the church, on Ash-Wednesday, by a great concourse of people of all persuasions, to whom Mr. Wetmore preached a sermon adapted to that day, and to the melancholly occasion."

In a letter of April, 1759, Mr. Wetmore acquaints the Society, that a very worthy person, a native of England (St. George Talbot, Esq.), but now being in New York, had put into his hands £600, currency of which he reserves to himself the interest during life, and hath left by his will, £400 more to be added after his death to purchase a covenient glebe, and other liberal legacies."—*Prop. Soc. Rep. Bolton, Hist. of Westchester.*

The date of Mr. Wetmore's marriage, and whom he married, we have not been able to discover, further than that he was a man of family during his residence in the city of New York, and that his wife's Christian name was Anna, and had issue by her, two sons and four daughters; their relative ages, we conjecture to be as he names them in his will, though this is a supposition only.

In 1731, he together with his brothers Judge Seth, Jeremiah and Josiah, deeded their right in their grandfather Stow's land in Westfield Society; and in 1733, he deeded to his brother Jeremiah, a lot of 196 acres on the east side of the Connecticut river (Chatham), which land he had also inherited jointly with his brothers from his grandfather, Rev. Samuel Stow.

He finished his pilgrimage upon earth, Thursday, May 15, 1760.

The last scene of his life was such as afforded the most pleasing prospect of the real Christian's hope. His views were clear, his love was strong, and his joy unspeakable and full of glory.

His remains lie interred in the old parish burial ground, on the northwest side of Blind brook. A plain monumental stone indicates the place, and bears the following inscription, written by his long-tried friend, and fellow-laborer in his Master's vineyard, the Rev. Samuel Johnson, D. D.

Sacred
to the Memory of
THE REV. MR. JAMES WETMORE,
the late
Worthy, learned and faithful Minister of the
Parish of Rye, for above 30 years,
Who having strenuously defended the Church with his pen
and adorned it by his Life and Doctrine,
at length being seized of the small-pox,
departed this life May 15, 1760,
Ætatis 65.
Cujus Memoriæ sit in
Benedictione sempiterna.

The *New York Mercury* of May 29, 1760, in noticing his death, says:

Rev. James, son of Izrahiah, son of Thomas.

This worthy clergyman was blessed with an extensive understanding, which he improved by a due application to the most important studies.   He was well versed in various parts of useful learning, and had a thorough knowledge of our happy constitution, both in church and state, of which he was a staunch friend and able advocate.

In the important duties of his ministerial office, he was zealous, constant and unwearied ; and though he observed with grief the great decay of true Christianity and genuine piety (which he often heartily lamented to his friends), yet he persevered warmly in the defence of the former, and in recommending the latter, both by precept and example.

His church has lost a faithful pastor, his wife and family an affectionate husband and a tender parent, and the public a worthy and useful member.   But

> "Blessed are the dead which die in the Lord."

The Rev. Dr. Sprague in his *Annals of the American Pulpit,* in a brief biographical notice of Rev. James Wetmore, says : " He is said to have been a man of highly respectable talents, and to have devoted himself with great zeal to the interests of the church with which he was fully connected."

Mr. Bolton in his *History of the Protestant Episcopal Church of Westchester co., N. Y.,* quotes from the Rev. Andrew Fowler's *Ms. Biog. of the Clergy,* II, 212 and 548.

I have (says Mr. Fowler) often heard some aged persons who recollected Mr. Wetmore, speak of him with great veneration, as a good man and sound divine.   He was not the eloquent orator, nor the fascinating speaker, but he was the rational and evangelical divine, and few clergymen in his day wrote better.   It is reported of him, that being in the city of New York on a visit, he was invited by the rector of Trinity Church, Dr. Ogilvie, to preach for him ; but no sooner was the sermon over, than a particular friend of the rector asked him privately, " how he could invite that old f—] into his pulpit," " why," said the rector, "did you not like him ?"   His friend replied : *"No ! never ..eard a more stupid sermon in my life."*   When the rector

came home, he desired Mr. Wetmore, to lend him the sermon he had preached that day, and promised to return it,
when he should see him again. Mr. Wetmore readily
complied with his request, and loaned him the discourse,
and not long after, the rector preached it, instead of his
own. His friend was pleased with the sermon, and told
him after church, that he had outshone himself, and that
his discourse was the best he had ever heard in his life.
The rector replied that he felt highly gratified to think
that he was well pleased with the sermon, but added, it
was none of his own; "it was the very one the old f—l, as
you called him at the time, delivered in my pulpit?" "Well,
said the rector's friend, "if he preaches such sermon as
that, I will never object to his preaching in your pulpit
again." So apt are people to condemn a clergyman for
what they themselves do not understand.

When a little work entitled: *The Englishman Directed
in the Choice of his Religion,* was republished in the city of
New York, he wrote a preface or introduction to it, which
was considered to be very good. He also wrote and printed several dialogues in answer to the Quakers, and in
defence of the doctrine and discipline of the Church of
England. One of his pamphlets I have in my possession,
which appears well calculated for the purpose it was intended; and I see not how the Quakers could answer it in
a rational and spiritual manner. I believe the Christian
church could never boast of better men, take them as a body,
than the Society's missionaries to this country. They
chose their profession from a pure love to religion and the
cause to Christ, not from the love of money or praise of
men. They sought for no honour but that which cometh
alone from God, and approving conscience. Like their
beloved Master, they were despised and rejected, and their
religion was every where spoken against and vilefied. As
the Apostles were a spectacle to men and angels, so were
these men, and if they suffered not as martyrs, it was because the civil authority protected them.

Among other writings published by Mr. Wetmore,
there were, *A Vindication of the Professors of the Church
of England in Connecticut, against Invectives contained
in a Sermon by Noah Hobart of Stamford,* Dec. 31,

Rev. James, son of Izrahiah, son of Thomas.

1746; *A Letter to a Friend,* 1747; *A Réjoinder to Ho-bart's Serious Address,* 1748; *Appendix &c., to Rev. J. Beach's Calm and Dispassionate Vindication of the Professors of the Church of England,* 1749, &c.

Mr. Wetmore's will (the subjoined being a copy), is recorded in the surrogate's office in the city of New York, book XXIV, pp. 125, 126.

THE LAST WILL AND TESTAMENT OF JAMES WETMORE, CLERK.

IN THE NAME OF GOD, AMEN. The sixth day of August, in the year of our Lord, 1759, I, James Wetmore, of Rye, in the County of Westchester, and Province of New York, Clerk, being of sound mind and memory; but calling to mind the uncertainty of life, and that 'tis appointed for man once to die, after that, the judgment; do make and ordain, and appoint this, my last will and testament, in manner following: That is to say: First of all, I bequeath my soul to God who gave it, hoping in his mercy, for everlasting life, through the alone merits of my blessed Redeemer; and my body to the earth, to be buried in a christianlike manner, at the discretion of my executors hereinafter named, in an assured expectation of its being raised up again at the last day by the Almighty power of my Redeemer, to a state of greater glory and perfection, to remain forever; and as to the small portion of my worldly estate, with which it has pleased God to bless me, I will bequeath, and dispose of the same in manner following, viz:

Imprimis: I give, and bequeath unto my loving wife, Anna Wetmore, instead of a legal dowry, the use and emolument of all that land, orchard, meadow, and pasture, which Samuel Lane sold to Raphael Jacobs, lying in the town of Rye, with the house thereon, and all appurtenances thereto belonging, and also that pasture lot adjoining thereto, which formerly belonged to Peter Brown, on the east side of the Road leading to Harrison's purchase, to the sole use of my said wife and her assigns, during the term of her natural life; also one equal half of linnen, bedding and other household furniture, and the priviledge of what firewood she shall have occasion for her own use; also three cows and one horse.

Item, I give, devise, and bequeath to my loving son, James Wetmore, the priviledge of the shop, and dam upon Blind brook, for accommodating a fulling mill, with the utensils belonging to such mill; also the wood and pasture lott above the first stone fence, to extend from Abraham Brundige's land, south-westerly, half the width of my land bought of Joseph Haight, and from the stone fence that runs across my land near Brundige's house, north-westerly to the next fence that now runs across my land, together with a privilege to cart and drive cattle thereto, from the bridge to the fulling mill, to him, his heirs, and assigns forever.

Item, I give and bequeath to my loving son, Timothy, that house, barn, and improvements, bought of Mr. Jacobs, lying in the town of Rye, with all the land lying on the west side of the road which formerly belonged to Peter Brown, and also that part of my land bought of Joseph Haight, on the west side of Blind brook, running from said brook, north-westerly to the stone fence that now runs cross my land, near Abraham Brundige's, and to extend northerly to the land I have sequestered for a glebe, which, at the upper end, by the stone fence, is to be half the width of my lot, to him, my said son Timothy, his heirs and assigns forever.

Item, I give and bequeath unto my loving daughter, Alethea, wife of the Rev. Joseph Lamson, £30, to be paid by my executors in one year after my decease.

Item, I give, devise, and bequeath to my loving daughter Anne, wife of Gilbert Brundige, so much of my land at Bullock's meadow, as will be included by a line bearing the same course with the line between said Gilbert Brundige's land and that part of my land he adjoins to, to begin at the south-east corner of said Brundige's lot, bought of Henry Strang, to run cross meadow and woods, the course before specified, unto the land of William Haight, comprising that part of my farm that is north of said line, unto my said daughter Anne Brundige, her heirs and assigns forever ; also £10, to be paid by my executors unto my said daughter, within a year after my decease.

Item, I give and bequeath unto my loving daughter, Charity, wife of Josiah Purdy, £30, to be paid by my executors in one year after my decease.

Item, I will devise and bequeath to my loving daughter, Esther Wetmore, the reversion of all that house, orchard, meadow, and pasture, which was formerly Samuel Lane's, and that pasture lot which did belong to Peter Brown, eastward of the road that leads to Harrison's purchase, with all the priviledges and appurtenances thereto belonging, after the decease of my wife, to whom I have given the use for life, the reversion and remainder to my said daughter, Esther Wetmore, to her heirs and assigns forever. I also give and bequeath unto my loving daughter, Esther, one half part of all my linnen bedding, and other household furniture, the same to be equally divided between my wife and said Daughter. All the residue and remainder of my estate, real and personal, after payment of above legacies, and all my just debts, I will devise and bequeath to my two loving sons, James Wetmore and Timothy Wetmore, to each in severalty, to be equally divided between them, after the sale of so much as shall be necessary for payment of my just debts and legacies, unto them, their heirs and assigns forever; and I do hereby nominate and appoint my said loving sons, James and Timothy, to be executors of this my last will and testament, disannulling all former wills by me made, or executors by me nominated, and do confirm this, contained in these two pages, alone, to be my last will and testament.

In witness whereof, I have hereunto affixed my name and seal.

JAMES WETMORE. [Seal.]

Signed, sealed, pronounced and declared to be his last will and testament, in disposing mind and memory.

In presence of
Hachaliah Brown,
Roger Park, Jr.,
Benjamin Brown, Jr.

Mr. Wetmore's widow survived him till February 28th, 1771.

The Rev. Ebenezer Punderson, a graduate of Yale College, 1726, succeeded Mr. Wetmore at Rye, July 1st, 1763. In the interim, the parish was without stated preaching of the Gospel.

FOURTH GENERATION.

Children of Rev. JAMES WETMORE,

Son of Izrahiah, Son of Thomas Whitmore.

JAMES, b. in Rye, N. Y., Dec, 19, 1727;[13] m. Elizabeth Abrahams, of Westchester co., N. Y., b. March 15, 1730, had Abraham, John, Izrahiah, James, David, Josiah, Caleb, Elizabeth, Susannah, Charity, Alithea and Esther.

---

[13] We have not been able after diligent search and inquiry, to obtain the dates of the births of the children of the Rev. James, save in the instance of his son James, above; hence we record them in the order that they are named in their father's will. Mr. Bolton in his *Hist. of the Ch. in Westchester*, speaks of James, second son of the Rev. James. * *. * * * * We think Mr. B. in error here, for if it be. true—as we are credibly informed—that Timothy died in 1820, aged 83 or 85 years, he would be the junior of his brother James, some eight years, and we conjecture that he was also the junior of his sisters Alethea and Anne.

He was for many years an influential citizen of Westchester co., N. Y. He remained loyal to the crown during the Revolution. To what extent he engaged in the controversy of those times, further than what we shall notice under the head of Timothy, we are unadvised. He removed with his family to New Brunswick in 1783, and settled at the mouth of St. John river, where he employed himself in teaching a school. He remained there but a short time, when he removed to Hammond river, distant about 20 miles from St. John, where he resided till his death, aged about 70 years. He was buried in the parish of Hampton, Kings co., N. B. His wife survived him seven years, and died at Hampton, and was interred by the side of the remains of her husband.

Mrs. Wetmore was the daughter of a Mr. Abrahams, a wealthy West India merchant. On a visit to New York he became enamored of a daughter of a Mrs. Bush, who was a native of Holland, whom he married, which led him to settle in that city, where he established himself in the East India trade, and added still further to his fortune. His wife was remarkable for her courage and muscular strength. It is said that one night she awoke from sleep and saw a black man, or one whose face was blackened, in her apartment, opening drawers, etc., she sprang up, seized him, and forced him out of the room; afterwards, a large knife was found on the floor near her bed.

A cartman on one occasion, in passing her door with a cask of molasses, had the misfortune to have the head of the cask started. The man stood with terror at witnessing the molasses fast discharging itself upon the ground. Mrs. Abrahams seeing the drayman's distress, rushed out of the house, seized the hogshead and set it upon its end.

Mr. Abrahams losing a number of his East India vessels with their valuable cargoes, without insurance, was obliged to suspend business. He removed from the city and settled in Rye; while residing there he experienced much pecuniary embarrassment, his necessities were such, that he had to dispose of his silver, and other valuable household articles, in order to provide his family with the necessaries of life. After his death, his widow removed to the vicinity of Philadelphia, where she was compelled to support herself from the products of a market garden.

TIMOTHY, b. ——; m. 1st, by the Rev. Joseph Lamson, Oct. 21, 1756, Jane Haviland of Rye, had James, Jane, Anna, Timothy, Fletcher, Thomas, Luther, Theodore, Robert Greffieth; m. 2d, ——, Rachel, wid. of Benjamin Ogden of N. Y.; no issue.

He was a highly respectable and influential citizen of the county of Westchester, N. Y.; was among the first graduates of Kings, now Columbia College, in the city of New York, 1758. He first studied for the Episcopal ministry, but circumstances prevented his going to England for ordination (tradition says, that his mother would not give her consent to his crossing the ocean). Subsequently he turned his attention to the study of law, and became a practitioner of considerable importance.

In 1753–4, he was appointed by the Society for Propagating the Gospel in Foreign Parts, successor to Mr. Samuel Purdy (dec'd.), as teacher for the parish of Rye; the appointment was made on the recommendation of the people of that town. Though he was without holy orders he nevertheless labored for the good of souls and the building up of Christ's kingdom upon earth. When a young man, his father was wont to send him out to destitute places to read the services of the church, and such sermons as were furnished him, which the Society in their records, note, that he continued his labors with pleasure, and that his efforts were received with good satisfaction, and promising hopes of promoting Christian knowledge.

In a letter to the secretary, dated Rye, May 6, 1761, he gives the following report of the parish for the year that followed the death of his father:

Rev. Sir:

It is now, I think, six or eight months since we have been favored with a sermon, or had either of the Sacraments administered in this Parish by a minister of the Church. The Parish being in this destitute condition, I have presumed, at the request of the people, to read service every Lord's day, and upon other convenient occasions, which appears to have a tendency, by the blessing of God, to keep up a spirit of religion, and as I have a singleness to the Glory of God and the good and comfort of my fellow creatures, I hope it may tend to the furtherance of the glorious designs of the Venerable Society. The people are constant in their attendance, descent in their deportment, and the temper of many of the Presbyterian congregation is such (who have no minister), that I am much inclined to think, if a popular man is settled in this parish, they will not call another preacher, but many of them may be brought into the Church.

The Constitution is such, that the minister must be called by the vestry and inducted by the Governour. The Vestry are chosen by all sects in the Parish, which is thirty miles in length. Mr. Thomas who is one of the representatives in this county, and who, in Governour DeLancey's time, being favoured with all the administration of all offices in the country, civil and military, by the help of which he has procured himself a large interest in the county, especially in the distant and new settlements, which abound with a set of people governed by vinality than by anything else. This gentleman, though one of the Society missionaries' sons, is so negligent and indifferent towards religion (in imitation of some of our great men), that it has been a steady method with him for years, not to attend publick worship, perhaps, more than once or twice in a year, whose example has been mischievous. This man is not only one of our Vestry (though very little esteemed by the true friends of the Church), but has procured that majority of the Vestry are not of the Church, and not one of them a communicant in the Church; accordingly, the church are not at all consulted with regard to a successor. It is, therefore, a mere chance will be pleased in this place, which will really be, if possible, a more melancholy in this Parish than others, from the peculiar circumstance of it. As our Governour depends, from year to year, upon the Assembly for his living, &c., and we have not so fully hopes of relief there, I have thought fit to give the Venerable Society a hint of these things, which they may possibly improve to the good of the Church.

Reverend Sir, &c.,
TIMOTHY WETMORE.

N. Y. Mss. from Arch. at Fulham, II, 286, 287, *Rev. Dr. Hawks.*

In answer to this letter (says Bolton in his *Hist. of the Ch. in Westchester*), the venerable Society expressed their readiness to send a missionary to Rye, if necessary, and did so by appointing the Rev. Mr. Palmer, in 1762. The vestry it seems not being aware of Mr. Palmer's appointment, called the Rev. Mr. Punderson of New Haven, as before stated.

Mr. Wetmore subsequently became a vestryman, and to him in connection with Peter Jay, Elisha Budd, Christopher Isinghart, Caleb, Joshua and Joseph Purdy, John Guion, Gilbert Willet, John Cahart, Thomas Sawyer, Gilbert Brundige, John Thomas, William Sutton, Anthony Miller, and John Adee, was the charter to the Rye Church granted by George the Third, Dec. 19, 1764.

Mr. Punderson having died the 22d of September previous, the parish was again without a rector, when Mr. Wetmore, it will be perceived by the following extract of a letter from him to the secretary, officiated.

RYE, June 1st, 1765.

Rev. Sir:

The Venerable Society have, doubtless, long since heard that our parish is again reduced to the melancholy state of being without a minister, exposed to the infection of schism, irreligion, profaneness and deism, or rather atheism. Mr. Smith, something of a popular dissenting preacher, is again introduced into Rye and the White Plains. I am sorry to say it, I think the appearances of religion, are not so favourable as they have heretofore been, and though the necessity is so great, the neighboring clergy are so attached to their proper missions, that we have not had, I think the sacrament but once, and but two sermons preached in our parish since the death of Mr. Punderson. This being the melancholy state of the church, and many manifestly verging towards an indifferency about public worship; to prevent which, and the dreadful consequences thereof, and also to prevent as far as lay in my power, as many as possible from being habituated to the dissenting meeting, taverns, and slothfulness on the Lord's day, vices to which many of our people are too much addicted, and which Mr. Punderson's successor might be obliged to struggle hard with, before he would be able to master, as also that we may have opportunity of publicly adoring our Great Creator, Redeemer, and Sanctifyer; I have presumed again to enter the sacred desk and read prayers at Rye and the White Plains, and elsewhere, occasionally, and such sermons, as I think, as are best calculated for these purposes, and to propagate the great doctrines and practice of Christians; and I have the satisfaction to think my weak endeavours are not without a blessing; many profess to be pleased, and established and comforted thereby in the blessed hopes of the Gospel.

The Reverend Ephraim, son of Rev. Ephraim Avery of Pomfret, Windham county, Conn., was appointed to the Mission at Rye, in the summer of the same year, and Mr. Wetmore was succeeded by a Mr. John Rand, as the Society's schoolmaster and catechist for the parish in 1769, though it would appear, from the Propagation Society's records, that he was a teacher to "ten or twelve; four children upon the bounty of the Society," as late as 1773 and 1774.

Mr. Wetmore being warmly attached to the English Church, from which his father had received much sympathy and material aid in his day of trial, as well as being of a loyal spirit, he naturally remained faithful to the mother country during the troublesome times of the Revolution.

Mr. L. Sabine, in his biographical sketches of American loyalists, in noticing Timothy Wetmore, says:

He was a person of consideration and influence. In September, 1774, the freeholders and inhabitants met at Rye, and declared that they were much concerned with the unhappy situation of public affairs, and that they considered it to be their duty to state, that they had no part in any resolution entered into, or measure taken, with regard to the disputes at present subsisting with the mother country; they also express their dislike to many hot and furious proceedings in consequence of said disputes, which in their opinion were more likely to ruin this happy country than to remove grievances, if they are. * * * * *

The following is the declaration alluded to above which we take from the *Am. Archives*, 4th Ser., I, 802:

RYE, New York, Sept. 24, 1774.

We the subscribers, Freeholders and Inhabitants of the town of Rye, in the county of Westchester, being much concerned in the unhappy situation of publick affairs, think it our duty to our king and country, to declare that we have not been concerned in any resolutions entered into or measures taken, with regard to the disputes at present subsisting with the mother country; we also testify our dislike to many hot and furious proceedings in consequence of said disputes, which we think more likely to ruin this once happy country, than remove grievances, if any there are.

We also declare our great desire and full resolution to live and die peaceable subjects of our gracious sovereign King George the Third, and his laws.

Signed by eighty-three of the influential citizens of Westchester, among them, the subject of this notice; also by his brother James, and his nephew Abraham Wetmore.

This appears not to have satisfied either of the parties. Subsequently Mr. Wetmore published the following explanation:

The above (quoting it) like many others being liable to misconstruction, and having been understood, by many to import a recognition of a right in the Parliament of Great Britain to bind America in all cases whatsoe'er, and to signify that the colonies labor under no grievances. I think it my duty to explain my sentiments upon the subject, and thereby prevent future mistakes.

It is my opinion that the Parliament have no right to tax America, though they have a right to regulate the trade of the Empire. I am further of opinion, that several acts of Parliament are grievances, and the execution of them ought to be opposed in such manner, as may be consistent with the duty of a subject to our Soverign; Though I can not help expressing my disapprobation of many violent proceedings in some of the colonies.

TIMOTHY WETMORE.

Nov. 3, 1774.

4th series, Am. Archives, I, 803.

This was in New York, and its vicinity, much like the more conservative Whigs view of the controversy.

Mr. Wetmore's loyal sentiments caused him to lose his property. At the close of the war (1783), he removed to Nova Scotia, where he practiced his profession for many years, and held numerous offices of public trust.

He educated his sons in the three professions in most of which, if not all, he was thoroughly educated himself.[14]

His wife, Jane Haviland, departed this life, in New York city, August 5th, 1777, at 3 o'clock in the morning; her remains, together with those of her daughter Anna, are buried beside each other a few rods north from Trinity Church, a few feet northward of a small stone of Mr. Shreve's children. "It pleased God, to enable them both to speak very distincly to the Saviour, at and near their departure, and to be very resigned to God's will."—*Old Family Bible Record.*

Mr. Wetmore returned from New Brunswick about 1800, and took up his residence in the city of New York, where he resided until his death, March, 1820, aged 83 or 85 years. His widow removed to New Brunswick, and died in Charlotte county, about 1826 or 1828. She had, by her marriage with her first husband, Benjamin, Andrew and Albert Odgen, who were at one time prominent and wealthy merchants in the city of New York.

ALETHEA, b. —; m. 1747, Rev. Joseph Lamson, son of William Lamson of Stratford, Ct.; b. about 1719; had I *A Dau.,* b. —; d. 1753: II *Anne,* b. —; m. Samuel Belden of Norwalk, Ct.; issue, Thomas, Samuel, William, Hezekiah: III *Esther,* b. —; m. Capt. Stephen Hoyt of the Prince of Wales regt.; issue Joseph Lamson, Stephen, Thomas; IV *Elizabeth:* V *William,* who was a physician to an American regt.: VI *John,* b. —; m. —— Hatfield; issue Elizabeth, Mary, William, Anne: VII —.

[14] We are informed that Mr. Wetmore studied medicine immediately after graduating.

He graduated at Yale College in 1741; declared for Episcopacy; studied for the ministry, and went out to England for holy orders in June, 1744; received his certificate of ordination from the bishop of London in 1745, and became assistant minister to his father-in-law.

The circumstances attending his voyage to England, and his appointment by the society, assistant to Mr, Wetmore, we quote from printed abstracts of the *Prop. Soc. Rep.*, which we find in *Bolton's Hist. of the Church in Westchester*.

Extract of letter from Rev. James Wetmore, to the secretary of the society, dated,

RYE, Dec. 13th, 1744.

Rev. Sir:

Mr. Lamson took a passage from Boston sometime in June last, and there being no account of his arrival in England, it is feared he is taken by a Spanish privateer and carried into some port in Spain. If that should prove to be his hard fortune, I hope, by the favour of divine Providence, he may find some way for redemption and get to London.

The Society's Abstracts for 1745, say:

Mr. Wetmore, the Society's missionary to the parish of Rye, in this Province, acquaints the Society that he is so fully employed in performing the duties of his holy function at Rye, Scarsdale and the White Plains, and he cannot attend the distant parts of his parish so often as he could wish, and therefore he humbly prays the Society, instead of appointing a successor to the late Mr. Dwight, the Societie's school master at the White Plains, they would grant him an assistant minister to officiate under him; and the good people of Bedford and North Castle, in which are four hundred families, that stand much in want, and are desirous of instruction in the true and sound principles of Christianity, and to those of Ridgefield adjoining to them, where a church is already built; and the inhabitants of those towns earnestly petitioning the

Society to the same purpose, and promising £30 per
annum towards the expense, the Society hath granted this
request and appointed the Rev. Mr. Lamson, lately arrived
from New England, with very ample testimonials from
the clergy of that province, to be upon his admission unto
holy orders, assistant minister to Mr. Wetmore, in officiating to the inhabitants of Bedford, North Castle and Ridgefield, with a salary of £20 per annum, besides a gratuity
of the same out of compassion to Mr. Lamson's sufferings
and necessities, who was taken a prisoner, stripped, and
carried into France, on his voyage towards England, and
afterwards in his way from Port Louis, in France, to London, was detained four months by a fever at Salisbury,
where he lost by that distemper, his companion and fellow
sufferer, Mr. Minor, another worthy candidate for the
Society's favour, and the Society hath lately had the satisfaction to be informed that Mr. Lamson arrived safe some
time since at New York, and went from thence to enter
upon the duties of his mission.

Some idea (says the Rev. M. H. Henderson) of the
great disadvantages under which the church labored during
our colonial existence, may be formed from the fact, that
beside the expense of the voyage (£100), and expense
which candidates for holy orders could ill afford to bear,
nearly one-fifth of all that went to England for ordination,
died, either from small pox, or the dangers of the deep.
The number, who had gone to England for ordination
from the northern colonies up to 1767, was 52; of these
42 only returned safely.—*Centennial Discourse.*[15]

The Society's Abstracts for 1746, say:

The society have had the satisfaction to be informed by
the Rev. Mr. Lamson, that he returned safe and in good
health; and the good people of Ridgefield, Bedford and
North Castle, the places of his mission, received him
gladly, and even as one risen from the dead, among whom
report had for some time placed him, and in his letter,
May 12, 1746, he writes:—"That he officiates by turns at
these three places to full congregations, and had baptized
eleven children, and three adults, well principled in Chris-

[15] Bolton's Hist. of Westchester co., II, 66.

tianity; and Mr. Wetmore, the Society's missionary in the populous parish of Rye, to whose assistance Mr. Lamson is appointed, returns his own hearty thanks, together with those of his parishioners, in his letter of April 3d, 1746, professing his hope that Mr. Lamson will do much good amongst them by his preaching and exemplary life, for which they very much respect him, and that as there are great numbers of people in the wilderness country northward of Bedford and Westchester, who have very little knowledge or sense of religion, Mr. Lamson's labors will be employed to good purpose among them.

Mr. Lamson writes to the secretary under date of

NORTH CASTLE, in the Parish of Rye, Feb. 10, 1746–7.
Rev. Sir:

I have endeavored since my arrival, to do what service I can among a great number of poor people, scattered about in the woods, who have little ability, and most of them little inclination to mind me. I compassionate their circumstances, and the more because so many of them have very little sense of the importance of religion and virtue.

The Rev. Mr. Wetmore has been treating with a very worthy young Gentleman, Mr. Thomas Bradbury Chandler, who is willing to perform the service of a lay catechist among these people, if the Honourable Society, upon my removal, will be please to bestow upon him the £10 sterling salary, that was formerly allowed to Mr. Kint Dwight, deceased. And I am of opinion that such a provision is as much as these people can expect at present, and I believe it may in a good measure supply the place of a minister in orders, considering that Mr. Wetmore, with Mr. Chandler's assistance, to read in the church at Rye, in his absence, may more frequently visit North Castle and Bedford, and administer the sacraments among them; and some of the people have expressed satisfaction in the hopes of having so ingenious a man as Mr. Chandler to labor among them, in such a method after my leaving them. They find as little fault as I could expect, at the talk of my removal, knowing that my present income is too small for a support.—*Conn. Mss. from Archives at Fulham, 282–3, Dr. Hawks.*

Soon after the date of this letter, Mr. Lamson took charge of the parish of Fairfield, Ct., where he continued to the time of his death, which took place in 1773. The register of the town of Fairfield contains a record of his marriage in 1747, to Alethia, daughter of the Rev. James Wetmore of Rye and of the birth of their six children, five daughters and one son. And the graves of the eldest daughter, who died in 1753, and Mrs. Lamson, who died 1766, are in the old burial place, near the Court House. But it appears from the proceedings of the society, that Mr. Lamson left a widow.—*Hist. of the Church in Westchester*, p. 534.

Mr. Lamson received his degree of master of arts at Kings College, New York, 1773; his family surname (says *Surtee's Hist. of the Co. of Durham*,) was originally written Lambton. Robert De Lambton, feudal Lord of Lambton Castle, in the county of Durham, died in 1350. "The Lampsons or Lamsons, were among the early settlers of New England. The will of William Lampson of Stratford, Ct., bears date Sept. 1754, proved Feb. 11, 1755. Wife Elizabeth, sons Joseph, Nathaniel and John; daughters, Elizabeth, Sarah and Mary (*Prob. Rec. Fairfield co.*, 1754-7)."—*Hist. of the Church in Westchester*, p. 532.

ANNE, b. —; m. Gilbert Brundige of Westchester co., N. Y.; had Timothy, Gilbert, who m. ——; had Mrs. Buckley of Rye.

Mr. Brundige was a man of influence in the county of Westchester, he (as before stated) receiving with others, the charter of the church at Rye from George the Third, in 1764.

CHARITY, b. in Rye; m. Josiah, son of Samuel[16] and Penelope (Strang) Purdy; had I *Seth*, proprietor of the homestead at Rye, who m. Pheobe Ketchum of L. I., and left Joshua, Seth, Josiah, Keziah, Alathea, Elizabeth, Charity, Melinda and

[16] Son of the first Francis Purdy. His wife Penelope was a daughter of Daniel L'Estrange, nat. 1656 at Paris; will dated 1706, vol. VII, 288, and Charlotte Hubert. *Arms*, gu, two lions, passant, guardant, arg. Crest, a lion, passant, guardant or.—*Chart, by Bolton*, II, 285.

Phoebe; II *Alathea*, who m. 1st Joseph Purdy, 2d William Purdy; III *Esther*, m. Henry Purdy of King street; IV *Hannah* (Anna?), m. Josiah Merritt.

Robert Bolton, Jr., in his *History of Westchester co.*, noticing the family of Purdy, says: Northeast of the village (Rye), bordering Purchase street, is the property of the late Josiah Purdy, Esq., now occupied by his son Josiah Purdy. The Purdy family were among the early settlers of Fairfield, Connecticut. Francis Purdy,[17] the first of the family of whom we have any account, died in 1658, at Fairfield. His sons Francis, John,[18] and Samuel, subsequently removed to Rye, p. 48. The Purdy estate is situated upon the eastern shore of Rye neck, bordering the Blind brook (Mock quams). A short distance from the house is the burial place of the Purdy family, p. 91.

ESTHER, b. in Rye; m. 1st David Brown; m. 2d Jesse Hunt, Esq., s. p.

Mr. Jesse Hunt was the high sheriff of Westchester county in 1780. "The family (says Bolton) are presumed to spring from one of the younger sons of Thomas Hunt of Shrewsbury, county of Shropshire, England, son of Richard Hunt, bailiff of Shrewsbury in 1613. Thomas was high sheriff of Shropshire in 1656, and a colonel in the parliament service; he died A. D. 1669."

Mr. Sheriff Hunt was the proprietor of Hunter's island; he had been previously, or was subsequently married to a Miss Staples, and had Capt. Thomas, Lieut. Jesse, Samuel, and a daughter who married a Gracie (*Bolton's Appendix*, 523). He was son of Thomas, son of Thomas Hunt, who removed to Westchester, and purchased the Grove farm, which was patented to him by Gov. Nicolls, 4th Dec., 1667 (*Bolton*, 523). Bolton in noticing the Hunt family says, p. 272:

[17] An inventory of the estate of Francis Purdy was taken, Oct. 14, 1686. *See Prob. Rec., Fairfield Co., Ct.*
[18] John Purdy was residing at Fairfield, 1658.

At the southeast extremity of the neck is situated Hunt's point. This property has been occupied by the Hunt family for nearly one hundred and sixty years, having passed into their hands by the marriage of Thomas Hunt with Elizabeth Jessup, daughter of Edward Jessup, son of the first patentees. In 1688, Thomas Hunt, of the Grove Farm, granted to his son Thomas Hunt, one hundred acres, lying on the south side of Gabriel Leggett's land, bounded eastwardly and southerly by Bronx river. It is now the property of Daniel Winship, who married Eliza, the widow of the late Richard Hunt, Esq. The old Grange, erected in 1688, occupies a beautiful situation near the termination of the point, overlooking the East river and Flushing bay.

This place was for many years the residence of Joseph R. Drake the poet, and it was here that he wrote his well known lines on the Bronx, on the neighboring banks of which he often wandered.

The burial place of the Hunt family, is located near the entrance of the point. The following inscriptions are copied from two of the monuments in this yard: In memory of Thomas Hunt, who departed this life July 4, 1808, in the 80th year of his age. He possessed the cardinal virtues in an eminent degree; he was temperate, brave and just.

> The solid rock shall sink beneath
> The iron hand of time,
> But virtue dwells with
> Immortality.[19]

[19] The other inscription alluded to, is one commemorative of Drake, who d. Sept. 21, 1825, ae. 25, with two lines taken from the poem written by Fitz Greene Halleck, on the death of his companion, Dr. Drake.
> "None knew thee but to love thee,
> None named thee but to praise."

FIFTH GENERATION.

· Children of JAMES.

ABRAHAM, b. in Rye, Nov. 29 (9?), 1747; m. Sarah Sniffers; had Josiah, William and Abraham.

He, on the breaking out of the Revolution, remained loyal to the crown. He signed the Manifesto, or Declaration, in company with his father and uncle. He removed to New Brunswick, at about the close of the war. He died in New York, Feb. 6, 1790. His widow subsequently married Sylvanus Whitney. She died in St. Johns, about 1804.

ELIZABETH, b. Rye, Aug. 30, 1750; m. David, son of David and Abigail Haight of Rye; had I *Abaigail*, b. Dec. 13, 1773; m. John Harris, about 1796; issue, 1' Elizabeth, m. Aug. 1837, Caleb Nelson, of Canada; had 4 chil.: 2, Thomas: 3, David, m. S. Smith (died): 4, Elijah, m. Lavinia P.—— of Canada; had Thomas, Elijah, John, ——: 5, James Wetmore, m. Jane Wilson, of Canada: 6, John Q., b. June 19, 1809: 7, Caleb, d. young: 8, Sarah, m. A. Morse, in Canada: 9, Moses Marshall. II *James*, b. Dec. 11, 1775. III *Susannah*, b. Dec. 1, 1777; m. Garret Williamson; issue, 1, Samuel, m. Levithea Doolittle, has 8 daus.: 2, Ezekiel Miller: 3, Abigail, m. Garnett Scott, had 4 chil.: 4, Ann Eliza: 5, William: 6, Susannah: 7, Markus: 8, Lavinia Jane: 9, Alithea. IV *Elizabeth*, b. Dec. 10, 1779; m. Elias B. Miller; issue, 1, Pheobe: 2, Esther, m. Perry Scott, of New York, has 2 sons: 3, David Williams: 4, Maria: 5, James: 6, Samuel. V *Esther*, b. Sept. 1781; m. Timothy Birdsall; had Jane Haight. VI *Alithea*, b. Aug. 23, 1783; unm. (1837). VII *Caleb*, b. Aug. 27, 1785; m. Elizabeth Whitlark; had 1, Elizabeth; m. 2d Maria Jackson; had 2, Nicholas: 3, Caleb Wetmore: 4, William (dead): 5, John; 6, Benjamin (dead): 7, Benjamin Ambler (dead): 8, William Marshall (dead): 9, Maria Banyan. VIII *Mary*, b. Dec. 27, 1787; m. Phineas Haight, May 25, 1808; had 1, Alvin Wetmore, b. Nov. 1809, who m. Patty Dibble, 1 dau.: 2, Millicent, b. May 18, 1811, m. Benjamin Green of Indiana, has 2 chil.: 3, James Lawrence, b. Aug. 27, 1814: 4, Thomas (dead):

5, David Edwin, b. May 26, 1819 : 6, Phineas, b. July 18, 1821 : 7, Mary Elizabeth, b. Oct. 7, 1824 : 8, Abraham Henry, b. April 23, 1827 : 9, Samuel Nicholson, b. — 18, 1829. IX *David* b. Feb. 1, 1790 ; m. Deborah Bailey March 8, 1815 ; had 1, Hester Jane, b. Dec. 18, 1815 : 2, David, b. Jan. 9, 1815 : 3, Thomas B., b. March 19, 1820 : 4, Infant, b. July 27, 1822 (died) : 5, Mary Lavinia, b. March 5, 1825 : 6, Anna Augusta, b. Oct. 21, 1828. Mrs. Deborah Bailey Haight d. March 3, 1835. X *Lavinia*, b. March 7, 1792 ; m. Moses Marshall, Aug. 21, 1815 ; had 1, Abby Jane, b. Dec. —: 2, William W., b. May, 1818 : 3, Moses H., b. July, 1819 : 4, Caroline Elizabeth, b. Sept., 1821 : 5, Charlotte Ann, b. Jan., 1824 : 6, James Henry, b. May, 1826 : 7, John Harris, b. Oct. 10, 1826 : 8, Emmery, b. March 20, 1831. XI *Jane*, b. March 20, 1795 : d. April 10, 1795.

Mr. and Mrs. Haight Sen, resided in New Bedford. She d. June 1843, in her 93d year.

SUSANNAH, b. in Rye, April 22, 1753 ; m. John Craft ; had I *Elizabeth*, m. Joseph Littlehall ; m. 2d James Brittian : II *John Thorn*, m. Pheobe Dunham : III *William*, m. Nancy McKinsey : IV *Polly*, m. Joseph Dunham : V *Sarah;* m. Griffeth Jenkins, s. p.

Mrs. Susannah Craft, died April 4, 1850, having attained 97 years, less 18 days.

JOHN, b. in Rye, July 7, 1755 ; m. 1st, about 1778, Anna Van Cott of Long Island ; had Elizabeth, James, Martha Van Cott, Caroline (Catherine ?), John, Ann, Jesse Lamereux, Daniel Van Cott, David, William, Edwin, Susannah, Joseph, Timothy, Hannah ; m. 2d Elizabeth Clark of Nova Scotia ; had Clark, Thomas and Sarah.

He removed to New Brunswick in 1783, where he was government land surveyor till an advanced age prevented his attending to the duties pertaining to the office. He was a magistrate of Kings county, N. B., for some years, received during the Revolution a lieutenant's commission in the British army ; was at the battle of White Plains, but was not engaged in the combat. On the King's troops removing to New Brunswick he was made a commandant of a company.

Capt. Wetmore was a strong Royalist, as well as an ardent Churchman, as will be seen by the following entry and declaration, made by himself on the fly leaf of his family Bible :

John Wetmore, born at Rye, state of New York, July 7, 1755. Baptized by the Rev. James Wetmore, Rector of Rye church. Landed at St. Johns, commanding a company of loyalists, with the rank of captain. Confirmed in Kingston Church by the Right Rev. Charles Inglish, D. D., Lord Bishop of Nova Scotia.

Declaration.

I, the above named John Wetmore, do hereby declare that I believe the United Church of England and Ireland, as by law established, to be a pure branch of Christ's Holy Catholic Church ; that for nearly seventy years I have lived in her communion, that in it I hope to die.

(Signed,)   JOHN WETMORE.

In the 89th year of age, in the year of our Lord, 1844.

He died at Yarmouth, N. S., May 4, 1848, aged 92 years and 10 month.

IZRAHIAH, b. in Rye, Oct. 15, 1757 ; m. March 12, 1782, Elizabeth Bush, b. March 20, 1761 ; had Nancy, Esther, Bush, Rebecca, Elizabeth, Anna, James Bush, Sarah Bush, Infant son, b. July 9, 1796, d. 16th of same month ; Gilbert Bush, Amelia, Izrahiah and Pheobe.

He resided at Rye. He was a loyalist and signed at White Plains, April 13, 1775, with three hundred other freeholders and inhabitants of the county of Westchester, the famous protest " against the assembling of all unlawful congresses and committees." (*Bolton Hist. of W.*, II, 351-2.) He died Feb. 7, 1838, and was buried in the old yard attached to Christ Church, not far from the grave of his grandfather, the Rev. James. His wife died in the fall of the year 1853, in her 93d year, and her remains rest besides those of her husband.

Descendants of Rev. James, son of Izrahiah, son of Thomas.

CHARITY, b. in Rye, Jan. 23, 1760; m. Daniel Lamereux, March 12, 1782; had I *Andrew Ogden*, who m. Sarah Wurt; res. in St. Johns, had a numerous family; his oldest son George, m. his cousin Susannah, dau. of Judge David Brown Wetmore; II *Daniel*, b. —; m. in N. Y.; III *Elizabeth*, b. —; m. in N. Y.; IV *Susannah*, b. —; m. in N. Y.; V *Thomas*, b. and m. in N. Y.; VI *James*, b. and m. in N. Y.; VII *David*, b. —; m. in N. Y.

She died ——.

JAMES, b. in Rye, May 23, 1762; m. ——; had Susan, Caleb, James, Hester, Elisha, Mary, John, Elizabeth.

He died March, 1850.

DAVID BROWN, Judge, b. in Rye, Nov. 4, 1764; m. Oct. 20, 1787, Ruth, dau. of Justus Sherwood at Hampton, N. B., b. at Cortlandt Manor, Westchester co., N. Y., Jan. 11, 1769; had Justus Sherwood, Martha Bashford, Elizabeth, Ruth Sherwood; m. 2d, Aug. 13, 1797, Elizabeth, dau. of Sylvanus Whitney, b. July 7, 1773; had Jane, James, David, Susannah Craft, Thomas, William Puddington, Henry Sylvanus, Elias Scovil, John, Huldah Butler, and Norton.

He was a loyalist, and removed with his father to New Brunswick in 1783, and resided for several years in the parish of Hampton; from thence he removed to St. Johns, where he lived a short time, from thence to Kingston, county of Kings, in 1820. He was a colonel of the first battalion of Kingston militia, and was a representative in the General Assembly of the Province for many years, and a Judge of the Common Pleas and Quarter Sessions. He died at Norton, Kings co., Dec. 17, 1845, in his 82d year. His wife, Ruth Sherwood, died Dec. 17, 1795. Her father Justus Sherwood, was a loyalist, and resided at Cortlandt Manor, Westchester co., N. Y. He, with his brothers Abijah and Jonathan, were grantees of St. John, N. B., in 1783; he died in Kings co., in 1836, at the age of eighty-four (*Am. Loyalists*, 612). Mrs. Elizabeth Whitney Wetmore, died ——; her father, Sylvanus Whitney, was also a loyalist, and resided in Stamford, Conn.

30

In June, 1775, (says the *American Loyalists*, p. 690), he was arraigned before the Committee of that town,. charged with the offence of buying and selling tea. He made a written confession of the fact, delivered up the tea remaining in his possession, and was allowed to depart. As the reader may be curious to learn how the Whigs disposed of this obnoxious article of drink, the following account of the destruction of that received of Mr. Whitney is here given : "At about eight o'clock in the evening a gallows was erected in the middle of the street. * * * * A large concourse of people soon collected, and were joined by a number of the soldiery quartered in the town. A grand procession soon began to move. In the first place a large guard under arms, headed by two captains, who led the van, with the unfortunate tea hung across a pole, sustained by two unarmed soldiers. Secondly, followed the Committee of Observation. Thirdly, the spectators who came to see the sight. And after parading through a part of the principal streets, with drums beating and fifes playing a most doleful sound ; they came to the gallows, where the common hangman soon performed his office, to the general satisfaction of the spectators. As it was thought dangerous to let the said tea hang all night, for fear of invasion of our tea lovers, a large bonfire was made under it, which soon reduced it to ashes ; and, after giving three loud huzzas, the people soon dispersed to their respective homes, without any bad consequences attending." Mr. Whitney was present during the execution, adds the writer, "and behaved himself as well as could be expected." He removed to St. John, at the peace, and was a magistrate and one of the aldermen of that city. He died at St. John in 1827, aged seventy-nine.

JOSIAH, b. in Rye, Dec. 5, 1766 ; d. June 15, 1767.

CALEB, b. in Rye, May 4, 1768 ; m. Deborah, dau. of Justus Sherwood Esq., formerly of Cortlandt Manor, Westchester co., N. Y.; had Ruth, Josiah Joseph, James, Caleb, Izrahiah, Joseph, Robert, Martha, Sarah, Elizabeth, Margeret, Infant, Deborah Jane.

He removed to St. Johns, N. B., with his father's family, in 1783. Was a colonel of the Kings co., N.

B., militia, and a member of the common council of
St. Johns for a number of years. He died Sept. 29,
1853. '

ALITHEA, b. in Rye, May 19, 1771; m. Ruben Craft; had I *Jerusha*,
II *James;* III *John;* IV *Charity;* V *William;* VI *Ruben:*
m. 2d, Walter Sherwood of N. B.; had VII *James 2d;* VIII
Charles; IX *Elizabeth;* X *Deborah;* XI *Esther;* XII *Jane.*

She died July 23, 1834, in her 64th year. Mr.
Craft was brother of John, he settled in N. B., ——;
died about 1801. Mr. Sherwood Sen., resided in N. B.,
was formerly from Pennsylvania.

ESTHER, b. in Rye, Aug. 16, 1774; m. April 9, 1793, at Carleton, N. B.,
William Puddington, b. in Edinburgh, Scotland, June 19, 1769 ;
had I *Infant dau.;* II *Mary,* b. March 20, 1794, who m. Nov.
4, 1813, Joseph Flewelling; had 1st William Puddington, who
m. 1st Susannah, dau. of John, son of James, son of Rev.
James Wetmore; had dau. d. y.; m. 2d, Esther Meritt, g. dau.
of Izrahiah, son of James, son of Rev. James Wetmore, had 3
sons and 2 daus.; 1 son (Osmond), m. 1861, Charlotte, dau. of
Brown Whelpley; m. 3d, Charlotte Whelpley, s. p.; Mrs.
Mary Flewelling d. Nov. 29, 1859; III *Elizabeth,* b. March
3, 1796, d. July 4, 1798; IV *James Wetmore,* b. Feb. 27,
1798 ; m. July 12, 1828, Elizabeth, dau. of Izrahiah Wetmore
of Rye; he d. Dec. 17, 1860, s. p.; V *Susannah Craft,* b.
Nov. 4, 1799, m. July 12, 1817, Thomas A. Flewelling; had 2
sons and 8 daus.; VI *William,* b. Feb. 13, 1802, m. March 13,
1828, Fanny Williams, have sons and daus.; VII *George,* b.
June 19, 1805, m. May 16, 1823, Debros Steward, dau. of
Alithea, dau. of James, son of Rev. James Wetmore; VIII
Clarissa Holmes, b. May 16, 1808, m. Oct. 22, 1829, Thomas,
son of Judge David Brown Wetmore (see issue under proper
head); IX *Esther Wetmore,* b. April 3, 1811, d. April 19, 1811;
X *David Wetmore,* b. Nov. 10, 1812, m. May 15, 1834; had
Edmond, who m. 1861, Eliza, dau. of David, son of Judge
David Brown Wetmore; XI *Caleb Wetmore,* b. May 13, 1815,
d. May 16, 1815; XII *Margeret Jane Gedney,* b. Jan. 26,
1818, m. Oct. 16, 1834, William Thomas Flewelling, had
Charlotte Flewelling.

Mrs. Esther Puddington Sen. removed with her
father's family to New Brunswick. She is still living,
and resides, as do most of her descendants, at or near

St. Johns. She is, we believe, the only one living of the grand children of the Rev. James of Rye. She is much loved and respected by her numerous connection.

Children of TIMOTHY.

JAMES, b. Rye, Oct. 21, 1757, and d. Nov. 26, 1758.

INFANT DAU., b. 1758; d. at time of birth.

JANE, b. in Rye, June 4, 1760; christened by Mr. Dibble, she m. Jesse Lamereux, and died in New York, leaving Timothy.

ANNA, b. in Rye, June 6, 1762, christened by Mr. Dibble.

She died aged 15 years, and was buried as has been stated, in Trinity Church yard, New York.

TIMOTHY FLETCHER, b. in Rye, Oct. 3, 1764; christened by Mr. Seabury of Jamaica.

He died in New York; was a physician of Columbia College. The following notice and tribute to him, we take from an autograph letter from his brother, Rev. Robert Griffith, addressed to his daughter Jane :

Your uncle Timothy F. Wetmore, studied Physic with Dr. Seabury (who was afterwards Bishop of Connecticut and Rhode Island), and practiced Physic a number of years in New Brunswick; he came to New York in 1793, attended the lectures of Columbia College for 3 years, wrote and published a dissertation on Puerperal Fever, and took the degree of M. D. with honor, but poor disappointed soul, he was cut off in youth, and in the most promising part of life, like many of his fellow mortals. He died in Jan., 1799; he was a dear brother to me ; his manners were pleasing and gentlemanly, and he was no less esteemed for his respect of religion than skill in his profession.

THOMAS, b. in Rye, Sept. 20, 1767; christened by the Rev. Mr. Ephraim Avery, Oct. 25; m. March 17, 1793, at Gagetown, N. B., by the Rev. Mr. Clarke, rector of G., Sarah, dau. of

Judge James Peters; had Margeret Lester, George Ludlow, Jane Haviland, Charles Peters, Ann Peters, Sarah, Timothy Robert, Thomas Allen, Susannah Mary, Eleanor, Emma, and Thomas Saunders.

He was a loyalist, and removed with his father to Nova Scotia, and from thence to N. Brunswick, where he studied law with the late Hon. Ward Chipman, son of the late Chief Justice Chipman, was admitted to the bar, and practiced with credit and success.

In 1792 he held the office of Deputy Surrogate of the Colony, was Master and Examiner in Chancery, Register of Wills and Deeds for the county of Queens, and was a member of the Council.—*Sabine's Am. Loyalists*, 683.

Was appointed Attorney General of the Province of N. B., July 26, 1809, which office he filled with signal reputation to the period of his death.

As a man, he was eminently distinguished for his talents, benevolence, kindness and hospitality. His hand was always open to the poor and needy, his heart always beat responsive to the cry of distress. He was a friend to all mankind. As a lawyer and an advocate he had no superiors in the Province. If he had equals he was a leader among them. No language we could use would be too strong to express the love and admiration in which he was held by his children and family, and the esteem and respect that he received from the community in which he lived. By the aid of his father's tuition and his own exertions he arose to the highest status in his profession. As it has been said of him "he never touched anything he did not adorn."

He was a communing member of the Established Church. While he was firm and steadfast in his own professed faith, he exercised forbearance and charity towards all denominations of Christians. That he was a true disciple of our blessed Redeemer, no one, we think, can doubt, after reading the following beautiful letter, written under painful circumstances, to his son Robert. We copy from the original lying before us.

These liable afflictions (my dear Robert), which are but for a moment, work for us a far more exceeding and eternal weight of glory. It is salutary for us to receive instruction in the school of adversity, and we ought to bear in mind that it happens, at least sometimes, that whom God loveth he chasteneth ; and it' is said, He scourgeth *every* son he receiveth. We all offend our maker daily, and certainly we have abundant cause to turn to him with our whole hearts. I have been most unfortunate in the eyes of all who are not disposed to admit that the hairs of our head are numbered, but from the moment the dreadful accident happened I have been fortunate far beyond expectation.

I had thought and presence of mind enough to place the broken bones together and so to hold them until the surgeons arrived, also to order the Bier out of the Graveyard to take me home. I was bro't quietly and comfortably out (2 miles) and placed on a Bed in the Drawing Room, whence I have not yet been removed (now the 17th day). I have been constantly and kindly visited by two skillful surgeons, and I have been blessed with my family around me. I have had very little Fever and the crippled Limb wears the most favorable appearance. For those and other Blessings I am really grateful. It is with very great pleasure I anticipate your return to us. On this day three weeks, should no accident happen, I hope to see you, and by that time I hope to be on crutches.

A very unexpected disappointment prevented your receiving a supply of cash before now. By the last Boat I took other steps which I hope will prove more successful to send you £65, a sum, sufficient, I trust, to discharge your Debts and to pay the expense of your journey here. Come, therefore, my dear son, the moment the Term closes, with all possible expedition, to the Bosom of your Father.

Bring with you (if you can obtain it) a certificate of the time of your Matriculation, and the Terms which you have kept, &c. Bring also a list of your Library. I can not use a pen as I am flat on my back.

Remember me respectfully and kindly to our Friends the Tonges and Dr. Cochran & Family. I am tired. May God Almighty protect and bless you my dear Boy, is the prayer of,

Your aff' Father,

· T. WETMORE.

Kingswood,
Saturday,
14 June, 1823,

He died without an enemy, March 22, 1828. The following notice of him appeared in *The Courier*, a paper published in New Brunswick, March 25, 1828.

Under the obituary head in to-day's *Gazette*, we have had the mournful task of inserting the death of Thomas Wetmore, Esq., his Majesty's late Attorney General for this Province, and whose loss, we have no doubt, will be greatly felt in that profession of which he was here, the distinguished head, so great an ornament and so profound a member. While at the same time, in a domestic view of this afflicting circumstance, we are confident, that all who had the pleasure of even a partial intimacy with the lamented deceased, will deeply sympathize in the bereavement thus sustained by his family circle.—*Royal Gazette.*

The following is a copy of the inscription upon his and his consort's tombstone :

The Honble. Thomas Wetmore,
Attorney General
of New Brunswick,
who died
22 March, A. D., 1828.

Also,
Sarah,
His wife, died
28 June,
A. D., 1827.
Aged 58 years.

The father of Mrs. Wetmore (Judge Peters), was a loyalist of New York. "He settled (says Sabine) in New

Brunswick in 1783, and was one of the agents to locate
lands granted to the loyalists, who removed to that colony.
Of the city of St. John he was a grantee. In 1792 he was
a magistrate of Queens county; also a member of the
House of Assembly for a long period. He died at his
seat at Gagetown, 1820, æ. 75. His son, the Hon.
Charles J. Peters, is the present (1847) Attorney General
of N. B.

LUTHER, b. in Rye, May 12, 1769, and christened June 25, by Mr.
Avery.

He died in the state of New York, May, 1813.

THEODORE, b. in Rye, June 28, 1771, and christened about 6 weeks
afterwards by Mr. Avery.

Rev. ROBERT GRIFFETH, A. M., b. in Rye, March 10, 1774; chris-
tened the Sunday next before Whitsunday, by the Rev. Mr.
Avery, Mr. Robert Griffeth and wife sponsors by proxy; m.
May 16, 1795, at St. Johns, N. B., by the Rev. M. Byles, rec-
tor of St. Johns, Jane Gidney, of Queens co.; had Jane, and
Abraham Kirsted Smedes.

To this good man and his good works we feel ourself wholly incompetent to do justice, and shall have
to be content with scarcely more than naming some of
the prominent acts of his short but eventful life.
In the tenth year of his age he removed with his
father to Nova Scotia and New Brunswick, where,
chiefly under his father's guidance and instruction, he
fitted himself for the study of the law, though his early
preferences were for the ministry. On completion of
the required number of years of preparation for the
bar, at the same time reaching his majority, he was
admitted an attorney in the courts of New Brunswick.[20]

[20] Copy of the certificate received by Mr. Wetmore:

In His Majesty's Supreme Court ⎫ Easter Term, in the thirty-fifth year
of Judicature for the Province ⎬ of our Soverign Lord, King George
of New Brunswick.   ⎭ the Third of Gt. Britain, &c.

It appearing to this Court, that Robert Griffeth Wetmore of Gagetown, in
Queens county, Gentleman, is duly qualified to act as an Attorney
[Seal.] of this Court; and he having this day in open court taken the
oaths of Allegiance and Supremacy and Abjuration, and taken and

Soon after, circumstances led to his removal to New York, where he superintended a classical school at New Rochelle. While thus engaged he was enabled to turn his attention to the study of theology, and fulfilling the requirements of the Protestant Episcopal Church, he was ordained deacon by the Rt. Rev. Samuel Provost, bishop of New York,[21] and immediately after received authority from the bishop, and was commissioned[22] to go into the western part of the state of New

subscribed the Declaration against transubstatiation and Popery; and also taken the oath of Attorney. Let him be admitted an Attorney of said Court, and his admission be enrolled. Given under the seal of said Court. Dated this sixth day of May, in the Year of our Lord one thousand seven hundred and ninety-five.

| Sworn in Court and Enrolled, this sixth day of May, 1795. | GEO. D. LUDLOW, ISAAC ALLEN, JOHN SAUNDERS. |

W. FRANKLIN ODELL,
　　　Dy. C'lk.

[21] By the Tender of these presents, be it known unto all Men, That We, Samuel Provost, by Divine Permission Bishop of the Protestant Episcopal Church in the State of New York, solemnly administering Holy Orders under the protection of Almighty God, in St. Paul's Chapel, on Sunday, the 21st day of May, of our Lord one thousand seven hundred and ninety-seven, did admit unto the Holy Order of Deacons, our well beloved in Christ Robert G. Wetmore, of whose virtuous and pious life and conversation, and competent Learning and Knowledge in the Holy Scriptures, we were well assured, and him, the said Robert G. Wetmore, did then and there rightly and canonically ordain a deacon. He having first in our presence made the subscription required by the General Ecclesiastical Constitution.

In witness whereof we have caused our Episcopal Seal hereunto affixed. Dated the day and year above written, and in the eleventh year of our Consecration.　　　　SAMUEL [Seal,] PROVOST.
　　　[Written on Parchment.]

[22] Be it Known by These Presents, That the bearer hereof, The Reverend Robert G. Wetmore, a Deacon of the Protestant Episcopal Church, has been engaged and employed by the Committee of the Protestant Ep. Church for propagating the Gospel in the state of New York, as a missionary, with authority to preach, to administer the sacrament of baptism, and to solemnize the matrimonial and funeral offices, and it is hereby recommended to the members of the Protestant Episcopal Church in all parts of this state where he may offer his services, to receive and respect him in the aforesaid character.

Signed in the Name and on Behalf of the Committee in the city of New York, on the twenty-fifth day of May, in the year of our Lord 1797.

Attest.　　　　　　　　　　　　　SAMUEL PROVOST.
J. BESSETT, Secy.　　　　　　Bp. of the Prot. Episc. Ch., N. Y.,
　[Written on Parchment.]　　　and Chairman of the Committee.

York, then a comparative wilderness, to preach the Gospel to that then destitute region. Of his services and of the extent of them, Bishop Chase, who succeeded him in his missionary labors, says : " To learn what good this pious man did by his ministrations through the State, one must travel where he traveled, converse with those with whom he conversed. The benefits arising to the Church of Christ and to individuals, were apparently many and great. He exhorted the indolent, comforted the desponding, and awakened the careless; in short, he so aroused the people from their lethargy and excited them to a sense of their religious duties, that in the year following there were incorporated in the state seven new congregations, and divine service began to be performed in many places, where people had never attempted it before."—See notice of the Rev. Mr. Wetmore, in Dr. Sprague's *Annals of American Pulpit*, v, 454.

The following year, he received from Columbia College, New York, the degree of Master of Arts. The diploma that was given him at the time, is before us, and has subscribed to it the celebrated names of William Samuel Johnson, LL. D., John Kemp, LL. D., P. Wilson, LL. D., Drs. Samuel L. Mitchel, David Hosack, Wright Post, and John R. B. Rodgers, Profs. John McKnight, and John Christopher Kunze, all members of the faculty.

His health failing him in a measure, he was obliged to give up his missionary work,[23] and to accept the

[23] Copy from the original.

In Committee of the Protestant Episcopal Church for propagating of the Gospel in the state of New York, June 2d, 1798.

The Rev. Mr. Wetmore having in the course of the year, travelled 2386 miles, performed divine service and preached 107 times, baptized 47 adults and 365 infants, and conducted himself with a degree of propriety becoming his character and office. Therefore,

Resolved, That the committee entertain a high sense of the fidelity and zeal, which Mr. Wetmore has displayed in the discharge of his duty as missionary.. J. BESSETT, Sec'y.
Extract from the Minutes.

more regular duties of a pastor. Receiving on the 10th of June, 1798, at the hands of Bishop Provost, his priest's ordination, he accepted a call from Christ's Church, Duanesburgh, N. Y., and was regularly instituted in that church,[24] on the 30th of the following month, and soon after, in addition, received and accepted the charge of St. George's Church, Schenectady.[25] To these two parishes he broke the bread of life, for three years. His health continuing to give way, he was obliged to resign his charge, temporarily.

Mr. Wetmore belonged to the Masonic fraternity, to which he was much attached. We give the various degrees that he received, which we take from an autograph record.

When and where Masonic Honors were conferred on Mr. Wetmore.

At Beeksmanstown, in Dutchess co., on the 14th of July, 1797, he rec[d] the degree of Entered Apprentice, and on the 18th of same month, in the same lodge, he rec[d] the degree of Fellow Craft.

On the 19th of July, af[d] in St. Simeon and St. Jude's Lodge at Fishkill, he was raised to the sublime degree of Master Mason.

[24] From the original, written and printed with a pen, on parchment:

By the Tenor of these Presents, Be it known unto all Men, that the Wardens and Vestry of Christ's Church in Duanesburg, did on the thirtieth day of July, in the year of our Lord one thousand seven hundred and ninety-eight, solemnly induct the Rev. Robert Griffeth Wetmore, A. M., Rector of Christ's Church aforesaid; and by the virtue of the Authority in them as a Body Corporate did place him in full Possession of all the Rights and Priviledges thereunto appertaining. Whereof the Delivery of the Key according to ancient usage is sufficient Testimony.

[Seal.]   In Witness whereof, I have hereunto set my Hand and affixed the Seal of the Corporation the day and year above written.

                                    EDWARD CUMPTON,
                                    Clerk to the Wardens and Vestry.

[25] A certificate before us of his induction, is written upon parchment, of similar tenor to the above, with the addition to the "delivery of key," the "tolling of the Bell according to ancient usage are sufficient testimonials," and signed, "29 day of September, A. D. 1798.

                                    WILLIAM CORLETT,
                                    Clerk to the Wardens and Vestry."

At the city of Schenectady in Saint George's Lodge, he was advanced to the Hon[ble] degree of Mark Master Mason on the 19th Aug., 1797.

At Poughkeepsie, in Feb. 1798, he rec[d] the degree of Past Master, from the Past Masters of Solomon's Lodge.

At Stamford, Delaware co., on the 1st of May following, he rec[d] the degree of Most Excellent Master, and was exalted to the degree of Royal Arch Mason in St. Andrew's Chapter.

The 5th July, 1798, he rec[d] 23 ineffable degrees from Major Augustin Prevost, duly anthorized and constituted Soverign Prince of Masons, &ca., &cal.

In January, 1800, was elected Most Excellent Grand Scribe of the Grand Royal Arch Chapter of the state of New York, and December following, he was unanimously appointed by the Royal Arch Bretheren of the city of Schenectady, High Priest of Cyrus's Chapter, and was warranted therein by the Royal Arch Chapter, af[d].

He was the earliest and the principal promoter of Masonry in Duanesburg; he performed the duties of Chaplain to Walton Lodge in that place, and for a considerable length of time governed the Orange Lodge.

By request, he published *An oration on the Festival of St. John the Evangelist,* June 17, 1797, Catskill, M. Croswell, *Address to Episcopal Congregation in Schenectady and Duanesborough,* July, 1798, Catskill, M. Croswell, 1800 : *An oration occasioned by the Death of Lieutenant General George Washington,* Delivered at the Lutheran Church in Schoharie, 15th Jan., 1800; Ellihu Phinney, Cooperstown; *Masonic Valedictory Address,* Duanesburg, 17 June, 1800; Chas. R. & George Webster, Albany, 1800 ; also *Extensive Charity in a Small Compass,* all of which, are creditable to his talents, and his heart.

The following, which we take from a small volume containing original addresses, genealogical records, &c., partly in print, and partly in autography, while it gives interesting historical matter respecting the family, it furnishes the reader an insight into the inner man, more than anything we can sketch, particularly that portion addressed to his daughter, respecting the principles that should govern her through life.

SOME ACCOUNT OF THE WETMORE FAMILY,

In a Letter from the Author of this Book to his Daughter.

My dear Jane:

Near one hundred and thirty years ago, Thomas Wetmore, your grandfather's great-grandfather, came from Wales, Great Britain, and settled in Middletown, in Connecticut; indeed he was one of the original patentees of that town, which perhaps accounts for the long continuance of his descendants in that place. For a considerable time our family spelt the name Whitmore, and why they afterwards converted it to Wetmore, I never could learn, nor is I suppose of any consequence to know. Although I have made much enquiry I can not learn anything very particular respecting the family before the time of your great-grandfather, the second of the six brothers in the third generation, and of him I have received a most pleasing account in the words following.

James Wetmore, A. M., of Yale College, was a Presbyterian minister at North Haven for five years, but possessing as much candor as discernment, he readily acknowledged himself to be without ministerial, or rather true apostolic authority, designed for the ministers of Christ, and therefore accompanied Dr. Johnson, Dr. Cutler and others to London, where with them he received holy orders from the Right Rev. Edmund Gibson, Bishop of London. When he returned he was assistant minister to the Rev. Mr. Vesey, rector of Trinity Church, New York. In this place he continued about two years, when preferring the country he removed to the parish of Rye, where he preached 36 years, and died about 36 years since. His Epitaph, or rather the inscription on his tomb stone, was penned by Dr. Johnson above named, and is a handsome eulogium, for which I respect the author. It announces that your great-grandfather was a sincere and able defender of the Church, both in the pulpit and with the pen. This Dr. Johnson was president of the College[26] in New York, and father to the late celebrated Dr. Johnson, president of the same college. It was remarked that the most perfect intimacy existed between him and your g. g. father from the age of five years until death broke the bond. I have reason to believe that they constitute a part of the church triumphant in heaven.

Your grandfather Timothy Wetmore, Esq., A. M., of Kings College, New York, was designed and educated for the ministerial office, but when on the point of departure for London, something intervened to prevent the journey, and he then turned his inclination to the study of the law; he was admitted attorney and counsellor in the Courts of the Province of New York, and practiced law for a considerable

[26] Kings College, now known as Columbia College.

period, but possessing loyalty in the Revolution of America, with many others, he fell a sacrifice to poverty, being deprived of a comfortable home. With a numerous family he experienced much trouble, and yet with a fortitude and an affection ever to be remembered he surmounted a multitude of difficulties; to him alone his children are indebted for education and subsistence, and I desire my Dr. child to possess a grateful remembrance of her grandfather's merit and always to manifest a willingness (if God shall enable her) to return love for love. Your g. father removed his family to Nova Scotia in the year 1783, and in that country practiced law 17 years with success, and filled sundry public offices with dignity.

As to myself, I cannot have much to say without sacrificing a propriety of thought, and yet boldly profess that I am in possession of some virtues, which I desire you to possess as long as heaven shall give you life.

1. A superior contempt for the world, and a wish to be in Heaven in God's own good Time.
2. An unfeigned and Cordial Esteem for the Righteous and Philanthropy for all men.
3. A never failing Disposition to " seek Peace and pursue it " to follow after it, so that the mind can be enabled to live by faith and meditation upon Divine Providence.
4 To pay " Honour to whom Honour is due," and never conceive yourself to be equal to all the world.
5. To love Learning, and above all to esteem the Fear of the Lord, as the first of all wisdom, and a departure from Evil real understanding.
6. To be spiritually and temporally prepared for Death [*Deo Volente*].

At an early time of life, I was inclined to the study of Divinity; this might have proceeded from the delicacy of constitution which I possessed, added to the frequent pious admonitions and instruction from my father, but after passing through my classical studies, it was found more convenient to embrace the Law. I was a student for five years, at the end of which time, that is to say in May, 1795, I was honorably admitted Attorney at Law in the Supreme Court of the Province of New Brunswick, the same year I came to New York, taught an academy at New Rochelle for 21 months with success, in which time, I was enabled to comply with the canons of the church, and in May received deacons orders ; four days after which I was appointed missionary for the state; travelled in a year 2386 miles on horseback, and discharged my duty satisfactorily to my conscience, and my employers. A little before the expiration of my mission, Columbia College was pleased to confer upon me, the degree of Master of Arts.

On the 10th of June, 1798, in St. Pauls Church, New York, received priests orders from the bishop aforesaid, and having received a call from Schenectady and Duanesburg, accepted the same, and was inducted rector, July, 1798. In these parishes, I preached for near three years, and was then obliged to withold ministrations and to travel for health, having suffered exceedingly with a pulmonary complaint.

Thus you have a few particulars respecting me. I am blessed with the friendship of many respectable characters in the state of New York, and if you shall be so happy as to conduct piously, prudently, and gracefully, you may experience their friendship also, and acquire more knowledge respecting me.

Your uncle, Thomas Wetmore, Esq., of New Brunswick, is a counsellor at law, of considerable note; it would be accounted vanity in me, should I say I have been credibly informed that he is esteemed one of the first in the province, in the civil and military list, he has filled very important offices, and discharged his duty with reputation. I have ever experienced unfeigned love from him. I believed him to be a *brother* and I have great reason to hope that if your conduct may merit his attention, that it will be shown with readiness and alacrity.

I hold myself under great obligations to him, and I beseech you to show all willingness to acknowledge as much for your father.

Mr. Wetmore's health continuing to fail, he sought a more genial climate, in hopes of being benefited, but such was not the will of his Master in Heaven.[27] His last sickness and circumstances attending his death, the reader will find detailed in the following letters:

Copy of letter from the Rev. Robert Smith, addressed to Mr. Wetmore's father, the Hon, Timothy Wetmore, then residing in New York.

SAVANNAH, Feb. 22d, 1803.

Hon^d Sir:

With swift emotions of sorrow and joy, you will, no doubt, receive the intelligence, which in the adorable Providence of God, we are called to communicate, your affectionate, your dutiful, your worthy son, the Rev. Robt. G. Wetmore, is no more. Alas, a father's heart can not but throb.

Yet, venerable Sir, " sorrow not as those who have no hope." In full confidence of eternal life, through Jesus Christ his Saviour, he finished his mortal course. Rejoice therefore, that he is discharged from the burden of his sorrows, and is gone to his Heavenly Father.

[27] He made two visits to Georgia, on his first visit he was accompanied by his wife.

Were his immortal spirit permitted to address you, would it not be in the language of our Lord, to the Daughters of Jerusalem, "weep not for me, weep not for me." May the compassionate Saviour who bedewed the grave of Lazarus with his tears, support your spirit and console your heart. May you adopt the language of the afflicted Job. "The Lord gave, the Lord taketh away; Blessed be the name of the Lord."

All the circumstances relating to your son's death, has been fully and accurately detailed by my worthy friend Judge Clay, whose communication accompanies this letter. Permit me, however, to add the assurance that your dear departed son, shortly before his death, made a choice of a text, as the subject of a funeral discourse, with psalmns adapted to the occasion. The text, Job, 27, 5, "Till I die, I will not remove my integrity from me." The Psalmns, 23 and 112.

On the Sabbath after his death, the ps. were sung and the discourse delivered to a very numerous and deeply affected audience. It was also his request, that I should transmit a copy of my sermon to his friends to the north, respecting which I shall consider more fully, and write you in some future period.

With sincere, &c.. &c.,.
ROBERT SMITH.

Copy of letter from the late Judge Joseph Clay, Jr., of Georgia, to the Hon. Timothy Wetmore:

SAVANNAH, Feb. 7th, 1803.

Respected Sir:

It is incumbent upon me to communicate the intelligence of an event, which is generally deemed a melancholly one, but which in the present case, has been attended by circumstances which I trust will not only afford you sufficient consolation, but will, notwithstanding the relenting of nature, be to you a subject of holy joy. Your son, the Rev. Robert G. Wetmore, died at my house on the 30th of last month, after having given repeated evidences of his reconciliation to God in Christ, and his unwavering and strong hopes of a blessed immortality. Knowing that the particulars which preceded and accompanied his last moments, will be interesting to you, I shall mention some of those which most attracted my attention, and which made the deepest impression upon my memory. He had never appeared to me since his last arrival from the northward, to be likely to survive the winter, and I have thought ever since our first interview, that I have perceived him declining very fast. He remained in this place somewhere about three weeks after his landing, and then went to my house, where he staid nearly as long, and then came back to this place. These alterations appeared most agreeable to him. He was making his second visit with me on the 19th of January, when we stopped at a house about fifteen miles from this place. He there sat about a quarter of an hour by the fire, and drank a little weak warm sangaree. He appeared to be refreshed, and we got into the carriage to proceed on our journey; very shortly after he was seated, he told me he was dying. I looked at him, and supposed he was. His temples were immediately rubbed with spirits, and they were applied to his nostrils, and he soon revived. He attributed his fainting fit, to the warmth of the fire and what he had drank, and his coming so soon into the open air. I expressed my great satisfaction at seeing him so much composed, when he supposed his dissolution was at hand. He replied that those who knew him best, knew it was an event which he anticipated with no uneasiness. I then requested him to determine whether we should remain where we were till the next day, or proceed to my house, which was between six and seven miles further. He preferred to go on, and as he seemed to be confident that he had strength enough, and the house near which we were, being an uncomfortable one, I thought his determination proper, and we continued our journey.

The day after, he continued all day in his chamber, but the following and every day after, until the 27th, he sat a part of the day in the parlour, where my family sit, and several of these days, in the middle of the day was carried in a large chair, up and down the walks of my garden. Hearing that the Rev. R. Smith was a friend, for whom he had great esteem, and in whom he much confided, I wrote to him on Thursday, the 20th, informing him of my apprehension, that he was near his end. Mr. Smith received my letter late in the morning and informed me that he had feelings then, which threatened a pluratic attack (he was also to preach on the Sabbath), but that he would come out as early the next week as his situation would admit. He was accordingly with us on Monday forenoon. Your son, within an hour or two after his arrival, desired us both to pray by his bed-side, and he requested me, I think both then and afterwards, to pray that no suffering might occasion his wavering, that he might be patient and submissive to the will of God, that if it pleased God, his pains might be of short duration, and that he might retain his reason to the last moment of his life, that I should pray for you, for his children, his congregation, and all that he was particularly bound to pray for. He told Mr. Smith and myself, that he placed his hopes of salvation on the Righteousness of his Redeemer alone. On Tuesday, he requested me to write Dr. Thollock, who had generally prescribed for him in Savannah, and to tell him, that if his business would admit, he wished the doctor would visit him, that he was desirous of seeing him that might say, whether he thought his end was very near, and if it was, that he might prescribe such things, as might mitigate the pains of dissolution; or if he thought it most proper, that he might be removed to Savananah. He said to me, at the same time, that he had no expectation of recovery, nor desire for life, but asked whether I did not think it was proper, that he should take every step which prudence dictated, as the most likely to produce benefit. I told him I viewed such conduct in the same light of duty he did. Dr. Thollock was with him on Wednesday afternoon. He had in the meantime been visited by two physicians of our neighborhood. Not long after the Dr. had been with him, and while Mr. Smith and myself were in the room, he said he was inclined to do whatever duty required, and he wished to be candidly informed whether we thought it best he should remain where he was, or be removed to Savannah by land, if he could bear it, and if not, whether it would be practical or prudent to make a removal by water. Being well acquainted with the state of your son's mind, I judged it proper, to make one or two remarks before the doctor gave his opinion, and observed that I had seen such evidence of composure in Mr. Wetmore on the subject of death, that I knew he was prepared for anything that the doctor could say, and that he would, I was sure be obliged by his candour, that I was thoroughly convinced that he had not strength to return by land, that I doubted whether he had, to be removed by water, of that, the doctor would be a better judge. That I would, if it were deemed proper, procure as comfortable a boat as could be got, but the time of its passage would be uncertain, from its winding course, and contrariety of tides, and that if there should a change of weather for the worse, his situation would be very uncomfortable, and he might not be able to support it. The doctor said he was convinced that it was best for him to remain where he was, that he did not think he could live many days, and did not believe he could bear a removal. That two days before Mr. Wetmore left Savannah, he perceived from the swelling of his feet, and the soreness of his throat and mouth, that his dissolution was fast approaching and that he had prepared to call on him, on that or the following day, to give him his opinion explicitly. Your son then said, "If my friend pleases then, ·I will die under his roof." I observed to him that I would repeat what I had said on a former occasion. He one evening, before he came last to my house to this place, said to me, that there was a question, which he thought it proper that he should propose to me.· You are willing I know my friend that I should live with you, can you be content that I should die with you? I answered· that if it was God's will that he should die in Georgia, I was willing that it should be at my house, and should rather prefer its taking place there. That from his acquaintance with our family, and ours with him, there was as great a probability of his last moments being made as comfortable as possible with us, as at any other place. He said a little after this that it would be very distressing to him, to know that he should continue to live two or three months, and that no intelligence would be more joyous, than to be assured that he should die by ten o'clock that night. Mr. Smith and myself lay in the room with him on Tuesday night; the doctor on Wednesday; I did on Thursday; a friend whom he esteemed on Friday; and I on Saturday. I had also two of my people each night with him in rotation, selected from the most intelligent. There was also one who could read, and the whole of those set up with him in turn, could sing psalmns and hymns, which they frequently did both by night and day, at his desire. I generally joined in these exercises, when in the room, and at his request, occasionally went to prayer. On Thursday morning he supposed he was dying, and desired me to be called to him. When I went to him he asked me to hand him a small looking glass, which was on a table near him. He looked a little at the glass, and then affectionately at me, and said, "My friend, how comfortable it is to die in Christ. When I have heard of people speaking of great comfort in dying, I thought it arose only from their great hopes of a happy immortality. It is true this does constitute much of it, but independent of these hopes, there is a pleasure in feeling that you are getting released from all your trouble, to go to another world," or to that effect. He paused a while and said: "I am disappointed. I thought I was going."

During the night of Thursday, he rested but little. He rested tolerably well two or three hours, after daylight, and said to me, about ten o'clock, as he had intimated the day before, that this day he thought would be his last, and that he had suffered a great deal since yesterday, without saying anything, yet he felt one hundred and fifty times more comfortable than he had done then. I supposed this to arise from the increased ardor of his hopes. He asked me not long after this, if there were not some prayers that that were comfortable and suitable to his case, in *Drelincourt on Death*. I told him I believed there were, but I was not sure, as I had never read him through, and that he had not been in my possession for a long time till lately, that I would bring him and look. I got Drelincourt and the title of several prayers, which seemed his consolatory chapters and asked him which of those I should read. He said, he suspected I misapprehended him, that he was not particularly anxious I should read any of them, from a preference that he had for them, that my own prayers were very agreeable, but he thought as his end was near, I might feel some pertubation from the interest which I took in it, and these acts of devotion might not be quite easy to me. I replied, that perceiving him to be so resigned, had given me a degree of composure, which I should not probably have felt otherwise, and that I did not imagine I should feel any difficulty in continuing to pray, when he desired, but that as I was a young pupil, in the school of Christ, many topics of consolation might not occur to me, and that it would perhaps be proper for me sometimes to pray of myself, and sometimes to read Drelincourt's prayers. He approved of this and I practiced according. He prayed himself at much length, this morning, with his head upon my knee. From its length and its being delivered with much difficulty of breathing, I should not be able to recal a good deal of it, if I desired. No small portion of it had relation to myself and family. Yourself and his children were, I think, other subjects of it. You were much I believe in his thoughts, his children he did not appear to be uneasy about. He seemed to rely much on God's care of them, but tho' he did not speak largely of you, yet when he mentioned you, it was with such tenderness of affection, as led me to suspect that he had some apprehension of your grieving too much on his account. I hope that the God which gave him such support, such constancy, such hopes in his Redeemer, will uphold you, and will sactify the manner of his death to you, so as to make it an abundant source of consolation and of humble rejoicing. His prayer, as it respected himself, was that he might be patient, that he might persevere to the end, that the period of his sufferings might be short, that when he came before the awful Bar of God, he might stand clothed in the righteousness of Christ. He said, that he had endeavored to keep God's commandments, but that he knew his obedience was very imperfect, and that after all he had done, he was obliged to confess, that he was an unprofitable servant and placed his hopes on the merits of his Redeemer. In the midst of this prayer he paused a considerable time, and when he spoke first, before commencing his prayer, he said, "I hoped just now, that I was going."

He sometimes lay and sometimes sat up in the bed, and was sometimes removed to a large chair by the fireside. As I was sitting by him this morning (Friday), he said: "There is no merit in a person wishing to die, merely to be relieved from pain, but rather a demerit, but I wish to depart, that I may go to Heaven, I shall see a mother whom I never saw, at least, not to remember; I shall see two sisters, and two brothers, and my wife, who I ought first to have mentioned. She was a dear and a good wife to me. But I desire to be patient, and would do whatever I knew to be proper."

The evening of this day, he said to me, and to those who were near his bed, "What a glorious expectation it is to be in Heaven, to see Abraham, Isaac and Jacob, and all the worthies whom God should think proper to take to Heaven." We acknowledged that it was. I remarked to him that, I had at different periods, particularly in the earlier part of my life, felt a great desire to visit those spots, which were still celebrated for the remains of ancient grandeur, such as Rome, Athens, Palmyra, &c., that I might be gratified by a view of the monuments of Genius, which still existed there, but tha this species of curiosity, had been for some time suppressed by the reflection, that death, which was not far from any of us, would remove me to scenes where I should behold things infinitely surpassing these in splendor and magnificence. He said he did not know, that precisely such a thought had ever occurred to him, that he thought it a pretty one.

I left him this evening at ten o'clock, having rest. not well the night before, and told him that I would be with him whenever he desired. When I went to him to see him in the morning, I found that he had not slept better than he had done the preceding night, but that he had then got into a doze. The first time of my going into the room this morning, when he was awake and saw me, he told me that he had been restless and was impatient; that he feared he should sin by his impatience. I told him that he had no cause to accuse himself on that account; that his entire resignation had been a subject of admiration to all who had been about him since his illness had become so great; that it was not wonderfull that the pains of his body should produce some little disquietude of mind, but rather that he should show so little. He asked me to go to prayer, and especially to pray that he might be patient. I went to prayer; and, very shortly after, he said that he already felt the comforts of that prayer.

On this day and at other times he thanked God for supporting him as he had done, and for his having as many comforts as the state of his disease would admit. I believe it was this day, or the day preceding, that he ventured one of his ejaculations, by saying, "Praise the Lord, oh my soul, and all that is within me praise the Lord! Praise the Lord, oh my soul" (something was added, but which I do not recollect).

After singing one or two hymns this day, he desired me to sing a hymn of thanksgiving. He did not rest well through Saturday night. He dozed a good deal on Sunday morning, generally leaning his head on some one's knee. Between one and two o'clock we sung several hymns and psalms by his desire, and at his particular request the one beginning with "Hark from the tombs a doleful cry." I went to prayer. We dined not long after this; after dinner I was reading in my chamber, and was told he wished to see me. I went to his bed side; he appeared to be in a doze. I took hold of his hand, and he immediately asked, "Is this the Judge?" I answered, "Yes." He said, "Farewell, my friend; I go to Christ." I observed to those who were near, "Hear Mr. Wetmore; he says he goes to Christ." I felt his pulse and said, "I believe, my friend, you are now going." He asked me where Mrs. Clay was. I said, "In the next room; shall I call her?" When she came and took hold of his hand, he bid her farewell, thanked her for her kindness, and prayed that God might bless her. He did so with Mrs. Gould, a friend who resided with us. He then desired to be raised up a little; and in about three minutes, without a groan, expired on my arm and that of one of my people.

I find that I omitted to mention that, on Saturday evening, Mr. Wetmore got into a copious perspiration. I had been engaged a little while in my garden, and he desired me to be called to him. When I went to him I felt his pulse. He asked me if I could give him no encouragement. I said, "You appear to be perspiring." He and the attendants said he had been perspiring very copiously; and he added, that the wind appeared to be rushing with some considerable coolness to every part of his body. He enquired whether I did not think that this cold sweat an evidence that his trouble was about over. On feeling his pulse with some attention, I told him I did not think he would live more than two or three days. He said it was good news, good news; so that he may be considered as having suffered death several times, and every time the idea of its being about to take place appeared to be the cause of comfort to him.

I have thus endeavoured with fidelity to relate the most interesting facts which immediately preceded and accompanied the death of your beloved son, and my dear (tho' I cannot add, considering his joyous death, lamented) friend. The length of this detail would be tiresome to an indifferent reader; but with you, it will be gratifying to a reasonable curiosity, furnishes grounds of consolation during your life, and confirm your hopes of spending a blessed immortality with him.

I might add other evidences of the temper in which he died, from his conversation with one of my children and with my servants. But it would swell this communication to a bulk too great, and for every useful purpose I perceive enough has been communicated.

I sent the body of your son from the place of my residence to this city, in the grave yard which is a general one for the different religious societies of this place.

His body was interred near the grave of the late pastor of the Episcopal Church of Savannah.

Mr. R. Smith has or will probably inform you of the circumstances of his funeral, and of the sermon which, by his desire, he preached on the subject of his death. I have only to add, that I feel an interest in whatever concerned your deceased son and my valued friend, and that I therefore desire to be enrolled among the number of the friends of his children, and that at a proper age they be informed of this my wish.

With much respect
and sympathy,
I am, respected Sir,
Your friend, &c.,
JOS. CLAY, Jun.

I have enclosed a memorandum, taken by your son's desire. Several letters, directed to him, have by his order been broken open, to see if anything was enclosed, and those will be returned.

Copy of letter written from New York by Timothy Wetmore to his son Thomas, accompanying a copy of the above letter of Judge Clay :

My Dear Son:

The ways of God are unsearchable and past finding out. These things that are revealed, belong to us and to our children.

Your brother was (I perceived) much respected throughout the State of New York. I hope he has done much good. Had health been granted, to a short-sighted mortal it seemed, he might have been serviceable in the vineyard. Precious in the sight of the Lord is the death of his saints.

You will not (I trust) regret the labour of love you bestowed. I hope the dear child is happy. He has passed the waves of this troublesome world. It is a matter of no consequence (as I know) to him, but to you especially, and also to me, it is a satisfaction, that he died in the bed of honour. But what a comfort to us is his resignation and joyful hopes.

It is a circumstance of great comfort to me that your good mother was perfectly resigned, and that her children have been so remarkably assisted at the awfull moment. I fear I never shall be so happy. Judge Clay's letter will afford you comfort. He is a man of wealth, and has been, or is one of the Supreme Judges. You will respect him highly, and I hope not fail to write to him. Oh ! what a comfort he has been to your dear brother. * * * *

I find he wished you to have a port-folio that he had from Judge Clay, which he supposed you would value the more on Judge Clay's account. * * * * *

I am in haste as the vessel is about sailing, and only add my love to Mrs. Wetmore and the dear children, and am

Your sympathizing and
affectionate Father,

March 23, 1803.   TIMOTHY WETMORE.

Judge Clay survived his guest till 1811, and we trust now enjoys a full measure of the reward of that hospitality concerning which our Lord Jesus hath said : " In as much as ye have done it unto one of the least of these my brethren, ye have done unto me."

While in Savannah, Mr. Wetmore was necessitated to accept pecuniary aid from some of the generous citizens of that place, and for the purpose of perpetuating the memory of those persons, as well as to return our (and we are confident we are only inscribing the sentiments of every living member of the Wetmore family, and especially this branch of it), grateful acknowledgments for the Christian love and charity bestowed upon the subject of our notice, while he was a sojourner among them.   We record their names in our pages, and pray that the *source* of all good and perfect gifts may bestow upon the *worthy* sons and daughters of those men, similar kindness in a like hour of need, and trust that they may at last go to that rest, that remaineth for the people of God.

(Copied from the original paper.)

Fearing that from continued indisposition the Rev. Mr. Wetmore may suffer some pecuniary embarrassment in a land blessed with abundance.   The subscribers request the Rev. Mr. Smith to present him the sums affixed to their names, in that manner which he may deem most acceptable to the feelings of Mr. Wetmore.

SAVANNAH, 10 March, 1802.

William Wallace,	$50,00
William Hunter,	50,00
[28] Robert Bolton,	25,00
John Bolton,	25,00
Ambrose Gordon,	10,00
Peyton Skipweth, Jr.	6,00
Joseph Clay,	50,00

[28] This Mr. Bolton was a merchant of Savannah, a grandson of Robert Bolton, Senior Warden of Christ Church, Philadelphia, 1727.   The branch of this family (says Bolton in his notice of the church in Westchester), to which Mr. Bolton (Rev. Robert Bolton) belongs, removed more than one hundred and eleven years since into Georgia, in which state his father was born A. D. 1757.   Rev. Robert Bolton, the first Rector of Christ Church, Pelham, Westchester county, and the Rev. Cornelius Winter Bolton, assistant Rector in the same church, 1847 to 1850, are sons of the first named Robert Bolton.   Robert Bolton, A. M., author of History of Westchester, and the Protestant Episcopal Church, in same county, and other works, we believe to be a grandson of Robert Bolton of Savannah.   They are a family long and favorably known in the Episcopal Church of the United States.

Descendants of Rev. James, son of Izrahiah, son of Thomas.

G. Woodruff, - - - - - -	$25,00
W. or N. V. Jones, - - - - - -	50,00
George Jones, - - - - - -	50,00
L. Kollock, - - - - - -	10,00
Philip D. Woolhopter, - - - - -	50,00
Isaac Minnis, - - - - - -	10,00
Samuel Howard, - - - - - -	10,00
Philetus Havens, - - - - - -	80,00
Benj. Brooks, - - - - - -	10,00
Gordon I. Seymour, - - - - - -	10,00
Joseph Machin, - - - - - -	10,00
From Mr. Telfair, - - - - - -	5,00
G. W. Nicholls, - - - - - -	20,00
Robert Smith, - - - - - -	80,00
	$536,00

Mrs. Jane Gidney, the wife of Rev. Robert Griffeth Wetmore, died at Rye, N. Y., Saturday, October 2, 1802, and her remains lie interred in the burial grounds of the Old Parsonage.

SIXTH GENERATION.

Children of ABRAHAM, .

Son of James.

JOSIAH, b. in Rye, Nov. 20, 1770; m. Rachel, dau. of Justus Sherwood, formerly of Cortlandt Manor, Westchester co., N. Y.; had Sally, William, Justus, Abraham, Josiah, Sarah.

At the age of 13, he removed with his father's family to New Brunswick, where he grew to manhood, much respected by the community in which he lived. He died ——.

WILLIAM, b. in Rye, Augt. 31, 1772; m. March 30, 1806, Mary, dau. of Weeden Fowler; had Weeden Fowler, Elizabeth, Isaac Sniffen, Mary, William, Sarah Craft, Deborah, Susannah,

33

Thomas Bashford, Ammon Henry, Ruth Ann, Joseph Abraham, Josiah.

He, also, removed to New Brunswick with his father in 1783, where he has ever since resided. He is, we believe, the oldest descendant now living of the Rev. James of Rye. His aunt, Mrs. Esther Puddington, being two years his junior. He may be truly called the patriarch of the family in New Brunswick.

ABRAHAM, b. Rye, 1774; d. —.

Children of JOHN,

Son of James.

ELIZABETH, b. Rye, Dec. 3, 1779; m. William Sherman in 1798.

Resided in N. B.

JAMES, b. Rye, Sept. 6, 1781; m. Susan Purdy, of Rye, Sept. 1803; had James Merritt, Stephen Purdy, John, Ann Maria, Matilda, Susanna Eliza, Edwin Jesse, Pheobe Caroline.

Resides in Carleton, St. Johns, N. B.

MARTHA VAN COTT, b. May 5, 1783.

CATHARINE, b. in N. B., Sept. 10, 1785.

JOHN, b. in N. B., Feb. 10, 1787.

Resides in Carrolton, N. B.

ANN, b. in N. B., May 31, 1788; m. —— Spring; lives in Penn.

JESSE LAMEREUX, b. in N. B., Mar. 31, 1790; m. Pheobe Clark; had Sally Ann, Catharine, Daniel, Jesse Lamereux, Pheobe, James Alexander, Joseph Clark, Catharine, Ward Chipman; William Puddington, John Saunders.

He died in 1853; resided in N. B.

DANIEL VAN COTT, b. in N. B., Nov. 13, 1791; d. about 1857.

Descendants of Rev. James, son of Izrahiah, son of Thomas.

DAVID, b. in N. B., Aug. 5, 1793; m. Deborah Saunders of Nova Scotia, Oct. 7, 1818; had Justus, James Edwin, Nathaniel Saunders, Lydia Ann, b. Feb. 16, 1824; d. Jan. 8, 1825; John Van Cott, Deborah Ann, William Nelson, Charles Enos, Elmira Jane, George Lamereux, Sarah Abigail, Elias Scovel, Susannah Elizabeth, Lydia Angeline and Emily Caroline.

Resides at Norton, King's county, N. B.

WILLIAM, b. in N. B., Sept. 4, 1795.

EDWIN, b. in N. B., April 9, 1797.

INFANT DAUGHTER, b. in N. B., May 16, 1799; d. —.

Children of IZRAHIAH,

Son of James.

NANCY, b. Jan. 21, 1783; d. June 24, 1783.

ESTHER, b. in N. B., July 9, 1784; m. April 5, 1823; Judge Justus Sherwood, son of Judge David Brown Wetmore; for her issue see under head of Justus S.

BUSH, b. in N. B., Dec. 24, 1785; m. in N. Y., Bethia Pierce, Aug. 29, 1805; had Olive Eliza, John Pierce, James, Esther Ann, Caroline, Daniel and Jane.

He died Dec. 13, 1827.

REBECCA, b. in N. B., Feb. 19, 1788; m. Feb. 12, 1806, Gabriel Merritt, at Rye, N. Y.; b. Dec. 1777; son of Josiah and Ann (Purdy) Merritt; had I *Elizabeth Wetmore*, b. Nov. 30, 1806; II *Rachel*, b. June 19, 1809; m. William Kelly, Nov. 22, 1828, and had 1, Amelia Jane, b. May 20 (died); 2, Catharine Elizabeth, b. April 22, 1831; 3, Merritt, b. Nov. 16, 1832; 4, Henry G., b. June 10, 1834; d. July 23, 1837; 5, William, b. Jan. 22, 1837; d. April 18, 1837; III *Amelia*, b. Jan. 31, 1811; m. James Henry Elting, Nov. 22, 1828; had William; IV *Izrahiah*, b. Aug. 2, 1812; d. Sept. 25, 1812; V *Esther Ann*, b. Nov. 2, 1813; VI *James D. M.*, b. May 4, 1816; VII *Edward Algar*, b. March 19, 1818; VIII *Rebecca Jane*, b. July 29, 1820; IX *Mary Montague*, b. Aug. 6, 1822; X *Gabriel*, b. Nov. 9, 1824; XI *Charles William*, b. March 21, 1827.

Mrs. Rebecca, wid. of Mr. Gabriel Merritt, resides at Marlborough, Ulster, co., N. Y. Josiah Merritt, the father of the above Mr. Gabriel Merritt, m. Ann Purdy, and had, I *Esther*, b. July 29, 1767 (dead): II *Gabriel*, b. Dec. 2, 1777; m. as above: III *Ann Carbenter*, b. Aug. 29, 1780: IV *Seth*, b. —; d. æ. 7 years: V *David*, b. —; d. æ. 7 years 6 months: VI *Josiah*, b. Dec. 2, 1783: VII *Alithea Brower*, b. July 19, 1785. Mrs. Ann Purdy d. Jan. 23, 1787; Josiah Merritt, Sen.; m. 2d Rachel Sherwood, Nov. 16, 1788. She was sister of Justus Sherwood, father of Ruth, 1st wife of Judge David Brown Wetmore.

ELIZABETH, b. in N. B., Oct. 6, 1789; m. July 12, 1828, James Wetmore Puddington, s. p.

Resides at Clifton, N. B.

ANNA, b. Sept. 21, 1791; d. Nov. 3, 1791.

JAMES BUSH, b. in N. B., Nov. 26, 1792; m. in New York, Jane, dau. of Rev. Robert Griffeth Wetmore, Dec. 21, 1816; had Robert Hodge, James Izrahiah, Abraham Kirstead Smedes, Henry Penfield, David Henry, Elizabeth Bush, John Griffeth, Charles R.; m. 2d, Isabella Smillie, Sept. 30, 1858, at Halifax, N. S.

For notice of Mrs. Jane, dau. of Rev. Robt. Griffeth W., see under proper head. Mr. Wetmore resides in Halifax, N. S.

SARAH BUSH, b. in N. B., Jan. 7, 1795; d. April 2, 1795.

INFANT SON, b. in N. B., July 9, 1796; d. July 16, 1796.

GILBERT BUSH, b. in N. B., Jan. 10, 1798; d. Jan. 20, 1798.

AMELIA, b. in N. B., Dec. 18, 1798; d. Dec. 12, 1799.

IZRAHIAH, b. in N. B., Jan. 15, 1801; m. Clorinda Porter, 1833; had Izrahiah (dead), a son, a dau.

PHEOBE, b. in N. B., May 21, 1803; m. Sept. 4, 1828, James, son of Judge David Brown Wetmore, for issue, see under proper head.

Resides at Kingston, N. B.

Children of JAMES,

Son of James.

SUSAN.

HESTER.

ELISHA.

MARY.

JOHN.

ELIZABETH.

Children of Judge DAVID BROWN,

Son of James.

Judge JUSTUS SHERWOOD, b. in Hampton, N. B., July 2, 1788; m.
April 5, 1823, his cousin, Esther, dau. of Izrahiah, son of
James Wetmore; had David, Izrahiah, Elizabeth Ruth, Mary
Ann De la Montagnie.

Resides at Clifton, Kings co., N. B. In early life
was extensively engaged in ship building. Served for
many years in the military service of the province,
holding the several offices in succession from a cornet
to major commanding 1st battalion Kings co. militia,
which latter office he still holds. About 1850, was
appointed one of the justices of the Common Pleas
Court of Kings co. Is a highly respected and much
esteemed citizen; enjoys the confidence and respect of
that branch of the Wetmore family residing in the
British provinces, where he is so well and favorably
known.

MARTHA BASHFORD, b. at Hampton, N. B., March 25, 1790; d.
May 12, 1807, at Kingston.

ELIZABETH, b. Nov. 29, 1791; m. Nov. 4, 1813, William Jewett
Flewelling of Kingston; had 8 children.

She died at Kingston, May 21, 1836.

RUTH SHERWOOD, b. in Carleton, N. B., Aug. 24, 1798; m. Sept. 3, 1826, David Pickett, of N. B.

JANE, b. in Kingston, Jan. 30, 1800; m. May 1, 1817, Joshua D. Gedney, of K.

JAMES, b. in Kingston, Oct. 29, 1801; m. at Rye, N. Y., Sept. 4, 1828, Pheobe, dau. of Izrahiah, son of James Wetmore; had William. Oliver, Justus Sherwood, Elizabeth Rebecca, Emma Olivia Miranda, Esther Pheobe Susannah, James Henry, Erasmus David Brunswick, Eliza Amelia and Sarah Ann.

DAVID, b. in Kingston, Sept. 12, 1803; m. Feb. 11, 1828, Eliza Whelpley, of K.; b. Nov. 2, 1806; had George Canning, Charlotte Annabella, Caroline Elizabeth, Mary Almira, Eliza Jane, Richard Whelpley, David Pickett, Wm. Wallace, Edwin Marshall, Charles Hiram, Agnes Lavinia, Howard Douglass, James Elias, Hannah Olive, Augustus Frederick, Celia Augusta, Julian Brunswick.

SUSANNAH CRAFT, b. in Kingston, Aug. 10, 1805; m. March 11, 1827, at Norton, N. B., George Lamereux; had —.

THOMAS, b. in Kingston, Aug. 13, 1807; m. Oct. 22, 1829, at K., Clarissa Holmes Puddington; had Esther, Elizabeth, David Brown, George Leverett, Mary Eliza Jane, William Albert, Thomas Alonzo, Oscar Avanda.

He died at Norton, Oct, 29, 1850; æ. 43.

WILLIAM PUDDINGTON, b. in. K., June 24, 1809; m. Oct. 14, 1830, at Springfield, N. B., Ruth Gillies, s. p.

HENRY SYLVANUS, b. in K., June 16, 1811; m. Feb. 17, 1833, at Hampton, N. B., Elizabeth Ann Fowler; had Mary Elizabeth, Ruth, Edwin Vail, Emeline Adela; m. 2d, Aug. 23, 1847, at Hampton, Esther Susannah Flewelling; had Helen Susannah, Gertrude, Thomas Henry Zobeiskie, John Leavitt, Herbert, Elsie Adelaide and Annie Almira (twins), David Brunswick.

ELIAS SCOVIL, b. in K., July 25, 1813; m. March 10, 1852, at Springfield, N. B., Sarah Matilda Scott; had Ada Eliza, Norman Arthur Leslie, Edward Clayton Scott.

JOHN, b. in K., July 25, 1815; d. Aug. 19, 1815.

HULDAH BUTLER, b. in K., June 17, 1816; d. at Norton, June 9, 1845.

NORTON, b. in K., Aug. 18, 1820; m. at St. Johns, March 24, 1847, Abby Caroline Morse; had Sarah Elizabeth, Charles Pembroke, Frances Caroline, George Stanton, Julia Maria, Emily Jane, Augusta Ruth, William Edmund.

Children of CALEB,

Son of James.

RUTH, b. June 5, 1794; m. Aug. 18, 1813, Benjamin F. Marsh; had Charles, John, and other chil.

Mr. Marsh was born in the state of Vermont; removed in his youth to St. Johns, where he followed mechanical pursuits; subsequently became engaged in commerce at St. Johns. About 1832 he retired from business with a competency. About the same time he returned to the states, and settled in Illinois. He purchased land to a considerable extent, we believe in the county of Hancock, near or upon the banks of the Mississippi, where he has since resided. His son Charles was a commissioned officer in the service during the war with Mexico. Soon after the peace, while out with a party of officers hunting, his gun accidently discharged its contents under one of his arms, and he died of the wound. *John* studied law, and is a practitioner. Mrs. Marsh died soon after hearing of the death of her son Charles.

JOSIAH JOSEPH, b. Dec. 25, 1795; d. Sept. 6, 1797.

JAMES, b. July 19, 1797; m. Rumah Hoyt; had William, George Lewis, Benjamin Franklin, Stephen Hoyt, Robert James, Sarah Jane, John Lockhart.

CALEB, b. March 23, 1799; m. Oct. 13, 1831, Ann, dau. of Richard Whelpley of Kings co., N. B.; had Augusta Sophia, Charles Frederick, William Walker, Caleb Newton, Charlotte Deborah, Richard Barton, Emma Caroline, Ann Adeliza, George Edwin, Alfred Brunswick.

IZRAHIAH, b. June 18, 1801; m. Elizabeth Fairweather; m. 2 Mrs. Mary Sherwood; had the following children, whether by

the first or second wife, we are unadvised, i. e. : William Caleb
West, Elias Scovil, Frances Amelia, Holland Amanda, Anna
Marsh, Catharine Deborah Jane.

He died Oct. 30, 1847.

JOSEPH, b. April 7, 1803 ; m. at St. Georges, Charlotte county, N.
B., Feb. 1831, Amy Clinch; m. 2, Sarah Clinch, Sept. 22,
1834 ; had Henrietta, Thomas Carleton, Wellesley, Josephine,
Frances Jane, Susan Henrietta, Sarah Hallett, Margaret Annabella, Robert Parker, Frances Augusta, Charlotte Annette.

ROBERT, b. April 4, 1805 ; m. in Sussex Vale, K. co., N. B., April
23, 1835, Annie Cougal (Cougle ?) ; had Oliver Cougal.

He died July 17, 1849.

MARTHA, b. May 24, 1807 ; m. at Hampton, March 16, 1825, Oliver
Hallett.

SARAH ELIZABETH, b. May 1, 1809 ; m. at Hampton, June 20,
1850, George Roberts.

MARGARET, b. Sept. 30, 1811 ; m. at H., Sept. 29, 1831, Josiah
Wetmore, son of Abraham.

DEBORAH JANE, b. Dec. 22, 1815 ; m. at H., Nov. 21, 1831, John
Lockhart ; m. 2, Feb. 17, 1848, George Flewelling.

Children of THOMAS,

Son of Timothy.

MARGARET LESTER, b. at Gagetown, Queens county, N. B., Feb. 2,
1794 ; christened in St. Johns, by the Rev. Mr. Clark, of G. ;
m. Oct. 17, 1814, the Hon. Thomas Carleton Lee ; had I
George, b. Oct. 27, 1816, was a graduate of Kings College, N.
B. ; thrice competed for and obtained the "Douglass Gold
Medal ;" studied law ; was admitted an attorney, and afterwards
called to the Bar and enrolled a Barrister, practiced with reputation and success ; was also clerk assistant of the House of
Assembly, and filled for several years, the office of counsellor
for the city of Fredericton ; m. Margaret dau. of William
B. Phair, Esq., an officer on half pay, of the 104th N. B. regt.,
and postmaster of Fredericton, by whom he had many chil. ;
he d. Sept. 12, 1849, much esteemed for ability and integrity.
II Thomas Wetmore, b. July 28, 1818 ; d. Feb. 1, 1829. III
Elizabeth Anna, b. Jan. 15, 1820 ; m. William H. Scovil Esq.,
a prominent and wealthy merchant of St. John, by whom she

has several children. IV *Frances*, b. Jan. 24, 1822; m. Rev.
William Elias Scovel, rector of Kingston, the capital of Kings
co., N. B., by whom she has many children. V *William Tyng
Peters*, b. Jan. 13, 1824; is a hardware merchant in St. Johns,
of the firm of Thorne & Lee; m. Harriet Phair, by whom he
has many children. VI *Charles*, b. Sept. 12, 1826; grad. at
Kings College, studied divinity, for many years presided as the
master of the Grammar School in Kingston; is now the rector
of the city of Fredericton; is much esteemed as a scholar and
a divine, and respected and beloved by the parishioners, among
whom he has been called to minister; m. a dau. of Henry
Bowyer Smith Esq., formerly collector and comptroller of His
Majesty's customs in St. Johns, by whom he has several chil.
VII *Sarah Peters*, b. Oct. 15, 1828; d. Jan. 16, 1839. VIII
John Head, b. Sept. 15, 1830; is a young merchant in the city
of Fredericton; unm. IX *Isabella*, b. June 13, 1833; d. Nov.
28, 1845. X *Thomas Wetmore*, b. March 18, 1835; graduate of
Kings College; succeeded his brother Charles, as master of the
Grammar School in Kingston, over which he presided for many
years; now teaches a High School in St. Johns. XI *A Son*, b.
Oct. 9, 1836; d. Oct. 24, 1836. XII *Margeret*, b. Dec. 18,
1840; d. Dec. 25, 1840.

The Hon. Thomas Carleton Lee, was appointed
receiver general of the province of New Brunswick,
Feb. 10, 1836, which office he filled with credit and
integrity to the day of his death, Aug. 31, 1859.

GEORGE LUDLOW, b. at Gagetown, Dec. 26, 1795; christened in
private, and afterwards presented in church, by Rev. Mr.
Clarke; m. Dec. 26, 1816, Harriet, dau. of Andrew Rainsford,
Esq., receiver general of N. B.; had Sarah Witter, James
Peters, Andrew Rainsford, George Ludlow Harriet.

He studied law with his father, was admitted an
attorney and enrolled a barrister; practised with great
ability and success; was appointed clerk of the House
of Assembly, was also clerk of the peace for Queens
co. He was killed in a duel with George F. Street,
Esq. (afterwards a judge of the Supreme Court), Oct.
2, 1821; was a man of much promise, if spared
would doubtless have risen to great eminence in his
profession.

34

JANE HAVILAND, b. at G., June 16, 1797 ; christened in Gagetown church, by Rev. Mr. Clarke, her parents as sponsors ; m. Nov. 6, 1826, Henry Bartlett Rainsford, Esq., son of Andrew Rainsford, receiver general ; had I *Andrew William*, b. Dec. 24, 1827 ; II *Sallie Peters*, b. Jan. 22, 1830 ; III *Eliza Baillie*, b. June 24, 1831 ; IV *Thomas Wetmore*, b. Aug. 30, 1832 ; was killed 23 Sept., 1854, at St. Johns, by the falling of a building, in which a ball was being held, in honor of the turning of the first sod of the European and North American Railway ; young in years, he was amiable, pleasing and gentlemanly in his manners, and was very generally esteemed and beloved, and his sad and tragical death was universally regretted ; V *Mary Ann*, b. March 17, 1836 ; VI *Henry Bartlett*, b. April 13, 1839 ; studied law and was recently admitted an attorney ; he possesses very much the character of his brother Thomas ; practices in Fredericton, and bids fair to rise in his profession ; holds the office of secretary and treasurer to the municipality of the county of York, of which county Fredericton is the capital ; unm.

CHARLES PETERS, b. at St. Johns, Dec. 16, 1798 ; christened in private, by Rev. Dr. Byles ; sponsors, Charles J. Peters, Esq., Valentine H. Peters and Mrs. Eliza Peters, wife of C. J. Peters, by Mrs. Horsefield, her proxy ; m. Nov. 15, 1823, Harriet Henrietta Minchin, dau. of Col. Minchin ; had infant, b. Aug. 21, 1824 ; died directly after ; Thomas George Robert Minchin ; m. 2, Oct. 29, 1830, Sarah Burr, dau. of the late Col. Ketchum ; had Thomas, Charlotte Elizabeth, Charles, Henry George Clopper, Edward Ludlow ; m. 3, Julia, daughter of the late Judge Valentine H. Peters, of Gagetown ; had infant dau. b. June, 1844 (d.) ; Julia Helen, Sarah Peters, Valentine Humboldt.

He also studied law with his father, was admitted an attorney and enrolled a barrister ; succeeded his late brother George Ludlow in the office of the House of Assembly, and was appointed Jan. 20, 1823, which office he still enjoys.   His first wife, Harriet H. Minchin, died March 22, 1828 ; his second wife, Sarah Burr Ketchum, died July, 1842.

ANN PETERS, b. at St. Johns, Tuesday, Aug. 19, 1800, noon ; christened All Saints Day, in Trinity church, St. Johns, by Rev. Dr. Byles ; sponsors, Mr. and Mrs. Horsefield ; m. Nov. 21, 1815, John Head, M. D. ; had I *Elizabeth*, b. Nov. 27,

1816, who m. the Rev. Wm. O. Ketchum, now Rector of St. Andrews, by whom she has several children; he is much respected and beloved by his parishoners. II *Emily Myers*, b. Dec. 29, 1818; d. Sept. 28, 1845. III *Sarah Wetmore*, b. June 25, 1820 ; d. Aug. 25, 1821.

Dr. Head died at St. Johns, Tuesday, March 11, 1823 ; he was much esteemed as a physician and surgeon.

SARAH, b. in St. Johns, Saturday Jan. 16, 1802; christened by the Rev. Dr. Byles, in private ; m. Aug. 7, 1819, George Pidgeon Bliss, Esq., barrister at law ; receiver general of Kings co., and son of the late Hon. John Murray Bliss, one of the judges of the Supreme Court of N. B.; he was b. 1798; and d. Jan. 20, 1836; had I *John Murray*, b. May 10, 1820 ; who after receiving a liberal education, manifested a predilection for a sea-faring life and turned his attention to that pursuit; was in the East India service ; perished in a merchantman that was lost at sea, while on a voyage to Sierra Leone, some few years ago. He was a spirited, daring, fine-hearted fellow, and destined to rise in his profession. II *Thomas Wetmore*, b. May 24, 1821; m. Aug. 20, 1851, at St. Pauls Church, Fredericton, by the Rev. Dr. Brook, Sarah Jane, 3d dau. of William Taylor, Esq., Ju. P. P., and coroner for York co.; had 1st, George William Murray, b. March 1, 1854; d. Aug. 6, 1854; 2d, Ella Maude, b. Oct. 4, 1855 ; 3d, William Taylor Ward Hatfield, b. Sept. 25, 1857; 4th, John Murray Upham, b. March 13, 1860; he grad. at Kings College; studied law; was admitted an attorney, and afterwards enrolled a barrister; practiced law for several years; appointed clerk of the peace, and keeper of the rolls for Sunbury co., which offices he resigned in 1854; removed to Kent co., and was appointed a justice of the peace, and a judge of common pleas in that co.; in March 1859, was gazetted high sheriff of Kent, which office he continues to fill. III *Sarah Jane*, b. Oct. 31, 1822 ; m. Oct. 31, 1842, Francis A. H. Stratton, Esq.. of Fredericton, barrister, register of probate for York co., and clerk of the executive council of N. B., by whom she has, 1st, John Matthew ; 2d, Sarah Isabella ; 3d, George Pidgeon Bliss; 4th, Frances Sophia Margaret; 5th, Mary Rebecca Harriet; 6th, Frank ; 7th, Barry ; 8th, James Murray ; 9th, Andrew William ; 10th, Frank 2d. IV *George Johnston*, b. Feb. 29, 1824; m. Oct. 8, 1851, Susan Mary, b. April 6, 1833, dau. of George I. Dibble Esq., barrister, and Susan Mary, dau. of Hon. Thomas Wetmore, by whom he has 1, Susan Mary, b. Sept. 8, 1852 : 2, Elizabeth Murray, b. July

26, 1854: 3, James Peters, b. Jan. 18, 1856: 4, George Samuel Thomson, b. May 31, 1858: 5, Helen, b. Sept. 16, 1860: he studied law, was admitted an attorney, and afterwards enrolled a barrister, practiced his profession at Oromocto, co. of Sunbury, where he resides; is clerk of the peace, and secretary treasurer to the municipality of said county; is also clerk assistant of the House of Assembly. V *Rev. Charles Parke*, A. M., b. July 26, 1825; m. Nov. 17, 1849, Dorothy Ann, dau. of Charles Vaughan Foster, Esq., of H. B. M. customs; had 1, George Pidgeon, b. Sept. 21, 1850: 2, Charles Vaughan Foster, b. May 12, 1853: 3, John Murray, b. Sept. 21, 1855: 4, Thomas Alder Dickson, b. June 28, 1857: 5, William Dickson, b. June 18, 1859. He is rector of Springfield, co. of Kings, where he resides; is much respected and beloved in the parish where he ministers. VI Rev. *Donald McQueen*, A. M., b. Jan. 16, 1827; m. Feb. 16, 1854, Sarah Hill, dau. of the Hon. Sir Alexander Stewart, of Halifax, N. S.; had 1, Allessandra Stewart: 2, Gerald Courtenay Wentworth; is rector of Westmoreland, N. B., and is a much esteemed and respected clergyman and citizen: VII *Sophia Isabella*, b. Oct. 26, 1828; m. William Carman, Esq., a barrister at law, and clerk of the pleas on the civil side of the Supreme Court; they reside at Fredericton. VIII *James Peters*, b. June 30, 1831; like his brother John Murray adopted a seafaring life; died 4th Nov. 1853, on the coast of Africa; he possessed very much the temperament and disposition, as well as the amiable and good qualities of his late brother. IX *Jean Hunter*, b. Nov. 15, 1832; unm. X *Henry*, b. May 25, 1834; is a farmer in the parish of Sunbury, N. B. XI *Emma Wetmore*, b. Jan. 8, 1836; m. June 7, 1857, Rev. George Goodridge Roberts, A. M., now rector of Sackville, N. B., by whom she had Charles George Douglass, b. Jan. 10, 1860.

TIMOTHY ROBERT, b. May 5, 1806, at St. Johns; christened in Trinity church, by the Rev. Dr. Byles; m. Jan. 13, 1829, Frances Sophia Margeret, eldest daughter of the late Captain John Stratton, of Her Majesty's Royal Artillery, and grand dau. of the late Andrew Phair, senior postmaster at Frederic, and half-pay officer in His Majesty's service; had Isabella Hailes, Harriet Margeret, Mary Elizabeth White, John Stratton, Charles Inglis, Frances Gustavia, Emily Myers; m. 2, Nov. 19, 1846, Mary Ann Sophia, b. Feb. 24, 1820, at Digby, N. S.; dau. of the late Wm. Franklin Bonnell, Esq.; had Anna Maria Bonnell, Thomas Medley, Sophia Maud, Emma Bedell, Susanna Grace, Margeret Lester, Jane Haviland.

He graduated at Kings College, Windsor, N. S., and

subsequently became B. C. L. of the University of Kings College, N. B., of which he is the first graduate. Studied law, was admitted an attorney and was afterwards enrolled a barrister; practiced his profession at Gagetown, the capital of Queens, of which county he is the clerk of the peace. His first wife, Frances S. M. Stratton, died at the family seat, Kingswood, near Fredericton, Oct. 2, 1840. Mr. William Franklin Bonnell was formerly a merchant, and filled with credit several important public offices in Nova Scotia.

THOMAS ALLEN, b. Saturday morning, Jan. 26, 1805, at St. Johns; christened ——, unfortunately (says the family record), this was deferred from time to time till too late, for after a week's illness, and after he was supposed to be upon the recovery, on Sunday, Sept. 22, 1805, a sudden and very unexpected change took place, and at 8½ he expired, a few minutes before the arrival of the rector, who was to have administered the sacrament of baptism; may this be an admonition not to neglect the discharge of an important duty.

SUSAN MARY, b. Friday, Oct. 3, 1806, at midnight, between that day and the 4th, at St. Johns; christened by the Rev. Dr. Byles; sponsors, Miss Mary G. White, Harry Peters, Esq., and her mother; m. June, 1829, George Jarvis Dibble, Esq., barrister and clerk of the peace of the county of York; had I *Emma Wetmore*, b. April 30, 1831; m. Wm. Tyng Peters, Esq., barrister, St. John; has several children. II *Susanna Mary*, b. March 6, 1833; m. her cousin, George I. Bliss, vide issue of Sarah, dau. of Thomas W. III *Sophia Isabella Bliss*, b. Oct. 12, 1834; m. Major Wm. Robinson of the British service; has 2 children. IV *Elizabeth Maria*, b. Feb. 12, 1836. V *Frederick Lewis*, b. Oct. 14, 1837; graduate of Kings College, profession, civil engineer. VI *Thomas Wetmore*, b. Dec. 29, 1839; graduate of Kings College, student at law. VII *Kathleen Head*, b. July 17, 1841. VIII *Grace Hailes*, b. May 8, 1843. IX *Sarah Peters*, b. Nov. 15, 1846.

Mrs. Dibble died Aug. 31, 1848, in her 42 year.

ELEANOR, b. Oct. 27, 1809, at St. Johns; christened 17 Nov., 1809, by the Rev. Mr. Roger Veats, Jr., assistant rector; sponsors, her parents and her sister Margaret.

Died Friday, May 10, 1810, after a week's illness.

EMMA, b. at St. Johns, Tuesday, Oct. 8, 1811; christened Oct. 22, by
the Rev. Mr. Veats; sponsors, her mother and sister Margaret,
and her uncle, Valentine H. Peters; m. William J., son of the
late John Bedell, Nov. 9, 1837; had I *John William*, b. Oct.
3, 1838; d. July 26, 1846. II *Alexander Rankin*, b. July 21,
1840.

Dr. THOMAS SAUNDERS, b. at Kingswood, parish of Kingsclear,
county of York, Friday, 26 Nov. 1813; m. Oct. 13, 1840,
Anna Dorathea, only dau. of the Hon. Frederick Philipse
Robinson, auditor general of the province of N. B., of
Nashwaakiss, near Frederick; had Jane Paddock.

Graduated at Kings College, N. B., in 1833, was for
some years clerk assistant of the House of Assembly
of New Brunswick. Studied medicine, and by his
own exertions and energy, he was enabled to proceed
to Scotland, in 1835, for the purpose of perfecting
himself in his profession, at the universities of Glasgow and Edinburg. He took the degree of M. D. at
Glasgow University, in 1839, and a diploma at the
Royal College of Surgeons in Edinburgh, the same
year. While in Glasgow he filled the clerkship of the
Fever Hospital and other departments of the Royal
Infirmary, in which institution he became house surgeon. He returned to New Brunswick about 1839-
40. Since which time he has been successfully engaged in his profession, in the city of St. Johns; has
been for 18 years surgeon to the Provincial Peniten-
tiary of New Brunswick, and it has been said of him
that he has conducted that institution as medical
officer without the use of mercury or bleeding; nor
has he used mercury in his private practice, 'tis said,
for 15 years.

Children of the Rev. ROBERT GRIFFETH,

Son of Timothy.

JANE, b. at Rye, Aug. 20, 1795; christened by Mr. Sands (parents
as sponsors); m. by the Rev. Dr. Rowan of New York, Dec.
21, 1816, James Bush Wetmore of Rye, son of Izrahiah, son of
James, son of Rev. James.

She died at Halifax, N. S., April 29, 1857, leaving her husband and 4 sons her survivors. (See under head of James Bush, &c.)

ABRAHAM KIRSTEAD SMEDES, Judge, b. June 6, 1802; bap. by the Rev. Evan Rogers of Rye; sponsors, the parents, Timothy Wetmore, A. K. Smedes and Esther Hunt; m. Sept. 30, 1824, Eliza, dau. of the Hon. Charles J. Peters, b. Dec. 1, 1798: had Matilda Jane, Charles Jeffery Peters, Elizabeth Baker, Robert Griffeth, Edwin, James Peters, Aldert Smedes, Jane Victoria and Henry George.

Prior to the death of Mr. Wetmore's father, Abrm K. Smedes, then a merchant of wealth in the city of New York (a gentleman who had been a sincere and devoted friend of the Rev. Robert Griffith W.), adopted the subject of this notice as his son, and from him it, will be perceived, he received his Christian names. From this noble specimen of the very best of men (now many years deceased), did Mr. W. receive his early education, and those principles which have so much contributed to the success that has attended him since that time. In 1819, Mr. Wetmore removed to the province of New Brunswick, and entered as a student the office of his uncle Thomas, the then attorney general. In 1823 was admitted an attorney of the Supreme Court, and in 1825 was called to the bar and enrolled as a barrister. In 1834 he received the appointment of clerk of the peace, and of the inferior court of Common Pleas, for the county of Carleton, where he has ever since resided. In 1850 the county of Carleton became divided into two counties, the new county known as that of Victoria. In the commissions of the peace and of the inferior court of Common Pleas for the new county, the distinguished position of senior justice was assigned to him; so that he now stands at the head of the two commissions, and has held other offices of minor importance. Is deputy provincial grand master of the grand lodge of New Brunswick. In that official capacity he had the honor of presenting the masonic address from the grand lodge to H. R. H. the Prince of Wales, in his recent visit to New Brunswick (1860). Judge Wetmore enjoys a large share of the confidence and respect of his fellow citizens, and we may add, is a worthy son of a worthy parent.

SEVENTH GENERATION.

Children of Josiah,

Son of Abraham, Son of James.

Sally.

Justus.

Abraham.

Josiah; m. at Hampton, Sept. 29, 1831, Margaret, dau. of Caleb, son of James Wetmore.

Sarah.

Children of William,

Son of Abraham, Son of James.

Weeden Fowler, b. Dec. 27, 1802; m. Mary Hatfield, Jan. 4, 1829: had Maria Thomas, Hilley Brower, Charles Henry, Samuel Bancroft, William, Fanny Hatfield, Elizabeth Ann, Emma, Joseph Hatfield, George Miles.

Resides in New Brunswick.

Elizabeth, b. May 8, 1804; m. May 7, 1837, Edward Spragg.

Resides in New Brunswick.

Issac Sniffen, b. Dec. 13, 1805; m. Jan. 12, 1855, Mary Campbell; had Emeline, Agnes Alithea, Catherine, Mary Lucretia, William Newton.

Resides in New Brunswick.

MARY, b. July 18, 1807, m. David Hatfield, Jan. 26, 1828.

She died June, 1858.

WILLIAM, b. March 25, 1809; m. June 12, 1832, Sarah Pickle; had Isaac Bashford, Weeden John, Mary Fowler, Judson Marshman, Esther Annable, Gilford Brunswick.

Resides in New Brunswick.

SARAH CRAFT, b. Dec. 30, 1812; m. Jan. 29, 1829, Charles Hughson.

Resides in New Brunswick.

DEBORAH, b. Sept. 23, 1814; m. Sept. 20, 1835, David Hatfield, Jr.

Resides in New Brunswick.

SUSANNAH, b. Oct. 23, 1816; m. March 20, 1843, Elijah Spragg.

Resides in New Brunswick.

THOMAS BASHFORD, b. Dec. 2, 1818; m. Jan. 15, 1841, Fanny Hatfield; had Lydia, Elias Gilbert, John Drake.

Resides in New Brunswick.

AMMON HENRY, b. Dec. 7, 1820; m. May 13, 1847, Mary Craft; had John Craft, Rainsford Henry, Elelia Emeline.

Resides in New Brunswick.

RUTH ANN, b. Dec. 9, 1823, m. Jan. 28, 1841, Stephen Craft.

Resides in New Brunswick.

JOSEPH ABRAHAM, b. March 23, 1826, m. July 20, 1848, Jane Mallery; had Josiah Smith, Joseph Abraham.

JOSIAH, b. July 15, 1830; m. July 10, 1855, Maria Smith; had Phœbe Alice, Mary Allova.

Children of JAMES,

Son of John, Son of James.

JAMES MERRITT, b. June 3, 1804; m. May 1, 1834, Rebecca Eliza Davison; had Oscar Davison, James Purdy Merritt, Elizabeth Lavinia Robertson, William Benjamin, Henry Alline, Frederick, Robert Purdy, Harriet Rebecca Merritt.

35

He died in Portland, St. Johns, N. B., July 18, 1850.

STEPHEN PURDY, b Nov. 9, 1806; m. Sarah Byles Littlehale of Carleton, N. B.; had Edwin Jesse, Susannah Elizabeth, Joseph Sherwood, Sarah Louisa, James, Francis Peters, Amelia Frances, Ann Littlehale, Stephen Merritt.

JOHN, b. Jan. 5' 1810; m. Margaret Flewelling.

ANN MARIA, b. Jan. 12, 1813'; m. Joseph H. Littlehale.

MATILDA, b. May 14, 1815; m. John H. Flewelling.

SUSANNAH ELIZA, b. Oct. 8, 1818; m. William Puddington Flewelling of Kingston, N. B.

He died November 9, 1835.

EDWIN JESSE, b. March 17, 1821; d. Jan. 10, 1825.

PHEOBE CAROLINE, b. Aug. 6, 1823; m. Hiram H. DeForest of Norton, N. B.

She died Nov. 29, 1857.

Children of JESSE LAMEREUX,

Son of John, Son of James.

SALLY ANN, b. July 30, 1816.

CATHERINE, b. Aug. 8, 1818.

DANIEL, b. April 8, 1820.

Resides in Liverpool, England.

JESSE LAMEREUX, b. Oct. 20, 1821; m. Matilda Hanmer.

Removed to San Francisco, California.

PHEOBE, b. April 14, 1823; m. Isaac O. Beatteay of Carleton, N. B.

JAMES ALEXANDER, b. July 3, 1825.

Resides in California.

JOSEPH CLARK, b. June 25, 1827; d. July 22, 1827.

CATHERINE, b. Sept. 20, 1828; m. James Beatteay of Carleton, N. B.

WARD CHIPMAN, b. June 25, 1830.

Resides in California.

WILLIAM PUDDINGTON, b. June 9, 1832.

JOHN SAUNDERS, b. May 8, 1834; died ——.

Children of DAVID,

Son of John, Son of James.

JUSTUS, b. in Norton, N. B., March 17, 1820; m. Jan. 31, 1845, Harriet Caroline Flewelling, of Kingston, N. B.; had Anna Elizabeth, Adino Paddock, George Beverly Bunyeat, Edna Charlotte Elting.

Resides in N. B.

JAMES EDWIN, b. in Norton, N. B., Aug. 18, 1821; m. in Boston, Mass., Maria Pickell; had Charles Frank, and others.

Resides in Westfield, Mass.

NATHANIEL SAUNDERS, b. in Norton, Oct. 16, 1822; m. in St. Johns, Mary Anderson; had Arthur Wellington, Herbert, Elizabeth, Alice.

Resides in Halifax, N. S.

LYDIA ANN, b. in N., April 14, 1824; d. Jan. 8, 1825.

JOHN VAN COTT, b. in Norton, April 14, 1825; m. June 30, 1853, Mary Puddington Flewelling; had Edwin Trevelyan, Charlotte Estella.

DEBORAH ANN, b. in N., Aug. 18, 1826; m. Dec. ——, Thomas Kierstead, of Hampton, N. B.; had several children.

WILLIAM NELSON, b. in N., March 26, 1828; m. May 23, 1855, Mary Conley, of New York, s. p.

Resides in California.

CHARLES ENOS, b. in N., July 17, 1829; m. May 19, 1859, Margerette ——.

Resides in Norton.

ELMIRA JANE, b. in N., Dec. 1, 1830 ; m. Dec., 1856, John Bentley Flewelling, of Kingston ; had 2 or 3 children.

GEORGE LAMEREUX, b. in N., July 15, 1832; m. Feb. 14, 1858, Martha P. Stratton, of Cincinnati, Ohio ; has George Melville.
Resides in Cincinnati.

SARAH ABIGAIL, b. in N., March 29, 1834; m. May 25, 1855, Samuel Whitney Saunders, s. p.

ELIAS SCOVIL, b. Jan. 22, 1836 ; unm.
Resides at Clifton, N. B.

SUSANNAH ELIZABETH, b. in N., Sept. 18, 1838 ; m. Charles Douglass Fairweather, of Norton, June 22, 1858 ; has Jessie.

LYDIA ANGELINE, b. in N., Nov. 25, 1840.
EMILY CAROLINE, b. in N., Feb. 5, 1845.

Children of BUSH,

Son of Izrahiah, Son of James.

OLIVE ELIZA, b. June 20, 1806.

JOHN PIERCE, b. Nov. 1, 1808.

JAMES, b. Dec. 11, 1816.

ESTHER ANN, b. July 31, 1818 ; d. April 2, 1826.

CAROLINE, b. Nov. 4, 1821 ; d. Nov. 6, 1826.

DANIEL, b. July 13, 1824.

JANE, b. Nov. 7, 1826.

Children of JAMES BUSH,

Son of Izrahiah, Son of James.

ROBERT HODGE, b. in New York city, Jan. 14, 1818; m. in New York, May 29, 1841, Eliza Laura Aylward ; b. in Waterford, Ireland ; she died in Halifax, N. S., June 21, 1846, leaving Butler Joseph, Frederick Robert; m. 2d, in Charlestown, Mass., April 20, 1853, Ann Proven Paul; b. in Aberdeen,

Scotland; had Paul Lessel, Henry Dunstan, James Alexander, John Griffeth.

Resides in Halifax, N. S.

JAMES IZRAHIAH, b. Oct. 20, 1819, in Marlborough, Ulster county, New York; m. in St. Johns, N. B., Warty Jane Dunstan, 1848; had son; dead.

Resides Frankfort, Me.

ABRAHAM KIERSTEAD SMEDES, Jr., b. Jan. 30, 1821; d. May 3, 1826.

HENRY PENFIELD, b. Oct. 30, 1822; d. July 12, 1823.

DAVID HENRY, b. Jan. 16, 1824; d. July, 1825.

ELIZABETH BUSH, b. Jan. 25, 1826; d. April 11, 1827.

JOHN GRIFFETH, b. in New York June 27, 1828; m. Frances Poad Drake, in Halifax, March 11, 1853; had 2 sons and 3 daughters..

CHARLES RAPELYEA, b. Oct. Oct. 27, 1831; m. April 27, 1859, Catherine May of Halifax; has a daughter.

Children of IZRAHIAH,

Son of Izrahiah, Son of James.

IZRAHIAH.

A SON.

A DAUGHTER.

Children of Judge JUSTUS SHERWOOD,

Son of Judge David Brown, Son of James.

Rev. DAVID IZRAHIAH, b. in Kingston, N. B., April 23, 1824; m. at Gagetown, N. B., Sept. 3, 1853, Harriet Margaret, dau. of Timothy Robert, son of Thomas, son of Timothy Wetmore; had Frances Sophia, Margaret Stratton, Justus Sherwood.

He matriculated at Kings College, Windsor, N. S., June 24, 1840. The degree of A. B. was conferred upon him, April 23, 1845. Studied divinity, and was ordained by the Right Rev. John Medley, Lord Bishop of Fredericton, March 15, 1848. Stationed at Weldford, N. B., the following month. Removed to Kingston in the spring of 1859, and took charge of the grammar school in that city.

ELIZABETH RUTH, b. in K. Oct. 5, 1825; m. Feb. 26, 1846, at Kingston, Edwin Pentreath of Penzance, Cornwall, England.

MARY ANN DE LA MONTAGNIE, b. in K. July 30, 1827.

Children of JAMES.

Son of Judge David Brown, Son of James.

WILLIAM OLIVE, b. in Kingston, June 24, 1829; d. June 25, 1829.

JUSTUS SHERWOOD, b. in Kingston, Aug. 21, 1850.

ELIZABETH, b. in Kingston, Dec. 12, 1832.

EMMA OLIVIA MIRANDA, b. in Kingston, Aug. 23, 1834; d. Jan. 25, 1836.

ESTHER PHEOBE SUSANNAH, b. in Kingston, Jan. 19, 1836.

JAMES HENRY, b. in Kingston, April 24, 1838.

ERASMUS DAVID BRUNSWICK, b. in K., April 8, 1840.

ELIZA AMELIA, b. in K., Oct. 20, 1842; d. April 7, 1848.

SARAH ANN, b. in K., Dec. 1, 1844.

Children of DAVID,

Son of Judge David Brown, Son of James.

GEORGE CANNING, b. in Kingston, Dec., 1828; m. in K., Feb. 28, 1855, Hannah Eliza Puddington; had Percy Colebrook, George Elmer, Edmund Stanley.

Resides in Kingston, N. B.

CHAROTTE ANNABELLA, b. in K., March 21, 1830; d. in K., Feb. 18, 1851.

Descendants of Rev. James, son of Izrahiah, son of Thomas.

CAROLINE ELIZABETH, b. in K., March 5, 1831.

MARY ALMIRA, b. in K., July 16, 1832.

ELIZA JANE, b. in K., Oct. 10, 1833; m. Jan. 1861, Edmund, son of David W., son of William and Esther (Wetmore) Puddington.

RICHARD WHELPLEY, b. in K., Dec. 28, 1834; m. Charlotte, dau. of Margaret J. G. and Wm. T. Flewelling, Jan. 25, 1861.

DAVID PICKETT, b. in K., May 9; 1836.

WILLIAM WALLACE, b, in K., May 20, 1837.

EDWIN MARSHALL, b. in K., July 6, 1838.

CHARLES HIRAM, b. in K., July 11, 1839; d. Sept. 10, 1839.

AGNES LAVINIA, b. in K., Oct. 25, 1840.

HOWARD DOUGLASS, b. in K., Nov. 19, 1841.

JAMES ELIAS, b. in K., Nov. 27, 1842.

HANNAH OLIVE, b. in K., Jan. 6, 1844.

AUGUSTUS FREDERICK, b. in K., April 7, 1845; d. July 12, 1845.

CELIA AUGUSTA, b. in K., May 1, 1846.

JULIAN BRUNSWICK, b. in K., May 25, 1847.

Children of THOMAS,

Son of Judge David Brown, Son of James.

ESTHER ELIZABETH, b. in Norton, N. B., August 25, 1830.

DAVID BROWN, b. in Norton, N. B., Feb. 12, 1833.

GEORGE LEVERETT, b. in Norton, N. B., Oct. 21, 1835; d. May 6, 1856.

MARY ELIZA JANE, b. in Norton, N. B., Dec. 19, 1837.

WILLIAM ALBERT, b. in Norton, N. B., June 16, 1840.

THOMAS ALONZO, b. in Norton, N. B., July 13, 1842.

OSCAR AVANDA, b. in Norton, N. B., Nov. 7, 1847.

Children of HENRY SYLVANUS,

Son of Judge David Brown, Son of James.

MARY ELIZABETH, b. in Norton, N. B., April 16, 1836; d. Jan. 24, 1845.

RUTH, b. in Norton, N. B., April 6, 1839.

EDWIN VALE, b. in Norton, N. B., April 20, 1841.

EMELINE ADELA, b. in Norton, N. B., May 10, 1843.

HELEN SUSANNAH, b. in Norton, N. B., July 25, 1848.

GERTRUDE, b. in Norton, N. B., April 4, 1850.

THOMAS HENRY ZOBEISKIE, b. in Norton, N. B., Oct. 17, 1851.

JOHN LEAVITT, b. in Norton, N. B., Nov. 8, 1853.

HERBERT, b. in Norton, N. B., June 18, 1855; d. Dec. 6, 1856.

ELSIE ADELAIDE, b. in Norton, N. B., May 15, 1857. } Twins.
ANNA ALMIRA, b. in Norton, N. B., May 17, 1857. }

DAVID BRUNSWICK, b. in Norton, N. B., April 13, 1859.

Children of ELIAS SCOVIL,

Son of Judge David Brown, Son of James.

ADA ELIZA, b. in Norton, Jan. 24, 1853.

NORMAN ARTHUR LESLIE, b. in N., Sept. 13, 1855.

EDWARD CLAYTON SCOTT, b. in N., Jan. 7, 1859.

Children of NORTON,

Son of Judge David Brown, Son of James.

SARAH ELIZABETH, b. in Norton, Jan. 6, 1848.

CHARLES PEMBROKE, b. in N., May 22, 1849.

FRANCES CAROLINE, b. in N., Nov. 13, 1850.

GEORGE STANTON, b. in N., April 11, 1852.

JULIA MARIA, b. in N., Dec. 17, 1853.

EMILY JANE, b. in N., July 3, 1855.

AUGUSTA RUTH, b. in N., April 3, 1857.

WILLIAM EDMUND, b. N., July 10, 1858.

Children of JAMES,

Son of Caleb, Son of James,

WILLIAM, b. — (dead).

GEORGE LEWIS.

BENJAMIN FRANKLIN.

STEPHEN HOYT.

ROBERT JAMES.

SARAH JANE.

JOHN LOCKHART.

Children of CALEB,

Son of Caleb, Son of James.

AUGUSTA SOPHIA, b. Aug. 7, 1832; d. April 13, 1854.

CHARLES FREDERICK, b. June 26, 1833.

Resides in New York city.

WILLIAM WALKER, b. June 8, 1834; d. Aug. 1, 1854.

CALEB NEWTON, b. June 16, 1835.

CHARLOTTE DEBORAH, b. Aug. 8, 1836; d. Aug. 18, 1837.

RICHARD BARTON, b. Feb. 9, 1838; d. Oct. 18, 1838.

EMMA CAROLINE, b. July 19, 1839.

ANN ADELIZA, b. Jan. 3, 1843.

GEORGE EDWIN, b. July 13, 1844; d. Sept. 13, 1844.

ALFRED BRUNSWICK, b. March 10, 1846.

Children of IZRAHIAH,

Son of Caleb, Son of James.

WILLIAM.

Resides in Iowa.

CALEB WEST.

Resides in Fredericton, N. B.

ELIAS SCOVIL.

Resides in New Orleans, La.

FRANCES AMELIA.

HOLLAND AMANDA.

ANNA MARSH.

CATHERINE DEBORAH JANE.

Children of JOSEPH,

Son of Caleb, Son of James.

HENRIETTA, b. March 10, 1835; d. March 25, 1844.

THOMAS CARLETON, b. Feb. 15, 1837.

WELLESLEY, b. May 9, 1839; d. April 5, 1840,

JOSEPHINE, b. March 29, 1841.

FRANCES JANE, b. Aug. 13, 1842; d. March 10, 1848.

SUSAN HENRIETTA, b. March 28, 1844; d. Sept. 5, 1844.

SARAH HALLETT, b. April 24, 1845.

MARGARET ANNABELLA, b. April 19, 1846; d. Sept. 3, 1847.

ROBERT PARKER, b. June 3, 1849.

FRANCES AUGUSTA, b. July 20 (26?), 1851.

CHARLOTTE ANNETTE, b. Nov. 28, 1854.

Son of ROBERT,

Son of Caleb, Son of James.

OLIVER COUGAL.

Children of GEORGE LUDLOW,

Son of Thomas, Son of Timothy.

SARAH WITTER, b. Nov. 22, 1817 ; m. Rev. John Black, rector of Kingsclear county, York, by whom she has a large family of children.

JAMES PETERS, b. March 21, 1819.

Studied law; was admitted an attorney and enrolled a barrister. Practises his profession at Fredericton, N. B. Is reputed a lawyer of excellent abilities.

ANDREW RAINSFORD, b. Aug. 16, 1820 ; m. Louisa, dau. of the late Thomas Lansdowne, Esq., high sheriff of the county of Kent, by whom he has Sarah, George, Louisa, Francis.

He studied law; was admitted an attorney and enrolled a barrister. Resides at St. Johns, where he practises with much ability and success. Has recently received the distinguished honor of being appointed a "Queen's Counsel."

GEORGE LUDLOW HARRIET, b. Oct. 29, 1821 ; m. Dr. Jasper Murphy, by whom she has many children.

They reside at Fredericton, N. B., where he practises, and is alike esteemed for his gentlemanly bearing as for skill in his profession.

Children of CHARLES PETERS,

Son of Thomas, Son of Timothy.

INFANT, b. Aug. 21, 1824 ; d. same day.

THOMAS, b. March 18, 1826 ; d. Sept. 18, 1828.

Descendants of Rev. James, son of Izrahiah, son of Thomas.

GEORGE ROBERT MINCHIN, b. June 2, 1827 ; d. 1851; killed by accidental discharge of a gun.

THOMAS, 2d, b. 1831; d. Oct. 1835.

CHARLOTTE ELIZABETH, b. May 14, 1834 ; d. May 8, 1856, by explosion of steamboat on river St. Johns; she was married to Thomas M. Johnston, Esq. (son of Hon. Hugh Johnston), who was drowned in the same river in 1858, while driving with his wife's sister, the horse running off the bank.

CHARLES, b. Sept. 1835; d. Oct. 1835.

HENRY GEORGE CLOPPER, b. March 17, 1837.

EDWARD LUDLOW, b. March 24, 1841.

INFANT (dau.) ; b. June 1844; died.

JULIA HELEN, b. Aug. 30, 1845; d. Feb. 18, 1846.

SARAH PETERS, b. Jan. 15, 1847.

VALENTINE HUMBOLDT, b. Sept. 1, 1848.

Children of TIMOTHY ROBERT,

Son of Thomas, Son of Timothy.

ISABELLA HAILES, b. at Fredericton, May 15, 1830 ; m. Jan. 12, 1850, Henry William Woodforde Plant, Esq., deputy commissary general of N. B.; now stationed at Quebec, Canada.

HARRIET MARGARET, b. at Gagetown, Nov. 19, 1831 ; m. Rev. David Izrahiah, son of Judge Justus Sherwood Wetmore. For issue of this marriage see under proper head.

MARY ELIZABETH WHITE, b. at Gagetown, Aug. 25, 1833 ; m. Jan. 10, 1861, at St. John's Church, Gagetown, John Head Lee, Esq.

JOHN STRATTON, b. May 11, 1834 ; d. Dec. 13, 1836.

CHARLES INGLIS, b. at G., Aug. 19, 1835.

FRANCES GUSTAVIA, b. at G.. June 9, 1837 ; m. John Lyster, Esq., June 9, 1860.

EMILY MYERS, b. at G., Sept. 26, 1838.

ANNA MARIA BONNELL, b. at Gagetown, N. B., Aug. 13, 1847.

THOMAS MEDLEY, b. Nov. 16, 1848, at Gagetown.

SOPHIA MAUDE, b. Jan. 19, 1850, at Gagetown.

EMMA BEDELL, b. Aug. 20, 1851, at Gagetown.

SUSANNA GRACE, b. April 20, 1853, at Gagetown.

MARGARET LESTER, b. June 15, 1855, at Gagetown.

JANE HAVILAND, b. July 15, 1859, at Gagetown.

Daughter of Dr. THOMAS SAUNDERS,

Son of Thomas, Son of Timothy.

JANE PADDOCK, b. Nov. 18, 1841; baptized in cathedral of Fredericton, by venerable Arch-deacon Coster, Feb. 1842; confirmed by bishop of Fredericton.

Children of Judge ABRAHAM K. SMEDES,

Son of Rev. Robert Griffeth, Son of Timothy.

MATILDA JANE, b. Aug. 14, 1825; d. Sept. 4, 1825.

CHARLES JEFFERY PETERS, b. Feb. 12, 1827; m. Sarah Jane Gidney; had Eliza Jane, Helen Louisa, Anne.

ELIZABETH BAKER, b. Dec. 8, 1829; m. Charles Harding English; had I *Richard Smedes*, b. March 31, 1853; d. July 28, 1854. II *Maud Marian*, b. July 12, 1855.

ROBERT GRIFFETH, b. Oct. 5, 1831.

EDWIN, b. Sept. 16, 1833; d. Oct. 13, 1833.

JAMES PETERS, b. March 31, 1835.

ALDERT SMEDES, b. June 10, 1836; d. Nov. 16, 1836.

JANE VICTORIA, b. Nov. 8, 1839; d. June 26, 1840.

HENRY GEORGE, b. Oct. 11, 1840.

EIGHTH GENERATION.

Children of WEEDEN FOWLER,

Son of William, Son of Abraham, Son of James.

MARIA THOMAS, b. Oct. 30, 1829 ; m. July 15, 1852, Israel Noble.

HILLEY BROWER, b. Sept. 13, 1833.

CHARLES HENRY, b. July 22, 1835 ; m. Jan. 25, 1859, Mary Davis.

SAMUEL BANCROFT, b. Jan. 18, 1838.

WILLIAM, b. April 30, 1841.

FANNY HATFIELD, b. Oct. 5, 1843.

ELIZABETH ANN, b. July 24, 1846.

EMMA, b. Sept. 26, 1848.

JOSEPH HATFIELD, b. Aug. 29, 1851.

GEORGE MILES, b. Jan. 22, 1854.

Children of ISAAC SNIFFEN,

Son of William, Son of Abraham, Son of James.

EMELINE, b. Dec. 20, 1843.

AGNES ALITHEA, b. Oct., 1845.

CATHARINE, b. June 6, 1848.

MARY LUCRETIA, b. May, 1852.

WILLIAM NEWTON, b. March, 1858.

Children of THOMAS BASHFORD,

Son of William, Son of Abraham, Son of James.

LYDIA, b. Dec., 1841.

ELIAS GILBERT, b. Dec., 1852.

JOHN DRAKE, b. May, 1857.

Children of AMMON HENRY,

Son of William, Son of Abraham, Son of James.

JOHN CRAFT, b. April, 1848.

RAINSFORD HENRY, b. Nov. 1856.

ELELIA EMELINE, b. Oct. 1858.

Children of JOSEPH ABRAHAM,

Son of William, Son of Abraham, Son of James.

JOSHUA SMITH, b. Sept. 1853.

JOSEPH ABRAHAM, b. Oct. 1855,

Children of JOSIAH,

Son of William, Son of Abraham, Son of James.

PHEOBE ALICE, b. June, 1857.

MARY ALLOVA, b. July, 1859.

Children of JAMES MERRITT,

Son of James, Son of John, Son of James.

OSCAR DAVIDSON, b. Feb. 18, 1835; m. Feb. 18, 1857, Janet Ann Hutchinson Stevens; has Maud Doulass, also son.

JAMES PURDY MERRITT, b. Feb. 8, 1857; d. Sept. 28, 1857.

ELIZABETH LAVINIA ROBERTSON, b. Feb. 3, 1839.

WILLIAM BENJAMIN, b. July 15, 1841.

HENRY ALLINE, b. Sept. 20, 1843; d. Aug. 13, 1846.

FREDERICK, b. Nov. 6, 1846; d. Jan. 24, 1860.

ROBERT PURDY, b. Nov. 6, 1848.

HARRIET REBECCA MERRITT, b. March 12, 1851; d. Oct. 19, 1851.

Children of STEPHEN PURDY,

Son of James, Son of John, Son of James.

EDWIN JESSE, b. July 1, 1829; m. April 29, 1851, Margeret Drake; had Walter Drake.

SUSANNAH ELIZABETH, b. Nov. 20, 1831; m. Thomas E. Streak.

JOSEPH SHERWOOD, b. March 4, 1834; m. Dec. 20, 1856, Charlotte M. Tilley; had Sarah, James Quinton.

SARAH LOUISA, b. Sept. 23, 1836; m. Edward J. Dennett.

JAMES, b. July 26, 1839.

FRANCIS PETERS, b. April 2, 1843; d. April 10, 1844.

AMELIA FRANCES, b. March 17, 1845; d. Nov. 12, 1846.

ANN LITTLEHALE, b. Aug. 31, 1847.

STEPHEN MERRITT, b. May 24, 1851.

Children of JUSTUS,

Son of David, Son of John, Son of James.

ANN ELIZABETH, b. Nov. 1, 1847.

ADINO PADDOCK, b. Aug. 28, 1853.

GEORGE BEVERLY BUNYEAT, b. Aug. 17, 1857.

EDNA CHARLOTTE ELTING, b. July 16, 1859.

Children of JAMES EDWIN,

Son of David, Son of John, Son of James.

MARIA PICKETT.

CHARLES.

FRANK, and others.

Children of NATHANIEL SAUNDERS,

Son of David, Son of John, Son of James.

ARTHUR WELLINGTON.

HERBERT.

ELIZABETH.

ALICE.

Children of JOHN VAN COTT,

Son of David, Son of John, Son of James.

EDWARD TREVELYAN, b. Aug. 8, 1856.

CHARLOTTE ESTELLA, b. May 22, 1859.

Children of GEORGE LAMEREUX,

Son of David, Son of John, Son of James.

GEORGE MELVILLE, b. in Cincinnati, Ohio, July 10, 1859.

Children of ROBERT HODGE,

Son of James Bush, Son of Izrahiah, Son of James.

BUTLER JOSEPH, b. in Kingston, N. B. Oct. 4, 1842.

FREDERICK ROBERT, b. Halifax, N. S., Jan. 13, 1845.

PAUL LESSEL, b. Feb. 9, 1854.

HENRY DUNSTAN, b. Nov. 1, 1855.

JAMES ALEXANDER, b. May 9, 1857; d. Nov. 4, 1859.

JOHN GRIFFETH, b. Nov. 20, 1859.

Children of Rev. DAVID IZRAHIAH,

Son of Judge Justus Sherwood, Son of Judge David Brown, Son of James.

FRANCES MARIA MARGERETTA STRATTON, b. July 4, 1854.

JUSTUS SHERWOOD, b. June 3, 1856.

Children of GEORGE CANNING,

Son of David, Son of Judge David Brown, Son of James.

PERCY COLEBROOK, b. Jan. 1, 1856.

GEORGE ELMER, b. Feb. 22, 1857.

EDMUND STANLEY, b. Jan. 31, 1859.

Children of CHARLES JEFFERY PETERS,

Son of Judge Abraham K. Smedes, Son of Rev. Robert Griffeth, Son of Timothy.

ELIZA JANE, b. Jan. 31, 1855.

HELEN LOUISA, b. Feb. 5, 1857.

ANNE, b. 1859.

Children of ANDREW RAINSFORD,

Son of George Ludlow, Son of Thomas, Son of Timothy.

GEORGE.

SARAH.

LOUISA.

FRANCES.

NINTH GENERATION.

Children of OSCAR DAVIDSON,

Son of James Merritt, Son of James, Son of John, Son of James.

MAUD DOUGLASS, b. Dec. 1, 1857.

INFANT SON, b. Feb. 26, 1859; d. March 12, 1859.

Son of EDWIN JESSE,

Son of Edwin Purdy, Son of James, Son of John, Son of James.

WALTER DRAKE, b. Feb. 21, 1859.

Children of JOSEPH SHERWOOD,

Son of Stephen Purdy, Son of James, Son of John, Son of James.

SARAH, b. Oct 22, 1857.

JAMES QUINTON, b. Nov. 28, 1858.

JUDGE SETH, SON OF IZRAHIAH, SON OF THOMAS,·
AND HIS DESCENDANTS.

THIRD GENERATION.

JUDGE SETH WETMORE,

Was the fifth son of Izrahiah and Rachel (Stow) Whitmore, born in Middletown, Ct., November 18, 1700 (o. s). He married 1, Margaret, widow of S. Gaylord, September 30, 1730. She died the sixth of November following. He married 2d, Hannah, daughter of Joseph[1], son of Francis[2], of Middletown ; son of Francis Whitmore, of Cambridge, Mass. ; born Dec. 25, 1715, by whom he had Jerusha and Seth. She died May 1, 1744, and he married 3, January 15, 1745–6, Hannah, daughter of the Rev. Timothy and Esther (Stoddard) Edwards, of East Windsor ; born February 8, 1713, and had born to him Lucy, Oliver and Hannah.

Of the early history of Judge Wetmore, we are ignorant. At what institution, or from whence he received his education, we have been unable to discover, further than that he studied law, and became a lawyer by profession, and that he was celebrated as a practitioner in his time. He was a deputy to the General Court of Connecticut from his native town, forty-eight terms, running from 1738 to 1771 ; magistrate of the

[1] Joseph Whitmore, b. Aug., 1687.
[2] Francis, Jr., b. Oct. 12, 1650; m. Hannah Harris, of Middletown, Feb. 8, 1674. Record of descendants of Francis Whitmore, of Cambridge, by William H. Whitmore, Boston, 1855.

town of Middletown; judge of the County Court of of Hartford county; he (together with Jabez Hamlin), was Justice of the Quorum for the same county, from 1761 to 1768. He was reputed a stern man, and had great reverence for all lawful enactments, and desired to see them obeyed by every citizen. It was unlawful in Connecticut in colonial times, as the reader is no doubt aware, to perform any out-door labor, or to travel on Sunday. The Sabbath was considered to have commenced at the going down of the sun on Saturday. On one occasion, the Judge had been attending court at the town of Meriden, and was returning home, on horseback on Saturday afternoon, and when within about three miles of his residence, the sun having sunk beneath the horizon, he spied a man chopping wood; he stopped his horse, and addressing the man, said: "Friend, do you not know that you are breaking the Sabbath?" "Oh, well," replied the wood chopper, "I guess I shall get through chopping my wood, by the time Judge Wetmore gets home."

At one time while riding in the main street of Middletown, he was met by a "hog howard," who stopped his horse, and said: "Judge Wetmore, I command you in the name of King George the Third, to get down from your horse, and help me to drive these hogs to pound." The judge could scarcely maintain his gravity, while he paid the howard to procure a substitute, to aid him in the performance of his duty.

Further, to illustrate the peculiarities of the times of our ancestors, as well as to relieve our pages of heaviness, we give the following amusing anecdote, which we received as we did the one just related, from a grand-daughter of Judge Wetmore.

It was the custom of Jonathan (son of President Edwards), subsequently president of Union College (Schenectady), and Timothy Dwight, afterwards president of Yale College (the former a nephew and the

latter a grand nephew of Mrs. Wetmore), to visit
"Staddle Hill" (the residence of Judge W.) during the
college vacations. They were not inclined to observe
strictly the custom of keeping Saturday night; and on
one occasion they proposed a plan to escape the vigil-
ance of the judge, and pay a visit to some young
ladies, living in the neighborhood. The supper for
Saturday night was invariably "hasty pudding" and
milk, for host, guest and servant. The pudding
was boiling in an enormous kettle, such as the old
fashioned, capacious kitchen fire places of those days
alone could hold. But the young men were impatient, stole into the kitchen (where the old negress
"Membo" was the acknowledged mistress). Calling,
in an undertone, "Membo, Membo, wont you give us
our supper?" and then admitted her to their confidence. "De Lor bress you," says Membo, "de hasy
puddin not done." "Never mind" (they replied),
"we will eat it," and into the pantry they went, and
brought out two large pewter plates, as bright as
silver, and with the ladles which they had provided
themselves with, they commenced dipping the pudding from the kettle. According to the custom of the
time, they were dressed in short breeches, with long
silk stockings and low-quartered shoes. Membo stood
aside, quite grieved, that her authority was so un-
ceremoniously interfered with, and particularly, to
see her young favorites helping themselves. "Now!
massa Ed'ards. Now! massa Dwight, see what you
gone and done." They had both dropped the boiling,
tenacious pudding upon their silk hose, and were
dancing around the floor with pain their impatience
had caused them. Membo assisted them in removing
the pudding, and applied a remedy to their burns, at
the same time giving them a lecture upon being in a
hurry, and the impropriety and sin of "gowin to see
de girls on Saturday night, de beginnin ob de Lor's

day." We trust the reverence the reader may have for Drs. Edwards and Dwight may not be lessened by this story of their "youthful indiscretion."

The judge would occasionally take the place of "tidings man" in church—a person appointed to look after the mischievous children, and would sometimes have a row of badly behaved boys arranged along upon the "deacons' bench" under the pulpit, to which they all had to march and face the congregation when they did not conduct properly. The boys were very shy of Judge Wetmore, but often got caught notwithstanding. Though rigid he was not forbidding, but tender and affectionate. His reverence and love of order and the rights of others constrained him to be ever respectful and courteous to those with whom he had intercourse, and expected the same in return. Among his professional brethren he had a commanding influence; he was respected for his talent as well as for his unbending integrity. As a Christian man he was foremost in all good works. His wife's nephews, Pierrepont Edwards and Aaron Burr, were members of his family and studied law under him. He acquired a large *personal* property, chiefly by his profession, having inherited much of his *real* estate. Slavery being recognized at that time in the colony he held slaves;[3] tradition says that he emancipated them, leaving each some property; this we think not entirely correct, for we have been informed by his grandson, Josiah Wetmore, and his grandaughter, Mrs. Clarissa Dodge, that his daughter, Mrs. Lucy Whittlesey, and his son, Deacon Oliver, held servants that had been bequeathed to them by their father, and that *they*, subsequently, enfranchised them. Membo, heretofore named, fell to Mrs. Whittlesey. Some of Membo's descendants live, or were living, not long since, in a small house on the left of the road leading from Staddle Hill to the city, and

[3] Slavery was abolished in Connecticut in 1784.

others live in different parts of the town, and are useful and respected in their sphere.

Judge W. resided, during the last half of his life on
his farm at Staddle Hill, near Middletown. The two
story double mansion, which he erected in 1746, is still
standing. The house and grounds are now owned and
occupied by his grandson, Chauncey Wetmore, Esq.,
and the widow of his grandson, Elisha Wetmore. He
died April 10th, 1778. His remains rest in the old
grave yard west of the city. A flat, brown free stone
slab, horizontally elevated some three feet above the
ground, and supported by six columns, marks the spot.
The following is a copy of the inscription upon the
stone, written by his pastor, the Rev. Enoch Huntington.

> "In memory of SETH WETMORE, Esq
> Who died of the small pox.
> April 10th A. D. 1778, Æ 78.
> Formed for public usefulness improved in various
> stations of civil life, an able Lawyer, a just
> judge, an affectionate head of his family,
> a faithful friend; having outlived most
> of his acquaintance of early life, was gathered
> to his Fathers in a good old age."

The same stone has also inscribed upon it,

> "In memory of
> HANNAH wife of Seth Wetmore Esq
> and daughtr of the Revd Timo.
> Edwards of Windsor who died
> June 1st A. D. 1773 Æ. 61."

> "In memory of
> HANNAH wife of
> Seth Wetmore Esqr
> who died, May 1st
> A D 1744."

> "Here dearest friends their kindred ashes blend,
> Clasped in the arms of death till time shall end;
> Then shall they rise and stand before the Lord,
> And ev'ry virtue meet a just reward."

Mr. Wetmore's second wife, Hannah Whitmore's
mother, was a Mary Warner, a descendant of the
family of that name, who were among the first settlers
and proprietors of Middletown. Note B. to Dr.

Field's address, says : " Andrew, Robert and John Warner, were sons of Andrew Warner, who emigrated from Hatfield, Eng., about 1630, who was at Cambridge in 1632, and at Hartford among the early settlers. He was a deacon in the Rev. Mr. Hooker's church, and an influential man of that town.   He removed to Hadley in 1659, where he died in 1684, at an advanced age. The three sons in Middletown were farmers.   Andrew Warner died Jan. 26, 1582.[4]   Robert repeatedly represented the town in the General Court; he died April 10, 1690.   John died in 1700.   The Warners in Chester and Lyme, are descendants of Daniel Warner, one of their brothers."

Her paternal grand-mother was Isabel, the daughter of Richard Parkes, of Cambridge, who is believed to have been the son of Henry Parke, a merchant of London.[5]

His third wife, Hannah Edwards, had those traits of character for which her family have been so remarkable ; highly intellectual ; deep and fervent piety ; never for an instant compromising truth and justice for the sake of expediency.   Her example and her precepts have long been felt by her descendants ; and the principles which she inculcated in the minds of her children, has already brought forth good fruit abundantly, and those of her lineage have the promise of a beneficent Creator, that he will bless to the third and fourth generations of them that love him, and keep his commandments.   This is their inheritance, which is of far more value, than title deeds or heraldric honors.

For the following biographical and genealogical notices of Mrs. Wetmore's father's family, we are indebted to *The Life of President Edwards,*" by Sereno Edwards Dwight, S. T. D., G. & C. & H. Carvill, New York, 1830.

[4] This is a probably a clerical error ; it should be 1682.— *Compiler.*

[5] Record of the descendants of Francis Whitmore, of Cambridge, by William H. Whitmore, Boston, 1855.

The family of EDWARDS is of Welsh origin.   The Rev. RICHARD
EDWARDS, *great great grandfather*, and earliest known ancestor
of President Edwards, [6] was a clergyman in London in the time
of Queen Elizabeth.   He came, according to the family tradition,
from Wales, to the metropolis, and was of the established church ;
but in what shire his family lived, or of what church in London he
was the minister, is not known.   His wife, Ann Edwards, after the
death of her husband, married Mr. James Coles, who, with her son,
Wm. Coles Edwards, then young and unmarried, accompanied her
to Hartford, Conn., about the year 1640, where they both died.

WILLIAM EDWARDS, Esquire, *the great grandfather*, resided in
Hartford, and is supposed to have been, by profession, a merchant.
His wife, whose Christian name was Agnes, and who came when a
young lady with her parents to America, had two brothers in England—one the mayor of Exeter, and the other the mayor of Barnstable.   Their marriage occurred probably about the year 1645.   It is
not known whether they had more than one child.

RICHARD EDWARDS, Esquire, *grandfather*, so far as can now be as-
certained, the only child of William and Agnes Edwards, was born at
Hartford in May, 1647, and resided in that town during his life.
He also was a merchant and a man of wealth and respectability. [7]

At an early age he became a communicant in the Presbyterian
Church at Hartford, and adorned his profession by a long life of
conscientious integrity, and unusual devotedness to the prosperity of
religion.

He married Elizabeth Tuthill, the daughter of William and Elizabeth Tuthill, who came from North Hamptonshire, England.   Mr.
Tuthill was a merchant of New Haven, and one of the proprietors of
the colony attempted at Delaware bay.—*Trumbull's History of Conn.*

By this connection Mr. Edwards had seven children, the eldest of
whom was Rev. Timothy Edwards, who had six children.   He died
April 20th, 1718, in the 71st year of his age, exhibiting during his
last sickness, a bright example of Christian and triumphant faith. [8]

The family of STODDARD is of English descent.   ANTHONY
STODDARD, Esquire, the maternal grandfather of President Edwards, and the first of the family in this country, emigrated from
the west of England to·Boston.   He had five wives ; the first of

[6] President Edwards and Mrs. Wetmore, as will be seen *post*, were brother
and sister.

. [7] These particulars were learned by Mr. Dwight at East Windsor, Ct., in
1823, from two parishioners of the father of Prest. and Hannah E.—the Rev.
Timothy Edwards—both of them (his informants) upwards of ninety years
of age.—*Compiler.*

[8] For a very interesting sketch of the life and death of Richard Edwards
we would refer the reader to Mr. Dwight's Appendix B. in his life of President Edwards, written by the Rev. Timothy Edwards.—*Compiler.*

whom, Mary Downing, the sister of Sir *George Downing*, was the mother of the R'ev. *Solomon Stoddard* of Northampton, Mass. His other children were Anthony, Simeon, Samson and Israel.

The Rev. SOLOMON STODDARD, his eldest child, and the *maternal grandfather* of President Edwards, was born in 1643, and received the degree of A. B. at Hartford College, in 1662.

Soon after his licensure, the first minister of Northampton, the Rev. Eleazer Mather, then a young man, died; Mr. Mather (says Mr. Dwight) was ordained June 18, 1661, and died July 24, 1669, and the parish applied to one of the ministers of Boston to designate a successor. He advised them at all hazards to secure Mr. Stoddard. When the parish committee applied to him he had already taken his passage for London and put his effects on board the ship with expectation of sailing the next day; but, through the earnest solicitation of the gentlemen who had recommended him, he was induced to relinquish the voyage and go to Northampton. He began to preach there in 1669, soon after the death of Mr. Mather, and on the 4th of March, 1670, received the unanimous call from the church and people of that village to become their minister, but was not ordained until Sept. 11, 1672. On the 8th of March, 1670, he married Mrs. Esther Mather, originally Miss Warham of Windsor, in Connecticut, and widow of his predecessor, who left three children. The Rev. John Warham, originally one of the ministers of Exeter, England, had four children, all daughters. He died April 1st, 1670. He was distinguished for piety and the strictest morals; yet, at times, was subject to great gloominess and religious melancholy. Such were his doubts and fears at times, that when he administered the Lord's Supper to his brethren he did not participate with them, fearing that the seals of the covenant did not belong to him. It is said he was the first preacher in New England who used *notes* in preaching.—*Trumbull's History of Connecticut.*

Mrs. Mather had three children by her first husband, Eunice, Warham and Eliakim. Eunice married Rev. John Williams, of Deersfield, who with his son (then a child), afterwards the Rev. Stephen Williams, D. D., of Long Meadow, was caried into captivity by the Indians in 1704.—*Dwight's App.*

Mr. and Mrs. Stoddard had twelve children, six sons and six daughters. The I *Mary* married the Rev. Stephen Mix, of Wethersfield. The II *Esther*, born 1672, married the Rev. Timothy Edwards (the father of Prest. Edwards), Samuel, Anthony, Aaron all died in infancy. The VI *Christian*, married Rev. Wm. Williams, of Hatfield. VII *Anthony*, born Aug. 9, 1678; A. B. of Harvard, 1697; the minister of Woodbury, in Connecticut; died Sept. 6, 1760. VIII *Sarah*, born April 1, 1680; married Rev. Samuel Whitman, of Farmington, Conn. They had five children: 1 Sarah, who married John Trumbull, of Westbury, and was mother of the Hon. John Trumbull, the poet. 2 Elizabeth, wife of Rev. Thomas Strong, of New Marlborough. 3 Elnathan, minister of Hartford, Ct. 4 Solomon. 5 Samuel. IX John, born Feb. 17, 1682; A. B. of Harvard, 1706; married Prudence, of Wethersfield. He was usually known as Col. Stoddard, of Northampton. They had six children: 1 Mary, born Nov. 12, 1732, and married Hon. John Worthington, LL. D., of Springfield, and died having no issue. 2 Prudence married Ezekial Williams, Esq., of Wethersfield. 3 Solomon. 4 Esther. 5 Israel. 6 Hannah. X Israel, born April 10, 1684; died in prison in France. XI Rebeckah, born in 1686; married Joseph Hawley, of Northampton; they had two children: 1 Joseph, A. B. of Yale, 1742, a distinguished lawyer and statesman. 2 Elisha, killed at the battle of Lake George, Sept. 4, 1755. XII Hannah, born April 21, 1688; married Rev. William Williams, of Weston, Mass; they had nine children: 1 William. 2 Elizabeth; m. Rev. Joseph Crocker, of Ipswich. 3 Anne. 4 Lucy; married Rev. Joseph Buckminster, of Rutland. 6 Mercy. 7 Esther. 8 Solomon. 9 Hannah.—*Dwight's Appendix.*

He (Rev. Solomon Stoddard, grandfather of Prest. E.), was celebrated throughout the colonies for his capacity, his knowledge of men, his influence in the churches, and his zeal for vital religion; and will long be remembered for his valuable writings, which have often been published on both sides of the Atlantic[9]; he was a minister of Northampton, from 1672, until his death in 1729, and left impressions of character strongly marked for originality, for talents, for energy, and for piety on the minds of its inhabitants, which the lapse of a century has scarcely begun to diminish.

We find the following, respecting the Rev. Mr. Mix's courtship in Mr. Nathaniel Goodwin's introduction to his Genealogical History of the descendants of Nathaniel Foote, of Wethersfield, which, we think, as he (Mr. G.) says, too amusing to be omitted. It is taken from a manuscript collection of Judge Franklin Comstock, late of Wethersfield, deceased.

Soon after his settlement, he (Mr. Mix) made a journey to Northampton, Mass., in search of a wife. On his arrival at Rev. Solomon Stoddard's, he made him acquainted with the object of his visit, and informed him that the pressure of duties at home made it necessary to proceed with all possible dispatch.

Mr. Stoddard took him into the room where his daughters were,

[9] For a list of Mr. Stoddard's writings, we would refer the reader to Dwight's *Life of President Edwards. Appendix F.*

---

and introduced him to Mary, Esther, Christiana, Sarah, Rebeckah and Hannah, and retired.   Mr. Mix lost no time in proceeding to business; but addressing Mary, the eldest daughter, said he had lately been settled in the ministry at Wethersfield, and was desirous of obtaining a wife, and concluded by offering her his heart and hand.

She, blushingly, replied, that the proposition was as unexpected as it was important, and required time for consideration.   He rejoined that he was not insensible of the marriage covenant, and was gratified to discover her unwillingness to enter into it without suitable time for reflection.   That in order to give her an opportunity to reflect upon the subject, he would walk into the other room, and smoke a pipe of tobacco with her father, and she could report to him.   Having smoked his pipe and sent a message to Mary that he was ready to receive her answer, she came into the room and asked for further time for consideration.   He replied that she could reflect longer upon the subject, and communicate her decision by letter, addressed to him at Wethersfield.   A few weeks afterwards he received the following laconic epistle, which concluded the courtship, and prepared the way of the marriage :

NORTHAMPTON, 1696.

Rev. Stephen Mix:
                    Yes.
                                     MARY STODDARD.
They were married Dec. 1, 1696.

Copy of inscriptions upon the tombstone erected to the memory of the Rev. Mr. Stoddard and his wife, at Northampton.

Here is intered
The Body of The
Rev. Solomon Stoddard, A. M.

Some time fellow of Harvard College, Pastor of yᵉ church in Northampton N. E. for near 60 years, who departed this life 11 Feb. 1729, and in the 86 year of his age ; A man of God, an able Minister of The New Testament, singularly qualified for that sacred office and faithful therein ; A light of the Churches in general, a peculiar blessing to this ; eminent for the holiness of his life as remarkable for his peace at death.

In Memory of
Mrs. Esther Stoddard
The virtuous Wdo. and Relict
of The
Rev. Solomon Stoddard
formerly Pastor of the Church
in This Town,
Who died Feb'ry 10th
A. D. 1736
in the 92 year of her age.

Northampton Epitaphs.

The Rev. TIMOTHY EDWARDS (father of President E.),
was born at Hartford, May 14, 1669, and pursued his
studies preparatory to his admission to college, under
the Rev. Mr. Glover of Springfield, a gentleman distinguished for his classical attainments. In 1687, he
entered Harvard College, at that time the only seminary in the colonies; and received the two degrees of
Bachelor and Master of Arts, on the same day, July
4th, 1691, one in the morning and the other in the
afternoon. "An uncommon mark of respect paid to
his extraordinary proficiency in learning" (*Rec. of East
Windsor*). After the usual course of theological study,
at that time longer and more thorough than it was
during the latter half of the following century, he was
ordained to the ministry of the gospel in the east
parish of Windsor, Conn., in May 1694. Windsor was
the earliest settlement in that colony, the first having
been erected there in 1633. The original inhabitants
came from Devonshire, Dorsetshire and Somersetshire,
Eng. They arrived in Boston, in the beginning of the
year 1630, and planting themselves at Dorchester,
Mass., where they formed into a Congregational Church,
on the 20th of March, when the Rev. John Warham
(already alluded to), previously a distinguished clergyman in Exeter, England, but ejected as a non-confor-
mist, was installed their pastor. Finding themselves
straightened for room at that place, in consequence of

the great number of emigrants from England, the church with their minister, left Dorchester, and planted themselves in Windsor, in the summer of 1635. This town lying immediately north of Hartford, and delightfully situated in the valley of the Connecticut, originally comprehended a very large tract of land on both sides of the river, and is distinguished for the fertility of its soil, and the beauty of its scenery. The inhabitants constituted one parish, until the year 1694, when those residing on the eastern side of the Connecticut, finding it inconvenient to cross the river, and being grown sufficiently numerous to support public worship among themselves, proceeded to build a church, which stood near the present burying ground, and invited Mr. Timothy Edwards, son of Richard Edwards, Esq., of Hartford, to be their minister.

Mr. Edwards was married on the 6th day of Nov., 1694, to Esther Stoddard, the second child of Rev. Solomon Stoddard, who was born in 1672. His father, immediately after his settlement, purchased for him a farm of moderate extent, and built him a house, which was regarded at the time of its erection, as a handsome residence. I (says Mr. Dwight) saw it in 1803. It was a substantial house of moderate dimensions, had one chimney in middle, and was entered like all other houses of that period, by stepping over the sill. In this house his children were born, and he and Mrs. Edwards resided during their lives.

He had one son and ten daughters, whose names follow in the order of their births: Esther, Elizabeth, Anne, Mary, Jonathan, Eunice, Abigal, Jerusha, Hannah, Lucy and Martha.

I. *Esther*, b. in 1695; m. Rev. Solomon Hopkins, of West Springfield. They had several children: Hannah; m. in 1740, to Hon. John Worthington, LL. D., of Springfield; they had two sons who died in infancy: Mary, who m. Hon. Jonathan Bliss, chief justice of the province of New Brunswick: Hannah, who m. Hon. Thomas Dwight, of Springfield: Frances, who m. Hon. Fisher Ames, LL. D.; and Sophia, who m. John Williams, Esq., of Wethersfield.

II. *Elizabeth*, b. April 14, 1697; m. Col. Jabez Huntington, of
Windham, June 30, 1724. They had four daughters: 1,
Jerusha, m. Dr. Clark, of Lebanon: 2, Sarah, m. *Hezekiah Wet-
more*,[10] of Middletown, and had two children; and after his
death m. Samuel Beers, of Stratford, and had three children.
Lucy, m. to George Smith, of Smith Town, Long Island. Sarah
Ann, m. David Burr, Esq., of Fairfield; and Wm. Pitt Beers,
of Albany, who m. Anne, daughter of Hon. Jonathan Sturges,
of Fairfield: 3, Elizabeth, m. Rev. Abraham Davenport, of
Stamford, and had two children: Hon. John Davenport, M. C.,
and Hon. James Davenport, a judge of the Supreme Court of
Connecticut.[11]

III. *Anne*, b. in 1699; m. John Ellsworth, Esq., of East Windsor,
and d. 1798, æ. 99. They had four children: 1, John, b.
Aug. 24, 1735, and had five children; 2, Solomon, b. April 3,
1737, and had twelve children; 3, Frederick; 4, Anne, who m.
Mr. John Stoughton, of East Windsor, and had six children.

IV. Mary, b. in 1701, and d. single, Sept. 17, 1776, in the 76th year
of her age.

V. *Jonathan* (President Edwards). For biographical and genealogical notices of him and his descendants, see Appendix D.

VI. *Eunice*, b. 1706; m. in Oct. 1729, Rev. Simon Backus of New-
ington, who was a chaplain of the Connecticut troops to Louisburg, in 1745, and d. there in 1746. They had seven children:
1, unknown; 2, Eunice, b. in 1732; d. unm., aged 75; 3, Elizabeth, b. 1734; m. David Bissel of East Windsor. They had
two children: 4, Esther, m. Benjamin Ely of West Springfield and had fourteen children; 5, Rev. Simon Backus, A. B.
of Yale, 1759; m. Rachel Mosley of East Haddam, and had
nine children; 6, Jerusha, m. Mr. Smith Bailey, and had four
children; 7, Mary; d. unm.

VII. *Abigail*, b. in 1708; m. William Metcalf, Esq., of Lebanon,
and A. B. of Harvard College; she died in 1754. They had
five children: 1, Abigail, m. Moses Bliss, Esq., of Springfield,
and had eight children: Hon. George Bliss Moses, William
Metcalf; Lucy, m. Dr. Hezekiah Clark of Lebanon; Abigail,
m. Hon. William Ely of Springfield; Frances, m. Rev. William Rowland of Windsor; Emily and Harriet; 2, William,
and 3, Eliphalet, who died young; 4, Lucy, who married Mr.
John Huntington of East Haddam, and had seven children; 5,

[10] This was a nephew of Hon. Seth Wetmore, who m. Hannah Edwards.
Hezekiah being a son of Jeremiah (brother of Seth), son of Izrahiah, son of
Thomas.
[11] Mrs. Elizabeth (Edwards) Huntington d. Sept. 21, 1733, æ. 36; m. 2d,
Widow Sarah Wetmore; he d. Sept. 26, 1752. Mrs. Sarah (Wetmore)
Huntington d. at Norwich, Ct., March 21, 1783, in her 83d year.—*Compiler.*

Eliphalet, b.· Dec. 6, 1748; m. Mary West of Lebanon, and had ten children.

VIII. *Jerusha*, b. in 1710, and died Dec. 22, 1729, aged about 19½ years.

IX. *Hannah*, b. in 1712, and m. Seth Wetmore, Esq., of Middle-town, Conn.   *   *   *   *   *]

X. *Lucy*, b. in 1715, and died unm.·in East Windsor, Aug. 21, 1736, aged 21.

XI. *Martha*, b. in 1716; m. Rev. Moses Tuthill of Granville, Mass., and died in Feb., 1794, aged 77. They had four children, all daughters. ·

In the spring of 1711, Mr. Edwards (Rev. Timothy) and the Rev. Mr. Buckingham of Milford, were appointed by the legislature of the colony the chaplains of·the Connecticut troops in a military expedition designed for Canada. He left Windsor for New Haven in July. ·A fleet, consisting of twenty men-of-war and eighty transports, sailed for Canada on the·30th of that month. Three companies, under the command of Lieut. Col. Livingston, marched from New Haven for Albany on the 9th of August, with whom went ·Mr. Edwards and Mr. Buckingham. The country through which their march lay was at that time chiefly uncleared, and the troops were obliged two nights to lie out in the forest. They reached Albany on the 15th and formed there, including their own regiment, 1100 white and 120 Indians. The following letter, addressed to Mrs. Edwards from Albany, not only details the state of the expedition, but· unfolds the character of the writer and the circumstances of· his family. ·

To Mrs.·Esther Edwards, on the East side of·the Connecticut river,
in Windsor.

ALBANY, August 17, 1711.

My dear and loving wife:

The last Wednesday we came to this place. That we might not travel too hard for the footmen of our troops (which consisted but of half of the regiment, the rest not marching out of ·New Haven when we did,) we spent seven days in the journey, which Col. Livingston judges to be about 160 miles, and I am apt to think it may not be much short of it. I lay with our troops two nights in the woods. I took cold in my journey, and have something of a cough, and am not otherwise much amiss. Notwithstanding this, I am able to travel, and hope I shall be so through the whole journey. Col.

Livingston has been very careful of me, so that through the whole march, both as to diet and lodging, I fared as well in the main as himself. The rest of the officers and troops carry themselves as well to me as I can expect or desire.

Here are about 1100 white men (or will be at least when the rest of the regiment come up, whom we expect to-night) and 120 Indians, besides what are expected of the Five Nations, which many here think will be 1600 or 1800 men, but Col. Schuyler told me he did not expect more than 1000. About 200 or 250 more whites .are expected; so that the whole army that goes to Canada is like to be about 2500 men; to carry whom over the lake, there are provided, as I am told here, 350 batteaux and 40 or 50 bark canoes. The Governor of New York and the General are here. The General is in great haste to have the forces on their march; so Col. Schuyler's regiment was, I understand, ordered to march out of town yesterday; but as I slept last night, and still am, on the east side of the river, I am uncertain whether they are yet gone. The General told Col. Livingston, and me also afterwards, that we must march for Wood creek to-morrow, but I am apt to think we shall hardly march till Monday.

Whether I shall have any time to write you after this, I know not; but however that may be, I would not have you discouraged and over anxious about me, for I am not so about myself. I have still strong hopes of seeing thee and our dear children once again. I can not but hope that I have had the gracious presence of God with me since I left home, encouraging and strengthening my soul, as well as preserving my life. I have been much cheered and refreshed respecting this great undertaking, in which I verily expect to proceed, and that I shall before many weeks are at an end see Canada; but I trust in the Lord he will have mercy on me, and thee, my dear, and all our dear children, and that God has more work for me to do in the place where I have dwelt for many years, and that you and I shall yet live together on earth, as well as dwell together in Heaven with the Lord Jesus Christ, and all his saints, with whom to be is best of all.

Remember my love to each of the children, to Esther, Elizabeth, Anne, Mary, Jonathan, Eunice and Abigail. The Lord have mercy on, and save them all, with our dear little Jerusha! The Lord bind up their souls with thine and mine in the bundle of life. Tell the children, that I would have them, if they desire to see their father again, to pray daily for me in secret; and above all things to seek the grace and favor of God in Christ, and that while they are young.

I would have you very careful of my books and account of rates. I sent you from New Haven a 40s. bill in a letter by Lieut. Willis, and since that ordered the treasurer to deliver to my father six pounds more for you. You call for it or send for it by some sure hand.

Descendants of Judge Seth, son of Izrahiah, son of Thomas.

Though for a while we must be absent from each other, yet I desire that we may often meet at the throne of grace in earnest prayers one for another, and have great hopes that God will hear our prayers. The God of Grace be with you.

I am thy loving husband,
TIMOTHY EDWARDS.

On Monday, August 20, they marched for Wood creek. At Saratoga, in consequence of the fatigues and exposure of the march, Mr. Edwards was taken severely ill. On the 4th of September, being unable to proceed with the army, he was conveyed in a boat to Stillwater. Thence he was carried back through the woods to Albany, where he arrived in three days in extreme danger. On the 10th he wrote to Mrs. Edwards as follows:

To Mrs. Esther Edwards, in Windsor, New England.

ALBANY, Sept. 10th, 1711.

My dear:

I came last Tuesday from Saratoga towards Albany, very ill, in order to return home, having been ill more than a month, and growing at last so weak that I could go no further than that place, which is near fifty miles above Albany. I came to Albany in a wagon, lying along, in a bed prepared for me, last Thursday night. Since then I have been at the house of Madam Van Dyke, a Dutch gentlewoman, where I have been so kindly taken care of, that I am much better, and daily gain strength, and my lost appetite is somewhat recovered. I hope to be able to ride homeward next week.

Last Friday I sent Mr. Hezekiah Mason to New England, to acquaint my father and my friends at Windsor how it is with me, and to desire three or four of them to come hither and to bring an easy horse with them for me to ride upon, and come provided to carry home my effects, and to bring a blanket or two with them, in case we should be forced to sleep in the woods. I should have written by him, but was too ill to do it. This is the first day I have been able to sit up. If the neighbors have not started when you receive this, speake to Mr. Drake that they set out as soon as possible.

I rejoice to learn by a letter from my father that you were all well on the 2d, and I hope in the mercy of God to see you all ere long.

Lieut. Silvy, sent over by the Queen to serve in the expedition, a stout active young man, who came sick with me in another waggon from the camp to Albany, died this evening, just by my lodgings; we came together from the camp sick, we lay together in one room by the way sick, we lodged just by one another several days in this town sick, but he is dead, and I am living and recovering. Blessed be God for his distinguishing and undeserved grace, and favor to me. Remember my love to all the children. Give my respects to Mr. Colton, who, I understand stays with you. I wish you to provide something for my cough, which is the worst I ever had in my life. Remember my love to sister Stoughton, and my duty to my father and mother, if you have opportunity.

I am your very affectionately
loving husband,
TIMOTHY EDWARDS.

Owing to the lateness of the season and to numerous disappointments, the expedition was soon after relinquished; and in the course of the month Mr. Edwards returned home.

Mr. and Mrs. Edwards lived together in the married state upwards of sixty-three years. Mr. Edwards was about five feet ten inches in height, of fair complexion, of a strong and robust frame, full, but not corpulent. He was a man of polished manners, particularly attentive to his dress, and to propriety of exterior, never appearing in public but in full dress of a clergyman.

The management, not only of his domestic concerns, but of his property generally, was intrusted to the care of Mrs. Edwards, who discharged the duty of a wife and a mother, with singular fidelity and success. In strength of character, she resembled her father; and like him she left behind her in the place where she resided for seventy-six years, that "good name, which is better than precious ointment." On a visit to East Windsor, in the summer of 1823, I found a considerable number of persons advanced in years, who had been well acquainted with Mrs. Edwards, and two, upwards of ninety, who had been pupils of her husband, from them I learned she had received a superior education in Boston, was tall, dignified and commanding in her appearance, affable and gentle in her manners, and was regarded as surpassing her husband in native vigor of understanding. They all united in speaking of her as possessed of remarkable judgment and prudence, of an exact sense of propriety, of extensive information, of thorough knowledge of the scriptures and of theology, and of singular conscienciousness, piety, excellency of character.

By her careful attention to all his domestic concerns, her husband was left at full liberty to devote himself to the proper duties of his profession. Like many of the clergy of that early period in New England, he was well acquainted with Hebrew literature, and was regarded as a man of more than usual learning; but was particularly distinguished for his accurate knowledge of the Greek and Roman classics. In addition to his other duties, he annually prepared a number of pupils for college, there being no academies, or public schools, endowed for that purpose. One of my aged informants, who pursued his preparatory studies under him, told me, that on his admission into college, when the officers had learned with whom he had studied, they remarked that there was no need of examining Mr. Edwards's scholars.

He was for that period, unusually liberal and enlightened with regard to education of his children, preparing not only his son, but each of his daughters, for college. In a letter bearing date Aug. 3, 1711, while absent on the expedition to Canada, he wishes Jonathan and the girls may continue to prosecute their study of Latin, and in another of Aug. 7, that he may continue to recite his Latin to his elder sisters. When his daughters were of a proper age, he sent them to Boston to finish their education. Both he and Mrs. Edwards were exemplary in their care of their religious instruction; and, as a reward of their paternal fidelity, were permitted to see the fruits of piety in them all, during their youth.

He always preached extemporaneously, and till he was upwards of seventy, without noting down the heads of his discourse.[12] After that time, he commonly wrote the divisions on small slips of paper, which, as they occasionally appeared beyond the leaves of the Bible that he held in his hand, his parishioners called "Mr. Edwards's thumb papers." Apologizing for this one day to one of his pupils, he remarked to him, that he found his memory beginning to fail, but that he thought his judgment as sound as ever; and this was likewise the opinion of his people, till near the close of his life. He is not known to have written out but one single sermon; which was preached at the general election, in 1732, and was published. It is a solemn and and faithful application of the doctrine of a general judg-

[12] This is an error of Mr. D's. We have in our possession, a number of Mr. E's sermons, written in a small, clear and beautiful hand.—*Compiler.*

ment to his hearers, particularly as legislators and magistrates. As he lived till within a few months of his son's decease, the latter often visited his father and preached in his desk. It was the customary remark of the people, that "although Mr. Edwards was the more learned man, and more animated in his manner, yet Mr. Jonathan was the deeper preacher."

His influence over his congregation was commanding, and was steadily exerted on the side of truth and righteousness. When he knew any division among them, he went immediately to see that the parties were reconciled, and when he heard of any improper conduct on the part of any individuals, it was his uniform custom to go and reprove them. Under his preaching, the gospel was attended with a regular uniform efficacy, and in frequent instances with revivals of religion; yet no record is preserved of the actual admissions in the church. From some of the family letters, I find incidental mention of a revival of religion as existing in 1715 and 1716, during which Mrs. Edwards, and two of her daughters, made a profession of their Christian faith; and several others of the family are spoken of, as "travelling towards Zion, with their faces thitherward." His son observes, in 1737, that he had known of no parish in New England, except Northampton, which had so often been favored with revivals of religion, as that of his father.

During the whole of his ministry he was regarded by his people with great respect and affection; no symptoms of dissatisfaction having been manifested by them for sixty-three years. In the summer of 1752, on account of his increasing infirmities, he proposed to them the settlement of a colleague, and they actually settled one, the Rev. Joseph Perry, June 11, 1755, but continued his salary until his death, which took place Jan. 27, 1758, when he was eighty-nine years of age.

. Mrs. Edwards survived him twelve years; her fourth daughter, Mary, residing with her and watching over the infirmities of age. From a lady in East Windsor, far advanced in life, I learned the following facts: Mrs. Edwards was always fond of books, and displayed a very extensive acquaintance with them in her conversation; particularly with the best theological writers. After the death of her husband, her family being small, a large portion of her time was devoted to reading.   A table always stood in the middle of her parlor, on which lay a large quarto bible and treatises on doctrinal and experimental religion.   In the afternoon at a stated hour, such of the ladies of the neighborhood, as found it convenient, went customarily to her house, accompanied, not unfrequently, by their children.   Her daughter regularly read a chapter of the bible, and then a passage from some religious author: but was often stopped by the remarks and comments of her mother, who always closed the interview with prayer.   On these occasions it was the favorite point with neighboring females, even with those who were young, to be present; all of them regularly attending them when they were able, and many of them, and among them my informant, dating their first permanent attention to religion from the impressions here made.   In this she was regarded with a respect bordering on veneration, and was spoken of by Mr. Perry as one of his most efficient auxilliaries.   She died Jan. 19, 1770, in the 99th year of her age, retaining her mental faculties until the close of her life.   Her daughter, Mary, spent many years of her early life at Northampton with Mr. and Mrs. Stoddard, and returning thence to her father's house.   She was the nurse and attendant, and I may almost say, support of her aged parents.   She was a woman of most amiable disposition, fine understanding and uncommon attainments ; had read much and appeared to have made the best improvement of the knowledge that she obtained.   She survived her mother six years.—*Dwight's Life of President Edwards.*

FOURTH GENERATION.

Children of Judge SETH.

JERUSHA, b. in Middletown, —, 1740; d. —, 1749.

SETH, b. in M., 1744; m. Nov. 16, 1768, Mary, dau. of William and Lucy (Downing) Wright; b. —, 1745 ; had Seth, William, Hannah, Samuel, Mary, Willard Wright, Titus, Josiah, Lucy, Nathaniel Downing ; m. 2, Lucretia Scott (widow) ; had Julia and Harriet.

He was a yeoman. The property inherited from his father enabled him to live upon his income, devoting himself more or less to public matters, in which he took a deep interest. He held the rank of captain in the colonial volunteer service during the revolution. In a town meeting, held January 7, 1777, he, together with Col. Comfort Sage and Capt. Samuel Russell, was appointed to petition Governor Trumbull, to remove William Franklin, the then late Tory Governor of New Jersey from the town, where he was a prisoner of war, on parol, it being deemed necessary to do so for the safety of the town and state. What is a little remarkable, this William Franklin, last royal Governor of New Jersey, was a son of Benjamin Franklin.

Though possessed usually of a good-natured, friendly and high-toned disposition, he was quick to repel indignities, and sometimes was overcome by a hasty temper, which "*it is said*" is a characteristic of the Wetmores generally. He was generous to a fault, and hospitable beyond the greatest hospitality which prevailed in his day. He was tender-hearted, and ever ready to relieve the distressed at any sacrifice. His descendants have a traditionary story of him, which, while it shows that characteristic trait of quickness of temperament, will evince at the same time his readiness to make the "amende honorable." It seems that a neighbor of Captain Wetmore had many geese that used to trespass upon the captain's premises, to his injury and annoyance. The neighbors were on the most friendly terms, but still all expostulation failed, so on one occasion catching two of the invading geese by their necks, down the road he ran, swinging them and exclaiming "keep your geese at home," "take care of your geese," &c. But by the time he had reached the gate of his neighbor, his temper had cooled off, and mortified at the exhibition he had made, without saying a word about the nuisance, he commenced, "really good neighbor *it is too bad*, for you to allow your geese to annoy me to such extent, as to cause me to act so foolishly, besides which, I have killed two of your geese, and must now compensate you."

The good feeling between the neighbors rendered a settlement easy, and the result of the ebullition of passion was a guarantee for the future.

He had a great veneration for the past, and was among the last of New England yeomanry who preserved the old custom, now almost obsolete, even in Old England, of the *harvest cup*.

His wife, Mary Wright, was of a highly honorable lineage, both paternally and maternally, she being 8th in direct descent from the Rev. John Rogers, the martyr; 5th in descent from George Wyllys (Willis), a deputy lieutenant governor and governor of the colony of Connecticut, from 1640 to 1643, and through him 22d in direct descent from Griffen de Warren, the 6th Earl of Warren and Surrey—the 2d Earl of Warren being a son of Grundred, daughter of William the Conqueror—and through these pedigrees back to Alfred the Great. She d. Dec. 24, 1790. Mrs. Lucretia (Scott) Wetmore, d. May 19, 1830, æ. 67 years. He died at Middletown, April 15, 1810; was buried at the old west yard of that city, and the following inscriptions appear upon his tombstone, and that of his wife Mary:

> Capt. SETH WETMORE,
> died April 15, 1810,
> in the 67th year of his age.
> MARY—his wife died Dec. 24, 1790,
> aged 45.
> In her the virtues of the daughter, wife
> and mother shine with peculiar brightness.

LUCY, b. at Staddle Hill, near Middletown, April 10, 1748; m. Feb. 14, 1770; had I *Lucy*, b. in M——; m. ——, Joseph W.

Alsop, Esq., of M——, who had 1, Lucy Wetmore, b. ——, m.
Henry Chauncey, Esq., of the highly responsible and honorable
mercantile house of Alsop & Co., of Valparaiso, and Alsop &
Chauncey, of New York; and had Henry, b. ——, m. Emily
Aspinwall, dau. of Samuel Shaw Howland, Esq., of New York,
who have Henry, Lucy: 2, Clara Pomeroy, d. young; 3, Charles
Richard, who m. Mary E. Armstrong; 4, Joseph Wright, who
m. Mary Oliver; 5, Clara Pomeroy 2d; 6, Elizabeth, b. ——,
m. George Hoppin, Esq., of Providence, R. I.; 7, Mary Wright,
b. ——, m. Dr. Thomas Mutter.   II *Hannah*, b. May, 1775.
III *Elizabeth*, b. ——; m. Josiah Williams.   IV Gen. *Chauncey*, b. June 18, 1783; m. Sarah Tracy.

Mrs. Whittlesey was a woman whose uncircum-
scribed and remarkable piety was widely known.

Her active benevolence knew no bounds.   She
sought out the poor; she provided them with work
and paid them from her own purse, and many were
the blessings showered upon her head from those who
were thus the recipients of her bounty.

It was her custom to take her servants young and
bring them up under her own eye and counsel; they
were reared in the principles of the gospel, and, through
her teachings, were made useful members of society.
Her household was managed in the fear of the Lord,
and it was esteemed a model Christian home.   In consequence of this gentle, kind and benevolent course of
action towards those dependent upon her, she enjoyed
the greatest deference and respect from them.   Her
counsel was sought by both young and old.   Her
brother, Deacon Oliver, looked to her for advice and
guidance in almost every important transaction of his
life, revering her judgment and abiding by it.   She in
return gave him her warmest affection and love.   She
had a just pride of distinction without being ostenta-
tious.   To her were her nephews and nieces often
indebted for letters advisory, both religious and political.   She continued the family altar after the death
of her husband, and the following form of *prayer*, composed by herself, she frequently used:

Infinitely blessed and most glorious God—We, thy unworthy creatures, desire humbly to present ourselves before *thee* this morning and unitedly to join our praise and supplication to thee, the author and giver of every mercy we enjoy. Grant us, we beseech thee, the influence of thy holy spirit that we may be enabled to worship thee who art a spirit in spirit and truth. Give us, we entreat Thee, worthy apprehensions of the great and glorious perfections of thy character, and may we bow before Thee with reverence and godly fear. We desire to adore thee for thy wonderful condescension manifested in allowing such guilty and defiled creatures as we are to approach into thy presence and to worship before Thee. We desire to take all encouragement in thy infinite goodness as evinced through the all-sufficient mediator, and to place our trust in His atoning blood and powerful intercession for our being heard and accepted.

We humbly beseech Thee, for his sake, to pardon and forgive all our sins, which we acknowledge have been many and great, and greatly aggravated. Remember not against us, the corruption of our hearts, or the sinfulness of our lives, transgressions of thy holy law, or our impenitence and unbelief under the call of the Gospel.

Most Merciful Father, enter not into judgment with us, for in thy sight we are not able to stand, but grant us redemption through the blood of thy Son, even the forgiveness of all our sins. We humbly pray that by the special influence of thy Holy Spirit, thou wilt work in us all those qualifications which accompany salvation ; teach us our dependence in Thee ; subdue our will, bring in subjection our evil propensities, give us hearts to mourn after a Godly sort for all our sins, and to turn from and forsake them ; enable us to trust our souls, with all our eternal concerns, in the hands of Jesus Christ our Saviour, who is able to save from the wrath to come, and may our faith work by love to God and man, and produce true holiness and obedience. Sanctify in us all the powers of our nature, and enable us in our whole conversation to adorn the religion that we profess; fill us with joy and peace and blessing; and grant that we may go on our way rejoicing in the God of our Salvation.

Be pleased, oh Lord, to bless us in the relation we

stand to one another; make us instruments of promoting each other's comforts and happiness, both temporal and eternal; grant that in living together on earth, it may be the means of preparing us to spend a happy eternity together in thy kingdom above. Let the smiles of thy providence and grace be continually upon us, and be graciously pleased to establish thy covenant with us. Do good to all our friends and acquaintances, reward them that have shewed us kindness, forgive those that have wronged us. Pity all that are under affliction and sorrow, teach them to profit by thy correction, and be thou entreated to remove the chastising rod. Dwell at all times in this place; bless them that minister in holy things; save thy people throughout the land from their sins and thy judgments. Succeed the ministry of thy Gospel. Water and increase thy church everywhere. May the set time for favoring Zion be hastened, when every tongue shall be brought to confess, and every knee to bow to Christ Jesus our Lord, to the Glory of God the Father.

We desire to thank Thee, Heavenly Father, for the innumerable blessings which we have been made the subjects of. We thank Thee, that we were born and educated under the light of the Gospel; for the preservation of our lives, that we have been kept from any fatal accident, and preserved in every danger. Accept our thank offerings for our preservation the last night, and for the comforts of this morning.

We humbly beseech Thee, to keep us all this day long from sin and every evil. Let us be in the fear of the Lord all the day long. Direct us in all our ways, preserve us in all our goings, smile on the labour of our hands, and prosper all our undertakings. Give us this day our daily bread, and guide us by Thy council all our days. Prepare us for the remaining services of life, and for all the trials, sorrows, and sufferings that we may meet with. Support and comfort us under the decays of nature and the approach of death. Order the time, and manner, and circumstances of our departure out of the world, in mercy for us, and receive us at last into Thy unchangeable kingdom above. To the praise of the rich grace in Jesus the Mediator of the new Covenant, for whose sake, be pleased to accept our prayers, and to whom, with the Father and Holy Spirit, be assented everlasting praises, Amen."

She died Jan. 23d, 1826, and the following is a copy of the inscription upon a marble monument.

Mrs. Lucy Whittlesey,
Relict of Chauncey Whittlesey Esqr
Distinguished for practical piety and
Benevolence died 23^d Jany 1826 Æ 78 years.

Mr. Whittlesey graduated at Yale College, in 1764. Studied divinity and was lincensed to preach by the Orthodox Congregational Church, but relinquished the ministry as his profession, without diminishing his attachment for the gospel.[12] He was of old Puritan stock. The family of Whittlesey have ever been remarkable for their talent, strong practical sense, and unflinching integrity, and the subject of this notice, was an inheritor of these virtues in an eminent degree.

He entered the mercantile business; was appointed by the Council of Safety, in 1776, commissary of subsistence to the army; was collector of the port of Middletown, from December, 1797 to 1801; magistrate of the town; a deputy to the General Court, 1809, 1810 and 1811; was elected deacon of the First Congregational Society, Sept. 17, 1778, which office he held till his decease.

A correspondent, noticing Mr. Whittlesey's death, in the *Connecticut Herald*, published at New Haven, March 29, 1812, says:

To the Editors :
I have observed in the various newspapers printed in this state, the late death of Chauncey Whittlesey, Esq., of Middletown, is barely mentioned without any further notice of the subject; this does not satisfy me.

I knew him well, and knew his worth. If the purest patriotism, manifested by a uniform zeal for the public good; if firmest integrity, exhibited in all his dealings with his fellow men; if the highest degree of benevolence and

[12] Dr. Field's Address.

charity, that ever delight to minister to the wants and comforts of all within his reach, deserves from *all men* esteem; then all should have esteemed *him* when living— should lament his death. If piety to God, made manifest by good works in all the various relations of life, meet from Christians love and respect, then Christians should have loved him while living, and should love to dwell upon his praises now that he has gone.

Dea. Whittlesey d. March 14, 1812, and his remains lie interred in the old west yard at Middletown; and the inscription upon a marble monument reads thus:

CHAUNCEY WHITTLESEY Esq
Died March 14th 1812
Aged 66 years.

Through vanquished agonies
What gleams of joy, what more than human peace!
His Lord sustains him in his final hour
His final hour brings glory to his God
Man's glory heaven vouchsafest to call her own.

Their daughter HANNAH, was highly intellectual, well read, and versed not only in polite literature, but in the history of her country. She had extensive correspondence with distinguished men of her time, both in this country and in Europe. Of fine conversational powers, ever courteous, polite and amiable, never forgetting the rights or feelings of others. To her kindred, especially, she entertained the liveliest sentiments of interest, both in their spiritual and temporal welfare. Always scrupulously neat in her personal appearance, dressing in good taste. She was what might be termed a lady of the old school. She died as she had lived, in the full assurance of a blessed immortality. Her remains were interred near those of her parents, and a brown stone shaft standing over her grave, bears this simple inscription:

Erected to the memory of
HANNAH WHITTLESEY
daughter of
Chauncey Whittlesey
born May 1775—Died Dec 21st 1855.

Their son, Gen. Chauncey Whittlesey, graduated at
Yale College in 1800. He studied law and settled at
Middletown. He represented that town in the state
Legislature, in 1817. Dr. Field, in his Centennial
Address, says :

From the close of 1804 until 1819, Chauncey Whittlesey, Esq., practised in this county, and though able
lawyers from Middletown and adjoining counties attended
the courts, he acquired an elevated rank among his brethren. He was also advanced in military life to the
command of a brigade. In the last mentioned year he
removed to Louisville, Ky., where he practised about four
years, and afterwards to New Orleans, where he practised
about four years more. His health having been seriously
injured while in the latter city, he returned to his native
town in 1827, and attended in a degree to official business
until the autumn of 1829, when his illness became distressing. His sight and other bodily powers were affected,
so that for the residue of his life he was almost helpless,
and often racked with severe pain. * * * * *

Gen. Whittlesey's early disappointments and sufferings
served to render the grace of God, in which he trusted,
the more conspicuous. Those who visited him in his
afflictions, were surprised in view of his weak and dis-
ordered body, at the continued vigor of his mind ;
were instructed by his conversation and improved by his
resignation to God, and his benevolence to men, and prospects of blessedness in the life to come.   .

An able writer in *The Philadelphian* of Jan. 8, 1835,
declares concerning him :

When almost every earthly comfort was withdrawn, he
was not cast down, for he looked to his inheritance among
the saints in light. When blindness and darkness came
over his bodily sense, the eye of his mind remained strong
and unclouded, and the light of Heaven still penetrated to

his soul and kept up a constant warmth in his heart.
While he was in a condition which would have made some
men forget all but self and suffering, his expansive benevolence worthy of his celestial origin, constantly flowed out
to his fellow beings. His intellect was still firm and vigorous after years of severe disease had taken from his body
almost all power, but that of endurance, and his feelings,
instead of being soured by disappointment and calamity,
grew more tender and affectionate, while one faculty and
enjoyment after another, in melancholy succession departed
from him. Thus through years of trial, he acted out the
faith and patience of the saints.

He died ——.

OLIVER, Dea, b. at Staddle Hill, near Middletown, May —, 1752;
baptized May 24, 1752; m. Oct. 13. 1773, Sarah, dau. of Capt.
Elisha Brewster,[13] b. 1754; had Oliver, Elisha, Sarah, Timothy,
Lucy, Hannah Edwards, Clarissa, Sophia, Chauncey and Emily.

He was in early life fitted for college, but delicate
health did not permit him to enter. He was a man
(says a correspondent who knew him well) of superior
talents, intellectual attainments, and sound judgment;
unbounded benevolence was a prevailing trait. He
was very dignified, yet accessible to all, both high
and low, rich and poor. He was a uniform christian,
and his example to his family and to the world was
truly such as to assure them he was ever abiding in
the Lord.. His cheerfulness was remarkable (in feeble
health as he was), especially in the social circle that
ever clustered around his board. His house was the
constant resort of visitors, who took a delight in his
society, while his amiable christian companion greatly
contributed to the comfort and happiness that ever
and brightly centered around their hearth-stone. His
benevolence was widely experienced; the widow and
fatherless had every reason to rejoice at his presence
in their midst, and for the provision bestowed upon
them from his granaries. His woodlands were open
to the poor. In the winter season *the bars* were

[13] For Brewster History and Genealogy, see Appendix.

let down, and all who were not able to provide for themselves, were free to enter and take as much fuel as they needed.

He consecrated his children to God in baptism, the very next Sabbath after their birth, believing it his duty so to do at the earliest possible moment of their existence. He was confined to his bed, for some weeks previous to his death, and during that time his views of God and eternity, were of the most exalted and consoling nature. His life was calm and peaceful, and peaceful and calm his death. He predicted the precise hour when his spirit would take its departure, viz : four o'clock in the morning; he looked at the clock *two* minutes before the hour, and exclaimed : " Come, sweet Jesus, come quickly," as the clock struck four, he turned his eyes to heaven and breathed his last sigh on earth. That dying scene, all through that night, was so solemn, so joyous and impressive, that it was not without its saving effect upon some of those who witnessed it. Such was the life, and such was the death of Deacon Wetmore, whose memory we all love to venerate and honor, and may we one and all, live as he lived, and may our last end be like his.

He united with the church, Nov. 8, 1772, was made deacon of the First Congregational Society of Middletown, March 4, 1784, which sacred office he held till he was removed by death.

It will be remembered by the reader, that to be chosen a deacon of the Church of New England in colonial times, was no ordinary honor. To be thus selected, was a sufficient guarantee that the recipient was without spot or blemish of character, and *prima facie* evidence, that the person so selected was a man of weight and influence in the community in which he lived. The late Gov. Treadwell of Connecticut, in his autobiography, in referring to the office of deacon, which office he held for many years, says : " happy

41

would he have been, if he could have honored the
office, as much as that honored him."

Deacon Wetmore, together with his sister Lucy
(Mrs. Whittlesey), and his half brother Seth, inherited the homestead and farm, together with the slaves
belonging to the estate.[14]   He, at the death of his

[14] As many of the slaves of Judge Seth were objects of interest, and care
to his children and grand-children for a term of years, it may not be considered out of place to detail a little of the history of some of them.   At
twenty-seven years of age the servants owned by Dea. W. were set at liberty,
but not without provision for their future comfort and welfare.   One of
them, Amos by name, ran away and hired himself out to Gen'l Morgan of
Hartford.   Amos was a good, faithful servant, but impatient under restraint ; he could not bear remonstrance, and so resolved to try whether he
could not gratify his own will among strangers.   Gen'l Morgan, finding
him a most excellent waiter, wrote Dea. W. requesting him to sell the unex-
pired term of his service to him.   Dea. W. consented, but before Amos's
time had expired Gen'l M. failed and his property was attached, and the
unfortunate runaway was taken by a creditor to the state of New York,
that being a slave state. at that time as well as Connecticut.   The creditor
also failed and poor Amos was again seized, sold and taken to South Carolina.   Dr. John Osborn, Jr., of Middletown, afterwards saw him in the
latter state and asked him if he was contented; he replied that he had a
kind master, " but," said he, " *I* would like to go back to Massa Wetmore's
once more."

Another servant, by the name of Toney, on receiving his freedom, chose
a seafaring life.   On his return from his voyages he made it his home with
his former master.   He had married a squaw, who was excessively intem-
perate, and her he could neither live with her or trust her with any of his hard
earned money.   So, with his old master's permission, he used to bury his
treasure in the cellar.   He had ever been a faithful servant and was
strongly attached to his old home and its inmates.

On a Sabbath morning, which was cold and blustering, after Toney's
return from one of his trips to sea, Dea. W. desired Toney to accompany
him to "meeting."   Toney demurred, saying, " that for some unaccounta-
ble reason he *must* stay home."   So he was permitted to remain with three
of the children, Hannah, Sophia and Clarissa.   In the course of the morning the children heaped upon the fire in the broad fireplace a quantity of
light wood chips.   The chimney caught fire and the roof was soon in a
blaze from the falling sparks.   Toney, with the alertness of a monkey,
ascended the south side of the house by the clapboards, mounted the roof
and tore the light shingles from their fastenings, and saved the dwelling
from destruction.   When Dea. W. returned and heard of the danger they
had encountered, Toney met him with a countenance beaming with delight
and self-satisfaction, and with many bows said, " Now, Massa Wetmore
want Toney to go to *meetin'*, but God want Toney to stay home.   Massa
Wetmore had no house now if Toney gone to meetin'."   And Massa Wetmore *was* sensible that an overruling Providence had put it into the heart
of Toney to stay at home that Sabbath to be the means of saving his property from the devouring element.

"Membo," whom we have already noticed, was born in Africa, and when
about nine years old was brought to this country with a cargo of slaves.

father, took charge of the homestead, where he continued to reside, giving attention to that portion of
the extensive farm of his father, that fell to his lot.
He died December 1st, 1798, and was buried among
his kindred, in the old grave yard, west from the city

Judge Seth purchased her with others and placed her in his family in the
capacity of waiting maid to his wife and daughter, and truly faithful she
proved to be. At Judge W.'s death, Membo fell to Mrs. Whittlesey's share.
When Mrs. Whittlesey died she left Membo to the care of her daughters,
Hannah and Elizabeth (Mrs. Williams), who faithfully fulfilled their trust.
Mrs. Whittlesey provided that Membo should be taken care of as long as
she lived; her freedom had been given her years before, but she remained
with her mistress who had given her a small house on the grounds attached
to her own mansion. She became blind and very feeble, and when the
winter came she was removed into the family dwelling and there taken
charge of in the kindest manner until the summer, when she returned to
her own humble home, still provided for and watched over by her benevolent Christian mistress.

Membo venerated, and was exceedingly attached to everything belonging
to the memory and estate of Judge Wetmore. She recognized his descendants, after becoming blind, by their voices. She was very tenacious of
"the rights of Oliver and Lucy." Her memory was remarkable, and she
had many anecdotes to relate of her own history, and of the sayings and
doings of "Massa (Judge) Wetmore." She remembered well the time she
was brought from Africa, and thanked God for bringing her to America,
where, she said, she had "learnt to lub Jesus," "for," said she, "if de
Lord had neber brought me here I should neber know Jesus who is so precious to me now." She mourned not the loss of her sight, but was cheerful
and resigned, and died rejoicing in her Redeemer. She was sincerely
mourned by the family. She was buried in the family lot at the foot of the
graves of her master and mistress.

The following anecdote has been related to us by an eye witness: Dea.
Wetmore had a small yellow dog, whose name was Penn, and it was Dea.
W.'s custom to conduct family worship in the south parlor, then used as
a sitting room, which communicated with the kitchen (now the dining
room) by a small entry. Leading from the sitting room to the kitchen was
a bell pull which summoned the servants to prayers morning and evening.
Invariably, without failure, dog Penn headed the servants as they proceeded
to the place of prayer, and took his position in a large wooden arm chair
that stood in the south east corner of the room, lying down while the master read the scriptures, and as he rose to pray (which he always did, standing at the back of his chair,) Penn would rise upon his hind legs, drop his
fore paws, close his eyes and remain in that position until the prayer was
ended; then he would alight from the chair, which no one else ever ventured to occupy, and precede the servants to the kitchen. Singular, that
although this bell summoned others to the sitting room at various times, yet
Penn never ventured in there at any other time, neither did he stay after
the prayer was ended. He lived to be very old, and was so blind that at
last it became necessary to kill him.

Penn and his "piety" has often been since the subject of remark, sympathy and wonder of the children around the fireside of that old mansion
at Staddle Hill.

of Middletown, and the following is a copy of the inscription upon a plain brown stone, placed over his grave.

> In Memory of Deacon Oliver Wetmore
> Who Died Dec. 1st A. D. 1798
> in the 47th year of his age.

With silent step he trac'd the way
To the fair courts of light, his wish'd abode,
   Nor could he ask a moment's stay,
Nor make the convoys wait, that call'd his soul to God;
   See the good man with head reclined,
And peaceful heart, resign his precious breath;
   No guilty thoughts oppress his mind,
Calm and serene his life, serene and calm his death.[15]

His wife, Sarah Brewster, was fifth in direct descent from Elder Wm. Brewster, of the Mayflower. She was a woman befitting her lineage, possessing much of the generous high mindedness of her noble ancestor. To her were her children greatly indebted for those virtues which adorned their characters. She died July 5, 1827, and was buried beside the remains of her husband. The inscription upon her tomb-stone is simply

> In memory of
> Sarah Wetmore, relict of
> Deacon Oliver Wetmore,
> who died July 5, 1827, in the
> 73d year of her age.

HANNAH, b. at Staddle Hill, near Middletown, 1753; d. July, 1756.

---

[15] These lines were selected, or composed by his daughter, Mrs. Whittlesey.

FIFTH GENERATION.

Children of SETH.

SETH, b. in Middletown, Sept. 10, 1769; m. Nancy, dau. of Gen.
   Wm. and Nancy (?) (Dewey) Shepard of Westfield, Mass.,
   Feb. 1, 1800; had William Shepard; m. 2d, Salome Smith of
   St. Albans, Vt.; had Charles Wright, Nancy Shepard, and
   Seth Downing; m. 3d, Mrs. Annie Goodrich, Jan. 11, 1817.

Was a lawyer by profession, and resided for many
years at St. Albans, Vt.; was sheriff of that county;
a member of the governor's council for about 20 years,
and judge of the court of probate, nearly as long.

He was an amiable, conscientious man, ever ready
to take a charitable view of things. While he always
felt indignant at the wrong doing of men, was willing
at all times to forget and forgive evil in others. Such
a nature could not but be susceptible to kindness, and
at the same time, sensitive in the extreme.

While on one of his professional tours, business
called him to the residence of Gen. Wm. Shepard,
where he was taken dangerously ill. He was prostrated by a fever, which was succeeded by delirium,
during which time, the general's daughter, Nancy, sat
by him, and ministered to his wants as only woman
can do under such circumstances. During his convalescence, these attentions were continued, until a feeling of gratitude on his part gave way to more tender
and lasting emotions, which resulted in the happy
union of himself and the fair daughter of the host,
before leaving his hospitable mansion.

He was a devoted Christian, and an active member
of the Methodist Episcopal Church.

It has been often said of him, that in prayer he was
eloquent, at the same time simple and solemn, carrying
those of his hearers, who were of a devotional mind,

before the Throne of grace, with great effect. His life was pure and holy, and like many a good man, whose energies have been devoted to "laying up treasure in heaven," pecuniary success in this world did not attend him.[16] He died at St. Albans, Aug. 29, 1830, in his 61st year. His wife, Nancy Shepard, died at the same place, Feb. 17, 1802.

Gen. William Shepard,

Her father, was born in Westfield, Mass., December 1st, 1737; he served six years as a captain in the Revolutionary army, and distinguished himself at Fort William Henry and Crown Point; in 1783, he was chosen a brigadier general, having fought twenty-two battles; he was subsequently a major general of militia; and a representative in congress, from 1797 to 1803.

The following letter addressed to General Washington, with Washington's reply, we take from *American Archives*, vol. II, fifth series, p. 603. We give them entire, to show the patriotic sentiments that animated the heart of Col. Shepard, and how they and his services were appreciated by the commander-in-chief.

To His Excellency George Washington, Esq., General-in-Chief of all the Forces in the thirteen free and United States of America, the petition of William Shepard, now Lieutenant-Colonel in the Third Regiment in the Continental Army, humbly showeth ;

That he, in early life, was called forth in defence of his country; that he cheerfully stepped forth, and for six years successively served in the late war in various capacities, from that of a private to a captain, in which station he served three years; during the whole of said term he was led to believe that he served with good reputation in said capacities; that early in the unhappy controversy between *Great Britain* and the now free States of America, he was again called to the field, and his mind being impressed with the importance of the cause in which he was engaged, and the duty he

---

[16] He was a purchaser of over 300,000 acres of the *Yazoo lands*, the titles to which, were repudiated by the state of Georgia. See *American State Papers, Land Claims*, i, 202, 203, 204 and 206; also *post* under head of, William, son of Seth, &c.

owed to God and his country, he thought himself under the strongest obligations to draw his sword against the unnatural enemies of his oppressed country to defend its sacred rights and liberties; which consideration alone induced him to enter the present service in the station he now holds.

Your petitioner further begs leave to observe that when he entered the service he expected the same advantages with regard to preferment, with officers of his rank in the army; but when he views the regiment to which he belongs, which has been destitute of a chief colonel for almost six months and not filled, and other regiments vacant but a few hours, before they are filled by advancements from their own corps.

Your petitioner is convinced that he is judged by the wise and prudent rulers of the states (whom he will honour and esteem), not to be an officer worthy of promotion, or the most flagrant injustice is done him. This being the case, your petitioner thinks himself compelled by every principle of justice to himself and to all his brethren who may continue in the service of their country (which has his best wishes, and which service he has no desire to leave, so long as the cause of his country shall require his assistance, or any other principle than those before noted, there being but little expected from a degraded officer), to beg Your Excellency to grant him liberty to resign his command.

And Your Excellency's petitioner, as in duty bound, shall ever pray, &c.   WILLIAM SHEPARD,
Bergen, Sept. 28, 1776.   Lieutenant Colonel.

General Washington to the President of Congress.

[Read October 2 ; referred to the Board of War.]

HEAD QUARTERS, HEIGHTS OF HARLEM, Sept. 30, 1776.
Sir :

Since I had the honour of addressing you last, nothing of importance has transpired, though from some movements yesterday on the part of the enemy, it would seem as if something was intended.

The enclosed memorial, from Lieutenant Colonel *Shepard*, of the *fourth* regiment, I beg leave to submit to the consideration of Congress ; and shall only add that I could wish that they would promote him to the command of the regiment, and send him a commission, being a good and valuable officer, and especially as the vacancy is of a pretty long standing; and I have had, nor has he, any intelligence from Colonel Learned, and himself, who had command, and who obtained a discharge on account of his indisposition, of his designs to return.

I have also enclosed a copy of a letter from Capt. *Ballard*, which

Congress will please determine on, the subject being new, and not within my authority.

I have the honour to be, Sir, your most

obedient servant,

Go. WASHINGTON.

P. S.—A commission was sent for Colonel *Learned*, which is now in my hands, having received no application or heard from him since it came.

From this postcript it is fair to presume that congress was unadvised till then, of there being a vacant colonelcy in the regiment which Lt. Col. Shepard was commanding.

We find by reference to the *Am. Archives*, that Col. S. was, on Nov. 3d, 1776, attached to Gen. Clinton's brigade, and his regiment contained 503 men, rank and file, and subsequently to Gen. Lee's division. He was commissioned by congress, colonel, on the 1st of December following.[17] At what time he was promoted to the rank of brigadier general we are unadvised. Gen. Shepard did his country signal service after the restoration of peace.

After the close of the war, and before the constitution had been framed, there was great pecuniary distress in New England, particularly in Massachusetts. The people very generally called upon the authorities for a stay of legal proceedings, and not having their wishes granted, they attempted, in Massachusetts, to take the law into their own hands.

This rebellion was known as *Shays's rebellion*, a Daniel Shays, formerly a captain in the revolutionary army, taking the command of some 1100 men, armed. After taking Worcester they assembled near Springfield with the design of taking possession of the

---

[17] He received a commission of lieutenant colonel in a regiment of foot, granted by the congress of the colony of the Massachusetts Bay, on the 19th of May, 1775, and signed by Joseph Warren, Prest. P. T., and by Samuel Freeman, secretary, P. T. He was wounded in the throat at the time of Burgoyne's defeat and capture.

arsenal at that place, then in charge of Gen'l Shepard, who had about 900 men under his command. Shays proposed to attack Gen'l S. on the 25th of January, 1787, and wrote a Luke Day and Eli Parsons, who had each 400 men under their direction, to meet him. Shays, confident of their coöperation, marched his men on the day appointed to the attack of Gen'l S., who had his raw militia drawn up to receive them. On Shays appearing in sight Gen'l S. sent an officer to warn him to desist. If the answer was favorable he was to file off to the right, if not, then in the opposite direction; the officer filed to the left. " Give them a shot to the right," said the general. The cannon was fired accordingly, no injury being done. Shays moved on. " Give them a shot to the left," said General Shepard. This was done, but instead of bringing the rebels to a halt, they pressed on more rapidly. " Give them a shot breast high," ordered General Shepard. It was done. The ball killed three men, wounding a fourth; the lawless body retreated in great confusion to a place some ten miles distant.

Had General Shepard been disposed to pursue he might easily have cut them to pieces. But the object was not to destroy, but to bring them to consideration and amendment.

The following day Major General Lincoln of Hingham, previously secretary of war, arriving with a large body of troops, the insurgents retreated towards Amherst. Gen'l Lincoln followed them, but they made good their retreat to Pelham, where they took post on two high hills, almost inaccessible by reason of the snow. The weather was very severe and Lincoln turned aside to Hadley to put his troops under cover. Negotiations ensued. The insurgents agreed to disperse on a general pardon, but Lincoln had no authority to make such a promise. While the negotiation was pending the insurgents, hard pressed for

provisions, broke up their camp, retreated to Peter-
sham on the borders of Worcester county.[18] Lincoln
pursued, and overtaking them, took 150 prisoners ;
the remainder scattered, taking refuge in the adjoining
states and Canada.

A free pardon on laying down their arms, and taking
the oath of allegiance, was offered all who had served
among the insurgents as privates merely, or as non-
commissioned officers, with deprivation however, for
three years, of the right to vote, to serve as jurymen,
or to be employed as schoolmasters, inn keepers, or
retailers of ardent spirits.[19] Gen. Shepard died at his
residence in Westfield, Mass., Nov. 11, 1817. Mrs.
Salome Smith Wetmore died at St. Albans, Vt.,
Dec. 11, 1815. Mrs. Annie Goodrich Wetmore
was much loved and respected by those who knew
her, and by none more than her step-children. She
proved to them a mother indeed. She died in Ohio
about 1855.

WILLIAM, Judge, b. in Middletown, Sept. 16, 1771; m. Nov. 28,
    1795, Anna Ogden, of Hartford, Ct.; had William Ogden,
    Edwin, Henry, Clarissa, Jacob Ogden, Infant Dau., and Har-
    riet: m. 2d, Jerusha Ogden, sister of his first wife.

Mr. Wetmore commenced his active business life as
merchant, in the city of Hartford, where he was successful and acquired some considerable wealth. He
became a purchaser to some extent of Gore lands, so
called, lying between the states of Connecticut and
New York, to which both states laid claim, and out
of which a civil war was threatened. The difficulty
however was settled, but not without loss to those who
had purchased the lands. About this time and before
the loss was known, certain parties from the state of
Georgia visited the north, for the purpose of disposing
of certain lands known as the Yazoo lands, lying in

18 Hildreth, *Hist. United States*, III, 475.
19 Hildreth, *Hist. United States*, III, 476.

---

the then territory of Mississippi, professed to be owned by a land company who received their title from the state of Georgia. As they showed the required papers with necessary vouchers with the *great* seal of the state attached, capitalists had no hesitation in making purchases; a large amount was bought by citizens of Connecticut. Mr. Wetmore, with Leonard Jarvis and Henry Newman became purchasers of an extensive tract.[20] The authority of the agents was subsequently denied, and the titles to the lands were repudiated by the state of Georgia. This infamous transaction was known, and will be long remembered as the "Yazoo frauds." This loss, together with the Gore land loss occurring about the same time compelled Mr. W. to suspend business at Hartford. He then returned to his native town, where he took the situation of deputy clerk in the county clerk's office. Here he had a proposition made him by John Stow, Esq., one of the Western Land Company (who had purchased the reserve from Connecticut) to remove to Ohio, for the purpose of acting as agent for the company, in the sale of their lands. He accepted the proposition and in June 1804, he with his family, consisting of his wife and four children, arrived in Stow township, then an unbroken wilderness, having been forty-two days, with a span of horses and a covered wagon in making the journey from Middletown. He built the second house in that township (says General Bierce, *Historical Reminiscences of Summit County, O.*), which was about 20 rods easterly from the north-west corner of lot 36, on which Gen. Cross's tavern stands. Three young men and their wives, and his brother Titus, then a single man, together with the subject of this notice and his family, were the first and only white inhabitants of the town for some time. Indians were

[20] For abstract of titles see table on next page, compiled from *Am. State Papers*, Public Lands, I, 202, 203, and 217.

An Abstract of all Evidences of Titles to Lands claimed under any Act, or pretended Act, of the State of Georgia, passed or pretended to be passed, in the years 1789 and 1795, recorded in office of this Department.

| DATE OF ACT. | DATE OF TITLE. | NAMES OF PARTIES | | QUANTITY OF LAND. | SPECIES OF WARRANTY. |
		FROM	TO		
Jan. 7, 1795,	Feb. 13, 1795,	Geo. Mathews, Governor of the State of Georgia,	Nicholas Long, Ambrose Gordon, and Thos. Cumming, and their associates, called the Georgia Mississippi Co.	Beginning on the Mississippi river at the place where the latitude of 31° 18′ north of the equator, then a due east course to the Don or Tombigbee river; thence up the middle of said river to where it intersects lat. 32° 40′; thence due west course along the Georgia Company's line to the river; thence down the middle of the same to the beginning; reserving out of the said tract of land 620,000 acres, to be subscribed for by other citizens of Georgia.	
	Feb. 13, 1796,	Georgia Mississippi Company, by their agents or attorneys, Williamson & Jackson.	William Wetmore, Leonard Jarvis, and Henry Newman.	For ditto.	Subject to same incumbrances, &c., while they remained the property of the Geo. Miss. Co.
	Feb. 17, 1797,	Confirmation deed, Geo. Miss. Co.	William Wetmore, Leonard Jarvis, and H. Newman.	For ditto.	Ditto.
	Feb. 28, 1798,	William Wetmore, Leonard Jarvis, and H. Newman.	John Peck in trust.	3,400,000 acres.	Ditto.
	Feb. 18, 1797,	William Wetmore, L. Jarvis, and H. Newman.	George Blake.	250,000 acres.	General.
	Nov. 24, 1795,	James Greenleaf.	William Wetmore.	320,000 acres.	J. Greenleaf warrants against all persons claiming under

then very numerous in that section of the country. Mr. W.'s conscientious dealings with them soon made them his faithful friends. It was his practice, always, to have the Indians, in a trade, name their own terms; if the terms suited, he would conclude the bargain, if not, he would not, never allowing himself to banter with them.

In this way he retained their confidence, and avoided the charge of "cheating poor Indian." As might be expected he enjoyed their friendship and esteem, so much so, they considered it a crime to steal from him.

He was elected the first justice of the peace, and postmaster of the township, Feb. 6, 1808; was appointed by the governor and senate associate justice of the court of common pleas for Portage co., which office he resigned the 6th Sept. of the following year. In 1810, he removed to Ravenna, and was elected clerk and recorder of the county. At the commencement of the war of 1812, he resigned and returned to Stow, and received the appointment of commissary of supplies to the army, which office he held during the war.

At about the time of the commencement of hostilities a British officer, in the disguise of an Indian, came to the chief of the Indian village, situated on Lake Pleasant, and not far from the residence of Judge Wetmore, and proposed to the chief to join the English, and for their services, they would restore all the land that the American government had bought from them, to which they assented, but when they were told it was necessary for them to massacre Judge Wetmore, and other Americans in the neighborhood, the chief and his warriors refused, saying that he "had been good to poor Indian."

Up to the time of his death, he was a general counsellor in matters of the law, especially to the poor, although he never appeared at the bar as an advocate. His counsel was always gratis, and was in effect

generally for his clients to keep out of the law, and
settle amicably.

In 1825, he and his sons William and Henry, made
the first survey of the river and grounds, now known
as that part of the village of Cuyahoga Falls, lying in
the town of Stow, being the one-half of the village.
Here he and his two sons commenced improvements
in the way of flouring, saw and oil mills, in company
with John Stow of Middletown, under the firm of
Stow & Wetmore. He was much respected in northern Ohio, and like his brother Seth, was truly conscientious, never pursuing the wrong, when he knew
the right. Among other enterprises the Judge was
engaged in, was that of *distilling*. On a certain Sunday morning, he was observed by his family, reading
a tract with much apparent interest. After dinner
he returned to the perusal of the same, and at supper
time, his assiduity in perusing the tract was explained.
Soon after sitting down to the tea table, the judge
says: "Boys," addressing his sons, "what sort of a
sheep pen, will the still house make, if moved upon
the rising ground?" The question puzzled his sons,
but after a little conversation, it was explained, and
it was decided to commence the following morning
removing the still house, for the purpose of a sheep
pen, instead of lighting the fires at midnight, as was
the custom. This was brought about, as the sequel
proved, by the judge having been engaged during the
day in reading the Rev. Dr. George B. Cheever's tract,
entitled, *Deacon Giles's Distillery*. He died Oct. 9,
1827; his wife, Anna Ogden, died June 20, 1825; and
his wife, Jerusha Ogden, died Aug. 9, 1854.

HANNAH, b. at Middletown, May 28, 1773; m. Judge Dyer White,
   of New Haven, Ct., b. May 20, 1762; had Henry, b. March 1,
   1803.

She was the second wife of Judge White of New
Haven (his first being a Whittlesey—his third was

Eunice Basset, a daughter of the principal of the Hebron Missionary Seminary). She was one of the best and purest of women; all was cheerfulness, hope and charity with her, thinking evil of no one. She was a woman of strong religious principles, seldom, if ever, doubting the goodness and mercy of God. She was called more particularly to the subject of personal piety on witnessing the cheerful and happy death of her uncle, Dea. Oliver. Wherever she .was, whether in society or by her own fireside, a delightful charm was thrown. She died June 30, 1820.

JUDGE WHITE was a lawyer of reputation and judge of one of the courts of Connecticut. Was a high toned honorable gentleman of the old puritan stamp, and during his long life deservedly received from his fellow-citizens their confidence and regard. He was a son of the Rev. Stephen White, born 1718; graduate of Yale College, 1736, and pastor of the church in Windham, Conn., 1740 to 1794, the date of his death; and Mary, daughter of Thomas and Lydia (Backus) Dyer, a sister of the Hon. Eliphalet Dyer, judge of the Superior Court of Connecticut, and member of Congress (1775–1777); and grand-son of John White, born 1692, died January 15, 1783, and Susannah, daughter of Judge John and Susannah Alling. Judge A. was a son of Roger and Mary (Nash) Alling; and great grand-son of Daniel White of Middletown, born February 23, 1661 (who died Dec. 18, 1739), and Susannah, daughter of Hugh and Marietta (Coit) Mold, both of New London, Connecticut. Marietta Coit was daughter of John and Mary (Jennis) Coit. They were among the first settlers of New London, Connecticut; and a great great grand-son of Nathaniel White, born about 1629, and one of the early settlers of Middletown, who was a representative to the General Court from that town for 86 terms, commencing October, 1659, and continuing a member, with the exception of 14 terms, till May, 1710.   He died August 27, 1711.   He (Nathaniel White) was a son of John White who came from England, 1632, and settled first in Cambridge, Mass., and removed to Hartford, 1636.   He died 1683–4.[21]   Judge Dyer White died Nov. 2, 1841.

HENRY WHITE, Esq., son of Judge Dyer and Hannah (Wetmore) White, graduated at Yale College, 1821, with marked honors.   He studied law in the office of his father, and was admitted to the bar about 1825, and has from that date to this been a counsellor of influence in the city of New Haven.   Few men in any community have ever been confided with more trusts than come under his charge, both by testamentary devise and by order of court.   He holds the office of Clerk of Probate. Whether in the performance, says a correspondent, of his religious duties as a deacon of the Old Center Church in New Haven, or as an honest and upright lawyer attending to the trusts devolving upon him, no one can be found more pure and unselfish.   He married Jan. 7, 1830, Martha Sherman, grand-daughter of Robert Sherman, one of the signers of the declaration of independence, and has 1, Henry Dyer, b. Sept. 20, 1830. 2, Charles Atwood, b. Nov. 11, 1833.   3, Willard Wetmore, b. Feb. 7, 1836.   4, Roger Sherman, b. Dec. 26, 1837.   5, Thomas Howell, b. Feb. 1840.   6, Oliver Sherman, b. Nov. 2, 1842.   7, George Edward, b. March 17, 1845.

Mr. White has always manifested a warm interest in the descendants of Thomas Wetmore, and has devoted much time and labor in collecting historical and genealogical matter relative to the family.

SAMUEL, b. at Middletown, Oct. 5, 1775 ; m. May 19, 1804, Elizabeth Wyatt, dau. of William and Hope (Phillips) Warner, b. Dec. 22, 1779 ; had Mary Wright, Esther Phillips, Samuel, Elizabeth Hoppin, George Phillips, Frances, and Edward Carrington.

[21] For a more extended genealogical record of the Whites, see White Genealogy by the Rev. Mr. Kellogg.

He was in early life engaged in the mercantile business, with his uncle, Chauncey Whittlesey, in the city of Middletown. He was interested in the politics of the day; was a magistrate of his native town; represented the place in the General Assembly in 1812, '13 and '14· It was said of him that he was always elected without regard to party.

At the solicitation of Gen'l Edward Carrington he took up his residence in Providence, R. I., in 1815, where he joined Gen'l C. in business. At a later period his brother, Willard Wright, joining them as a partner, the firm became extensively engaged in foreign commerce, particularly with China, the East Indies, west coast of South America, and the continent of Europe. Under the auspices of this firm, and of Cyrus Butler and Benj. and Thos. C. Hoppin, Mr. Samuel Russel went out to China, where he founded the house of Russel & Co., which firm has since established a world wide reputation. At a later period, the absorbing power of New York, as a commercial emporium, was such, that the Providence firm were forced, from time to time, to send their ships to that port, till at last their foreign business centered there entirely, and for a greater convenience, Mr. Wetmore, the subject of this notice, removed thither, establishing the house of Wetmore, Hoppin & Co. (his brother Willard Wright, John Griswold and Samuel Russel being partners), in connection with the Providence firm.

He was of a tall and commanding figure, in personal appearance was what might be termed a handsome man, not generally as easy of approach, perhaps, as the other sons of Seth 2d, but kind and affable to his friends and acquaintances, and very affectionate towards his family.

His wife, Elizabeth Wyatt Warner, was sixth in in descent from the Rev. John Cotton,[22] first minister of

[22] The Rev. John Cotton (son of Roland Cotton, a barrister of Derby,

.Boston, Mass., and in compliment to whom, that city received its name. She died in the city of New York, May 22, 1849. He died in the same city, Dec. 12, 1851.

MARY, b. at Middletown, Sept. 14, 1777; m. Capt. Abel Denison of New Haven, June 6, 1802; had 1, *Charles*, b. April 6, 1803; m. Parmelia Skinner, of Euclid, O., Feb. 9, 1834; had 1, Mary, who m. Mr. E. R. Horton; 2, Lucy Wetmore, b. May 21, 1840; he d. Feb. 5, 1841. II *Zina*, b. Aug. 21, 1804; d. Sept. 5, 1805. III *Zina 2d*, b. March 17, 1807; grad. Yale College, 1826; d. Nov. 4, 1852. IV *George*, b. April 10, 1809; d. Nov. 13, 1809. .V *Mary Wetmore*, b. Oct. 15, 1810; m. Dr. John B. Robertson, of Charleston, S. C.; had 1, Samuel, b. Oct. 21, 1832; 2, Mary Wetmore, and 3, Ann Thomas (twins), b: Jan. 22, 1855: she d. Feb. 1, 1835, æ. 25 years. VI *Ann Elizabeth*, b. April, 1813; d. Sept. 28, 1815.

Mr. Denison was a captain in the mercantile

England,) was born at Derby, England, Dec. 4, 1585; B. D. at Cambridge, Fellow, Head Lecturer and Dean of Emanuel College; minister of Boston, Linconshire, England, for twenty years, when he dissented from the established church party. He left England and arrived in Boston, New England, Sept. 3, 1633, and died Dec. 23, 1652, aged 67. He married first, Mrs. Elizabeth sister of Mr. James Horrocks, a celebrated minister of Lancashire. She died without issue; he m. 2d, Mrs. Sarah Story, widow, and had I a dau. who m. an Egginton, a merchant. II Roland, d. Jan. 29, 1649. III Sarah, b. Sept. 12, 1635; d. Jan. 20, 1649. IV Rev. Seaborn, who m. 'l, Dorothy, dau. of Gov. Bradstreet, and had issue; and m. 2, Prudence, wid. of Dr. Anthony Crosby. V Rev. John (the ancestor of the subject of this notice), b. at Boston, March 15, 1639-40; graduated at Harvard College, 1657; m. Joanna, dau. of Dr. Brian Rossiter of Guilford, Conn., Nov. 7, 1660; b. July, 1642; d. at Sandwich, Oct. 12, 1702; had, 1, Rev. John, b. Aug. 3, 1661; grad. at Harvard College, 1681; m. Sarah, dau. of Richard Hubbard of Ipswich; 2d, Elizabeth, who m. James Alling and had issue; 3, Sarah; 4, Rev. Roland who m. Elizabeth, only dau. of Col. N. Saltonstall, sister of Gov. Saltonstall; 5, Sarah, m. Wm. Bradbury, b. ——; 7, a son; 8, Josiah, d. young; 9, Samuel, d. young; 10, Judge Josiah (ancestor of Mrs. W.); b. Jan. 8, 1680; grad. Harvard College, 1698; d. at Plymouth Aug. 19, 1756; m. Hannah Sturtevant, grand-dau. of Gov. Josiah Winslow; b. Jan. 8, 1708; d. May 27, 1756; had Hannah; b. April, 1709; d. in Boston 1781; who m. 1, Thompson Phillips; had Hannah; b. July 20, 1728; d. March 4, 1769; who m. her cousin, George Phillips; b. Oct. 22, 1717; d. Feb. 26, 1778; had Hope, b. Nov. 30, 1756; m. Aug. 31, 1776, William, son of Oliver Ring Warner, b. July 3, 1754. He was lost at sea, returning home from Guadaloupe in the Bunker Hill privateer, March, 1781, then had Elizabeth Wyatt, the subject of the above notice. Mrs. Hope Warner m. 2, Samuel Johnston, formerly of Boston, afterwards of Middletown, Conn. No issue by this marriage. She died in Providence, R. I., Sept. 24, 1820, aged 64 years.

marine, which occupation, together with his commercial adventures to foreign ports, enabled him to amass a handsome fortune. He died at New Haven, Feb. 15, 1813, aged 37, leaving his widow a fine residence, where she lived many years to dispense hospitality and benevolence. If the knowledge of want or destitution came to her, her heart expanded and her purse strings were loosened to afford relief.

She was a devoted member of the Episcopal church. The clergy were at all times welcome guests at her hospitable board. One of our correspondents in detailing her many virtues, says: "Her house was the Elysian home, where the warm and hearty welcome made all feel joyful, and caused the soul to enlarge with fond hopes and high aspirations."

She died Nov. 29, 1829.

WILLARD WRIGHT, b. in Middletown, Oct. 19, 1779.

He was in his younger days, a sea captain, subsequently a merchant, engaged in business with his brother Samuel, as before noted.

A correspondent, who knew him well, says, " He was of a disposition as amiable as his brother Seth ; was possessed of indefatigable industry, and unceasing application ; it was a rule with him to do all that he did, well. If any unusual duty presented itself, he would reflect and well mature his plans before he would *act*. Like all his father's family, he had a great aversion to the use of profane language ; he lost no opportunity to rebuke any indulgence in that sin, and so remarkable was the influence ·which he had over men in that particular, that I am told while around any ship where he was interested, and any longshoreman or ship's officer gave vent to his feelings in oaths, he would call the offender aside, and after a few moments, the man would return to his duty, and his conduct would show that an *impression* of a beneficial character had been made upon him."

He was associated in the house of E. Carrington & Co., of Providence, and was a partner with his brother Samuel, Mr. John Griswold and Mr. Samuel Russel in the New York house.

He had a commanding influence with his brothers, and was much revered and respected by them, as well as by the community in which he lived. He died of apoplexy, Dec. 14, 1833, in the 55th year of his age; unmarried.

TITUS, b. in Middletown, July 16, 1781; m. Sally Hamlin, dau. of Caleb Wetmore, of Stow, O., b. Dec. 28, 1791; had Seth, Willard Wright, and Josiah.

He removed to the Western Reserve, Ohio, in 1804, and was postmaster at Stow twenty years. He died Sept. 20, 1837; his wife survived him till Oct. 18, 1843.

JOSIAH, b. in Middletown, July 21, 1783; m. Nancy, dau. of Moses and Lydia (Farwell) Willard, of Charlestown, N. H., Jan. 17, 1808; had Nancy Shepard, Nathaniel Downing, Lucy Wright, Moses Willard, William Hastings, Josiah Farnsworth, Samuel Farwell, Robert Courtney, and George Henry.

At seventeen years of age he removed to Charlestown, N. H. where he was engaged one year in the mercantile business. He then returned to the homestead of his father and his own birth-place, Staddle Hill, pursuing the occupation of farming, which was more congenial to his tastes. His father, at his death, left the settlement of the estate to his brother Samuel and himself. In the division of the property by will, the farm remained in his possession, until he removed to Stow, Ohio, in 1818. He remained in S. till 1824, experiencing all the privations to which pioneer settlers were subjected, when he returned to New England, and for a time resided at St. Albans, Vt. About 1840 he returned to the village of Cuyahoga Falls, where he now resides, much beloved by his numerous family, and respected by his fellow citizens.

Descendants of Judge Seth, son of Izrahiah, son of Thomas.

During the late war with Great Britain, he commanded a company of volunteer militia at Middletown, and was anxious to serve his country in the field, but was prevented on account of his commission being of a more recent date, than those held by others. He is, in old age, as he was in youth, remarkable for his good nature, and lively turn of mind; his wit and ready humor have always made him popular with old and young.

He usually declined the honor of office when tendered him, but was once persuaded to act as magistrate of Cuyahoga Falls, and was several times, trustee of the township. His wife is of a quiet and retiring nature. In the trials of her pioneer life in Ohio, she has had a consolation and a hope, which looked beyond the fitful scenes of this world; she has viewed this world's afflictions and sorrows, as sent for some good purpose. The more severe her suffering, the brighter her Christian character has shone. She has always been warmly attached to the Episcopal Church. Her bible and prayer book have been her solace in the darkest moments of tribulation. Now that her hearing precludes her from attending worship in the sanctuary, the regular appointed services of the church are performed in her own house, in company with any who may be present, and disposed to join in them, otherwise, *alone.*

Episcopal missionaries who used occasionally to pass through that section of the country, held service a few miles distant from her husband's log cabin, which occasions were to her heart an oasis in her secluded life. The missionary usually making her humble dwelling his abiding place, his presence was always enthusiastically greeted by every member of the family, as the young members used to express it, "wish missionary would come all the while."

She has taught her children self respect, independence, and propriety of conduct. Her life has been

spent for the good of others. She is still left to her
descendants, as a blessing of more value than count-
less rubies, a bright Christian example to be imitated.
As we shall have occasion to speak of her hereafter,
we will merely add in this connection, that she belonged to a family in New Hampshire, that did much
to bring about and secure peace to New England in
colonial times; and her descendants have good reason
to honor their maternal ancestry. Her father's blood
flowed in defence of the then frontier from incursions
of the Indians and French, made in ignorance of the
fact that the party attacked was one they held in reverence and veneration, for knowingly, the Indian would
not infringe upon anything that belonged to Moses
Willard, the Quaker. While others would not leave
anything in their fields for fear of depredation, his cattle and farming utensils were safe anywhere.

After the close of the French war, he, by his
energy and the fortunate relation in which he stood
toward the aborigines, did much to bring about a
better state of feeling between the settlers, and the
red men of the forest, consequently, to develop that
part of New England.

A portion of his house was at all times open to the
Indian or traveler, without fee or hindrance. The
wood pile and oven[23] were ever at the disposal of his
less fortunate neighbor, and the wayfarer.

Lucy, b. in Middletown, April 16, 1786.

She was an influential member of her father's family,
prudent and cautious in family counsel, which gave
weight to her advice. She was like her sister Mary, a
devoted member of the Episcopal Church, and was
active in her Christian duties. She dispensed for a

[23] The family oven in those days, was built of brick or "adobe" and
stood in the open yard or lot, as they may now be seen in some parts of our
rural districts.

number of years the hospitalities of her nephew, William Shepard Wetmore, Esq., at his *Chateau sur Mer*, at Newport, R. I., where she died *unm.*, of paralysis, Sept. 14, 1858. Her remains were interred at New Haven.

NATHANIEL DOWNING, b. in Middletown, Oct. 30, 1790; d. at M. unm. Oct. 27, 1810; was buried in the old west yard.

He was a young man of fine promise; he had remarkable natural mathematical powers. On one occasion he was sent to an academy, under the charge of a Mr. Nichols, who had had twenty years' experience in teaching. On the teacher subsequently meeting the father, he said: "You may as well keep your son at home, as I can not instruct him in mathematics; in truth he puzzles me with his problems." He was then in his sixteenth year. He died from a fever, produced by exposure, while obtaining leeches for a sick brother.

JULIA, b. in Middletown, Jan. 22, 1792; m. Dec. 3, 1812, John Churchill Bush, of New Haven; had I *Robert Wasson*, b. Nov. 18, 1813; m. Oct. 29, 1846, Catharine Udall, of Hartford, Vt.; had 1, Julia Sophia, b. at Ogdensburg, N. Y., Aug. 12, 1848; 2, Robert Wallace, b. at Naples, Ill., April 22, 1851; d. at N. Feb. 5, 1853; 3, John James, b. at Ogdensburgh, Nov. 8, 1854; 4, Henry Kirk Brown, b. at O., April 21, 1857. II *Harriet Wetmore*, b. April 25, 1815; m. at Ogdensburg, May 27, 1840, Gen. Elihu William Nathan Starr, son of Nathan and Grace Townsend Starr, of New Haven, b. Aug. 10, 1812; had 1, William Edwards, b. at Middletown, Aug. 3, 1841; 2, Julia Wetmore, b. Dec. 20, 1843, d. Aug. 24, 1845; 3, Robert Wetmore, b. Feb. 14, 1846, d. May 23, 1847; 4, Henry Barnard, b. June 3, 1848; 5, Frank Farnesworth, b. Nov. 11, 1852; 6, Grace Townsend, b. April 21, 1857.

Mr. Bush was a merchant, and served his clerkship with Birdsey Norton, of Goshen, Conn.; while there he introduced the manufacture of the pine apple cheese, which has become so celebrated. He commenced business on his own account, in company with a friend in New Haven, and was engaged in the

West India trade, when the war of 1812 broke up
their business.   In 1813 he removed to Montreal,
Canada; while engaged in business there, he started
the plan of a bank of deposit, from which arose the
first chartered bank in Canada.   In 1819 he removed
to Ogdensburg, N. Y., where he remained until his
death, which occurred Dec. 26, 1859, in his 80th year,
Mrs. Bush is still living, though in feeble health.
waiting patiently for her Heavenly Father to take
her unto himself.[24]   Her son-in-law Mr. Starr resides
in Middletown, where he has enjoyed the confidence
and respect of the people for many years.   He has
held the office of recorder of M. since 1851.

HARRIET, b. in Middletown, Sept. 23, 1794; m. Henry Sylvester
    Ward, of M.   She d. March 1, 1823, s. p.

Children of Deacon OLIVER.

OLIVER, Rev., b. at Staddle Hill near Middletown, Ct., Dec. 15,
    1774; m. Jan. 15, 1797, Esther Arnold, dau. of Capt. Jonathan
    and Martha Southmayd, b. July 6, 1770 ; had Edmund Arnold :
    m. 2d, Sept. 23, 1807, Chloe, dau. of Capt. Asa and Abigail
    Benton, of Hartford, b. March 27, 1774 ; had Edward Perkins,
    Infant Son, James Carnahan, and Abigail Sarah.

For the following biographical notice, we are indebted to the Rev. P. H. Fowler, D. D., of Utica, N. Y.
"The Rev. Oliver Wetmore was a lineal descendant
of Elder Brewster, so conspicuous among the Pilgrims
of the Mayflower, and a great grandson of the Rev.
Timothy Edwards, the father of Pres. Jonathan Edwards.   His early life was spent in his native place in
the enjoyment of its literary advantages, and in business pursuits.

[24] Mrs. Bush died at M., April 11, 1860.

"In the twenty-fifth year of his age, he entered upon the study of divinity with the Rev. Nathan Perkins, D. D., for sixty years the pastor of the church in West Hartford, and who was in high repute, and much resorted to as a theological instructor. In 1802, Mr. Wetmore was licensed by the Hartford Association, and traveled for two years as a missionary in the portions of Vermont and New York lying on Lake Champlain. He subsequently prosecuted the same work in central New York, and very extensively laid the foundations on which others built. In 1805 and 1806, he went to Holland Patent, Oneida co., N. Y., where he was ordained in 1807, his revered preceptor Dr. Perkins, preaching the sermon on that occasion. On leaving this his first pastoral charge, he labored for several years at Norwich and Trenton village, where he was permitted to rejoice in precious and powerful revivals of religion.

"His missionary toils and exposures begot an ailment from which he never recovered, and for thirty years, he was denied the much coveted privilege of proclaiming Christ from the pulpit. He spent the most of this space in the city of Utica, and though unable to preach in public, he assiduously labored in private, and keeping himself well informed about movements in the world, religious, reformatory and benevolent, and remaining to the last, deeply interested in them, he prayed earnestly for every good cause, and as his circustances allowed vigorously helped it on.

"Mr. Wetmore belonged to a class who are rapidly disappearing from among us, and the like of whom the world has not seen since the days of the apostles. He was a Puritan in spirit and principles, as he was a Puritan by descent; a man beneath whose stern exterior innocent humor played and warm affections glowed, of the most unbending integrity, and above all meanness; while upright and honorable himself, indignant at aught else in others; an ardent friend of humanity, of public spirit as a citizen, faithful and tender as a husband and parent, undaunted in courage and perfectly unyielding in his deliberate and intelligent convictions of righteousness and truth. He may be described in a single sentence, as a man of deep feeling and fearless and persistent adherence to principle.

"His last sickness was of but a week's continuance, and from the first excited alarm among his friends; very kindly was it ordered that his mind should remain undistracted and undimmed, and still more kindly was it ordered that he should receive a large measure of divine grace. At times it was difficult to check the outflow of his blissful feelings, and he poured them forth in "words that burned." It is the language of soberness to say that he enjoyed dying. The writer of this having been with him one morning during a faintness which precluded his speaking, on reviving he requested him to be sent for, observing, "I wish to tell him what a privilege it is for a Christian to die. Previously to that he had said that he was never so happy, and so great was his joy, that he feared for a moment that he might be laboring under some delusion, and rather anxiously enquired if it was right to feel as he did. The morning before his death he was in a pre-eminently blissful frame. A few verses of the fifth chapter of Romans which were read to him, seemed to thrill his whole soul. The fire flashed from his eyes, and with clasped and uplifted hands he made exclamations, as the reader proceeded, and at the close, added: 'What a precious apostle! How I love his writings! It seems sometimes as if I must worship him, but I shall see him in Heaven.'

"He sent special messages to different friends and spoke of the affection he had for all he knew, who loved the Saviour, and begged that Christians everywhere might be entreated to be faithful, and that the impenitent, and especially impenitent youth, might be urged to make their peace with God.

"He said but little after this, and between four and five o'clock the next morning he fell asleep.

> So fades a summer cloud away,
>   So sinks the gale when storms are o'er,
> So gently shuts the eye of day,
>   So dies a wave along the shore.

"His life was occupied to its latest hour in the active prosecution of his master's work. He has been for the last thirty years the senior member of the Oneida Presbytery. His active mind led him to take strong interest in the moral and political topics of the day, nor was his voice or pen ever wanting on the side which he deemed the right."

He died in Utica, on Thursday morning, the 1st day of January, 1852.

Owing to the church to which he belonged (the First Presbyterian) being in the process of rebuilding, his funeral services were held at the Dutch Reformed Church on Broad street, where there was congregated a large assemblage of sympathizing friends and citizens.

His remains were taken to the Ever-Green Cemetery for interment, a spot that he took great pleasure in visiting for a number of years before his death, and where he took part in its consecration, as a resting place for the dead, by offering the dedicatory prayer. His grave is situated on a point commanding a view of the Mohawk and Nail creek valleys. A stone with the simple inscription, "Oliver Wetmore," with date of birth and death, marks the spot.

Mrs. Esther Arnold Wetmore was of an old and highly respectable family of Middletown. She died January 17, 1804, after seven days' illness.

Mrs. Chloe (Benton) Wetmore's ancestry, were among the early settlers and proprietors of Hartford; her paternal ancestor, Andrew Benton, settled at Milford in 1639, and removed to Hartford in 1660. He owned property and lived on Wethersfield lane in 1664; he died 1683, Thomas Lambert says 1681, leaving by his first wife, Andrew, Samuel, Joseph, Mary and Dorothy, and by a second wife Ann, who died in 1686, Ebenezer, Lydia and Hannah.[25]

Mrs. W.'s father, Capt. Asa Benton, was for many years engaged in a seafaring life and in the West India trade, in both of which occupations he was remarkably fortunate; while on the sea he never met with an accident. After retiring from service he sent out a son and a nephew as supercargo. The vessel and cargo were never heard from after being out of sight of land. He retired from active business, and made his residence on what was known as the "Meadows," below and adjoining the city of Hartford. He died, leaving a comfortable estate to his family.

Mrs. Wetmore's maternal ancestry were Bigelows, who were also early settlers and proprietors of Hartford. John Bigelow, [26] in H. (says Porter in his

[25] Hannah, dau. of Andrew Benton, m. Edward Scofield of Haddam. Daniel (Benton) Guilford, 1669. Edward Guilford, 1650, was of Hartford, 1659, and again of Guilford, 1669. Edward Wethersfield, 1660, perhaps son of preced.; d. Feb. 19, 1698, aged 60; by W., Mary left Samuel, Edward, Rebecca, Mary, Ellen and Dorothy, all of full ages except Edward; but his youngest child Daniel, b. March, 1682, d. at 4 months; Joseph Milford, son of Andrew, m., Feb. 10, 1698, Sarah, dau. of Bevil Waters of Hartford. This surname is found in New Hampshire.—*Savage Gen. Dict.*

[26] Bigelow, Baguley or Biglow, Daniel; Sudbury of that place which became Farmingham, son of the first John, m. Abial, dau. of Thomas Pratt of Watertown; had Abigail, b. Oct. 28, 1689; Daniel, Nov. 24, 1691; Abiel, Jan. 20, 1693; Susanna, May 4, 1696; Ephraim, May 12, 1698; and Lydia, Jan 2, 1702. James, Watertown, youngest brother, of preced., m. March 25, 1687, Patience, dau. of Jonathan Brown; had James; bap. May 6, 1688. His w. d. soon, and he m. July 3, 1693, Eliz. Child, youngest dau. of John of the same; had John, Nov. 15, 1694; Patience, Sept. 30, 1695, and Abraham, Nov. 12, 1699. His second w. d. April 20, 1697, and he m. next, June 15, 1708, Joanna Erickson of Boston, and d. Jan. 20, 1728. His wife m. within a year Adam Smith.

John, Watertown, 1636, blacksmith, found by Mr. Somerby to be son of Randle of Wrentham, in county Suffolk, and bap. Feb. 1617, of course by the hand of Rev. John Phillip, the rector, who came to our country two years after B. and lived sometime at Dedham, but on the overthrow of the Bishop's domination in England went back to his old living. He m. Oct. 30, 1642, Mary, dau. of John Warren, who, Bond says, was the earliest m.

Hist. Notices), in 1669, and owned lot 52 on Cooper lane, and Jonathan Bigelow lived and owned land on Wethersfield lane in 1677.

Mrs. W. is still living, now 87 years of age. She enjoys her physical and mental faculties in a wonderful degree. She takes a lively interest, as she always has, in the affairs of the day. She recognises her Maker's hand in all the events of life. Her benevolence and charity for the human family knows no bounds; the strength of her love and devotion to her children and those who are near to her by ties of consanguinity is peculiarly strong.

As a professing Christian, she follows "the golden rule" with fidelity. While she is properly jealous of that which is her due, she is acknowledged to be *wholly unselfish*. Her sister, Mrs. Abigail Wells, widow of Capt. Wells, resided in the city of New Haven. She died April 1, 1860, at the age of about ninety years. She retained her bodily and intellectual powers to the end of her life. She was an earnest and devoted

on town rec.; had John; b. Oct. 27 foll.; Jonathan, Dec. 11, 1646; Mary, May 14 or March 18, 1649; Daniel, Dec. 1, 1650; Samuel, Oct. 28, 1653; Joshua, Nov. 5, 1655; Eliza, June 15 or 18, 1657; Sarah, 1659; James; Martha, April 1, 1662; Abigail, Feb. 4, 1664; Hannah, March, 1666; d. very soon, as did also a son without a name, in 1667. His w. d. Oct. 19, 1691, and he m. Oct. 2, 1694, Sarah, dau. of Joseph Bemis of W. and d. July 14, 1703. His will of June 4 of that year was proved July 28, foll. His inventory shows good estate.

John of Hartford, 1688, son of the preceed., m. Rebecca, dau., as Bond says, of Jonathan Butler, but an old friend has taught me that it was George Butler, and died without issue, 1722; giv. his estate to Jonathan, son of Samuel Butler. By one report his w. was Mary.

Jonathan, Hartford, brother of the preceed., m. 1671, Rebecca, dau. of Serg't John Shepard; by her had Jonathan; b. 1673; Rebecca; John; Mary, who, by Goodwin was erron. call. dau. of the sec. w. Sarah, and Violet, whose dates are not known, but all three lived to m.; for second w. he took Mary, dau. of Samuel Olcott, and by her had Samuel; b. bap. March 13, 1687; d. soon; Abigail, Nov. 2; 1690; Daniel, March 26, 1693; and Samuel, again, March 31, 1695; besides an infant, b. March 5, 1697, two days bef. its mo. He m. third w. Mary Benton, but had no children by her, who, after his death, m. March 1713, Dea. John Shepard, and died Dec. 23, 1752. * * * * * " Many variat. in spell. of this fam. name will be found in early records, but the gr. at Harv. in 1834, either with two or three syllab. amount to eighteen, two at Yale, one at Dart. and five at other N. E. Coll."—*Savage's Geneal. Dictionary.*

Christian, experiencing during a long and eventful life a lively interest in all that concerned her Redeemer's kingdom.

ELISHA, b. at Staddle Hill, near M., Oct. 1, 1776; m. Mary Bacon, June 25, 1809; had Samuel Brewster, and Elisha Brewster.

He was a farmer, and resided at Staddle Hill, and cultivated a part of the farm left by his father. He died from wounds received from falling upon a scythe, Feb. 16, 1855. He was a warm hearted generous man, and had strong love and affection for all who bore his name.

SARAH, b. at Staddle Hill, near M., Oct. 3, 1778; m. Feb. 26, 1799, John Stoughton, Esq., of East Windsor, b. Feb. 2, 1772; had I *John Wetmore*, b. Nov. 5, 1799; d. Sept. 15, 1801. II *Sarah*, b. Sept. 5, 1801; m. Thomas Potwin, of E. W., May 22, 1828; had 1, Thomas Stoughton; 2, Lemuel Stoughton; 3, Sarah Wetmore: Mrs. Potwin d. Dec. 14, 1841, æ. 40. III *John Wetmore 2d*, b. June 20, 1803; d. Nov. 13, 1812. IV *Lucy Wetmore*, b. July 18, 1806; m. Abner M. Ellsworth, of E. W., April, 1832; had 1, Frederick; 2, Samuel Hayden (dead); 3, Lucy Stoughton; 4, Sarah Elsie (dead); 5, Stoughton; 6, John; 7, Hugh Thompson. V *Lemuel*, b. March 5, 1808; m. Dec. 31, 1841, Hannah Blodget; had 1, Hannah Edwards; 2, Lemuel (dead); 3, Oliver Wetmore: m. 2d, Mary Moody, of Granby, Mass., Dec. 4, 1851; had 4, Susan Amanda (dead). VI *Ann Ellsworth*, b. May 25, 1810; m. Oct. 27, 1842, Frederick William Grant, of E. W.; had 1, Frederick Wm. (dead); 2, Anna Stoughton; 3, Roswell; 4, Lucy Elizabeth (dead); 5, Elizabeth (dead). VII *John Wetmore 3d*, b. Oct. 18, 1813; m. Mary E. Ellsworth, of E. W., Feb. 17, 1847; had 1, John Alden; 2, Mary Brewster: m. 2d, Mary Buckley Ellsworth, of E. W., June 4, 1856. VIII *Frederick Ellsworth*, b. July 23, 1817; d. Sept. 16, 1839. IX *Martha Jane*, b. Jan. 23, 1821; m. her cousin Charles Southmayd of Middletown, June 17, 1846; had Sophia (dead), Anna, John, Mary, Charles Everett (dead).

Mrs. Sarah (Wetmore) Stoughton, died at East Windsor, Nov. 12, 1836. She was a woman of clear intellect, strong religious principles, devotedly attached to the church (Presbyterian) to which she belonged;

charitable, ever excusing the faults of others; a devoted wife, and affectionate and faithful mother. She enjoyed the confidence and respect not only of her own family, but of the society of which she was a worthy member.

Mr. Stoughton, son of Lemuel, son of Nathaniel, son of John Stoughton, was an independent farmer on the banks of the Connecticut, in East Windsor; he was from a highly honorable family, his ancestry had enjoyed an enviable reputation in colonial times for their talent and moral worth. His father, Lemuel Stoughton held a commission, during the revolution, in the Connecticut forces at the city of New York; his great grandfather, John Stoughton, was one of the petitioners for a church organization, on the east side of the Connecticut river opposite Windsor, in 1694; he was also on the committee of the society, east of the river, in 1699, called then the Second Society of Windsor, of which the Rev. Timothy Edwards was first pastor. Mr. Stoughton was a man of great kindness of heart, he never suffered wrong to be done in his presence if he could prevent it; he was of a mirthful disposition, full of wit without bitterness; his hospitable dwelling was a spot his numerous kindred took great delight in visiting; plenty and good cheer, together with Christian graces ever abounded there. He died much lamented Sept. 19, 1841.

His sons, Lemuel and John W., still reside in East Windsor and are independent farmers and public spirited men, and receive much of that confidence from their fellow-citizens that their ancestors received before them. The latter has represented his native town in the state Legislature.

Thomas Stoughton Potwin and Lemuel Stoughton Potwin, grandsons of John and Sarah (Wetmore) Stoughton, are graduates of Yale College, the former in 1851, the latter in 1854. Thomas was made tutor in Yale in 1855, and Lemuel at a later date. They have since studied for the ministry, and are now Orthodox Congregational clergymen; the former residing at Franklin, Delaware co., N. Y.

TIMOTHY, b. at Staddle Hill, near M., Aug. 8 (2 ?), 1780, m. April 26, 1808, Hannah, dau. of Samuel Ward of Middletown; b. April 26, 1781; had Oliver and Timothy Edwards.

He was a farmer; removed with his family to Volney, N. Y., in 1821, where he resided some fourteen years, when he removed to Genesee county, N. Y., where he lived six years, from thence to the town of Alden, Erie county, N. Y., where he died from effects of injuries received from falling from a scaffold in his barn, July 25, 1848. He was an earnest Christian minded man, a member of the Close Communion Bap-'tists, in which society he held the post of deacon for many years. His widow resides with her son Oliver in Middleville township, Michigan.

LUCY, b. at Staddle Hill near M., Augt., 1782. She d. unm. Jan. 30, 1806.

The old west grave yard at M. contains her remains; a plain brown stone with her name inscribed, together with date of birth and death, indicates the place.

HANNAH EDWARDS, b. at Staddle Hill, near M., Aug., 1784; m. Feb. 13, 1805, John Pomeroy, son of Gov. John Treadwell of Farmington, Ct., b. Oct. 19, 1778; had I Oliver Wetmore, b. Dec. 31, 1806. He grad. at —— College in ——. He removed to the vicinity of Baltimore, about ——, where he established and carried into successful operation, the Mount Hope Seminary for young ladies. In order to the better educate his children, he removed to New Haven, Ct., where he now resides. In his life, he has rather avoided the obtrusive eye of the public; seeking pleasures and interest chiefly in literary pursuits. He m. July 31, 1834, Anna Helena, dau. of Frederick Kramer Bremen, Germany, b. Oct. 10, 1810; had 1st, Anna Helena Dorothea, b. Oct. 21, 1837, who m. Thos. Wilson Longstreet of Montgomery co., Md., Nov. 4, 1856; chil.

Helena Treadwell, b. Aug. 28, 1857, and Arthur Treadwell, b. July 20, 1859; 2d, Oliver Ferdinand, b. June 25, 1841; 3d, George Edwards, b. March 9, 1843; 4th, Lucy Whittlesey, b. Dec. 12, 1847. II *Eunice Gay*, b. July 23, 1808; d. Nov. 24, 1808. III *John Goodwin*, b. Jan. 26, 1811; m. April 30, 1841, Ellen Tinker, dau. of Jacob Holmes of New London, Ct.; had 1, Hannah Wetmore, b. Jan. 20, 1842; 2, Ellen Holmes, b. Aug. 10, 1843: d. July 31, 1844; 3, Sarah Wetmore, b. Aug. 15, 1845; 4, Mary Treby, b. March 22, 1847; 5, John Goodwin, b.. Nov. 23, 1848; d. infant; 6, John Pomeroy, b. Dec. 7, 1852; 7, Thomas, b. Nov. 18, 1854; d. Nov. 21, 1854; 8, Edward Norton, b. Sept. 7, 1856. Mr. Treadwell is of the firm of Treadwells & Perry, Albany, N. Y. IV *William Brewster*, b. Jan. 26, 1813; m. May 14, 1844, Mary Elizabeth, dau. of Richard Adams of Albany, N. Y.; had 1, Elizabeth, b. 1845; 2, Frederick (dead); 3, Franklin Adams, b. July, 1849. Mr. Treadwell is a partner of his brother, John G., and he, as well as his brother, has enjoyed for many years, an enviable reputation for high moral worth and integrity in his business and social relations. V Dr. *Samuel Edwards*, b. Dec. 17, 1815; m. Sept. 12, 1836, Anna, dau. of Mordecai Stamp of Talbot co., Md.; had 1, Helena; 2, Alice; 3, Lucy Wetmore; 4, Sarah, 5, Martha   Dr. T. was for many years in the practice of medicine at Havre de Grace, Md.   He died of typhoid fever, in the city of New York, April 30, 1860. VI *Sarah Wetmore*, b. May 20, 1818; d. in the city of New York, May 18, 1845; her remains were taken to Middletown for interment, and now rest near those of her maternal ancestry in the old west yard of that city.   She was a young lady of many virtues, personal charms and Christian graces.   Her death caused a void in her mother's heart, that was never subsequently filled. VII *Edward Francis*, b. Aug. 29, 1820; m. April 21, 1847, Rosina, dau. of Thomas Hamill, of Baltimore, Md; had 1, William Brewster; 2, Rosina; 3, Cornelia La Tourette; 4, James Wetmore; 5, Bertha Frances. Mr. E. F. T. is an attorney and counsellor at law in the city of New York. He has many of those sterling traits of character, that were so conspicuous in his grandfather, Gov. Treadwell.

Mrs. Hannah (Wetmore) Treadwell died Sept. 5, 1857; her husband the 11th of Oct., 1839. We have been furnished with the following sketch of Mr. and Mrs. Treadwell, which we insert in these pages. with more than ordinary satisfaction. We remember Mrs. Treadwell with feelings of love and admiration. Her

45

retentive memory, strong and well stored mind, high moral principle, with a faculty for imparting to others of her store of knowledge, her cheerful and kind disposition, made her a welcome guest in every circle where she was known. She had a just pride of family, and was ever ready to extend a hearty welcome to all who might claim kindred with her.

In this short notice of Mrs. Hannah Edwards Treadwell, it is not intended to eulogize alone, although that were a grateful task, nay, duty, on which one might linger with tender affection, but to depict some phases of her character which remoter generations of her posterity, may contemplate with admiration, though mingled with sorrow.

Of her life previous to her marriage, we have nothing to unfold. Surrounded with all the comforts of life, and enjoying the advantages of the most refined society which New England could boast, we can picture to ourselves very readily how such an intellect would have been employed.

The genealogical record states her marriage at the early age of 19, with John Pomeroy Treadwell, the eldest son of the then lieutenant governor of Connecticut. [27] Her residence, for ten years after, was in Burlington, Ct., where her husband was engaged in mercantile pursuits. Here four of her children were born, and her second child was buried. Unsuccessful in business, the firm of Treadwell & Gay, was dissolved, and her husband removed his family to the city of New York, in the hopes of permanent and renumerative employment which were never realized. Here two more children were born. The breaking out of the yellow fever in that city, drove the family to Middletown, Ct., where her youngest child was born, and where she continued to reside for many years. Afterwards, as her second and fifth sons became fixed there in business, the family again took up their abode in New York, where they continued to remain, until the death of her husband in 1839, at the residence of her eldest son in Baltimore, Md., and the decease of her only daughter in 1844, induced her to break up house-keeping and dwell with her

[27] For a biographical notice of Gov. Treadwell, see Appendix.

sons in Albany, New York or Baltimore, as might suit her pleasure or convenience.

She died September 5th, 1857, at the age of 73, at the old homestead in Middletown, Ct., and in the very room in which she had been born and married.

Such is the epitome of her life, on the surface appearing to be in no respect uncommon. But, in truth, there was much uncommon in her pilgrimage, not, it is true, in the outward circumstances which environed her, for multitudes have been called on to endure in this world, more than was her lot to encounter, but in the spirit and resolution with which she met her difficulties. Her life was a chequered one, full of vicissitude and trial and sorrow, yet not wanting, especially in the latter part of it, in joy and consolation.

The failure in business of her husband at Burlington, and his want of success afterwards in New York, made it a matter of necessity on the part of both husband and wife, to maintain the strictest economy, and to exercise the most untiring personal labor. The wants of a growing family were sometimes severely pressing, yet she met these wants without shrinking, presenting a firm and unshaken front. By her incessant toil, she furnished her children with all that they needed, both for body and soul : giving them the best education which the country could afford, and training them in their duties to God and man.

And for this abnegation of self, she, in her after life, met her reward. She lived, in God's loving mercy, to see in her own family, the verification of the maxim of Solomon, "Train up a child in the way he should go, and when he is old he will not depart from it." She was permitted to behold before her death, all of her children but one, members of the church of Christ, and all of them in positions of eminent usefulness and influence. By their success in the world, her sons were enabled to smooth her passage to the grave, and to show by unswerving devotion their tenderness for her who had done and suffered so much for them.

In saying, in this direction, thus much of this most excellent woman, it must not be supposed that there was the least direlection of duty on the part of the husband and the

father.   On the contrary, he was everything that the most
devoted husband and affectionate father could be: He was
truly one of the most loving and lovable of men, calm,
gentle, and tender in the extreme.   His earnest and laborious exertions for the honorable support of his family,
made him an old man before his time, for he died with the
constitution of a man of eighty, at the age of sixty-one.

Mrs. Treadwell was a woman of uncommon mental
ability.   She had the education which, when she was a
child, was accorded, at least in this country, to her sex.
And this, all who know anything of that period are aware,
was very limited.   Yet her reading was very extensive,
and whatever she read she retained.   She was exceedingly
well acquainted with the history of her times, and as they
dated back to those of the French revolution, her accounts
of the events of that stirring period, especially in connection with its influences on our own institutions and on the
character of our people, was eminently entertaining and
instructive.

Her colloquial powers were, indeed, unrivaled.   Her
abilities in argument, on any subject with which she was
familiar, could not be carelessly encountered by any one.
Her facts were always at her command.   Her assertions
with reference to historical matters, could seldom be successfully denied, or her conclusions refuted.

As a Christian woman her memory is sweet.   To say .
that she had no faults would not be true.   Let them be
" hid in the bosom of her Father and her God."   Let us
look only to her life of usefulness and honor, and bless
God for the recollections which it clusters around our
hearts.

CLARISSA, b. at Staddle Hill near M., July 25 (5 ?), 1786; m.
    Oct. 26, 1808, Capt. Gale Goodwin, b. in Middletown, July 22,
    1785; had I Emily Gale, b. in M. Oct. 16, 1809, who m. in Hart-
    ford, Nov. 27, 1830, Prof. Benj. Spilsbury Barclay, b. in Wor-
    cester, Eng., 1806; had 1, Thomas Spilsbury, b. in H. Feb.
    18, 1833, d. in Philadelphia, July 10, 1834; 2, Emily Eliza-
    beth, b. in Phila. Feb. 1, 1835, m. April 16, 1857, George
    Stuart, b. in Saratoga co., N. Y., Oct. 14, 1831, had William
    Barclay, b. in Phila. March 1, 1858, d. same day, Edward Gale, ′
    b. in Phila. Oct 1, 1859, d. inf,; 3, Ida Williams, b. in Phila.
    Nov. 29, 1836, m. Clement C. Moore of Fulton, Miss.; she d.
    at Fulton, Oct. 19, 1855; 4, Edwards Wetmore, b. in Phila.

Jan. 3, 1842; 5, Clara Hannah, b. in Camden, N. J., July 8,
1845 : Mrs. Emily Gale Barclay d. at Athens, Ala., Sept. 4,
1848. · Mrs. Clarissa (Wetmore) Goodwin m. 2d, Oct. 12, 1813,
Stephen Dodge of Colchester, Ct., b. Feb. 22, 1771; had II
Elizabeth Whitney, b. in Middletown, Aug. 27, 1814 ; m. Jan. 4,
1840, John Milward, b. in Halifax, N. S., Feb. 9, 1814, s. p.
III *Harriet Clara,* b. in New York city, Feb. 7, 1818; m.
Feb. 19, 1840, Dr. Thomas Greenleaf Chase, b. in Bolton,
Mass., March 3, 1793 ; had 1, Clara Annie, b. in Phila. Nov. 12,
1840 ; 2, Thomas, b. in Phila. June 11, 1843 ; 3, Alleyn Gar-
diner, b. in Phila. March 26, 1849 ; 4, George Emanuel, b. in
Phila. March 8, 1852 ; 5, Emeline Goodwin, b. in Phila. March
27, 1854, d. Aug. 15, 1856. IV *Clara Harriet*, twin sister of
Harriet Clara, b. in New York Feb. 7, 1818 ; m. Oct, 20, 1840,
Dr. John Fondey, of Albany, N. Y., b. Dec. 22, 1815 ; had 1,
Martha Townsend, b. in A. May 15, 1843 ; 2, William Hunn,
b. in A. Jan. 25, 1848, d. Aug. 6, 1850 ; 3, Clara Edwards, b.
in A. April 3, 1850 ; 4, Helena Wetmore, b. in Philadelphia
Oct. 14, 1857, d. Aug. 28, 1859 : Mrs. Fondey d. in Phila.,
Dec. 3, 1859. V *Stephen Larned*, b. in New Haven, Ct., Jan.
25, 1821 ; m. March 29, 1848, Elizabeth McCalvey, b. in
Phila. April 3, 1823 ; had Emily Milward, b. in Phila. June
30, 1849 ; and Henry Clay, b. in Paducah, Ky., Nov. 28,
1851. He d. in Philadelphia, April 26, 1855, in his 35th year.
VI *William Henry*, b. in Hartford, Ct., Sept. 6, 1824 ; m. in
Philadelphia, Oct. 14, 1852, Caroline Brown Ryan, b. in Rich-
mond, Va., Jan. 26, 1827. VII *Edwards Wetmore*, b. in
Hartford, Sept. 7, 1826, d. Sept. 8, 1826.

Capt. Gale Goodwin was lost at sea, during a severe
storm, *supposed* Jan. 15, 1810. The vessel, the
"Patty," of New London, encountered a gale in the
gulf stream ; she was subsequently seen in the Ber-
mudas, bottom up.

· Mr. Stephen Dodge, died at Hartford, Feb. 5, 1827.
Mrs. Dodge Sr., resides in Philadelphia. She has during
her life been visited with many trials and afflictions in
the loss of different members of her family. Her
strong faith and confidence in the promises of her
risen Saviour, has been her stay and hope in hours of
darkness. Her daughter, Mrs. Barclay, was a lady of
large benevolence and amiability, as well beauty of
person and manner. · To her half sisters and brothers

she was all their hearts could desire; she was their
counsellor, friend and dearest companion; her writings
shadowed forth the purity of her soul. The editor of
the *Pennsylvania Enquirer*, under date of Sept. 16,
1848, noticing her demise, says: "The subject of the
above brief and melancholy announcement, was a devoted daughter, a fond and faithful wife, a tender and
affectionate parent. She was highly accomplished,
possessed many noble qualities, and was esteemed and
beloved in the social and domestic circle, of which she
was at once the charm and the pride. * * * * *
Her dying bed surrounded by endearing affection,
was one of resignation and peace. She died the death
of a Christian."

The *Philadelphia Saturday Courier*, of Sept. 23,
1848, editorially on the same subject, says: "We
regret to recognize, in the name of the deceased, one
of our admired correspondents, author of "Song of the
Spring Time," "I Know the Spot," &c., and sincerely
sympathize with the bereaved husband and family,
who are left to mourn her irreparable loss."

We regret we have only space for the following, referred to above :

A SONG FOR THE SPRING TIME.

Oh! let us sing to the beautiful spring
A carol of welcome to-day;
　　She comes! she is here,
　　And her voices so clear,
Bids stern winter vanish away.

Hail to the Spring—the sportive Spring—
In her wild and frolicsome glee;
　　The streamlets play
　　In the sunbeam's ray;
Let us join in revelry;

Hail to the Spring—the mirthful Spring—
And the blossoming shrub and tree;

Birds are singing,
Forests ringing
With harmonious melody.

Hail to the Spring—the blooming Spring,
In her roses so fresh and gay;
The budding flowers
In garden bowers,
Are keeping nature's holiday.

Hail to the Spring—the tearful Spring—
With her gentle falling showers;
Now clouds appear,
Now skies are clear,
While swiftly speed the golden hours.

Hail to the Spring—the joyful Spring—
As she trips with footsteps light,
Strewing around
On the teeming ground
Her jewelry green and bright.

Hail to the Spring—the blessed Spring—
Displaying the power of God;
Throughout the land,
With a lavish hand,
She scatters His gifts abroad.

Then let us sing to the beautiful spring,
A carol of welcome to-day;
She comes! she is here!
And her voice so clear,
Bids stern winter vanish away.

PHILADELPHIA, March, 1848.

Mrs. Dodge's last sad bereavement, has been in the
removal of her much loved daughter, Mrs. Fondey.
The *Phila. Christian Observer*, in noticing the event,
says: "After months of suffering, which she endured
with patience and resignation, such as is seldom witnessed, this Christian woman has gone to her reward.
She was a devoted wife and mother, a fond affection-

ate daughter, a tender, loving, idolized sister. She possessed an amiable, loving disposition, surpassed by no one, whom the writer has ever known. Her character was one of child-like innocence, so pure and free from guile, that the thought of evil in others never entered her heart; from her infancy, she was remarkable for her love of truth, and therefore, was the favorite of every youthful circle in which she mingled. In mature life, no enemy sped its shaft, for none knew her, but to love and praise her.

" The scenes around her death bed, her triumphant hope of going to Jesus, will never be forgotten by those who witnessed them.

"As death approached, when asked if she was easy, she replied : 'Very pleasant, going to Jesus,' and as the last words died upon her lips, the spirit fled to the arms of her Saviour, with whom she so longed to be at rest. 'Blessed are the dead that die in the Lord.'"

Her sufferings during an illness of five months, she counted as nothing, when compare with the sufferings of her Redeemer for her; with her arms thrown around her sister's neck, she exclaimed : "I shall eat of meat that you know not of," then pausing for breath, "oh! my dear sister, I shall drink it anew in my Father's kingdom!" With such thoughts and expressions she was constantly occupied. While conversing on one occasion with her nephews and nieces, endeavoring to impress upon them the importance of coming to Christ, she said : "I gave my heart to God, when I was but thirteen years old, and I have never, no never, regretted it."

While Mrs. Dodge has had many things to sadden her life, she has had much to cause her to rejoice. Her children have ever been dutiful and affectionate, and have given her great satisfaction in their Christian life and character, as well as in their marriage relations.

Mr. Thomas Spilsbury Barclay's family were of high standing in England. He, as well as his brothers, is a graduate of Oxford University. Dr. Chase is a grand-nephew of Gov. John Hancock, his mother being a Quincy; his father, Thomas Chase, was a colonel in the revolutionary army, and he is descended paternally, in a direct line from William the Conqueror. Dr. Fondey is a Huguenot, both paternally and maternally; his ancestors settled in Holland, after fleeing from their prosecutors in France; and subsequently emigrated to America, his father's ancestors settling in the state of New York, his branch at and near Albany, and his mother's settled in New Jersey. Mr. John Milward's family were of Nova Scotia. His paternal grand-father was a resident of Brooklyn, Long Island, a man of high, moral and social standing, and honored by all who knew him. His mother was of German descent, and a woman most lovely in person and character. She was a devoted noble Christian, endeared to all who knew her, for her virtues, her charity, her tenderness and kindness to those who came within her reach. When God took her home, her children had to mourn a mother indeed, society its purest gem, the poor their friend, and the church one of its brightest ornaments. The widow of Stephen Larned Dodge is a descendant of the Abbotts of England, by her maternal side. Isaac Abbott, her great uncle, was lord high chancellor and speaker of the House of Lords for many years. Stephen Dodge, Sr., was a great grandson of Lord Gardiner, his grandmother Elizabeth, daughter of Lord G., and the wife of the late Mr. —— Whitney.

SOPHIA, b. at Staddle Hill, near M., May 25, 1788; m. Feb. 2, 1814, Giles Southmayd, of M.; had I *John D.*, b. May 8, 1815, m. Aug. 14, 1844, Harriet H. North, had Frederick Giles. He d. Oct. 11, 1847, in his 32d year. II *Thomas*, b. June 11, 1817; m. Aug. 31, 1846, Mary A. Mathus, s. p.; resides in Wilmington, N. C. III *Elizabeth*, b. July 12, 1819; m. May

5, 1853, Samuel Brown; had Thomas Southmayd, Lina Cone. He resides in Colchester, Ct. IV *Charles*, b. Oct. 1, 1821; m. June 17, 1845, his cousin Martha Jane Stoughton; had 1, Sophia (dead); 2, Anna; 3, John; 4, Mary; 5, Charles Everett (dead). Resides in Middletown, Ct. V *Timothy W.*, b. Sept. 27, 1823. VI *Lucy*, b. Oct. 19, 1825; d. Dec. 1, 1829. VII *Sarah*, b. Feb. 5, 1828; m. June 5, 1860, Rev. John Hartwell, of Leverett, Mass. VIII *William*, b. April 29, 1830; d. May 12, 1832. IX *Lucy 2d*, b. Nov. 4, 1833.

Mrs. Sophia Southmayd died March 15, 1841. She lived and died a consistent Christian, leaving a bright example of devotion to her principles, and affection for her family. Mr. Southmayd is of an old family of Middletown, and a much esteemed and respected citizen of that place.

CHAUNCEY, b. at Staddle Hill, near M.. June 5, 1790; m. Rebecca Hubbard, Oct. 9, 1817; had Chauncey Edwards, Lucy, Harriet, Cornelia Lyman, Henry Goodwin, Cornelia Hubbard, and Mary Ellen.

Mr. Wetmore resides on, and is proprietor of a part of the Staddle Hill farm, the homestead of his grandfather, Judge Seth. His dwelling is the same that was built by his grandfather in 1746. The exterior of the house is much the same, as it was when first erected, save that the gambrel roof has been changed for a more modern one. In the interior, the most of the apartments have the same finish they had in the days of their original occupant. The carved mantles and cornices, with water colored paintings over the fireplaces, are still to be seen.

Mr. Wetmore leads the quiet and retired life of an independent farmer; conscientious and generous in all his dealings with his friends and neighbors. He has always evinced a warm attachment for his kindred, and takes a lively interest in all that concerns their welfare. While he has a just appreciation of the rights of others, he hates oppression by what ever name it may be known; he never knowingly justifies any man or party, or church, in doing wrong for expediency's sake. He has long been a member of the First Congregational Church of his native town, and is a worthy representative of a worthy ancestry. May he long be spared to represent the family of Wetmores at Middletown, the home of the paternal ancestor of all of the name, and when he is called hence, may the place on which the head of this branch of the family established, and where he spent so many years of honorable life, be retained by some one of the descendants of the founder, bearing the surname of Wetmore. In our castle building in Spain, we have thought how well an asylum, or some charitable institution, or a college of learning, to be made free to such as could be accommodated of the descendants of Thomas Whitmore (Wetmore), who might need such advantages, would look on Staddle Hill. Why will not some one or more of the wealthy Wetmores, take into consideration the establishing out of their abundance, some such institution? What more lasting memorial could they establish of their ancestor, or of themselves?

EMILY, b. at Staddle Hill, near M., Jan. 1, 1795; m. April 6, 1815, Samuel B. Smith, of M.; had I *Lucy Beers*, b. April 9, 1816; res. in M. II *Emily Wetmore*, b. Sept. 13, 1817; res. in M. III *Henry Charles*, b. June 13, 1819; m. Jan. 16, 1843, Julia Burr, of Fairfield, Ct. He d. at Nevada, Cal., May 4, 1851, leaving Mary Eliza, b. Jan., 1844, and Julia Burr, b. Sept. 1846; his widow resides in Fairfield, Ct. IV *Samuel George*, b. July 16, 1821; res. in M. V *Julia Burr*, b. Feb. 28, 1823; d. while on a visit to East Windsor, Nov. 1845.

Mrs. Emily (Wetmore) Smith died April 27, 1852. She possessed much firmness of character; was a consistent Christian woman, and took a lively interest in all religious and benevolent enterprises. She was strongly attached to her kindred, and was always ready to meet them with a cordial welcome.

Mr. Smith was a farmer, and resided with his family

at Staddle Hill, and enjoyed the confidence and esteem
of his fellow citizens. He died in July, 1843, aged
53.

SIXTH GENERATION.

Children of SETH,

Son of Seth.

WILLIAM SHEPARD, b. in St. Albans, Vt. Jan. 26, 1801; m. in the
   city of London, Oct. 24, 1837, Esther Phillips, dau. of Samuel
   Wetmore Esq. of New York; had infant dau., d. Oct. 12, 1838:
   m. 2d, Anstice Rogers, of Salem, Mass.; had William Shepard,
   George Peabody, and Annie Derby Rogers.

That the subject of the above record deserves more
than ordinary mention at our hands, will we think be
admitted, when we state that so far as we are informed,
no one of the descendants of Thomas Whitmore, has
manifested more interest in the welfare of all those
bearing the name, than has he. He has done much
to bring about a fraternal feeling among the different
branches, by his efforts to collect together genealogical
records of the various families; and while we would
not detract from others, we may add that no one of
the sixth generation has, as yet, done more to honor
the name, at home and abroad, by a high-toned, upright, benevolent, and gentlemanly course of life than
has the subject of our notice.

That our readers may the more fully understand
his character, we will commence our sketch, by detailing a few circumstances connected with his childhood.

The first occasion for his leaving the home of his
youth, at St. Albans, was when one of his uncles and
aunts were on a visit to his father. It was then proposed that the " good and trusty William " should re-

turn with them to Middletown, preparatory to his being sent to school, and from thence to active employment. On the arrival of his uncle and aunt at St. A., he was enquired for; his father replied that he did not know where William was, but that he would return in safety. Night approached and he was enquired for again, with some feelings of uneasiness, but his father replied as before, that there was no cause for anxiety, that it frequently occurred that he was gone for a day or two and that he was not afraid of his intruding where he would not be a welcome guest. Late the following afternoon, William returned. Very large of his years, he had grown out of his clothes; a hat on his head, that presented the appearance of having seen very hard usage, and as if originally intended for a much larger head than his. Somewhat bashful and timid, such an appearance did not augur well for one who should subsequently stand the first merchant in a great city of the East; to be consulted by high officials both in the Indies and in England[28] upon state policy; and to amass wealth far beyond that possessed by any one of his name.

It took but a short time for his uncle to become convinced that the father's estimate of the boy was not the mere dictate of the heart of a fond parent, but was deserved. Before the visit was finished, plans were matured for William to accompany his aunt and uncle to Middletown — which he did. As soon as his acquaintance was made at M., all seemed to agree that he was a *clever* boy. His grandfather's family took a particular interest in him. He fell more immediately under the supervision of his uncle Willard Wright, who sent him to school at Cheshire,

[28] He was (while on a visit in England, at the commencement of the late famine,) in Ireland, and was invited by the ministry, to a cabinet meeting, held for the purpose of consulting upon the best method to be adopted, to supply food to that distressed land.

Ct., where he demeaned himself with great propriety, and made good progress. Though he was not remarkable as a scholar, his industry and perseverence gave him the respect of his teachers and friends. He was always very observing, learned accurately, not alone from the printed page, but from events and incidents as they came under his observation. He was, after going to school at Cheshire in a store in Middletown, and the following anecdote has been related to us, as evincing "William's readiness to adopt himself to circumstances," which has ever been characteristic with him. "The wife of the merchant with whom he was engaged as a clerk, happened. to have pancakes, the first day that he entered into his employer's service, and having a boy's appetite, he ate very heartily. So Mrs. V— gave him pancakes to eat daily and constantly, till he became tired of the sight of them. No complaint was made, however, by the boy, but when, of a Saturday, he used to get out to Staddle Hill, and his aunt's pantry was at his service, he made an onslaught, and told his aunt how tired he was of the ever recurring pancakes. His aunt thought his fare hard, and told him he ought to ask Mrs. V— to give him something else. "Oh! no," he said, "it will only make trouble, if I say anything about it, and besides Mrs. V— thinks I am very fond of them, for if the neighbors happen to make any remark, about what a pancake eater I am, she says: 'Oh, yes, I never saw any one so fond of *pancakes*, and it seemed on the first day as if I could not cook enough for him.'"

On one occasion he was desirous of going to a party of some kind, but not being supplied with proper shoes, and seeing no way of obtaining a pair without intruding upon his uncle, or in some degree compromising his feelings of independence, he concluded to forego the gratification; his aunt told him he was welcome to her slippers, and he willingly accepted the offer, saying he was glad to be able to go, *because* it would disappoint certain friends if he were not there; thus showing that consideration for the gratification of others was stronger than his own personal pleasure. After the entertainment, his aunt was informed that William called attention to the excellence of the fit of his aunt's slippers. Success in life, since, has not changed his character in this respect; what he was then, he still is, perfectly free from false pride and vain glory; accessible to every one, be he ever so humble; all he wants to know is, is he honest, is he deserving?

On his leaving Middletown, he went to Providence, R. I., in the employ of Messrs. Carrington & Co.—his uncles, Samuel and Willard Wright, being partners—where he acquitted himself so entirely to their satisfaction, he was entrusted by them, jointly with the captain, with the responsible position of supercargo of one of their ships, the Fame, on a voyage to England, the west coast of South America, and the East Indies. This, his first voyage around the world, was not a profitable one, though satisfactory to his principals, so far as he was concerned. His next voyage, in the employ of the same firm, was to the west coast of South America, in the ship Lion. On the vessel arriving off the West coast, she was totally lost, but her cargo was saved, in a damaged state. After disposing of the goods, etc., he sought employment in Valparaiso, which was soon found, and resulted in his forming, in 1823, in connection with Mr. Richard Alsop, of Middletown, the house of Alsop & Wetmore. The firm became very extensively engaged in business, enjoying, for a period, all the United States and a good part of the English trade to that port. In 1825, they were joined by Mr. John Cryder, of Philadelphia, and the firm became Alsop, Wetmore & Cryder. In 1829, Mr. W. retired from the firm, and returned to the

United States with what was considered at that time an ample fortune.

After his return his health became impaired, and, on advising with his physician, he concluded to go out to China, and there engage in business, hoping that the climate and an active life might again establish his health. Soon after his arrival in Canton, 1833, the late Nathan Dunn, of the house of Dunn & Co., retiring, he became his successor, associating with him Mr. Joseph Archer, of Philadelphia, who had been a junior partner of the late firm of Dunn & Co. The old house was highly respectable, but afterwards, under the style of Wetmore & Co., it became one of the largest houses in the East Indies.

During the time of his being engaged in business in China, the difficulties concerning the opium trade arose. He was opposed—as it was well known by the friends of the house and the Chinese authorities—to trading in opium or any other contraband article. If any opium came consigned to his house, it was received and taken care of, until after the destruction of the opium by the government, subsequent to which the house received none.

The English, by bribery of officials, smuggling, &c., carried on an immense trade in the article; and the English government, to their shame let it ever be said, protected their subjects in the traffic, justifying themselves by the specious plea, that "the conduct of the Chinese authorities, or executive officials, legitimatized the trade, in spite of the decrees and laws against the importation."

Mr. Wetmore's well-known reputation, as an honorable and high-minded merchant, caused him to stand favorably with the authorities of the empire, and, during the troubles growing out of the opium trade, he was invited to their counsels. After and during the war, great benefit resulted to the firm, in consequence of the general and constant conservative course adopted by the house.

In 1837, he returned to the United States for a short visit, stopping in England on his way back to China. While there, he married his first wife, the marriage festivities taking place at the residence of the bride's brother-in-law, Mr. John Cryder, Gloucester Lodge, Regent's park, London. As it was his intention to remain at Canton but a short time, his bride did not accompany him, but returned to her father's, in New York. On his arranging his business in the East, he finally returned to this country.

While Mr. Wetmore was abroad, he was in the constant practice of supplying his father with abundant means for his support, and, on his return, liquidated every reasonable claim that was made against his father's estate.

In 1844, he established in New York, in connection with Mr. John Cryder, the house of Wetmore & Cryder. In 1847, he withdrew his interests from the firm of Wetmore & Co., of Canton, having, by his connection with it, added very largely to his previous handsome fortune. The same year he retired from the firm of Wetmore & Cryder, Mr. Samuel Wetmore, Jun., succeeding him.

Possessed of ample means, with a reputation the most enviable, he, immediately after establishing himself in New York, took his stand among the leading merchants and bankers of that city. .

With a hand ever ready to relieve the wants and necessities of others, and so long accustomed to munificence in all his dealings, he became at once a valuable acquisition to benevolent and philanthropic circles.

Mr. Wetmore, soon after retiring from active business in New York, removed to Newport, R. I., where he built an elegant and very commodious marine villa, which is known as *Chateau sur Mer*. Here, in August,

1857, he gave a famous *fête champetre* in compliment to his friend, George Peabody, Esq., the wealthy and munificent American banker of London. This entertainment was pronounced, by the public journalists of the day, as quite the most grand and *recherché* private entertainment ever given on this continent. Distinguished strangers from Europe, the British provinces and the different states of the Union were present; and the whole affair was said to be worthy of the generous host and the distinguished gentleman for whose honor it was given.

Mr. Wetmore has declined public offices, preferring the real pleasures afforded him in private to the uncertain gratification of a public life. He is in stature full six feet, and of commanding figure; his head large, with a broad forehead, indicating strong mental faculties; his eyes light blue; his hair auburn; in his person he is said to resemble his late grandfather, Gen. Shepard.

CHARLES WRIGHT, b. at St. Albans, Sept. 8, 1803; m. Sophia
Hazeltine, Aug. 3, 1824; had Salome Smith, William Shepard,
Nancy Shepard, Sophia Hazeltine, Maria Louisa.

He removed to Stow township, Ohio, where he has frequently served as magistrate, as well as postmaster of Cuyahoga Falls. He and his uncle, Josiah Wetmore, were the first justices of Cuyahoga Falls.

NANCY SHEPARD, b. in St. Albans, Feb. 21, 1805.

She died at St. Albans, Jan. 18, 1830.

A circumstance of some interest occurred in connection with her death. Her cousin of the same name (dau. of Josiah Wetmore), and nearly the same age, died the same day, and nearly at the same hour; they were but a few miles apart, and although each knew that the other's situation was critical, yet neither was aware that the other was near her end, and the first consciousness of the fact, was when their souls met in the world beyond the grave.

SALOME SMITH, b. in St. Albans, April 10, 1809; d. June, 1810.

SETH DOWNING, b. in St. Albans, Dec. 28, 1811; m. Sophronia Burroughs of Portage co., Ohio, March 15, 1835; had Helen Frances.

He died at Massillon, O., May 13, 1853.

Children of Judge WILLIAM,

Son of Seth.

WILLIAM OGDEN, b. in Hartford, Sept. 5, 1796; m. Elizabeth Wallace, Oct. 2, 1822; had Henry, Edward, Edward 2d, Mary, Frederick, Julia and Eliza.

He resided at Cuyahoga Falls, where he was extensively engaged in manufacturing. He, with his brother Henry, built the first paper mill in Ohio, to spin out paper by machinery on the wet felt, as now universally used. They were public spirited men, and, while attending to the welfare of their own families, have always had the public good in view. He represented the counties of Portage and Summit in the state senate, in 1844 and 5. He died January 12, 1852, from exposure to extreme cold.

EDWIN, b. in Hartford, Sept. 25, 1798; m. Polly, dau. of Caleb, son of John, son of Dea. Caleb Wetmore, Aug. 24, 1820; had Silas, Charles, Luther; m. 2d, Polly Bell, Jan. 12, 1844; had Clarissa P. and Harriet B.

He is a farmer, and resides near the site of the old homestead, on the banks of Lake Pleasant. He has been a commissioner of Summit county for eight years, and a magistrate of the town for a number of years.

Descendants of Judge Seth, son of Izrahiah, son of Thomas.

HENRY, b. in Hartford, Feb. 10, 1801; m. Eliza B. Price, Dec. 8, 1830; had Henry W. and George Prentiss.

He resides at Cuyahoga Falls, where he is much respected. He is engaged in manufactures; he, with his father, and his brother William were, as it has been stated, the founders of that flourishing manufacturing town. He is the only survivor of the firm of Stow & Wetmores, to which firm the town of Stow and village of Cuyahoga Falls are greatly indebted for works of public utility. He has some of the characteristics of his father, advises, when asked, his neighbors and friends to compromise, rather than try the uncertainties of the law.

CLARISSA, b. in Middletown, Ct., March 18, 1804; m. Oct., 1827, Cyrus Prentiss, b. at Francistown, Hillsboro co., N. H., Feb. 10, 1797; [29] had I *Harriet*, b. April 20, 1829; II *Eliza C.*, b. Sept. 20, 1838.

Mr. Prentiss, removed with his father's family to Cuyahoga co., O., in 1804, where on arriving to "man's estate" he took a prominent position among his fellow citizens, in maturing the resources of the then new country. He died at Ravenna, after a short illness, on Friday the 29th July, 1859, much lamented by a wide circle of friends and relatives. The *Ravenna Democrat*, in noticing his death, says: "The announcement of his alarming illness, and sudden death startled our entire community, and produced a deep and prevailing sensation of sorrow and sadness. * * *" Wherever Mr. Prentiss was known, all hearts were touched with sorrow at his sudden decease, and all felt it a duty to offer to his honored memory the last tribute of respect that can be paid to man. The banks, stores, post office and all business places in Ravenna, were closed during the hours in which the

[29] For a history and genealogy of the Prentiss or Prentice family, see C. J. F. Binney's genealogy of those families, Boston, 1852.

funeral took place. The attendance of the elderly citizens of the place was very large. Those who had been intimate with the deceased in other days, could not resist the impulse to come forward and show emotions of respect to the departed man, whom it was a pleasure to meet when life's vigor animated his frame. A long procession escorted the remains to the house appointed for all living, the pleasant and well filled God's Acre, on the hill overlooking the lovely village, which Mr. Prentiss had done so much to improve and beautify. Solemn funeral service were read by the Rev. Mr. Baker, and ' dust was committed to dust, to share the holy rest that awaits a life well spent.' "

JACOB OGDEN, b. in Stow, Ohio, Jan. 29, 1807; m. Julia Newberry; d. s. p., June 8, 1841.

He was a highly respected, public spirited citizen, and his death was universally regretted.

HARRIET, b. in Stow, O., Feb. 17, 1816; d. Sept. 27, 1823.

Children of SAMUEL,

Son of Seth.

MARY WRIGHT, b. in Middletown, Ct.; m. at Providence, R. I., Oct. 7, 1830, John Cryder, Esq., of Phila.; had I *Samuel Wetmore*, b. in Phila., Dec. 1, 1831; d. at Poughkeepsie, N. Y., while at school, June 5, 1842. II *Anna Elizabeth*, b. in London, Eng. III *William Wetmore*, b. in London. IV *Elizabeth*, b. in London; d. infant. V and VI, *George* and *Mary* (twins), b. in London; d. infants. VII *Mary*, b. at Newport, R. I. VIII *Duncan*, b. in New York. IX *Edward*, b. in Phila. X *Esther Wetmore*, b. in New York. XI *Julia*, b. in New York: d. young.

Mr. Cryder resides in or near the city of New York; his life has been chiefly spent in matters pertaining to commerce. In 1825 he went out to Lima,

and joined, as partner, the house of Alsop & Wetmore;
subsequently they established the house of Alsop,
Wetmore & Cryder, of Valparaiso. The two houses
having a common interest, the Lima firm was changed
to Alsop, Wetmore & Co. In 1829, on the retirement
of Mr. Wm. S. Wetmore and himself from those firms,
as active partners, the style of both houses was
changed to Alsop & Co. He returned to the United
States; Mr. Alsop residing in Philadelphia, as representative of the firms in South America.

Mr. Cryder removed to London, and established
himself as a banker. In 1835, he, with Mr. James
Morrison, opened the banking house of Morrison,
Cryder & Co. Mr. Cryder's residence was in Gloucester
Lodge, Regent's park, where the hospitalities of his
mansion were dispensed by his accomplished lady,
whose natural sprightliness, remarkable conversational
powers, and amiability of manner, together with her
beauty of person, made her a charming hostess and
much-courted member of society in the *west end* of
that great metropolis.

In 1840, the firm of M., C. & Co. was dissolved,
and Mr. Cryder returned to the United States. The
firms of Wetmore & Co., of China, and Morrison,
Cryder & Co., of London, were in their business relations closely and intimately connected with the South
American houses, and Mr. Richard Alsop, of Philadelphia.

In 1844, the house of Wetmore & Cryder, of New
York (as before stated), was established, Mr. Wm.
Shepard Wetmore and Mr. Cryder composing the firm.
This house had close and intimate business relations
with Mr. George Peabody, banker, of London.

The firm of Wetmore & Cryder was dissolved in
1856. While in business, Mr. C. stood high, as an
honorable merchant and banker. He is, *paternally*, of
an old and highly respectable Delaware family; and
maternally, of an old Pennsylvania family.

ESTHER PHILLIPS, b. in Middletown; m. in London, Oct. 24, 1837,
    William Shepard Wetmore; had infant, b. in New York; d.
    Oct. 12, 1838.

She died in New York, Oct. 26, 1838.

It was our good fortune, when a youth, to make,
through the family of the late Hon. Henry R. Storrs,
her acquaintance. Her kindliness of manner, courteous
bearing and generosity, as well as her lady-like accomplishments, convinced us that she was a *truly* noble
woman. The feelings of respect with which she
inspired us we have never forgotten.

She was peculiarly strong in her family attachments,
and we have understood she often expressed the wish
that she were able to relieve the necessities of all who
bore the name of Wetmore, while she ever treated
them with marked kindness and consideration. Her
generosity and kindness of heart did not stop with
those of her own kindred, for she was constantly, as
she had opportunity, administering to the wants and
necessities of others. Her sympathies were ever alive
to those in distress.

Some months after marriage she returned from London to New York, where, it may truly be said, she
sacrificed her life in acting the part of a good Sama-
ritan to her own waiting maid, who was dangerously
ill, and died a short time before her mistress.

SAMUEL, b. in Middletown; m. at the residence of Col. René Ed-
    ward de Russy, U. S. corps of Engineers, Fortress Monroe,
    Old Point Comfort, Va., July 12, 1848, Sarah Tayler, dau. of
    Capt. William Boerum, U. S. N., and his wife, Emily Browne,
    b. at Fort Hamilton, N. Y.; had William Boerum, Wyatt.

He turned his attention in early life to commerce,
not however till he had fitted himself by study to
become an accomplished merchant. He first went
abroad in one of his father's ships to the west coast of
South America and China. Soon after his return
home, he embarked again for the East, with the inten-

tion of remaining there for a term of years.   In 1837 he joined the house of Wetmore & Co., of Canton, and on the departure of the senior member of the firm, for the United States, in 1839, he became the head of the house; he continued a partner till 1853, when he retired, withdrawing his interests.   In 1847 he succeeded Mr. Wm. S. Wetmore in the house of Wetmore & Cryder in the city of New York, which firm continued till the close of the year 1856, when he retired from all active business.

On the return of Mr. Wetmore to the United States, he commenced a very general correspondence with the various branches of the Wetmore family, for the purpose of collecting the history and genealogy of Thomas Whitmore and his descendants, that the same might be preserved in some permanent form.   He expended money liberally for this purpose, and the Wetmores are under obligations to him for stimulating the various branches with a spirit of inquiry respecting their common ancestry.

He secured a handsome fortune by his industry and judicious commercial adventures, and is now enjoying the fruits of his labors in the city of New York.   His wife Sarah Tayler Boerum, is of a highly honorable family; her great-grandfather, William Boerum, nephew of the patroon Simeon Boerum, equipped at his own expense, a company of dragoons during the Revolutionary war, and commanded them in person.   Her great-grandmother, the wife of the above Capt. B., was a heroine, and did her part towards bringing about an honorable peace.   On one occasion she passed through the enemy's camp, with £500 about her person, the proceeds of a sale of wheat.   This money she appropriated towards the maintainance of her husband's troops.

The patroon was a member of the first convention for the call of the first Congress.   He came direct from Holland. Her grandfather Martin Boerum inherited a large property, and married Jane Fox, of English parentage, a most exemplary Christian woman. She was one of the first communicants of the old St. Ann's (Epis.) church of Brooklyn, N. Y. She had large dower rights which she never availed herself of. She died Dec., 1848, aged 77.

Capt. WILLIAM BOERUM, U. S. N., the father of Mrs. W., was appointed a midshipman in the U. S. Navy, Oct. 15, 1811, and ordered to the sloop of war Hornet, 18 guns, on the 16th of the following month.

On the 21st of June, 1812, the frigates President, 44, Com. Rodgers; Congress, 38, Capt. Smith; brigs, Essex, 32, Capt. Porter; Hornet, 18, Capt. Lawrence, and Argus, 16 guns, Capt. Sinclair, sailed from New York Harbor in quest of a British fleet of merchantmen, bound from Jamaica to England. On the 23d, at an early hour of the morning, a sail was discovered to the northward and eastward, all sail was made for her and at half past four P. M., the forecastle gun of the President was discharged; this was the first hostile shot fired afloat in the war of 1812. The enemy's vessel proved to be the Belvidere frigate, 36 guns, Capt. Byram. The B., being the sharpest sailer, was enabled to get out of reach, not however without receiving a shot from the President, which killed one man and wounded sixteen others. The President lost twenty-two killed and wounded, sixteen of whom suffered by the bursting of a gun on board; Com. Rodgers having a leg fractured. "The squadron hauled up to its course in pursuit of the Jamaica men, and on the 9th July, the Hornet captured an English letter of marque; her master reported having seen the Jamaica vessels the previous evening, under convoy of a two deck frigate, a sloop of war, and a brig. He had counted 85 sail. The chase was continued with all possible speed, but without success. Com. Rodgers, finding himself within a day's sail of the British Channel, stood to the southward, passing Madeira, and going into Boston by the way of the Western Islands and the Grand Banks. Seven merchant-men were taken and one American recaptured."—*Cooper's Naval History*.

The Constitution, 44, and Hornet, 18, Capt. Lawrence, sailed Oct. 24th from Boston, under command of Com. Bainbridge, with orders to rendezvous at Port Praya, St. Jago. Midshipman Boerum, being on board the Hornet as before, says, in a letter to his father, dated

U. S. Hornet, Boston, Oct. 24, 1812.

We are now under way, the Constitution in company, I expect for a six months' cruise; we have provisions for that time, and also the Constitution for eight months. It is not known where we are going for a certainty, but Com. Bainbridge has ordered Capt. Lawrence to get charts for the coast of Brazil, and river Laplata, the Cape of Good Hope, Island of Bermuda, and both sides of the Mediterranean, besides the charts we have on board. * *

The same letter contains the following, although the report made by the captain of the schooner did not prove to be correct, we nevertheless give it, to show the commendable spirit that prevailed on board the Hornet:

The Captain has just spoken a schooner, who informs us that Commodore Rodgers has taken with the President, before the rest of the squadron came up, a large 64. Huzza! for the old Commodore. I have not the least doubt that if the Hornet comes alongside of a frigate, but we will take her or sink alongside, such is the spirit of our little crew.

The foundation of the schooner skipper's report, probably rose out of Commodore Rodgers giving chase to the Nymph frigate, but did not succeed in engaging her.

The vessels arrived off St. Salvador on the 13th of December, and the Hornet was sent in to communicate with the Consul where she found the British sloop of war Bonne Citoyenne, 18, Capt. Green, about to sail for England, with a large amount of specie on board. The British captain was invited outside, with the assurance that the Constitution should not interfere, but declined. The Constitution left the Hornet to blockade the Bonne Citoyenne alone, while she stood to the southward, when she came across the British frigate Java, 38, Capt. Lambert, which she captured.

The Hornet was left with discretionary orders. She remained off the port eighteen days, when she was chased into the harbor by the Montagu, 74, which vessel had come to relieve the B. C.[30] It was late in the evening when the Montagu approached, and the Hornet availed herself of the darkness to wear ship and stand out again, passing into the offing without further molestation. She stood northward and eastward, with the intention of going off Pernambuco. She made a few prizes, and continued up the coast until the 24th of February, 1813, when, near the mouth of the Demerara river, she gave chase to a brig, which drew in to land; just without the bar another vessel hove in sight, which proved a man of war brig, showing English colors. The Hornet was cleared for action. The two vessels were now, 5 P. M., standing towards each other, with their heads different ways, both close by the wind. They passed within half pistol shot, delivering their broadsides as the guns bore, each vessel discharging their larboard battery. As soon as they were clear, the Englishman put his helm hard up, with the intention to wear short round

[30] Cooper's Naval History.

and get a raking fire at the American, but the man-
œuvre was closely watched and promptly imitated,
and, firing his starboard guns, he was obliged to right
his helm, as the Hornet was coming down on his
quarter; the latter closed, and maintained the position
she had got, poured in shot with such vigor that, a
little before 5:40, the enemy not only lowered his
ensign but hoisted it union down. She proved to be
the sloop of war Peacock, 18, Capt. Peake; she sunk
before all of her men could be got off. The Hornet
returned to New York, via Martha's Vineyard and
Long Island Sound.[31]

We quote from Midshipman Boerum to his father:

UNITED STATES SHIP HORNET, }
NEAR NEW LONDON, AUG. 2, 1813. }

This morning Mr. Montandevert arrived with the money
for the Peacock; my share amounted two hundred and
fifty-seven dollars.   *   *   *   *

We have no particular news here, except that two of the
United States' boats, and two of the Macedonian's went
out on an expedition, but returned without being as successful as we expected, one of the Macedonian's getting
separated, went on shore at Gardner's Island, where they
found the first and third lieutenants of the Ramillies, one
midshipman and five men. Mr. Tenike, midshipman, who
commanded the Macedonian's boat with eight men, made
them prisoners and paroled them. * * * *

The commodore expects to get out in about six weeks.
I heard him offer to bet Capt. Biddle a new coat, that he
would have another frigate in some of our northern ports
this winter.

Subsequently Captain (afterwards Commodore) Biddle
succeeded Capt. Lawrence in command of the Hornet,
young Boerum continuing to serve on the H.

Capt. Biddle succeeded in evading the British squadron, and joined Com. Decatur at New York, who was
preparing the President flag ship, and sloop of war

---

[31] *Cooper's Nav. Hist.; Wilson's Nav. Heroes.*

Peacock, Capt. Warrington, for a cruise in the East Indies. Com. Decatur sailed in the President on the 14th of January, 1815, leaving the Peacock and Hornet to convoy the store ship, which was not then in readiness to sail.

They did not get out till the 23d of January, and separated a few days after in consequence of the Hornet chasing a vessel, which, on being overhauled, proved to be a Portuguése. From this they proceeded singly for their first rendezvous, which was the Island of Tristan d'Acunha; what immediately followed we will leave the young midshipman, Boerum, to narrate, which he does in the following graphic and patriotic dispatch to his father, dated

U. S. Ship Hornet, }
Off the Island of Tristan De Acunha, }
April 8th, 1815. }

We have had another action, and the Hornet is again triumphant. After leaving New York we had a continued series of ill luck, having seen only five sail, all of which proved to be neutrals. We parted with Peacock and Tom Bowline four days after we left New York, in chase. On the evening of the 22d of March we made the Island of Tristan De Acunha in latitude 37° 7′ south; longitude 11°. 38′ east. The next morning whilst preparing to bring the ship to anchor, we discovered a strange sail; we supposed her to be either the President, Peacock, or brig Macedonian, that sailed in company with the President. We however stood off a short distance from the shore, hove to and cleared the ship for action. About half-past, the strange sail, being within pistol shot to windward, hoisted a British ensign, and fired a gun, but no sooner did our brave tars see the enemy's flag, than they gave three hearty cheers, the Yankee stripes were unfurled aloft. We gave them a bloody broad-side, and the action commenced, which was continued with great spirit. But in the short space of twenty-two minutes their pride was humbled, and their flag came down. She proved to be His Majesty's sloop-of-war Penguin of 20 guns, James Dickenson, Esq., commander, who was killed in the latter part of the action.

She lost her foremast and bowsprit, had 28 wounded, and they acknowledged 14 killed, but from all accounts she must have had more. A number of her wounded have died since they have been on board. Her upper works were completely cut to pieces, two of her ports were knocked into one, and five shot struck her mainmast. Our loss was trifling, 1 killed and 11 wounded, nothing but grape shot touched our ship ; our rigging was considerably cut, and our spanker-boom was carried away by the enemy's running afoul of us.

Some tutelary angel certainly hovers over the American flag, and where's the youth whose bosom is fired with the righteous cause of liberty that don't aspire to be foremost in guarding the sacred banner of his Columbia ? When men fight for freedom they must be victorious. The next morning we took our prize in tow, and stood off from land, till we got everything that was of service to us out of her, and then sunk her. We had kept Capt. Dickenson on board, that we might bury him on shore, but on the third day we were standing in for the land, when we discovered two strange sail, one of which was plainly distinguished to be a man-of-war. The ship was immediately cleared for action, which obliged us to commit the body of our gallant enemy to the deep. The vanquished, if brave, are renowned. They are like the sun when he hides his face in a cloud, but shines again with redoubled splendor. He was buried with all the honors of war.

The two strangers proved to be the Peacock and Tom Bowline. The Peacock had been more unfortunate than we were before we fell in with the Penguin, having seen only one sail since we separated. We have made a cartel of the Tom Bowline. She will take the prisoners to South America, from thence she proceeds to the United States. We have watered here, and shall continue our cruise with the Peacock. * * * *

N. B.—Captain Biddle and Lieutenant Connor are among the wounded.

The Penguin had by their own account, 132 men, but I am confident she had more ; they had twelve additional marines from the Medway 74.

The combat between the Hornet and the Penguin, says Cooper, in his *Naval History*, was one of the most creditable to the character of the American marine that occurred in the course of the war. The vessels were fairly matched; and when it is remembered that an English flag officer had sent the Penguin on special service, against a ship believed to be materially heavier than the vessel she actually encountered, it is fair to presume she was thought to be in every respect, in her own service, an efficient cruiser, yet, with the advantage of the wind, this ship was taken in twenty-two minutes, including the time lost while she hung on the Hornet's quarter and while the latter was wearing. The neatness and dispatch (continues Cooper) with which the American sloop did her work, the coolness with which she met the attempt to board, and the accuracy of her fire and handling, are all proofs of her being a disciplined man of war, and of the high condition of that service in which she was one of the favorites. It is by such exploits that the character of a marine is most effectually proved.

The President, that sailed from the port of New York in advance of the Hornet and her companion, the Peacock, had been taken by the English. Notwithstanding this misfortune, Capt. Warrington, the senior officer, determined to proceed on the original cruise with the remaining vessels, and on the 12th April set sail for the Cape of Good Hope. On the 27th of the same month they fell in with a strange sail and gave chase, and at break of day the following morning they found themselves in close proximity to a line of battle ship, and she an enemy. The Peacock got ahead, the Hornet tacked to the westward, and the enemy commenced a chase which continued for a day and a half, and, to get clear of her, the Hornet had to throw overboard much of the store taken from the Penguin and his heavy anchors, together with six of his heavy guns, the ship coming up at times within three-quarters to a mile distant, casting shot all the while, which, fortunately for the H., but three struck her. To throw off his persistent enemy, Capt. Biddle had to continue casting overboard all the spare material on deck. A favorable change of the wind brought the Hornet to the windward, when she began to make space between herself and her too familiar companion, and the next day, at meridian, she was fairly clear of danger. The H. had now but one gun, no cable, anchor or boat, and she made her way to New York, where she arrived June 9th, 1815.[32]—*Cooper's Naval Hist.*

Capt. Biddle gained nearly as much reputation for the steadiness and skill with which he saved his ship on this occasion, as for the fine manner in which he had fought her a few weeks earlier. The vessel that chased the Hornet was the Cornwallis 74, bearing the flag of an officer to the West Indies. * * * *

The battle between the Penguin and the Hornet was the last regular action of the war.—*Cooper's Naval History.*

November 16, 1815, Mr. Boerum was granted a leave of absence, for six months; was appointed lieutenant, March 5, 1819; ordered to the Nonsuch, June 24, 1817, and to New York for duty March 28, 1818; to the navy department, Feb. 4, 1820; to the New York station, Oct. 26, 1820, and to the Constitution, March 17, 1821; granted leave of absence for six months, Oct. 29, 1824; ordered to the brig Shark, Dec. 8, 1824; leave of one month, July 12, 1825; ordered to the Macedonian, April 26, 1826; leave unlimited, Nov. 1, 1828; ordered to the Erie, Oct. 7, 1829; detached from command of schooner Shark, July 18, 1833, and leave of three months; ordered to the Constitution, July 31, 1835; appointed to the command of the schooner Shark in the Mediterranean, by Com. Elliott, Dec. 24, 1835; promoted to a *commander*, Aug.

[32] Wilson in his *History of Naval Heroes* reports the Hornet to have arrived at New York July 30.

4, 1838; detached from the Constitution and three
months leave; ordered to the command of the sloop-
of-war Concord, and on the 2d of Nov., 1842, was
drowned on the bar at the mouth of Loango river,
Portuguese province of Quillemane.[33]

It was to the Concord, which had been wrecked off
the mouth of the Loango river that Capt. B. was returning, when his boat was capsized, and he lost his
life.

But few officers of the navy saw more active service
than did Commander Boerum, and he died in the faithful discharge of his duty.

ELIZABETH HOPPIN, b. in Middletown, m. in New York, Nov. 21,
1845, Rev. George B. Cheever, D. D.; had George Wetmore,
b. at Newport, R. I., Aug., 1856; d. Aug. 23, 1856.

She deserves more at our hands than we have the
data to give. She is mild and gentle, modest and unassuming. In her girlhood she was of a strong conscientious and religious turn of mind, and preserves
these characteristics in her womanhood.

Dr. Cheever's biography we could hardly presume
to sketch. His bold, fearless preaching and writings,
have made him many enemies; he has, however,
daguerreotyped living principles upon the hearts and
minds of thousands, that will never be effaced either
in this world, or in the world to come. For many
years he has been the courageous and faithful pastor
of the church of the Puritans in the city of New York,
which was erected especially for his ministry.

GEORGE PHILLIPS, b. in Providence, R. I.

He was prevented by an impaired vision during his
years of study from developing a naturally strong and

[33] For these dates of orders, &c., of the Navy Department, we are indebted
to Hon. Secretary Toucey, under date of his favor of the 8th of September;
1860.

brilliant mind.   The skill of a London oculist enables
him to see to an extent sufficient for all ordinary
wants of life, and he has acquired a more general
knowledge than often falls to the lot of students who
are blessed with perfect sight.   He possesses an ample
fortune, acquired by judicious adventures to the East
Indies, and fortunate investments of their net proceeds.

FRANCES, b. in Providence, R. I.; m. in New York, Oct. 25, 1842,
John Jacob Taylor; had I *Jacob Bloome*, d. 1843; II *John
Jacob*, b. in New York; III *Amelia Mott*, b. at Saratoga Springs
d. April 5, 1855; IV *Elizabeth Cheever*, b. in New York; Mr.
Taylor d. June, 1852; m. 2d, Thomas Robinson, son of Hon.
William Hunter of Newport, R. I.; had V *William Robinson*,
b. in Newport; VI *Elizabeth Wetmore*.

Mr. Hunter resides at Newport.   He represented in
part that city in the General Assembly of Rhode Island
in 1852, '53 and '54, and was mayor *pro tem* of Newport in 1853, and member of the board of aldermen in
1854 and 1855.   He was for a time attached to the
U. S. Legation at the court of the Tuilleries during
the Hon. William C. Rives' embassy.   His father, the
late Hon. William Hunter, was a distinguished citizen
of Rhode Island.   We quote from Lanman's *Dictionary of Congress:* William Hunter, born at Newport,
Rhode Island, November 23, 1775; graduated at
Brown University in 1791; went to London and
studied medicine, but soon changed to the law, and
entered at the Inner Temple in London; and on his
return to Newport, at the age of twenty-one, was admitted to the bar.   In 1799 he was a representative
in the General Assembly of Rhode Island, and reëlect-
ed at different periods from that time to the year 1811,
when he was chosen a senator in Congress, and held
his seat till 1821.   His speeches, especially those on
the acquisition of Florida, and the Missouri compromise, won him a high reputation as a sagacious states-

man, and a finished orator. In 1834 he was chargé to Brazil, an office which was in 1842 raised to a full mission, and he was continued as Minister till 1845, when he retired from public life, and resided at Newport until his death, which occurred December 3, 1849.

EDWARD CARRINGTON, b. in Providence, R. I., Oct. 18, 1824; d. unm. in New York, Sept. 13, 1846.

Children of TITUS,

Son of Seth.

SETH, b. Nov. 10 (16?), 1808; d. unm. May 8, 1831.

WILLARD WRIGHT, b. Oct., 18—; d. unm. June 1, 1830.

JOSIAH, b. May 13, 1816; m. Oct. 29, 1839, Elizabeth R. Brainerd, b. July 18, 1821; had Morris, Henry.

Children of JOSIAH,

Son of Seth,

NANCY SHEPARD, b. at Middletown, Oct. 18, 1808: m. about Dec. 1828, Col. William L. Sowles of Alburg, Vt.; had Henry Shepard, b. Jan. 10, 1830; d. aged about 19 months.

She died Jan. 18, 1830. Remarkable for her mild and gentle nature, her purity of character endeared her to all with whom she associated. The privations incident to a life in an unsettled country, and fevers to which she was exposed, undermined her constitution, and brought her to an early grave. It was she, to whom we alluded in our notice of the circumstances attending the death of Nancy Shepard, daughter of Seth 3d. The similarity of name, character and time of decease of each, at a short distance from each other, being a coincidence of special interest to their relatives and friends.

NATHANIEL DOWNING, b. in Middletown, Dec. 4, 1810; m. Lydia
Ann Hanson McIntosh; had Nathaniel Downing, Emily Amanda, Henry Shepard, Lucy Ann, Lydia Amelia.

Is an honest, upright man. At thirteen years of age,
he had the misfortune to sever his knee pan, and has
consequently been more or less a cripple since that
time. This circumstance we notice, as it gave occasion for his mother to show those resolute qualities of
which she is possessed. A correspondent in relating
the affair, says:

"While the lad lay on the bed in the log house
where his parents lived, his father, together with
other members of the family, were prostrated with
typhoid fever, then prevalent in the western reserve.
The knee grew worse from day to day, till it assumed
a frightful form. The physician in that neighborhood,
was coarse and rough. In spite of his daily attention,
it was evident that no improvement was taking place,
but everything indicated actual approach of mortification. One morning the doctor called about the usual
hour, accompanied by two stalwart young men. The
mother observed a little more than usual unpacking,
as the doctor dismounted from his horse, but she was
still unsuspicious what was about to be undertaken;
walking into the house, placing his parcels on the
table, the doctor said, "Good morning, Mrs. Wetmore,
I have come to take off that boy's leg, and these young
men have come to assist me." The mother knew that
the boy's strength was almost gone, and felt that the
terrible operation could not be effected and he survive,
or if he lived, there came instantly to her mind, the
idea of a poor crippled child for a whole life time.
The sudden and abrupt manner in which the suggestion was made, horrified and shocked her feelings;
for a moment she was stupified and could only mechanically give utterance to the exclamation, " *Oh!*

doctor, I don't know about that." " Of course," says
the doctor, " *you don't* know, and I shall *insist* upon
doing what is justice to my patient, and demanded of
me as a practitioner." The bluntness of the doctor
aroused the feelings of the mother, and there being no
time to lose, she replied with great firmness : " Doctor,
I am able to take the responsibility on *my* shoulders.
I do not approve the course you intend to pursue ; it
can not be done, unless the boy desires it ;" and leaning over the lips, which could hardly move to utter
the words, she received the reply, " Let me lie in the
grave, mother, with my limbs on." The young men
were much affected, but the doctor was unmoved, and
said, " Pooh, pooh. How can the boy know what is
for the best ?" " *It can not be done,*" said the mother.
" *It shall not,*" said the young men. . The doctor finding himself overruled, hastily placed the instruments
(which he had all the time been arranging) in the
case, picked up his saddle-bags, and said "Take charge
of matters then, you know *better* than I do." " What
shall I do for that little boy (alluding to one lying
sick of fever), and for my husband," asked the mother ?
" Oh, *you* know best," replied the doctor, and rode
away. Messengers were immediately sent to a young
physician who had lately come into that part of the
country, and when he arrived he declared that the
operation would certainly have proved fatal. Youth
and nature did more than the young doctor dared to
hope for, and he survived.

This was a trying position to place a mother in, but
as the sequel has shown she was equal to the emerg-
ency."

We will give one more incident to illustrate Mrs.
Wetmore's self-possession in the hour of peril, for
which we are also indebted to the same correspondent.

* * * Many years after the foregoing incident, her husband was taken with severe illness. She had no one around her but her little children. The delirium which ensued was so violent, that constant care was necessary, and the wife had watched, till almost worn out. The doctor found it necessary to bleed his patient. This quieted him, and he lay sleeping calmly. The wife had not removed her clothing for many days, and as her husband appeared so comfortable, she thought she would seek some repose herself. Naturally, she fell asleep. It was 10 o'clock when she retired; about 1 she awoke, and as her husband was so quiet, she placed her hand on him, but found him *cold* and *motionless*. In turning, and insensible of what he was doing, he had rubbed the bandage from the arm, which caused the lance wound to bleed so freely, that the bed became a pool of blood. Examining the wound, she perceived that all compression was removed, and that the vein had oozed out from the incision. She procured a small knife, and taking the arm, inserted the pouted vein, and firmly bandaging on a small slip of wood, called one of her sons, and sent for the physician. The doctor arriving, could not discover any signs of life; as all had been done that man could do, he sat silently by awaiting the issue. About noon, which was nearly twelve hours, from the time the patient's situation had been discovered, evidences of circulation were observable, a slight blur on a looking glass had been the only evidences of vitality; from this moment, he gradually recovered.

Mr. Nathaniel D. Wetmore embarked in business early in life, which has caused him to remove severally to Canada, Dover, N. H., Rochester, N. H., and Cuyahoga Falls, Ohio, where he now resides, at all of which places, he has been esteemed a correct business man, and one who would rather submit to a wrong himself, than be suspected even of committing a wrong upon another.

He was a member of the general assembly of New Hampshire in 1846, 7 and 8, and having had previous pleasant intercourse with the Hon. John P. Hale, he gave point and direction to the movement which resulted in the election of Mr. Hale to the United States senate. He has much of that unselfishness of character, for which many of the descendants of Judge Seth, have been remarkable. We regret that we have not space to illustrate this trait of his character, by giving at least one of the many examples that he has furnished to his cost. He was U. S. marshal for a census district in New Hampshire in 1850, and was treasurer of the county of Stratford, N. H.

LUCY WRIGHT, b. in Middletown, July 13, 1812; m. Dr. Chester W. Rice of Cuyahoga Falls, Nov. 6, 1834; had I *Sarah Frances*, b. Aug. 24, 1835, who m. Edwin J. Howard, Aug. 31, 1858 : II *William Olney*, b. May, 1837; III *George Wetmore*, b. Nov. 7, 1845.

Dr. Rice resides at Cuyahoga Falls, where he is a successful practitioner.

MOSES WILLARD, b. in Middletown, Jan. 19, 1814; m. in Cincinnati, O., April 3, 1834, Julia, dau. of Norman and Ruth Dexter, of New Haven, Ct.; had Henry Stanley; m. 2d, Sept. 15, 1836, Mrs. Jane Eliza Heddington of Louisville, Ky., dau. of Maj. Richard Oldham; had Julian Neville, Florence Lorelle, William Calhoun Stewart, Mary Thomas, Oldham Bryson, John Edgerton, Jeannie Elise, Leona Matilda.

He commenced his business career at an early age, and has experienced what may be termed an eventful life.

The following story of him has been related to us. We give it to show the principle by which he was governed, when he started in life; at the same time furnish a good example to others. He was on one occasion, when a young man, traveling in a stage coach from Charlestown, N. H., to New Haven, Ct., with one of his brothers. In the same stage was an Irishman, in thread-bare apparel, shriveled up with the cold, which was intense, for it was early in January. The poor fellow sat alone on the seat he occupied, shaking, and his teeth chattering as if he had the ague. The two brothers were warmly clad, and had with them a heavy bear skin. Moses asked the man some questions, but the son of Erin could give no satisfactory account of himself, further than to say that it was so cold in that region he was going to meet warm weather. He told him he would freeze before morning in the condition he was, and begged him to come over to the seat which he and his brother were occupying, and share the benefits of the bear skin. This the poor fellow did, and his benefactor saw how nearly perished the man was; he requested his brother to sit the other side of the coach, and let the man sit between them. Thus the three rode all night. The next morning at breakfast his brother remarked to him, " That (alluding to the Irishman), is a strange man. I would not ask him to sit on the seat again, for I have been thinking that it is very probable he is the Irishman who committed that horrible murder a day or two since at Clermont, now fleeing from justice; for his story is strange, and his manner so remarkable." " Brother," says Moses, " never take such measure of a charitable act, the man was in distress, and if I had *known* he was the murderer, I would have warmed him when shivering and suffering as he was, if I had the power to relieve, and I will always do so, be the sufferer who or what he may."

Mr. Wetmore removed to Tennessee some years since, where he has acquired an independence. He now resides in the city of Nashville.

WILLIAM HASTINGS, b. in Middletown, June 13, 1816; m. March 9, 1849, Mrs. Eleanor, widow of Timothy Keyser of Nashville, Tenn.; had William Angelo Keyser, Charles Williard Shepard, Sarah Florence Eleanor, and Anna Cora Willard.

His older brothers leaving their father's roof, left William Hastings to see to the welfare of the family, and by his industry and labor on the farm during summer, and keeping school in the winter, he was enabled to be of essential service to his parents.

He afterwards left home while still a young man, and took up his residence in the state of Tennessee. He now resides in the town of Wetmore, Polk county, where he is the postmaster. The town of Wetmore was first established by his brother, Moses Willard, and his cousin, William Shepard Wetmore. He, with his cousin, William S., and his brother, Moses W., and others, owned large tracts of mineral lands in the vicinity of the town. He is a gentleman of punctilious habits and religious principles.

· Mrs. Wetmore's father was Samuel Henry Laughlin, of Western Virginia, whose father removed to Tennessee when he was quite young. The son acquired a liberal. education by his own· exertions, and distinguished himself as a lawyer, and a political writer and leader. His wife was a Miss Bass, of Tennessee; his death occurred in Washington, D. C., about 1850, his wife having deceased before him.

JOSIAH FARNSWORTH, b. in Middletown, May 8, 1818; m. June 22, 1841, Sarah Ann, dau. of Griffen Green, Esq., of New York; had Robert Dean, Mary Denison, Thomas Townsend, Edward Griffen, George Townsend.

He was but an infant when his parents removed from Middletown to Stow, Ohio, where he spent his days of childhood, suffering much sickness and many privations incident to an unsettled country. At seven or eight years of age, his aunt, Mrs. Denison, made him a member of her family, where everything conspired to make life joyous; he attended to his studies, having the care and assistance of his cousin, Charles Denison.

When it became necessary for him to prepare for a business life, he attended a boarding school till the time fixed for his departure to China, where he was to be under the care and mercantile instruction of his cousin, Wm. Shepard Wetmore. In 1835 he sailed from Providence. On his arrival in Canton, his cousin found him too immature in years to be confined strictly to business; so, with his cousin's accustomed liberality and large-heartedness, he conceived the idea of sending him to London, there to acquaint himself with the tea trade and business generally. He spent three years in L., profitably as well as pleasantly, and everything indicated a prosperous career; but misfortune was in store for him. The time arrived for him to return to China, taking New York en route.

In bidding adieu to his London friends, he was made the recipient of many marks of their esteem. The excitement attending his leaving England caused him to feel much debilitated; he expected that the quiet of a sea voyage would fully recruit his health and strength. On board ship he made the acquaintance of an old gentleman, a Quaker, who was intelligent and affable, and the two soon found themselves close companions.

After a few days out the old man was taken violently ill; the captain being enfeebled in health, and from the want of proper feeling on the part of certain Boston, Scotch and English passengers on board, the care of the invalid was left wholly to our young friend. Each night the sick man would not rest without his new-made friend by his side; so it continued, from day to day, till the termination of a long voyage, and when the vessel arrived at the port of New York the young man was broken down in health and strength, instead of being recruited, as he had anticipated. His friend, Daniel Wheeler, for that was his name, died of dropsy on the chest soon after arriving.

Before sailing for the East, Josiah desired to pay a visit to his parents at Cuyahoga Falls. On the way

he was seized with a cold, which settled into a fever
and a disease of the eyes, so that when he arrived at
his paternal home he was in a precarious situation,
and quite blind.

After many months' detention on the Reserve, he
returned to New York, where his eyes were treated by
a celebrated oculist; his right eye was lost. During
his long confinement and suffering, he had the *kindest*
attention of the lady who subsequently became his
wife. The long delay caused by his sickness rendered
it impracticable for him to return to Canton. Thus,
falling in with his Quaker friend gave a turn to his
whole life. It may be truly said in his, as in all cases,
" Man proposes and God disposes." The Christian
example of his mother, and his aunts Denison and
White, were not lost upon him, which was, not to
distrust Providence; this simple trust enabled him
not only then but has constantly since, to bear up
under all his disappointments in life.

He was inspector of the customs for the port of
New York during Presidents Taylor and Fillmore's
administrations. He resides in Brooklyn—doing business in Wall street, N. Y.

SAMUEL FARWELL, b. at Stow, O., May 3, 1820; m. Lydia Leonard
    Wadleigh, Sept. 18, 1845; had Willie Courtney, Harriet Wil-
    lard, Mary Frances Molineux, Ralph.

In his early youth he formed a partiality for printing and publishing, which he chose for his business,
on arriving at a proper age; he became the editor and
publisher of the *Manchester* (*N. H.*) *American*, etc.
He was the deputy secretary of state of New Hampshire for 1847.

ROBERT COURTNEY, b. at Stow, O., Nov. 30, 1822.

He died unmarried at Cuyahoga Falls, Aug. 2, 1853.
He was amiable, benevolent and kind in his disposi-

tion ; was a printer by profession, and for a time published a newspaper at Concord, N. H. He was a ready and forcible writer, indulging at times in wit and satire. A writer in a Cleveland paper, noticing his death, says:

Though strictly a moral man, he had not till his last sickness, so realized his need of something higher and more enduring than morality, as to seek with earnestness and perseverance an interest in a crucified Saviour. But God in his mercy visited him with that *slow*, though sure disease, consumption, and thus gave him time to review the past, and prepare for the future. And he gave us cause to hope that it was well employed. He felt that he could but look back with shame to the past because of a neglected Saviour, and that salvation so needful to all.

After much earnest wrestling with God in prayer, the prospect for the future brightened, and he was finally enabled to appropriate, "by faith," the promises of God to his soul. The patience with which he was able to endure his closing and protracted sufferings, and to wait God's time and will, was a strong evidence of, and a witness for the power and triumph of faith. And yet he realized the folly of delaying to prepare for death to the eleventh hour. May we all take warning and "watch."   H.

GEORGE HENRY, b. at St. Albans, Vt., Jan. 5, 1825.

He resides at Polo, Ogle county, Illinois. He, like most of his family, has great kindness of heart and amiability. A fund of wit and anecdote, together with benevolence and good feeling, conspires to make him, as he is, popular among his friends and acquaintances.

Children of Rev. OLIVER,

Son of Deacon Oliver.

EDMUND ARNOLD, b. in Middletown, Ct., Aug. 6, 1798; "baptized Lord's day, March 6, 1803, by the Rev. Nathan Strong, D. D.;" m. in Utica, N. Y., June 3, 1829, Mary Ann, dau. of

John Hosmer and Jerusha (Kirkland) Lothrop, b. in Utica, Oct. 16, 1806; had Mary Buckminister, Cornelia Lothrop and Edmund.

He resides in the city of Utica; graduated at Hamilton College in 1817; studied the profession of law, in the office of Messrs. Gold & Sill, Whitestown, N. Y. He commenced the practice of his profession in Utica, in connection with the late Hon. Morris Miller. For the following notice of Mr. Wetmore, we are indebted to an eminent member of the Oneida county (N. Y.) bar.

He practised law many years successfully as a partner of the present judge, Hiram Denio, but after the latter entered judicial life, he gradually withdrew from the active part of his profession, being engaged in somewhat extensive land agencies.[34]

Some years since he was elected treasurer of the New York State Lunatic Asylum, a position of great responsibility, and requiring a large devotion of time and labor to fulfill its duties, which he discharges with marked fidelity. His fellow citizens have not been unmindful of his merits as a public servant; he was twice elected alderman of the city; and in 1845, was chosen by the people mayor, and re-elected with great unanimity the following year.

Soon after the organization of the public school system, he was elected one of the six school commissioners, who have charge of that great interest. In this cause his labors have been abundant, and are so well appreciated by the public, that he has been constantly re-elected, and we should as soon think of taking out the main column of an edifice by which it is in good part supported, as permitting him to retire from his honorable, although onerous post.

He was also one of the commissioners for building the City Hall, a large edifice, which is an ornament to the city.

For many years he has been a trustee of Hamilton Col-

[34] He was agent for the Holland Land Company; also late Stephen B. Munn, of New York, and others.

lege, and performed, in connection with that institution, a great amount of most valuable, though unrequited service.

These are a few of his public duties and labors. Of his private life, it is only necessary to say, that he is a model husband, father, neighbor and friend; and if the phrase be true, "An honest man is the noblest work of God," then it is true, that he stands fairly and squarely upon that platform.

In Mr. Wetmore's social and private relations of life, has his nobleness of character been the better reflected. To his aged and infirm father, he was the chief stay for more than twenty years, and no parent could have been more tender or considerate of the wants of a child, than was he of his father's, and his father in return gave him all the affection and confidence which he was possessed of. To his step-mother and half-brothers and sister, he has been alike considerate. They who survive, owe him for his aid and good counsel much more than they have, or will ever be able to return.

He has been warmly seconded in his deeds of kindness and benevolence by the partner of his joys and his sorrows. His wife is the fourth child, and second daughter of John H. and Jerusha (Kirkland) Lothrop. She has largely inherited the virtues and accomplishments of her ancestry, and she has cultivated her inheritance with a diligent assiduity. During her minority she enjoyed the benefits of education and society at the town of Cambridge, the seat of Harvard University; her uncle, John Thornton Kirkland, D. D., LL. D., being at that time president of that institution, gave her an unusual opportunity to acquire useful knowledge and accomplishments pertaining to a highly cultivated and refined society, which advantages were not lost upon her. In society, she has ever been a valued member and an ornament; by her fireside have her virtues been the most conspicuous; there that which graces a family circle have always been found. Her father, the late John Hosmer Lothrop, was born at New Haven, May 20, 1769. He graduated at Yale College, 1787. He was a classmate of the Rev. Azel Backus, D. D., first president of Hamilton College, and of the Rev. Dr. Chester, of Albany, and was an intimate and warm friend of both during their lives. Mr. Lothrop studied law in New Haven and Hartford, and was admitted to practice in the courts of Connecticut. He removed to the state of Georgia, where he was successful in acquiring property. He married Feb. 1, 1797, Jerusha, daughter of the Rev. Samuel Kirkland.[35] After his marriage he removed to Oneida county, N. Y., where he purchased a valuable estate, and a very pleasant residence in the village of Oriskany, where he resided for a short period. In consequence of embarrassments caused by heavy endorsements for a friend, he sold his property and removed to Utica. He was one of the leaders of the old federal party in that part of the state of New York, and was for some time the editor of the *Utica Patriot*, during the turbulent period of the embargo and non-intercourse acts preceding the war of 1812.

He subsequently removed to New Hartford, N. Y., where he was the law partner of Gen. Joseph Kirkland (now deceased). In 1816, he returned to Utica having been appointed cashier of the Ontario Branch Bank, which office he held until a short time before his death, in the summer of 1829.

He was a member of the first board of trustees of Hamilton College, and was active and influential in founding and establishing that institution.

He was distinguished as a classical and belles lettres scholar, and was during his whole life a diligent and extensive reader, and his mind was stored with such

[35] For a biographical notice of Mr. Kirkland, see Appendix.

knowledge as made his conversation exceedingly
agreeable and instructive.

He possessed striking personal accomplishments, and
was always the charm of the social circle. He was
generous and hospitable, his dwelling was the resort of
the educated and the refined. He was a man of unsullied purity and integrity of character, and his removal by death was an irreparable loss to the community in which he had so long resided. His wife and
six children survived him. · Mrs. Lothrop is sixth in
descent from Miles Standish.[36] She enjoyed previous
to her marriage, the privileges of the seminaries and
society of Boston, and her accomplishments made her
a befitting companion for her intelligent husband.
She has ever evinced that true love and charity to
those who have come under her notice, which so distinguished her father during his life, and in rearing
her family she has striven successfully to impart to
them like virtues. In the early settlement of Oneida
county, she was a lady whose society was much court-
ed, and she has lived to see the maturity of seats of
learning, churches, and their attendant blessings which
her lamented father spent the best of his life and his
money, and endured the privations and hardships of
a pioneer, to establish.

EDWARD PERKINS, b. in Hartford, Ct., Sept. 20, 1808; "bap. Lord's
    day, Nov. 13, 1808;" m. in Cincinnati, O., March, 1851, Mrs.
    Harriet Frances (Norton) Dockstader of Cleveland O., s. p.

He resides near Cheviot, Hamilton county, O., has
been engaged, till of late years, in the business of
bookselling and binding in the cities of Cleveland and
Cincinnati, and has been esteemed as highly honorable and liberal in all his dealings. His generosity and
kindness of heart knows no bounds; his attachments

---

[36] For biography of Capt. Standish, see Appendix.

for kindred and friends are of the strongest nature; his hospitality and benevolence he limits only by his means.

JAMES CARNAHAN, b. in Whitestown, Oneida co., N. Y., May 1, 1813; bapt. July 9, 1813, by the Rev. John Frost; m. by the Rev. E. Channing Moore, rector of St. John's Church, May 29, 1851, Catharine Mary De Hart, dau. of the Hon. William and Mary (Barber) Chetwood of Elizabethtown, N. J., b. in Elizabethtown, Jan. 16, 1822; had John Chetwood.

He was named after the late Pres. Carnahan of Princeton College. Owing to the want of means, his father was unable to give him much more than a common school education. The district school of his native town, and two or three terms spent at an academy in the town of Remsen, Oneida co., N..Y., and at a high school in Utica, kept by Mr. Chas. Bartlett, was all the opportunity afforded him when a youth, to acquire an education. So that whatever knowledge he may possess, has been obtained since, by reading and observation. At fifteen years of age, he was placed by his father and oldest brother, in a store in Utica, kept by Mr. B. B. Lansing now deceased, where he spent two years. The restraints and *discipline* of a younger clerk, did not well suit his nature, but as he had no other alternative, he had to submit. His employer, at the end of two years, failing in business, he had to seek another situation, which he soon obtained. Having acquired some experience in "cutting goods," he was elevated from "a boy in the store," to a junior clerkship, which relieved him "carrying bundles," "sweeping out store," and "sweeping the street in front." This favorable change reconciled him somewhat to the fate of a dry goods clerk. At the end of two years, his then employer suspended business, when he was once more afloat. This rendered him heartily sick and disgusted with the retail dry goods trade, and he mustered up the resolution of trying his fortune in the great city of Gotham. After providing himself with sundry letters introductory, he left his native county, and proceeded to the city for the purpose of finding employment in some wholesale or importing dry goods establishment. On his arrival in New York, he found business almost wholly suspended, in consequence of the cholera, which was then raging (Aug., 1832). With a palpitating heart and trembling hand, he presented his letters of introduction; by some of those to whom he had letters, he was treated courteously, by others quite the reverse. The different interviews that he had with the "merchant princes," left anything but a favorable impression on his mind, as it respected their good breeding or intelligence.[37]

After some days awaiting replies to his applications for employment, fortune favored him, and he was offered a situation by a Mr. Zachariah Griswold, a worthy man, now deceased, who was a jobber of cotton goods in Maiden lane; near Pearl street, and into whose family he was taken, and where he was treated with great kindness and consideration, by his employer's wife (now no more), a lady of great goodness of heart and general benevolence. At the end of two years, his employer meeting with one of those "reverses" to which business men in the Metropolis are so accustomed, he was again without employment. This compelled the young man to renew his not very agreeable acquaintanceship with his "friends" to whom he had previously brought letters, and his second intercourse with them rather confirmed him in his first impressions of them. It was not long before he obtained a place in a jobbing house in Pearl street, near Hanover square. Here he

[37] The reader will bear in mind that the time narrated, was thirty years ago, before rail roads, electric telegraphs, ocean steamships; and before the time that quarterlies and monthlies, could be purchased at the corners of the streets, and newspapers delivered at one's door, at two cents a copy.

remained for about two years, when he removed to the state of Mississippi. The chief cause of this step was, he had on a visit to Utica met with a severe injury from being thrown from a buggy while the horse which was attached was running away. The injury compelled him to keep his bed and room some six or eight weeks.. On his getting out, he found himself much debilitated, and winter approaching, he conceived it would be well to seek a more genial clime. This, together with being offered a larger salary than he was receiving, induced him to leave New York, which he did in October, 1835. On his arrival in Mississippi, he took charge of the business of his employer. The following year he was offered an equal partnership in the house in which he was engaged. Being promised the use of all needful capital, he returned to New York, where he purchased goods to some considerable extent.

At this time (1836), everything in the way of business and property throughout the country, especially at the South, was greatly inflated. In the fall of that year, Gen. Jackson, who was then President, issued his famous specie circular. This caused the banks to curtail their discounts, which was followed in the winter ensuing by a panic and a crash, the like of which had never been seen before or since in this country. The cotton states became almost wholly bankrupt; real and personal property commanding but nominal prices. Of the $20,000 that Mr. W.'s firm entrusted out the year preceding, they collected but about $2,000 when due. Mr. W.'s partner becoming embarrassed, he withdrew his capital; property that was received from debtors by the firm, either depreciated in value, or the titles were found worthless. The result was an utter failure. The general bankrupt law relieved Mr. W., after which he set about mending his fortunes. By some years of laborious efforts, he was enabled to make and collect together some $10,000 or $12,000, which he devoted to paying obligations that he had been previously relieved from by the bankrupt law. Tiring of a life in Mississippi, he removed to New Orleans.

Before leaving this part of the narrative, it may be well to say that during his residence in Mississippi, he received from its citizens marks of respect and confidence. While there he endeavored to act the part of a useful and upright citizen. The river on which he was living—the Tchula, a branch of the Yazoo—requiring a short canal to connect it with the Upper Yazoo, also the removal of driftwood, fallen timber, etc. from the bottom and the banks of the river, to make the stream navigable, he with the aid of some of his enterprising neighbors, obtained the passage of a law, requiring the planters living within a certain distance of the river, to furnish their hands during the summer months, to work on the river instead of the roads. After the authority was obtained, it required some one to take the matter in hand and carry the work on. No one could be found to risk his life in the bed of that pestilent stream in the summer, and the undertaking was about to fall through, when Mr. Wetmore volunteered to take upon himself the overseeing and directing the negroes in cutting the timber and brush on the banks and the bottom of the then dry stream, so that when the water rose the obstruction would float out. After a long and tedious summer's labor, the work was accomplished, from one end of the river to the other, distance 60 miles, and the following winter, the planters had the satisfaction of getting their cotton to the New Orleans market, at $1 per bale freight, where they had previously been paying $3 per bale; up freights were proportionably lower. Where steamers of a small class, were heretofore only able to run during day-light, steamers of a large class were able to run night or day. The cutting of the canal at the head of the river, enabled boats bound to the Upper Yazoo, to take the Tchula river enroute. For this, Mr. Wetmore was voted by his fellow citizens a piece of plate, with a suitable inscription engraved thereon, as a token of their obligations to him, for the services he had rendered the community. His exposure in the bed of the river, as was expected, brought its fruit, in the way of an attack of bilious fever. By the aid of kind friends, and the care of an attentive and skillful physician in the person of Dr. James Maynard, formerly of Baltimore, Md., he recovered after a few weeks' confinement.

In New Orleans, he obtained agencies from New York houses, for the purchase of sugar and molasses. The war of Mexico occurring, one of the houses who had given but a verbal order, withdrew their order for cistern bottom sugars, giving as an excuse, that they had fears that the privateers would take the vessels and cargoes in transitu. The real truth was, sugars had fallen in market. The sugars which had been engaged on plantations, were received by Mr. W., and resold by him at a loss of some thousands of dollars. Soon after the opening of the war with Mexico, he joined a party who had been long a resident of that country, in the shipment of goods suited to the market, and opened mercantile establishments, as the American army advanced, at the several towns of Camargo, Monterey and Saltillo. On the advance of Gen. Santa Aña upon Gen. Taylor, Mr. W. placed his goods in the charge of United States officers, and volunteered his services for active duty, and at the battle of Buena Vista, acted as a volunteer aid to Capt. Rodgers of Col. Jefferson Davis's regiment of Mississippi Rifles, who was senior officer commanding detachment for the purpose of watching the enemy's cavalry, about

Descendants of Judge Seth, son of Izrahiah, son of Thomas.

2500 strong, under Gen. Miñon, who entered the valley of Buena Vista, by a narrow pass in the rear of Gen. Taylor's forces. This cavalry force made several attempts to drive Capt. Rodgers's command from their position; not succeeding, they retired in the direction Agua Frio, a pass in the Sierra Madre, some twelve miles to the east of Saltillo. Mr. W., accompanied by two young men, followed the enemy in order to discover their intentions. The enemy at about 4 P. M., halted and went into camp at an English factory, distance some ten miles in rear of Buena Vista. In hastening back, the little party were fired upon from ranches they had to pass, they however escaped untouched. Mr. W. lost no time in communicating[38] the intelligence of the whereabouts of Gen. Miñon, to headquarters on the field. The dispatch was received by Gen. Wool, who subsequently remarked to Col. Davis, that the officer who communicated such important information, deserved to be breveted.[39]

Soon after the close of the war, Mr. W. made an expedition to San Luis Potosi, passing with his caravan through pass Agua Nueva, from thence through the desert of one hundred and fifty miles, running south to real de Catorce mountain, the same desert through which Santa Aña passed, on his march from the city of Mexico to attack Gen. Taylor, and where so many of his troops perished from want of water and proper food. The cholera broke out in Mr. W.'s company, and proved fatal to a number of his men. He had fortunately furnished himself with a medicine chest, the contents of which he found of great service in staying the epidemic. Santa Aña in his retreat had left many of his men on the road,

[38] Mr. Wetmore wrote his dispatch in pencil, and signed it by consent, "Capt. Rodgers commanding."

[39] Mr. W. subsequently met Capt. Rodgers in Washington, who informed Mr. W. that he was "after that brevet of Gen. Wool's." Capt. R. was rewarded with the office of U. S. Consul at Vera Cruz.

who turned their attention to robbery and pillage, which together with the Apache Indians that were overrunning the country, made it very unsafe to travelers. Mr. W., by drawing up his wagons and stacking *los cargoes* (bales of goods suited for mule transportation) at night, in a manner to afford breastworks, and by keeping a constant guard by night, and a watch while under way by day, reached his place of destination in safety. On his arrival at San Luis, he found that he was the first American to bring goods by that route to that city. The usual course of transit from the coast to that mountainous region, was by the way of Tampico. After some few months' tarry in San Luis, Mr. W. sold out his goods, receiving his pay in Mexican dollars fresh from the mint, returning to the Rio Grande by the same route he had come; after which he returned to New York, continuing his consignments to Mexico for some considerable time. After the withdrawing of the American army from Mexico, the country became much disturbed, and consequently the trade very hazardous, and it was not without its losses to him; whereupon he gave up shipments to the Gulf and opened an office in Wall street, encountering the usual vicissitudes incident to that street. In 1847 he removed to Ohio, where he now resides. Whatever virtues Mr. W. may be possessed of, if worth naming at all, he prefers that they be recorded in some other connection than the present.

Mrs. Wetmore is the twelfth and youngest child of Major William and Mary (Barber) Chetwood. Her life previous to marriage was spent in her native town, where she enjoyed those advantages of education and society for which that old borough has been so long celebrated. The influences by which she was surrounded, were of the most pleasing and improving nature, and these circumstances were not without their beneficial effect upon her mind and character. She became, early in life, a communicant of the church (St. John's Episcopal) in which she had been made, by baptism, a member in her infancy. To this church she has ever since given her heart's best affection and devotion. Its doors have seldom if ever opened for service, when she was in the town and able to leave her dwelling, without her being found within its portals. In its prosperity or its adversity, she has always been constant in her attachment to it; though she is now deprived, for portions of the year, from its ministrations, it nevertheless has her prayers and her offerings. In her life she governs herself by a strict sense of religious duty. Truth, at whatever cost, is strictly adhered to by her. Her attachments for kindred, home and country, are of the strongest nature. To her the author is greatly indebted for assistance in compiling the various records and biographies forming this volume.

MAJOR WILLIAM CHETWOOD, father of Mrs. Wetmore, was born in Elizabethtown, N. J., Monday, June 17, 1771; christened in St. John's Church, by the Rev. Thomas Bradbury Chandler, July 21, 1771; he graduated at Princeton College, 1792; commenced the study of law with his father, Judge John Chetwood; which studies were soon after interrupted by a disturbance in the country, growing out of a rebellion in Western Pennsylvania, which became historical as the "Whiskey rebellion." Having much of that patriotic enthusiasm for which the citizens of New Jersey have ever been conspicuous, he enlisted as a volunteer in the force called out by the Governor of that state, in response to a requisition from the President of the United States—Gen. Washington—to go, in connection with troops from other states, to put down, by force of arms, those who had revolted against the constituted authorities of the land. He was appointed on the staff of Maj. Gen. Lee. The army consisted of about 15,000 men, composed of volunteers from Pennsylvania, New Jersey, Virginia, and Maryland. Gov. Lee of Virginia commanding, assisted by Gov. Mifflin of Pennsylvania, Gov. Howell of New Jersey, Gen. Daniel Morgan, and Adj. Gen. Hand. The army arrived in Pittsburg in November, 1794. The forces being too strong for the rebels, they dispersed, not however, till many were arrested and held to answer.[40]

After the troops were disbanded, Major Chetwood returned to the law, and was admitted to the bar in 1798, commencing at once the practice of his profession, to which he was ardently attached. He generally avoided a public life, preferring the interests and pleasures that his profession and his own fireside afforded him, to the blandishments of office and emoluments. He was chosen by his fellow citizens as mayor of the town, representative to the General Assembly, and to represent them in Congress during the administration of President Jackson, &c. Lanman, in his *Dictionary of Congress,* in speaking of him says, that he "was an able lawyer, practicing his profession till his seventieth year." His cotemporaries at the New Jersey bar were the late Judge John McLean of the U. S. Supreme Bench, ex-Chief Justices Hornblower and Green, Hon. Theodore Frelinghuysen, &c., &c.

He was married March 24th, 1801, by the Rev. Dr. Kollock, to Mary, daughter of Col. Francis Barber and Nancy his wife, daughter of Moses and Nancy Ogden.

He always experienced a lively interest in all that concerned the welfare of his country, state, and native town, and was conservative in all his views of public policy. Though confined for some years almost entire-

[40] For information respecting the Whiskey Rebellion, see *American State Papers,* vol. xx; *Miscellaneous,* vol. i, pp. 83, 113; *Hugh Breckenridge's Incidents of the Western Insurrection; William Findlay's His. of the Insurrection; Memoirs of Judge Breckenridge; So. Lit. Messenger,* Jan., 1842, and *American Pioneer,* 1842.

ly to the house by physical weakness, he retained his mental faculties until the time of his death, which occurred Dec. 17, 1857, in the 87th year of his age. The *Newark Daily Advertiser* in noticing his demise, said:

The funeral of Major Chetwood was attended by a large concourse of citizens, in St. John's church. The Rev. Samuel A. Clark, rector of the church officiated on the occasion. Having read 1 Cor. xv., he made the sublime topics there discussed, the theme of his address. In the course of his remarks, he stated that the deceased was baptized in that church before the Declaration of Independence, by the missionary from the mother country, sent by the Society for Propagating the Gospel in Foreign Parts. The members of the bar in attendance at the County Court were present, as also several distinguished citizens of Newark, and other neighboring cities. Among the pall bearers were noticed the Hon. Theodore Frelinghuysen, Ex-Chief Justice Hornblower, Chancellor Williamson, and others. The remains were deposited in the Ever Green Cemetery. A member of the bar pronouncing his eulogy a few days since before the court, stated that several years ago, when party strife ran high, two prominent men were candidates for speaker of the legislative council of the state. So equally divided were the council, that neither could be elected. Both parties united however, on Major Chetwood who presided, notwithstanding the bitterness of party feeling, with great ability, and entire acceptance to all parties. His urbanity of manner and unblemished character have ever secured for him universal confidence and respect. It is said when Gen. Lafayette visited Elizabeth, Major C.'s twelve children, whose grandfather on the mother's side, Col. Barber, had served under Gen. Lafayette, were taken and introduced to the distinguished guest.

The vestry of St. John's church, to which he had been devoted during his long life, and of which he was the senior warden at the time, and for many years prior to his death, passed befitting resolves.

Major Chetwood's father, John Chetwood, a distinguished lawyer of New Jersey, in colonial times and the early days of the republic, was judge of one of the higher courts of that state for a number of years; he was married by the Rev. T. B. Chandler, June 3, 1759 (Whitsunday), to Mary, dau. of John and Mary Emott; had I *John*, who became a successful medical practitioner and highly respected and honored citizen of Elizabethtown; he died 1832, from an attack of cholera, brought on by unceasing labors in his profession; he acted as surgeon to the New Jersey troops in their expedition to quell the rebellion in western Pennsylvania, 1794; II *William*, already noticed; III *Elizabeth*, who became the wife of Col. Aaron Ogden of the Revolutionary army, governor of New Jersey, United States senator, 1801 and 1803, and president of the Cincinnati society; IV *Philip*. Judge Chetwood descended from a family of honorable note in England, Sir John being the head. Mrs. Mary Emott Chetwood was of a family of high repute in New Jersey.

Mrs. Mary (Barber) Chetwood, the relict of Major Chetwood, was born in Elizabethtown, Nov. 1, 1780, where she has ever since continued to reside, and now occupies the old homestead, where her entire married life has been spent, and around which so many fond memories cluster, and where her children love to assemble on every Christmas festival, bringing with them their children's children, representatives of the fourth generation. Her father dying in her infancy, she shared the domestic duties, and cheered the retirement of her mother.

Elizabethtown having the advantages of a seminary and schools of learning, which were not then very numerous, drew to that point, families of wealth and influence. They constituted a society that was remarkable for its refinement and high cultivation. It was in that circle she matured into womanhood. Her father having been an officer in the Continental army, and an aid to Gen. Washington, made the home of her

mother a very general resort of the surviving officers
and patriots of the Revolution, and her recollection of
them has ever inspired her with love and reverence
for "the revolutionary fathers," and the school in
which she was reared, has made her keenly appreciate
an exalted patriotism.   She is a devoted member of
the Episcopal church, and her unostentatious piety is
exhibited in acts of secret benevolence, as well as
more demonstrative associations with charitable institutions of the town, in which she has long taken a prominent and active part.

What has been said of another of her sex, a lady
of the Revolution, long since passed away, may with
truth be said of her.   "She possesses a fine, cultivated
and delicate mind; a temper gentle and sweet; a spirit
composed in difficulty, and patient in suffering, humble in prosperity, cheerful in adversity; a demeanor
chastened and regulated by clear perceptions of duty
and a high sense of propriety.   As a child, exemplary
for filial reverence ; as a wife for conjugal tenderness ;
as a mother for parental affection.   Forgetful of herself, and studious of the happiness of others."   May
her life long be spared to animate by her presence and
improve by her counsel, her numerous family.   We
take the following biographical sketch of her father
from the *National Portrait Gallery* :

Col. Francis Barber

Was the son of Patrick Barber, Esq., who was born in
the county of Longford in Ireland, at a place called the
Scotch Quarters.   His maternal ancestors were Scots, of
the name of Frazer, some years before his immigration to
America, in 1749 or 1750.   After a short residence in New
York he removed to the then small village of Princeton, in
New Jersey, where the subject of this memoir was born,
in the year 1751.   After Francis had entered the college,
or classical school attached to it, his father removed to

the county of Orange, in the state of New York. He received appointments to civil offices under colonial and state governments of New York, and his ashes now repose in the family cemetery in Orange county, beside the untimely grave of his gallant and lamented son.

After Francis Barber had finished his education at Princeton, he took charge of the academy at Elizabethtown, New Jersey; and the classical department under his charge was soon distinguished. He was charged with the instruction of several young men, who in after life rose to the highest eminence. Among others Alexander Hamilton was placed at this school by Governor Livingston, himself a ripe scholar, whose preference for this school is the best evidence of his confidence in the teacher. Upon the breaking out of the revolutionary war, Francis Barber, with his two younger brothers, John and William, were officers in the New Jersey line. Francis received a commission from congress, bearing date the 9th of February, 1776, as major of the third battalion of the New Jersey troops. On the 8th of November of the same year he was appointed, by the legislature of New Jersey, lieutenant-colonel of the third Jersey regiment, and was commissioned by congress on the 1st of January, 1777. Not long after the office of inspector-general of the army was conferred upon Baron Steuben, and Colonel Francis Barber received that of assistant inspector-general. In a letter addressed to him by the baron at the time, he says:

"I make no doubt but with a gentleman of your zeal and capacity, the troops, under your inspection will make great progress in the military discipline, and the good order prescribed in the regulations."

Colonel Barber was in constant service during the whole war. Although a strict, nay a rigid disciplinarian, always scrupulously performing his own duty, and requiring it from all under his command, yet so bland were his manners, and his whole conduct so tempered with justice, and strict propriety, that he was the favorite of all the officers and men, and possessed the friendship and confidence, not only of the general officers, but of the commander-in-chief. He served with his regiment in the northern army under Gen. Schuyler. He marched with the army from Ticonderoga to join General Washington previous to the battle of Trenton.

Colonel Barber was in that battle and also in that of Prince-ton, which so soon followed it.   He was engaged in the battles of Brandywine, Germantown and Monmouth, and in the latter was severely wounded.   Even when unable to remain in the field, his active spirit was employed in devis-ing means of usefulness, as it is shown by the following letter from the commander-in-chief, dated July 9th, 1778 :

Dear Sir—I was favored this afternoon with your letter of the 8th inst.; while you are at Elizabethtown, I wish you to obtain the best intelligence you can from time to time of the enemy's situation, and of any movement they may seem to have in view.   For this purpose you will em-ploy the persons you mention, or such others as you may judge necessary.   Whatever expenses you are at upon this occasion, will be repaid at the earliest notice.   I am ex-tremely happy to hear your wound is in so favorable way. I hope it will be better every day.   Though I wish for your services, I would not have you to rejoin the army be-fore your condition will admit of it with the most perfect safety.   I am dear sir

Your most obedient servant,
GEORGE WASHINGTON.

On the 14th of the same month (July) the commander-in-chief acknowledged the receipt of another letter of Colonel Barber's of the 13th inst., expresses his obligation for the intelligence it contains, begs him to continue his endeavors to procure every information he can concerning the enemy, and closes with his best wishes for his recovery, and with much regard, &c.   In 1779 Colonel Barber served as adjutant general with General Sullivan in his memorable expedition against the Indians, and was slight-ly wounded at the battle of Newtown ; at the close of the campaign he received from the general a highly compli-mentary testimonial of his conduct in that department of the army.   During the expedition Colonel Barber kept his wife constantly informed, not only of his per-sonal safety, but of the movements, progress and suc-cess of the army, and the letters preserved of that corre-spondence furnish probably, as particular and detailed an account of the expedition as is anywhere to be found.   On the 8th of January, 1780, Washington entrusted to him the important and highly delicate duty of enforcing in the county of Gloucester, in west Jersey, the necessary requisition made throughout the state for grain and cattle, to relieve the distresses of the army.

The Jersey brigade was again conspicuous at the battle of Springfield, where Colonel Barber was actively engaged. In this battle fell that high-minded, and gallant youth, Lieutenant Moses Ogden, the brother-in-law of Colonel Barber. When the meeting first of the Pennsylvania, and afterwards of the Jersey line, threatened the dissolution of the army Colonel Barber received from the commander-in-chief the following in the hand writing of Gen. Hamilton:

New Windsor, January 21st, 1781.

Dear Sir—With no less pain than you communicated it I receive the information contained in your letter of yesterday. This affair if possible, must be brought to an issue, favorable subordination, or the army is ruined. I shall therefore immediately march a detachment to quell the mutineers, Colonel Frelinghuysen will impart to you what I have written to him. In addition to that, I am to desire you will endeavor to collect all those of your regiments who have had virtue enough to resist the pernicious example of their associates. If the revolt has not become general, and if you have force enough to do it, I wish you to compel the mutineers to unconditional submission. The more decidedly your able to act the better.

Your most obedient servant,

GEORGE WASHINGTON.

The mutineers had threatened to shoot any officer who should attempt to restrain, or in any way molest them. Notwithstanding this threat, it was supposed by many of the officers, that the Jersey troops entertained so high a regard for Colonel Barber, and his influence over them was such, that he might safely appeal to their patriotism, and honor as soldiers, and in this way lead them to submission. The popularity of the officer had an influence in restraining many, and the decisive measures of Washington, together with the partial relief afforded by a timely supply of money, soon restored the Jersey line to order. In August, 1781, he accompanied the Jersey line, on their march to Virginia, and was at the investment and capture of the British at Yorktown. During the march of the army Colonel Barber, as before, kept his wife informed by letters of the daily movements of the American and British armies, so far as the latter could be ascertained. One of these letters so correctly foretold the glorious termination of the contest, as to seem almost in a spirit of prophecy, it proves at least the accuracy of his judgment; speaking of the enemy, he says:

"Sometimes their movements indicate the design of embarking from some southern port, probably to return to New York; others of proceeding to Yorktown. If they pursue the first alternative, the struggle may yet be protracted for some time, if the latter, I think it will be brought to a speedy and glorious termination."

The latter was adopted, and the auspicious result soon followed; peace was concluded, and the independence of the country was confirmed.

The day on which the commander-in-chief intended to communicate these joyful tidings to his army, was the day on which this high-minded soldier was summoned from this to witness the more glorious realities of another world, on that day many of the officers, and such of their wives as were in camp, were invited to dine with the commander-in-chief at New Windsor,[41] and among the rest Col. Barber and his wife. He was acting at the time, as officer of the day in place of a friend. While on duty and passing by the edge of a wood, where some soldiers were cutting down a tree, it fell on him, and both the rider and the horse were instantly crushed to death. He had received an intimation that the commander-in-chief intended to communicate to the officers, at the table, the intelligence of peace, before it appeared in general orders. His afflicted and disconsolate widow received letters of condolence from many of the officers upon this mournful event. It was in truth a cloud that not only shrouded her mansion in mourning, but appeared to eclipse forever the brightness of her future prospects.

To the honor of his native state its legislature allowed to her during life the half pay of a colonel. The death, the untimely death of this gallant officer was not only lamented by all his companions in arms, but long after

[41] Orange county, N. Y.

sorrow was soothed by the lapse of time, many a war-worn soldier has *halted* at the mansion of his widow, to recount his virtues, and consecrate his memory with a tear.

W. C.

ABIGAIL SARAH, b. in Utica, N. Y., Jan. 8, 1816; bap. Aug. 18, 1816, by the Rev. Henry Dwight, D. D.

She died at Utica, May 16, 1856.

Miss Wetmore united herself early in life with the First Presbyterian Church of her native place, and ever lived a consistent professor of religion. Her love and sincere benevolence of heart, endeared her to all those who chanced to come within her sphere. She suffered for many years previous to her death from a disease of the heart, which finally terminated her existence. She bore patiently and meekly the trials put upon her by a merciful Providence, and when her last sickness (which was about two weeks duration), came upon her, she seemed to rejoice in the thought that her pilgrimage upon earth was so soon to terminate, and that she was to exchange *sorrows* here for *joys* in Heaven, and there to dwell with her Redeemer, as well as to meet those "whom she had loved and lost." Her only regret was expressed at parting with her aged mother, who had been wont to receive from her those tender attentions, which only a daughter can render to a parent; but through faith she had assurances that God would care for and protect her, and in due time would gather *her too*, to those "blessed mansions not made with hands," to which she was going a little in advance. Her death was calm and happy. To those near and dear to her that stood about her bed, after sending messages of love to absent ones, she said (just before expiring), with a smile, "we shall all soon be together, I trust, in Heaven, with father." Her remains were deposited beside those of her father in Ever-Green Cemetery, at Utica.

53

Children of ELISHA,

Son of Deacon Oliver.

SAMUEL BREWSTER, b. at Staddle Hill, near M., Jan. 19, 1811;
m. Eliza Bridgham, April 25, 1833; had Elisha Brewster,
Caroline Tudor.

Resides at the place of his nativity.

ELISHA BREWSTER, b. at Staddle Hill, Jan. 23, 1815; d. Nov. 7,
1829.

Children of TIMOTHY,

Son of Deacon Oliver.

OLIVER, b. Middletown, March 19, 1814; m. at Hannibalville, Os-
wego county, N. Y., Parmelia Mason, of Saratoga county, N. Y.;
had Mary Jané, Esther Ann.

He is an independent farmer. Resides in the township of Middleville, Barry county, Michigan.

TIMOTHY EDWARDS, b. at Butler Creek, below Middletown, Ct.,
Feb. 17, 1821; m. Elizabeth, dau. of Rev. H. Halsey, of East
Wilson, Niagara county, N. Y., April 26, 1848; had Warren
Halsey, Walter Ely, Samuel Buel, Charles Edwards.

He died after a short but painful illness, at the residence of his father-in-law, in the town of East Wilson,
June 30th, 1856. Mr. Wetmore was removed during
his infancy from the place of his nativity, to Volney,
N. Y., where his father resided for some years, from
thence to Genesee county, same state, where he finished
his minority, attending the schools and academies
which that section of country afforded, at the same
time giving what assistance he could to his father in his
farming pursuits. It was here he acquired that love
and knowledge of agriculture, and its attendant characteristics, that so marked his subsequent life.

The editor of *Moore's Rural New Yorker*, a periodical published at Rochester, and devoted chiefly to agricultural interests, says in noticing his death :

It becomes our painful duty to announce the decease of T. E. Wetmore, Esq., of Kent co., Mich., for several years an able and acceptable contributor to the pages of this journal. An appropriate obituary notice, giving some particulars of this mournful event, will be found on our next page.

Though our personal acquaintance with the deceased was somewhat limited, we had long esteemed him as an upright and honorable man in the various relations of life, and as an especially able and influential advocate and promoter of rural improvement. We, therefore, regard his loss, ere he had scarcely reached the meridian of life and usefulness, as a public calamity. In a letter announcing Mr. W.'s death, a mutual friend justly remarks :—" I have known and have been intimate with him from childhood, and know that few excelled him in all those qualities which constitute true manhood, and render one truly great and good. He was so modest and retiring, however, that it was only by intimate acquaintance that we discovered all the good qualities of his head and heart."

The following obituary, is the one alluded too, above :

* * * * It was here (Genesee co., N. Y.) that he began to develop that industry and energy of character, and that thirst of knowledge, which enabled him to attain the high rank as a citizen and scholar, as a contributor for the press, which he held at the time of his decease. He rarely spent an hour idly, but occupied his leisure moments, either in reading or study. While busily engaged in agricultural pursuits, he found time, unaided, to obtain a thorough practical knowledge of botany, and collected and arranged a herbarium, more full and complete than any other in western New York. Here he also commenced a diary, which he kept up till the day of his death.

In May, 1844, he entered the academy at Yates, Orleans co., where he soon became distinguished for his industry and ability, and ranked as one of the most thorough and talented students of the institution. He here formed many warm friendships.

In the spring of 1846, he entered the Collegiate Institute at Wilson. His career here, I can not better express than in the language of one who knew him well. "He at once took a high rank among the most talented members of the seminary, which rank he maintained during his connection with it. He early took a very active and prominent part in the literary societies of the institute, and it may, in truth, be said, that no member was more liberal or efficient in their support, and the death of no one, will be more deeply and sincerely lamented."

After leaving the seminary, Mr. Wetmore engaged in business, and remained in Wilson till the summer of 1850, at which time he removed to Kent co., Mich., where he has ever since resided. While he remained in Wilson, his character and course are so well known, as to make remarks unnecessary. It is sufficient to say that he was active, patriotic and eminently public-spirited. In his dealings he was just and honorable, in his acts upright and conscientious, in his feelings benevolent and humane. After his removal to Michigan, he devoted himself mainly to agricultural pursuits, but amidst all his toils, he did not forget the cultivation of his mind. He kept himself supplied with a large number of the standard journals and magazines of the country. He maintained a very extensive correspondence with his numerous friends in all parts of the country, and also contributed frequently to the public journals.

At the time of his death, Mr. Wetmore was editor of agricultural department of the *Grand River Eagle*, and a special contributor for *Moore's Rural New Yorker*, and the readers of both those journals, will miss the genial articles which flowed from his prolific pen. As a writer, Mr. W. particularly excelled; he wrote with ease and dispatch, and his style was clear, terse and forcible, and very free from verbiage and useless rhetorical display. The aim of his writings seemed to be to benefit and instruct, and his thoughts, as expressed in his various compositions, indicate a mind well cultivated, and of singular purity.

Perhaps a word should be said of Mr. W.'s religious

character. We are not aware that he ever made a public profession of religion, yet from our own intimate acquaintance with him, and from the general tone of his letters, we feel no hesitation in saying that he was a man of decided religious opinions and sentiments. He loved the character of God; he admired his attributes and perfections; he was an ardent student of nature, and looked through nature up to its great Author. He regarded the bible as the great rule of faith and duty, and in reference to his children, he expressed an earnest wish that they might be educated upon the basis of the Christian faith. His moral character was above reproach; his habits were singularly pure and correct, and his whole course of life, was such as might be safely held up to young men, as a model of excellence. He was a dutiful son, an affectionate brother, a faithful husband, a kind partner, a respected and beloved citizen, and a truly good man.

He has left an aged and beloved mother, a kind brother, an affectionate wife, and four little sons, to mourn his early death. May the God of the widow and the orphan abundantly sustain and comfort them under this heavy bereavement. He has been called from earth just as he had acquired for himself an extended and enviable reputation, just as hope and promise beckoned him onward in the noble career which he had marked out for himself.

R. B. W.

Children of CHAUNCEY,

Son of Deacon Oliver.

CHAUNCEY EDWARDS, b. at Staddle Hill, near M., Dec. 28, 1818; m. Oct. 8, 1845, Mary Mix Buck, of Wethersfield, Ct.; had Edith F., William Brewster, Henry Claverence.

Resides near Martinez, California, where he removed from Baltimore, Md., with his brother-in-law, John W. Jones, previous to the discovery of gold in California. They took with them machinery for flouring mills, and it was not till they arrived at the Sandwich Islands, that they heard of the gold discovery. He is an enterprising and industrious citizen, and is worthy of success in life.

LUCY, b. at Staddle Hill, near M., Dec. 24, 1820; m. Dec. 14, 1847, Samuel Cotton Gray; b. in Boston, Oct. 11, 1816; had I *Edward*, b. Nov. 17, 1849. II *Franklin Henry*, b. Aug. 20, 1851; d. Jan. 18, 1852. III *Samuel Arthur*, b. Nov. 24, 1853. IV *Theodore*, b. Oct. 24, 1855. All born in California.

He resides in Benicia, Cal., where he has acquired property and influence. He is a son of Samuel (b. 1784), son of Samuel (b. 1738), son of Samuel (b. 1711) Gray; all natives of Boston. Mr. S. C. Gray's grandmother's maiden name was Hannah Cotton, a lineal descendant of the Rev. John Cotton, pastor of the First Church in Boston, and in compliment to whom that city was named. Mrs. Gray is a lady of energy of character, and fine natural abilities, faithful and conscientious in all her relations of life.

HARRIET, b. at Staddle Hill, April 15, 1823; m. John Wesley Jones, June 8, 1852; had I *Walter*, b. in California, July 2, 1856. II, a dau., b. in C., Jan. 16, 1859.

Resides in Benicia, Cal.

CORNELIA LYMAN, b. at Staddle Hill, Sept. 30, 1825; d. June 27, 1829.

HENRY GOODWIN, b. at Staddle Hill, Jan. 19, 1828; m. April 6, 1852, Mary Townsend Winn; had Franklin Henry, Charles, Chauncey, Lucy.

Is a farmer. Resides in Suisin Valley, Rockville P. O., Solano county, Cal.

CORNELIA HUBBARD, b. as above, Jan. 31, 1830.

MARY ELLEN, b. as above, March 29, 1834.

SEVENTH GENERATION.

Children of WILLIAM SHEPARD,

Son of Seth, Son of Seth.

WILLIAM SHEPARD, b. in New York, ——; d. at Newport, R. I., June 1, 1858.

GEORGE PEABODY, b. in London, Eng.

ANNIE DERBY RODGERS, b. in London, Eng.

Children of CHARLES WRIGHT,

Son of Seth, Son of Seth.

SALOME SMITH, b. May 7, 1825, ——.

WILLIAM SHEPARD, b. Feb. 26, 1827: graduated at New York University, ——; and Harvard College, 1849.

NANCY SHEPARD, b. March 15, 1830; d. May 23, 1851.

SOPHIA HAZELTINE, b. Feb. 17, 1831.

MARIA LOUISA, b. May 11, 1838.

Daughter of SETH DOWNING,

Son of Seth, Son of Seth.

HELEN FRANCES, b. at Cuyahoga Falls, Feb. 6, 1836; m. Albert Jenks, Esq., banker, Aurora, Illinois, Nov. 1, 1853; had I *William Wetmore*, b. at A., Jan. 13, 1855; d. Aug. 16, 1856. II *Kittie Wetmore*, b. Dec. 5, 1856.

Children of WILLIAM OGDEN,

Son of Judge William, Son of Seth.

HENRY, b. in Portage co., Ohio, July 20, 1823.

EDWARD, b. in Portage co., O., April 16, 1825; d. about 1826, being the first death in the town of Cuyahoga Falls, O.

EDWARD 2d, b. in Portage co., O., March 16, 1827; he was the first child born in Cuyahoga Falls.

MARY, b. Portage co., O., Sept. 27, 1829; m. —— Collier.

FREDERICK, b. in Portage co., O., March 6, 1835,

JULIA, b. in Portage co., O., March 13, 1838.

ELIZA, b. in Portage co., O., Sept. 25, 1841.

Children of EDWIN,

Son of Judge William, Son of Seth.

SILAS, b. in Western Reserve, O., July 4, 1821.

CHARLES, b. in Western Reserve, O., Dec. 24, 1822; d. Oct. 7, 1845.

LUTHER, b. in Western Reserve, O., Oct. 10, 1825; d. Sept. 1847.

CLARISSA P., b. in Western Reserve, O., Feb. 13, 1847.

HARRIET B., b. in Western Reserve, O., July 2, 1855.

Sons of HENRY,

Son of Judge William, Son of Seth.

HENRY W., b. in Western Reserve, O., Nov. 16, 1834.

Resides in Milwaukee, Wis.

GEORGE PRENTISS, b. in Western Reserve, O., Sept. 19, 1836.

Land Agent, St. Louis, Mo.

Sons of SAMUEL,

Son of Samuel, Son of Seth.

WILLIAM BOERUM, b. in London, Eng.; christened at St. George's Church, Hanover square, London.

WYATT, b. in New York, Oct. 1, 1854; christened at Calvary Church, N. Y., by the Rev. Francis L. Hawks, D. D.; d. April 21, 1855.

Sons of JOSIAH,

Son of Titus, Son of Seth.

MORRIS, b. in Stow township, Ohio.

HENRY, b. in Stow township, Ohio.

Children of NATHANIEL DOWNING,

Son of Josiah, Son of Seth.

NATHANIEL DOWNING, b. in Dover, N, H., Feb. 5, 1838 ; m. Susan Maria Bruce, April, 1855.

Wholesale grocer, Memphis, Tenn.

EMILY AMANDA, b. in Dover, N. H., April 8, 1840.

HENRY SHEPARD, b. in Rochester, N. H., Nov. 23, 1841.

Cadet at West Point U. S. Military Academy, where he has distinguished himself as a mathematical scholar.

LUCY ANN, b, July 14, 1843.

LYDIA AMELIA, b. Jan. 13, 1845.

Children of MOSES WILLARD,

Son of Josiah, Son of Seth.

HENRY STANLEY, b. in Cincinnati, O., Jan. 12, 1835.

JULIAN NEVILLE, b. in Newport, Ky., July 2, 1837.

FLORENCE LORELLE, b. in Newport, Ky., Nov. 2, 1848 ; m. Sept. 9, 1856, Thomas Edward Sumner Russwurm of Cleveland, Tenn., son of Sumner Russwurm of Rutherford co., Tenn.; had I

Lorelle, b. in Cleveland, Tenn., July 14, 1857; II *John Willard*, b. in Murfreesboro, Tenn., April 12, 1859.

WILLIAM CALHOUN STEWART, b. in Covington, Ky., July 12, 1840.

MARY THOMAS, b. in Covington, Ky., March 18, 1842.

OLDHAM BRYSON, b. in Cinn., O., March 12, 1844.

JOHN EDGERTON, b. in Edgefield, Tenn., April 29, 1846.

JEANIE ELISE, b. in Nashville, Tenn., Feb. 16, 1848; d. Aug. 24, 1852.

LEONA MATILDA, b. in Edgefield, Tenn., Feb. 7, 1850.

Children of WILLIAM HASTINGS,

Son of Josiah, Son of Seth.

WILLIAM ANGELO KEYSER, b. in Tenn., June 24, 1850.

CHARLES WILLARD SHEPARD, b. in Tenn., Feb. 18, 1853.

SARA ELEANOR FLORENCE, b. in Tenn., Nov. 27, 1856.

ANNA CORA WILLARD, b. in Tenn., April 3, 1860.

Children of JOSIAH FARNSWORTH,

Son of Josiah, Son of Seth.

ROBERT DEAN, b. in New York, Nov. 1, 1843.

MARY DENISON, b. in N. Y., Dec. 23, 1844.

THOMAS TOWNSEND, b. in N. Y., June 15, 1848.

EDWARD GRIFFEN, b. in N. Y., July 13, 1851.

GEORGE TOWNSEND, b. in N. Y., Dec. 25, 1853.

Children of SAMUEL FARWELL,

Son of Josiah, Son of Seth.

WILLIE COURTNEY, b. March 16, 1846.

HARRIET WILLARD, b. July 20, 1848.

MARY FRANCES MOLINEUX, b. June 26, 1852.

RALPH, b. Nov. 5, 1855.

Children of EDMUND ARNOLD,

Son of Rev. Oliver, Son of Deacon Oliver.

MARY BUCKMINSTER, b. in Utica, N. Y., Sept. 2, 1830; m. Sept.
6, 1854, Dr. John P. Gray, b. at Half Moon Center, Penn.,
Aug. 6, 1825; had I *Edmund Wetmore*, b. in Utica, Sunday,
July 29, 1855; II *Dorsey*, b. in Utica, Friday, Jan. 8, 1858;
III *John P.*, b. in Utica, May 27, 1860.

𝔇𝔦𝔢𝔡.

Wednesday, June 5, 1861, of diptheria, EDMUND WETMORE, and on Wednesday, June 19, 1861, of the same disease, DORSEY, sons of Dr. JOHN P. and MARY BUCKMINSTER GRAY.

These children who were removed after a few days'
illness, were of unusual intellectual promise and loveliness of character. When the first was taken, the
younger could hardly reconcile himself to the absence
of his brother, but when disease fastened upon *him*,
he seemed to be anxious how *he* should get from hence
to his "Neddy" in Heaven, and as death approached,
he wondered why God did not send for him, and why
Neddy didn't call for him, and as his spirit was about
taking its flight, in a whisper he repeated Neddy's
name, as if calling for him to meet him.

"NOT LOST, BUT GONE BEFORE."

How mournful seems, in broken dreams,
　　The memory of the day,
When icy death hath seal'd the breath
　　Of some dear form of clay.

When pale, unmoved, the face we loved,
　　The face we thought so fair,
And the hands lie cold, whose fervent hold
　　Once charmed away despair.

Oh, what could heal the grief we feel
　For hopes that come no more,
Had we ne'er heard the scripture word,
　" Not lost, but gone before."

*　　*　　*　　*　　*　　*　　*

Oh! world wherein, nor death, nor sin
　Nor weary warfare dwells,
Their blessed home we parted from
　With sobs and sad farewells.

Where eyes awake, for whose. dear sake
　Our own with tears grow dim,
And faint accords of dying words
　Are changed for heaven's sweet hymn;

Oh! then at last, life's trials past,
　We'll meet our loved once more,
Whose feet have trod the path to God,
　" Not lost, but gone before."

Hon. Mrs. Norton.

Dr. Gray is the well known and worthy superintendent of the New York State Lunatic Asylum at Utica.
He commenced his preparatory studies for a collegiate
course at the Bellefonte (Pa.) Academy, graduating
at Dickinson College in 1845; and received his medical instruction at the Pennsylvania University, and
his degree of M. D. in 1849. He was for a year
one of the associate physicians of Blockly Hospital.
Removed to Utica and obtained the appointment of
third assistant superintendent of the above asylum in
1850, and second assistant Feb. 1852; first assistant
in June the same year, and superintendent in July
1854, since which time his labors have been incessant
in bringing that noble institution to that high state of
perfection, to which it has arrived.

In Dr. G.'s arduous and philanthropic duties, he enjoys the sympathies of his wife, a lady whose mind
has been carefully cultured, and whose sensibilities are
ever alive to the wants and misfortunes of others.

CORNELIA LOTHROP, b. in Utica, Dec. 4, 1831.

Miss Wetmore received her christian name in compliment to her aunt, the late Mrs. Cornelia G., wife of Hon. Charles P. Kirkland, and daughter of the late John H. Lothrop, Esq., of Utica. As we remember Mrs. K. with feelings of great respect and admiration, we desire and deem it not inappropriate to record, in this connection, a copy of an obituary of her that was published in a Utica paper, soon after her decease, which occurred in July, 1831:

Died at Mr. Voorhees', near New Brunswick, N. J., Mrs. Cornelia G., wife of Charles P. Kirkland, Esq., of this village, aged 29 years.

Mrs. Kirkland had been under the charge of Dr. Physic, of Philadelphia, and her friends finding medical aid of no avail, began their return towards home, when her extreme illness compelled them to stop at a stranger's, where she died. Her remains were conveyed to this village, and accompanied to the grave by her friends and acquaintances. Mrs. Kirkland died of consumption. The delusive character of this disease is well known. Those who have watched its progress, are well aware how insiduous are its approaches, and apt it is to beguile one's fears, until the sufferer is beyond the reach of art. In ordinary circumstances, its peculiar and treacherous nature invests the subject with more than usual interest. From day to day, its advance towards the grave, though sure, is silent and scarcely perceptible, and the eye of watchful affection fancies it discerns returning health, while the hectic of the cheek, and the bright lustre of the eye presage with melancholy certainty its fatal termination. The disease seized in this instance upon one for its prey, whose personal attractions and grace of manners, whose purity of feeling, cultivated mind and happy disposition, rendered her the charm of the domestic circle, and the cherished object of affection to her friends. It has been said (and the reflection was perhaps inspired by a similar privation), that death seemed to pass the old, the infirm and the unfortunate, to smite her, upon whom life had

comparatively hardly dawned, whose maturer age was
yielding the happy fruits of seed sown in childhood by paternal affection, and whose circumstances gave her the promise of the highest enjoyment. This lady possessed great
benevolence of disposition and simplicity and gentleness
of feeling. In her domestic relations she was assiduous
and exact, and discharged them under the most trying
circumstances of health, with cheerfulness and patience.
A native delicacy of moral feeling, and an acute sense of
propriety, secured her against any deviation from the
nicest standard of moral rectitude; but she aspired to a
higher and a surer guide. She found in the consolations of
religion a more certain reliance, and a cheering assurance
which enabled her to meet with serenity the gloomy approaches of death. In those last moments, when human
resources avail nothing, she was strong in her faith and
bright in her hope, and passed away "refreshed by the
dews of heaven."

Mrs. Kirkland died leaving three young children,
two daughters and a son, viz: Julia, Cornelia Lothrop
and John Lothrop. The former resides with her
father, on Gramercy Park, New York; the second
married Alex. Seward, Esq., of Utica; she has those
Christian, feminine and endearing characteristics for
which her mother was so remarkable. The son, John
L., graduated at Harvard College in 1849; studied
law with his father, at Utica, and being threatened
with pulmonary disease, he removed to Florida, where
he practiced law till the summer of 1860, when he
returned north for the purpose of spending a few
months, and while on a visit to his sister, Mrs. Seward, he was taken with a hemorrhage, which ended
his existence in a few minutes. He was much beloved
by his family and acquaintances, and by none, more
than the sister, who had the privilege of supporting
him in his last moments.

Miss Wetmore has much of that *bel esprit* for which
her maternal grandfather was remarkable; this, to-

gether with her literary tastes and amiability of temperament, causes her to be a favorite in educated and polite circles. ·

EDMUND, b. in Utica, June 3, 1838.

He made his preparation for a collegiate course, chiefly in the Utica Academy, and entered the freshman class at Harvard University in 1856, and graduated with credit to himself, and satisfaction to his friends, in 1860, having received during his college term, the honor of two Shattuck, and one Thayer scholarship. He has commenced the study of the law, with Hon. Charles P. Kirkland, in the city of New York.

Son of JAMES CARNAHAN,

Son of Rev. Oliver, Son of Deacon Oliver.

JOHN CHETWOOD, b. in Elizabethtown, N. J., Aug. 22, 1856; christened at St. John's Episcopal Church, by the Rev. Samuel A. Clark, his father, his uncle, Francis B. Chetwood, and his aunt, Mrs. Sarah Robert (the latter by proxy), acting as sponsors.

His Christian name was given him by his mother, as a token of affection that she bore the memory of her deceased brother, John Chetwood, who died in San Francisco, Cal., Sept. 17, 1852. That the child may ever have before him, on a printed page, the recorded virtues of his uncle, whose name he bears, as an example, as well as to place in an enduring form "memorials" of the esteem in which the departed was held, we give place to the following which we extract from a pamphlet entitled *A Memorial of the late John Chetwood:* New York, Baker, Godwin & Co., 1853. The collection was compiled and edited by William G. Bull, Esq., of New York (since deceased), for private circulation only :

* * * Mr. Chetwood was one of the most eminent lawyers of the state of California, and although quite a young man, he was selected, unanimously, by the whig state central committee, on the 8th inst., as the whig candidate for judgeship on the supreme bench of the state. As a man he was deeply esteemed; and the void now felt in the large circle of which he was an honored and prominent member, can not easily be filled. But while his friends and society mourn their bereavement, we can not but express, in common, with the great party of which we are humble members, the profound regrets we experience in the loss of so able an advocate of the principles we profess. Although the dispensation which removed him from the midst of life, to us, who are left behind seems severe, we must yet remember that it is the common lot of humanity; a dispensation to which, sooner or later, we must bow. It should be ours to see that we depart from the vale of tears, with minds as pure, and souls as full of noble emotions, as his whom we mourn.—*San Francisco Eve. Journal.*

* * * His faithful attention to business confided to his hands, his thorough acquaintance with the science which he professed, his upright and honest character, and his courteous demeanor soon made him a most successful practitioner, and the possessor of a lucrative business, and the esteem and confidence of the community. A proof of this was lately shown in the action of the whig state central committee, who unanimously nominated him as a candidate to fill one of the vacancies on the supreme bench of the state.—*Alta California.*

* * * His death is one of those afflicting dispensations to which we can only bow in silence, and though regrets are unavailing, they will be deeply felt. Sincere and heartfelt sorrow will be experienced at his early death. Few persons like John Chetwood, had the power to endear and attach to themselves personal friends by stronger ties. He was beloved by all who knew him, respected by all. His was a name never mentioned save in honorable connection; whether in politics, in his profession or private life, he was the same estimable high-minded man. In the language of one of his warmest friends, we may say, "It is not for him we mourn, but for his friends." His loss leaves a void which none can fill, an absence which none can supply, a sorrow which nothing can assuage.—*San Francisco paper.*

PROCEEDINGS OF THE WHIG STATE CENTRAL COMMITTEE.

At a meeting of the California Whig State Central Committee, on Saturday, the 18th inst., the death of John Chetwood being announced by the President, on motion, Messrs. Billings, Kewen and Wilson were appointed a committee to present resolutions appropriate to the occasion.

The committee reported the following resolutions which were unanimously adopted:

Resolved, That this Committee have heard with profound sorrow of the death of John Chetwood, who, at their last meeting, was unanimously and cordially selected as the worthy candidate of the Whig party, for the highest judicial office in the state.

That his death is a public calamity ; that, far above all party considerations, we mourn over his sudden departure. The eminent and conscientious lawyer, the upright citizen, the gentle and the honest man, John Chetwood, was a treasure and an ornament to the Bar, Society and the State,

That we tender to his stricken relatives our earnest sympathies in their affliction, and assure them in their great grief, they have the consolation of knowing that if an unsullied life, a most distinguished position in his profession and society, the respect and affection of all who knew him, if virtue and honor, and success and friends, could have saved John Chetwood from death, they and we, and the community, would have been spared this melancholy occasion.

That we will, in a body, attend his funeral to-morrow, from his late residence.

That the Chairman transmit to his relatives a copy of these resolutions. C. J. BRENHAM, President

H. M. GRAY, Secretary. Whig State Central Com.

PROCEEDINGS OF THE DISTRICT COURT.

At the opening of this court yesterday, ex-Gov. Smith brought to the notice of Judge Lake the decease of the lamented Mr. Chetwood. He did so in the following remarks:

May it please your Honor: Since the adjournment of the court yesterday, death has been busy amongst us, and has stricken to the earth one of the most accomplished and brilliant members of our profession. John Chetwood, who had gained a most enviable position in this community, and who but a few hours since was living, full of hope, and with a bright and brilliant prospect before him, is no more! Disease, that was not viewed with apprehension in the beginning, traveled with unexpected force over his feeble form; and he has fallen before a power that no one can resist. It is a painful subject of contemplation, at all times, to witness the strong and powerful crumbling away before the march of time; but it is particularly painful and melancholy when we see the gentle, the amiable, and pure spirit stricken down in our midst. John Chetwood was well known in this community, and, while living, had not perhaps a single enemy. Coming, as many of us have come, to this land to better his fortune, he had nearly realized all his hopes: when his purposes, in a temporal sense, were accomplished, when he was beginning to look for the honors of his country, when he had received a strong manifestation of the high confidence reposed in him by a great political party—in the midst of all this, it has been the pleasure of Providence to manifest its dispensation in the trying incident to which I am now referring. I may say there is not a single person in the community who will not view his death with regret. I will go further and say, in reference to the honor proposed to be conferred upon him, that there is not a man, be he whig or democrat, who would view his success with one single regret. His was the glorious province to live among us, amidst the feeling that affects the public mind in regard to public men, without suspicion; and, had he lived, he would have been elected to the high office to which he was nominated, with the profound conviction that with him integrity would sit enthroned in the judgment seat. But it has pleased Him who rules the thunders to strike from among us one of the humblest, gentlest and purest spirits. He has been called for wise purposes from among us, to "that bourne whence no traveler returns." The only thing left us is to cherish his recollection within our inmost soul, and to be ambitious to pursue the high career that he attained. Under these circumstances, I move that this court, and the members of the bar, in regard to the memory of the distinguished deceased, wear crape around the arm for the space of thirty days; and if it be the pleasure of the court to adopt the resolution, I ask that it may be spread upon the minutes; and, out of respect to his memory, that the court do now adjourn.

Judge Lake.—It is not necessary for the court to add anything in relation to this dispensation of Providence. It has come upon us in such a manner as to unfit us for the ordinary business of the court; and as a mark of respect to the lamented deceased, we will adjourn; and the motion will be entered on the minutes.

PROCEEDINGS OF THE SUPERIOR COURT.

At the opening of the court on Saturday, John W. Dwinelle, Esq., rose and remarked:

May it please the Court: It becomes my painful duty, without premeditation, but in accordance with the wish of the members of the bar now present, to announce to this court the decease of John Chetwood, Esq., which took place yesterday in this city Mr. Chetwood was one of the most distinguished and successful practitioners at this bar. There was no member of the bar whose intimacy and friendship I enjoyed and valued in a higher degree; and this intimacy and friendship only enable me to bring to a closer test, and place a higher estimate upon, the enlarged learning, the unerring legal logic, the skillful tact, the energetic perseverance, the graceful professional courtesy, and the gentle amenities in private life, for which he was so eminently distinguished. But he has now gone from among us, and we shall see him no more!

Sir, it is one of the first lessons which is taught to us, that of DEATH! In our earliest infancy we are taught that God created us, and that he will surely take us away. But it is not until some dear friend is removed from our midst—not until our companion is smitten down by our side, that we for the first time appreciate the awful reality of death, and of the "remarkable retirement" of the grave. And that reality is now brought home to our hearts with a sense which cannot be mistaken. Our friend who, as it were, but yesterday stood in our midst, honored in the retrospect of a useful and stainless life, happy in the enjoyment of reputation and of the gifts of fortune, and distinguished by the unsolicited honors with which a great political party had associated his name, has gone forever from among us, and left nothing but the remembrance of his abilities and his worth. Yes! he who, but on the afternoon of yesterday, wasted by disease and attenuated by suffering, as he lay upon the bed of death, still retained to the last moment of that awful crisis his clearness of intellect and legal acumen, which he devoted to the settlement of his affairs—our friend, our brother—his pulse has ceased to throb, and it will never beat again! In the pride of his prime, in the height of his reputation, in the midst of his usefulness, while his armor was still buckled on, and he breasted the battle in the foremost rank of forensic strife, death beckoned to him at a distance with his silent finger, and he wrapped the drapery of the grave about him and obeyed the summons.

May it please the Court: I but express the unanimous and profound sentiment of the members of the bar, in view of this afflictive dispensation, in moving that this court do now adjourn.

Judge Satterlee said that he had always entertained a high appreciation of the learning, the abilities and the private virtues of Mr. Chetwood; and that he deeply sympathised with the members of the bar under the calamity which had afflicted them, the court and the whole community. The court would therefore, in accordance with the motion which had just been made, stand adjourned until Monday next.

PROCEEDINGS OF THE UNITED STATES COURT.

On the opening of the court yesterday morning, Calhoun Benham, Esq., U. S. District Attorney, arose and made the following announcement:

If your Honor please: It is my duty to announce the death of one of the members of the bar and a practicing attorney of this honorable court, Mr. John Chetwood.

This is, indeed, a mournful duty.

It is always sad to announce the death of one whom we have known, of one who has walked the daily routine of common life, associated in its duties and shared its pains with us. But it is still more melancholy to make this announcement.

There were circumstances attending the death of the deceased, which were somewhat peculiar.

As your Honor knows, he was but young, in the full vigor, indeed, of early manhood. He was a man of learning and ability, of zeal and fidelity and courtesy in his profession. He had been successful in it.

In the two short years he had passed amongst us, he had laid the foundations, as I am pleased to learn, of a competent fortune by his professional exertions alone. And, satisfied with what he had so honorably reaped of worldly goods, and strong in the teachings of the patience he had so sedulously practiced in gathering them, he was just preparing for a strife which, if successful, would have placed him on a yet more exalted and honorable eminence, where, it is no disparagement to the living to say, he would have shone. Nominated for the most responsible, delicate and confidential office in the gift of the people of the state—a place on the Supreme Bench—he was hailed with acclamation by his party, and just respect by his opponents. All agreed that he was worthy; and had he been promoted by the popular suffrage, his rivals might well have consoled themselves in defeat in the knowledge that they had succumbed to so upright a citizen and so accomplished a jurist.

But, sir, it was not to be. He was called from the possible fruition of this hope, and compelled to turn his thoughts to that

future state, of which the mysteries are so inscrutable to man, and
even divine revelation is dim.

He died. His fate was but as that of the lowliest—the least.
He died *here*, sir—away from his aged father—away from his fond
old mother—away from the tender care of his gentle sisters—here
in California, where there is many a solitary exit—where many a
one has died—where many a one must die.

Sir, the theme is too painful to pursue; nor is this the proper
place to pursue it. It is fitting we should send a word of comfort
to his friends at home, and pay the mark of decent respect to his
memory here.

I move your Honor to suspend the business of the court until
to-morrow morning.

Judge Campbell then arose and said:

I rise to second the motion of the District Attorney. The loss
occasioned by the unexpected decease of Mr. Chetwood falls not
only upon the immediate circle of his family and friends, but upon
the entire community in which he lived. It was my good fortune
to become acquainted with him several years since, in the state of
his nativity; to know that he there possessed a high reputation, not
only as an accomplished lawyer, but as a high-minded, honorable
gentleman; and to see him among those with whom he was connected by the ties of consanguinity and early association. There,
where he had spent the earliest years of his life, where he had
passed from infancy to manhood and mature age, and where all the
noblest traits of his character were most familiar, he gained the
esteem, respect and affection of all who knew him. His career here
is known to those who are now uniting in this last tribute of respect
to his memory. For upwards of two years he practiced at the bar
in this city with distinguished success: while his ability, industry
and profound learning were universally acknowledged, his gentle
courtesy, amiable temper and strict sense of honor were not less
generally admired and esteemed. He had justly earned all the
honors of the bar, and, had he lived, might in a few months have
taken his seat as a member of the highest judicial tribunal of the
state—honoring the station as much as it could have honored him.

But a few days before his death, he was nominated for the
Supreme Court; and while the nomination was hailed with enthusiasm by his political associates, those who differed with him were
fully satisfied that, in the event of his election, justice would be
faithfully, ably and impartially administered by him.

But it has pleased Providence to take him from us. While we
feel most deeply his loss, and sympathize warmly with the absent
relatives and friends, upon whom the news of his unexpected death
will fall most heavily, let us cherish in our hearts the memory of

those virtues which endeared him to us while living, and which cannot readily be forgotten, though he is now separated from us by the grave.

After Mr. Campbell had concluded, Judge Parsons arose and addressed the court as follows :

May it please the Court: I rise to pay what I deem but a just tribute to the accomplished lawyer, the honest man and the sterling friend. My acquaintance with Mr. Chetwood commenced some two years since. In that period I have known him at this bar as standing in the foremost ranks of his profession; and as a man governed invariably by the dictates of honesty; but it was as the sterling friend that he most bound himself to me. It will be remembered that at a time when some portions of this community seemed to vie with each other in their maledictions of myself, and when some individuals seemed to care for nothing but my ruin, both as a man and as an officer of this state, and while many persons, owing to the popular tumult, were afraid to avow their real sentiments and convictions, Mr. Chetwood came forward, and after a mature examination of the subject, threw the whole weight of his professional position, his character as an honest and intelligent man, into the scale, and in the court, in the community, and before the legislature vindicated the correctness of the positions taken by myself; and it is his readiness on that occasion to vindicate the right, his utter disregard of popular prejudice, that has bound him to me by feelings of more than ordinary friendship.

It is now melancholy to reflect that he, after having arrived at the culminating point of his hopes, being about to return to that circle of which he was the center, should have been stricken down. But there is a moral lesson to us all in contemplating the end of the just and the good man. Its teachings are, that we should cultivate the like virtues, and always keep before our minds the principles of virtue and of truth.

His end is a notice to us all of the final termination of all earthly pursuits; and it is well for us to pause as we here stand amid the hum and bustle of the great world around us, and that each one should ask himself what the chief end of life is. Let us all learn from this, to cultivate principles of justice and truth—that like him, when our last hour may come, we may wrap the drapery of our couch around us, and lie down as to pleasant dreams.'

His Honor, Judge Hoffman, made the following appropriate and feeling reply:

It seems but a cold formality in me to adjourn this court as a mark of respect to an eminent lawyer, when I lament him in my heart as a valued friend.

If varied and thorough knowledge of his profession, if the most scrupulous integrity, the nicest and most refined sense of honor, if a most sweet and gentle nature could command respect or win affection, Mr. Chetwood must have secured both.

His death has produced a profound impression on this community. But it is not merely his acute and disciplined mind, his habitual industry, or his care and devotion to the interests of his clients, which have elicited the ·feeling. It is the sense of his sterling honesty, his truth, candor and justice, which have made his loss felt as a public misfortune.

All who hear me knew and respected him as a lawyer, occupying a position second I may say to none in this state. To some of us he was united by ·nearer ties of friendship and affection. That equanimity of temper, those kind and gentle manners, which distinguished him in his daily life, he retained until his last moments.

Throughout an illness protracted and often painful, he betrayed no irritation, he made no complaints, but in all things "sweetly showed a most noble patience;" and when his last hour drew nigh, he exhibited a serene composure, a genuine and unpretending courage, as worthy of himself as it was affecting to all who beheld it.

One tribute to him I cannot withhold, for it is at least sincere. Had I desired the counsel of a friend to regulate my own conduct, had I sought to be advised what the purest integrity could sanction, or the most refined sense of honor dictate, by no man's opinion would I have been more willingly governed than by that of John Chetwood.

The bar has paid its last tribute to him at his grave. But he will long be remembered by us, as one who added dignity to the profession, whose character largely contributed to raise it above the imputations so often cast upon it by the ignorant and unreflecting, and as one of the ablest, the most eminent, and the purest men who adorned the early bar of California.

PROCEEDINGS OF THE SAN FRANCISCO BAR.

At a meeting of the Members of the Bar, of the city of San Francisco, held in the court room of the U. S. District Court, to express their affection and respect for the character and memory of their deceased brother, John Chetwood, Mr. M. H. McAllister was called to the chair, and Frederick Billings appointed secretary.

After remarks by the chairman and Mr. Hager, on motion of the latter gentleman, a committee of six was appointed to present to the meeting resolutions appropriate to the occasion.

The committee, consisting of Messrs. Hager, Benham, Yale, Crockett, McHenry and Baker, through their chairman, reported the following, which were unanimously adopted:

Resolved, That we have heard with unfeigned sorrow of the death of our lamented brother, John Chetwood.

That in his death we not only deplore the loss of an eminent lawyer, whose life was marked by a scrupulous integrity, profound learning and a high sense of honor, but we mourn the departure of a friend endeared to us by those generous sympathies, that singleness of purpose, and that purity of heart for which our deceased brother was distinguished;

That, whether we regard him as a lawyer who had already achieved distinction, or as a citizen always zealous for the public good, or in his social relations, as a friend, a brother or a son, he was eminently worthy of regard, and his death may justly be esteemed a public misfortune;

That we deeply sympathize with his bereaved relatives in their incomparable loss; knowing the excellence of his character, we can well appreciate the strength of those ties by which he was bound to the members of his household;

That, as a token of respect to the memory of our departed brother, we will attend his funeral in a body, and will wear the usual badge of mourning for the space of thirty days;

That a copy of these proceedings be transmitted by the chairman to the family of the deceased;

That the secretary cause these proceedings to be published in the city papers.

On motion of Mr. Casserly, the following resolution was adopted:

Resolved, That the members of the bar of the city of San Francisco will proceed in a body from the U. S. District Court Room, at a quarter past three, P. M., on the 19th inst., to the late residence of Mr. Chetwood, for the purpose of attending his funeral.

The meeting then adjourned.

M. H. McALLISTER, Chairman.

FREDERICK BILLINGS, Secretary.

MONUMENT TO MR. CHETWOOD.—MEETING OF THE BAR.

Upon the adjournment of the U. S. District Court, on the morning of the 20th inst., the members of the bar present organized a meeting by the appointment of Judge Hoffman as chairman, and Levi Parsons, secretary.

The object was stated by the chair to be the adoption of a further testimonial of respect to the memory of John Chetwood, on the part of the Bar of San Francisco, by the erection of a monument.

Frederick Billings, Esq., made a motion to that effect, accompanying it with the relation of frequent interviews held with the deceased, in which the latter always testified the most affectionate remembrance of his family in New Jersey, to return to whom would be to him a greater gratification than the most brilliant successes in California. He therefore hoped that Mr. Chetwood's remains would be taken to his old home in New Jersey, and buried near the family he loved and who loved him so well; and that the Bar of San Francisco would also erect there this monument, to show, though his remains were thousands of miles distant, how he was loved by them while living and remembered when dead.

Judge Parsons seconded the proposition of Mr. Billings, and it was unanimously adopted.

On motion to that effect, the chair appointed the following gentlemen a committee to receive subscriptions from members of the bar, and to superintend the erection of the monument: Levi Parsons, Frederick Billings, Hall McAllister, Judge Campbell and J. S. Hager.

THE LATE MR. CHETWOOD.

At a meeting of the Vestry of Trinity Church, held on the 18th of September, 1852, to manifest respect for the memory of their late associate vestryman, John Chetwood, Esq., the following resolutions were unanimously adopted:

Resolved, That in the death of Mr. Chetwood we recognize a bereavement equally to be deplored by his surviving friends, the church, the state and the city of his adoption.

Resolved, That in the character of the deceased we were made acquainted with an example of *unsurpassed integrity*, *a sterling sense of justice, high intellectual endowments*, with great cultivation, *gentleness of manners*, and *kindness of heart*, and *sobriety of conduct*, with *many charities*.

Resolved, That while we would convey to the aged parents of our departed friend our most heartfelt condolence, we may temper the cup of their affliction with the assurance that the virtues and pre-eminent worth of their son were known and honored in this distant state, where his death is bewailed as a public calamity by all good citizens.

Resolved, That these resolutions be published in the San Francisco papers, and that a copy of them be transmitted to his family, in Elizabethtown, N. J.

(Signed)   E. D. KEYES, Chairman.

D. H. HASKELL, Secretary.

DEATH OF JOHN CHETWOOD, ESQ.—Sad indeed are the emotions produced by this announcement, the truth of which is but too fully confirmed by our letters and papers from California, on the 30th; and most heavily does it fall upon venerable parents, a large circle of heart-stricken relatives, who have been watching his disease with trembling anxiety; and a still larger association of deeply sympathizing friends, to whom he was endeared from earliest youth by evidences of the best sympathies of our nature, rare instincts of honor, and the most delicate sensibilities of a true gentleman.

Nearly three years ago, he broke away from a wide circle of steadfast friends, and a large and growing practice at the bar, in this city, prompted only by an innate consciousness of his own power to encounter the risks of a strange land. At San Francisco he at once began a career of success and usefulness in his profession almost unexampled even in that state of remarkable vicissitudes; and, having achieved both fortune and honor, he was just contemplating a visit to the land where all his affections centered, when all his prospects for the future were thus changed by a mysterious Providence. * * *—*Newark Daily Advertiser.*

The announcement of the decease of our late townsman, John Chetwood, Esq., which occurred at San Francisco on the 17th ult., produced a marked effect upon our citizens on Saturday morning; and the expressions of sincere condolence with his mourning relatives, together with the sadness which oppressed the hearts of his numerous personal friends, were most affecting. Our whole community deplore the loss of one whose early years were passed in this his native town, and whose buds of early promise had gradually unfolded into full and brilliant development here, among the companions of his childhood and the devoted friends of his riper years. A very large proportion of our young men were, like ourselves, closely attached to him by the strongest ties of personal friendship, and—having felt warmly interested in his unusually brilliant career in the far-off El Dorado—were accustomed to watch the arrival of every steamer, in the fond anticipation of seeing his name honorably connected with some new triumph in the strife of fame and fortune. We were never disappointed, and the mention of his name recalls the memory of a success almost unparalleled even in the golden regions of the Pacific. Fortune never showered her favors upon a more worthy recipient; honor never rested upon the head of one who had more fairly won her smiles; friendship never rewarded with her choicest blessings one whose gentle kindness and manly sincerity were more attractive to all who knew him; the world's approval was never bestowed upon one whose sterling worth and inflexible integrity ever shone more conspicuously than did those qualities in the character and conduct of John Chetwood. The hearts of hundreds, who were not connected with him by the ties of kindred, beat more heavily upon receiving the sad tidings of his death; but among them all, no one will cherish his memory with more fond regret or more sincerely mourn his loss than we, who knew him intimately, and loved him as men always love true manliness.—*New Jersey (Elizabethtown) Journal.*

ESSEX COUNTY BAR.

A meeting of the Essex County (N. J.) Bar was held at the Court House yesterday, ex-Chief Justice Hornblower, in the chair, when the following resolutions were passed:

Whereas, Intelligence has been received of the death of John Chetwood, Esq., of California, a native of this county, and for thirteen years a successful and honorable practitioner of this Bar. Therefore,

Resolved, That we receive the intelligence of the death of our late associate and friend, with profound sorrow.

Resolved, That by his decease, the Bar of San Francisco, in California, has sustained a loss they will find it difficult to repair.

Resolved, That in his professional and private character he was worthy of our regard, as a sagacious lawyer, a successful advocate, a safe counselor, a sympathizing friend and affectionate brother and a dutiful son; a man of noble instincts and generous, he was known in this community, and was thus esteemed wherever known.

Resolved, That from our knowledge of his character as a lawyer and a gentleman, we feel assured, if length of days had been added to his other gifts, and by the suffrages of the people he had obtained judicial station in the state of his adoption, he would have adorned the office by his ability, courtesy, patience, application and spotless integrity.

Resolved, That the Circuit Court in and for this county, at the next term, be requested to order these proceedings to be spread upon its minutes.

Resolved, That in token of respect to the memory of our deceased brother, we will wear crape upon the left arm for thirty days.

Resolved, That a copy of these proceedings be forwarded to the parents and family of the deceased, and be published in the papers of the county.

Eloquent and impressive remarks were then made by Messrs. D. A. Hayes, William K. McDonald, Courtlandt Parker, Asa Whitehead, and ex-Governor Pennington, all of which evinced the sincere grief of the speakers at the loss of one who was an ornament to the Bar, and deeply beloved in social life; and the occasion was one which evidently created a deep impression on those who had formerly associated with the deceased. Touching tributes were paid to his character; and the high gratitude and pride which was felt for his eminent success, was forcibly expressed.

Essex County Courts.

The Essex County Courts opened this morning, Chief Justice Green presiding, with Associate Judges Haines, Crane, King, Davis and Kirkpatrick.

Upon the retirement of the Grand Jury, ex-Gov. Pennington rose and delivered the following address:

May it please the Court: When the news of the death of John Chetwood, Esq., at San Francisco, in the state of California, reached this place, a meeting of the Bar of Essex was held in this room, and resolutions passed sympathizing in that sad and melancholy event. By one of those resolutions, I was requested to present them to the Court at this time, and to ask that they be placed on their records. I now perform that duty.

Descendants of Judge Seth, son of Izrahiah, son of Thomas.

Mr. Chetwood was well known to the Court, and to the community here. He was a young man of high promise, of untiring industry, of laudable ambition, and of untarnished reputation. As a lawyer he was discriminating and able ; and as a gentleman and friend, a man of the highest honor. Born and educated among us, we knew his origin, and had witnessed with great pleasure his progress and advancement. His sudden death—far from his home, in a land of strangers, whither his enterprising character had led him to advance his fortune and his fame—fell heavily and mournfully upon a large circle of estimable relatives and friends. His father, William Chetwood, Esq., now venerable for his years, as he has been upright and excellent in his life, felt as the aged feel when their prop falls beneath them. A fond mother wept at the untimely death of her son. A brother, and an only brother, felt that the companion of his youth, one with whom he had passed the days of boyhood, had gone whence he could never return ; and a large circle of amiable and accomplished sisters mourned a most affectionate, kind, and generous friend and brother. To these near and dear relatives who mourned his loss, should be added a large number of associates, and the society here, to which he had formerly added so much by his personal courtesies, his correct and amiable manners, and by the brilliancy of his genius and talents.

The death of such a man is a public loss; but the sorrow seemed to be the more serious as it was sudden and unexpected. His last letters, before the sad intelligence reached us, were full of the brightest anticipations. He had made his mark upon the new theatre upon which he had entered. His character as a lawyer was established ; and he had received a nomination to the high office of Justice of the Supreme Court of California, and that too upon the earnest solicitation of the members of the Bar at San Francisco, who could best estimate his character for such a station. It may be said, he had passed the difficult period of his life ; he had earned a reputation, and all before him seemed brilliant and prosperous.

But Providence, by an inscrutable decree, had directed that his labors on earth should cease,—that he should die *there*, without one more look on his near and dear friends, or his native place. Mysterious as are these dealings, we have but one duty,—to bow submissively to the divine will. We trust his spirit has gone from a pure life on earth, to that blessed abode where no more troubles come, and where the weary are at rest.

I ask, sir, that the resolutions I hold in my hand, and which I will now read, may be placed on your records, as a memorial of the high character our friend has left among his old companions, and in the former scenes of his usefulness.

The Chief Justice expressed his sympathies with the

Bar, and ordered the resolutions to be entered on the minutes.—*Newark Daily Advertiser.*

SAN FRANCISCO, CALIFORNIA, Feb. 27, 1853.

GENTLEMEN : The undersigned, a committee appointed by the Bar of San Francisco, take a melancholy pleasure in transmitting to you the sum of two thousand dollars, contributed by the bar, to erect, in New Jersey, a monument to the memory of John Chetwood. The committee have thought they could best carry out the wishes of the Bar by forwarding the amount to you, and asking you, who were his friends, and who live so near the place where his remains will lie, to superintend the expenditure of the money, and the erection of the monument. Assured that you will fully appreciate the spirit and object of this testimonial to the private and professional character of Mr. Chetwood, and will take a deep interest in seeing the design of the Bar accomplished, the committee confide the matter to your discretion, with the single suggestion, that upon the monument should be marked the time and place of Mr. Chetwood's birth, and the time and place of his death, and in addition, the simple inscription, "To the memory of John Chetwood, by the Bar of San Francisco." They will be glad to hear of the completion and erection of the monument.

In behalf of the Bar of San Francisco,
Very respectfully, your ob't servants,
FREDERIC BILLINGS,
LEVI PARSONS,
JOHN S. HAGER,
ALEX'R. CAMPBELL,
HALL MCALLISTER.

Hon. Wm. Pennington, Hon. Joseph C. Hornblower, David A. Hayes, Esq., Newark, New Jersey.

P. S.—It is due to Burgoyne & Co., to say that the within draft is furnished free of charge by that house.

REPLY OF NEWARK COMMITTEE.

Gentlemen : Permit the undersigned in the use of your own appropriate language, to say, "we take a melancholy pleasure" in acknowledging your letter of the 27th of

February last, together with a draft for the sum of two
thousand dollars, so generously contributed, by the Bar of
San Francisco, to erect a monument, in this state, to the
memory of the lamented John Chetwood. It is a "melancholy" duty, because a recurrence to the death of our
esteemed friend and professional brother, fills our hearts
with sadness on the one hand; while on the other, it gives
us heartfelt "pleasure," and the most unfeigned gratification, to be assured, by your liberal donation, that you justly
appreciated, while he was permitted to be with you, the
many social virtues, the high integrity, the moral excellence, the courteous and gentlemanly bearing, and the professional learning, of our departed friend.

Accept, gentlemen, for yourselves and your constituents,
the Bar of San Francisco, our unfeigned thanks for this
fraternal and generous expression of your regard for the
memory of Mr. Chetwood. We consider your tribute of
respect to his memory as an honor done to us, and to our
fellow brethren of the Bar of this state, by all of whom
he was beloved and respected. Your wishes, gentlemen,
in connection with those of his bereaved parents and family, you may rest assured, shall be carried into effect as far
as may be in our power. The inhabitants of Elizabethtown are about erecting a cemetery in an eligible situation
in the vicinity of that place ; in which, we presume, the
family will desire the proposed monument to be erected.
Their wishes, however, will be consulted and complied
with.   With great sincerity and respect,

We remain your obedient servants,

JOS. C. HORNBLOWER,
WM. PENNINGTON,
DAVID A. HAYES.

Frederick Billings, Levi Parsons, John S. Hager, Alexander Campbell, Hall McAllister.

Mr. Chetwood's remains were removed from San
Francisco, and reinterred in the New Cemetery at
Elizabethtown, where the monument contemplated
by his professional brethren has been erected. It is
a tall shaft of white Italian marble, resting upon a
square base of like material, upon which is engraved :

"To the Memory of John Chetwood, by the Bar of San Francisco," together with the date of birth and death of the deceased.

Children of SAMUEL BREWSTER,

Son of Elisha, Son of Deacon Oliver.

ELISHA BREWSTER, b. in Middlet   Jan. 22, 1835; m. Josephine Spencer; had Frederick Brewster.

Resides at Seymour, Ind.

CAROLINE TUDOR, b. in M., April 6, 1842.

Children of OLIVER,

Son of Timothy, Son of Deacon Oliver.

MARY JANE, b. Sept. 14, 1839; m. Feb. 22, 1859, Thomas Wilkin of Yates co., N. Y.

ESTHER ANN, b. Aug. 18, 1845.

Children of TIMOTHY EDWARDS,

Son of Timothy, Son of Deacon Oliver.

WARREN HALSEY, b. at Wilson, Niagara co., N. Y., July 4, 1849.

WALTER ELY, b. at Cannon, Kent co., Mich., Sept. 5, 1851.

SAMUEL BUEL, b. at Cannon, Kent co., Mich., Aug. 16, 1853.

CHARLES EDWARDS, b. at Cannon, Kent co., Mich., Dec. 7, 1855.

Children of CHAUNCEY EDWARDS,

Son of Chauncey, Son of Deacon Oliver.

EDITH F., b. in California, Sept. 24, 1848.

WILLIAM BREWSTER, b. in C., April 1, 1851.

HENRY CLAVERENCE, b. in C., April, 1856.

Children of HENRY GOODWIN,

Son of Chauncey, Son of Deacon Oliver.

FRANKLIN HENRY, b. in California, Dec. 1, 1852.

CHARLES, b. in C., Jan. 26, 1855.

CHAUNCEY, b. in C., Dec. 1856.

LUCY, b. in C., June 15, 1859.

EIGHTH GENERATION.

Son of ELISHA BREWSTER,

Son of Samuel Brewster, Son of Elisha, Son of Deacon Oliver.

FREDERICK BREWSTER, b. June 3, 1856.

57

JEREMIAH, SON OF IZRAHIAH, SON OF THOMAS.

THIRD GENERATION.

JEREMIAH WETMORE,

Was the sixth son of Izrahiah and Rachel (Stow) Whitmore, born in Middletown, Nov. 8, 1703; m. Abigail Butler, of Wethersfield, Ct., Feb. 25, 1724–5; had Hezekiah, Jeremiah, Abigail, Anna, Ichabod, Elizabeth, Rachel, Rachel 2d, and Thankful. He died at Middletown, October 2, 1753.

We have been unable to obtain as complete a biographical record of him as we could wish. He inherited a large landed property from his father and his grandfather, Rev. Samuel Stow. His wife, we conjecture, is the grand daughter of Joseph Butler,[1] of Wethersfield, and his wife, Mary Goodrich.[2] Both

---

[1] RICHARD (Butler), Cambridge; 1632, freem. 14 May, 1634; rem. to Hartford before 1643; was rep. 1656–60, a deac. and d. 6 Aug., 1684. By first *w.* he had Thomas, Samuel and Nathaniel; by sec. *w.* Eliz., had Joseph, Daniel, Mary, wh. m. 29 Sept. 1659, Samuel Wright; Eliz. wh. m. an Olmsted; and Hannah wh. m. Green. His wid. d. 11 Sep. 1691. JOSEPH, Wethersfield, s. prob. of Richard of Hartford, m. about 1667, Mary d. of William Goodrich; had Richard, b. 1667; Benjamin, a. 1673; Joseph, ab. 1675; Mary, a. 1677; Gershom, ab. 1683; and Charles, ab. 1686; all nam. in his will. He d. 10 Dec. 1732, aged 84; his wid. d. 1 June, 1735. NATHANIEL of Wethersfield, br. of Joseph, of wh. no more is told. SAMUEL of Wethersfield, son of Richard, was deac., and of him I can tell no more, but that his dau. Mary m. 21 Jan. 1692, Ebenezer Hopkins, of Hartford.—*Savage's Geneal. Dict.*

[2] WILLIAM (Goodrich), of Wethersfield * * *; m. Oct. 4, 1648, Sarah, d. of Matthew Marvin, wh. outliv. him; had William, b. 8 Aug. 1649, beside eight others ment. below, and d. 1676, leav. good est. to wid. daus. respeliv. ws. of Robert Wells (wh. was Eliz. b. 1658, m. 9 June, 1675); Abigail, of Thomas Fitch; Mary, of Joseph Butler, and eldest dau. Sarah,

these families have long been distinguished in Connecticut for respectability and talent.

FOURTH GENERATION.

Children of JEREMIAH.

HEZEKIAH, Capt., b. in Middletown, Aug. 22, 1726; m. Sarah, dau. of Col. Jabez and Elizabeth (Edwards) Huntington of Windham, Ct., and grand dau. of Rev. Timothy Edwards of East Windsor, and niece of president Jonathan Edwards; had Hezekiah and Tryphenia.

He died in the West Indies.

JEREMIAH, b. in M., Nov. 25, 1727; m. Hannah, dau. of Josiah Hobbs of Weston, Mass.,[3] b. in Boston, Jan. 5, 1729; d. Aug.

b. 1649; m. 20 Nov., 1667, John Hollister, and s. John, b. 20 May, 1653; William again, 8 Feb., 1661; Ephraim, 2 June, 1666; and David, March 4, 1667. He was early an ens. rep. 1660, 2, 5, and 6, but prob. not progenit. of the emin. men of the state of Conn., bearing his name, His wid. bec. sec. w. of Capt. William Curtiss, of Stratford. It is some times spelt, in conform. with sound, Goodridge and Guttridge on careless rec. WILLIAM, of Wethersfield, son of preced. by w. Grace Riley; m. 22 Nov., 1680, wh. d. 23 Oct. 1712; had William, b. 3 Aug., 1681; d. at 3 mos.; William again, 2 or 23 July, 1686; Benjamin, 29 Sept., 1688; Joseph, 29 July, 1691, or 29 Feb., 1692; Isaac, 18 Aug., 1693; Ann, 25 Mar., 1697; Ephraim, 12 Sep., 1699; and Ethan, 3 June, 1702. He had by sec. w. Mary Ann, wid. of Dr. Nicholas Ayrault, Eliz., Lucencia and Eunice; and d. 1737. This fam. of wh. fifteen had 20 years since been grad. at Yale Coll. was from Suffolk, Eng. Rev. William, br. prob. by m. of Rebecca, a sis. of John and of William, the first comers, gave them by will, 1678, all his est. at Hegesset, a village near Bury St. Edmunds."—*Savage's Geneal. Dict.*

[3] JOSIAH (Hobbs), came to Boston in the Arabella, 1671, a passenger from London, lived at Woburn. By w. Mary, had Josiah, b. Aug. 6, 1685, Mary, 16 March, 1687, Susanna, 24 Nov., 1688; but the family tradition in Geneal. Reg., IX, 255, makes the eldest s. Josiah, b. in Boston, 1684, and the f. there to have liv. eighteen years after coming. In 1690, says the geneal reg., he rem. to Lexington, then called Cambridge Farms, and with w. Tabitha, join. the ch. there, Aug., 1699; had Josiah, Tabitha and Mary, bapt. 17 Sept. 1799; Matthew and Susanna, Oct. 1700; Ebenezer, 8 Jan., 1710; and Tabitha again, 13 April, 1712; and he d. 30 May, 1741, aged 92 years. JOSIAH, Boston, s. of the preced.; m. 1708, Esther, dau. of Ebenezer Davenport; had Ebenezer, b. 1709, Tabitha, 10 July, 1715,

5, 1802; had William, George, Hannah, Josiah, Sarah, Jeremiah, Esther, Mary, Butler, Frances, Butler 2d, Rachel, Tryphenia.

He died at Middletown, March 26, 1790.

He resided at Middletown, and was engaged in the West India trade, at a time when there was considerable foreign commerce carried on from that place.

It appears from the following, which are taken from the *Am. Archives*, vol. v, 4th series, that Mr. Wetmore was a loser during the Revolution, by seizure on the high seas. The statement itself, we deem a curiosity, and one of general interest. The persons named as owners and consignees, are heads of well known families of the present day.

An account of the brigantine Polly, vessel and cargo, Giles Sage, Master, taken by His Majesty's ship Nautilus, commanded by Captain John Collins on the 20th of Sept. last (1775), carried into Boston and converted to the use of the Ministerial Army and Navy there; in which is contained the value of said brigantine, the particular articles of which her cargo consisted, with names of the persons to whom each article in particular did belong; as follows, to wit:

The property of Matthew Talcott, Esq., and Captain Jeremiah Wadsworth, merchants:

The brigantine Polly, 110 tons burden, valued..................£500. 0. 0
Sundries named, rum, sugar, canvass, beef, etc., ... 752.16. 5
————————£1,252.16. 5

Josiah and John, tw. 1721, on Governor's Isl., it is said in the tradition tale. Esther, 22 Oct., 1722; Sarah, bapt. 10 May, 1724, in right of her mo. who had 12 April, preceed. united with Mather's ch. (the old North, not new North, as Geneal. Reg., ix, 255, reads), Dorcas, 8 May, 1726; Hannah (Mrs. Wetmore above), Jan. 5, 1829, tho' the fam. geneal. makes the b. 20 days later than the bapt., and tells that at Mather's ch. "all his chil. but one were bapt., when only three of the nine enjoy that rite in that place. He rem. to Weston, 1730; there had Nathan, b. next yr. He d. 27 Feb., 1779, aged 94 years, and his wid. d. the preceed. 29 Nov., if the accounts be correct."—*Savage's Geneal. Dict.*

The property of Richard Alsop, Esq. :
Eight hogsheads best Muscavato
   sugar, contng 9,882 ℔s ; weight
   is 88 cwt., 26@60s, ... £264.13.10
Two puncheons Jamaica rum, B.
   P., No. 38, 39, contg 227 gals.,
   4s,...................... 45. 8. 0
Twenty bags of cotton wool, contg
   2,214 ℔s., at 2s6d ℔ ℔.,....... 276. 1.10
Sundries (named), ... 62.10. 0
                          ————— 649.1. 10

The property of Titus Hosmer :
Sugar, rum and French ware,.............. 74. 7. 0

The property of Elisha Brewster :
Indigo 50 to 125, and checked linen, 23 yds.,
   3s, ... 34. 1. 0

The property of Samuel Russel :
Two puncheons Jamaica rum, B. P., No. 30, 31,
   225 gals., 4s,............................ 45. 0. 0

The property of Return Meigs :
One puncheon of Jam. rum,................ 21. 4. 0

The property of Stephen Ranney :
2 puncheons rum, and 2 hogs. Sugar,........ 110.10. 3

The property of Jeremiah Wetmore :
One puncheon Jam. rum, 109
   gals., 4s,..................... £21.16. 0
Three bbls. mess beef, 60s. ℔ bbl.,. 9. 0. 0
                         ————— 30.16. 0

The property of Giles Sage :
326 ℔. Indigo, 12s. ℔., 1 hhd. sugar, 13
   cwt., 1. 9. 16. 60s.; 80 ℔s. ginger, 50s. ℔
   cwt.; 1 ℔. nutmegs, 1.10, and sundries,
   making in all an invoice of 334.11. 0

The property of —— :
Sundry other parties named; seaman's wages,
   making a total of loss on vessel and cargo,
   of................................£3,034.19. 2

The captain's wages were rated at 50s. per month; seamen's at 35s. and 45s. per month. Affidavits, dated March 2, 1776, and signed by George Starr and Giles Sage, on the part of vessel and cargo, and Eleazer Treadwell, on the part of seamen, before Titus Hosmer, Justice of the Peace.

The vessel was owned by Talcott & Wadsworth, and it appears that she sailed from Middletown, in May, 1775, for New London, where she took in a cargo of horses, provisions and lumber for Kingston, Jamaica, W. I. ; arrived at latter port, July 6, 1775, and sailed thence for New York, the 20th of August. On the 20th of Sept., when on soundings S. W. from Long Island and standing in for New York, was captured by His Majesty's ship Nautilus. The captain and men were taken prisoners to Boston, preparatory to being sent to England. Capt. Sage made his escape at Dorchester Point, and from thence returned home.

It appears from a map of Middletown made before the revolution, that there were at that time three families of the name of Wetmore residing within the limits of the city, viz: Ichabod, Jeremiah and Josiah Wetmore. " Jeremiah, *sea captain*," is inscribed on lot next west of Ichabod on Washington street, west of Main street, and before Broad street, north side, now or late, the residence of Thomas Addison, Esq.

ABIGAIL, b. in M., Sept. 18, 1729.

ANNA, b. in M., March 6, 1731–2.

ICHABOD, b. in M., Aug., 1734 ; m. Elizabeth Starr, of New London, Ct., Nov. 10, 1757 ; had Ichabod ; m. 2, Elizabeth Christophers, Nov. 24, 1783 ; had Elizabeth, Maria, Harriet Lydia, Sarah Christophers, Ichabod 2d.

He, in early life, followed the sea, and became master of a merchant vessel. On the old map of Middletown, alluded to above, his name is recorded Ichabod Wetmore, "Seafaring." He occupied a house in Washington street, west of Main. He was a warden in the first Episcopal church of M., and was highly esteemed (says a correspondent who knew him in his old age) for his excellence and integrity of character. He died May 27, 1807. His first wife, Elizabeth Starr, died March 12, 1778. His second wife, Elizabeth Christophers, was of an old family of New London.[4]

ELIZABETH, b. in Middletown, July 29, 1736.

RACHEL, b. in M., May 28, 1738; d. Jan. 18, 1739.

RACHEL 2d, b. in M., Feb. 11, 1739–40.

THANKFUL, b. in M., Feb. 14, 1743; d. Nov. 2, 1753.

[4] CHRISTOPHER (Christophers), New London, 1667, mariner of Devonshire, brot. from Barbadoes, w. Mary, and chil. Richard, John and Mary. His w. d. July 13, 1676, aged 54, and he m. Elizabeth, wid. of Peter Bradley, dau. of Jonathan Brewster, and d. 23 or 25 July, 1687, aged 55, if the grave stone wh. makes his age ten yrs. less than that of his w. be correct. Perhaps the best change would be that on that of his w.'s stone as she might well be thot. younger; but the evidence is strong, that the inequality was real, and she felt the disadvant. CHRISTOPHER, New London, son of Richard of the same; was Judge of the Co. Ct., and asst.; had Christopher, who fill. the same offices after his f. JEFFREY, New London, br. of Christopher the first, came ab. the same time with him; had daus. Margaret, Joanna, and ano., beside only s. Jeffrey, wh. m. and d. 1690, of small-pox, with his w. within three wks., leav. no chil. He was call. 55 yrs. old in 1676, and rem. in old age with two daus., liv. in 1700 at Southold, L. I. Margaret, m. Abraham Coney; Joanna, m. 25 Dec., 1676, John Mayhew, of New London; and the other dau. m. a Packer, of S. JOHN, New London, mariner, younger s. of Christopher the first; m. 28 July, 1696, Eliz., perhaps dau. of John Mulford, and d. at Barbadoes, Feb. 3, 1703, leav. a wid and four chil. His wid. m. 21 Oct., 1706, John Picket. RICHARD, New London, elder br. of the preced., b., says a fam. reg., 13 July, 1662, at Cherton Ferrers, Torbay, Devonsh., ab. 6 mos. from Dartmouth; m. 26 Jan., 1682, Lucretia, d. of Peter Bradlee; had Christopher, bef. ment., b. 2 Dec. 1683, H. C. 1702, and other ch., but their names and dates have not been seen. His w. d. 7 Jan., 1691, and he m. 3 Sep. foll. Grace Turner of Scituate, perhaps a dau. of John, by wh. he had more chil., in all fifteen, and d. 9 June, 1726. The name bec. extinct at N. L. a doz. years ago, but descend. in fem. lines are there."—*Savage's Geneal. Dict.*

FIFTH GENERATION.

Children of Capt. HEZEKIAH.

HEZEKIAH, b. in Middletown; —; m. —— ——; had George and Sarah.

He resided in 1793, in Fairfield, Ct.

TRYPHENIA, b. in M. about 1750.

She died and was buried at Stratford, the following being a copy of the inscription upon her tombstone:

Mrs. TRYPHENIA WETMORE
daughter of Capt. Hezekiah Wetmore.
of Middletown.   Died July 11, 1772, æ. 22.

It will be remembered that the title of Mrs. or Mistress was given in colonial times to unmarried ladies that were of age, and of elevated social rank. The custom still prevails, we believe, in some parts of Europe.

Children of JEREMIAH.

WILLIAM, Judge, b. in M., Oct. 30, 1749; m. Nov. 5, 1776, Catherine, second dau. of Wm. Pynchon, of Salem, Mass., who d. July 28, 1778, leaving William. He m. 2d, Oct. 8, 1782, Sally, dau. of Samuel Waldo; had Sarah Waldo, Caroline Lucy, Augusta, Hester Ann, Thomas and Samuel Waldo, twins.

He graduated at Harvard College, 1770, and settled in Salem, Mass., where he practiced his profession and represented that town in the General Court in 1777. He was one of the original founders of the Massachusetts Historical Society, and was named with twenty-eight other distinguished citizens of that commonwealth, in the act of incorporation of that honorable society in 1794.   He ever after took a warm interest in the welfare of the society; and was engaged with the Rev. Dr. Morse, Dr. Aaron Dexter, Dr. William Spooner, and others, in superintending the publishing of one or more volumes of the Society's collections. He resigned his official connection with the Society, the 29th of August, 1815. He was judge of the court of common pleas of Boston, for a number of years.

In an autograph sheet before us, containing genealogical and biographical notices of a number of Wetmore families, arranged and sent by him to the Rev. Robert Griffeth Wetmore, in March, 1793, he says:

William, eldest son of Jeremiah, 2d son of Jer^e, 6th son of Iz. 1st, 4th son of Thomas, rec^d a liberal education at Harvard College, took the degree of A. B., July, ——, his degree of A. M., July ——; noticed in ye public performances by having comp * * * parts assigned him in ye English exercises on ye commencement days ——; removed to Salem, Massachusetts; studied law under Wm. Pynchon esq^r, an emminent Barrister 3 years, was admitted to ye court of common pleas; 1st Ap., 1774, to ye Sup. Judicial Court, 2 years after was called Barrister & power accordingly. His practice was extensive & embraced all the business he desired, till he quited it altogether in 1792, having acquired a fortune to gratify all his desires, the foundation of wc^h he laid in ye study & practice of ye com & civil law. He married 1st on 5 Nov. 1776 Catherine, 2^d daughter of Wm Pynchon esq^r of Salem, by whom had one son born Aug. 7, 1777, who is now at Harvard University, where he entered a student, July, 1792. She died 28 July, 1778. He remained a widower till ye 8 Oct., 1782, when he married *Sarah*, eldest daughter of Co^l Samuel Waldo of Falmouth, Massachusetts, dec^d; by her he had Sarah Waldo, a daughter, born at Salem, 24 May, 1784. Caroline Lucy, another daughter born at Boston, 5 Aug., 1786, died there 24 July, 1792, to the inexpressable grief of her parents, on acc^o of their unreasonable expectation from her heavenly temper and disposition and personal graces. Augusta, another daughter born 17 Feb. 1788.

He removed to Boston, 1785, where he now lives, occasionally visiting Middletown, the seat of his ancestors, where he possessed much of the old family estate for wch he feels the strongest attachment."

On the back of the paper, of which the above is taken, is inscribed, "Notices of Family of Wetmore, settled at Middletown in Connecticut, rec^d from Wm Wetmore esq., 2^d March, 1793."

Judge Wetmore died Nov. 1830. The isle at the mouth of the Penobscot river, known as " Wetmore's Island," was a part of the grant from the English government to Gen. Waldo, and received its name in compliment to Judge Wetmore, and was a part of his wife's inheritance, and where they resided for some time. The island was sold to the Messrs. Cary by his heirs in 1836 or 7, for $56,000.

His wife, Sarah Waldo, died Aug. 5, 1805. She was of a highly respectable ancestry; her paternal grandfather was Gen. Samuel Waldo, a distinguished officer during the Indian and French wars. The section of country, 10 leagues square, now composing a part of Waldo county, in the state of Maine, was patented to him, and is still known as the Waldo grant, and where he resided, and to whose heirs it descended.

Gen. Waldo was a son of Jonathan Waldo, a respectable merchant in Boston, who died in 1731, leaving a large estate to his five children. He was interested in eastern lands, and his son Samuel was connected with him in these speculations. On his death; Samuel came into possession of large tracts here and further east. The general was the largest proprietor of land in this town for many years, having purchased the rights of old proprietors, previous to 1730. In 1730, he bought 800 acres of the proprietors committee, and seized every opportunity to extend his interest here. He was an active intelligent and persevering man, and spent much time in town. He died at the age of 63, leaving two sons, Samuel and Francis, who lived in this town, and daughters, Hannah, married Isaac Winslow

of Roxbury, and Lucy married to Thomas Flucker of
Boston, who were the parents of the late Gen. Knox's wife;
a third son Ralph, died young. Gen. Waldo went to
England in 1729, to defend the Lincoln proprietors, and
published a pamphlet in vindication of their rights.— *Williamson's Hist. of Me.*, II, 338.

The same authority details the circumstances of his
death, as follows :

As soon as the laborers had commenced work,[5] the
Governor,[6] attended by Gen. Samuel Waldo, with guard
of 136 men, ascended the river near the head of tide water,
and below the bend, and May 23, (1759), went ashore on
the westerly side of the river. From this place he sent a
message to the Tarratin tribe, giving them notice of the
enterprise undertaken at the fort point, and assuring them
if they should fall upon the English, and kill any of them,
the whole tribe should be hunted and driven from the
country. But, added he, though we neither fear your re-
sentment, nor seek your favor, we pity your distress; and
if you will become the subjects of his Majesty and live
near the fort, you shall have our protection, and enjoy
your planting grounds, and your hunting berths, without
molestation.

Gen. Waldo took great interest in the expedition, ex-
pecting that the Musconges (or Waldo) patent extended
to some place near the spot then visited by them; and that
he and his co-proprietors would derive essential advantage
from the projected fortification. Withdrawing a few paces
he looked around and exclaimed, " here is my bound,"
and instantly fell dead, of apoplexy.[7] *   *   *   *

To commemorate the spot, the Governor buried a leaden

[5] Gen. W. was on an expedition up the Penobscot river. The work
about to be commenced was the building of a fort on the west side of the
river below Orphan's Island.

[6] Gov. Pownal.

[7] Council Rec. 1756 to 1767. Governor Pownal says "he went up to
the first falls, four miles and a half from the first ledge, found cleared
lands on the western side of the river, where Gen. Waldo dropt down,
May 23, just above the fall, of an apoplexy, and expired in a few minutes;"
the place is not known, supposed to be not far from Fort Hill, in Bangor,
some say it was on the eastern side.

plate, bearing an inscription of the melancholy event. Gen. Waldo was a gentleman of great enterprise and worth; and the conspicuous part he acted in the first capture of Louisburg, will be long recollected with intermingled pleasure and praise. His sons, Samuel and Francis, and the husbands of his two daughters, were the testamentary executors of his large estate, much of which was in the last mentioned patent.

Mrs. Wetmore's father, Col. Samuel Waldo, graduated at Harvard College in 1743; he represented Falmouth in the General Court, 1765, when the question of the stamp act was being agitated in the colonies, and was "directed to use his utmost endeavors to prevent the stamp act taking place in that province;" being unfavorable to the popular party was not returned the second time.

Francis, 2d son of Gen. Waldo, was also a graduate of Harvard (1747). He never married (says a note in *Hist. of Portland*, p. 112), a disappointment in that quarter in 1768, induced him to abandon the idea; he writes in Sept. of that year, "Miss —— has behaved in a manner so base, ungrateful and false, that I don't expect any further connection there." He was a representative of the town in 1762 and 1763; at the commencement of the revolution he went to England and never returned. His estates here were confiscated under the absentee act in 1782, and sold. He died in London.

GEORGE, b. in Middletown, July 31, 1751; m. by Bishop Seabury, Rachel, only dau. of Benjamin Ogden, Esq., of New York city; had Rachel Ogden, George Curgerven, Alexander Ogden, William Henry, Sophia Maria, Charles, Jeremiah, Thomas George, Harriet Augusta, Cornelia Charlotte, Mary Ann.

He was educated in his native place, and at an early age embarked in the West India trade, by which he amassed a considerable property. He continued in that trade until the commencement of the Revolutionary war. Remaining loyal to the crown, he enlisted a company of 48 men at his own expense, called the Independent Volunteers, attaching his company to Brig. Gen. Browne's brigade; from Gen. Browne he received his first commission of lieutenant, Jan. 1, 1777, and afterwards that of captain in the 2d battalion, March 25, 1777. He served his sovereign until 1783, when the regiment was disbanded. He then took up lands at Antigonish, Nova Scotia, where he resided many years, after which he returned to the United States, and settled at Troy, N. J., where he died soon after, Nov. 2, 1800. His remains are entombed, together with his wife's, at Morristown, N. J.

HANNAH, b. in M., March 22, 1753; m. Mr. —— Douglass of M.; d. Sept. 20, 1810.

JOSIAH, b. in M., Jan. 11, 1755; "went to sea; was taken to Halifax; put on board of a British guard ship; caught a putrid fever, and died Oct. 12, 1778."[8]

SARAH, b. in M., Jan. 10, 1757; m. Mr. —— Hart of M., d. Sept. 19, 1789.

JEREMIAH, b. in M., Feb. 17, 1759. " He also went to sea, was in y[e] service of the Dutch, during y[e] late war; was taken and confined in y[e] Mill Prison, England, where he continued till y[e] peace; what became of him we[ed] never learn."[8]

He died in 1803.

ESTHER, b. in M., March 5, 1761; d Oct. 13, 1810; unm.

MARY, b. in M., Nov. 20, 1762; single.

BUTLER, b. in M., July 16, 1765; d. Aug. 16, 1766.

FRANCES, b. in M., May 20, 1767; m. Mr. —— Clark of M.

BUTLER 2d, b. in M., Nov. 20, 1768; d. Nov. 24, ——.

RACHEL, b. in M., July 1, 1770, lived with her brother, Judge William, in Boston; d. unm., Jan. 16, 1814.

TRYPHENIA, b. Nov. 29, 1772 (single).

[8] From an original record made by his elder brother, Judge William (as was most of the above gen. record), dated March, 1793.

Children of ICHABOD.

ICHABOD, b. in Middletown, Feb. 12, 1759; grad. at Yale Coll., 1778; d. unm. Aug. 9, 1786.

ELIZABETH, b. in M., Aug. 23, 1784; m. John Hinsdale, May 26, 1804; had I *Sarah Wetmore*, b. June 1, 1805, who m. E. H. Kimball, of N. Y. II *Elizabeth Christophers*, b. June 17, 1807; m. E. H. Kimball, of N. Y.; d. Sept. 1, 1828.

Mrs. Hinsdale d. Oct. 25, 1808.

MARIA, b. in M., May 28, 1786; m. Capt. John (Andrew?) of the U. S. revenue service, at New London, July 7, 1810; had I *John P. C.*, b. Sept. 26, 1816.

HARRIET LYDIA, b. in M., Oct. 27, 1787; m. Benjamin Williams, July 19, 1807.

Resides in New London.

SARAH CHRISTOPHERS, b. in M., March 9, 1789; d. Oct. 13, 1805.

ICHABOD 2d, b. in M., March 14, 1792; m. in Newbern, N. C., Jan. 23, 1817, Elizabeth Ann, dau. of Thomas Badger, Esq.; had Laura Jane, Elizabeth Cogdell, Thomas Badger, George Badger, Frances Rebecca, Lydia Cogdell, and William Robards.

He removed to North Carolina about the time of his majority, where he settled and married, and where, by his integrity and uprightness of character, he established a reputable name, and received that confidence and respect from the citizens of the "old North State" that his worth and honorable ancestry entitled him to. He was for many years cashier of the State Bank of North Carolina, at Fayetteville.

He died at the latter place, Oct. 7th, 1857. A plain stone, with name, date of birth and death inscribed thereon, erected in the grave yard of that city, marks the place where his remains repose. His widow continues to reside in Fayetteville, much honored and loved by her numerous family, as well as highly respected and revered by the citizens generally. She is a daughter (as before noted) of the late Thomas Badger,[9] of North Carolina, who was a native of Windham, Conn.; he settled in North Carolina in early life, and married Lydia, daughter of Richard Cogdell, Esq., of Newbern. He was an attorney and counsellor, was esteemed for his probity and trustworthiness, and became one of the most eminent lawyers of that state. He died of yellow fever in 1799, leaving three small children—George E., Elizabeth Ann, and a daughter who died young. The son, the

Hon. GEORGE E. BADGER, we may truly say, has well sustained the reputation and honorable name that he inherited. He was born in 1795. His maternal grandfather, Richard Cogdell, with Dr. Alexander Gaston, was of the Council of Safety for the Newbern district. He graduated at Yale College in 1813; studied law with the Hon. John Stanley, who was a near relative; was a representative in the N. C. state legislature in 1816; judge of the superior court from 1820 to 1825, when he resigned; was secretary of the navy under President Harrison, which office he resigned on the incoming of President Tyler. In 1846 he was elected U. S. senator, and again in 1848 for a term of six years, serving on committees on military and naval affairs. Of late years he has been most exclusively engaged in the practice of his profession in

[9] "GILES (Badger), Newbury, 1635; m. Elizabeth, dau. of Edmund Greenleaf; had John, b. June 30, 1643; and d. 10 July, 1647. His will, of 29 June, was pro. in Sept. and his wid. m. 16 Feb. foll. Richd. Brown. JOHN, Newbury, son of the preced. by w. Eliz. wh. d. 8 Apr. 1669; had John, b. 4 Apr., 1664; d. soon; John, again, 26 Apr., 1665; Sarah, 25 Jan., 1667; and James, 19 Mar., 1669. For sec. w. he m. 23 Feb., 1671, Hannah, dau. of Stephen Swett; had Stephen, 13 Dec. foll.; Hannah, 3 Dec., 1673; Nathaniel, 16 Jan., 1676; Mary, 2 May, 1678; Eliz., 30 Apr. 1680; Ruth, 10 Feb., 1683; a. s. 9 Mar., 1685; d. soon; Abigail, 29 June, 1687; and Lydia, 30 Apr., 1690. He d. 31 Mar., 1691, and his w. at near the same date, both small pox. NATHANIEL, Newbury, 1635, br. of Giles, perhaps elder; had w. Hannah, but I can no more of him, or ano. br. Richard."—*Savage's Gen. Dict.*

In 1857, three grad. of this name had come from Harvard, in 1856; five from Yale; and in 1834, two from other N. E. Coll.—*Compiler.*

the higher courts of his own state, and of the Supreme Court at Washington.

In politics he has always been a Whig, as was his father in the early days of the Republic; always conservative in his views. He is one of the few of that school of Clay and Webster statesmen left among us. As might be expected from such a man, he is a *Union loving man*, and as the *crowning glory* of his life it may be *here* recorded, that he is, during this momentous crisis in our country's history, using his commanding influence and forensic powers in endeavoring to stay revolution and all its attendant horrors. If his descendants in generations yet to come, should have no other birthright of which to be proud and to entitle them to heraldric honors, the simple fact that their ancestor, George E. Badger, was in *sentiment* and in *deed* against disunion, of itself will be *sufficient*.[10] As a citizen and neighbor, Mr. Badger stands deservedly high, enjoying the confidence and esteem of those opposed, as well as of his own, political faith. Many is the young student of limited means, as well as others, who has been made the recipient of Senator Badger's kindly aid and countenance.

He married, first a daughter of Geo. Turner, second a daughter of Col. Polk, and third Mrs. Williams, a daughter of the late Sherwood Haywood, Esq., of Raleigh, N. C.

[10] We are pained beyond expression, in having to note here that Mr. Badger has given way to the revolutionary storm, that is devastating the southern states. We have ever been a political admirer of Senator Badger, and we wish it could have been so ordered, that he should stand firm with those sturdy oaks, his cotemporaries in times past, John J. Crittenden of Kentucky, Edward Bates of Missouri and Edward Everett of Massachusetts.

SIXTH GENERATION.

Children of HEZEKIAH,

Son of Jeremiah.

SARAH.

GEORGE.

Children of Judge WILLIAM,

Son of Jeremiah.

WILLIAM, b. Aug. 7, 1777; grad. at Harvard College, 1797; d. unm., Feb. 1807.

SARAH WALDO, b. at Salem, Mass., May 24, 1784; m. in Boston, Aug. 28, 1808, Judge Joseph Story, LL. D.; b. Sept. 18, 1779; had Caroline, Joseph, Caroline Wetmore, Mary, William Wetmore, Louisa, and Mary Oliver.

Sarah Waldo Wetmore was the 2d wife of Judge Story. His first wife was Mary Lynde Oliver, " whose intellect (says his son) commanded his respect, as her greatness and amiability had won his heart." * * * " She was an elegant and accomplished woman, full of fine sense, and interesting in her person and manners" (*Judge S.'s Autobiography*). They were married Sunday, Dec. 9th, 1804, and she died the 22d of June, 1805.

The following history and circumstances attending the subsequent marriage and wedded life of Judge Story, we take from the *Life and Letters of Joseph Story*, edited by his son, Wm. W. Story; Boston: Little & Brown. 1851.

* * * * * To a nature so social and demonstrative, the idea of a solitary life was repulsive. As his grief wore away and he became interested in society his desires

stretched forward timidly, but decidedly towards a life
which should not be without its

> "Intimate delights,
> Fireside enjoyments, home-born happiness."

In his solitude he longed for a home and for the charms
of sympathy and love. The prize' of office and fame,
grateful as they were to his ambition, did not satisfy the
demands of his heart. His aimless affections required to
be concentrated, and though doubtingly at first, he soon
listened to the flattering voice of 'hope. From beneath
the cloud of sorrow the sunlight began to gleam.

In the beginning of the year 1808, he became interested in Miss Sarah Waldo Wetmore (my mother), and before
it had elapsed he was affianced to her. Her father, Hon.
William Wetmore, was a lawyer of distinction in Boston,
and a judge of the Court of Common Pleas. Her mother
was the granddaughter of Brigadier General Waldo, so
well known in the provincial annals of this country. She
had been the intimate friend of my father's first wife, and
was related to her by marriage, and the esteem and affection, which had begun during his previous marriage, now
matured into love. The news of his engagement he thus
announces to his brother-in-law, Joseph White, Jr.

BOSTON, May 28, 1808.

My Dear Brother :

If you are in company, home or abroad, when you receive this
letter, perhaps you may as well fold it up in silence. Will it be a
surprise to you that again I am awakening to the influence of love,
and again am seeking the happiness of domestic life ? I have long
wished to change this irksome state for one more congenial to my
feelings and my habits, but a thousand circumstances have repress-
ed the consideration. My difficulty in meeting with an individual
to whom I could offer the free homage of my heart in sincerity, has
opposed an insuperable obstacle. No motive but that of affection
could ever find a place in guiding my choice, and how few, how
very few, in the circles of polite life, unite the qualities to form
domestic felicity. Thanks be to God ! all my doubts and apprehensions have vanished. I am now an affianced lover, to one my heart
most sincerely reverences and admires. Shall I tell you that this
gentle being is Sally Wetmore ? I have known her long, very long,
and have always respected her excellent character. Esteem has
ripened into affection, and she, whom in the circles of friendship

I always sought with delight, has now become the first in my heart. I ask your congratulations to me on this occasion, and I know that you will feel pleasure in learning that I shall soon have a home, to which to welcome you and yours.   Yours affectionately,
JOSEPH STORY.

A letter of later date, to Samuel P. P. Fay, Esq., announces his marriage.

Monday, August 28th, 1808.
My Dear Friend :
I bless my stars that, at half-past six yesterday morning, I received from the hands of Parson Eaton a wife. We were married at the North Church, dined in Boston, and drank tea in Salem, at our own house. Here we shall rejoice to welcome you and Harriet, and believe me in truth, we love you and her very sincerely. May our friendship find in this new connection an additional tie to fix its everlasting permanence. My wife is at my elbow, with my sister Harriet. They are happy. Heaven grant that we may all long be so ! ,   Yours affectionately, .
JOSEPH STORY.

P. S.—There is a small package containing a piece of bridal cake, which is left at Judge Wetmore's in Winter street ; pray if in town get it for our young friends to dream over.

His son continues : His domestic happiness was crowned by the birth of his daughter Caroline, subsequently of his son Joseph.
The following letter to Mr. Williams gives us a glimpse into the household :

BOSTON, February 20th, 1811.
My Dear Friend :
I rejoice in the acknowledgement of your recent letter, though I have been a little more charitable than usual in accounting for your silence. The necessary arrangements of the profession, the accumulation of domestic cares, and the delightful task of sporting with your boy, were all considered as no mean apology for a half year's epistolary negligence.
My wife and myself take great interest in the picture which you have given us of your family group, and learn with peculiar satisfaction that our young friend is lively, elegant and sensible. By the by I do not well discern how he could have been otherwise. Can a good tree bring forth bad fruit ? In return we assure you, that our dear little Caroline is very healthy, and very handsome ; as fine a specimen of New England's red and white, as ever graced the visions of a northern poet. She is a source of perpetual interest

and anxiety, and amply, and very amply, repays our endearments, by becoming every day more affectionate and playful. * * * * I have just published Lawes on Assumpsit, with notes, and I have preserved a copy for you, which I shall transmit by the first convenient opportunity.   *   *   *   *   *   *   *   *

Yours affectionately,
To Nathaniel Williams, Esq.   JOSEPH STORY.

But these golden days were not destined to last.   On the 28th of February, 1811, Caroline died and a cloud of sorrow darkened over the house.   My father was almost inconsolable; but he devoted himself to study and labor as the best alleviation of his sorrow, and sought, by creating other interests, to forget his loss.

His son Joseph still was left, for whom, with all a father's pride, he laid out future visionary plans of joy and fame— never, alas, to be realized.

The following verses he wrote on the death of Caroline:

Sweet, patient sufferer, gone at last
    To a far happier shore,
All thy sick hours of pain are past,
    Thy earthly anguish o'er.

And yet if aught or fair or bright
    Might hope to linger here,
Long, long had shone thy modest light,
    And never caused a tear.

In temper, how serene and meek!
    How touching every grace!
The smile that played upon thy cheek
    Might warm an angel's face.

A heart how full of filial love!
    How delicate, how good!
Thy feelings served intent to prove
    The bliss of gratitude.

So quiet and so sweet thy death,
    It seemed a holy sleep,—
Scarce heard, scarce felt, thy parting breath,
    Then silence fixed and deep.

Who can the utter wretchedness
  Of such a scene portray,
When the last look, the last caress
  Is felt, and dies away.

I kissed the faded lips and cheek,
  And bent my knees in prayer,
Bent—but there was no voice to speak,
  It choked in still despair.

Ah! never, never, from my heart
  Thine image, child, shall flee—
'Tis soothing from the world to part,
  'Tis bliss to think on thee.

*   *   *   *   *   *   *

The following letters contain another picture of domestic grief. His daughter Mary, who was born on the
9th of April, 1814, died March 28, 1815; and scarce had
this wound began to heal, when on the 19th of October,
in the same year, Joseph, then in his 6th year—a bright,
handsome and promising boy, in whose growing childhood
my father had watched with delight the tender reflections
of his own early life and feelings, and whose future career
he had painted with sanguine hopes—died:

SALEM, May 8th, 1815.
My Dear Friend:
  I feel very much obliged to you for your late kind letter. When
I reached home it was but a melancholy meeting. My youngest
daughter, Mary, about eleven months old, was very ill, and in about
a week she expired, to our unspeakable sorrow. This was indeed a
most cutting affliction to my wife; the little girl was uncommonly
handsome and intelligent, and promised us many days of future
happiness. I may well exclaim, in the words of Young—

"Early, light, transient, chaste as morning dew,
    She sparkled, was exhaled, and went to heaven."

My wife has been very melancholy since this unfortunate event,
and so indifferent is her health, that I propose to make a short journey into the country, with a hope of her convalescence. May you
long be shielded from the pangs and sorrows of losses of this kind,
though it will be almost miraculous if you should escape for any
considerable length of time from an evil which seems the fate of all

human connections. I know of no sorrow more bitter or more piercing than the sudden removal of the children of our love. This is the second time that I have buried a lovely daughter. As a parent, you cannot but sympathize with us. Alas! this is the only consolation which the loss admits, and it is truly precious from the hands of friendship.

With a view to dissipate my grief, for it is unavailing, I have been latterly engaged in drawing up my dissenting opinion in the case of *Nereide* (9 Cranch's R. 449.) I have now completed it; and never in my whole life was I more entirely satisfied that the court were wrong in their judgment. I hope Mr. Pinckney will prepare and publish his admirable argument in that case; it will do him immortal honor.   Your affectionate friend,

To Hon. Nathaniel Williams.   JOSEPH STORY.

SALEM, Sept. 28th, 1815.
My Dear Friend:
I owe you an apology for not answering your interesting letter, but in truth I have been overwhelmed with public, private and domestic business. My wife has been severely sick during the greatest part of the summer, and has hardly yet recovered any considerable portion of health. To add to my anxiety and afflictions, my little boy has been again seized with the same disorder as in the last year, except that the symptoms have been, if possible, more alarming. He has now been ill about two months, and we have hopes (alas, they are but hopes), that he is now slowly on the recovery.

These two events have completely broken up all my studies and pleasures during the whole summer, and have exhausted and employed my time in the most anxious occupations. The few moments which I have been able to spare from the chamber of sickness, have been devoted to necessary judicial concerns.

You, too, have been placed in most trying circumstances, and have felt what indeed has often been my lot, the dreadful horror of losing children in the very bloom and brightness of youth. * * * How frail is the tenure of our happiness, and how little of our joys and sorrows is within our own control?

For myself I can truly say, that my personal experience has greatly tended

> " To damp my brainless ardor, and abate
> The glare of life which sometimes blinds the wise."

These are melancholy reflections, and though they sometimes press on my anxious hours, I am glad to say that they have not robbed me of many cheerful days.   *   *   *   *   *

                         Your affectionate friend,
To Hon. Nathaniel Williams.   JOSEPH STORY.

Descendants of Jeremiah, son of Izrahiah, son of Thomas.

SALEM, December 3d, 1815.

My Dear Friend :

Since I wrote you last, I have undergone great and severe anxieties, and have sustained what I must ever deem an irreparable loss. My dear little boy, after suffering in a most melancholy manner from a gradual decline, died towards the close of October. It was my painful duty to attend him almost exclusively during the last months of his illness, and what with almost incessant watchfulness, anxiety, and sorrow, my very soul sank within me. It is impossible to describe to you, or to any other human being, who has not passed through such a bitter scene, how much I loved him, and how much his death has worn upon my feelings. I loved him indeed for what he was, a most intelligent and promising boy; I loved him most because *he* loved *me* most dearly; never could a child cling more fondly to a parent. But I forbear to trouble you with these useless and melancholy details; I bear the loss, as well as I may; I fly to business to stifle my recollection of the past, and I find, what I always believed, that employment is the only relief under the severe losses of human life. It has fortunately happened, that the session of the Circuit Court has compelled me to more than usual labor. My mind has been occupied, and I have been obliged to run away from the indulgence of grief.

Human happiness is held by so feeble a tenure, that we should not add to our sorrows, by treasuring up for solitary musings. We shall have as many griefs as we can well struggle under, without looking backward on the past. I feel myself bound, therefore, by my duties to my yet remaining family, a wife and daughter, to shake off the gloom, and to press into the cares of business, where I may gather smiles from those who in the sunshine can amuse and instruct us. But never, never, my dear friend, can the wound in my soul, be healed; I shall carry to the grave the memory of my dear boy, whom I fondly doted on. I am again forgetting my purposes and leading you into a path in which I am not willing to travel.   *   *   *   *   *   *   *   *   *   *

Adieu my dear friend, I am as ever,

Yours affectionately,

To Hon. Nathaniel Williams.   JOSEPH STORY.

The domestic sorrows of this period of his life gave a sadness to his meditations, which showed itself in the verses he wrote in later days; and although they have not the power permanently to depress his natural light-heartedness, they chastened his enthusiasm and sobered his imagination. The loss of his children afflicted him deeply, and the first burst of his grief completely overwhelmed him. The memory of these days was always a pain, and he could never bear any allusions to the children he had lost.

But, as these letters indicate, he did not surrender himself to despondency or to vain lamentations over what was irretrievable. Cheerfulness he cultivated as a duty. It was his creed that we should keep our mind serene, bear up against misfortunes, avoid repinings and look upon the sunny side of things. Early in life he read in the *Spectator* a series of essays on this subject, by Addison, which made a deep impression upon him, and thenceforward he saw it "writ down in his duty" to dwell upon the compensations of every disappointment, and to preserve, as far as possible, an equable and enjoying spirit. Moments of gloom and despondency fall to the lot of all, especially of the sensitive, and

> "There is often found,
> In mournful thoughts, and always may be found,
> A power to virtue friendly;"

but such moments and thoughts are for seclusion, not for society. He was not without his sorrows. But he strove to keep them to himself, so as not to overshadow with them the happiness of others. Even in solitude and meditation he studied to banish moroseness and melancholy from his thoughts, not only as being injurious but unchristian. At once cheerful by temperament and by principle, he sought not only to do his duty, but to enjoy doing it, and to accept life as a favor granted, and not a penalty imposed. Happy indeed is he

> "That can translate the stubbornness of fortune
> Into so quiet and so sweet a style."

Henceforward he was compelled annually to absent himself from his family during the three winter months, in order to attend the sessions of the Supreme Court at Washington. The change of scene, the vivacity of political action and intrigue, and the many distinguished men he met, gave a new turn to his thoughts and habits, and rendered his temporary residence there in many respects interesting. But he would gladly have surrendered all the attractions of Washington for those quiet, fireside enjoyments of home which he prized so much more highly.

Still, it is probable that the exchange of the stern New England winter for a warmer and more equable climate, together with the double journey, and the excitements of new objects and persons, had a beneficial influence on his health, prolonged his life, and, on the whole, promoted his happiness.

During succeeding years, he devoted himself to judicial duties with great assiduity, and took his full share in the labors of the court at Washington.

* * * * * * * * *

In 1819, Judge Story was again visited by another severe affliction, of which he gives an account in a journal that he kept.

What a melancholy interval since I last wrote; a year has elapsed and nothing is recorded.

On Thursday, the 1st day of April, 1819, at ten o'clock in the evening, died my dear little daughter, Caroline Wetmore Story, aged 6 years. This day (the 4th) is her birthday. But she is gone forever. She was a most kind, affectionate and intelligent child; and has endeared herself to me by a thousand ties. She continued cheerful, affectionate and interesting to the last; I never saw a more delicate, chaste and modest being. She seemed instinctively to shrink from everything which might expose the frailties of our nature. Her intellectual powers were great, her desire of knowledge insatiable, and her curiosity rapid and perpetually alive. We were obliged to restrain her ardor for knowledge, lest the exertion should be unfavorable to her health; yet child as she was, she manifested at every turn a penetrating intellect. I dwell, however, with most satisfaction, if that may be so called, which is but a deep and melancholy recollection, of her gentleness, her unbounded love for her parents, her affectionate tenderness to her friends, and her gratitude for all the kindness which she received. It is a consolation—a melancholy consolation—that until within a few days of her death she was able to enjoy the pleasures of her age; that she was cheerful, and having no fears of the future, happy. In her last sickness she suffered but little pain; her principal difficulties arose from extreme debility and exhaustion. She died

60

perfectly sensible to the last. A moment before she asked her aunt Hester to lift her up higher in the bed, and immediately sunk away into a gentle sleep, holding her aunt's hand until she had ceased to breathe.   *   *   * The dear little child, however, had no dread of death, for she knew nothing of it. It was a blessing. Her ignorance was bliss. Would to God my exit might be as calm, as sweet, as pure as her's. Life daily loses its charms in my eyes; I feel less and less the power of its pleasures, and even when I struggle most to mingle with the business of life, I often feel my heart sink within me. It requires no ordinary effort now even to brace myself up to perform duties. Yet with the world, I dare say I pass for a cheerful man, and so I am, but my cheerfulness is the effect of labor and exertion to fly from melancholy recollections and to catch a momentary joy. While we live we are bound to do all the good we can; life was not meant to be passed in gloom, yet how difficult is the task to act up to duty in this respect. He who feels that he has but a short hold upon life (and how feeble it is), drags slowly on, for his ambition for distinction is perpetually liable to be extinguished by that melancholy consideration. God, without doubt, has wisely ordered all things in his providence as to our present and future being; but his ways are inscrutable, and his doings are mysterious beyond human comprehension. I repose myself entirely upon his mercy, his wisdom, his omnipotence, and his infinite goodness. He will temper the wind to the shorn lamb.

His life was thus gliding on smoothly and busily, when his home was stricken by another domestic calamity. Louisa, the youngest of his children—most lovely and attractive in person and mind, and who had been the pride and joy of my father's heart, as he watched her rapidly-developing graces and powers—was taken ill of a scarlet fever, and, after a very short illness, died on May 10th, 1831. This blow, which was wholly unanticipated, desolated our home and entirely prostrated him. With great determination, however, he immediately betook himself to earnest labor, striving thus to attain to forgetfulness of his great loss. But it was very long before the world looked glad to him, and, to his death, this sorrow he carried like an arrow in his heart. The following letters show the condition of mind in which this bereavement left him:

CAMBRIDGE, May 25, 1831.

My Dear Sir:

I have just received your kind letter, and reply gratefully to it at this moment, not knowing when I shall find more leisure. You did exactly as I should have done under like circumstances, and from the same considerations. When we are overwhelmed by a recent sorrow we are incapable of consolation, and even of communion with other minds. We must be left to our own thoughts, and to the solitude of our own sorrow, until the heart has exhausted itself of its anguish and despair.

I have been very, very wretched. The calamity came upon us so suddenly and so awfully that it quite stunned me, and for a while, I was sunk in utter desolation and despair. I have now become tranquil and collected. My official duties have compelled me to enter upon the business of common life, and this for a part of every day, has diverted my thoughts from my immediate griefs. When, however, I am alone, I voluntarily relapse with a settled and miserable gloom. My dear little daughter was one of the best, purest, and most affectionate of human beings. She was as perfect as anything (at least to my eyes) on earth could be. The Providence which has removed her from us, is to me truly mysterious; but having a firm and unfaltering belief in the goodness of God, and his parental wisdom, I can not doubt that it is for the best, though I am incapable of perceiving how it is so. Indeed, my dear sir, life would be to me a burden, a grievous burden, if it were not for the belief in another and better state of existence. The hope of a glorious immortality, and of a re-union with those from whom we have parted here, seems to me the only real source of consolation; and I trust that after the anguish of my affliction shall have diminished, by time and distance, I shall be able to realize the full force of it. At present, I am unable to do more than to bring the truth to my mind, without the power of giving it the mastery over my feelings.   *   *   *   *   *   *   *   *

And now I beg to thank you again and again for your sympathy. Mrs. Story and myself have had occasion several times to say that we were sure of your kind remembrance, and that of Mrs. Brazer in our affliction. God grant that your little family may be preserved to you, and that, as parents, such a bitter cup may pass by you without being tasted. Mrs. Story sends her love to Mrs. Brazer, and I cordially join in it, being her and

Your affectionate,

though afflicted friend,

To Rev. John Brazer: JOSEPH STORY.

CAMBRIDGE, June 24, 1831.

My Dear Sir:

The last evening's mail brought me your kind and consolatory letter, and it was, indeed, very soothing to me. I thank you again, and again for it. I have indeed been made very wretched by this to me irreparable loss. My little daughter was one of the most beautiful and attractive of human beings, and at ten years of age everything her parents could wish. She was in our eyes absolutely perfect, and we lost her so suddenly, that we were at first stunned and overwhelmed with the blow. At present, Mrs. Story and myself are quite calm and tranquilized, as wretched as we well can be, and as well disposed as we can be, if we know how, to see a consolation and a healing balm in any direction. I have been driven, by the pressure of my official duties, to escape from my own sorrows, and for some hours every day have been required to think for others and not for myself; and this occupation, though painful, has, I doubt not, been useful to me.

The mysteries of God's providence are to me inscrutable. But I have the firmest belief in His parental character, and that all he does is in mercy as well as in wisdom. The immortality of the soul—the Christian doctrine of a life to come, which shall adjust all the irregularities here, seems to me the only natural ground of comfort and consolation. Without this hope and this belief life would be a burden.

My sorrows have lately led me (as we are naturally led on such occasions) to look at the sources of consolations to which the wisest and best of the heathens were accustomed to resort, to solace their own griefs. I was especially attracted to Cicero, to the topics by which his friends endeavored to assuage his griefs, and he theirs. I was surprised to see how few and desolate, and unsatisfactory were all their grounds of consolation, and I could not but feel that death then must have been, even in its mildest forms, most afflictive and terrific. In the treatise of Cicero, to which you refer, we see more of our own private thoughts and reasonings, and we can not but admire his anxious eloquence in support of the immortality of the soul. But it is most manifest, that it was, at best, a cold and lifeless and hesitating confidence, with which he pressed his arguments. If Christianity had done no more for mankind than to make known to us the immortality of the soul and the parental character of God, it seems to me that it would be the first of blessings. * * * *

Most truly and affectionately yours,

To Hon. Chancellor Kent: JOSEPH STORY.

This is the true spirit of Christian resignation. None but a truly religious nature could meekly bend to affliction with such trust and faith, looking forward to a reunion in

Descendants of Jeremiah, son of Izrahiah, son of Thomas.

another state of existence with her whom he had lost; and forgetting, in his grief for the dead, his daily duties and the claims of the living upon his activity and cheerfulness.

The following beautiful lines, written by my father, are those alluded to in the last letter :

Farewell, my darling child, a sad farewell!
Thou 'rt gone from earth, in heavenly scenes to dwell;
For sure, if ever being formed from dust
Might hope for bliss, thine is that holy trust.
Spotless and pure, from God thy spirit came;
Spotless it has returned, a brighter flame.
Thy last, soft prayer was heard—No more to roam;
Thou art ('t was all thy wish) thou art gone home.[11]
Ours are the loss, and agonizing grief,
The slow, dead hours, the sighs without relief,
The lingering nights, the thoughts of pleasure past,
Memory, that wounds and darkens to the last,
How desolate the space, how deep the line,
That part our hopes, our fates, our paths, from thine!
We tread with faltering steps, the shadowy shore;
Thou art at rest, where storms can vex no more.
When shall we meet again, and kiss away
The tears of joy in one eternal day?

Most lovely thou! in beauty's rarest truth!
A cherub's face; the breathing blush of youth;
A smile more sweet than seemed to mortal given;
An eye that spoke, and beamed the light of heaven;
A temper like the balmy, summer sky,
That soothes, and warms, and cheers, when life beats high;
Abounding spirit, which in sportive chase,
Gave, as it moved, a fresh and varying grace;
A voice, whose music warbled notes of mirth,
Its tones unearthly, or scarce formed for earth;
A mind, which kindled with each passing thought;
And gathered treasures, where they least were sought;
These were thy bright attractions; these had power
To spread a nameless charm o'er every hour.

[11] The last words, uttered but a few moments before her death, were "I want to go home."

But that, which more than all, could bliss impart,
Was thy warm love, thy tender, buoyant heart,
The ceaseless flow of feeling, like the rill,
That fills its sunny banks, and deepens still;
Thy chief delight to fix thy parent's gaze,
Win their fond kiss, or gain their modest praise.

When sickness came, though short and hurried o'er,
It made thee more an angel than before.
How patient, tender, gentle, though disease
Preyed on thy life!—how anxious still to please!
How oft around thy mother's neck entwined,
Thy arms were folded, as to Heaven resigned!
How oft thy kisses on her pallid cheek
Spoke all thy love, as language ne'er could speak!
E'en the last whisper of thy parting breath
Asked and received, a mother's kiss in death.

But oh! how vain by art or words to tell,
What ne'er was told,—affection's magic spell!
More vain to tell that sorrow of the soul,
That works in secret, works beyond control,
When death strikes down, with sudden crush and power,
Parental hope and blasts its opening flower.
Most vain to tell, how deep that long despair,
Which time ne'er heals, which time can scarce impair.

Yet still I love to linger on the strain—
'Tis grief's sad privilege. While we complain,
Our hearts are eased of burdens hard to bear;
We mourn our loss and feel a comfort there.

My child, my darling child, how oft with thee
Have I passed hours of blameless ecstacy!
How oft have wandered, oft have paused to hear
Thy playful thoughts fall sweetly on my ear!
How oft have caught a hint beyond thy age,
Fit to instruct the wise or charm the sage!
How oft, with pure delight, have turned to see
Thy beauty felt by all, except by thee;
Thy modest kindness, and thy searching glance!
Thy eager movements, and thy graceful dance;
And while I gazed with all a father's pride,
Concealed a joy, worth all on earth beside.

Descendants of Jeremiah, son of Izrahiah, son of Thomas.

How changed the scene! In every favorite walk
I miss thy flying steps, thy artless talk;
Where'er I turn, I feel thee ever near;
Some frail memorial comes, some image dear.
Each spot still breathes of thee—each garden flower
Tells of the past, in sunshine, or in shower;
And here the chair, and there the sofa stands,
Pressed by thy form, or polished by thy hands.
My home, how full of thee!—But where art thou?
Gone, like the sunbeam from the mountain's brow;
But, unlike that, once passed the fated bourn,
Bright beam of heaven, thou never shalt return.
Yet, yet, it soothes my heart on thee to dwell;
LOUISA, darling child, farewell, farewell!"

The following prayer, written while under the immediate influence of this affliction, was found in his common-place-book:

A PRAYER, WRITTEN IN MAY, 1831.

O! Almighty God, our merciful Father, who dost not afflict the children of men but for wise ends, we humbly entreat thee to look down with thy favor upon us thy afflicted servants, bowed down with sorrow for the loss of a dearly beloved child.

Pour comfort into our hearts; teach us the ways of consolation; enable us to be resigned to thy will, and to feel in this sad event the workings of thy mysterious but beneficent Providence. O! heal the wounds which by thy will now make our souls to bleed. Give us to know more of thee and of ourselves. Let us receive light from thy blessed influences on our broken spirits. Show us the paths of true religion and peace, and direct our steps therein. Thou knowest our misery and despair; Thou alone canst succor and support us. May we learn that, even in this calamity, Thou hast in store blessings for us. O! preserve, protect, and keep in Thy holy care the two remaining children who are left to us. May they grow up and become blessings to their parents, and their friends, and their country, and serve Thee with true and devout hearts.

Thou art teaching us what shadows we are and what shadows we pursue. O! may we improve this afflicting event, by more humility and devout affection, more ardent piety, and more love to mankind, and grant us that spirit of gratitude which shall lead us to Thee, the Source of all wisdom and power and goodness, and to adore and bless Thy holy name ever more. Amen.

It was at this time that Mr. Story made a translation of
the beautiful epitaph on Miss Dolman, written by Shen-
stone. The epitaph and translation are as follows:

Ah! Maria,
Puellarum elegantissima,
Ah! flora venustatis abrepta!
Heu, quanto minus
Cum reliquis versari,
Quam tui meminisse.

TRANSLATION:

Maria, ah! most lovely! snatched away,
E'en in the flower of beauty's rare display,
To dwell with Thee, in thought, how much more dear,
Than to hold converse with the living here."

Mr. Story says that his father earnestly pursued his
labors to bury in them his sorrows.

Judge Joseph Story was the senior of eleven sons of
Dr. Elisha and Mehitable (Pedrick) Story, of Marble-
head, Mass. (His mother was born in 1759, and his
father in 1743. The latter was a man of mark and
influence in colonial times; was an ardent Whig, and
one of the " Boston Tea Party," and a surgeon in the
Revolutionary Army.) He graduated at Harvard
College in 1798; immediately after commenced the
study of the law in the office of Mr. Samuel Sewall, of
Salem, then a celebrated lawyer of that town, and a
member of Congress, afterwards Chief Justice of Massachusetts. He began the practice of his profession in
1801. In 1804 he published *Power of Solitude*, a
poem, in two parts; also, *Selections of Pleadings in
Civil Actions*. In 1805 he was chosen to represent
the town of Salem in the State Legislature, where he
was a leading member of the Republican (Jeffersonian)
party, in the House, and where he served three sessions.
In the fall of 1808 he was elected, without opposition,
to fill a vacancy in Congress occasioned by the death

of the Hon. Jacob Crowninshield, where he distinguished himself by his speeches on the embargo, non-intercourse, war, &c.. He remained in Congress but one session, viz : 1808–9. On his return home he was again returned to the State General Assembly. In January, 1811, he was chosen Speaker of the House, and again at the May session in the same year, and in November following was appointed by President Madison Associate Justice of the Supreme Court of the United States, which he accepted at a great pecuniary sacrifice, When he took his seat upon the bench, he was but thirty-two years of age, quite the youngest man, with but one exception, perhaps, that of Mr. Justice Butler of the King's Bench, that was ever called to the highest judicial station of this or the mother country. The United States Supreme Court at that time was composed of John Marshall, Chief Justice; Bushrod Washington, William Johnson, Brockholst Livingston, Thomas Todd and Gabriel Duval, Justices; William Pinckney, of Maryland, Attorney General.

From the time he took his seat on the bench up to 1819, he was constant in his judicial labors and correspondence arising therefrom. In only one instance, says his son, during his whole judicial life, was he present at a political meeting, or publicly engaged in the discussion of a political question. The time alluded to, was on the occasion of the great agitation in the country respecting the admission of Missouri into the Union. There was a meeting called at Salem in December, 1819, at which Mr. Story was present, where he declared himself, in an eloquent and powerful speech, in favor of the absolute prohibition of slavery by express act of Congress in all the territories of the United States, and against the admission of any new slaveholding state, except on the unalterable condition of the abolition of slavery.

61

These views he advocated as being founded on the declaration of independence, the constitution of the United States, and the principles of freedom by which the government was originally inspired ; * * * * he felt that his duty to himself, his country and the world, required him to overstep the limits he had set for himself on ordinary occasions, and to throw the whole weight of his influence and opinions upon the side of liberty and law.

In 1818, he was elected a member of the Board of Overseers of Harvard College, and in 1825 a Fellow, and in 1830 was made Dane Professor in the Law School of the same institution. A committee of the Board of Overseers, in 1849, consisting of the Hon. Peleg Sprague, Hon. Wm. Kent, Hon. Charles Sumner, Hon. Albert H. Nelson and Peleg W. Chandler, Esq., in closing their report, say :

It may well be a question whether the services of Professor Story—important in every respect, shedding upon the Law School a lasting fame, and securing to it pecuniary competence, an extensive library and a commodious hall—can be commemorated with more appropriate academic honors than by giving his name to that department of the University, of which he has been the truest founder. The World, in advance of any formal action of the University, has already placed the Law School in the illumination of his name. It is by the name of STORY that this seat of legal education has become known, wherever jurisprudence is cultivated as a science. By his name it has been crowned abroad."

It was his intention, early in 1845, to resign his seat on the bench, so soon as he had written out his opinions on the cases that had been argued before him, in order that he might give his whole time to his professorship at Harvard, and with this view he labored unusually hard during the summer of that year ; which so exhausted his physical frame, that, on taking a slight cold in the beginning of September, it was followed by interruption of the intestinal canal, which produced great bodily suffering and prostration, to all of which he manifested an entire resignation. While the domestic was arranging his bed, in order to make it more comfortable, he said with a smile, "Well, David, they are trying. to patch up this good-for-nothing body, but I think it is scarcely worth while." Soon after he called his wife to his bed side, and said, "I think it my duty to say to you that I have no belief that I can recover; it is vain to hope it; but I shall die content, and with a firm faith in the goodness of God; we shall meet again."

He then ceased, and lay as in prayer, with uplifted eyes. In this calm state, and very feeble, he continued for about two days, not regaining his strength, but apparently not losing it. All prescription failed in reviving him. During the early part of Wednesday, he gradually lost his strength, and he lay calm and peaceful, and without taking heed of the objects and friends around him. At about eleven o'clock, to a question, whether he recognized me, he opened his eyes and feebly smiled, stretching out his hands towards me, and murmuring some indistinct words, and shortly after this he breathed the name of God; and this was the last word that was ever heard from his lips. Gradually he lost his consciousness; and without pain fell away into the arms of the good angel. At about nine o'clock in the evening of the 10th of September, 1845, at the age of sixty-six, he breathed his last. Thus he died full of honors and years; before age had robbed him of a single happiness, or dimmed in the least, the perfectness of his powers. His work was complete—nothing was wanting to the entire completion of his judicial life, but to finish a single half written judgment. * * * * * * During his illness, the alternations of his condition were the engrossing subjects of interest in Cambridge and Boston. And most touching instances of the affectionate feeling which his kindly nature had created, were manifested among the townsfolk. Many of them thronged the gate, lingering around it, or returning from hour to hour, to learn the tidings of his health, and cautiously refraining from noise. Tears stood in the eyes of the roughest, while they asked of him. All felt that they were about to lose a friend, or as one expressed it to me, "that a part of the sunlight of the town would pass away with him." Every where a cloud hung over the village; business stopped in the streets, and even over the busy stir of the city, his illness seem to cast a shadow.

His funeral, which was strictly private, in compliance with his wishes, took place on the 12th of September, but a large concourse of persons attended the hearse, in which his body was carried to Mount Auburn, and clustered around his grave, when to earth we gave back what belonged to it, yet what we had loved so much. Among them were the most distinguished men of Boston and its vicinity, and of all the members of the Law School. The townsfolk also closed their shops and suspended their business for the day. He lies in the cemetery of "Mount Auburn," beneath the shadow of forest trees, and over his remains stands a marble monument, erected by him, on which the names of the children he had lost are recorded. On the one side of this monument is the motto—

Sorrow not as those without hope.

And on the other—

Of such is the kingdom of heaven.

On the front now stands the following inscription:

JOSEPH STORY,
BORN, SEPTEMBER 18TH, 1779,
DIED, SEPTEMBER 10TH, 1845.
He is not here—he hath departed.

On the receipt of the intelligence of his death, resolutions were passed and speeches made in commemoration of his talents, his virtues, and his great legal and literary acquirements, by the Supreme Court of the United States; the Bar of Massachusetts in general meeting, assembled at the Circuit Court Room in

Boston ; the Bar of the U. S. Court of Maine, and by various Courts in New Hampshire, Rhode Island, New York, Pennsylvania, Tennessee, Louisiana, Mississippi, etc.

Judge Story received the degree of LL. D. from Harvard, Dartmouth and Brown Universities.

He acquired a large fortune from his practice as lawyer, and the income from the sale of his legal writings, which are numerous and of the highest order, numbering twenty-seven volumes, with thirty-four volumes of decisions, has amounted to ten thousand dollars per annum.—*Lanman's Congressional Dict.*

It could hardly be expected of us, in our limited space, to give even the title of his works, much less to note their contents. We have felt a delicacy in bringing his illustrious name under notice. Knowing and fully realizing our inability to do this eminent man justice, we have therefore kept ourself confined to that which more particularly related to his domestic life, leaving his public life and character to abler and more worthy hands than our's. His son, William Wetmore Story, Esq., has published two volumes entitled *Life and Letters of Joseph Story*, &c. (Little & Brown, Boston, 8vo, 1851), "a full, genial, biography (says *Cyclopedia of American Literature*), written with enthusiasm and fidelity." The two volumes alluded to, he dedicated in the following beautiful and affectionate style to his mother:

TO

MY MOTHER,

SARAH WALDO STORY.

THESE memorials of my father I dedicate to you. Of our home group, that lived in the sunshine of his familiar presence, you and I alone are left; and love, gratitude, the losses we in common have sustained, and the happy memories of the past which bind us so closely together, conspire to make the inscription of these pages to you at once most appropriate in itself and most grateful to my feelings.

Your sympathy has lightened my labor and cheered me in my progress; and however others may look upon this work, in your eyes I know it will seem well done. To you, therefore, I bring it with the loving regards of an affectionate son.   W. W. STORY.

MARY OLIVER, the daughter of Mr. and Mrs. Joseph Story, married George Ticknor Curtiss, Esq., a lawyer of repute in Boston; she died in 1849, leaving two children.

WILLIAM WETMORE STORY was born in Salem, Mass., Feb. 19, 1819; graduated at Harvard, 1838; married Emeline Eldredge, of Boston, Oct., 1843; read law under his father, and was for several years a frequent contributor to various literary periodicals. He published, in 1842–5, *Reports of Cases Argued and Determined in the Circuit Court of the United States;* in 1844, *A Treatise on the Law of Contracts not under Seal;* and in 1847, Messrs. Little & Brown, of Boston, published a volume of his poems, which were spoken of as "the production of a man of cultivated taste, and of a quick susceptibility to impressions of the ideal."

At an early period he evinced a marked taste for the fine arts, particularly that of sculpture, and has since acquired high reputation in that art. "Among his works as an artist (says the *Cyclopedia of Am. Literature*) are an admired statue of his father, and various busts in marble, including one of his friend, Mr. J. R. Lowell. He has modeled a Shepherd Boy, Little Red Riding Hood, and other works. Besides achieving success in these varied pursuits of law, letters and art, Mr. Story is an accomplished musician." He is now in Italy, pursuing his favorite art studies.

Descendants of Jeremiah, son of Izrahiah, son of Thomas.

CAROLINE LUCY, b. Aug. 5, 1786; d. July 24, 1792.

AUGUSTA, b. May 19, 1788; m. July 14, 1824, her cousin, Jeremiah, son of George Wetmore; had Hester Ann, George and Charles.

She died May 13, 1846, æ. 58 years.

HESTER ANN, b. Feb. 19, 1790; d. Jan. 25, 1835.

THOMAS, b. Aug. 31, 1794, in the city of Boston.

He died of dropsy, March 30, 1860; unm. After graduating, studied law, and was admitted attorney and counsellor of the Suffolk County (Massachusetts) Bar. The *Boston Daily Advertiser* noticing his decease, says:

We are pained to announce the death of Thomas Wetmore, Esq. He died at his residence (Dwight street) in this city yesterday, at the age of 64 years and 7 months. Mr. Wetmore was a native of Boston, and was born the 31st August, 1795.[12] He graduated at Harvard College in 1814, being a classmate with President Walker, Rev. Andrew Bigelow, D. D., Rev. Alvan Lamson, D. D., Hon. Pliny Merrick. LL. D., the late Rev. Dr. Greenwood, and the late William H. Prescott. This is the fourth death which has occurred in this class within a year. Mr. Wetmore was a lawyer by profession, but retired from practice many years since, with an ample competence of worldly estate. He has been a most useful and highly respected citizen, and was devoted many years of his life to interests of the city. He was a member of the common council from 1829 to 1832; was an alderman in 1833–5, 1837–9, 1841–4 and 1847. He was for several years a member of the Board of Water Commissioners. He was once a candidate for the office of Mayor, but there being two other candidates, and as a majority of all the votes cast was necessary for a choice, there was no election, and he then withdrew from the contest. He has left behind him a good name, and an unsullied reputation. His death is a loss to the community. He was never married.

[12] This is an error of the writer. Mr. Wetmore, in a letter to us, dated Feb. 1st, 1860, gave the date of his birth, Aug. 31, 1794.

SAMUEL WALDO, twin bro. to Thomas, b, in Boston, August 31, 1794.

He graduated at West Point Military Academy, April, 1813, second lieutenant Artillery, July 21, 1814, resigned 16th July, 1816 (*Dicty. of the Army*). He died November, 1817.

Children of GEORGE,

Son of Jeremiah.

RACHEL OGDEN, b. in New York, Nov. 1, 1778; m. at Morristown, N. J., Israel Canfield, Esq.; had I *Alfred Washington*; II *Israel*; III *William Cummings*; IV *Benjamin Ogden*; V *Cornelia*.

GEORGE CURGENVEN, b. in Halifax, N. S., May 11, 1783; m. at Pecon Point, Red river; had two daughters.

He graduated at Andover College. Died January, 1828.

ALEXANDER OGDEN, b. in Middletown, Ct., April 14, 1785; m. at Pecan Point.

He graduated at Andover College. Died Aug, 13, 1826.

WILLIAM HENRY, b. at Antigonish, N. S., Dec. 16, 1786; m. Jane Ross, of Morristown, N. J.; had James Wood, Emily.

SOPHIA MARIA, b. at Antigonish, Feb. 12, 1789; m. Joseph Lovell; had Mary, who married Capt. Wm. Radford, of the U. S. Navy.

CHARLES JEREMIAH, b. at A., April 24, 1791; m. in Trinity Church, Boston, by the Rev. Dr. Gardner, July 14, 1824, his cousin, Augusta, dau. of Judge William Wetmore; had Hester Anne, George and Charles.

He died June 7, 1837, in his 47th year. She died at Morristown, N. J., May 13, 1846.

THOMAS GEORGE, b. in Dorchester, N. S., June 12, 1793; d. at Morristown, N. J., unm., Feb. 16, 1830.

HARRIET AUGUSTA, b. in Penobscot, Maine (Dorchester, N. S.?) Feb. 7, 1795; m. Aug. 4, 1821, in St. Paul's church, Baltimore, by the Rt. Rev. Bishop Kemp, James Colles, Esq., merchant of New Orleans, formerly of New York; had I *Harriet Augusta*, b. in Morristown, N. J., Aug. 28, 1822; christened in St. Paul's church, Baltimore, by the Rev. Dr. Wyatt, Oct. 23, 1822; m. at St. Peter's church, Morristown, N. J., Dr. John Metcalfe (eldest son of Dr. James Metcalfe, of Montrose plantation, near Natchez, Miss.), professor in N. Y. Univ. Medical College, Aug. 14, 1845, by the Rev. William I. Kip, rector of St. Peter's church, Morristown, N. J.; had 1 James Colles (d.); 2 Henry; 3 Mary Gertrude; 4 Francis Johnston; 5 Edith Caroline. II *Mary Gertrude*, b. in Morristown, N. J., Sept. 1, 1824; christened in Trinity church, N. Y., by the Rev. Dr. Schroeder, Oct. 27, 1824; d. in New Orleans, June 29, 1828, and buried in the Protestant cemetery of that city. III *Frances*, b. in New Orleans, April 29, 1826; christened in Christ church, N. O., July 2, 1826, by the Rev. James F. Hull; m. in St. Mark's church, N. Y., by the Rev. Henry Anthon, D. D., May 15, 1830, John Taylor, eldest son of John Johnston, of New York, formerly of Scotland; resides in New York; had Emily, Colles, John Herbert and Frances. IV *James*, b. in N. O., July 10, 1828; christened in Christ church, March 1, 1829, by the Rev. James F. Hull; m. in St. Mark's church, New York, by Rev. Henry Anthon, D. D., Oct. 18, 1855, Mary Josephine, dau. of Oliver Blackley, of Cincinnati, O.; had Elizabeth and Christopher John; he is a merchant. V *John Henry*, b. in Morristown, N. J., Oct. 13, 1831; chris. in M. by the Rev. Mr. Peters; unm.; merchant in New Orleans. VI *George Wetmore*, b. in New Orleans, April 10, 1834; chris. in Christ church, by the Rev. James F. Hull; d. at Morristown, N. J., July 24, 1836, from the effects of measles and whooping cough. VII *George Wetmore* 2d, b. in N. O., March 13, 1836; chris. at Morristown, by the Rev. William Ingraham Kip, July, 1836; grad. at Yale College, grad. N. Y. University Law School, 1857; subsequently entered Harvard Law School, where he is at present (1860) engaged in his studies; unm.

CORNELIA CHARLOTTE, b. July 23, 1797; m. July 16, 1833, Dayton J. Canfield, Esq., of Morristown, N. J.; had I *Frances Dayton*, b. April 26, 1834, who m. Eliza Ann Wurts, b. Jan. 4, 1859, and had Henry Wurts, b. Oct. 22, 1859; II *Joseph Lovell*, b. Dec. 20, 1835; III *Hobart*, b. Jan. 10, 1841.

MARY ANN, b. in Troy, N. J., April 27, 1799; m. Albigence Waldo Hayward, of Boston; had I *James Colles*, d. in St. Louis, Mo.,

1836; II *George Albigence*, who m. Ellen Erwin, of Nashville, Tenn.

Children of ICHABOD,

Son of Ichabod.

LAURA JANE, b. in New London, Ct., Oct. 17, 1817; m. Major Theophilus Hunter Holmes, U. S. A., June 16, 1841; had I *Elizabeth Wetmore*, b. May 16, 1842. II *Mary Maria*, b. Dec. 25, 1843; d. few days after. III *Theophilus H.*, b. Dec. 17, 1844; appointed by President Buchanan, Feb. 13, 1861, "cadet at large," in the U. S. Military Academy at West Point, being in consideration of his father's gallant conduct at the battle of Monterey. IV *Gabriel*, b. Jan. 25, 1848. V *Wetmore*, b. March 2, 1850; VI *Laura Lydia*, b. Nov. 18, 1851; d. Jan. 29, 1857. VII *Hardy Lucien*, b. June 15, 1855.

Mrs. Holmes died on Governor's Island, New York harbor, March 7, 1860, in her 43d year.

Major Holmes is a son of Gov. Gabriel Holmes of North Carolina. Was born Nov. 11, 1804; "entered U. S. Military Academy, West Point, in 1825; graduated and breveted 2d lieutenant, July 1, 1829; appointed 2d lieutenant of dragoons, March, 1833; which he declined; adjutant ——; 1st lieutenant, March, 1835; captain, Dec., 1838; made brevet major, "for gallant and meritorious conduct in several conflicts at Monterey, Mexico, 23d Sept., 1846 (April, 1847)."— *Dict. of the Army.* Is commanding officer at Governor's Island, N. Y.[13]

His father was educated at Harvard College. Read and made law his profession; returned to the state senate in 1807; elected governor in 1821, and member of congress in 1825, and re-elected in 1827.

ELIZABETH COGDELL, b. in Newbern, N. C., March 6, 1819; m. Sept., 1841, Samuel Johnson Hinsdale, Esq., b. in Middletown, Ct.; had I *John Wetmore;* II *Frances Broadfoot.*

Resides at Fayetteville, N. C.

[13] Major Holmes resigned his commission in the army, April, 1861.

THOMAS BADGER, b. in Newbern, N. C., April 7, 1821; m. Octavia
T. Hill of Livingston, Ala.; had Robert Smith.

He graduated at Chapel Hill, N. C., University,
1841; studied law; he removed to North Alabama,
where he has achieved a high reputation at the bar.
He now resides at Selma, in that state.

GEORGE BADGER, Rev., b. in Newbern, Feb. 16, 1823; m. in
Fayetteville, N. C., June, 1850, Rose Hall; had William Hall,
George Badger, Annie Troy, Samuel Hinsdale.

He graduated at the University of North Carolina,
at Chapel Hill, June, 1844; studied law under his
uncle, the Hon. George E. Badger; was admitted an
attorney in 1847; practiced his profession a few years,
when he turned his attention to divinity; was ordained deacon in Christ Church, Raleigh, Jan., 1855, by
. the Rt. Rev. Thomas Atkinson, bishop of the Protestant Episcopal Church of North Carolina, and priest
at Salisbury, N. C., May 31, 1857, since which time
he has been the rector of Christ Church, Wood Leaf,
Rowan co., N. C., and adjacent Episcopal parishes and
missionary stations.

FRANCES REBECCA, b. in Raleigh, March 4, 1825; m. William
Gillis Broadfoot, Esq., native of Virginia; had I *Charles Wet-
more;* II *George Badger;* III *William Wilson;* IV *Thomas
Wetmore;* V *James Baker;* VI *Andrew;* VII *Frank Hinsdale;*
VIII *John Barrett.*

Resides in Fayetteville, N. C.

LYDIA COGDELL, b. in Raleigh, Nov. 28, 1829; m. Philip Augustus
Wiley, Esq., of N. C., June, 1856.

WILLIAM ROBARDS, b. in Releigh, Nov. 8, 1833.

He graduated at the University of North Carolina,
June, 1854; was tutor in same institution, 1855 and
1856; read law; was admitted an attorney and counselor, and for a time practiced his profession in connection with his brother, Thomas Badger, at Livingston,

Ala. He is now studying for the ministry, preparatory to being ordained in 1861, a clergyman of the Protestant Episcopal. Church. Resides at Selma, Ala.,

SEVENTH GENERATION.

Children of WILLIAM HENRY,

Son of George, Son of Jeremiah.

JAMES WOOD.

EMILY, b. ——; m. Dr. T. Burtiss Flagler of Morristown, N. J.

Children of CHARLES JEREMIAH,

Son of George, Son of Jeremiah.

HESTER ANN, b. Oct. 5, 1826; m. Dec. 11, 1849, Dr. Henry Van Arsdale of Newark, N. J.; had I *Henry*, b. Dec. 26, 1851; II *William Waldo*, b. Nov. 17, 1855.

Mrs. Van Arsdale is a devoted church woman, having in early life become a member of St. Peter's Church, Morristown, N. J., whose growth and interests have ever held a warm place in her heart. With its services she has long been identified, lending her vocal and instrumental abilities in leading and assisting the praises of the congregation. Dr. Van Arsdale belongs to an old and highly respectable family of New Jersey; he removed to Morristown soon after his marriage where he now resides.

GEORGE, b. on Wetmore Isle, Maine, March 11, 1828; d. Sept. 14, 1835.

Buried at Bucksport, Me.

CHARLES, b. June 15, 1831; m. Mary Ludlow of New York city Oct. 7, 1852; had Augusta Ludlow, Mary.

Resides in New York.

Son of THOMAS BADGER,

Son of Ichabod, Son of Ichabod.

ROBERT SMITH, b. July 1, 1856.

Children of Rev. GEORGE BADGER,

Son of Ichabod, Son of Ichabod.

WILLIAM HALL, b. in Richmond co., N. C., April 7, 1852.

GEORGE BADGER, b. in Fayetteville, N. C., Dec. 26, 1853.

ANNIE TROY, b. in Fayetteville, Jan. 9, 1856.

SAMUEL HILLSDALE, b. in Rowan co., N. C., July 14, 1858.

EIGHTH GENERATION.

Children of CHARLES,

Son of Charles Jeremiah, Son of George, Son of Jeremiah.

AUGUSTA LUDLOW, b. Dec. 21, 1853.

MARY, b. June 7, 1856.

CALEB, SON OF IZRAHIAH, SON OF THOMAS,
AND HIS DESCENDANTS.

THIRD GENERATION.

Deacon CALEB WETMORE,

The seventh son, and child of Izrahiah and Rachel
(Stow) Whitmore, was born in Middletown, July 5,
1706. Married Mary ———; had John, Elizabeth,
Seth, Mary, and Eunice.

We have been unable to trace out his history as
fully as we could wish. From *Historical Sketches of
Middletown*, by the Rev. David D. Field, D. D., we
find his name recorded, with others, as head of a family, and attached to the Middlefield Society in 1744.
As Dr. Field states that "almost all the persons
named were farmers," we conjecture that he was one.
His title of Deacon is traditionary. He died in Middletown in 1788; his wife died July 20th, 1742.

FOURTH GENERATION.

Children of Deacon CALEB.

JOHN, b. in Middletown, Oct. 25 (Oct. 1 ?), 1733; m. Oct. 26,
1760, Lois, dau. of Samuel (son of Thomas) Wetmore; b.
April 18, 1742; had Sarah, Lois, Caleb, John, Mary, Azariah,
Timothy, James, Elizabeth, Josiah.

He died in Litchfield, Ct., March 31, 1815. She died Jan. 10, 1796.

ELIZABETH, b. in M., Nov. 6 (8 ?), 1734; d. unm.

SETH, b. in M., Feb. 5, 1736; d. Feb. 4, 1741.

MARY, b. in M., June 1, 1738; d. Sept. 5, 1742.

EUNICE, b. in M., June 10 (May 10 ?), 1742; m. Asahel Johnson, b. Sept. 25, 1743; he d. June 26, 1818; she d. March 24, 1816; they had I *Horace*, b. Sept. 28, 1766, who m. Catharine Thorn, and had 1 Edward Henry, b. —; d. 1819; 2 Margaret Eliza, b. 1801, who m. June 1, 1830, William Twinning; had 1 Almira, b. July, 1831; m. Charles Marshall, 1852; 2 Edward; 3 Catharine Anna, b. 1838; 4 William Johnson; 5 Helen; 6 Charles; 7 Mary. II *Seth*, b. Nov. 2, 1767; d. Dec. 7, 1802; m. Mary Storer; had 1 Charles John, who m. Mary Noel Neilson, he d. April 6, 1843; she d. March 1, 1844. III *William*, b. Oct. 17, 1769; m. Maria Templeton, June 17, 1809; he d. June 25, 1828; had 1 Maria, b. June 22, 1810; d. July 13, 1810; 2 Maria Catharine, b. July 4, 1811; 3 Eliza Frances, b. Oct. 19, 1812, who m. May 14, 1839, Horace Binney, Jr., Esq., of Philadelphia, and had Horace, b. March 11, 1840; William Johnson, b. Feb. 5, 1842; John, b. Feb. 23, 1844; Maria Templeton, b. Sept. 20, 1846; Elizabeth Cox, b. Feb. 11, 1850; Julia Hope, b. May 7, 1852; Charles Chauncey, b. Oct. 20, 1855; 4 William Templeton (of Phila.), b. May 22, 1814; m. Laura Winthrop, June 10, 1846; had Elizabeth Winthrop, b. Jan. 12, 1850; Oliver Templeton, b. June 29, 1851. William Johnson, Esq., was counsellor-at-law in the state of New York, and a distinguished reporter of the decisions of the Supreme Court, and the Court of Chancery of that state. IV *John*, b. Nov. 23, 1772; d. —. V *Eunice*, b. March 2, 1776; d. 1776. VI *Richard*, b. May 2, 1777; d. 1852; m. ——; had William. VII *Fanny*, b. April 12, 1779; d. 1851. VIII *Henry*, b. Dec. 5, 1781. IX *Edward*, b. June 11, 1785; d. Nov. 12, 1785.

Arms—Gules, three spear heads argent, a chief ermine. *Crest*—A spear's head argent, between two bunches laurel, vert, crossing each other over the spear's head.

For the following, taken from the *Litchfield (Ct.) Town Records*, we have no connecting link, but conjecture David Wetmore to be a son of Deacon Caleb.

SARÀH, dau. of *David* and *Sarah* Wetmore, b. April 12, 1772. David Wetmore died June 15, 1774.

FIFTH GENERATION.

Children of JOHN.

SARAH, b. Oct. 20, 1762; d. in Middlefield or Middletown, Ct., Aug. 26, 1794 (April 10, 1791 ?).

LOIS, b. June 13, 1764; d. Jan. 24 (June 14 ?), 1794.

CALEB, b. in Middletown, Jan. 27 (June 27 ?), 1766; m. Mary Hamlin, b. Feb. 11, 1770; had Sally Hamlin, Maria, Charles Hamlin, William, Polly, Anna, Electa, Marilla, Abigail.

He removed to Western Reserve, Ohio, about 1800, settling in the town of Canfield; and removed to Stow township about 1810, and died at the latter place about 1851. He was a successful farmer, and a much respected citizen.

JOHN, b. in Middletown, Nov. 13, 1767; m. June 5, 1795, Ann Hamlin of M., b. 1771; had Ebenezer Brown, Frederick; she d. March, 1804; m. 2, Anne Seymour, of West Hartford, Ct.; b. Feb. 25, 1798; had Evelina Ann, Mary Ann, Timothy Seymour, Henry, John, Edward, Rachel Elizabeth, Charles Hamlin.

. He died Oct. 26, 1847; his widow resides in Litchfield, Ct.

MARY, b. Dec. 30, 1769; d. unm., Dec. 10, 1792.

AZARIAH, b. in Middlefield, Middlesex county, Ct., Feb. 4, 1772; m. in Canfield, O., Feb. 5, 1804, Belinda Sprague, b. in Sharon, Ct., Feb. 9, 1782; had Caroline, Harriet, Cornelia Sarah, William, Elizabeth, Henry and George.

He removed to the Western Reserve, O., at about the close of the last or commencement of the present century. He was employed by the general govern-

ment, during the war of 1812, to transport military
stores and ordnance for the army. He died Sept. 16,
1856, æ. 84. His widow died March 18, 1857. We
have been favored with the following notice of him,
written by Judge E. Newton, of Canfield:

Mr. Azariah Wetmore came from Litchfield, Conn., in
1800, and drove an ox-team, for Gen. Elijah Wadsworth,
and was forty-two days on the road. From the time of
his arrival to the time of his death, he resided in this township. He raised a large family, five daughters and three
sons who survive him, all highly respectable and industrious.
Mr. Wetmore was a man of strong mind, unimpeachable
character, amiable in all of his relations of life, a kind
husband, father and neighbor. He was well versed in history generally, and particularly our own, in which he took
a deep interest. He attended every annual election, and I
presume never failed for more than fifty years. I was intimately acquainted with him for nearly thirty-four years,
during that time he was hard of hearing. During that
time I never met him until the day of his death that he did
not manifest a desire to enter into conversation upon the
subjects of the day.

He lived through a long life, an example of sobriety,
industry and economy, and acquired a large property for a
farmer. I called to see him two days before his death, his
intellect was clear and vigorous, and his memory very
tenacious for an old man. He died regretted and without
an enemy.

TIMOTHY, b. Feb. 20, 1774; d. in Litchfield, Ct., unm.

JAMES, b. June 1, 1776; m. June 13, 1805, Elizabeth Gardner, b.
    June 13, 1785; had Louisa, John Daniel, Elizabeth, Catherine,
    Ann, Nancy, Huldah Ann, Arrietta, James Henry.

She died May 20, 1835, in her 50th year; he m. 2d,
Mrs. Brown (wid. of ——), June 28, 1837.
He removed from Connecticut to Holland Patent,
Oneida co., N. Y., in 1802. At that time, that now
densely settled region was almost an unbroken wilder-

ness. He still resides in that town, engaged in farming, and is much respected.

ELIZABETH, b. Dec. 4, 1779; d. in Litchfield, Ct., March 2, 1818 (1819?); unm.

JOSIAH, b. May 19, 1782 (1783?), m. Jan. 2, 1810, Elizabeth Ramsey, b. Jan. 28, 1789; had Clark, John, Margeret, Lois, Oliver Perry, Eliza Jane, Charles, Josiah, Henry Wallace, Rebecca A.

Resided in Canfield; d. Oct. 1, 1828.

SIXTH GENERATION.

Children of CALEB,

Son of John.

SARAH HAMLIN, b. in Conn., Dec. 28, 1791; m. Titus Wetmore of Stow, O., about 1808; had Seth H., Willard W., and Josiah. (See descendants of this marriage under head of Titus, son of Judge Seth.)

She died Oct. 19, 1843. He died Sept. 20, 1837.

MARIA, b. in Conn., March 14, 1794; m. George Hartle of Stow, Feb. 20, 1817; had I *John*, b. Nov. 18, 1818, who m. Mary Morris of Stow, May 10, 1844; a farmer; II *Mary*, b. Sept. 19, 1820; m. Joseph Nickerson of Boston, Mass., June 28, 1840; he d. March 1, 1852; III *Susan*, b. Oct. 17, 1822; m. Clark Wetmore, March 20, 1846; IV *Lotan*, b. Feb. 12, 1824; m. Delia Buel, May 20, 1846; she d. April 28, 1848; he m. 2d, Diana Buel, Sept. 25, 1848; V *Betsey*, b. March 21, 1826; m. Robert Morris, Jan. 6, 1847.

The above named sons and sons-in-law of Mrs. Hartle, are residents of Summit co., O.; independent farmers and respected citizens.

Descendants of Caleb, son of Izrahiah, son of Thomas.

CHARLES HAMLIN, b. in Conn., April 14, 1796 ; m. Ann Rodgers, Oct. 28, 1830 (of Stow) ; had Sarah.

Farmer, resides in Missouri.

WILLIAM, b. in Conn., May 22, 1798 ; m. Lois Beckley, March 28, 1821 ; had Lotan ; she d. Sept. 23, 1823 ; m. 2d, Rebecca Fletcher, of Boston, Portage co., O., Jan. 31, 1826 ; had Seth H., Lucy Angeline.

A farmer, resides at Stow, O.

POLLY, b. June 4, 1800 ; m. Edwin, son of Judge William Wetmore, Aug. 24, 1820 ; had Silas, Charles and. Luther. (See under head of Edwin, descendants of Judge Seth.)

ANNA, b. in Canfield, O., Oct. 23, 1802 ; m. Erastus Southmayd ; had I *Lucy*, b. Jan. 23, 1823 ; d. Feb. 17, 1840 ; II *Charles*, b. Feb. 4, 1824 ; III *Leonard*, b. Dec. 19, 1826 ; m. Jan. 1, 1850, Elizabeth Starks of Stow.

Mrs. Anna Southmayd d. Dec. 26, 1826. Mr. Southmayd is an intelligent and influential farmer, residing in Stow township, O.

ELECTA, b. in Canfield, O., Jan. 9, 1805 ; d. May 28, 1805.

MARRILLA, b. in Randolph, O., Nov. 14, 1808 ; m. in Stow, Oct. 12, 1834, Joseph C. Butler of Hartford, Ct.; had I *Mary M.* b. in Stow, Sept. 29, 1835 ; II *Fanny C.*, b. in Stow, Nov. 10, 1838 ; m. Daniel W. Storer of S., Sept. 20, 1859 ; III *William C.*, b. in S. Feb. 25, 1845.

ABIGAIL, b. in Stow township, Mar. 9, 1812 ; d. July 2, 1830 ;

Children of JOHN,

Son of John.

EBENEZER BROWN, b. June 2, 1798 ; m. Sarah Pettibone, May 15, 1823 ; she d. July 29, 1849, leaving Charles Pettibone, Edward Abijah, and Hiram Pease; he m. 2d, Marietta Noble, April 7, 1851.

Resides in New Britain, Ct.

Descendants of Caleb, son of Izrahiah, son of Thomas.

FREDERICK, b. Feb. 23, 1800; m.. Erelina Blackburn, Oct. 20, 1836; had D. Simmons, Mary Louise, Erelina.

Resides in Troy, N. Y.

ERELINA ANN, b. Dec. 30, 1806; m. Feb. 24, 1824, Cyrus Catlin of Litchfield, Ct.; had I *Clarinda*, b. June 17, 1825; m: Justin Hotchkiss; II *Mary Cordelia*, b. Sept. 8, 1828; III *Arthur D.*, b. June 17, 1830; m. Eliza Buel, April 26, 1853; IV *Eleanor S.*, b. April 12, 1834; died May 3, 1837; V *Emma*, b. Aug. 16, 1836; d. Aug. 30, 1837; VI *Ellen*, b. April 16, 1838; VII *Truman*, b. April 21, 1842.

Mr. Catlin is a farmer, residing near Litchfield, Ct.

MARY ANN, b. Nov. 2, 1808; m. ——; d. April 18, 1857.

TIMOTHY SEYMOUR, b. July 16, 1810; m. May 18, 1836, Mary Clark, b. Jan. 18, 1814; had Dwight Erwin, Junius Marcellus, Mary Seymour, Frederick Henry.

Resides in New Britain, Ct.

HENRY, b. Feb. 23, 1812; m. Mary (Jane ?) Goodwin in 1837, s. p.

Resides in Hartford, Ct.

JOHN, b. May 22, 1814; d. in Litchfield, unm., Mar. 23, 1852.

EDWARD, b. Dec. 8, 1816; m. May 6, 1849, Adeline Williams of New Preston, Ct.; b. March 14, 1821; had Ann M., Emeline and John Stanley (twins); Albert, Mary Adeline.

Resides at the "old homestead," in Litchfield, Ct.

RACHEL ELIZABETH, b. Feb. 6, 1818; m. John S. Seymour of Davenport, Iowa, Dec. 25, 1854.

CHARLES HAMLIN, b. Nov. 28, 1821; m. Clara W. Knight, Oct. 24, 1850; had Alice C., Frank K., Charles E., Henry S.

Resides in New Britain, Ct.

Children of AZARIAH,

Son of John.

CAROLINE, b. in Canfield, O., Dec. 7, 1805; d. May 27, 1832.

Descendants of Caleb, son of Izrahiah, son of Thomas.

HARRIET, b. in Canfield, O., Dec. 27, 1806; m. July 5, 1832, Horace Byington Brainerd, Esq., of Canfield, b. at Saratoga Springs, N. Y., March 26, 1808; had I *Belinda Caroline*, b. May 16, 1833, d. Aug 29, 1855; II *Seth Wetmore*, b. Mar 24, 1836.

Mr. B., senior, resides at Canfield.

CORNELIA, b. Jan. 1809; unm.

Resides at Canfield, O.

SARAH, b. Nov. 18, 1810; unm.

Resides at Canfield.

WILLIAM, b. in Canfield, Dec. 16, 1814; m. Aug. 29, 1838, Susan Edwards of Hudson, Summit co , O.; had William Walden, Luther Edwards, Henry Pratt.

Resides at Canfield.

ELIZABETH, b. in C., March 5, 1817; m. Sept. 1, 1842, Chauncey Gunn Beardsley; s. p.

Mr. B. is a farmer. Resides at Lordstown, Trumbull co., O.

HENRY, b. in C., Aug. 1, 1820; m. Jan. 27, 1859, Lovina Patterson.

Farmer. Resides in Mayville, Dodge co., Wis.

GEORGE, b. in C., Jan. 2, 1823; m. Oct. 30, 1850, Caroline Marrilla Crane; had Charles R., Harriet Belinda.

A farmer; resides at Canfield.

Children of JAMES,

Son of John.

LOUISA, b. Nov. 22, 1805; d. June 1, 1832.

JOHN DANIEL, b. Nov. 26, 1807; d. Dec 4, 1811.

ELIZABETH, b. Oct. 28, 1809; d. Jan. 16, 1832.

CATHERINE ANN, b. Jan. 3, 1812; d. Nov. 13, 1814.

NANCY, b. May 9, 1814; d. Nov. 8, 1814.

HULDAH ANN B., b. Oct. 27, 1815; d. April 11, 1838.

ARIETTA, b. March 4, 1818; m. Joseph Combs, Sept. 30, 1856.

JAMES HENRY, b. Nov. 16, 1820; m. Jan. 14, 1846, Mary Strickland, b. May 19, 1818; had Mary Elizabeth, Eunice Louisa, George Henry, Emma Arietta.

A farmer at Holland Patent, Oneida co., N. Y.

Children of JOSIAH,

Son of John.

CLARK, b. in Canfield, O., Dec. 14, 1811; m. Oct. 8, 1845, Susan dau. of George and Maria (Wetmore) Hartell of Stow; b. Oct. 8, 1822; had Ogden E., Elizabeth M., Rebecca Amber, Annie C., Mary Ella, Jenny, Rebecca Amber.

JOHN, b. in C., Dec. 5, 1813; m. March 1, 1850, Minerva Wallace, b. Feb. 25, 1826; had Eliza Jane, Lucy Wallace, Margeret Chamber.

He resides at Canfield, O.; is vice-president of the Ashtabula and New Lisbon R. R. Co.; is an extensive property holder, and public-spirited citizen.

MARGERET, b. in C., July 8, 1815; m. Lorain L. Bostwick, May 29, 1834; had I *Mary Elizabeth*, b. July 25, 1836; II *Charles Edward*, b. April 22, 1840; III *Julia Clandes*, b. March 3, 1842.

Resides in Canfield, O.

LOIS, b. in C., March 8, 1817; m. Jonathan H. Cunningham, May 30, 1841; had I *Flora Rebecca*, b. Nov. 3, 1844; d. March 8, 1859; II *Jane Elizabeth*, b. Sept. 12, 1846.

OLIVER PERRY, b. in C., Jan. 3, 1819; m. Amina Cilley, July 3, 1851.

She died, s. p., in Wisconsin, Sept. 5, 1852.

Descendants of Caleb, son of Izrahiah, son of Thomas.

ELIZA JANE, b. in C., Nov. 1820.

CHARLES, b. in C., March 14, 1823; m. Abigail Dubal, June 2, 1851; had Charles.

JOSIAH, b. in C., May 10, 1824; d. Sept. 5, 1827.

HENRY WALLACE, b. in C., April 16, 1826.

Merchant, Akron, Ohio.

REBECCA A., b. in C., April 1, 1828; m. T. D. Wheeler, of Marlboro, Mass., April 15, 1860.

SEVENTH GENERATION.

Daughter of CHARLES HAMLIN,

Son of Caleb, Son of John.

SARAH, b. March 12, 1836; m. James Wilson, Jan. 1, 1856.

He died May 28, 1856.

Children of WILLIAM,

Son of Caleb, Son of John.

LOTAN, b. Dec. 29, 1821.

SETH H., b. April 29, 1828; m. Lucy Whitman, May 5, 1853.

Farmer. Resides in Stow township.

LUCY ANGELINE, b. May 19, 1842.

Children of EBENEZER BROWN,

Son of John, Son of John.

CHARLES PETTIBONE, b. Oct. 27, 1824; m. Sarah F. Pierce, May 9, 1850.

He died Feb. 4, 1856, at Millbury, Mass., leaving Rosabella Sarah.

EDWARD AHIJAH, b. Jan. 30, 1827.

Resides in Springfield, Mass.

HIRAM PEASE, b. May 22, 1829.

Salesman in New York city.

Children of FREDERICK,

Son of John, Son of John.

D. SIMMONS, b. Sept. 5, 1837.

MARY LOUISA, b. July 10, 1841.

EVELINE, b. June 10, 1848; d. July 23, 1855.

Children of TIMOTHY SEYMOUR,

Son of John, Son of John.

DWIGHT ERWIN, b. Aug. 12, 1837.

Resides in New York.

JUNIUS MARCELLUS, b. June 13, 1839.

Resides in New Britain, Ct.

MARY SEYMOUR, b. Nov. 6, 1850.

Resides in N. Britain, Ct.

FREDERICK HENRY, b. Nov. 7, 1853.

Resides in N. Britain, Ct.

Children of EDWARD,

Son of John, Son of John.

ANN M., b. in Litchfield, Ct., Feb. 9, 1850 ; d. Feb. 28, 1856.

EMELINE, b. in L., Ct., Feb. 28, 1852 ; d. March 7, 1856, ⎫
⎬ Twins.
JOHN STANLEY, b. in L., Ct., Feb. 28, 1852, ⎭

ALBERT, b. in L., Ct., Dec. 21, 1855.

MARY ADELINE, b. in L., Ct., Nov. 29, 1858.

Children of CHARLES HAMLIN,

Son of John, Son of John.

ALLACE C., b. in N. Britain, Ct., Nov. 18, 1851.

FRANK K., b. in N. Britain, Nov. 17, 1853.

CHARLES E., b. in N. Britain, Sept. 30, 1855.

HENRY S., b. in N. Britain, June 5, 1858.

Children of WILLIAM,

Son of Azariah, Son of John.

WILLIAM WALDEN, b. in Canfield, Nov. 15, 1841 ; d. Jan. 25, 1857.

LUTHER EDWARDS, b. in C., April 30, 1846.

HENRY PRATT, b. in C., April 29, 1849.

Children of GEORGE,

Son of Azariah, Son of John.

CHARLES R., b. in Canfield, Nov. 5, 1851.

HARRIET BELINDA, b. in C., Mar. 27, 1857.

64

Children of JAMES HENRY,

Son of James, Son of John.

MARY ELIZABETH, b. Dec. 9, 1846.

EUNICE LOUISA, b. Sept. 18, 1849.

GEORGE HENRY, b. Feb. 11, 1855.

EMMA ARIETTA, b. Jan. 14, 1858.

Children of CLARK,

Son of Josiah, Son of John.

OGDEN E., b. Aug. 25, 1846.

ELIZABETH M., b. April 10, 1849.

REBECCA AMBER, b. May 26, 1851; d. Jan. 27, 1852.

ANNIE C., b. Aug. 27, 1853.

MARY ELLA, b. Aug. 27, 1853.

JENNY, b. Feb. 12, 1860.

Children of JOHN,

Son of Josiah, Son of John.

ELIZA JANE, b. in Canfield, O., April, 1852; d. Dec. 11, 1858.

LUCY WALLACE, b. in C., May 11, 1855.

MARGARET CHAMBER, b. in C., Mar., 1859.

Son of CHARLES,

Son of Josiah, Son of John.

CHARLES, b. Nov. 1, 1852.

Descendants of Caleb, son of Izrahiah, son of Thomas.

EIGHTH GENERATION.

Daughter of CHARLES PETTIBONE,

Son of Ebenezer Brown, Son of John, Son of John.

ROSABELLA SARAH, b. Dec. 12, 1855.

SON OF IZRAHIAH, SON OF THOMAS.

THIRD GENERATION.

JOSIAH WETMORE,

The eighth, and youngest son and child of Izrahiah and Rachel (Stow) Whitmore, was born in Middletown, March 1, 1708–9. He married and had two daughters, Martha and Esther. He resided in Middletown, in a small house north side of Spring street, a little west of the present Roman Catholic church. He was a merchant. " He died Sept. 27, 1751, æ. 42, of a broken heart, on acc° of misfortunes in trade, owing to impositions of servants & agents, & his too great confidence in yᵉ honesty of others—left two daughters—he was buried in yᵉ east yard by yᵉ side of his father.[14]   *   *   *   *   *

FOURTH GENERATION.

Children of JOSIAH.

MARTHA, b. —— ; m. Dec. 9, 1770, Gen. George, son of George and Hannah (Phillips) Phillips of Middletown, b. April 4, 1750; had I George, b. Oct. 14, 1771; d. Oct. 10, 1775; II

[14] Manuscript letter of Judge William Wetmore (son of Jeremiah &c.) of Boston, addressed to the Rev. Robert G. Wetmore, and received by the latter March 2, 1793.

Samuel, b. Aug. 20, 1773; d. unm.; III *Martha,* b. March 20, 1776; d. Sept. 19, 1779; IV *Hannah Cushing,* b. Oct. 15, 1778; m. Mr. Palfrey of New Orleans; she d. at N. O., Nov. 18, 1808, aged 30 yrs.; V *George Thompson,* b. Feb. 20, 1782; m. Emily Stillman of Mass.; he d. at N. O., Sept. 17, 1808; aged 27 yrs.; VI *Martha 2d,* b. Dec. 9, 1784; m. Chester Holmes of Conn.

Gen. Phillips died at Savannah, Ga., Oct. 14, 1802, aged 52 years. The collection district of Middletown was established in 1795, and he was the first collector appointed, receiving his commission in June of the same year.

His grandfather, George Phillips, came to America from England with a brother, Thompson Phillips; he married Hope Stow, daughter of John and Esther, and grand daughter of Rev. Samuel Stow of Middletown; he in part represented that town in the general court from 1729 to 1738; he had 1 *George,* b. Feb. 6, 1709, d. April 18, 1709; 2 *Hope,* b. March 17, 1711, m. E. Lord of Wethersfield, Ct., a member of the general court from that town; 3 *Margeret,* b. Jan. 13, 1713, m. the Hon. Jabez Hamlin (grandson of Giles Hamlin) who was commissioner of the peace in 1733; justice of the quorum for Hartford county from 1745 to 1754; judge of the court thirty years; a representative to the to the general court forty-three terms; member of the council of safety; judge of probate from 1752 to 1789; mayor of the city from its incorporation in 1784 till his death; was colonel of colonial militia (Giles Hamlin was one of the early settlers of Middletown, many times a representative to the general court); 4 *Samuel,* b. Nov. 20, 1716; 5 *George 2d,* b. Aug. 22, 1717, m. May 5, 1748, his cousin Hannah, dau. of Thompson and Hannah (Cotton) Phillips, b. July 20, 1728, who had I *infant son,* b. Jan. 18, 1749; II *Gen. George,* b. April 4, 1750 (o. s.), m. Dec. 9, 1770, Martha, dau. of Josiah Wetmore, had as above; III *Thompson,* b. Oct. 1752 (o. s.), m. March 17, 1776,

Esther Arnold (1st wife) b. March 26, 1735 ; m. 2d
Nov. 22, 1776, Abigail Cheesbrough Mumford, grand
daughter of Gov. Saltonstall and great grand daughter
of Gov. Winthrop ; they had 1 Abby Martha, who m.
John Porter (lawyer), who had Charles Talbot, m. Harriet Morgan ; Anna Phillips m. Alonzo Beardsley ; 2
Ann Duryea who m. David Lee and had Anna Phillips.
Abby Mumford m. Augustus Charles Murray of Scotland, an officer in the British army ; 3 Josephine
Louisa, m. Baron de Waechter-Lautenback, envoy
extraordinary and minister plenipotentiary from the
kingdom of Wurtemburg to the court of the Tuilleries ; 4 David Bradley ; 5 Mary Esther ; 6 George
Thompson ; IV *Hannah*, b. July 31, 1754, m. Oct.
1774, her cousin William Cushing of Scituate, Mass.,
judge of the U. S. supreme court, and son of Judge
John and Mary (Cotton) Cushing ; V *Hope*, b. Nov. 30,
1756, m. Aug. 31, 1777, William, son of Oliver Ring
and Elizabeth (Wyatt) Warner ; she d. Sept. 24, 1820,
had 1 Esther Phillips, b. July 18, 1778, m. Benjamin Hoppin of Providence, R. I., d. Jan. 1842 ; 2
Elizabeth Wyatt, b. Dec. 22, 1779 ; m. May 19, 1804,
Samuel son of Seth and grandson of Judge Seth Wetmore of Middletown (for issue of this marriage see
under proper head) ; VI *Margeret*, b. April 7, 1759 ; m.
Oct. 8, 1777, Lloyd Bowers of Somerset, Mass.; she d.
Dec. 16, 1831 ; issue 1 Margeret, b. ——; 2 Henry,
b. Sept. 20, 1781, m. ——; 3 George Phillips, m.
Laura Florian of New Orleans ; 4 Hannah Cushing,
m. Samuel Cooper of Middletown ; 5 Lloyd, b. ——,
m. Ann Bowers of Providence, R. I.; 6. John ; 7
William Cushing, also four other children d. in infancy ; VII *Samuel*, b. March 9, 1763, d. July 25,
1766 ; VIII *Esther*, b. April 10, 1764, m. Jan. 9, 1783,
William Walter Parsons of Middletown, had William
W. ; m. 2d William Jackson, had 2 Esther Phillips,
b. Dec. 9, 1785, m. —— Hammett, had Esther Phil-

lips Parsons now of Bangor, Maine; 3 Infant Son, b.
July 31, 1787, d. Aug. 1787.

ESTHER, b. ——; m. Arthur Magill, merchant of Middletown; had
I *Arthur*, who m. Fanny Wolcott. II *Esther*, who m. John
Williams, Esq. of M., and had 1 William; d. ——; 2 John, d.
——; 3 Caroline, who m. Mr. Joyner of Pensacola, Florida; 4
Mary; d. ——; 5 Margaret; m. Theodore E. Parmelee of Buffalo, N. Y.; 6 Elizabeth; m. Capt. Ebenezer Farrand, U. S.
Navy;[15] 7 Edward.   Mr. Williams came from the Bermu-
das, where his family are ranked among the most respectable
on the Islands. III *Mary*, b. ——; m. Josiah, brother of John
Williams above; had 1 Arthur McGill; d. ——; 2 Stephen
Clay; 3 Martha Malvina; 4 Emily Matilda; d. ——; 5 Frederick Claudius; d. ——. IV *Elizabeth*; d. unm. V *Martha*,
b. ——, m. Samuel, bro. of the above John and Josiah Williams; had 1 Frederica, who m. Samuel Barstow, Esq., of Detroit, Mich. (dead); 2 Elizabeth; m. Hon. Mark Skinner of
Chicago; 3 Mary Ann.

[15] A native of New Jersey; resigning his commission, at the commencement of the rebellion of 1861, he joined the Confederate forces at Pensacola!

SON OF THOMAS.

THIRD GENERATION.

Children of DEACON BERIAH,

The fifth Son. and ninth Child of Thomas and Sarah (Hall) Whitmore.

SARAH, b. May 6; 1693.

HOPE, b. Oct. 27, 1695.

THOMAS, b. Feb. 8, 1698; d. Mar. 2, 1698.

MARGARET, b. July 16, 1700; m. Samuel Allen, Feb. 25, 1724-5; had I *Margaret*, b. Feb. 8, 1725-6. II *Mary*, b. Oct. 9, 1727. III A *Son*, b. April 10, 1729; d. 4 days old. IV *Rebecca*, b. April 21, 1730. V *Sarah*, b. July 24, 1732; VI *Noadiah*, b. Oct 11, 1736. He died Sept. 4, 1759. He was attached to the Middlefield Society. See under head of Samuel son of Thomas, and for Geneal of the Allen and Allyns prior to 1693, See *Dr. Savage's Gen. Dict.*

HANNAH, b. May 2, 1703; m. Ebenezer Hubbard, Feb. 25, 1724-5; had I. *Hannah*, b. Nov. 30, 1725-6. II *Ebenezer*, b. Aug. 1, 1727. III *Hope*, born Feb. 22, 1729-30. IV *Josiah*, born March 6, 1732. V *Jedediah*, b. July 12, 1734; VI *Elijah*, b. July 16, 1736-7. VII *Hezekiah*, b. Sept. 2, 1745; d. Oct. 28, 1762. She d. May 22, 1761; he m. 2d Lydia daughter of Joseph and Lydia Wetmore, Feb. 14, 1764. He belonged to the Middlefield Society. His ancestors were among the first settlers of Middletown. He d. Mar. 30, 1776.

BETHIAH (dau.), b. Nov. 12, 1705; d. Jan. 5, 1706.

BERIAH, b. April 23, 1707; m. Hannah Bowman, Feb. 7, 1737-8; had Beriah, Mary, Samuel Bowman, Hope, Hannah, Thomas, Andrew, Susannah and Margaret. (For genealogy of the Bowmans prior to 1693, see *Dr. Savage's Gen. Dictionary.*)

MARY, b. Oct. 6, 1715; d. Dec. 11, 1715.

FOURTH GENERATION.

Children of BERIAH,

BERIAH, b. Nov. 13, 1738; m. Abigail Bacon, June 2, 1763; had
Nathan, Andrew, Mary, Philip, Nathaniel, Asahel, Lemuel.

MARY, b. Feb. 13, 1739–40.

SAMUEL BOWMAN, b. Aug. 19, 1742; m. Ann, dau. of Gideon
Canfield, of Durham, Ct.; had Nathan, Asher, Rachel, Hannah,
Anna.

He had lands recorded at East Haddam, Feb. 20,
1776; also Feb. 17, 1776, records the name of his
wife as daughter of Gideon Canfield, of Durham.

HOPE, b. Nov. 13, 1743; m. ——; had Lament Stow; b. March
27, 1768; d. April 4, 1772.

HANNAH, b. June 3, 1745.

THOMAS, b. Aug. 10, 1747; m. ——; had Thomas, Raplephe
(Rapelyea?).

ANDREW, b. Aug. 24, 1750; d. Sept. 5, 1750.

SUSANNAH, b. Aug. 25, 1752.

MARGARET, b. Feb. 10, 1756.

FIFTH GENERATION.

Children of BERIAH,

Son of Beriah.

NATHAN, b. Oct. 5, 1767.

ANDREW, b. April 16, 1768.

MARY.

65

PHILIP.

NATHANIEL.

ASAHEL.

LEMUEL.

Children of SAMUEL BOWMAN,

Son of Beriah.

NATHAN.

ASHER.

RACHEL.

HANNAH.

ANNA.

Children of THOMAS,

Son of Beriah,

THOMAS.

RAPELYE.

SON OF THOMAS.

THIRD GENERATION.

Children of NATHANIEL,

The sixth Son and tenth Child of Thomas and Sarah (Hall) Whitmore.

THOMAS, b. in Middletown.

MOSES, b. in M.; m. Margeret, dau. of Isaac Johnson, Sept. 16, 1722–3; had Moses, Elizabeth, Isaac, Reuben, Content, Comfort and Stephen.

He resided in East Haddam as late as 1729, and in Middletown in 1731. He, with his sons Moses and Isaac, were lost at sea in 1739.

DEBORAH, b. Sept. 22, 1704.

ESTHER, b. in M., Feb. 13, 1705–6; m. Daniel Meeky or McKee of Wethersfield, Jan. 14, 1729–30; had I *Mary*, b. May 1, 1731; II *Deborah*, b. Nov. 9, 1732; III *Elizabeth*; IV *Esther*, b. Dec. 18, 1737; V *Daniel*, b. April, 1740; VI *Elizabeth 2d*, b. Feb. 8, 1742; VII *Rachel*, b. July 23, 1744; VIII *Eunice*, b. Jan. 26, 1748–9; d. same year.

FOURTH GENERATION.

Children of MOSES WETMORE.

MOSES, b. in East Haddam, Dec. 15, 1723; lost at sea 1739.

MARCY, b. in East Haddam, Aug. 13, 1725.

ELIZABETH, b. in East Haddam, Jan. 2, 1727–8; d. April 30, 1731.

ISAAC, b. Oct. 7, 1730; lost at sea, 1739.

REUBEN, b. in Middletown, March 30 (April 10?), 1733; m. Hannah Foster, June 24, 1753; she d. 1782; had Margaret, Hannah, Mehitable, Elizabeth, Content, Mary, Zephora, Moses, Reuben B., Patience; m. 2, Chloe Johnson, Dec. 20, 1783; had Lois, Stephen, Isaac, Chloe.

He removed to Hillsdale, Columbia, N. Y. He d., æ. 96 years.

CONTENT, b. Sept. 27, 1735.

COMFORT, b. Sept. 20, 1737.

Reported died in infancy.

STEPHEN, b. Jan. 12, 1739–40.

FIFTH GENERATION.

Children of REUBEN,

Son of Moses.

MARGARET, b. April 8, 1757; m. Seba Norton.

HANNAH, b. Dec. 31, 1758; m. Andrew Webb.

MEHITABLE, b. Nov. 7, 1760; m. Zephaniah Holcom.

ELIZABETH, b. Oct. 3, 1762, m. Judah Lawrence, a magistrate, afterwards judge.

Resided at Spencertown, Col. co., N. Y.; had Jacob.

CONTENT, b. March 17, 1766; m. David Newtown.

MARY, b. May 28, 1768; m. John Blair.

ZEPHORA, b. Feb. 27, 1771; m. Jesse Wilcox.

MOSES, b. Jan. 18, 1772; m. Elnor Guiles.

REUBEN B., b. in Middletown, Dec. 28, 1773 (4?); m. July 30,

1794, Sylvia Howard, b. Columbia co., N. Y., May 16 (14 ?), 1774; had Lucinda, Reuben C., Cynthia, Moses, Cynthia 2d, Lydia Louisa, Almira, Elisha Howard.

He died in St. Lawrence co., N. Y., June 16, 1823, aged 49. The " B." in his Christian name was used to distinguished his name from his father's. His wid. resides with her son, Reuben C., at Moultonville, Ill.

PATIENCE, b. Nov. 22, 1777; m. Eliphaz Spencer.

LOIS, b. Feb. 14, 1785; m. Jonathan Close (Clost?).

STEPHEN, b. March 10, 1787; m. Hannah Dingman.

ISAAC, b. March 23, 1790; m. Aug. 3, 1817, Nancy Butler, b. Jan. 14, 1798; had Jehiel R., Martin B., Harriet, Ira, Harry; m. 2d, Oct. 13, 1831, Lucinda Hall, b. June 22, 1801; had Aretas, Louisa, Cynthia.

Mrs. Nancy (Butler) Wetmore, died March 19, 1831. He died Sept. 11, 1853.

CHLOE, b. June 25, 1792; m. William Read.

SIXTH GENERATION.

Children of REUBEN B.,

Son of Reuben, Son of Moses.

LUCINDA, b. Jan. 12, 1796; m. Friend Gibbs.

REUBEN C., b. in Columbia co., N. Y., Dec. 28, 1797 (1798?); m. Martha Olmsted of Maryland, Otsego co., N. Y., Sept. 14, 1822, had Stephen R., Reuben D., d. young; Cynthia Ann, Cornelia, Lucinda, Martha, Reuben E., Lovina, Mary, Minerva P.

Was in early life a merchant in Schoharie co., N. Y.; removed to Morgan co., Ill., in 1837. When Scott county was organized out of Morgan, he was one of the first magistrates elected in the new county.

The " C." in his name was given to distinguish his address from that of his father and grandfather.

CYNTHIA, b. April 11, 1800; d. young.

MOSES, b. June 1 (7 ?), 1801; m. Balsora White, 1825; had John J., Polly Ann, Almira, Orvilla, Reuben.

He resides in Scott co.; Ill., where he was Judge of the County Court in 1850.

CYNTHIA 2d, Jan. 28, 1805; m. Ezekiel Gallup; had I *Levi;* II *Celinda* (Lucinda?); III *Ezekiel.*

Resides in Jefferson, Schoharie co., N. Y.

LYDIA LOUISA, b. Feb. 9, 1809.

ALMIRA, b. April 20, 1810; m. in Summit, Schoharie co., N. Y., July 20, 1833, Treat, son of Philo M. Durand, b. in Hartford, Ct., July 4, 1813; had I *Sylvia,* b. April 16, 1835; d. Sept. 12, 1840; II *Harvey,* b. May 22, 1838. Is general bookkeeper in the National Bank at Albany, N. Y.

Mrs. Durand died in the spring of 1848 or 1849. Mr. Durand was for some years High Sheriff of Schoharie county, where he now resides (Schoharie C. H. P. O.). His father, Philo M. Durand, of Oxford, New Haven co., Ct., married Harriet, dau. of William and Elizabeth (Dykeman) Livingston, of Livingston's Manor, Albany co., N. Y., b. Sept. 30, 1792; had Almira, b. Dec. 10, 1811; Treat, b. July 4, 1813; Amanda, b. April 3, 1820; his maternal grandfather, William Livingston, was b. 1738; d. Dec. 24, 1798, and his wife Elizabeth (Dykeman) Livingston, was b. 1748 (1728 ?); d. 1851; aged 103 (123?) years. They had I *Catherine,* b. Nov. 16, 1772; II *Lydia,* b. Nov. 20, 1774; III *Elizabeth,* b. Nov. 29, 1776; IV *Cornelius,* b. Dec. 28, 1778; V *James,* b. Jan. 17, 1780; d. —— ; VI *John,* b. Jan. 4, 1782; VII *Richard,* b. March 10, ——; VIII *Samuel;* IX *Harriet,* b. Sept. 30, 1792.; X *Ezekiel;* XI *William;* this family show remarkable longevity. Mr. Durand's grandfather was Ebenezer

Durand, who came from France in 1768, had Polly, Andrew, Philo M., Isaac Philander, David, Ebenezer, William, Samuel, Hiram.

ELISHA HOWARD, b. Aug. 30, 1817 ; m. Polly Rankin.

He is a merchant at Du Quoin, Ill.

Children of ISAAC,

Son of Reuben, Son of Moses.

JEHIEL R., b. May 1, 1818; m. Jan. 1849, Alvina Bacon, b. Jan. 24, 1830 ; had Sylvester J., Stephen B.

He resides in Watson, Lewis county, N. Y.

MARTIN B., b. Tuesday, April 18, 1820.

HARRIET, b. Saturday, Feb. 16, 1822.

IRA, b. Friday, Feb. 13, 1824.

HARRY, b. Sunday, March 26, 1826.

ARETAS, b. Feb. 28, 1833.

LOUISA, b. March 8, 1855.

CYNTHIA, b. Sept. 12, 1837.

SEVENTH GENERATION.

Children of REUBEN C.,

Son of Reuben B., Son of Reuben, Son of Moses.

STEPHEN R., b. June 29, 1823 ; m. April 13, 1849, Lucy A., dau. of Dr. N. Barron ; b. in Auburn, N. Y., Dec. 9, 1832 ; had Barron, Eugene, Mary Helen.

He was a volunteer during the Mexican war, was 1st sergeant of 1st dragoons, and with the head-quarters' staff from Vera Cruz to the city of Mexico. After his return, settled at Moultonville, Ill. ; was made postmaster at that place in 1851, which office he continues to hold, though he has removed his place of business to Du Quoin, Ill., where he has coal mine and merchandise interests.

CYNTHIA ANN, b. Sept. 14, 1825 ; m. William Crabb ; had dau. ; d. Oct. 6, 1847.

She died July 31, 1849. He died in California, Dec. 13, 1849.

CORNELIA, b. Oct. 25, 1827 ; m. J. Russell Auberry, 1846 ; had I *Stephen*, b. 1847 ; II *Almira*, b. 1849 ; III *Emma*, b. 1850 ; IV *Ella*, b. 1854.

Resides at Moultonville, Ill.

LUCINDA, b. Feb. 10, 1830 ; m. Jacob Mock ; had I *Charles*, b. 1853 ; II *Edward*, b. 1857.

Resides in Moultonville, Ill.

MARTHA, b. March 29, 1832 ; m. William Barron.

, REUBEN E., b. Aug. 23, 1836 ; m. Octavia Lee ; had Mary. The " E." in his name he received according to the custom of his family, viz : adding a letter of the alphabet to those of the same christian name in chronological order.

He resides at Moultonville.

LOVINA, b. April 28, 1839 ; m. Franklin Galy ; had Irene, b. 1856.

MARY, b. Oct. 5, 1841.

MINERVA P., b. April 21, 1844.

Children of MOSES,

Son of Reuben B., Son of Reuben, Son of Moses.

JOHN J., b. Jan. 17, 1826 ; m. Sept. 9, 1845, Amanda Malvina, dau. of Royal N. and Polly Lee, b. Sept. 31, 1831 ; had Mary Corrinda, Byron L., Mary M., George Warren.

He resides at Nokomis, Ill.

Descendants of Nathaniel, son of Thomas.

POLLY ANN, b. Dec. 28, 1828; m. William Lee.

ALMIRA ORVILLA, b. Jan. 28, 1830; m. about 1850 or '51, Marshall Lee; had I *Rodolph*, b. Jan. 28, 1852; II *Fannie*, b. Feb. 10 (6?), 1858.

Resides in Nokomis, Ill.

REUBEN, b. 1835.

Children of JEHIEL R.,

Son of Isaac, Son of Reuben, Son of Moses.

SYLVESTER J., b. Feb. 6, 1852.

SYDNEY B., b. Aug. 6, 1855.

EIGHTH GENERATION.

Children of STEPHEN R.,

Son of Reuben C., Son of Reuben B., Son of Reuben, Son of Moses.

BARRON EUGENE, b. March 24, 1850,

MARY HELEN, b. Nov. 18, 1857.

Daughter of REUBEN E.,

Son of Reuben C., Son of Reuben B., Son of Reuben, Son of Moses.

MARY, b. April 18, 1857.

Children of JOHN J.,

Son of Moses, Son of Reuben B., Son of Reuben, Son of Moses.

MARY CORRINDA, b. 1847.

BYRON L., b. 1848.

MARY M., b. 1850.

GEORGE WARREN, b. 1851.

66

SON OF THOMAS.

THIRD GENERATION.

Children of JOSEPH,

Seventh Son and Eleventh Child of Thomas and Sarah (Hall) Whitmore.

JOSEPH, b. in Middletown, March 19, 1706–7 ; m. Abigail Roberts, June 28, 1733 ; had Abigail, Joseph, Amos, Itha (Ithama?), Ebenezer, Timothy, Nathaniel, Anna, Lydia, Sarah, Nathaniel 2d. She d. Nov. 18, 1760 ; he m. 2 Rebecca Blake, Oct. 12, 1761.

He belonged to the Middlefield Society, as will be seen by reference to notice of Samuel, son of Thomas.

LYDIA, b. Sept. 22, 1708 ; m. Ebenezer Hubbard, Feb. 14, 1764 ; she d. ——.

His first wife was Hannah, dau. of Deacon Beriah, son of Thomas Whitmore, Sen.; he died March 30, 1776.

ANN, b. in M., Feb. 11, 1711 ; died same year.

ANN 2d, b. in M., March 14, 1712–13 ; m. John Boam, March 28, 1733 ; had I *Joseph*, b. Feb. 28, 1734 ; II *Ann*, b. Jan. 6, 1735–6 ; III *Elizabeth*, b. Nov. 14, 1737 ; d. 1738 ; IV *John*, b. Aug. 25, 1739 ; she d. Aug. 11, 1741, aged 29.

NATHANIEL, b. in M., Feb. 22, 1715–16 ; m. Ruth Allyn, Dec. 17, 1741 ; had Ruth, Lydia, Nathaniel.

He died Nov. 1774 ; was buried in the West grave-yard at Middletown; his widow died Jan. 24, 1849–50.

FOURTH GENERATION.

Children of JOSEPH WETMORE.

ABIGAIL, b. in Middletown, Feb. 2, 1734–5 ;

JOSEPH, b. in M., Feb. 3, 1738–9 ; m. ——— ; had Joseph, Nathaniel, Polly, Luman (Lyman ?), Bela, Lucy, Lydia ; he d. in Otsego co., N. Y.

AMOS, b. in M., Oct. 14, 1740 ; m. Rachel Parsons, Nov. 11, 1765 ;
had Grace, Parsons, Rachel, Amos, Asher, Ezra, Eunice, Jehial.

He removed to Whitestown, N. Y., about 1790 ; he
d. 1807–8, æ. 67 ; his wife d. ———; aged 82 years.

ITHA, b. in M., Sept. 30, 1742 ; m. Dorathy Webster, Nov. 16,
1768 ; had Abigail, Dolly, Itha, Susannah, Ada, Ebenezer,
Ada 2d, Ruth, Lois, Asel, Pheobe, Asher.

He was a sea captain ; he d. about 1793 or 4.

EBENEZER, b. in M., June 16, 1744.

TIMOTHY, b. in M., April 9, 1746 ; m. Dec. 21, 1768, Martha Eggleston ; had Timothy, Clark, James and Martha; he d. in Otsego co., N. Y.

NATHANIEL, b. Dec. 14, 1748 ; d. young.

ANNA, b. in M., Feb. 8, 1749–50 ; m. Mr. Blake of Conn.; had
Deacon Blake of Whitestown ; she, married 2d, Hezekiah Hale
of Conn., all deceased.

LYDIA, b. in M., Mar. 9, 1753.

SARAH, b. in M., April 1, 1755.

NATHANIEL 2d, b. in M., Mar. 9, 1759.

Children of NATHANIEL.

RUTH, b. April 25, 1743.

LYDIA, b. July 7, 1747; d. Sept. 24, 1752.

NATHANIEL, b. Nov. 29, 1749; d. ——; was buried beside the grave of his father, in the West graveyard of Middletown.

FIFTH GENERATION.

Children of JOSEPH,

Son of Joseph.

JOSEPH, m. ——; had Sanford, Louisa, Howell, Clarissa, Maria.

NATHANIEL, m. ——; had Pheobe; lived in Camden, Oneida co., N. Y.

LUMAN, or Lyman, m. ——; had Jemima and Emeline.

POLLY.

BELLA.

LUCY.

LYDIA.

Children of AMOS,

Son of Joseph.

GRACE, b. in Middletown, Dec. 3, 1766; m. Gen. George Doolittle; she d. æ. 68 years.

PARSONS, b. in M., Aug. 10, 1768; m. 1787, Aurelia, dau. of Judge Hugh White of Whitesboro, N. Y., b. July 22, 1770; had Betsey, Lois, Lansing, Parsons, Aurelia White, Aurelia White 2d, Melancton Clark, Daniel White, Leonard, Angeline, Mary Louisa, Zephaniah Davenport and Vincent Stone.

He was a farmer in Whitestown; in the autumn of

1815, removed with his family to Warren county, Pa.,
then a wilderness, where he opened up a farm; subsequently sold his land and removed, via the Alleghany
and Ohio rivers, to Western Virginia, near Wellsburg;
from thence, after a brief residence, to Steubenville,
Ohio, and finally in the fall of 1827, to Rochester,
where he continued, mainly, until his decease; closing
a long and eventful life, marked by much of enterprise, patience and hardy endurance, equaled by few.
He died September 22, 1852, in possession of a cheering hope of a blessed immortality. His wife died at
Rochester, July 18, 1846. Mrs. Wetmore's father,

Judge HUGH WHITE, was a native of Middletown,
Conn., and was a g. grandson of Nathaniel White, one
of the original proprietors of that town. He, together
with Zephaniah Platt, Melancton Smith, and Ezra
L'Hommedieu, became in 1784, joint owners of a
tract of land on the banks of the Mohawk river, and
along the Oriskany and Sauquoit creeks, west of the
German Flats, in the state of New York, then known
as the Sadaqhuadate Patent, where they established a
settlement and gave the place the name of Whitestown,
in compliment to Mr. White who was first to move on
the ground with four of his sons, a daughter and a
daughter-in-law, in the month of June of that year.
They ascended the Mohawk from Schenectady in a
barge, and landed at the mouth of the Sauquoit, where
they erected a shanty for their temporary accommodation. After having finished a survey of the lands, a
partition was made, and Judge White proceeded to
erect a log house. The site fixed upon was the slight
rise of ground which forms the eastern boundary of
the village. Early the following year he returned to
his native town, and brought his wife and the remainder of his family. Some three or four years subsequently he erected the house still standing (we presume, at least it was when we visited Whitesboro, our

native place, a few years since) on the southeastern corner of the village green. About 1809 or 1810, he removed to a dwelling of his own on the hill (south) overlooking the town. At the time of the establishing of Herkimer county, he was appointed a judge, which office he afterwards held in Oneida county.

For the first two years of Judge White's residence at W., the nearest mill was situated at Palatine, a distance of about forty miles (east). The distance was traversed by an Indian path impassable to a wheel carriage. The wants of animal food induced the first settlers to salt down a barrel or two of the breasts of pigeons, which they separated from the remainder of these birds, which were caught in great numbers. In 1786 the settlement of Whitestown had so far increased, that its inhabitants formed a religious society and employed as a minister the Rev. Dr. Hillyer of Orange, New Jersey, and organized the first Presbyterian church west of Albany. In 1788, when Whitestown was organized, its limits were laid off by a line crossing the Mohawk at a small log cabin which stood upon the site occupied by the rail road depot in Utica, and running north and south to the boundaries of the state, and comprehending all the state lying westward—a territory which at present (1842) is inhabited by more than a million of inhabitants. The first town meeting was held in a barn owned by Needham Maynard, Esq., on the road leading from Whitesborough to Middle settlement.[16]

For a number of years after Judge White's arrival, quite a number of the Oneida Indians resided in his vicinity. The following interesting incident, which took place during this period, is copied from William Tracy's *Lectures :*

An old chief, named Han Yerry, who, during the war, had acted with the royal party, and now resided at Oriskany in a log wigwam which stood on this (east) side of the creek, just back of the house, until recently, occupied by Mr. Charles Green, one day called at Judge White's with his wife and a mulatto woman who belonged to

[16] Barber & Holmes's *Hist. Coll. N. Y.*

him, and who acted at his interpreter. After conversing with him a little while, the Indian asked him—"Are you my friend?" "Yes," said he. "Well then," said the Indian, "do you believe I am your friend?" "Yes, Han Yerry," replied he, "I believe you are." The Indian then rejoined, "Well, if you are my friend, and you believe I am your friend, I will tell you what I want, and then I shall know whether you speak true words." "And what is that you want?" said Mr. White. The Indian pointed to a little grand child, the daughter of one of his sons, then between two and three years old, and said, "my squaw wants to take this pappoose home to stay with us one night, and bring it home to-morrow; if you are my friend, you will now show me." The feelings of the grand-father at once uprose in his bosom, and the child's mother with horror and alarm at the thought of intrusting her darling prattler with the rude tenants of the forest. The question was full of interest. On the one hand the necessity of placing unlimited confidence in the savage, and intrusting the welfare and the life of his grandchild with him; on the other, the certain enmity of a man of influence and consequence in his nation, and one who had been the open enemy of his countrymen in their recent struggle. But he made the decision with a sagacity that showed that he properly estimated the character of the person he was dealing with. He believed that by placing implicit confidence in him, he should command the sense of honor which seems peculiar to the uncontaminated Indian. He told him to take the child; and as the mother, scarcely suffering it to be parted from her, relinquished it into the hands of the old man's wife, he soothed her fears with his assurance of confidence in their promises. That night, however, was a long one; and during the whole of the next morning many and often were the anxious glances cast up the pathway leading from Oriskany, if possible to discover the Indians and their little charge, upon their return to his home. But no Indian came in sight. It became high noon; all a mother's fears were aroused; she could scarcely be persuaded from rushing in pursuit of her loved one. But her father represented to her the gross indignity which a suspicion of their intentions would arouse in the breast of the chief; and half frantic though she was, she was restrained. The afternoon slowly wore away, and still nothing was seen of her child. The sun had nearly reached the horizon, and the mother's heart had swolen beyond further endurance, when the forms of the friendly chief and his wife, bearing upon her shoulders their little visitor, greeted her mother's vision. The dress which the child had worn from home had been removed, and in its place its Indian friends had substituted a complete suit of Indian garments, so as completely to metamorphose it into a little squaw. The sequel of this adventure was the establishment of a most ardent attachment and regard on the part of the Indian and his friends for the white settlers. The child now Mrs. Eells of Missouri, the widow of the late Nathaniel Eells of Whitesboro, still remembers some incidents occurring on the night of her stay in the wigwam, and the kindness of her Indian hostess.

Judge White had issue Daniel, Hugh, Joseph, Ansel, Philo, Rachel, Aurelia and Mary;[17] he died April 16, 1812, and was buried in the old grave yard upon the hill overlooking the town of which he was the founder, the following being the inscription upon the stone that identifies the spot :

> Here sleep the mortal remains of
> HUGH WHITE,
> Who was born 5th February, 1733,
> at Middletown, Connecticut,
> and died 16th April, 1812.

In the year 1784, he removed to Sedaghquate, now Whitesborough ; where he was the first white inhabitant in the state of New York, west of the German settlers on the Mohawk. He was distinguished for energy and decision of character, and may justly be regarded as a *Patriarch* who led the children of New England into the wilderness. As a magistrate, a citizen and a man, his character for truth and integrity was proverbial. This humble monument is reared and inscribed by the affectionate partner of his joys and sorrows, May 15, 1826.

RACHEL, b. in M., March 9, 1770.

AMOS, b. in M., Nov. 5, 1772 ; m. dau. of Timothy Olmstead, ——
—— ; d. 1855–6.

ASHER, b. Dec. 10, 1774.

EUNICE, m. William Cheever; d. aged about 50 years.

EZRA, m. a dau. of Mr. Palmer, of Rhode Island.

JEHIAL, b. in M., March 28, 1785 ; m. Harriet Gilbert of Newfield, Ct. ; had Curtiss G., Edward B., Mary, Harriet, and two chil-

17 For a more complete genealogy of Judge White and his family see the White Genealogy, by the Rev. Allyn S. Kellogg ; for copies of the work apply to Henry White, Esq., New Haven, or Norman White, Esq., New York.

dren, who d. infants. She died about 1850 ; he m. 2 Emeline Newcomb, of Whitestown, N. Y.; had Elizabeth, Emma and Anna.

He is a farmer. Resides at Whitestown.

Children of ITHA,

Son of Joseph.

ABIGAIL, b. in Middletown, Aug. 27, 1769.

DOLLY, b. in M., April 2, 1771.

ITHA, b. in M., May 5, 1773; m. Lucy Talcott, 1803–4; had Leander, Ira, Morris, George W., Lucy, and Orlow E.

He removed from Middletown to Leyden, N. Y., when young. In 1815 or 1818, he emigrated to the Western Reserve, Ohio, where he entered land to a considerable extent. He was one of the contractors for the building of the Pennsylvania and Ohio canal, where he lost a large sum of money by the absconding of a paymaster. He died September, 1829.

SUSANNAH, b. in M., Mar. 5, 1775.

ADA, b. in M., Nov. 12, 1776; d. Dec. 17, 1779.

EBENEZER, b. in M., Nov. 6, 1778; m. ——; removed to Leyden, N. Y., where many of his descendants, we are informed, are now living.

ADA 2d, b. May 16, 1780; m. in Turin, Black River, N. Y., Samuel Hart; had I *Samuel W.*, b. Jan. 1, 1800, who resides in Rochester, N. Y.; he d. ——; she m. 2d, Dr. Manly Wellman; had II *Delia P.*, b. Oct. 30, 1803, who m. Isaac Castle in 1820, and had Dr. Wellman; d —— ; Mrs. Delia P. Castle d. in 1823. III *Harriet D.*, b. May 13, 1807, m. Isaac Castle (before named); had 1 Wellman D., b. March 24, 1825, who m., Aug. 1845, Francis Ferry, and had Isaac Nelson, b. Aug. 10, 1846, Manly Chapman, Aug. 11, 1848; d. Aug. 20, 1851, æ. 3 years. William D. Castle removed with his family to California, where he resides ; 2 *Ada Elizabeth*, b. Sept. 26, 1828 ; d. Jan. 26, 1830 ; 3 Asa E., b. Sept. 19, 1831 ; d. Jan. 24, 1849 ; 4 Hart W., b. Aug. 15, 1835, who m. Feb., 1856, in

California, Harriet Vantine, and had Ada; d. young; 5 Delia
C., b. Dec. 26, 1839; d. May 14, 1848; 6 Lemuel J., b. April
20, 1844; Mrs. Ada Wetmore Hart d. Jan. 14, 1845.

RUTH, b. in M., Aug. 22, 1782.

LOIS, b. in M., May 17, 1784.

ASEL, b. in M., Aug. 15, 1786; d. Nov. 14, 1788.

PHEOBE, b. in M., July 13, 1788.

ASHER, b. in M., May 10, 1790; m. Nov. 1815, Martha Platt of
Leyden, Lewis co., N. Y; she died six weeks afterward; he
m. 2d, Electa S. Talcott, Jan. 1, 1825; had Electa S., Delos A.,
Orlando E., Alson L. and Lucy Ann; she d. ——; he m. 3d,
Susannah Whitcomb, Oct. 24, 1843; had Charles A., Ira N.
and Marcella Electa.

He removed with his father to Lewis county about
1793–4, and about 1829 he removed with his own
family to Stow, Ohio, and to Shiawassie, Mich., Sept.,
1841.

Children of TIMOTHY,

Son of Joseph.

TIMOTHY CLARK, b. July 23, 1769.

JAMES ——, b. May 2, 1772.

MARTHA, b. 1774.

SIXTH GENERATION.

Children of JOSEPH,

Son of Joseph, Son of Joseph.

SANFORD.

LOUISA.

HOWELL.

CLARISSA.

MARIA.

Daughter of NATHANIEL,

Son of Joseph, Son of Joseph.

PHEOBE.

Resides at Camden, Oneida county, N. Y.

Children of LUMAN or LYMAN,

Son of Joseph, Son of Joseph.

JEMIMA.

EMELINE, m. —— Cook.

Children of PARSONS,

BETSEY, b. at Whitesboro, Oneida county, N Y., March 31, 1789;
m. at same place, Dyer Fitch, merchant of Auburn, 1817; she
d. at Charleston, now Wellsburg, Va., May 30, 1818, leaving
Dyer Wetmore, b. at Charleston, Brook county, Va., April 6,
1818, who m. Sept. 24, 1849, Julia Ann, eldest dau. of Watson and Ann G. Miller, of Erie county, Pa., s. p.

Dyer W. Fitch resides at Erie, Pa.

LOIS, b. at W., Aug. 26, 1790; d. unm. Aug. 8, 1808.

JUDGE LANSING, b. at W., Aug. 28, 1792; m. in Warren county,
Pa., Nov. 16, 1816, Caroline Ditmars; had Lansing Ditmars, Je-
rome White, Augustus Parsons, Albert Abraham, Caroline
Louisa, Sydney A., Sarah Maria, Charles Canvass, Catharine
Bridget, George Rapelyea.

He was, with his father, one of the early settlers of
Warren co., Pa., and there became one of its most
prominent and honored citizens. He died at Warren,
Pa., Nov. 15, 1857. The subjoined biographical
notice and proceedings we copy from the *Warren*
(*Pa.*) *Ledger:*

"At a meeting of the members of the bar and officers
of the court of Warren county, held at the office of John-

son & Brown on the evening of the 16th November, 1857, on motion, the Hon. G. Merrill was chosen chairman, and John F. McPherson, Secretary.

The object of the meeting being stated to have reference to the death of Hon. L. Wetmore, on motion, S. P. Johnson, G. W. Scofield and R. Brown, Esqs. were appointed a committee to make report and draft resolutions expressive of the purpose and sentiments of the meeting.

S. P. Johnson on behalf of the committee, presented the following obituary notice of deceased, and the accompanying resolutions:

The Hon. Lansing Wetmore was born at Whitesboro, Oneida county, N. Y., on the 28th of August, 1792, making him at the time of his decease, in his 66th year. In the year 1815, he emigrated to Warren county, and settled on the head waters of the Little Brockenstraw, where he was married to Caroline Ditmars, now his bereaved widow. After living awhile at Pine Grove, he removed in 1819 to Warren, where, and in the vicinity of which, he resided until his death.

On the 25th of September, 1819, soon after the organization of this county, he was appointed its first prothonotary, by Gov. Findly; which office, together with those of register and recorder and clerk of the several courts, he held until the spring of 1821. On the 23d of January, 1824, he was again appointed by Gov. Shultz to the several offices of prothonotary, recorder, &c., which he continued until superseded by the appointment of Robert Miles, in the winter of 1830.

About the year 1831 he was admitted to the bar of Warren county as a lawyer, the functions of which he continued to exercise until he retired to his farm in Cinewango in 1842. In the fall of 1851 he was elected as one of the associate judges of the county, the duties of which he ably and faithfully discharged during his term of five years. Between 1825 and 1850, for several years, he assisted and was interested in the publication of the Warren *Gazette*, in which enterprise he expended considerable time and money. The latter years of his life were devoted to agricultural pursuits, in which he always felt a deep interest, and to the advancement of which, he perhaps contributed more than any one in the county.

Without ostentation, he was always found with the foremost in every enterprise that promised progress in the improvement in society and the development of the county, and was ever ready to bestow liberally of his time, toil and money to further educational and literary projects, as also, all enterprises for the material improvement of the country in roads, bridges, &c.

Judge Wetmore was one of the oldest and most honored citizens of Warren county.   Having emigrated to its wilderness among its early pioneers, he was a gratified witness of its prosperity, and an active participant in all measures tending to its development and improvement.

Both his pen and personal toil were devoted to this purpose many years.   He commenced as a tiller of the soil, and often spending a considerable time in the discharge of public and professional duties, closed his career while engaged in his favorite pursuit of agriculture.

Without fortune or patronizing friends, his early life was characterised by those struggles with hardships and deprivations incident to pioneer life.   His courage in braving them, attest the energy and perseverance of his character. For more than forty years he was prominent as a citizen, filling many important positions in the social organization of society.   In all the relations of life, personal, professional and official, he exhibited an evenness of temper and uniformity of character seldom seen.   Always calm, conscientious and unimpassioned, whatever it became his duty to do, he did with such quietude and competency as to disarm opposition and reflect credit on his fairness of purpose and soundness of judgment.

As a citizen, his influence was always found and felt on the side of order, sobriety, morality and progress ; as a public officer, his duties were all discharged with promptness and fidelity ; as a lawyer, his conduct was characterised by integrity of purpose and urbanity of manners ; as a judge he was patient and impartial, and as a Christian, he was earnest and consistent ; while as a husband and a father, he has left after him a widow and numerous family to reflect his virtues and revere his memory, whose characters and positions in society are enduring monuments to his virtues in the domestic relations.

The following resolutions were then read, and on motion of B. W. Lacy, Esq., adopted :

Resolved, That we have heard with emotions of profound regret of the decease of our esteemed friend and professional associate the Hon. Lansing Wetmore, and in sorrow unite, with our fellow citizens of all classes, in rendering our tribute of respect to the memory of unassuming merit.

Resolved, That our long acquaintance with the deceased, enables us to bear testimony to his integrity as a man, his fidelity as an officer, his courteous and honorable bearing as a lawyer, his ready and impartial action as a judge, his benevolence to the needy, and his zeal and industry as an agriculturalist.

Resolved, That his conduct as a spirited citizen, his uniform and efficient zeal in favor of all measures to improve the moral condition of society, his impartial and conscientious discharge of all the duties that devolved upon him, and his consistent perseverance in the observance of all the proprieties that belonged to his profession as a lawyer, and his character as a Christian, he has left us an example worthy of all imitation.

Resolved, That we extend to the afflicted relations of the deceased, our sincere sympathy and condolence in the bereavement which it has pleased an all-wise Providence to inflict on their household, suggesting only by way of consolation, that their loss is the eternal gain of him they mourn.

Resolved, That the proceedings of this meeting be published in the Warren papers and that the Secretary be instructed to furnish a copy of the foregoing resolutions to the family of the deceased.

PARSONS, b. at Whitesboro, N. Y., Aug. 1794; d. unm., Feb. 3, 1835.

He lived for some years in Utica, where acquired a knowledge of the jewelry business, and removed to Warren co., Pa., from thence to Mexico, to recruit his health, at the same time to engage in his accustomed business. After a protracted sojourn of fifteen years, among the several towns of Mexico, he returned to the States and arrived at Steubenville, Ohio, much enfeebled in health, in expectation of meeting his kindred there, but who had removed in 1827 to Rochester, N. Y. He survived but a few days.

Descendants of Joseph, son of Thomas.

AURELIA WHITE, b. at Whitesboro, Sept. 30, 1797; d. æ. 6 weeks.

AURELIA WHITE 2d, b. at Whitesboro, Nov. 16, 1798; m. Dyer Fitch of Wellsburg, Va., the widower of her deceased sister, Betsey, Sept. 22, 1819; had I *Mary Elizabeth*, b. Sept. 21, 1820; m. and resides in Robinson, Ill.; II *Charles Dewitt*, b. May 8, 1822; m. and resides in Robinson; III *George Clinton*, b. Aug. 29, 1824; m. ——; resides in California; IV *Maria Louisa*, b. July 29, 1827; m. ——; resides in Ohio; V *Elisha Parsons*, b. Oct. 30, 1832; resides in Robinson. VI *Samuel Augustus*, born Nov. 30, 1835; resides in Robinson. Mr. Dyer Fitch resides in Robinson, Crawford co., Ill. Aurelia White Wetmore is the third wife of Mr. Fitch; her sister Betsey was the second; who was the first we are not informed.

MELANCTON CLARK, b. in Whitesboro, N. Y., Feb. 1, 1801; m. Feb. 1, 1827, Octavia Parker of Madison, N. Y.; had George Parker, Hugh White.

He is a highly respected citizen of Rochester, N. Y. He is kept in some office of trust or honor by his fellow citizens, most of his time; holding at different periods the office of supervisor, assessor, overseer of the poor, school trustee, commissioner of highways, etc.; is an influential and consistent member and class leader of the Methodist Episcopal church.

DANIEL WHITE, b. in Whitesboro, Aug. 11, 1803; m. in 1832 (3?) Margeret Wiley of Rochester.

Resides in Buffalo, N. Y.

LEONARD, b. in Whitesboro, July 10, 1805; m. Sophronia Barber of Rochester; had Mary Louisa.

Resides in Dayton, Ohio.

ANGELINE, b. in Whitesboro, Sept. 8, 1807; m. in 1834, Abraham De Kroyft of Rochester; had I *Abraham W.*, b. 1834; II *Parker*, b. 1836; III *William*, b. 1839.

Resides in Rochester.

MARY LOUISA, b. in Whitesboro, Feb. 8, 1810; m. George S. Williams, Nov. 11, 1830; had I *Mary Louisa*, b. April 28, 1832; m. at Buffalo, Bradley D. Rodgers, April 4, 1855, and had I

Mary Louisa, b. April 6, 1852 ; 2 Emily, b. May 13, 1857 ; 3 George Bradley, b. Feb. 1, 1859 ; d. Mar. 29, 1859 ; 4 Charles Otis, b. July 3, 1860. II *George Otis*, b. in Rochester, Jan. 26, 1834 ; d. in R., Jan. 24, 1835. III *Albert Parsons*, b. in Buffalo, Dec. 9, 1835.

They reside in Buffalo, N. Y.

ZEPHANIAH DAVENPORT, b. in Whitesboro, Oct. 18, 1812; d. unm. at Steubenville, Ohio, Sept., 1823.

VINCENT STONE, b. in Warren co., Pa., May 12, 1816; d. at Buffalo, N. Y., Aug, 16, 1840.

Children of JEHIAL,

Son of Amos, Son of Joseph.

CURTISS G., b. about 1825.

Resides in Dansville.

EDWARD B., b. about 1828.

Resides in Westmoreland, Oneida co., N. Y.

MARY, b. about 1829; m. George Hovey.

HARRIET, b. about 1831; m. Albert Pier of California, and has 2 children.

ELIZABETH, b. in Whitesboro, N. Y.

EMMA, b. in W., N. Y.

ANNA, b. in W., N. Y.

Children of ITHA,

Son of Itha, Son of Joseph.

LEANDER, b. in Leyden, Lewis co., N. Y., April 4, 1805 ; m. Betsey Lindsay, Nov. 8, 1833 ; had May.

IRA, b. at Leyden, May 8, 1807; m. Mary McGregor of Rochester ; had Etta, Henry, Charles H.

He died of small pox at Rochester, Dec. 17, 1847.

MORRIS, b. in L., April 16, 1809; m. 1839, Polly Pendleton; had Julia; m. 2d, Fanny McGregor Pendleton, sister of his deceased wife; had Alson, Ella; m. 3d; ——.

He died at Stow, May 16, 1850.

GEORGE W., b. in L., July 16, 1813; m. 1839, Elizabeth Parks.

Died in Illinois from a kick of a horse, May 23, 1857, s. p.

LUCY, b. in L., Feb. 16, 1815; m. Charles G. Barnes, 1837; had one child; m. 2d, J. Carr, 1844; had Alice, Elva, Alta.

She died March 20, 1853, in her 39th year.

ORLOW E., b. in Stow, Ohio, April 7, 1819; m. Nov. 24, 1847, Mary F. Williamson of Stow; had Henry Clay, Wilber, Pestor (Preston?), Ade Elno, Jennie May.

He died at Stow, of typhoid fever, Nov. 27, 1856.

Children of ASHER,

Son of Itha, Son of Itha, Son of Joseph.

ELECTA S., b. in Leyden, N. Y., 1826; d. infant.

DELOS A., b. in L., June 22, 1827; m. March 17, 1850, Mahala A. Doty; had Asher.

He resides at Shiàwassie, Mich.

ORLANDO E., b. in Stow, O., Jan. 1, 1830; unm.

ALSON L., b. in S., Jan. 9, 1832; m. Jan. 7, 1858, Lucy A. Doty, sister of Mahala next above.

LUCY ANN, b. in Stow, Sept. 29, 1837; m. Dec. 31, 1858, Russell Webb.

CHARLES A, b. in Shiawassie, Mich., Oct. 14, 1844.

IRA N., b. in S., May 11, 1847; d. Jan. 4, 1848.

MARCELLA ELECTA, b. in S., Jan. 27, 1854.

68

SEVENTH GENERATION.

Children of Judge LANSING,

Son of Parsons, Son of Amos, Son of Joseph.

LANSING DITMARS, b. at Pine Grove, Warren co., Pa., Oct. 1818; m. June 24, 1852, Betsey Wetherby, of Warren co.; had Alice M. Mrs. W. d. May 7, 1856; he m. 2d, Maria C. Shattuck, of Groton, Mass., 1858.

He graduated at Union College, Schenectady, N. Y.; studied law, and practices his profession at Warren, Pa.

JEROME WHITE, b. at Warren, Pa., May 1, 1820.

He graduated at Union College; attorney-at-law, Erie, Pa.; unm.

AUGUSTUS PARSONS, b. in W., Pa., July 22, 1822; m. Oct. 15, 1846, Catharine Kidder, of W. co., Pa.; had Sidney Lansing, Mary Louisa, Kate Lilian, Augustus Ditmars.

He is a farmer, having large lumber interests in Pennsylvania.

SIDNEY A., b. at Warren, Pa., Jan. 18, 1825; m. Oct. 14, 1858, H. Aurelia Buckfield, of Morristown, N. J.; had child, b. Jan. 8, 1859 (name not given us.)

He is a farmer and woolen manufacturer at Conewango, Pa.

ALBERT ABRAHAM, b. March 26, 1827; d. Jan. 30, 1828.

CHARLES CANVASS, b. at W., Pa., June 23, 1829; m. Dec. 15, 1857, Rose E. Hall, of Warren, Pa.; had Chapin Hall.

He graduated at Union College; merchant and rail road contractor.

SARAH MARIA, b. at Warren, Pa., Sept. 6, 1831; m. Jan. 29, 1859, Charles F. Reese, of W. co.; had Charles Jerome, b. May 4, 1860, at Conewango, Pa.

Descendants of Joseph, son of Thomas.

CAROLINE LOUISA, b. April 14, 1834; d. April 21, 1837.

CATHARINE BRIDGET, b. May 1, 1836; m. June 24, 1856, George S. Hutchinson.

Merchant of Albion, N. Y.

GEORGE RAPELYEA, b. at W., Pa., Jan. 29, 1841.

Children of MELANCTON CLARK,

Son of Parsons, Son of Amos, Son of Joseph.

GEORGE PARKER, b. in Rochester, N. Y., Dec. 18, 1827; m. Eleanor R. V. Bosley of R; had George M.

HUGH WHITE, b. Dec. 15, 1830; d. Mar. 7, 1831.

Daughter of LEONARD,

Son of Parsons, Son of Amos, Son of Joseph.

MARY LOUISA, b. ——; m. —— Bunstine, merchant, in Dayton, O.

Daughter of LEANDER,

Son of Itha, Son of Itha, Son of Joseph.

MAY.

Children of IRA,

Son of Itha, Son of Itha, Son of Joseph.

ETTA.
HENRY.
CHARLES H.

Children of MORRIS,

Son of Itha, Son of Itha, Son of Joseph.

JULIA.
ALSEN.
ELLA.

Children of ORLOW E.,

Son of Itha, Son of Itha, Son of Joseph.

HENRY CLAY.

WILBER.

PESTOR or PRESTON.

ADE ELNO.

JENNIE MAY.

Son of DELOS A.,

Son of Itha, Son of Itha, Son of Joseph.

ASHER, b. April 18, 1852.

EIGHTH GENERATION.

Children of LANSING DITMARS,

Son of Judge Lansing, Son of Parsons, Son of Amos, Son of Joseph.

ALICE M., b. at Warren, Pa., May 2, 1853.

Children of AUGUSTUS PARSONS,

Son of Judge Lansing, Son of Parsons, Son of Amos, Son of Joseph.

SIDNEY LANSING, b. at Pine Grove, Warren co., Pa., Dec. 15, 1849.

MARY LOUISA, b. at Pine Grove, Warren co., Pa., Sept. 10, 1851.

KATE LILIAN, b. at Pine Grove, Warren co., Pa., June 3, 1857.

AUGUSTUS DITMARS, b. at Pine Grove, Warren co., Pa., July 4, 1860.

APPENDIX.

A.

HISTORICAL SKETCHES OF JOHN WHITMORE,
of Stamford. 1639–45.

John Whitmore was a representative in the General Court of New Haven. He was murdered at Stamford, where he lived, while in search of cattle in the woods. An Indian, the son of a Sachem, brought in a report of his death, which he charged to Taquatoes. His body was sought for in vain, until that Indian led the way to the spot, and it was very evident that he was one of the murderers: but he made his escape.[1]

For the following we are indebted to a pamphlet entitled *Record of the Descendants of Francis Whitmore, of Cambridge, Mass.*, compiled by William H. Whitmore, Esq., of Boston, 1855:

John Whitmore was of Weathersfield, Conn., in 1640, as in February of that year, Richard Westcoat, for misleading him, was fined ten shillings. In 1641, he removed to Stamford, with others, who settled under the direction of Rev. Richard Dunton, and had been sojourners at Western Mass. A list of his farms in Weathersfield is here given:

The second month and fifth day, 1641, the lands of Jo. Whitmore, lying in Weathersfield, on Connecticut river.

One piece whereon his house and barn standeth, containing twelve acres and half, more or less: bounds and abut against the common, or landing place, and against the house-lot of Robert Batts, west, and the meadow of Francis —— east; the sides against the lands of Rob. Batts and Tho. Curtice, north, and the lands of Tho. Whitmore, Francis ——, Mr. Denton, Jo. ——, and Tho. Coleman, south.

One piece of meadow and swamp lying in the Great Meadow, containing three acres three roods, more or less: bounds abut against the highway, west, and Connecticut river, east; the sides against the meadow of Mr. Evarts, south, and Rich. ——, north.

[1] T. Dwight's *Hist. of Conn.*

One piece lying in Beaver Meadow, containing two acres, more or less : bounds abut against a highway, north, and the lands of Mr. Talcott, south; the sides against the lands of Fran. Horton, east, and Sam. Smith, west.

One piece lying in the wet swamp, containing four acres, more or less : bounds abut against a way leading to Beaver Meadow, west, and swamp of Gov. Hubbard, east ; the sides against the land of Mr. Evarts, north, and Mr. Sherman, south.

One piece in the east side of Eastfield, being dry swamp, containing seven acres three roods, more or less : bounds abut against a way leading from Beaver Meadow into Mile Meadow, west, and the middle land, east; the sides against the lands of Ro. Gildersleeve, south, and Ro. Parker, north.

One piece lying on the east side of Connecticut river, containing four and fifth acres, more or less : bounds abut the river, west, and lands of ——, east ; the sides against the lands of John Robins, south, and Jeffery ——, north.

One piece lying in penny wise, containing three acres, more or less : bounds abut against the highway, west, and the Great river, east ; the sides against the lands of John Nott, south, and Jonab Weed, north.

One piece lying in the west field, containing —— acres two roods, more or less : bounds abut against the highway, south, and Hartford bounds, north; the sides against the lands of John ——, east, and Ro. Abott, west.

One other piece also lying in the west field, containing fifteen acres and a half, more or less : bounds abut against the highway, south, and Hartford bounds, north ; the sides against the lands of Robt. Abott, east, and John Jesiopt, west.

(1649) The commissioners of New Haven informed the rest of the commissioners, that in or about October last, John Whitmore, one of the deputies of Stanford, a peaceable, inoffensive man, not apt to quarrel or provoke any of the Indians, going forth to seek his cattell, returned not according to expectation, nor could be found by the English that sought him ; but, quickly after, the son of a Sogamore who lives near Stanford came to the towne, and told the English that John Whitmore was murdered by one Torquatoes, had some of his cloths, and particularly his shirt, made of cotton-linen. Hereupon the English and some Indians went into the woods to take the murthered body for buriall ; but, though they bestowed much time and labore, could not find it. Divers of the English at Stanford suspected Songamore's son to be either the author or the accessory of this murder, but had not the satisfying grounds to seize and charge him.

About two or three months after, Uncas coming to Stanford, calling the Indians thither, and inquiring after the murdered body, the fore-mentioned Songamore's son, and one Rohoron, another suspected Indian, led some of the English, and some of Uncas his men, to the place where the murdered body, or the relicts of it lay. The carcase was brought to Stanford. The Sogamore's son and Rohoron fell on trembling, and thereby confirmed the suspicion of the English, and wrought suspicion in some of the Mohegin Indians, so they said those two Indians were nought, meaning they were guilty.

John Whitmore's widow, both by messengers and letters, presses for justice ; and other Indians grow more insolent, and censure the English for want of due prosecution in such a case.—*Hazard's State Paper, p.* 127. *W. H. Whitmore.*

March 7, 1649. The teſtimony of John Whitmore his wife, being no . . . Goodwife Whitmore affirmeth yᵗ her huſband ſold to her ſon John . . . five acres land on yᵉ plane . . .

Another from the same source (both being defective and partly illegible on the records), says:

... Y^t Bro. Whitmore told him he had fold his fon John five acres, in ye Eaft Field on ye playne; and if it not come to fo much, he would make it up in ye other plain, and fo make it good; in lay in y^t plain; and this land was Ro. Fifher's by gift from ye Corte.—*Stamford Records, W. H. Whitmore.*

"Feby the 6th 1639.
A P'ticular Court.

" Jno Haynes Efq^r,
Rodger Ludlow, Efq^r, Mr Miles, Mr Hopkins, Mr Wells, Mr Webfter, Mr Phelps.

Jno Porter was fworne a conftable for Windfore, Nathan Eli for Hartford, Robert Rofe for Weatherffield, for the yeare enfueing." * * * * * * * and Richard Weftcoat, for mifleading Jno *Whit*more, was fined 10s to the cuntrey."—*Col. Rec. of Conn, by J. H. Trumbull.*

" [33] A Gen^{rll} Courte the 6th of the 2^d moneth, 1642, * * * * Mr Mitchell and *John Whitmore* of Rippowarms was alfo admitted members of this Co^{rt}, and accepted the charge of Freemen."

" [73] A Gen^{rll} Courte held at New Haven for the Jurifdiétio the 27th of Oét. 1643.
Prefent.

MAGISTRATES.	DEPUTYES.	
Theophilus Eaton, Gouerno^r,	George Lamberton, N. Haven,	
Stephen Goodyear, Deputy,	John Aftwood, John Shirman,	Milford,
Thomas Gregfon,	Wm. Leete, Sam Difbbrow,	Guilford,
William Towler,	Richd Gilderfleeve,	Stamford.
Edward Tapp;	*John Whitmore,*	

" Itt was agreed and concluded as a foundamentall order nott to be difputed or queftioned hereafter, That none fhall be admitted to free burgeffes in any plantations w^{t}hin this jurifdiction for the future, butt fuch planters as members of fome or óther of the approved churches of New England, nor fhall any butt fuch free burgeffes have any vote in any election,.&c."—*Hoadley's New Haven Col. Rec.*

" A General Courte in Hartford, the 13^{nth} of September, 1649.
John Haynes, Efqr, Gou^{r}no^r.
Edward Hopkins, Efq^r, Deputy.
Magiftrates: Roger Ludlow, Efqr, Mr Wells, Mr Woolcott, Mr Webfter, Mr Cullick.
Deputyes: Mr Taylecoate, Mr Steele, Mr Trott, Mr Allen, Mr Phelps, Mr Gayler, Mr Clarke, Mr Warde and fix others, four abfent." * * *
" This Courte taking into ferious cohfideration what may bee done according to *God* in way of reuenge of the bloude of John Whitmore, late of Stamford, and well weighing all circumftances, together with the carriages of the Indians (bordering therevppon) in and about the premiffes: doe declare themfelues that doe judge it lawful and according to God to make warr vppon them."—*Colonial Records.*

The court defired the Deputy Govenor Mr Ludlow, and Mr Talcott to ride the next day to New Haven and confer with Mr Eaton and the reft of the magiftrates there about fending out againft the Indians, and on Sept. 18^nth fent out 45 men, to affift the Colony of New Haven. Thefe fpirited meafures appear to have had the defired effect. The Indians at Stamford foon became peaceable.—*Trumbull's N. H. Col. Rec.*

[105] At a Courte of Magiftrates held at New Haven for this jurifdiction, the 26th of May, 1656.

Prefent,

Theophilus Eaton, Efq^r, Gouernor,
Mr Stephen Goodyeare,
Francis Newman,
Mr William Leete, } Magiftrates.
Mr. Benjamin Fenn, }

*   *   *   *   *   *   *

An inuentorie of ye eftate of Jno Whitmore was prefented from Stamford, amount to two hundred and feuenteene pound, foure fhilling two penc, made the 8th December, 1648, prifed by Robert Huftis & Jefferey Ferris." * * * *New Haven Col. Rec.*

" At a Courte of Magiftrates held at New Haven the 15^nth of Oct. 1662.

Prefent,

The Gouern^r, De' Govr, Mr Jones, Mr Fenn, Mr Treate & Mr Crane.

Taphanfe an Indian was brought before ye Courte who^e hath a long lay vnder a fufpicion of being guilty of ye death of one John Whitmore of Stamford, but by his flieing (as was informed by ye Govern^r) hath euaded comeing to a triall, but of late haueing intelligence that he might be taken the gouerno^r f^d he gave order for his apprhending, according to order of ye commiffion^rs formerly, which was accordingly done, & hath been kept in durance for fome fpace of time. The Gouern^r alfoe informed ye court y^t he had acquainted ye comiffion^rs lately wth what was done, which they well approued & defired ye matter might be brought to an iffue concerning him, for which caufe he was now called before ye Court, & there was Mr Minor p^rfent to be interp^rter betwixt them, who firft informed ye Indian vpon w^t account he was there, to p^ruent any p^rjudice againft him ; then he was wifhed to tell Taphanfe that ye Court was met to attend the bufinefs for which he was examined about at Stamford was prefented and read ; then fome queftions was put to him vnto which he was to give anfw^r. 1 Que, whether he was guilty or not guilty of ye death of John Whitmore. He anfwered not guilty. 2 Que, then why did he fly away ? He anfwered y^t he did not run away but was fent to ye place where the murder was & did not at all run away. The Gouern^r told him y^t y^t was not according to his former anfwr, for he being with fome others giuen them ye flip.

Taphanfe that y^t might be cleared, for while fome teftimonies was read, & firft the teftimony of John Mead, which is as followeth, viz :

That he being at goodman Lawes houfe about funrifing ye fecond morning after goodman Whitmore's miffing, in fhort time after him Taphanfe came in & told goodman Law y^t Ponas had fent him & told him y^t there was an Englifhman kild; goodman Lawes afkt him where it was y^t ye Englifh man was kild, Taphanfe anfwered y^t he knew not how far off, whether ten, twety or thirty miles off, but pointed to good-man Law y^t it was vp the riverward. Goodman Laws afkt him whoe or w^t Indian it was y^t kild ye man, Taphanfe f^d it was an Indian y^t liued vp neare the Mohawkes & y^t y^t Indian told them at their wigwams y^t he would kill an Englifh man, and y^t they pferred him wampom but went away very angrie, & further y^t upon goodman Lawes queftioning wth him f^d y^t this Indian (naming him Taquatoes) went away in hafte & left a ftocking at their wigwams; goodman Laws fpoke to him to ftay and he would goe wth him to the wigwam, & as they were goeing he trembled and fhake foe y^t feuerall of vs tooke notice of it & goodman Laws tooke notice of it wth ye reft & f^d y^t his carriage argued guilt, & when they came to the wigwam, Taphanfe fhewed them the ftocking (which he faid) Taquatoes left behind, and further faith y^t Taphanfe flipt into anoth^r wigwom, & foe from wigwom to wigwom, and foe flipt away from y^m & returned not wth them to helpe looke ye man man y^t was killd as he had promifed to doe at good man Lawes houfe, came from thence wth them to helpe looke ye man as they p'tended Stamford.

July 2^d 1666, attefted vpon oath,

JOHN MEADE, } FRA: BELL,

before vs

his I marke. } RICHARD LAW.

" The teftimony of Richard Ambler, he affimeth as followeth, viz : That he wth goodman Jeffop came to goodman Laws y^t morning Taphanfe brought the newes of an Englifhman being killd, and y^t goodman Lawes afkt Taphanfe how he knew there was an Englifh man killd, & y^t Taphanfe anfwered y^t there was an Indian at their wigwom before & f^d he would kill an Englifh man, & y^t after he had killd him ye Indian came againe & brought with him a fhirt & a paire of ftockings, & y^t fome ye things was bloody; this Richard Ambler affirmeth y^t good man Lawes ·declared to them whoe was there as interp^{r}ting w^t Taphanfe f^d, and y^t in reference to their goeing to the wigwoms y^t Taphanfe pmifed to returne wth them againe & helpe looke the Englifh man, & in their goeing he was very feareful, & trembled and quaked much, foe y^t he & ye reft tooke [324] great notice of it & f^d often one to anoth^r & goodman Law with the reft, & y^t when they came to ye wigwoms, Taphanfe fhewed them a ftocking which he f^d Taquatoes left there, & notwithftanding his promife to returne with them he gave them ye flip & returned not, yet feuerall oth^r Indians came thenze to helpe looke ye man with them. Furthermore he faith y^t the ftocking which Taphanfe fhewed them and told them y^t Taquatoes there was bloody.

This 2^d of ye 5th m^o 1662, given before vs vpon oath,

RICHARD LAW,
FRANCIS BELL.·

"Thefe being read & told him by ye interp^rter, Taphanfe anfwered that he is not guilty of thefe things, viz of his runing away at y^t time, & denied thofe things about ye ftockings & f^d alfoe it was a miftake y^t euer they fee any of thofe things foe far as they went with him, & further f^d that after this men vp further into ye country. But to cleare ye firft of his runing away the gouern^r told him y^t one time Vncus he was fent tc feeke the dead body, & this Taphanfe was with him wth oth^r Indians and as they rofting venifon, Taphanfe goeing a little from them ron away foe ye Vncus brought word that Taphanfe was matchet, Taphanfe being told of this, he acknowledged it y^t it was foe & that he did very ill in foe doeing, and being afkt the reafon of it, he f^d that an Indian came and told him. y^t Vncus would take him & carry him away & therefore bid him run away & foe he did. Then it was put to him why he fhould run away more then another Indian if he was cleare, the Govern^r f^d they had neuer any good anfw^r of it, he anfwrd if he knew him felfe guilty he would fpeake, but he was afrayd & therefore did fly, & is forry he foe did, for he did euill & gaue juft caufe of fufpicion.

Then he was afkt how he knew y^t Toquatoes did ye murder, becaufe he always f^d it, was he by? He anfwer^d he had it from an Indian, and named his name, and f^d ye fachem of crowton fent an Indian to Ponas (the next day after Jno Whitmore was killd) to tell him y^t an Englifh man was killd, & it was funfet & they aduefied Taphanfe not to come and tell ye Englifh while next morning.

Now this Crowton is nearely forty miles from thence, which caufed this queftion to him. How Toquatoes could do this murder y^t day & after goe to Crowton (feeing it was about eleven o'clock when John Whitmore went out of Stamford) & then fend downe this word the next day to Ponas? Taphanfe anfwered that it was not a halfe days journie if he ftir betimes. Then he was afkt if he faw Toquatoes that day Jno Whitmore was killd? He anfwrd that two dayes before he was at Nor-walke & faw him there, but whither he went he knewe not & that he knew nothing of his intendment & fd he gave them his heart in this. Then he was afkt whether he was at John Whitmore houfe y^t day he was killd? He anfwered noe, nor at Stamford at all that day, and being afked where he was then, he f^d at his fathers making wampom. Now he was a teftimony of Anne Akerly read, which is as ·followeth, viz: [325] The teftimony of Anne Akerly, widdow of about feventy-five years of age. The f^d deponent vpon oath teftifieth that ye fame day (a little in ye afternoone) that goodman Whitmore was killed, fhee did fee the Indian called Taphanfe at goodman Whitmores houfe with oth^r Indians & ye f^d Taphanfe fhooke her (the wife of goodman Whitmore) by ye hand, and afked her netop was, for he foe big loued her netop, then fhe replied that fhe could not tell.

This depofed vnto vpon the 2^d July, 1662,
before vs   FRA: BELL,
                                  RICH: LAW.

"And it was ſd vpon this goodwife Whitmore was in ſuch an extacy that ſhee feared ſome miſchiefe was befallen her huſband, & it was ſd yt feuerall at Stamford faith ye fame that goodeô: Whitmore ſd ſoe, & yt Taphanſe lies in this buſineſs. He anſwered, what ſhall he ſay if teſtimony come in againſt him, but if he ſpeake the truth he muſt ſay he was not there & yt it was a miſtake & yt ſhe would not ſpeake it, to his face, & this (ye interprter ſd) he ſpoke in ſuch a phraſe as noted his confirmation of it more than ordinary, that if Manatue were here he would ſay the fame as he doth. Then he was queſtioned about another paſſage that rendered him very ſuſpicious yt he knowing himſelfe & Taquatoes vnder ſuſpicion in this buſineſs & yet he ſeeing Taquatoes at Stamford ye laſt winter & yet did not diſcouer (which might have been fayre way to have cleared himſelfe) but hides the guilty pſon. He anſwered that was very true that caſe might make him ſuſpicious, but the Engliſh neuer ſpoke to him to doe it, & if he had done it it had been a faire way, he confeſt hee did fooliſhly. Then he was aſkt how he came to goe ſoe readily to the place when they went tô look the body. When he had ſhewed a ſtrange-ners before as if he knew nothing? He anſwered yt he knew it well enough, for Taquatoes told him ye very place of ground. He was aſkt how he came to know it? He ſd that Mr Lawes ſent him to know it of Taquatoes & being at Mattatuckes he was weary & ſd ſent by an Indian to wiſh Taquatoes to meet him there, ſoe he did & told him ye place; and further ſd he thincs many Engliſh here knowes the murderer & that neither Engliſh nor Indian could ſay that two kild the man. Then Taphanſe was aſkt if had any thing elſe to ſay? He anſwrd all he had to ſay is yt he is inocent. Then the whole examination was read, & Mr Minor ye interprter was aſked if it was according to truth. He anſwered it was fully expreſſed, not more nor leſſe, but very wel. The Taphanſe was aſkt how he came to have ſuch correſpondence with Taquatoes about this thing more than another Indian? He anſwrd as before, that Mr Lawes ſent him to know it of Taquatoes, &c. He was aſkt if the Indians at Mattachuckes was friends to Taquatoes? He anſwrd that it was all one his owne countrie. Then Mr Minor ſd that he had been often among the Indians when miſchiefe was done among ye Engliſh, & that thoſe Indians that was inocent would tremble from feare.

The Courte conſidering the caſe pceeded to ſentence which the gouernor in the name of ye court declared thus as followeth, viz:

[326] That it appears to them & to all ſtanders by againſt him, that he is by his owne acknowledgement to be ſuſpeſted of being acceſſary to this mans murder, both in his trembling & comeing to the wigwom that he flipt away contrary to his pmiſe of helpe, & another time vpon ye fame account wth Vncus both of trembling & runing away, & this to be added that he is guilty of lieing about ye ſtockings, &c. & in yt othr paſſage as is teſtified by one vpon oath & was ſd by many at Stamford that the children and wife of John Whitmore often ſd it that he was at their houſe that day in ſuch a fauning way & that comeing of Taquatoes to meete him at Mattacuckes ſhewes correſpondencie with him & yt this (as he ſaith) of Mr Lawes ſending him, was neuer brought to them at Stamford, alſoe

that other paſſage of his not diſcouering of Taquatoes when he was at
Stamford, which was a duty vpon him for his owne cleareing whoe ſtoode
ſuſpicious of guilt that in yᵉ whole there ſtands a bloṭt upon him óf ſuſpicion that there was ground for his apʳhending and commiting to durance
& all yᵗ he hath ſᵈ at this time canot cleare him of a ſtayne of ſuſpicion;
but as being guilty of yᵉ murder direétly or acceſſary he did pronounce
him not guilty in point of death, but yet muſt declare him to ſtand bound
to pay all charges that hath been about him & leaue him guilty of ſuſpicion & obtaine yᵉ murderer, & now to remaine in durance vntill yᵉ next
ſceſſion of yᵉ court about a fortnighte hence, except he can giue ſome
aſſurance of his payinge the charge before, which charge was concluded
to be ten pound.

Taphanſe anſwered that he would · do his utmoſt endeauʳ to procure
Taquatoes, & for the charge he is poore but he will ſend to his friends to
ſee wᵗ may be done in it, but deſired his chaine may be taken off. He
was told then he would run away. He anſwʳᵈ that vpon his runing away
he confeſſes himſelfe guilty & · ſᵈ they ſhould kill him. Vpon this he was
granted to be at liberty ſoe yᵗ he appeare at the next meeting of yᵉ court,
which he promiſed ſoe to doe although he could not obtaine the money."
Hoadley's N. H. Col. Rec.

Hannah, daughter of William Harris, was married Feb. 8th, 1654-5, to
Lieut. Francis Wetmore, of Middletown, and had ten children, the oldest
of whom was named Edith. The child Edith,[2] daughter of Lieut. Francis
Wetmore of Middletown, dec'd, and grand-daughter of William Harris, late
of same town, dec'd, aged 10 years on the 9th of Sept. 1700.

On the 30th of August, 1722, there was a distribution of property of
Wm. Harris, dec'd, to the heirs of Mary Gilbert, dec'd, to heirs of Martha
Coit, dec'd, to Elizabeth Foster, Hannah Whitmore and Patience Markham.
—*New England Gen. and Hist. Register.*

Lieut. Francis Whitmore of Middletown (says Mr. W. H. Whitmore of
Boston, in relation to Mr. E. P. Whitmore of N. Y.), was the oldest son of
Francis, of Cambridge. Of this, I have full proof. He married, in 1674,
not 1654, as the Register printed it by a clerical mistake.

> Here lyes yᵉ body
> of *Francis Whit-*
> more, aged 62
> years deceased
> October 12,
> 1663.

Francis Whitmore, Cambridge, 1653, member of the church; his first
wife, Isabel, died March 31st, 1665 (o. s.), and he married Margeret Harty,
Nov. 10, 1666. The date of death of Francis Whitmore (or Whittemore) in
the town records is Oct. 12, 1685.—*Cambridge Epitaphs.*

Francis Whitmore, of Cambridge, the year 1653, had sons: Francis;
John, born Oct., 1654; Samuel, May 1, 1658.

Samuel, son of Francis and Isabel Whitmore, married Rebekah Gardner,
March 31, 1686, and died Sept. 15, 1726, æ. about 79.—*Farmer's Geneal.
Reg.*

2 Edith was married March 3, 1692, and died Sept. 9, 1700. Her age, as stated above by N. E.
Register, is an error.

Here lyes ye body
of Mr. Samuel
Whittemore,
who died Sept^r
ye 15th, 1726
aged about 79
years.   —*Cambridge Epitaphs.*

Francis Whitmore, sen., of Cambridge, died Oct. 12, 1685; his birth is ascertained, by two affidavits on file at Cambridge, to have been in 1625.— *W. H. W.'s Record, &c.*

Concerning the three families of *Whitmore*, *Wetmore*, and Whittemore, all researches show the present bearers of the first name to be descended from Francis Whitmore, of Cambridge; of the second name, from Thomas Whitmore of Middletown; of the last name, from Thomas Whittemore, of Malden. I regard the first two as descended from the same stock; but the third is, and has been, a distinct name in England.   *   /   *   *   * —*Appendix to W. H. W.'s Record of the Descendants of Francis Whitmore.*

B.

ARMORIAL BEARINGS;

Of the Families of Whitmore in England, taken from Burke's Encyclopædia of Heraldry, &c.; London, 1847.

Whitmore, Apley, co. Salop; originally seated at Whyttemere, subsequently removed to Claverly, and acquired considerable possessions there; derived from John, Lord of Whyttemere, *temp.* Henry III, and Edward I. The tenth in descent from whom, Sir William Whitmore of London, *knt.* purchased the estate of Apley, and was high sheriff of Salop in 1620: he was father of *Thomas Whitmore* of Apley, created a Baronet in 1641; but the latter's son, Sir William Whitmore, the second d. s. p. in 1699, when the title become extinct. The present representative of the family, is *Thomas Whitmore* of Apley, Esqr., a magistrate and deputy-lieutenant for Salop, formerly M. P. for Bridgnorth and high sheriff in 1805, eldest son and heir of late *Thomas Whitmore* of Apley, Esqr., M. P. for Bridgnorth by Mary his second wife, daughter of Thomas Foley, Esq., Capt. R. N., and great-grandson of William Whitmore of Low Slanghter, Esqr., M. P. for Bridgnorth who succeeded to Apley upon the death s. p. of his kinsman, Sir William Whitmore, second bart. by his wife Elizabeth daughter of Roger Pope of Wolstaston, co. Salop, Esqr , and sister and (in his issue) eventual heir to her brother, Bromwich Pope, Esq., vert, fretty or, quartering *Whitmore*, additional arms and crest granted to the descendants of William Whitmore of London, 1593, *Weld of Willey, Wettenhall, Le Gras, Fitz Hugh of Congleton, Greswold, Groome, Grange, Bromley, Hawe,* &c. &c. &c. Crests. First, a falcon, sitting on a stump of a tree, with a branch proceeding from the dexter side, all ppr.; second an arm, couped at the elbow, and erect, habited or, turned up ppr.; holding in the hand ppr.; a cinquefoil of the first, leaved vert, all with two wings expanded of the fourth.

Whitmore, Dudmaston, co. Salop; a branch of Whitmores of Apley, William Whitmore, Esq., grandson of William Whitmore, of Apley, Esqr., M. P., by Elizabeth his wife, sister of Bromwich Pope, Esq., of Wolstaston, inherited the estate of Dudmaston at the demise of Lieutenant-Colonel Weld, and was father of the present William Volryche Whitmore of Dudmaston, Esqr). Arms, &c., as Whitmore of Apley.

Whitmore, Thurstanton, co. Chester. Ar, a chief az. crest—out of a ducal coronet or a lion's head ar. gorged with a plain collar az. tied behind with a bow.

Whitmore (London) vert, fretty or ; on a canton of the second a cinquefoil, pierced az. *Crest*—An arm erect, couped at the elbow, habited or ; turned up az. holding in the hand ppr. a cinquefoil of the first, leaved vert ; all within two wings expanded of the fourth.

Whitmore (London) Ar. fretty sa.

LINEAGE[1]

Of the English Family of Whitmore.

JOHN, LORD OF WHYTEMERE, in the reign of Henry III, Edward I, was father of

PHILIP DE WHYTEMERE, who died in 1300, and was S. by his son,

JOHN DE WHYTEMERE, living in 1361, whose son,

RICHARD DE WHYTEMERE, of Claverley and Whytemere, *m.* Margery, dau. and heir of William Atterall, of Claverley, and dying about 1386, left a son and heir,

RICHARD DE WHYTEMERE, father of another

RICHARD DE WHYTEMERE, who *m.* a lady named Joan, but of what family is not ascertained, and was S. at his decease, in 1442, by his son,

THOMAS WHYTEMERE, of Claverley, who died in 1483, his son,

RICHARD WHYTEMERE, left at his demise in 1504, by his wife Agnes, who died 1522, a son and successor,

RICHARD WHITMORE, of Claverley, born in 1495, who *m.* Frances Barker, and had two sons,

WILLIAM, his heir,

THOMAS, ancestor of the Whitmores of Ludstone, in Claverley.

RICHARD WHITMORE died in 1549, and was S. by his son,

WILLIAM WHITMORE, Esq., of London, merchant, who *m.* Anne dau. of Alderman William Bond, of that city, and by her (who died Oct. 9, 1615) had issue : 1 William (Sir), his heir ; 2 Thomas, died s. p. ; 3 George (Sir), Knight of·Balmes, in Hackney parish, Middlesex. He died Dec. 12, 1654.

From the above, the several families of Whitmore, in England, trace their ancestry.

[1] Burke's *Landed Gentry.*

C.

ABSTRACT OF WILLS,

Copied from Various Records in England, by Mr. A. S. Somerby.

Stephen Brown, of Brampton, in Yorkshire, in his will, dated March 20, 1597, speaks of Rowland Whitmore, and of his brother Whitmore and his wife Ellen.

Abstract from the Will Office at Chelmsford:

Richard Whytmore, of Curringham, yeoman; will dated May 27, 1569; wife Jane, daughter Agnes, brother Thomas Whytmore.

Abstract from the Registry of the Archdeaconry of Norwich, co. Norfolk:

Richard Whitmar, of Aylsham, in Norfolk; will dated in 1604; wife Alice, son Edward, daughter Agnes; wife's son, Robert Coye.

Marian Whitmer, of Longham, widow; will, nuncupative, dated 1620; sons William, Henry and John Whitmere. '

In the index of wills, proved in the Archdeacon's Court at Exeter, in Devonshire, John Whitemore of Norleigh, 1615, and Richard Whitmore of Axminster, 1640. The wills are lost.

Abstract from the Register of Wills at Chester:

Christian Whitemore, daughter of William Whitmore, of Leighton, in the county of Chester, Esquire, deceased; will dated Dec. 14, 1625; sister Jane, wife of William Burnet, brother William, his wife and two daughters, brother Richard, brother Thomas, and his wife; appoints Hugh Anderton, of Pendlehall, co. Lancaster, Gen'l. Executor.

William Whitmore, the elder of Leighton, co. Chester, Esquire; will dated March 1, 1619; desires to be buried in the parish church of Newton, near his late wife; son William, heir apparent; reputed son, Thomas Whitmore, to whom he gives considerable real estate; daughter Christian; son-in-law William Burnet, and his wife Jane; daughter Eleanor Whitmore, deceased wife, Katherine, kinsman, John Hough; kinsman, William Coventree, of London.
Proved Jan. 16, 1620.

Abstracts from Prerogative Office in London, England:

John Whytmor, parson of Stowe, in the Diocese of Rochester. Will dated April 25, 1498. Desires to be buried in the Chapel of Our Lady, in the Abbey of Manning; mentions his cousin Thomas Whitmore.
Proved May 17, 1498.

Richard Whitmore, of Willbrighton in the Parish of Gnosall, co. Stafford. Husbandman. Will dated Dec. 20, 1557. Wife Isabel. son Thomas. Daughters Ellen, Beatrice and Joan. Children by his first wife Francis, Humphey, and William. Witnessed by Thomas and Mary Whitmore. Proved January 27, 1588.

Robert Watmore, of Stratfield Mortimer, in Berkshire. Yeoman. Will dated Sept. 20, 1608. Wife Margaret, son Robert, daughter Elizabeth wife of Wm. Cowper, sister Elizabeth Richards. Brothers George, John, and William. Speaks of his father. Proved March 7, 1611.

Anne Whitmore, of London. Widow. Will dated Jan. 21, 1613. Desires to be buried in the Parish of St. Edmunds, in Lombard street. Sons, George and William. Speaks of her late husband William Whitmore. (She was highly connected, and her will is long.)

James Watmore, of Chortley, in the Parish of Stotesdon, in the Diocese of Hereford. Husbandman. Will dated Oct. 20, 1614. Wife Joice, sons William and Francis. Daughters Joice and Margaret, son-in-law John Cromp. Brother William Watmore. Proved Feb. 9, 1614–15.

William Whitmore, of Wittlesea, in the Isle of Edy, co. Cambridge. Will dated April 2, 1632. To be buried in the church yard of St. Mary. Gives to sons, Thomas, Ralph and William; £10 each. To daughter Joan £10. Wife Isabel. Proved May 29, 1632.

Richard Weadmore, Master of the Reformation. Will dated May 29, 1623. Mentions Richard Weadmore of Blackwell, co. Somerset, Husbandman, and cousin Thomas Weadmore. Wife Mary.

William Watmore of Mortimer, co. Berks, will dated April 26, 1635, son William, grandson William, brother John (deceased), sons-in-law Robert Turner and James Wirdman, wife Joan. Proved May 5, 1635.

Richard Whitmore of the Parish of Drayton, co. Berks, will dated Nov. 12, 1559. Sons Robert, John, Richard, and Henry; daughter Joan. Proved Oct. 19, 1560.

Abstract from the Will office at York :

Cecilia Whitmore of Eastwood, in the Parish of Rotheram, in Yorkshire, widow. Will dated Oct. 5, 1610. No Whitmores mentioned.

Helen Whitmore of the town and county of Nottingham, widow. Will dated 1612. No Whitmores named.

William Whytmore of Rotherham, in Yorkshire, gentleman. Will dated Aug. 16, 1568. Desires to be buried in the church. To his son and heir apparent Richard Whytmore, all his houses, lands, &c., in Caunton, Kirksall, Newark, and Beasthorp, in Nottinghamshire: wife Cicely, daughter Elizabeth, wife of Stephen Browne, daughter-in-law Frances Parker, speaks of his wife's father, John Parker, deceased; sister Elizabeth Howtost and Jane Richardson.

Charles Watmore of Tuxforth, in Yorkshire. Will dated June 23, 1568. Sons Robert, John, Thomas, Richard, William, Roger, Christopher, and James : daughters Lettis or Lettris, Dorathy, Barbara and Elizabeth. Mentions lands heretofore given to his sons ; speaks of his wife and "the child she is withal," His executors, Roger and Christopher, to have the tuition of John and William.

William Watmore of Normanton in Nottinghamshire. Husbandman. Will dated Aug. 3, 1582 ; wife Agnes, eldest son William, youngest son James, eldest daughter Margery, youngest daughter Lettice, son-in-law Richard Cowper. Gives to each of his sons a house and lands, and appoints them executors.

Proved Oct. 10, 1582.

D.

PRES. JONATHAN EDWARDS[1]

Was born at East Windsor, Conn., Oct. 5, 1703; received his preparatory classical instruction from his father; entered Yale College when thirteen years of age, and graduated from same institution in 1720; commenced preaching the gospel in his nineteenth year; was tutor in Yale College, —— to 1726; at the latter date was ordained a minister, and settled as a colleague with his maternal grandfather, at Northampton. He married July 28, 1727, Sarah, daughter of Rev. James and Mary (Hooker) Pierrepont, of New Haven, Conn., a young lady of eighteen, of rare beauty and excellence of character.

Mr. Edwards preached in Northampton till 1750, when a difficulty arose between him and his congregation, respecting church government, and he was dismissed by an ecclesiastical council; the following year he was called to Stockbridge, among the Indians, preaching to and teaching them with great success, till he was invited to succeed his son-in-law, the Rev. Aaron Burr, D. D., as president of Princeton College, where he was installed in Jan. 1758. The following March he was inoculated, agreeably to the advice of his physician and the faculty of the college, for the small pox; in consequence of this act of precaution, he lost his life, March 22, 1758.

From the time he was first installed at Northampton, to 1757, he was actively engaged in writing and publishing his theological works, which have made his name so illustrious.

The *Cyclopedia of American Literature*, in noticing Pres. Edwards, says:

"It is impossible to study the portrait of Jonathan Edwards without noticing an air of purity, a tinge, perhaps, of feminine character, a look of thorough earnestness, and expression of native delicacy, energy and reserve, all seem to be happily blended in his countenance. On reading the narrative of his youthful studies, and early developments of intellect and piety, we see an exuberance in both which indicate a richly endowed nature.

" Education, whatever it may be with such a man, is simply the mould to be filled by his genius. In other places, in other relations, he would always be a man of mark. In the field of Belles lettres, if he had cultivated them, he would have shown as an acute

1 Biographical sketch of, with genealogical notices of some of his descendants.

critic and poet; among men of science, as a profound and original observer; among wits, as a subtle philosopher. As it was; born in New England, of the ghostly line of Puritanism, all his powers were confined to Christian morals and metaphysics.

"The religious element was developed in him very early At the age of seven or eight, in a period of religious excitement in his father's congregation, he attained a height of devotional fervor, and built a booth in a retired swamp for secret prayer, with some of his school companions.

"His account of his 'early religious life, is pure and fervent, re-calling the sublime imagination of Sir Thomas Browne of those who have understood Christian annihilation, gustation of God, and in-gression into the divine shadow, and have had already an handsome anticipation of heaven.' Nature at that time was transfigured be-fore him. It was the thorough consecration of a mind of the strong-est and finest temper. His love of nature was a trait of his boyhood. Before the age of twelve, he had written a minute account of the habits of a forest spider. When the world gained a great metaphy-sician, it perhaps lost an admirable natural historian."

His remains were interred at Princeton, where a suitable monu-ment was erected by the faculty.

The following is a copy of inscription on a mural stone at North-ampton, Mass. :

Rev. Jonathan Edwards

- The American Divine

Born

Oct. 5, 1703,

Ordained College Pastor with

Rev. Solomon Stoddard, in this town,

Died of small pox in New Jersey

March 22, 1758.

NOTE.—This monument was erected June, 1850 ; just 100 years after his dismissal.—*Northampton Epitaphs.*

FAMILY OF PRESIDENT EDWARDS.

The following is a copy of the Family Record, in his own hand, in the Family Bible :

Jonathan Edwards, son of Timothy and Esther Edwards, of Windsor, in Connecticut.

I was born Oct. 5, 1703.

I was ordained at Northampton, Feb. 15, 1727.

I was married to Miss Sarah Pierrepont, July 28, 1727.

My wife was born Jan. 9, 1710.

My daughter Sarah was born on Sabbath day, between 2 and 3 o'clock in the afternoon, Aug. 25, 1728.

My daughter Jerusha was born on a Sabbath day, towards the conclusion of the afternoon exercises, April 26, 1730.

My daughter Esther was born on a Sabbath day, between 9 and 10 o'clock in the forenoon, Feb. 13, 1732.

My daughter Mary was born April 7th, 1734, being Sabbath day, the sun being about an hour and a half high, in the morning.

My daughter Lucy was born on Tuesday, the last day of Aug., 1736, between 2 and 3 o'clock in the morning.

My son Timothy was born on Tuesday, July 25, 1738, between 6 and 7 o'clock in the morning.

My daughter Susannah was born on Friday, June 20, 1740, at about 3 o'clock in the morning.

All the family above named had the measles, at the latter end of the year 1740.

My duaghter Eunice was born on Monday morning, May 9, 1743, about half an hour after midnight, and was baptized the Sabbath following.

My son Jonathan was born on a Sabbath day-night, May, 26, 1745, between 9 and 10 o'clock, and was baptized the Sabbath following.

My daughter Jerusha died on a Sabbath day, Feb. 14, 1747, about 5 o'clock in the morning, aged 17.[2]

My daughter Elizabeth was born on Wednesday, May 6, 1747, between 10 and 11 o'clock at night, and was baptized the Sabbath following.

My son Pierrepont was born on a Sabbath day-night, April 8, 1750, between 8 and 9 o'clock, and was baptized the Sabbath following.

I was dismissed from my pastoral relation to the first church in Northampton, June 22, 1750.

My daughter Sarah was married to Elihu Parsons, June 11, 1750.

My daughter Esther was married to Timothy Dwight, Esq., of Northampton, Nov. 8, 1750.

My daughter Mary was married to the Rev. Aaron Burr of Newark, June 29, 1752.

Mr. Burr aforesaid, President of the New Jersey College, died at Princeton, Sept. 24, 1757, of the Nervous Fever. Mr. Burr was born Jan. 4, 1715.

I was properly initiated President of New Jersey College, by taking the previous oaths, Feb. 16, 1758.

Rev. Jonathan Edwards, President of Nassau Hall, died of small pox, March 22, 1748, and was buried March 24th.

Esther Burr, wife of the Rev. Aaron Burr, died at Princeton, April 7, 1758, of a short illness, aged 26.

Sarah Edwards, wife of Jonathan Edwards, died Oct. 2, 1758, about 12 o'clock, and was buried at Princeton the day following.

Elizabeth, daughter of Sarah and Jonathan Edwards, died at Northampton, Jan. 1, 1762, aged 14 years.

Lucy Woodbridge died at Stockbridge in Oct. 1786, aged 50.

Rev. Jonathan Edwards, D. D., died at Schenectady, August 1, 1801, aged 56.

Susannah Porter died at Hadley in the spring of 1812, aged 61.

2 The brief and beautiful career of this young lady is concisely and feelingly given in the following note by the father:

Since it has pleased a holy and sovereign God to take away this my dear child by death, on the 14th of February next following, after a short illness of five days, in the eighteenth year of her age. She was much the same spirit as Brainerd. She had constantly taken care of and attended him (Rev. David Brainerd, the missionary—Compiler) in his sickness for nineteen weeks before his death, devoting herself to it with great delight, because she looked upon him as an eminent servant of Jesus Christ. In this time he had much conversation with her on the things of religion, and in his dying state often expressed to us, her parents, his great satisfaction concerning her true piety, and in his confidence that he should meet her in Heaven, and his high opinion of her not only as a true christian but a very eminent saint, one whose soul was uncommonly fed and entertained with things which appertain to the most spiritual, experimental and distinguishing parts of religion, and one who, by the temper of her mind, was fitted to deny herself for God, and to be good, beyond any young woman whatsoever whom he knew She had manifested a heart uncommonly devoted to God in the course of her life, many years before her death, and said on her death-bed that she "had not seen one minute for several Years wherein she had desired to live one minute longer for the sake of any other good in life but doing ood, living to God, and doing what might be for His glory.—*Cyclo. of Am. Lit.* vol. I, page 14½

Sarah Parsons died at Goshen, Mass., May 15, 1805, aged 76.
Mary Dwight died at Northampton, Feb. 1807, aged 72.
Timothy Edwards died at Stockbridge in the autumn of 1813, aged 75.
Eunice Hunt, died at Newbern, N. C. in the autumn of 1822, aged 79.
Pierrepont Edwards, died at Bridgeport, Ct., April 14, 1826, aged 76.—
Dwight's Life of Jno. Edwards.

Children of President Edwards,

With some of their Descendants.

SARAH, m. Elihu Parsons, June 11, 1750; lived at Stockbridge, subsequently at Goshen; had 1 Ebenezer, d. in infancy; 2 Esther, b. May 17, 1752; d. at Stockbridge, Nov. 17, 1774; 3 Elihu, b. Dec. 9, 1753; m. Rhoda Hinsdale, of Lenox; he d. at Goshen, in Aug. 1804; had 6 children; 4 Eliphalet, b. Jan. 1756; m. Martha Young, of Long Island; he d. at Chenango, N. Y., in Jan. 1813; had 5 children; 5 Lydia, b. Jan. 15, 1757; m. Aaron Ingersoll, of Lee; they had 4 children; 6 Lucretia, b. Aug. 3, 1759; m. Rev. Justin Parsons, of Pittsfield, Vt.; she d. at Goshen, in Dec. 1786; had 1 child; 7 Sarah, b. Sept. 8, 1760; m. David Ingersoll, of Lee, Dec. 13, 1781; had 13 children; 8 Lucy, b. Oct. 14, 1762; m. Joshua Ketchum; had 3 children; 9 Jonathan, d. an infant; 10 Jerusha, d. an infant; 11 Jerusha, b. May, 1766; m. Ira Seymour, of Victor, N. Y.; had 5 children.

ESTHER, m. Rev. Aaron Burr, D. D., June 29, 1752; lived at Newark and Princeton, N. J.; he d. Aug. 1757; she d. 1758; had 1 Sarah, b. May 3, 1754; m. Hon. Tapping Reeve, of Litchfield, Conn.; had Aaron Burr; 2 Aaron, b. Feb. 6, 1756, who was Vice President of the United States; m. Theodosia Provost;[1] had Theodosia; Col. Burr m. 2 Mad. Jumel, wid. of ——.

3 Theodosia Prevost was the widow of Colonel Prevost of the British army. She was said to have been an accomplished and intelligent lady. Her first husband died early in the revolutionary war in the West Indies, where he was with his regiment.
It was her son, the Hon. John B. Prevost, who in 1802 was Recorder of the city of New York, and subsequently district judge of the United States Court in Louisiana. The house of Mrs. Prevost was the resort of the most accomplished officers in the American army when they were in the vicinity of it. She was highly respected by her neighbors, and visited by the most genteel people of the surrounding country. Her situation was one of great delicacy and constant apprehension. The wife of a British officer. and connected with the adherents of the crown, naturally became an object of political suspicion, notwithstanding great circumspection on her part. Under such circumstances a strong sympathy was excited in her behalf. Yet there were those among the Whigs who were inclined to force the laws of the state against her, whereby she would be compelled to withdraw within the lines of the enemy.
In this family Colonel Burr became intimate in 1777, and in 1782 married the widow Prevost. —*Davis' Memoirs of Col. Burr.*

The following year (1783) Mr. and Mrs. Col. Burr had born to them a daughter, subsequently the unfortunate Mrs. Theodosia Burr Alston. The following beautiful and touching epistle relative to the infant Theodosia, we find in Mr. Davis' *Memoirs:*

From Mrs. Burr.

ALBANY, Aug. 14th, 1783.
How unfortunate, my dearest Aaron, is our present separation. I never shall have resolution to consent to another. We must not be guided by others, we are certainly formed of different materials, and our undertakings must coincide with them.
A few hours after I wrote you by Col. Lewis our sweet infant was taken ill, very ill. My mind and spirits have been on the rack from that moment to this. When she sleeps, I watch anxiously; when she wakes, anxious fears accompany every motion. I talked of my love towards her, but I knew it not until put to this unhappy test. I know not whether to give her medicine or to withhold it, doubt and terror are all the sensations of which I am sensible. She has slept better last night, and appears more lively this morning than since her illness. This has induced me to postpone an express to you which I have had in readiness since yesterday. If this meets you I need not dwell upon my wish.
I will only put an injunction on your riding so fast, or in the heat or dew. Remember your presence is to support, to console your Theo., perhaps to rejoice with her at the restoration of our much-loved child. Let us encourage this hope; encourage it at least till you see me, which I flatter myself will be before this can reach you. Some kind spirit will whisper to my Aaron how much his tender attention is wanted to support his Theo., how much his love is necessary

MARY, m. Timothy Dwight, Nov. 8, 1750; they lived at Northampton; he d. in Natchez in 1776, and she in Feb. 1807, at Northampton; had 1 Rev. Timothy, D. D., LL. D., President of Yale College, b. May

to give her that fortitude, that resolution, which nature has denied her but through his medium. Adieu.   THEODOSIA.

The reader would hardly expect us in these circumscribed pages to follow this child from her infancy to womanhood; suffice it to say, she was reared by her parents with great care and affection, and received a superior education; grew up an elegant and accomplished lady. At the age of nine years her reading was chiefly in the French language of which she was particularly fond, so much so, her father found it difficult to keep her supplied with reading in that language. She was remarkable for her beauty of person and classic profile. She married Joseph Alston of South Carolina, in January, 1801, "a gentleman of talents and fortune, and a few years after his marriage was chosen governor." They had a boy born to them in the spring of 1802, he died June 30th, 1812, aged ten years. The following from its father to Col Burr, announces the death:

                                                                                         · July 26, 1812.
A few miserable weeks, my dear sir, and in spite of all embarrassments, the troubles and disappointments, which have fallen to our lot since we parted, I would have congratulated you on your return in the language of happiness (Col. Burr had just returned from a trip to Europe), with my wife on one side and my boy on the other, I felt myself superior to depression. The present was enjoyed, the future was anticipated with enthusiasm. One dreadful blow has destroyed us; reduce us to the veriest, the most sublimated wretchedness   That boy on whom all rested; our companion, our friend—he was to have transmitted down the mingled blood of Theodosia and myself—he who was to have redeemed all your glory, and shed new lustre upon our families—that boy, at once our happiness and our pride, is taken from us—*is dead.* We saw, him dead. My own hands surrendered him to the grave; yet we are alive. But it is past. I will not conceal from you that life is a burden, which heavy as it is, we both shall support if not with dignity, at least with decency and firmness. Theodosia has endured all that a human being could endure; but her admirable mind will triumph. She supports herself in a manner worthy of your daughter. *   *   *   *   *   *   *   *   *
                                        [Signed.]   JOSEPH ALSTON.
—*Davis' Mem. of Col. Burr.*

Mrs. Alston's health became very much impaired consequent upon the death of her son. During the summer and autumn that followed she suffered from an almost incessant nervous fever. In December it was thought advisable by her father and family physician that she should try the benefits of a voyage from Charleston to New York, and accordingly, a small pilot boat schooner called the Patriot (Capt. Overstocks), was chartered for her special accommodation, which vessel sailed from Charleston the last Thursday of December (1812), with Mrs. Alston and Dr. Timothy Green, her medical attendant, as passengers, since which time no tidings either of the vessel, crew or its passengers have been received. Many were the rumors at the time, and since respecting the fate of the vessel, that she was "captured by pirates," "the crew had mutinied," "was lost in a severe gale," &c. The latter is most likely the truth, as there was a severe gale along the coast soon after the Patriot's sailing from Charleston. The letters that followed between Colonels Burr and Alston, were as may be easily imagined, of the most affecting nature. In one of Mr. Alston's letters to Col. Burr he says: *   *   "My boy—my wife—gone, both! This then is the end of all the hopes we have formed   You may well observe that you feel severed from the human race. She was the last tie that bound us to our species. What have we left?   *   *   *   *   *   *   *   *   *
I visited the grave of my boy. The little plans we had all three formed rushed upon my memory   Where now was the boy? The mother I cherished with so much pride? I felt like the very spirit of desolation. *   *   *   *   *   *   *   *
You are the only person in the world with whom I can commune on the subject, for you are the only person whose feelings can have any community with mine. You knew those we loved. With you, therefore, it will be no weakness to feel their loss. Here none knew them, none valued them as they deserved. The talents of my boy, his rare elevation of character, his extensive reputation for so early an age, made his death regretted by the pride of my family; but, though of the loss of my son not less admirable wife they seem to think it like the loss of an ordinary woman   Alas! they know nothing of my heart. They have never known anything of it. Yet after all he is a poor actor who cannot sustain his little hour upon the stage, be his part what it may. But the man who has been deemed worthy of the heart of *Theodosia Burr,* and has felt what it was to be blessed with such a woman's, will never forget his elevation !
February 25, 1813.   JOSEPH ALSTON.

In Mrs. Alston and her son were centered all of Col. Burr's affections. all the ties that bound him to this life. The effect upon him, as these events occurred, can better be imagined than described. His biographer says that "In his intercourse with the world (subsequent to the loss of his daughter) and in his business pursuits, there was a promptitude and an apparent cheerfulness which seemed to indicate a tranquility of mind. But not so in lone and solitary hours in the society of a single friend; if an accidental reference was made to the event, the manly tear would be seen to steal down his furroughed cheeks until, as if awakening from a slumber, he would suddenly check those emotions of his heart, and all again would be become subdued." Mrs. Burr died in the spring of 1794.

Col. Burr lived to his eighty-first year, having died on Wednesday, the 14th of Sept., 1836, near the village of Richmond, Staten Island, N Y. His body was taken to Princeton, N. J., where it was interred on the 16th of the same month, near the remains of his ancestors. Funeral services were held at College Chapel, attended by professors, collegians, military and citizens. The funeral sermon was preached by the president of the college. Since then a befitting monument has been erected over his grave by some one or more of President Edwards' descendants.

For further interesting sketches of the life of Col. Burr and his daughter Theodosia, we would refer the reader to *Memoirs of Aaron Burr,* by Matthew L. Davis. Harper & Brothers, New York, 1837

14, 1752; m. the daughter of Benjamin Woolsey, Esq., of Dorsons, L. I.; they had 7 children; he d. at New Haven, Jan. 11, 1817; 2 Dr. Sereno Edwards, b. 1753; m. Miss Lyman; had 2 children; he was lost at sea, on the coast of Nova Scotia in 1799; 3 Jonathan, b. 1755; m. Miss Wright; had 2 children; he d. in 180–; 4 Erastus, b. 1756; d. unm. in 1825; 5 Dr. Maurice William, b. May 29, 1758; m. Margaret Dewitt; had 2 children; 6 Sarah, b. May 29, 1760; m. Seth Storrs, of Northampton; she d. at Northampton in 1805; 7 Hon. Theodore, b. in 1762; m. Abby Alsop; had 3 children; 8 Mary, 1764; m. Lewis R. Morris; had 1 child; 9 Delia, b. 1766; m. Jonathan Edwards Porter, Esq.; had 3 children; 10 Dr. Nathaniel, b. in 1769; m. Miss Robins; had 4 children; 11 Elizabeth, b. 1771; m. William W. Woolsey, Esq.; had 8 children; she d. at New Haven in the fall of 1812; 12 Cecil, b. June 10, 1774; m. Mary Clap; had 11 children; 13 Henry Edwin, b. in 1776; m. Electa Keyes; had 6 children.

Lucy, m. June 1764, Jahleel Woodbridge, Esq.; they lived at Stockbridge; had 1 Jonathan, b. 1766; m. Sarah Meach; had 8 children; 2 Stephen, b. 1778; had several children; 3 Joseph, b. in 1770; m. Louisa Hopkins; had 4 children; 4 Lucy, b. in 1772; m. Henry Brown; had 9 or 10 children; 5 John; 6 Sarah, m. a Mr. Leicister of Griswold, Ct.; had 5 children; 7 Rev. Timothy of Green River, N. Y.

Hon. TIMOTHY, m. Sept. 25, 1760, Rhoda Ogden; they lived at Stockbridge; children, 15; two d. young; 1 Sarah; 2 Edward; 3 Jonathan; 4 Richard; 5 Pheobe; 6 William; 7 Robert Ogden; 8 Timothy; 9 Mary Ogden; 10 Rhoda; 11 Mary; 12 Anna; 13 Robert.

SUSANNAH, m. Sept. 1761, Eleazer Porter, Esq.; they lived at Hadley; had 1 Eleazer; 2 William; 3 Jonathan Edwards; 4 Moses; 5 Pierrepont.

EUNICE, m. Jan. 1764, Thomas Pollock, Esq.; they lived at Elizabethtown, N. J.; had 1 Elizabeth, m. —— Williams, Esq.; 2 Hester, d. unm.; 3 Thomas; 4 Frances, m. John Devereux, Esq.; they had 3 children; 5 George.

Rev. JONATHAN, graduated at Yale College, 1767; President Union College, ——; m. Sarah Porter; they lived at New Haven and Schenectady; had 1 Mary, m. Mr. Hoit, of Schenectady; 2 Jonathan Walter, Esq., m. Elizabeth Tryon; 3 Jerusha, m. Rev. Calvin Chapin, D. D., of Stepney; 4 child., d. infant.

ELIZABETH, d., æ. 14.

Hon. PIERREPONT, Judge U. S. Court for Conn.; m. Frances Ogden, May, 1769; he d. at Bridgeport, Conn., 1826; had I *Susan*, m. Samuel W. Johnson of Stratford; had 1 Frances, d. ——; 2 William, m. Laura Woolsey, who had Susan, William, m. Frances Sanders, Laura, Woolsey; 3 Elizabeth, m. George Devereux; had Elizabeth, m. —— Umsted; have two chil.; Georgiana; 4 Edwards, m. Ann Doudall; had Frances, d.; Edwards, George, Samuel; 5 Robert Charles, m. M. Pumpelly. II Hon. *John Starkes*, m. Louisa Morris; had 1 William, m. Mary ——; had 1 dau.; 2 ——; 3 ——. III Hon. *Henry Waggoner*, m. Lydia Miller; had 1 John, m. ——; had three chil.; 2 Judge Henry P——; d. unm., ab. 1855–6; 3 Alfred, late U. S. Consul to Manilla, m. Mary, dau. of Nathaniel Griswold of New York; d. ab. 1857, s. p.; 4 Frances, m. Wm. S. Hoyt; had Henrietta, m. Henry Shelton; James, William; 5 Henrietta, m. Prof. Hooker of New Haven. IV Hon. *Ogden* of N. Y.; m. Harriet Penfield; had 1 Ogden P.; m. Maria

Sayles of Boston; had Amy, Pierrepont; 2 Jonathan, grad. Yale Coll. 1840; m. Mary Morris of New York; had Gerard Morris, Mary; 3 Alfred; 4 William; m. Sarah Bush; had Minnié; 5 Mary; 6 Frances, and 4 others, d. unm. V *Alfred*, m. Deborah Glover; had Alice, who m. Dyer Vinton of Providence, R. I.; had Alfred; two other chil. VI Henrietta Frances, m. Eli Whitney, Esq., of New Haven, the inventor of the cotton gin; had 1 Frances, m. Charles Chaplin; had Henrietta, William, Fanny, Elizabeth; 2 Elizabeth, d. unm.; 3 Eli, m. Sarah Dalaber; had Susan, Eli, Henrietta; resides at New Haven.[4]

4 Dwight's *Life Pres. E.* and correspondents.

E.

ELDER WILLIAM BREWSTER[1]

Was born (it is supposed) in Scrooby, in the county of Suffolk, England, in the year of our Lord, 1559–60. He received his education at the University of Cambridge, where he became impressed with the truth of the necessity of personal piety; those impressions never left him, and had the effect of influencing his whole subsequent life. He left the university before receiving his degree, and went into the service of William Davison, secretary of state to Queen Elizabeth, and ambassador to Holland, and shared with him the vicissitudes of fortune which befel that statesman. "Davison (says Dr. Belknap) esteemed him as a son, and conversed with him in private, both on religious and political subjects with the greatest familiarity, and when anything required secresy, Brewster was his confidential friend."[2]

When the Queen entered into a league with the United Provinces (1584), and received possession of several towns and forts, as security for her expenses in defending their liberties; Davison who negociated the matter, entrusted Brewster with the keys of Flushing, one of those cautionary towns,[3] and the states of Holland were so sensible of his merit as to present him with the ornament of a golden chain.

He returned with the ambassador to England, and continued in his service, till Davison having incurred the hypocritical displeasure of his arbitrary mistress, was imprisoned, fined and ruined. Davison is said to have been a man of abilities and integrity, but easy to be imposed upon, and for that reason was made secretary of state.

When Mary, the unfortunate Queen of Scotland, had been tried and condemned, and the Parliament of England had petitioned their sovereign for her execution, Elizabeth privately ordered Davison to

---

1 His life and character, embracing historical, biographical and genealogical notices of some of his descendants. In making up this record, we have had occasion to refer to the *Mass. His. So. Coll.*, *Plymouth Colony Records, His. of Duxbury*, by Justin Winsor; Mitchell's *His. of Bridgewater*, Thacher's *His. of the Town of Plymouth, Chronicles of the Pilgrims, N. E. Register*, etc.

2 Mr. Brewster had for a colleague in office under Davison, George Cranmer, the pupil and friend of the judicious Hooker. Walton's *Lives*, p. 179, Major's Edition; Judge Davis justly remarks that there seems to have been a similarity of character between Mr. Brewster and his patron.—*Morton Memorial*, p. 221.

3 Elizabeth advanced the United Provinces money to enable them to maintain their independence of Spain, her rival in power and ambition; she very prudently got consigned into her hands the three important fortresses of Fushing. the Brille, and Rammekins, as pledges of the reimbursement of the money which she furnished them, in defence of their liberties. They were accordingly called "the cautionary towns." They were surrendered by King James in 1616.—Sir Dudley Carleton's *Letters*, pp. 27, 35.

draw a death warrant, which she signed, and sent him with it to the Chancellor to have the great seal annexed. Having performed his duty, she blamed him for precipitancy. Davison acquainted the council with the whole transaction; they knew the Queen's real sentiments, and persuaded him to send the warrants to the Earls of Kent and Shrewsbury, promising to justify his conduct and take the blame on themselves. These Earls attended the execution of Mary, but when Elizabeth heard of it, she affected surprise and indignation; threw all the blame on the innocent Secretary, and committed him to the Tower, where he became the subject of raillery from those very counsellors who had promised to countenance and protect him. He was tried in the Star Chamber, and fined ten thousand pounds, which being rigorously levied upon him, reduced him to poverty.

A letter to King James from the Earl of Essex, dated 18th April, 1587, while interceding for him says: "he is beloved of the best and most religious of this land. His sufficiency in council and matters of state is such, as the Queen herself confesseth in her kingdom, she hath not such another; his virtue, religion and worth in all degrees are of the world taken to be so great, as no man in his good fortune hath had more general love than this gentleman in his disgrace. Lord Burleigh, in a petition to the Queen, 13th Feb. 1586, writes: I know not a man in the land so finished universally for the place he had, neither know I any that can come near him."[4]

Brewster did not desert his friend, as we might expect from the class of politicians of the present day, but remained as true to him as in the hey day of his political power and influence, assisting him with his money and kindly offices. His own fortune which had been large, becoming somewhat impaired—he sought retirement in the north of England where he improved his time in making himself acquainted with the scriptures, and practising its precepts. The conduct of the established church party at this time being so full of persecution, corruption and bigotry, caused him to look more closely into their pretensions of ecclesiastical authority, and finding so much that was at variance with the simple teachings of Christ, he withdrew from their communion, and joined others of the same sentiments, and organized a separate church, the aged Richard Clifton and Mr. Robinson officiating as pastors, meeting at his own house where he provided for them in Christian love and kindness, till they were driven by James the First, to seek refuge on the continent.[5]

4 Supp. to the *Cabala*, p. 23; Strype's *Annals*, iii, p. 373.

5 At a conference held at Hampton Court, Jan. 14, 1604, King James declared "I will none of that liberty as to ceremonies; I will have one doctrine and one discipline, one religion in substance and ceremony. I shall make them [the Puritans] conform themselves, or I will harry them out of the land, or else do worse. If any would not be quiet, and show his obedience, he were worthy to be hanged." In his speech at the opening of his first Parliament, March 19, 1604, he "professed the sect Puritans or Novelists were not to be suffered in any well governed community." In a private letter written about the same time he said: "I had rather live a hermit in the forest, than be a king over such a people as a pack of Puritans that overrules the lower house." He had previously written by his son in the *Basilicon Doron*, "Take heed, my son, to such Puritans, very pests in the church and commoweal. I protest before the great God, that ye shall never find with Highland or border thieves greater ingrati-

He made use of his means for their removal, and when on board of the vessel in the harbor of Boston (Lincolnshire), he with the whole party were seized at night and carried to prison, from which they were not released till after paying oppressive fines, he having means was made to suffer most. When liberated he assisted the needy to embark, and followed them soon after.

After arriving in Holland, his family being large, he began to experience pecuniary embarrassment. The money that he had given for the relief of others, he now needed to supply his own daily wants. He was not suited to either mercantile, mechanical or agricultural pursuits, and was compelled to turn his attention to teaching the languages, of which he had acquired a perfect knowledge at the University, and with the assistance of a few friends established a printing office, from which he issued several works against the hierarchy in England. Among the books printed by him in Leyden were, " *Commentarii Succincti et Dilucidi in Proverbia Salmonsis; Authore Thomâ Cartwrightis, S. S.; Theologiæ in Academiâ Cantabrigiensi quondam Professore; Quibus attribita est Preafatio clarissimi viri Johannis Polyandri; S. Theologiæ Professoris Liedensis ; Lugduni Batavorum ; Apud Gulielmum Brewsterum*, in vice Chorali. 1617. 8vo. pp. 1513. A copy of this work is now in the possession of the pastor of the First Church in Plymouth, the same having been presented to that church in 1828 by the Hon John Davis, LL. D. Another copy is in the Library of the Pilgrim Society at Plymouth."—Thacher's *Plymouth, p.* 270.

His moral excellence, his talent and capability was acknowledged by the church in appointing him their ruling elder, and they confided to him their temporal as well as their ecclesiastical affairs.

When a portion of their number volunteered to go to America to establish a colony, preparatory to the whole church following, he was chosen their spiritual guide and instructor, while their pastor, John Robinson, remained at home.

He was not with them when they left Delft Haven,[6] July 22, -1620, in the Speedwell, a vessel of only 60 tons, being in England making preparations privately for the voyage. The wind being fair, the vessel soon arrived at Southampton, where they found waiting the bark Mayflower, of London, with others to accompany them, among whom was Elder Brewster. Both vessels sailed on the 5th of August, 1620. They were not long at sea before the master of the smaller vessel, complained that he found his craft leaky, and re-

tude and more lies and vile injuries than with these fanatic spirits."—Barlow's *Sum and Substance*, pp. 71, 83, 92; Calderon's *Hist. Ch. Scotland*, p. 478; *Hallam*, I, 419.
    In conformity to these views on the 5th of March, 1604, he issued a proclamation, that the same religion with common prayer, and Episcopal jurisdiction, shall be fully and only be publicly exercised, in all respects as in the reign of Queen Elizabeth, without hope of toleration of any other; and on the 6th of July he issued another proclamation in which he ordered the Puritan ministers either to conform before the last of November, or dispose of themselves or families some other way; as being unfit, for their obstinacy and contempt, to occupy such places. The consequence of this was, that after November of the next year more than three hundred ministers were ejected, silenced or suspended, some of whom were imprisoned and others driven into exile.—Neal's *Hist. of the Puritans*, I, p. 232; *Prince*, pp. 107, 108 and 110.

    6 Delft Haven is on the north side of the Meuse, two miles S. W. from Rotterdam, eight miles from Delft, and about fourteen from Leyden.

fused to go further, so accordingly both vessels were headed to the eastward, and made the port of Dartmouth, after being out eight days. The Speedwell was examined and corked where it was deemed necessary, and they again sailed on the 21st of August. When they had reached some three hundred miles on their course, the captain (Reynolds) of the S., again pronounced his vessel leaky, so much so that he feared she would founder at sea; they then bore up and went into Plymouth. On examination it was found that the craft could have crossed to America had the captain so desired, he and the owners having conspired to throw up the voyage, and plotted this way of freeing themselves. It was then determined to place all in the larger vessel and proceed. Some twenty passengers on board the Speedwell declined going, and returned home.

All arrangements being made, they set sail about the 6th of Sept. with 101 persons on board, besides the crew of the vessel. The weather for a time was propitious, but before they reached the end of their voyage they met with head winds and severe equinoxial gales, which strained their bark so much as to cause her decks to leak badly, but the hull proving staunch, they determined to continue their course, and made Cape Cod November 9th, and entered the harbor of Cape Cod the 11th, and on that day drew up and signed the following

Compact:

In the Name of God, Amen.—We whose names are underwritten, the dread subjects of our dread sovereign lord, King James, by the Grace of God, of Great Britain, France and Ireland King, defender of the faith, &c., having undertaken for the glory of God, and advancement of the Christian faith, and honour of our king and country, a voyage to plant the first colony in the Northern parts of Virginia, do, by these presents solemnly and mutually, in the presence of God and one another, covenant and combine ourselves together into a civil body politic, for our better ordering and preservation, and furtherance of the end aforesaid; and by virtue hereof to enact, constitute and frame such just and equal laws, ordinances, acts, constitutions and offices, from time to time, as shall be thought most meet and convenient for the general good of the colony; unto which we promise all due submission and obedience.

In witness whereof we have hereunder subscribed our names, at Cape Cod, the 11th of November, in the year of the reign of our sovereign lord, King James, of England, France and Ireland the eighteenth, and of Scotland the fifty-fourth, Anno Domini 1620:

Mr. John Carver, -	-	8	Thomas Tinker, - - - 3
William Bradford, - -	-	2	John Ridgdale, - - - - 2
Mr. Edward Winslow, -	-	5	Edward Fuller, - - - 3
Mr. William Brewster,	-	6	John Turner, - - - - 3
Mr. Isaac Allerton,	-	6	Francis Eaton - - - 3
Capt. Miles Standish,	-	2	James Chilton, - - - - 3
John Howland, - - -	-	—	John Crackston, - - - 2
Mr. Stephen Hopkins,	-	8	John Billington, - - - 4
Edward Tilly, - -	-	4	Moses Fletcher, - - - 1
John Tilley, - - -	-	3	John Alden, - - - - 1
Francis Cook, - -	-	2	Mr. Samuel Fuller, - - 2
Thomas Rogers, - -	-	2	Mr. Christopher Martin, - - 4

Mr. William Mullens,	- -	5
Mr. William White, -	- -	5
Mr. Richard Warren,	- -	1
John Goodman, -	- - -	1
Degory Priest,	- - -	1
Thomas Williams, -	- -	1
Gilbert Winslow, -	- -	1
Edmund Margeson, -	- -	1
Peter Brown,	- - -	1

Richard Britterage, -	- -	1
George Soule,	- - -	—
Richard Clarke,	- -	1
Richard Gardiner, -	- -	1
John Allerton, -	- - -	1
Thomas English, -	- -	1
Edward Dotey, -	- - -	—
Edward Leister, -	- -	—

Total number, - - - 101

The list includes a servant that died, and a child that was born at sea.

From the date of the compact to the 20th of the following month, was occupied in exploring the country, and their explorations resulted in their determining to land on a point of rock on the south-west side of a harbor which they had named Plymouth Bay, and on the land adjacent to take up their abode and establish their colony; and these were the founders of the Colony of Plymouth.

We shall not attempt to follow the subject of our notice through all his labors and trials to the time of his death; he was as one writer justly remarks the very soul of the colony. He was proffered the office of governor, at the time Gov. Carver was chosen, which he declined; he esteemed his mission not of this world, only so far as to prepare himself and his fellow men for another and better beyond the grave.

The church had no regular minister for four years after their pastor Robinson died at Leyden, making nine years that they were without having the sacrament of the Lord's Supper administered to them. In 1629 they settled Ralph Smith, a man said to have been of "low gifts," he resigned at the end of about five years, when they had Roger Williams of "bright accomplishments but offensive errors," he officiated three years and was followed in 1636 by John Reyner, an "able and godly man, of meek and humble spirit, sound in the truth, and unreprovable in his life and conversation," he resigned in 1654, and removed to Dover, N. H.

Mr. Brewster continued in uninterrupted good health, attending to all his domestic and religious duties till within a few days of his death. On the fourteenth day of April, 1644, he was confined to his bed, and the following day he died in the eighty-fourth year of his age.

"He had been (says Dr. Belknap) remarkably temperate during his whole life, having drank no liquor but water, till within the last five or six years. For many months together he had lived, through necessity without bread; having nothing but fish for his sustenance, and sometimes was destitute of that. Yet being of a pliant and a cheerful temper he easily accommodated himself to his circumstances. When nothing but oysters or clams were set upon his table he would give thanks, with his family, that they could "suck of the abundance of the seas, and of the treasures hid in the sand."

When we take into consideration that Mr. Brewster had been born in affluence, received his education at one of the most aristocratic institutions of England; companion to ministers of state; an attaché to a foreign embassy; familiar with the elegance and abundance of a court life, we can say with truth that the world has furnished but few such instances of cheerful Christian resignation, humility and gratitude to God for even the least of his mercies, as was exhibited by him. It was with him as with Moses of old, " choosing rather to suffer affliction with the people of God, than enjoy the pleasures of sin for a season, esteeming the reproach of Christ," or persecution for Christ's sake " greater riches than treasures of Egypt for he had respect to the recompense of reward."

" In his public discourses (says Dr. Belknap), Mr. Brewster was very clear and distinguishing, as well as pathetic; addressing himself first to the understanding, and then to the affections of his audience ; convincing and persuading them of the superior excellence of true religion. Such a kind of teaching, was well adapted, and in many instances effectual to the real instruction and benefit of his hearers. What a pity that such a man could not have been persuaded to take on him the pastoral office!"

Why he did not assume the robes of priesthood has always appeared strange. It is only left for those who now study his life and character to speculate upon the subject. Some suppose it arose wholly from his natural diffidence. We are unable to see that his character warrants such a conclusion, for wherever *duty* called, there he had the *boldness to be found*. We can not account for this *seeming* neglect of duty in him, upon any other grounds, than that he had been early trained to reverence the holy office, and to hold it a sacrilege for any one but those solemnly and properly ordained to officiate in ." sacred things." Such an ordination he could not obtain in the colony at the time that his services were particularly needed, and his going to England to receive ordination was wholly impracticable.

We here give a memoir of Elder Brewster, written by his friend and fellow pilgrim, Gov. Bradford, originally entered on *MS. Records of Plymouth*, book 1, p. 30, by Secretary Morton:

" Now followeth that which was matter of great sadness and mourning unto this church. About the tenth of April, in the year 1644, died their reverend Elder, our dear and loving friend, Mr. William Brewster; a man that had done and suffered much for the Lord Jesus and the Gospel's sake, and borne his part in weal and woe with this poor persecuted church about thirty-six years in England, Holland, and in this wilderness, and done the Lord and them faithful service in his place and calling; and notwithstanding the many troubles and sorrows he passed through, the Lord upheld him to a great age. He was near four score years of age, if not all out when he died. He had his blessing added by the Lord to all the rest, to die in his bed, in peace, amongst the midst of his friends,

who mourned and wept over him, and administered what help and
comfort they could unto him, and he again recomforted them whilst
he could. His sickness was not long. Until the last day thereof
he did not wholly keep his bed. His speech continued until somewhat more than half a day before his death, and then failed him;
and about nine or ten of the clock that evening, he died without a
pang at all. A few hours before, he drew his breath short, and
some minutes before his last, he drew his breath long, as a man
fallen into a sound sleep, without any pangs or gaspings; so sweetly
departed this life unto a better.

"I would now demand of any what he was the worse for any
former sufferings. What do I say? The worse? Nay, surely he
was the better, and they now add to his honor. 'It is a manifest
token,' saith the Apostle, 'of the righteous judgment of God, for
which ye also suffer; seeing it is a righteous thing with God to
recompense tribulation to them that troubled you; and to you who
are troubled, rest with us when the Lord Jesus shall be revealed
from Heaven with his mighty angels' (2 Thess., i, 5–7). And
'If ye be reproached for the name of Christ, happy are ye; for the
spirit of God and glory resteth upon you' (I Pet. iv, 14). What
though he wanted riches and pleasures of the world in his life, and
pompous monuments at his funeral, yet the memorial of the just
shall be blessed when the name of the wicked shall not (Prov.
x, 7).

"I should say something of his life, if to say a little were not
worse than to be silent. But I cannot wholly forbear, though happily more may be done hereafter. After he had attained some
learning, viz: the knowledge of the Latin tongue and some insight
into the Greek, and spent some small time in Cambridge, and then
being first seasoned with seeds of grace and virtue, he went to the
court, and served that religious and godly gentleman, Mr. Davison,
divers year, when he was Secretary of State, who found him so discreet and faithful, as he trusted him above all others that were about
him and only employed him in matters of greatest trust and secrecy.
He esteemed him rather as a son than a servant, and for his wisdom
and godliness, in private, he could converse with him more like a
familiar than a master. He attended his master when he was sent
in embassage by the Queen into the Low Countries (in the Earl of
Lecister's time, 1585), as for other weighty affairs of State, so to
receive possession of the cautionary towns; and in token and sign
thereof, the keys of Flushing being delivered to him in her majesty's name, he kept them some time and committed them to his servant, who kept them under his pillow on which he slept, the first
night. And, at his return, the States honored him with a gold
chain, and his master committed it to him, and commanded him to
wear it when they arrived in England, as they rode through the
country, until they came to the Court. He afterwards remained
with him until his troubles, when he was put from his place about

the death of the Queen of Scots, and some good time after doing
him many offices of services in the time of his troubles. Afterwards
he went and lived in the country, in good esteem amongst friends
and the good gentlemen of those parts, especially the godly and religious.

" He did much good in the country where he lived, in promoting
and furthering religion; and not only by his practice and example,
and provoking and encouraging of others, but by procuring of good
preachers thereabouts, and drawing on of others to assist and help
to forward in such a work; he himself most commonly deepest in
the charge, and sometimes above his ability. And in this state he
continued many years, doing the best good he could and walking
according to the light he saw, until the Lord revealed further unto
him. And in the end, by the tyranny of the bishops against godly
preachers and people, in silencing the one and persecuting the other,
he and many more of those times began to look further into particulars, and to see into the unlawfulness of their callings, and the
burden of many anti-christian corruptions, which both he and they
endeavored to cast off, as they also did, as in the beginning of this
treatise is to be seen. After they were joined together into communion (1602), he was a special store and help to them. They
ordinarily met at his house on the Lord's day, which was a manor
of the bishop's, and with great love he entertained them when they
came, making provision for them to his great charge; and continued
so to do whilst they could stay in England. And when they were
to remove out of the country, he was one of the first in·all adventures, and forwardest in any. He was the chief of those that were
taken at Boston, in Lincolnshire (1607), and suffered the greatest
loss; and [one] of the seven that were kept longest in prison, and
after bound over to the assizes.

" After he came into Holland, he suffered much hardship after he
had spent the most of his means, having a great charge and many
children; and, in regard of his former breeding and course of life,
not so fit for many employments as others were, especially such as
were toilsome and laborious. Yet he ever bore his condition with
much cheerfulness and contentment. Towards the latter part of those
twelve years spent in Holland, his outward condition was mended,
and he lived well and plentifully; for he fell into a way, by reason
he had the Latin tongue, to teach many students who had a desire
to learn the English tongue to teach them English, and by this
method they quickly attained it with great facility; for he drew
rules to learn it by, after the Latin manner; and many gentlemen, both Danes and Germans, resorted to him as they had
time from other studies, some of them being great men's sons. He
had also means to set up printing[7] by the help of some friends, and

---

7 The following extracts of letters written by Sir Dudley Carleton to Secretary Naunton,
from the Hague in 1619-20, shows that Mr. Brewster was at this time an object of suspicion and
pursuit, to the English government on account of obnoxious books which he had printed.
" July 22. One William Brewster a Brownist, hath been for some years an inhabitant and

so had employment enough; and by reason of many books which would not be allowed to be printed in England, they might have had more than they could do.

" But now removing into this country, all these things were laid aside again, as a new course of living must be submitted to; in which he was no way unwilling to take his part and to bear his burden with the rest, living many times without bread or corn many months together, having many times nothing but fish, and often wanting that also; and drank nothing but water for many years together, yea until five or six years of his death. And yet he lived by the blessing of God, in health till very old age; and besides that he labored with his hands in the fields as long as he was able. And yet when the church had no other minister, he taught twice every Sabbath, and that both powerfully and profitably, to the great contentment of the hearers, and their comfortable edification. Yea many were brought to God by his ministry. He did more in their behalf in a year, that many that have their hundreds a year do in all their lives.

" For his personal abilities, he was qualified above many. He was wise and discreet and well spoken, having a grave and deliberate utterance; of a very cheerful spirit, very sociable and pleasant among his friends, of an humble and a modest mind, of a peaceable disposition, undervaluing himself and his own abilities, and sometimes overlooking others; inoffensive and innocent in his life and conversation, which gained him the love of those without as well as those within. Yet he would tell them plainly of their faults and evils, both publicly and privately; but in such a manner as usually was well taken from him. He was tender hearted, and compassionate of such as were in misery, but especially of such as had been of good estate and rank, and were fallen into want and poverty, either for

printer at Leyden, but is now within three weeks removed from thence and gone back to dwell in London, where he may be found out and examined, not only of this book, *De Regimine Ecclesiæ Scoticaniæ*, but likewise of *Perth Assembly*, of which if he was not the printer and author; for as I am informed he hath had, whilst he remained here, his hand in all such books as have been sent over into England and Scotland; as particularly a book in folio, entitled a *Confutation of the Rhemists' Translation, Glosses and Annotations of the New Testament*, anno 1618, was printed by him. So was another in 18mo., *De verâ et genuinâ Jesu Christi Domini et Salvatoris nostri Religione*, of which I send your honor herewith the title page likewise, you will find it is the same character; and the one being confessed (as that De verâ et genuinâ Jesu Christi, &c., Religione, Brewster doth openly avow), the other can not well be denied."

" Aug. 20. I have made good inquiry after William Brewster at Leyden, and am well assured that he hath not returned thither; neither is it likely he will, having removed from thence both his family and goods."

Sept. 12. In my last I advertised your honor that Brewster was taken at Leyden; which proved an error, in that the schout, who was employed by the magistrates for his apprehension being a drunken fellow, took one man for another. But Brewer, who sent him on work, and being a man of means bare the charge of his printing letters, which were found in his house in a garrett, where he had hid them, and his books and papers are all seized, and sealed up. I expect tomorrow to receive his voluntary confession of such books as he hath caused to be printed by Brewster for this year and a half or two years past, and then I intend to send one expressly to visit his books and papers, and to examine him particularly touching *Perth Assembly*, the discourse *De Regime Ecclesiæ Scoticanæ*, and other Puritan pamphlets, which I newly discovered."

" Sept. 18. It appears that this Brewer and Brewster, whom this man set on work, having kept no open shop, do printed many books fit for sale in these provinces, their practice was to print prohibited books to be vented underhand in his Majesty's Kingdom."

Jan. 19, 1620. Unless Brewer undertakes to do his utermost in finding out Brewster (wherein I will not fail likewise of all other endeavors) it is not like to be at liberty; the suspicion whereof keeps him from hence, for as yet he appears not in these parts."

From a letter from Robert Cushman, dated London, May 8th, 1619, to " His Loving Friends," it seems that Mr. Brewster was in England at the date of his letter, and the probability is that he did not return to Leyden again but remained secluded till the sailing of the Mayflower.

goodness or religion's sake, or by the injury or oppression of others. He would say, of all men these deserved to be most pitied; and did more offend and displease him, than such as would haughtily and proudly lift up themselves being risen from nothing, and having little else in them but a few fine clothes or a little riches--more than others.

"In teaching, he was stirring, and moving the affections; also very plain and distinct in what he taught; by which means he became the more profitable to the hearers. He had a singular good gift in prayer, both public and private, in the humble confession of sin, and begging the mercies of God in Christ for the pardon thereof. He always thought it better for ministers to pray oftener, and divide their prayers, than to be long and tedious in the same; except upon solemn and special occasions, as on days of humiliation and the like. His reasons was that the heart and spirits of all especially the weak could hardly continue and stand bent (as it were), so long towards God, as they ought to do in that duty, without flagging and falling off.

"For the government of the church, which was most proper to his office, he was careful to preserve good order in the same, and to preserve purity both in the doctrine and communion of the same, and to suppress any error or contention that might begin to arise amongst them; and accordingly God gave good success to his endeavors herein all his days, and he saw the fruit of his labors in that behalf. But I must break off, having thus touched a few heads of things "—*Chronicles of the Pilgrims*, pp. 462 *to* 469

The following respecting Elder Brewster, his ancestry and his early history, we extract from an interesting paper, relative to the Plymouth Puritans, by Joseph Hunter, Esq., Fellow of the Society of Antiquaries, London, to the Massachusetts Historical Society, and published in their collections of 1852.

* * * "But we must now turn our attention to a person who was not a minister, but who, more than any other person, exerted himself to collect into a church the different persons in the neighborhood who were willing to go the length of Separation. He was at that time neither the pastor nor the teacher, though afterwards, when they were settled on the shores of America, he was both, but was content to take upon himself the subordinate office of elder. This was WILLIAM BREWSTER, the most eminent person in the movement, and who, if that honor is to be given to any single person, must be regarded as the Father of New England.

"I cannot find that Brewster has ever been the object of biographical curiosity in England. I know of nothing relating to him, either in printed books or in manuscript collections, but what has been copied from the writings of Bradford or from those who have derived their information from him. Yet, independently of his connection with the movement of which we are speaking, there is enough in the connections which he had formed in this country to make him an object of interest.

* * * "It was in 1587 that Davison's ruin was completed, and it was in 1608 that he was advanced so far ahead of the principles of the Church of England, as professed by those in whom the power of the times was vested, that he was an object of animadversion by them, and formed the determination of escaping from what he deemed their tyranny, and following Smith to Holland, where was then toleration for all forms of Protestant worship.

" Here then we find a person, acquainted with the world, and accustomed to the best society it afforded, not a mere rural esquire, who in a country retirement had contracted a fondness for religious enquiry, and seeking, perhaps notoriety, by peculiarities in his religious profession and practice; but one who, while he had lived in the world, and borne a share in some of its fiercest contentions, had yet been throughout subject to religious influences, first in the university, and afterwards in his connection with Davison, who was noted in the court of Elizabeth for his religious spirit. And we may easily conceive the amount of influence he would obtain in such a region as Bassetlaw, where, it is probable, there were a few laymen like him, and few clergymen who could contend with him in controversies which it was for so many years the business of his life to master; and where not a few of the clergy had come to the same conclusion with himself, even in respect of points which were deemed by the authorities unfit to be meddled with. But the circumstances in which he had retired from the world, must have led him to distrust the authorities of the times; for there can hardly now be a doubt that his master was the sufferer from court chicanery of the most desperate kind, and that it was by this improper use of authority that his own progress in the course of life in which he had originally been set, was so fatally interrupted.

"It is remarkable that Bradford should have left unnamed the place to which Brewster retired. That may, however, now be considered as determined; and I shall proceed to two or three minor points on which some trifling additional information may be given respecting him. And first the date of his birth, which Bradford seem to make the year 1564; but Morton, writing as it seems on some authority derived from Bradford, speaks of him as being eighty-four at the time of his death in 1643.

"This would throw back his birth to 1559, the first year of the reign of Elizabeth, and this seems to be the true date. His baptism could not be found at Scrooby, for the earlier registers are lost; and if they were in existence, it is hardly probable that his baptism would be found in them, as the earliest period at which I have found any Brewsters at Scrooby is 1571, where there is a William Brewster one of three persons who are charged to the Subsidy of that year in the township of Scrooby cum Ranskill.

" This could hardly be he who was afterwards Elder Brewster ; but it might be his father, with whose Christian name we are not acquainted. We have the misfortune not only of having no register of Scrooby parish, but we have no wills of the Brewsters of that place. The other two persons assessed with Brewster were Thomas Wentworth, who called himself in his will an Esquire, and William Dawson. Dawson was assessed on twenty shillings, land, Wentworth on forty shillings, land, Brewster on sixty shillings, goods, as if he had no freehold. This shows that he was a man of good substance, paying to the tax, which was a species of income tax, more than his neighbor, the Esquire.

" The name of Brewster is an old Nottinghamshire name, and the circumstances which brought them to Scrooby can only be a matter of conjecture. It could not be any connection with the family of Sandys, for Sandys did not become Archbishop of York till 1576 ; and in the absence of any more plausible theory, it might be suggested that they were brought into those parts of Nottinghamshire as a consequence of the acquisition of an estate at Sutton upon Lound, the adjoining parish to Scrooby, by one of the Welbecks, who had other large possessions in those parts of Nottinghamshire—the Welbecks being a Suffolk family, in which county there were many Brewsters of the rank to which the Nottinghamshire Brewsters belonged, and there having been a marriage between a Brewster and a Welbeck.

" We do not, however, find in any account of the Brewsters of Suffolk any notice of the settlement of any part of the family in Nottinghamshire. Yet it seems little probable that any other family of the name, beside that in Suffolk, should have sent a son to the university, and then have placed him in so advantageous a position as that of an under-secretary of State, which is usually the first step in political advancement. However, as at present this is only a conjecture, a very brief notice of the Brewsters of Suffolk, who were contemporary with Elder Brewster, may suffice. · Their chief places of residence were Rushmore and Wrentham. Robert of Rushmore married one of the co-heiresses of Christopher Edmonds, of Cressing Temple, in Essex, and had two sons, Henry and James. The latter died without issue ; but Henry, who transferred his residence to Wrentham, had four daughters and two sons, Francis, who succeeded him at Wrentham, and Humphrey, who died at Hadley in 1614. Francis married Elizabeth Snelling, a daughter of Robert Snelling of Whatfield, near Ipswich (of which family of Snelling were the wives of Edmund Calamy and Mathew Newcomen, two of the most eminent Puritan divines of the reign of Charles the First, and both concerned in the *Smectymnuus*), and had Robert of Wrentham, who was a member of Cromwell's Parliament. We see, therefore, that the political leaning of the Suffolk Brewsters would coincide with that of your venerable elder.

" The descent of the Welbecks from Suffolk is shown in *Harl.*

MS. 891; but they were rather possessors of estates in the neighborhood of Scrooby, than residents upon them, the person who acquired dying in early life in 1556, leaving an infant daughter an heir, who became married in the great Yorkshire family of Savill."

* * * " Returning, then, to William Brewster, and his connections and affairs, we may observe that this story of the Bawtry Hospital comes in aid of the fact that the Brewsters were tenants of the family of Sandys, to show that long before there was any thought of calling in the aid of any member of that family in the project of settling a colony on the American shores, there had been a friendly correspondence between the Brewsters and Sandyses, who may justly be considered as persons at this time of near equality of position. Sir Edwin Sandys could not but, even in the times before Brewster left England, have observed the course which a gentleman, whom no doubt he esteemed, was taking, and if we may rely upon certain passages in his *Europæ Speculum*, written by him at Paris in 1599, he must then have been to a considerable extent like minded with Brewster. There was another link between them ; for Cranmer, who had been with Brewster in the service of Davison, accompanied Sir Edwin Sandys in his continental tour, undertaken for the purpose of observing the state of religion in the different countries of Europe, of which the *Speculum* exhibits the result. Whether Brewster out ran Sandys, or Sandys out ran Brewster, there seems to have been a friendly race between them for a time, though ultimately Brewster's was the more decided conduct. Even the old archbishop was not himself averse to further changes in the church in the way of reformation.[8]

* * * " Let us consider how this bears on the question at what time he became one of the officers of Brewster's church. He was at Mundham in 1603, and after this was for some time at Norwich ; so that we may assign with much probability the beginning of his connection with the church to the year 1666 or 1667. Perhaps even the formation of the church in the regular order may have risen out of the opportunity of securing his services.

"Of the persons who composed Brewster's church without holding office in it, we may mention in the first place, two persons, whose names only are known, and the fact that, when active efforts were being made to put down the church, they were singled out together with Brewster as objects of attack. Their names were RICHARD JACKSON and ROBERT ROCHESTER, and they appear to have resided at the village of Scrooby itself. We get their names from the certificate of Tobias, Archbishop of York, dated November 13, 1608, to the Treasurer and Barons of the Exchequer of fines unpaid which had been imposed by the commissioners for causes ecclesiastical in the Province of York. 'Richard Jackson, William Brewster, and Robert Rochester of Scrooby, in the county of Nottingham, Brownists or Separatists, for a fine or amercement of £20

---

8 As may be seen in his will. See *Collins' Supplement to his Peerage*, 1750, vol. II, p. 582.

a piece, set and imposed upon every of them by Robert Abbott and Robert Snowden, Doctors of Divinity, and Matthew Dodsworth, Bachelor of Law, Commissioners for Causes Ecclesiastical within the Province of York, for not appearing before them upon lawful summons, at the Collegiate Church of Southwell, the 22d day of April, anno Domini, 1608—£60.' I have seen no account of any proceedings of the officers of Exchequer to recover this money. The parties were probably out of the jurisdiction of the court." * *

COATS OF ARMS of the Brewster Families mentioned by Mr. Hunter:

"BREWSTER (Withfield, co. Essex). *Az. chev. erm. between three etoiles ar. Crest*—A demi lion, holding in his dexter paw a club over his shoulder.

BREWSTER (Suffolk). *Sa. a chev. erm. between etoiles ar. Crest*— *A bear's head erased az.—Burke's Heraldry, London*, 1847.

WELBECK ARMS—"WELBECK ABBEY (Nottinghamshire). *Gu. three lozenges conjoined in fesse az. each charged with a rose of the first."—Ibid.*

" Elder Brewster's estate (says Mr. Winsor), occupied the south eastern part of the nook adjoining the farm of Capt. Standish. Some years ago, on a piece of land which was originally included in the limits of his farm, was found a small silver spoon bearing the initials ' J. B.' Elder Brewster it is said traditionally, planted the first apple tree in New England. In the time of the revolution the original tree was gone ; but there had sprung up from its roots another, which was then of large size, and known as the ' Brewster tree.' "

Elder Brewster was buried at Duxbury, at what particular spot is not known.

His eldest sons, Love and Jonathan, it appears from the following, were his administrators :

1644 LRES, of adminiftracon of all goods and Cattells of Mr Willm Brew-
5 June fter, deceafed are graunted by the Court to Jonathan Brewfter and Loue
Winflowe Brewfter, and a true inventory thereof was exhibited to the court vpon
Gounor. the oathes of faid Jonathan and Loue.—*Plymouth Col. Rec.*, II, p. 73.

The following is a copy of the Inventory of Elder Brewster's property, as rendered by his sons Jonathan and Love (adm'rs) to the court :

Wearing apparell, household utensils, &c., appraised by Capt. Standish and Jone Done, May 10th, 1644. - - - -	28. 8.10
Articles at his house in Duxbury, by Standish and Prence, May 18th. - - - - - - - - - -	107. 0. 8
His Latin Books by Mr. Bradford, Mr. Prence, and Mr. Reyner, May 18 ; sixty-three volumes, - - - - - -	15.19. 4
His English Books by Mr. Bradford and Mr. Prence ; between three and four hundred volumes, - - - - - -	27. 0. 7
Latin and English Books, - - - - - 42.19.11	
Total sum of goods - - - - - -	150. 0. 7

—*N. E. Reg.*

" Elder Brewster left a considerable library, many volumes of which were in the learned languages. He had eight children, two of whom were born in America. His two oldest daughters did not arrive until 1623. The first married Isaac Allerton, one of the most distinguished among the pilgrims. The last married Gov. Prince (Prence). His other daughters bore the names of Lucretia and Mary. His sons were Love, Wrestling, Jonathan and William. " Wrestling and William died before their father."—*Memoir of Plymouth Colony*.

Jonathan Brewster, son of Elder William, arrived in the ship Fortune, 1621; was frequently deputy from the town of Duxbury to the General Court, and he appears, from the Colonial records, to have been a man of marked influence both in the formation of the colony and the church. He practiced before the court as an attorney, and was also styled a " gentleman."

History of Duxbury says that he sold his house to Dr. Comfort Starr in 1638. He went to New London, Conn., and from that place he seems to have returned to England, in 1656, or contemplated so doing, judging from the following letter, addressed to the widow of his brother Love, which we give here, as it relates to the death of one in the line of ancestry :

" Loveing and kind Sister :
" I thanke you for Youer letter I received, being glad to heare of youer well doeing in youer widdowhood ; the Lord will make up youer losses and healp you to bee thankfull for raiseing youer good brother to bee insteaa of an husband to you. In my judgement I would advise to marry one whom you could love. I would to God I was nearer you, I should doe something for you ; but I fear I shall thee next year go further from you, for I with my whole family resolve for old England, and then I shall bee able to do a little for you and youers, whom I love and respect being glad to hear of your daughters improvement, both in spirituall and temporall thinges ; the Lord bestow his further blessing upon her and the rest of youers ; I doe heerby this give unto her all my interest in the pcells of Land, which was left by my father, lying near Plymouth, to her and her heires for ever. I pray you remember my love and Respects to the Capt. and his wife and children with the rest of my friends with you, to whom I cannot write; excuse me to them all ; those with my best love remember to you and youers ; I pray to the Lord to blesse you and keep you in all youer ways in his feare. Amen, and doe rest.
" Mooheeken, this 1 of   Your unfeigned brother,
September, 1656.   JONATHAN BREWSTER.

Love Brewster (son of Elder B.), married Sarah Collier, daughter of William Collier, "who was eminently (says Mr. Winsor) distinguished in the affairs of the colony. He (Mr. Collier) was one of the merchant adventurers in England, a wealthy merchant, and quite early came to Plymouth and soon removed to Duxbury, and settled in the south-eastern part, near Standish and Brewster. He also had land west of North Hill (granted 1635), and a tract called Billingsgate. He was an enterprising man, and engaged much in business, and during most of his life employed in the government of the colony, as assistant and otherwise. In 1658, "the court ordered a servant to him, because he can not easily come to business." Mr. Collier was appointed with Gov. Winslow, commissioner to treat on the subject as will be seen by the following colonial record, taken from *History of Duxbury:*

"1642. This year, the Indians under Miantinsomo, of the Narraganset tribe, meditated the extirpation of the English; but their plot was discovered, and the court ordered and agreed to "pᵉ vide forces against them for an offensive and defensive warr;" and the following were appointed on the part of Duxbury a committee for raising the forces: Capt. Standish, Mr. Alden, *Jnoa Brewster*, Mr. C. Starr, Mr. William Witherell, William Bassett, C. Wadsworth and George Soule. The court afterwards considered it proper to make further preparations for defence, and a committee consisting of *Mr. Collier*, Mr. Winslow, Mr. Hatherly and Capt. Standish, were sent to Massachusetts Bay, to conclude on a junction with them in their present state of affairs, and of this number *Winslow* and *Collier* were afterwards authorized to subscribe the articles of confederation. This union was fully consummated and concluded, and the articles signed at Boston, May 19, 1643, Connecticut and New Hampshire being also included in the compact; and this era of the confederate union of the colonies, may be properly looked upon as the grand epoch, when the present American republic first appeared in embryo."

Of the forces raised, Capt. *Standish* was appointed the commander; William Palmer the lieutenant; Peregrine White the "ancient bearer;" and Mr. Prence was joined to them as counsellor. Of every £25 expense of the war, the proportion of Duxbury was to be £3.10s. And the following were constituted a *council of war:* the governor, Mr. Winslow, Mr. Prence, *Mr. Collier*, Mr. Hatherly, Mr. John Brown, Mr. William Thomas, Mr. Edmund Freeman, Mr. William Vassel, Capt. Standish, Mr. Thomas Dimmack, Mr. Anthony Thacher. A sale of moose skins was then ordered to furnish means for procuring powder and lead; and then they passed the following order: "The first Tewsday in July the maᵗʳᵃᵗˢ meete and eich Towne are to send such men as they shall think fit to joyne wᵗʰ them in consult about a course to saveguard ourselves from surprisall by an enemie."

1634		⎧ Jobe Cole and Rebecka Collier ⎫	
New Plymouth	May 15, 1634. ⎨	⎬ were married.
Prince Gounor		⎩ Loue Brewſter & Sarah Collier ⎭	
15 May			—*Plym. Rec.*, I, 30.

Loue Brewster early moved from Plymouth to Duxbury, and settled with his father by the bayside.

1669	In anſware vnto the petition of William Brewſter and Wraſtling Brew-
5 July	ſter (two grandchildren of the Reverend Mʳ William Brewſter, deceaſed)
Prence	requeſting accomodations of Lands, the Court haue granted that in caſe
Gounor	they, the ſaid William and Wraſtling Brewſter, ſhall ſee cauſe to goe to

73

liue att Swanſey, that they be accomodated with lands there, as beirg ſuch as are comended vnto them by the goument for that end, as aboue expreſſed.—*Plymouth Col. Rec.*, v, 24.

GENEALOGICAL RECORD OF THE BREWSTERS.

Elder WILLIAM BREWSTER,[9] b. 1559–60; m: Mary ——; she d. ʃ 1627; had I *Patience*, b. in England; arrived in America, 1623; m. Thomas Prence,[10] governor of the colony of New ·Plymouth; she d. 1634; he d. 1673; II *Fear*, b. in England, arrived in America, 1623; m. Mr. Isaac Allerton, in 1626; d. in 1633; had Isaac; III *Love*, b. in England; IV *Wrestling*, b. in England; d. before his father, unm.; V *Jonathan*; VI *Lucretia*; VII *Mary.*

LOVE (son of Elder William), Plymouth; b. probably in Holland, possibly in England; he settled in Bridgewater, Mass., 1645; was óne of the original prop.; his will is dated Oct. 1, 1650; m. Sarah Collier, May 15, 1634, and .had issue I *Nathaniel;* owned land·about the old Tarpits, and d. 1676; II *William;* III *Wrestling;* IV *Sarah;* m. ·Benjamin Bartlett, 1656; his widow m. a (John?) Parks.—(*Col. Rec.* VI, 1679.)

JONATHAN (son of Elder William)[11] m. *Lucretia* ——, and had I *William*, b. in Holland, was in the Indian wars in 1645; II *Mary*, b. probably in Holland, m. John Turner, of Scituate, Nov. 12, 1645; III *Jonathan*, 1627; IV *Benjamin*, who removed from Duxbury after 1648, to Norwich, then to New London, where he m. Ann Dart, 1659, and had Ann, September, 1662; Jonathan, 1664; Daniel, 1667; William, 1669; and Benjamin, 1673; Grace m. Aug. 4, 1659, Daniel Wetherill; Ruth m. John Pickett, and 2d Charles Hill, and d. April 30, 1677; Hannah (and perhaps Elizabeth); m. 1654, Peter Bradley.

9 WILLIAM (Brewster), the famous Elder, claims of liberal Christians everlasting gratitude, as the earliest of distinguished Puritan Laymen in Eng., came, &c., with his two younger s. the w. of the eldest, and he s. Wm. He was b. 1563 (prob., but earlier by some computations). at Scrooby, in Nottinghamshire at the Manor Hall of wh. village belonged to the archbp. of York; He afterwards long resided at the same house at wh. Cardinal Wolsey had made his last stop, before reaching home to his final journey, on compulsory retirement from Court, after banishment by Henry VIII, thirty years earlier. His family, probably William, was tenant under liberal lease from Archbishop Sandys, and the s. was educated sometime at Cambridge, and his family became a sub-tenant of Scrooby manor, the possessor of that very residence of the Cardinal, and the s. therein worshipd. * * * * He was in the employment of the crown, however, as postmaster, before April, 1594, above a dozen years before leaving London; then he married the wife Mary.—*Dr. Savage's Gen. Dict.*

10 "The 9th marriage of New Plimouth is Mr. Thos. Prince, with Mrs. Patience Brewster (bg)." —*New Eng. Chronology, Boston*, 1736.

11 Dr. Savage says he was the oldest son and b. at Scrooby, co. Notts, on the road to Doncaster, in Yorkshire, from 12 to 13 miles distant; had been instructed only by his glorious father, either in his native land or the doz. yrs. resid. in Holland, where he was left by the Elder to take care of two sisters, with his own family; he came in 1621 in the Fortune without his sisters; in June 1636, was in command of the Plymouth trading house on Conn. river, and gave notice to John Winthrop, Gov. of the fort at Saybrook, in a letter in my (Dr. S.) possession of 18 June of the evil designs of the Pequots; rem. to Dux. of wh he was rep. 1639—the earliest Assembly of Deputies in that Col., thence to New London bef. 1649; there was selectman; d. bef. Sep. 1659; having in Sep. 1656 projected ret. to Eng. with his family.—*Dr. Savage.*

APPENDIX. 569

Dea. WILLIAM (son of Love, son of Elder Willlam), d. Nov. 3, 1723, æ. nearly 78, having served in the office of deacon for many years; * * * a worthy man, who was often employed to good advantage in the civil affairs of the town; he m. Lydia Patridge,[12] Jan. 2, 1672 (3?); she d. Feb. 2, 1732; had *Sarah*, April 25, 1674; m. Caleb Stetson, 1705; *Nathaniel*, Nov. 8, 1676; *Joseph*, March 17, 1694; *William*, and according to Mitchel, a *Benjamin*.

WRESTLING (son of Love, son of Elder William), Dux., a carpenter; d. Jan. 1, 1667, leaving an estate of £330, "13 Dec., 1689, the town did engage to Wrestling Brewster that if he in curtesy did take Nathaniel Cole into his house, they would secure him from.burthened with keeping of him said Cole."— *Town Records*. He m. Mary, who is probably the Mary who m. John Partridge, 1700; he had Jonathan, m. Mary Partridge, May 6, 1710; went to Windham, Ct., after 1728; she was alive 1733; Wrestling, probably the one of Plymouth, who m. July 12, 1722, Hannah Thomas; a deacon of K.; had Wrestling, 1724; m. at K., Feb. 8, 1810, æ. 86; *Thomas, Isaac, Elisha, John, Mary, Sarah, Abigail, Elizabeth* and *Hannah*.

NATHANIEL (son of Dea. William, son of Love, son of Elder William), Dux.; m. Mary Dewelley, of Scituate, Dec. 24, 1705, who d. July 29, 1764, æ. 80; had *Samuel* and *Mercy* (twins), April 5, 1708; *Ruth*, Dec. 9, 1711; m. Joseph Morgan, of Preston, Ct., May 8, 1735; *William*, b. Feb. 14, 1747, and had *Daniel*, ab. 1746; *Nathaniel*, ab. 1748; and *Stephen*, ab. 1750; *Joseph*, b. July 3, 1718.

JOSEPH (son of Dea. William, son of Love, son of Elder William), Dux.; m. Elizabeth, who d. April, 1786, æ. 82; he d. April 26, 1766; had Lemuel, bap. 1740; Eunice, m. Timothy Walker, 1758; Truelove, 1737. "January 18, 1757, Truelove Brewster fell through the ice, attempting to come over Oakman's ferry, and was drowned."—*Church Rec.*

WILLIAM (son of Dea. William, son of Love, son of Elder William), Dux.; m. Hopestill Wadsworth,[13] May 20, 1708; had *Olive; Ichabod*, Jan. 15, 1711; m. Lydia Brewster, of Pembroke, June 3, 1735; Capt. *Elisha*, Oct. 29, 1715; *Seth*, Dec. 20, 1720; *Lot*, March 25, 1724; *Huldah*, Feb. 20, 1726; m. John Goold of Hull (for genealogy of this family, see *Hist. Dict.*, etc.), June 13, 1745; she d. April 27, 1750.

12 "PARTRIDGE, George (Duxbury), Yeoman, 1636; married Sarah Tracy, Nov. 1638, died about 1695; had *John*, Nov. 29, 1657; *Lydia*, m. Dea Wm. Brewster, 1672, and died Feb. 3, 1743; *Ruth*, m. Rodolphus Thacher, Jan. 1, 1669; *Treiphosa*, m. Samuel West, Sept. 2b, 1668; *Mercy; Sarah*, 1639, m. Dea. samuel Allen of Bridgew.; *James*; * * *.
George Partridge. His name is spelled Partrich, Partick, and Patrick. He was one of the most respectable yeomanry of the Colony, and came from the county of Kent, England, about 1636, where he was possessed of an estate which he mentions in his will. * * * His will witnessed by Alexander and Josiah Standish is dated June 26, 1682. * * * His descendants have not been numerous."—*Hist. of Duxbury*.

JOHN, son of Wrestling, son of Love, son of Elder William), Dux.; had Joseph and Job, who served in the old French war.

Family of Capt. Elisha.

Capt. ELISHA (son of William, son of Dea. William, son of Love, son of Elder William), b. Oct. 29, 1715; m. Miss Fosdick of New Hampshire; had I *Lucy*, b. ——; m. Willis, a relative of Gen. Willis of Charter Oak place, Hartford, Ct.; II *Lucretia*, b. ——; m. Dr. Elihu Tudor,[14] and had issue; III *Sarah*, b. 1755.; m. Dea. Oliver Wetmore of Middleton, Ct. (for their descendants see under head of Dea. Oliver, son of Judge Seth Wetmore, p. 334); IV *Hopestill*, b. 1760; m. Capt. Hardy of the Revolution; was killed in an engagement at Lex.; he left a dau.; b. 1788; she m. 2d —— Morrison; had John, b. in N. Y. city, March 20, 1790; m. Nov. 7, 1813, Betsey Palmer of Hebron, Ct.; had Charles F. and Maria L. (twins), b. Aug. 13, 1815; Edward, b. June 1, 1818; Albert, b. March 13, 1820; Clarissa E., b. Feb. 28, 1822; John H., b. Feb. 21, 1821; Catharine, b. Feb. 3, 1828; Catharine, b. Dec. 15, 1830; Frederick and Fanny (twins), b. May, 22, 1831. Mr. John Morrison resides at Willimantic, Conn. (Mansfield Cen. P. O.).

13 Hopestill Wadsworth was a daughter of John, son of Christopher Wadsworth, the first of the Wadsworths at Duxbury, Mass., his will is dated July 31, 1667. Justin Winsor in *History of Duxbury* says! "It is not known whence they came. The family of Wadsworth is a Yorkshire family of some antiquity." Burke's *Heraldry* gives their arms. "Wadsworth (Yorkshire) Gu. three fleur de lis stalked and slipped ar. "Wadsworth same *arms*. *Crest*—On a Globe of the world, winged ppr, an eagle rising or."

14 Dr. Tudor, son of Rev. Samuel, and great grandson of Owen Tudor, a first settler of Windsor, was born in that town February 3d, 1732. Graduated from Yale College, where he was esteemed an excellent Greek scholar, in 1750. and studied under the then famous Dr. Benjamin Gale of Killingworth. He entered the army during the French war—probably in August, 1759 —as surgeon's mate, with the rank of a 2d lieutenant.—Barber's *Hist.* Coll.

In this capacity he served with General Wolfe in Canada, and at the capture of Havana. From 1762 to 1764 he seems to have lived in London, engaged in the hospitals and the active pursuit of his professional studies. Returning then to his native land, with a mind richly stored by research and observation, he established himself in practice at East Windsor. His first introduction to surgical practice, we have been told, was on the occasion of the accidental blowing up of the Hartford school house on the 8th of June 1766, on the day of rejoicing for the repeal of the Stamp Act. The skill displayed by him in treating the sufferers by this deplorable accident gave him an excellent start. In the following year we find in the *Connecticut Courant*, under date of June 15, 1767, the following advertisement:

Dr. Tudor, lately from London, begs leave to acquaint the public that he sets out on the 22d instant to visit the Mineral Springs at Stafford, in Connecticut, where he will be ready to give his Advice to those that choose to consult him in drinking the Waters.

Upon the breaking out of the revolutionary war, Doctor Tudor was a pensioner of the British government. It is said that the British government, thinking that the doctor was stretching out his life to an unconscionable length, actually sent an agent over to see "whether the old cuss was really alive" It is a remarkable fact that very many of the pensioners of England lived to such an advanced age as to induce suspicion on the part of the Home government that there was some trickery in the matter. His popularity, however, visibly declined, and his practice, which was favorable to the loyalist cause, and fell under the suspicion of his neighbors at East Windsor. Indeed a party once attempted "to ride him on a rail," but the cool determination of the doctor completely overawed them, and he met with no further annoyance. His popularity, however, visibly declined, and his practice, which was chiefly surgical, was, in his latter days, not very extensive.

His reputation as a surgeon was, at one time, equal, if not superior, to any in New England. In person he was of medium height, and upright form, near sighted, always very neat in his dress, wearing ruffles, fine silver buckles, and a nosegay in his button hole. He died in 1826 at the advanced age of 93.

Previous to his death, in 1790, he received from Dartmouth College the degree of Doctor of Medicine, which in that day was a compliment and honor which can scarcely be appreciated in these days of indiscriminate diploma-giving. He was one of the founders and second vice-president of the Connecticut Medical Society.

In his commission as surgeon's mate in the 43d Regt. of Foot, dated in September, 1763, his name was by some mistake written *Edward Tudor*. As he had always disliked his name of Elihu, he always afterward wrote and drew his pension under the name of *Edward.*—*App. to Dr. Stiles' His. of Windsor.*

Mrs. Hopestill Morrison resided at Geneva, N. Y. V *Lydia*, b. ——; m. Peter Van Deusen of Albany. VI *Ruby*, b. ——; m. William Kippen of Bridgeport, Ct. VII *Elisha*, b. ——; m. Margaret Curtiss of Wethersfield, Ct.; had 1 Betsey, b. Feb., 1781; 2 William, b. June, 1783; m. ——; had William, Oliver, Elisha, and 5 daus.; 3 Sally, b. June, 1787; 4 Dea. Elisha C., b. Feb. 8, 1791; m. ——; had Noah L., and 3 daus. Dea. Elisha C., in a letter to us, in speaking of his and his brother and sister's families, says: "I believe all hopefully pious, inheriting as we trust something of the spirit professed by our venerated ancestor of the Mayflower." Dea. Elisha C. Brewster resides at Bristol, Ct. VIII *William*, b. ——; d. in Philadelphia, 1832, of the cholera; he was owner and master of vessels, and was at one time a man of considerable wealth. He lost a vessel and cargo by pirates; he married and had a daughter, who, though eccentric, was a lady of considerable talent, author of many poetical pieces, as well as works of romance. She removed to Cincinnati, where she died. IX *Lott*, b. ——.

Capt. Elisha Brewster, Sen., married a second time, a Boston lady, said to have been a very handsome woman, graceful and elegant in her person, and a woman of superior education and intellect. He was engaged in commerce.

JOSEPH (son of Nathaniel, son of Dea. William, son of Love, son of Elder William), Dux. and Attleboro; m. Jedidah ——, who d. March 26, 1794; æ. 72; he d. Sept. 3, 1791; æ. 73; had Zadock, baptized, 1742; had Cyrus, Dec. 7, 1772; m. Ruth Sampson, April 5, 1798, and who had Zadock, Darius and Sarah; Mary m. Silas Freeman, 1763; Joseph, m. Deborah Hunt, April 13, 1773; Ruth; Nathaniel, baptized 1755; Truelove, baptized, 1760.

NATHAN (son of ——), Dux., b. 1723; m. Hannah, who d. June 4, 1776; he d. Nov. 1807; æ. 84; had Anne, baptized, 1756.

JOSHUA (son of ——), Dux.; m. Lydia Weston, who d. Oct. 22, 1841; had Daniel W., 1788; Job E., 1799; Sarah C., 1801; Warren W., Priscilla, Harriet.

JOSHUA (son of ——), Dux.; had Deborah, 1787; Rachel, 1790; Sarah, 1792; Nathan, 1796; Hannah, 1798; Joshua, 1801; Ruth, 1803.—*Duxbury History*.

NOTES.

"Mr. Benjamin Brewster was grandson of Elder William Brewster of Mayflower memory. Jonathan the third son of the Elders removed to New London, where 1649, he was acting as one of the townsmen. His son Benjamin was old enough to convey a tract of land by deed in 1654, and 1659 was married at New London to Anna Dart. He removed to Norwich very soon after the settlement. The birth of his daughter Ann is recorded there September, 1662, his sons were Jonathan, 1664; Daniel, 1667; William, born 1669; Benjamin, 1673. Mr. Brewster was an active and highly respected member of the infant plantation. In 1693 he succeeded Mr. Burchard as commissioner of the peace. His descendants are still to be found in Norwich and vicinity, In 1779 there were eleven families of the name in "East Society."

The venerable Mr. Seabury Brewster, now living in Norwich city, and one of the Patriarchs of the place, is not, however, descended from *Benjamin* but from *Wrestling*, the second son of Elder Brewster. He was born at Plymouth in 1755, and emigrated to Norwich when about 22 years of age. He is the father of Sir Christopher Brewster, an eminent dentist who has resided a number of years in Paris and St. Petersburgh, and has been knighted by the Emperor of Russia.—*Hist. of Norwich* by Miss F. M. Caulkins.

Capt. Brewster (son of ——), was captain of 8th company 20th Regiment Connecticut Militia, commanded by Maj. Rogers.

Saw Pitts, Nov. 1, 1776, weekly returns. Ebenezer Brewster was appointed captain in May, Gen. Wooster Division, no date.

A letter from Samuel Brewster, Esquire, chairman of the committee of New Windsor, covering an affidavit relating to one *Conner* and Montgomery, was read. The said letter and affidavit set forth sundry matters which rendered it very probable that certain quantities of butter and flour purchased by the said Conner and Montgomery, were purchased with the intent to supply the enemy.

Ordered, That the said papers be referred to a committee, say the committee for detecting conspiracies.

Elisha Brewster, Assistant Commissioner, Dec. 17, 1776.

Henry Brewster, Jr., Lieut., Dec. 1776.

Capt. Jonathan Brewster, ordered to take charge of prisoners by the Connecticut Council of Safety, Nov. 15, 1776.

Capt. Jnoa Brewster, list of officers and men, 27th August, 1776.—*U. S. Archives,* 5th Series, vol. iii. 1776.

Joshua, 1698, d. March 27, 1776, æ. 78; Rachel, 1727, d. April 26, 1757; Deborah, 1704, d. Sept. 1, 1769, æ. 65; Mary m. Edward Arnold, 1706; Sarah, m. Joseph Wright of Plympton; Jane, m. Asa Weston, 1777; Elizabeth, m. Samuel Walker, 1784; Nathan, m. Diadema Dawes, 1784; Joseph, drowned while returning from the Gurnet, 1807. Yong Joseph Brewster bore arms in Dux. 1643.—*Dux. History.*

John Alden of Dux.; married a Brewster, April 14, 1713.

Joseph (son of ——), Dux.; married Almine Baker about 1800.

Nathan (son of ——), Dux.; married Julia Norris, daughter of Samuel Loring, seventh in descent from Dea. Thomas Loring from Aixminster, Devonshire, Eng., 1635.

Leonice Soule, a descendant of John Soule of Dux.; 1620, married a Mr. Brewster of Dux.; Simeon Soule married Acenith Brewster, who was born March 8, 1778; he died Dec. 21, 1831.

The name of Sole, Soal, Soul, and Soule is an ancient English name.—*Dux. History.*

F.

HON. JOHN TREADWELL, LL. D.[1]

" It has long been supposed that military achievements, or literary eminence or romantic adventures furnish the only suitable themes for biography. The experiment of several popular writers has proved that simple *goodness*, when its portraiture is faithfully drawn, possesses inherent charms, which even in the creation of fiction, fasten to the heart of the reader the more in proportion as its lineaments are more distinctly preserved. If, then, the picture of goodness, even in its simplest forms, is naturally so pleasing to the eye, much more do we love to view it when it is radiant with all the nobler virtues which illustrate and adorn a public life of unsullied integrity, pure patriotism, fervent piety, and' enlarged usefulness. Such a life was that of the late Governor TREADWELL.

" He was the last of' the Puritan governors of Connecticut; the last example afforded by their annals of the Union, in the person of the chief magistrate, of the statesman and the theologian. His exclusion from office, after many years of tried and faithful services to the state, constituted the first departure from the line of ' steady habits' of Connecticut, and was the commencement of a new order of things, retaining but few characteristics of the ancient connection between church and state.

" His history, therefore, involves that of the last days of the Puritan dynasty, and of a revolution which although bloodless, and for the most part peaceful, produced a change in the political aspect of the commonwealth as marked and real, as those which overturn the most powerful empires. His history, moreover, is intimately connected with the rise of those great efforts, which have been institu‑ted, and are now in progress, for the propagation of the gospel, and the conversion of the world; and to him, more perhaps than to any other individual, Connecticut owes the possession of such an ample fund for the support of her primary schools. Let us then take' a concise review of the life and character of this venerable and excellent man.

" JOHN TREADWELL was born at Farmington, Connecticut, Nov. 23d (o. s.), 1745. His father was a mechanic by profession, of a

---

[1]. *Memoir of John Treadwell, LL. D., late Governor of Connecticut,* by Prof. Olmsted, of Yale College.

competent fortune, and a standing among the most respectable yeomanry of the town. Both parents were pious, and both lived to an advanced age, and after serene and useful lives, died in peace and in the faith of the Gospel. Young Treadwell received the rudiments of an English education at the common village school; but when about sixteen years of age, his father gave him the offer of a liberal education, with one week to deliberate on the choice. At the end of the prescribed time, he accepted the offer and entered immediately upon the preparatory studies, under the instruction of the minister of the place, the Rev. Timothy Pitkin. From the earliest settlement of the country to a recent period, it was the practice of the clergy to prepare for college the youth of their respective parishes, who received a liberal education.

* * * * "The Rev. Mr. Pitkin was among the number of those clergymen who gained an intimate knowledge of such Latin and Greek authors as were required for entering college. Indeed, it is believed that he went much further; for most of the Latin poets seemed quite familiar to him at the age of eighty and upwards. * * * * * * * *

"The account which Mr. Pitkin gave of the earliest studies of young Treadwell, coincided with that which the latter gave of himself, namely: that his progress was at first slow and discouraging, but that, through dint of perseverance, they grew more and more easy, and at last delightful. After a few months close application, he read before his father and the family a chapter in the Greek testament, and not rendering it precisely in the words of the common translation, his father expressed much dissatisfaction, and told him he grew worse and worse in reading the English language the more he studied Latin and Greek; but when his son informed him that he read from the Greek Testament, he was delighted to find him already so skilled in the original Scriptures. At the close of fifteen months, his preceptor pronounced him fitted for the freshman class of Yale College, and at the ensuing commencement, in 1763, he was approved and admitted accordingly, being then in the eighteenth year of his age.

* * * "The class of which Treadwell was a member is distinguished in the annals of the college for the large proportion of eminent alumni which it produced; among whom, besides Gov. Treadwell, were Judge Trumbull, author of MacFingal, Doctor Wales, professor of divinity in Yale College, Doctor Joseph Lyman, of Hatfield, and the celebrated Dr. Emmons. With these distinguished men Gov. Treadwell maintained a friendly and intimate relation during their lives. * * * * *

"In his college studies, Mr. Treadwell was patient, persevering and thorough, but unambitious of distinction, and rather solid than brilliant. Locke *On the Human Understanding* and Edwards *On the Will* were then studied classically. To these profound works he applied his mind with ardor and avidity, being exactly suited to his taste; and they gave a permanent complexion to his mode of thinking and reasoning on the faculties and operations of the mind.

"Mr. Treadwell considered his advantages for religious instruction and improvement as far more valuable than those for pursuits merely scientific, in the same proportion as the objects of religion are superior to those of science. He highly prized the truly apostolic teachings, counsels and exhortations of President Clapp, and systematic and discriminating sermons of Professor Daggett. These solemn religious seasons he constantly attended, and in view of the great things of *God*, he was often if not habitually impressed; but having imbibed the sentiments of President Edwards, on the terms of church communion, and doubting with respect to his qualifications, he neglected to make a profession of religion while he was a member of college. At the public commencement in 1767, he was admitted to the degree of bachelor of arts, and returned, to his father's house.[2]

"On leaving college, Mr. Treadwell, finding himself presumptive heir of a considerable patrimony, and his father advanced in life and needing his society and aid, relinquished all views of a professional life, for which he supposed himself not well qualified by nature, having few of the gifts of oratory, and being diffident of his powers of acting to advantage as a public speaker. Still he read law with an eminent jurist (Judge Hosmer, of Middletown), who pronounced him qualified for the practice; but having it in view to enable himself the better to act the part of a useful citizen, he gave up all thoughts of professional life, and took up his abode with his father, laboring on the farm in the summer and keeping school in the winter." *   *   *   *   *   *   *

Prof. Olmsted here enlarges upon the character of Gov. Treadwell as a *scholar*, which we regret we have not the room to give in full.

"Having at his disposal an income sufficient for a moderate support, he turned his thoughts towards the family state, and contracted an alliance with Miss Dorothy Pomeroy, a young lady of Northampton, of good family and high personal accomplishments, and not the less precious in his eyes, for having when young, listened to the preaching of the great President Edwards. Feeling now the necessity of some fixed and productive employment, and encouraged by the success in trade experienced by several merchants of his native town, he resorted to the same employment. But through want of experience and probable want of a natural tact for such business, his adventure was unsuccessful, and he came near sacrificing in this experiment a large part or the whole of his fortune. By a happy expedient in the manufacture of nitre, then in great demand for the use of the army, near the commencement of the revolutionary war, he extricated himself from his pecuniary liabili-

2 *Autobiography.*

ties, but gave up all thoughts of further prosecuting the business
of a merchant.

"On the birth and early death of his first child, an event which
produced a remarkable impression upon his character, we find in his
autobiography the following account: On the 28th of November,
1771, he[3] was presented with a daughter, who, to the fond partiality
of the parents, appeared to be uncommonly forward and engaging.
Her health was perfect until she was about two years and three
months old, when she was seized with a fever which proved incura-
ble. She languished under extreme distress for twenty days and
then expired. The anxiety of and grief of the parents, witnessing
the fatal progress of the malady, can be better conceived than expressed. The father, especially, was deeply sensible that the hand
of God was upon him. He had neglected to dedicate himself and
his dear offspring to God in the bonds of the gospel covenant. He
knew that his child inherited from him a sinful nature, a child of
wrath; that if it was saved it must be as a sinner through the
atonement of Christ, and sanctification of the spirit; that although
God is sovereign, and might, through the all sufficient atonement of
Christ, save all infants, and indeed all men without the intervention
of means, if he were pleased so to do, yet he was not bound in
justice to do it, nor was it certain that any were saved without the
use of means, either employed by themselves personally, or if incapable of this, by their constituted representatives. He was persuaded that the infant children of believers are proper subjects of
baptism; that when dedicated to God in that ordinance, the dedica-
tion would be the answer of a good conscience in the parent, and also
a mean of salvation to the offspring, which God might bless for
that purpose, and hopefully would, especially if taken away in infancy; and to neglect this mean of salvation, was in the parent the
worst of cruelty. In this extremity he could do nothing more, and
certainly nothing less, than in an act of solemn worship with his
wife by themselves, dedicate himself and his dying child to God
through Christ, committing it, so far as he was able, into his hands,
and fervently begging for its sanctification and eternal salvation;
and that his sinful neglect might not be imputed to him, or issue in
the eternal loss of his dear offspring. His peace of mind was, in a
good measure, restored, and the child soon after died; and the
parents hope in God that it has gone to rest. The result of this
trying scene was so thorough a conviction of his duty, that soon
after, although with a trembling heart, he made a public profession
of his faith in Christ, and joined the church then under the care of
the Rev. Timothy Pitkin."

About this time the scenes of the American revolution were
opening. He was inspired with a high sense of the value of civil
liberty, and accordingly exercised all his energies in the "grand

3 Gov. Treadwell in his *Autobiography*, speaks of himself in the third person.

and glorious struggle for freedom," among his neighbors and towns-people, as the records of his native town—Farmington—bear evidence. The part he took then introduced him to political life, and "opened to him unexpectedly a career of civil offices (says Prof. O.) more numerous, and in the aggregate perhaps more important, than were ever held by any individual in the state of Connecticut."

In his autobiography, Gov. T. says: "In the year 1774 and 1775, Mr. Treadwell, having thoroughly imbibed the principles of the revolution, entered with zeal into the measures adopted to carry into effect the 'Association' recommended by the Continental Congress, and took an active part in the proceedings of the *Committee of Inspection and Correspondence*, who, in every part of the country, exercised a new and extensive jurisdiction over the conduct of the people, to compel them, by withdrawing from them social intercourse, or publishing their names as enemies of the common cause, to comply with the recommendations of Congress. In two instances, he joined numerous bodies of the mobility to discipline tories, and extort from them a humble retraction of their errors in principle and practice. He was, however soon convinced of the pernicious tendency of such violent and tumultuous proceedings, and thenceforth declined aiding or countenancing such assemblies. This for a time clouded his popularity ; but in the end it had a salutary influence, and rather elevated than depressed the estimation in which he was held. In September, 1776, he was elected *a representative from the town of Farmington in the General Assembly*, a situation which he held by successive elections, with the exception of one session, until 1785, when he was appointed by the House one of the *Assistants*, a name then given to the Senators or Governor's council."

The council consisted of only twelve men besides the Governor and Lieutenant-Governor, and was usually selected from those of the most enlarged public experience in legislation, and of undoubted integrity. Mr. Treadwell continued by annual elections one of the *Assistants* until 1798, when he was made Lieut.-Governor, still occupying his seat in the council, his seat being at the right hand of the Governor. He remained Lieut.-Governor till he was elected Governor of the state in 1809.

During the time above named he held many posts of honor and trust. He received the honorary degree of doctor of laws from Yale College in 1800. In the year 1777 he was appointed *Clerk of the Court of Probate*, for Farmington, &c., which office he held till May, 1784, when he became a Judge of the Court of Probate by an act of the legislature, which office, says Prof. O., "he held till 1810, a period of twenty-six years, making the previous period of seven years of his clerkship, thirty-three years of service in this important and interesting station. Of all the civil offices with which Gov. Treadwell was interested this was to him the most agreeable."

" In 1795, Mr. Treadwell was appointed *Judge of the County Court* of Hartford county, having been for many years one of the justices of the quorum in the same court. After he was elected Lieut. Governor, in 1798, the appointment of Judge of the County Court was still renewed; but having at this time numerous public employment, he declined serving further in that capacity. At the time he was chosen *Assistant*, in 1785, the Governor and council were the *Supreme Court of Errors*, and the dernier resort in all questions of law and equity, brought before them by writ of error or complaint. Of course he was ex-officio, a Judge of this Court, and continued such until it was reorganized in 1806, embracing a period of twenty years.   *   *   *   *   *   *   *

" Being, in the year 1792, one of the six senior Assistants, who, together w.th the Governor and Lieut. Governor, constituted the civil part of the *corporation of Yale College*, he became ex-officio a member of that board, and continued for eighteen years. During a greater part of that time, he was a member of the *Prudential Committee*, a committee consisting of three members of the corporation, besides the President, to whom the care and interests of the College are especially confided during the recess of the board, and upon whom, in fact, devolves a very large portion of all the concerns and management of the institution, except the immediate government and instructions, which are delegated to the faculty.

Gov. T. took an active part in all that concerned Yale College, and the cause of Education generally. To him may be ascribed much of that efficient discipline that characterized the management of the *old State Prison of Connecticut;* he was one of the three who constituted the *Board of Overseers;* was a member of the board for nineteen years.

To Gov. Treadwell may be awarded much of the honor of founding the Connecticut common school system on a permanent basis. The money that constitutes the common school fund of Connecticut, was received from the sale of lands owned by the state of Connecticut, lying in the western reserve of Ohio. The sale of those lands was made in 1795, for $1,200,000.[4] What use to make of that sum was a matter of great interest to the people of Connecticut at that time. After much debate in the General Assembly, it was finally set apart for school purposes, and when the present constitution of the state was formed, the fund was irrevocably placed to the same object.

" In these negotiations, Gov. Treadwell had a most important agency. He drew the bill for the application of the fund; was the leading commissioner in effecting the sale of the lands; took the original bonds, and after reporting to the legislature the results of these laborious and responsible transactions, received strong testimonials of their approbation and was appointed one of the Board

4 *North American Review*, 1823, p. 379.

of Managers of the School Fund, who were invested with extensive powers, which they continued to exercise until the extent and complication of the transactions required the whole time of an agent, when the Hon. James Hillhouse, then Senator in Congress, was appointed Commissioner of the Common School Fund and devoted himself to its interests with his well known faithfulness and energy.

"In the midst of numerous and responsible civil employments Lieut.-Gov. Treadwell was extensively engaged in *theological writings* and *ecclesiastical* proceedings. He had from early life been fond of his pen. He says of himself in reviewing his life, that his most delightful employment had been writing, as occasions prompted, on the great and distinguishing truths of revealed religion."

In forming and sustaining the Connecticut Missionary Society, Gov. T. was most active. That society was formed about 1792, and by legislative enactment authorized the several churches in the state to take up collections. The first year collections amounted to £380 13s. 1¼d. It would hardly be expected of us here to notice the many regligious and other topics that Governor Treadwell wrote upon. He was decidedly Calvinistic in his theology; his favorite authors on religious subjects, were President Edwards, Dr. Bellamy, Dr. Hopkins, Dr. Smalley and Dr. Edwards. At one time there was considerable prejudice against him under the belief that he was hostile to the Episcopalians; regarding these misrepresentations he himself says : " It was circulated, and to some extent believed, that he was an enemy to the Episcopal church. This, however, was asserted not only without, but against evidence. He always thought and spoke of that church in respectful terms, as truly evangelical, and as the great bulwark of the doctrines of the reformation. In its articles he considered it Calvinistic, and its teachers and writers the greatest lights in Christendom. He did not, indeed, believe in the divine right of diocesan episcopacy, maintained by some members of that church, nor did he approve of all her ceremonial, much less did he approve all those Armenian doctrines introduced in modern times by some Episcopal divines, but viewed them as a departure from the original principles of that church."

Gov. Trumbull died in August, 1809. At the meeting of the legislature at New Haven, in October, he opened the session with the usual message, the legislature subsequently investing him with the authority of governor till the time for holding the next annual election. At the next spring election, votes were much divided, Roger Griswold being his chief competitor for the gubernatorial chair. Gov. Treadwell had a plurality, but lacked a clear majority. The duty of appointing the governor falling upon the legislature, Gov. Treadwell was appointed chief magistrate for the ensuing year, and Mr. Griswold was made lieutenant governor. In 1811, there being a division in the Federal party, Mr. Griswold was elected governor by the opposition, then known as Jeffersonian Republicans, throwing their votes for Mr. G., instead of for one of their own party. The consequence was, Gov. T. was defeated.

The opposition, though largely in the minority at that time in Connecticut, were never wearied in their efforts to gain ascendancy. They contrived to turn Governor T.'s excellencies against him, by calling his want of the art of pleasing the multitude, " haughtiness and reserve (says Prof. Olmsted), and his deep and fervent piety, superstition and bigotry."

The usual imposing procession on election day at Hartford (which under the old regime was more formal than at present), presented a spectacle never before witnessed in the state of Connecticut, of its chief magistrate superseded and disgraced. It was the concluding scene of the age of "steady habits," a term which denoted a constant re-election to office of those who had once gained the confidence of the freemen by tried services. Gov. Treadwell was also the last of the Puritan governors of Connecticut, in whom the character of deep and fervent piety, no less than judicial experience and wisdom, was considered an essential requisite for the office of chief magistrate; and the state was now to witness, for the first time in the gubernatorial chair, a man who, although of the most respectable character, was not a professor of religion. From the earliest settlement of Connecticut, although the elections were annual, yet it had been almost uniform practice of the freemen to continue a man in office by successive elections; so that while the frame of government seemed to render it liable to great and constant fluctuations in the holders of public offices, yet in fact the " steady habits " of the people secured to these appointments an unusual measure of stability. As this system extended not only to the chief magistrate but also to the members of the council, the latter was composed chiefly of men who had been elevated to that rank after a long and successful probation in the lower house. From this body, with which he had been so long associated, Gov. Treadwell parted with much emotion, as from the companions and tried friends of his best days. Both houses united in strong testimonies of regard, and appointed a joint committee to tender him their affectionate respects, and accompany him to his home.

" After having been a representative to the General Assembly from his native town nine years, a member of the Council twenty-four years, for eleven of which he held the place of Lieutenant Governor, and one and a half years Governor ; having in the meantime, been twenty-six years Judge of the Court of Probate, three years Judge of the County Court, twenty years a Judge in the Supreme Court of Errors, and nineteen years one of the corporation of Yale College ; and having sustained numerous other and important relations to the State, as one of the Board of Overseers of the State prison, and one of the managers of the school fund, he now suddenly found himself stripped of every civil office, and after so industrious and useful a life devoted to the public service, he experienced the reward for which republics have long been proverbial. The words which Thomson applies to a patriot of another age, had too literal an application to our venerable friend :

> "'Like Cato firm, like Aristides just,
> Like rigid Cincinnatus *nobly poor.*'

"After all these varied and laborious services, performed for the commonwealth through a period of thirty-five years, he returned to private life without any increase of his property; and this, although adequate to his expenses when a young man, was wholly inadequate to meet the claims now made upon him. The emoluments he received from all his offices were so small as to require the constant addition of all his private income derived from his paternal inheritance, to maintain his family even in style, considering their rank, uncommonly plain and frugal. * * * * Unambitious of distinction, he would have been glad to resume almost any of those subordinate employments which had successfully occupied him, especially the office of Judge of Probate (which was always his favorite) ; but this he had resigned on being appointed Governor, deeming it incompatible with the high and responsible duties of that office, and this, as well as the other offices he held, had now passed into other hands, and were beyond his reach. He did not even refuse the token of respect offered him by his townsmen, who elected him their *representative to the Legislature;* and after thirty years absence from the lower House of the Assembly, he returned to it and served for several sessions in the comparatively humble but useful capacity of delegate from the town of Farmington. Also, in 1818, he was appointed by the same electors, in conjunction with his respected fellow citizen, Hon. Timothy Pitkin, member of the *Convention* assembled to form the present Constitution of Connecticut. This appointment gave great pleasure to his old friends throughout the State, several of whom addressed him letters on the occasion. One of these, now before me, was from the venerable historian of Connecticut, the late Dr. Trumbull, and evinces that deep regard for the preservation of the liberties and institutions of the State, which at the age of nearly four score and ten, still animated this excellent divine and pure patriot. This was the last occasion that Gov. Treadwell appeared in the councils of the state, in which he had served, as we have seen, in very various capacities, with slight intermissions, for more than forty years.

"After his retirement from the chief magistracy, he alloted most of his time, except at short intervals devoted to the public service, to what had always constituted his chief delights, namely : reading and writing on abstruse subjects of Theology, and practicing the various offices of Christian duty and benevolence. He commenced

and advanced towards the completion of a volume of ' Theological
Essays,' and issued proposals for publishing it by subscription ; but
the distressed state of the country on account of the war that was
but just closed, prevented his receiving the encouragement necessary
to warrant the expense, and the publication was abandoned. A partial perusal of the manuscript has been sufficient to assure me, that
the work would have been esteemed by the religious public one of
standard value.

" On the formation of the *American Board of Commissioners for
Foreign Missions*, in 1810, Gov. Treadwell was appointed president,
and was afterwards re-appointed to the same office annually until
his death. The conversion of the world was an object suited above
all others to this enlarged spirit of benevolence."

He died August 18, 1823, in his 79th year.

CHILDREN AND DESCENDANTS OF GOV. TREADWELL.

DOLLY, b. Sept 28, 1771; d. aged about 28½ months.

DOLLY 2d; m. Romanta Norton; had I *John Treadwell*, who m.
Mary, dau. of Hon. Timothy Pitkin; had 1 John Pitkin, b. in
Albany, July 19, 1822; analytical and agricultural professor,
Yale College; m. Elizabeth, dau. of Alexander Marvin of
Albany, N. Y.; had Alexander Marvin; d. inft.; John Tread-
well. Prof. N. d. at Farmington, Ct., Sept. 5, 1852. 2, Ed-
ward; 3, Elizabeth, d. y.; 4, Mary, d. inft.; 5, Mary 2d, d.
inft.; Mrs. Mary (Pitkin) Norton, d. 1829; he m. 2d, Eliza-
beth, dau. of Dr. Mason Cogswell of Hartford, Ct.; had 6,
Charles.

JOHN POMEROY, b. Oct. 19, 1778; m. Feb. 13, 1805, Hannah Edwards, dau. of Dea. Oliver Wetmore of Middletown, Ct. For
descendants of this marriage, see page 342.

EUNICE; m. Erastus Gay of Farmington; had I *Fisher*; m. Harriet,
dau. of Luke Wadsworth of F.; the latter d. —— ; m. 2d,
Lucy, dau. of Jonathan Thompson; had Julius; II *Pheobe*, m.
Thomas Mygatt; had William, who m. ——, and had 2 chil.; d.
y.; III *Mary*, m. Henry Root; had 1, Jane, d. y.; 2d, Charles;
m. Sarah Walker of Buffalo; d. —— ; she had Henry and
Sarah; d. inft.; IV *William*, m. Ruth Holmes of Albany; had
1, Richard; m. Gertrude Palmer of Orange, N. J., they had
Mary, Margeret; 2, Caroline; 3, Erastus; 4, William; V *Almira*. Mrs. Eunice (Treadwell) Gay; d. —— ; he m. 2d, Elizabeth Perkins; had VI *Charles*; m. Elizabeth Hall of Albany;
who had Mary, Harriet; VII *Eliza*.

Lucy; m. Amasa Jerome; had George and Lucy; d. y.

George; m. Nancy Curtiss; had I *Lucy;* m. Augustus Cowles of Farmington; Mrs. C. d. 1833, s. p.; Mr. C. d. ——; II *Eunice;* m. Daniel Sparhawk of New Hampshire; he d. s. p., 1859; III *George Curtiss;* m. 1836, Amy, dau. of Eli Roberts of Albany; had 1, George Hooker; 2 Lucy; d. y.; 3 Julia; 4, Charles; 5 Edgar; d. y.; 6 Ezra Prentice; 7 Emma; 8 Alice, d. y.; 9 Howard; IV *Jane;* V *Ann;* VI *Henry;* m. Eliza Roberts of Albany; had 1 Ada; 2 Walter; 3 Florence.

Mary; m. Erastus Perry; had I *John Strong,* b. 1815; m. Mary Jane, dau. of Josiah Willard of Plattsburg, N. Y.; had 1, Harriet Willard, b. 1847; d. at Albany; 2, Florence, b. 1849; 3, Henry Webb, b. ——; d. at A., 1852; 4, John Treadwell, b. 1853; 5, Willard Ellmore, b. 1855; 6, Jessie May, b. 1857; 7, Edith, b. 1859; II *Roger Hooker,* b. 1817; d. about 1818; III *Samuel,* b. 1819; d. about 1820; IV *Mary,* b. 1821; d. 1821; V *Mary 2d,* b. 1823; the four latter deceased at Albany. Mrs. Mary (Treadwell) Perry; d. at Farmington, 1823; he m. 2d, Clarinda, dau. of Levi Crittenden of Richmond, Berkshire co., Mass.; had VI *Mary Norton,* b. Dec., 1828. Mr. Erastus Perry d. at Albany, 1858.

G.

REV. SAMUEL KIRKLAND,[1]

The missionary to the Indians inhabiting the valley of the Mohawk from 1764 to 1797, was born Dec. 1, 1741, at Norwich, Conn.; his great grandfather John Kirkland was of Scotch descent and came from London, and was one of the early settlers at Saybrook, Ct; his father Daniel Kirkland (b. at S. 1701), graduated at Yale College in 1720, and became a orthodox Congregational minister, and settled at Norwich in 1773, where he preached some thirty years, removing from thence to Groton, Ct., in May 1773; he enjoyed a high reputation, as a pastor and a man of learning. He married Hannah Perkins of Windsor, Ct., her family were among the most respectable in that vicinity; by her he had issue twelve children, the subject of this notice being the tenth. Samuel received the benefit of his father's instruction till he was removed to Lebanon and became a pupil of Dr. Wheelock's, where he endeared to him all those who made his acquaintance. In 1762 he entered the Sophomore class in Princeton College, and gained a high reputation as a scholar and a gentleman. Being early impressed with the command of our Saviour, to go into all the world and preach the Gospel to every creature, he could not be persuaded to remain in college to the end of his term, but left in his senior year, the degree A. B. being conferred upon him subsequently. About this time he met with the celebrated Whitefield; making known to him his wishes to become a missionary, he encouraged him in the idea, and he immediately made preparations for a mission to the Senecas, then a powerful tribe in Western New York.

Receiving aid and counsel from his old principal, Dr. Wheelock, and assistance from a missionary society whose head was established at Boston, he departed in the fall of 1764. Sir William Johnson at this time represented the Home government, among the six tribes, having his headquarters at Jamestown, to him Mr. Kirkland made known his intentions and received from Sir William every possible encouragement. This his first attempt to preach and teach the blessing of a true religion, was full of toil and danger. The Indians, naturally suspicious, watched him with all the intensity of the savage, and made several efforts to put him out of the way, but he was preserved, and lived to see good fruits arise from his planting.

1 *Annals of the Am. Pulpit; Life of Rev. Samuel Kirkland*, by Rev. Samuel K. Lothrop, D. D.

In the spring of 1766 he returned to Connecticut and Massachusetts, accompanied by one of the Seneca chiefs. On their arrival at Hartford, they found the general court in session, and were invited to appear within the bar where the governor welcomed the chief in a speech suited to the occasion, which he replied to, Mr. Kirkland acting as interpreter; the court testified their pleasure by presenting him with twenty pounds, which was gratefully received.

During this visit to the east Mr. Kirkland was ordained at Lebanon) a minister, and was commissioned by a Scotch Missionary Society as a missionary to the Indians generally.

He immediately returned to his field of labor, selecting a place among the Oneidas—they being the most central to the six tribes, at the same time esteeming them the most friendly and the most susceptible to religious instruction of any of the surrounding " Nations." Here he established a church and had the gratification of seeing it gradually enlarged. His field of labor extended from the residence of the Governor-General at Jamestown to the Seneca tribe.

He returned to Connecticut early in the fall of 1769, and married on the 19th of September, Jerusha, daughter of —— Bingham, a niece of his old preceptor and patron Dr. Wheelock. She was (says the Rev. Dr. Asahel Norton) a lady of high intellectual, moral and Christian qualities, and was eminently qualified to share with her husband the labors and sacrifices incident to a mission among the Indians. She was to him a most efficient auxiliary. Up to the time of the revolution he was remarkably blessed in his labors. Some six years after Mr. Kirkland established the mission Dr. Wheelock withdrew his material aid. This compelled Mr. Kirkland to seek further assistance from the London Board of Correspondence in Boston, and they voted him a salary of £130, which arrangement gave Mr. K. a fresh impetus in his work.

In 1773, the country becoming disturbed, and the conduct of the Indians threatening, Mrs. Kirkland removed to Stockbridge where she purchased a house with money she had received from the Missionary Board in Boston; here she remained employing her time in educating her children, till the close of the war, her husband laboring among the Indians and troops in the Continental army, and visiting his family at stated periods.

Sir William Johnson at his death in 1773 was succeeded by his son-in-law Col. Guy Johnson, who proved unfriendly to Mr. Kirkland's mission. Mr. Kirkland remonstrated by letter in a respectful manner. During the revolution the missionary work proper was almost wholly suspended. At the commencement of the troubles Mr. Kirkland used all his influence to preserve a neutrality among the six nations, this occasioned him to visit their various councils at Albany and other places. In this he and the colonial patriots were disappointed, the influence brought to bear by the officers of the crown being more potent than the missionary's moral suasion, and in the fall and winter of 1775 the Mohawk valley resounded with the war cry of the red man.

In 1779 he was chaplain to General Sullivan's division, in their campaign down the valley of the Susquehanna, after which he was stationed at Fort Schuyler, save occasional visits to Connecticut and Massachusetts. After the war closed the mission was revived; the board at Boston recognizing his services, subsequently liquidated their indebtedness to him. Congress, also, recognizing his services as chaplain, as well his efforts for peace among the Indians, voted him a liberal grant.

Harvard College which had from time to time previous to the war contributed to his support, also voted him a considerable sum of money (upwards of £300), all of which contributed in some measure to repay him for the sufferings and dangers that he had experienced.

In 1784, he returned to his field of labor in Oneida with renewed zeal. The conversion of an aged Indian who had more than ordinary influence among his tribe, was the beginning of revival among them. This brought out much opposition from a haughty chief who had had intercourse with the more warlike Western Indians. He conspired against the life of Mr. K., but his scheme providentially failed. This persecution enlisted the mass of the Indians more warmly in his favor.

In 1788, he received from the government and the Indians jointly, a grant of a large tract of land in the vicinity of Oneida, which he took possession of the following year, building himself a log habitation, and otherwise improving it.

In 1791, he was sent as a commissioner to Philadelphia to aid the Senecas in making communications to Congress regarding the introduction of civilized life among them. The object of his mission was successful, and while engaged in this business his heart was made glad by the conversion, through his influence, of the noted chief *Cornplanter*.

In 1791, he made a census of the Six Nations, and completed "A statement of the numbers and situation of the Six United Nations of Indians in North America," contributing a copy to the American Academy of Arts and Sciences, of which he was a member.

In the summer of this year he attended the commencement at Dartmouth College, accompanied by the Indian chief Onondego, where his son, George Whitefield, graduated. Before returning he visited Boston for the purpose of conferring with the Missionary Board; returning to Oneida in the autumn, where he met with fresh encouragement in his religious duties.

In the fall of 1791, he removed his family to Oneida. The following winter he accompanied, agreeable to the request of the Secretary of War, forty chiefs and warriors to Philadelphia, further to consult with Congress respecting the welfare of the Six Nations, at the same time to establish a better understanding between the Indians and the government. The visit was attended with highly beneficial results.

"It had long been (says Dr. Norton) a favorite object with Mr. Kirkland to establish a high school or an academy in the vicinity of Oneida, and contiguous to some English settlement, at which both English and Indian youth might be educated.

"In his journey to New York and Philadelphia, he did much to aid in this object; and, as a result of a conference with the Governor and Regents of the University at New York, he took the initiatory steps towards procuring a charter for the institution. The charter was granted in 1793, and the institution incorporated under the name of Hamilton-Oneida Academy. He subsequently made to the institution a valuable donation in lands. This Academy went into successful operation, and exerted a powerful and benign influence on the whole surrounding region. In 1810, it was elevated to the rank of a college. The agency that Mr. Kirkland had in the original establishment and subsequent growth of this institution, would of itself justly entitle him to a place among public benefactors."

In January, 1788, his wife, Jerusha Bingham, died. He remained a widower till 1796, when he married Miss Mary Donally, a lady who had long been intimate in his family, and who had had charge of his children. "She proved (says Dr. Norton) a rich blessing to him, and enjoyed a high degree of the affectionate confidence of his children. She died at Clinton, N. Y., August, 1839, æ. 84."

In 1797, his connection with the Scotch Missionary Society was closed. In 1799, his son, George Whitefield, who was a merchant, failing in business, and for account of whom he was obligated, he lost all his property save his homestead farm. In 1805, his youngest son died in Boston, and the following year his son George Whitefield died in Jamaica. These bereavements weighed heavily upon him till his death, which occurred February 28, 1808. His remains were taken to the church in the village of Clinton, where a sermon was preached by his old friend and cotemporary in the ministry, the Rev. Dr. Norton.

Mr. Kirkland had six children. Rev. John Thornton, D. D., LL. D., late President of Harvard College; George Whitefield; Samuel; Jerusha, who married John H. Lothrop, Esq., of Utica, noticed pp. 389, 390; Eliza, who married Prof. Robinson, D. D., of the New York Presbyterian Theological Seminary; and ——, all deceased, except Mrs. Lothrop.

H.

CÁPTAIN MYLES STANDISH

Was "a gentleman born in Lancashire (says Nathaniel Morton, Secretary to the Colony of New Plymouth, 1645), and was heir apparent to a large estate of lands and livings, surreptitiously detained from him, his great grandfather being a second or younger brother from the house of Standish."

There are two ancient houses of Standish in England. The one known as of Standish Hall, county Lancashire; the other of Duxbury Park, same county, both families tracing their descent from Ralph de Standish—1251. The subject of our notice appears to have inherited the military. spirit for which he was so celebrated. The chronicles of Froissart giving the memorable meeting of Richard II and Wat Tyler, at Smithfield (1381), after the rebel was struck from his horse by William Walworth, the mayor of London, says, "then a squyer of the Kynges alyted, called John Standysshe, and he drewe out his sworde, and put into Wat Tyler's belye and so he dyed." For this he was knighted. Another Sir John Standish fought at the battle of Agincourt, 1415.

Of the family of Standish Hall, Burke in his *Encyclopedia of Heraldry*, says: "derived (Arms) from Thurston de Standish, living 6 Henry III, who inherited lands in Shevington, from his mother Margaret de Standish, daughter and coheiress of Robert de Hulton. The present (1847) representative of this ancient house is Charles Strickland Standish of Standish, Esq., eldest son, by Anastasia his wife, daughter and coheiress of Brough, bart., of the late Thomas Strickland of Sizergh, county Westmoreland, Esq.,who took the name and arms of STANDISH on inheriting the Standish estates. Sa. three standing dishes ar. *Crest.*—An owl, with a rat in its talons ppr."

Of the Duxbury Park family, the same authority says : " Arms derived from Hugh Standish, living 34 Edward I, second son of Ralph Standish, and grandson of Thurston de Standish living 6 Henry III. The representative of the family, 1667, Sir Richard Standish of Duxbury, was created a Baronet ; but the title expired with his great grandson, Sir Frank Standish, the third Baronet, in 1812 ; the estate devolving on his cousin, Frank Háll, Esq., great grandson of Sir Thomas Standish, the second Baronet, through that gentleman's daughter Margaret. Mr. Hall assumed on inheriting

the name and arms of STANDISH, but d. s. p. in 1841, and was succeeded by his cousin William Standish Carr, of Cocken Hall, county
Durham, Esq., grandson of Rev. Ralph Carr, M. A., Rector of Al-
derleigh, county Chester, by Ann his wife, daughter of Anthony
Hall, of Flass, county Durham, Esq., and Margaret his wife, daughter of Sir Thomas Standish of Duxbury, bart. Mr. Carr assumed
by sign manual, 6th May, 1841, the surname and arms of STANDISH
only, and is the present WILLIAM STANDISH STANDISH of Duxbury Park, Esq. Az. three standing dishes, two and one ar. *Crest.—*
A cock ar. combed and wattled gu."[1]

" All which I (says Rev. Dr. Belknap[2]) have been able to collect
relative to the family of Standish, is as follows :

" *Henry Standish*, a Franciscan, D. D., of Cambridge, Bishop of
St. Asaph, before the reformation, was a bigot to Popery. Falling
down on his knees, before King Henry VIII, he petitioned him to
continue the religious establishment of his ancestors. This prelate
died A. D. 1535, at a very advanced age.

" *John Standish*, nephew to Henry, wrote a book against the
translation of the bible into the English language, and presented it
to the Parliament. He died in 1556 in the reign of Queen Mary.
—Fuller's *Worthies of England*.

Sir Richard Standish, of Whittle, near Chorley. In his grounds
a lead mine was discovered, not long before 1695, and wrought
with good success. Near the same place is a quarry of mill stones.
—Camden's *Brittania*.

The village of *Standish*, and seat called *Standish Hall*, are situ-
ate near the river Douglass, in Lancashire, between the towns of
Chorley and Wigan, which are about six miles distant. Wigan is
nine miles north of Warrington on the southern side of the country."

This family (says Benham in his *Baronetcy of England*), is of
good antiquity and note, being denominated from the lordship of
Standish in Lancashire in their possession for many ages. But
many of the ancient records and evidences of the family are so worn
out by time, and wrote in such strange hands, that no more can be
gathered from them than that follows." * * * * *

1 STANDISH, Lancaster, a parish in the hund. and deanery of Leyland, union of Wigan; the
parish includes the townships of Adlington, Anderton, Charnock-Heath, Charnock-Richard,
Coppul, Duxbury, Shevington, Standish with Langtree, Welsh-Whittle, and Worthington; 199
miles from London (coach road 204), 4 from Wigan, 13 from Preston. Nor. West Rail. through
Crewe to Wigan, thence 3 miles; from Derby, through Crewe, &c., 99 miles. * * * * The
church is one of the finest in Lancashire. The free grammar school, founded in 1603 by Mrs.
Mary Langton, is endowed for the sustenance of a master and usher; and in 1794, Mrs. Mary
Smalley bequeathed £1,000 for the endowment of a school in which 20 girls are educated. The
other annuities produce about £20 per annum. There are several seams of coal in the parish,
and hand-loom weaving is, for the size of the place, rather extensively carried on. The living, a
rectory in the diocese of Manchester, is valued at £45.16s 8d; present net income, £1 874; patron, Dr. Brandreth, 1841; present incumbent, W. H. Brandreth, 1841: contains 15,190 acres,
1,313 houses; population in 1841. 8 686; do. in 1851, 9.989; assessed property £33,170; poor
rates in 1848, £890. Standish Hall is the seat of Charles Standish, Esq.; Duxbury Park that of
W. S. Standish. Esq."—*British Gazetteer*, London.
STANDISH, a parish of England, co of Lancaster, 3½ m. N. N. W. of Wigan, on the Preston and
Wyre Railway. Population employed in manufactures of cotton and linen, and in coal mines.—
Lippincott's Gazetteer, 1855.

2 *American Biography*, or an historical account of those persons who have been distinguished
in America, as adventurers, statesmen, philosophers, divines. warriors, authors, &c." by Jeremy
Belknap, D. D. Isaiah Thomas and E. T. Andrews, Boston, July 1798.

Burke in his *Dormant Baronetages* traces the families of Stan-
dishes of Standish and Duxbury, to the same ancestor. Jordon,
son of Ralph, son of Thurstin de Standish, is the founder of the
family of Standish, while Hugh, his brother, is the progenitor of
the house of Duxbury These two families became respectively
Catholics and Protestants.

Miles Standish was of the family of Standish Hall.
The precise date of his birth is not known. From evidence obtained by J. W. R. BROMLEY, Esq., in England in 1846, it is conjectured that he was born in 1584. He went to the Netherlands in
the army sent over by Queen Elizabeth to assist the Dutch in their
struggle against the troops of Philip III, King of Spain. On or
soon after the coming of the Rev. John Robinson and his fellow
separatists into Holland, he made their acquaintance and became a
member of their church, and he and his wife Rose embarked with
the Pilgrims in the Speedwell at Delft Haven, for America,
where they finally arrived in the Mayflower, and landed on Plymouth
rock, the ever memorable 20th of December, 1620, he having been
previously appointed commander of a party of sixteen men to land
and make discoveries. His wife died the 29th of the succeeding
month. Very soon after her decease, tradition says, he set about
seeking another companion. His young friend and fellow voyager,
John Alden,[3] who was a member of his family, a young man of
agreeable manner and fine personal appearance, was chosen by him
to visit a neighbor, one William Mullins, a worthy man, for the purpose of asking of him in the name of his principal the privilege of
paying court to his daughter, who was fair and comely. He went,
it is said, and faithfully made known the captain's wishes. The lady's
father did not object, as might have been expected from the recent
bereavement of the suitor, as well as from the unfriendly terms that
had unfortunately existed between them ; but he unhesitatingly gave
his consent, saying at the same time, that his daughter must be first
consulted. So accordingly the fair damsel was called into the room ;
and on her entering the young and handsome ambassador arose, and
with all the self possession he could command, made known the object of his mission. The interview is thus happily described by
Henry W. Longfellow in his poem entitled *Courtship of Miles
Standish*. Ticknor & Fields, Boston, 1858.

"So I have come to you, now with an offer and proffer of marriage
Made by a good man and true, Miles Standish the Captain of Plymouth !"

Thus he delivered his message, the dexterous writer of letters;
Did not embellish the theme, nor array it in beautiful phrases,
But came straight to the point, and blurted it out like a schoolboy;

3 " He professed much native talent, was decided, ardeut, resolute and persevering, indifferent
to danger, a bold and hardy man, stern, austere, and unyielding; of exemplary piety, and of
incorruptible integrity; an iron nerved Puritan, who could hew down forests and live on
crumbs."—Thacher's *Hist. of the Town of P.*
N. B.—The above quoted words are used in describing the character of Capt. Standish in a note
to an article entitled the *History of the Pilgrim Society*, p. 119 *N. E. Rec.*, 1847, which we think
more befitting than in connection with Alden.

Even the Captain himself could hardly have said it more bluntly.
Mute with amazement and sorrow, Priscilla the Puritan maiden
Looked into Alden's face, her eyes dilated with wonder,
Feeling his words like a blow, that stunned her and rendered her speech-
    less;
Till at length she exclaimed, interrupting the ominous silence:
"If the great Captain of Plymouth is so very eager to wed me,
Why does he not come himself, and take the trouble to woo me?
If I am not worth the wooing, I surely am not worth the winning!"
Then John Alden began explaining and smoothing the matter,
Making it worse as he went, by saying the Captain was busy,—
Had no time for such things;—such things! the words grating harshly
Fell on the ears of Priscilla; and swift as a flash she made answer:
"Has he no time for such things, as you call it, before he is married?
Would he be likely to find it, or make it after the wedding?
That is the way with you men; you don't understand us, you can not.
When you have made up your minds, after thinking of this one, and that
    one,
Choosing, selecting, rejecting, comparing one with another,
Then you make known your desire, with abrupt and sudden avowal,
And are offended and hurt, and indignant, perhaps, that a woman
Does not respond at once to a love that she never suspected,
Does not attain at a bound the height to which you have been climbing.
This is not right or just; for surely a woman's affection
Is not a thing to be asked for, and for only the asking.
When one is truly in love, one not only says it, but shows it.
Had he but waited a while, had he only showed that he loved me,
Even this Captain of yours—who knows? at last might have won me,
Old and rough as he is; but now never can happen?"
Still John Alden went on, unheeding the words of Priscilla,
Urging the suit of his friend, explaining, persuading, expanding;
Spoke of his courage and skill, and of all his battles in Flanders,
How with the people of God he had chosen to suffer affliction,
How in return for his zeal, they had made him Captain of Plymouth;
He was a gentleman born, could trace his pedigree plainly
Back to Hugh Standish of Duxbury Hall, in Lancashire, England,
Who was the son of Ralph, and the grandson of Thurston de Standish;
Heir unto vast estates, of which he was basely defrauded,
Still bore the family arms, and had for his crest a cock argent
Combed wattled gules, and all the rest of the blazon.
He was a man of honor, of noble and generous nature;
Though he was rough, he was kindly; she knew him during the winter
He attended the sick, with a hand as gentle as woman's;
Somewhat hasty and hot, he could not deny it, and headstrong,
Stern as a soldier might be, but hearty, and placable always,
Not to be laughed at and scorned, because he was little of stature;
For he was great of heart, magnanimous, courtly, courageous;
Any woman in Plymouth, nay, any woman in England,
Might be happy and proud to be called the wife of Miles Standish!

But as he warmed and he glowed, in his simple and eloquent language,
Quite forgetful of self, and full of praise of his rival,
Archly the maiden smiled, and, with eyes overrunning with laughter,
Said in a tremulous voice, "Why don't you speak for yourself, John?"

Into the open air, John Alden, perplexed and bewildered,
Rushed like a man insane, and wandered alone by the seaside;
Paced up and down the sands, and bared his head to the east wind,

76

Slowly as out of the heaven, apocalyptical splendors,
Sank the city of God, in the vision of John, the Apostle,
So, with its cloudy walls of chrysolite, jasper and sapphire,
Sank the broad red sun, and over its turrets uplifted,
Glimmered the golden reed of the angel who measured the city.

*   *   *   *   *   *   *   *   *   *

We here leave John Alden, adding only that they were made,
after much tribulation, one.[4]

Tradition says that the captain never forgave his young friend.
As he married soon after a lady by the Christian name of Barbara,
who it is supposed came over in the second vessel in 1621, their
long intercourse in the government of the colony, the intermarriage
of their children, and their church connections, would lead us to
suppose that time, the healer of all wounds (even of the heart), did
its work with the impetuous Standish.

On the 17th of March, 1621, the colonists met to establish a military organization among themselves, when he was regularly chosen
as their captain, and he was very soon called into active service.
For his expeditions among the treacherous inhabitants of the forest,
he seldom selected more than a score of men to·accompany him.
In this way, he was enabled to enter unobserved into their midst,
and by bold and decisive action strike terror among them. In 1622
the settlement of Plymouth was enclosed and fortified, and the defence of the place was committed to his charge. He organized
the adult male inhabitants into four divisions, selecting from the
most reliable suitable officers to act under his orders. In February
1623, he was sent with six men on a trading voyage to Matachiest,
an Indian settlement, between what is now Barnstable and Yarmouth ; a storm came up during the first night, filling the harbor
with ice and compelling him and his men to seek refuge in a hut belonging to the Indians. They collected in numbers with seeming
friendship, but he like a true soldier kept a part of his men on
watch while others slept. In the morning it was discovered that
they had committed depredations upon his shallop. He immediately
went with his entire force, surrounded the house of their chief
Ianough, and obliged him to find the depredators and restore the
stolen property. This decided action on the part of Standish, gave
the savages to understand that he was a man not to be trifled with,
and they furnished him with a load of corn, when he departed for
Plymouth where he arrived safely.

These circumstances caused the colonists to suspect that all was not
right among their red brethren, and the following month discovered

---

4 Horses not being in use in the Colony at this time. it was common for the people to ride on
bulls, and there is a tradition (says Thacher). when John Alden went to Cape Cod to be married
to Priscilla Mullens, he covered his bull with a handsome piece of broadcloth and rode on his
back. On his return he seated his bride on the bull, and led the uncouth animal by a rope fixed
in the nosing. This sample of primitive gallantry would ill compare with Abraham's servant,
when, by proxy, he gallanted Rebekah on her journey with a splendid retiome of damsels
and servants seated on camels (Gen. ch. 24). Had the servant employed bulls, instead of
camels, it may be doubted whether Rebekah would have been quite so prompt in accepting his
proposals.

a conspiracy existing among them to destroy the whites. At this time the captain was sent to Manomet, a creek which runs through the town of Sandwich, and empties into the upper part of Buzzards Bay. He was not received with that cordiality which he had been led to expect from the manner they had welcomed Gov. Bradford the fall before, when the governor was there to engage the corn that he had now come to receive. Two Indians (we quote from Belknap) from Massachusetts were there, one of whom had an iron dagger, which he had gotten from some of Weston's people at Wessagusset (Weymouth), and which he gave to Canacum, the sachem of Manomet, in the view of Standish. The present was accompanied with a speech, which the captain did not then perfectly understand, but the purport of it was, "that the English were too strong for the Massachusetts Indians to attack without help from others; because if they should cut off the people in their bay, yet they feared that those of Plymouth would revenge their death. He therefore invited the Sachem to join with them, and destroy both colonies. He magnified his strength and courage, derided the Europeans because he had seen them die, crying and making faces like children."

An Indian of Paomet, was present who had formerly been friendly, and now professed the same kindness, offering his personal service to get the corn on board the shallop, though he had never done such work before; and inviting the captain to lodge in his hut, as the weather was cold. Standish passed the night by his fire, but though earnestly pressed to take his rest, kept himself continually in motion, and the next day, by the help of the squaws, got his corn on board, and returned to Plymouth. It was afterwards discovered that this Indian intended to kill him if he had fallen asleep.

The conspiracy was discovered by Winslow while on a visit to Massasoit. The first victims of the slaughter were to have been the colonists sent out by Weston, at Wessagusset. John Sanders, overseer of Weston's colony, was absent at the time on the coast in pursuit of provisions. The Indians, taking advantage of his absence, became openly hostile, so much so that it became necessary to send a force there not only to protect the colonists, but to crush the conspiracy; a party, under command of Standish, was accordingly sent. Mr. Winslow, in his narrative, gives the following account of the expedition :

"The 23d of March [1623] being yearly court day, we came to this conclusion, that Captain Standish should take as many men as he thought sufficient to make his party good against all the Indians in the Massachusetts Bay; because it is impossible to deal with them upon open defiance, but to take them in such traps as they lay for others, therefore that he should pretend, as at other times; but first go to the English and acquaint them with the plot and the end of his own coming, that by comparing it with their own carriage toward them he might better judge of the certainty of it, and more fitly take opportunity to revenge the same, but should forbear, if it were possible, till at such time as he could make sure of Wittuwa-mat, a bloody and bold villian, whose head he had orders to bring with him. Upon this Captain Standish made choice of eight men, and would not take more because he would prevent jealousy. On the next day, before he could go, came one[5] of Weston's company to us, with a pack on his back, who made a pitiful narration of their lamentable and weak estate, and of the Indians' carriage, whose bold-ness increased abundantly, insomuch that they would take the vic-tuals out of their pots and eat before their faces; yea, if in anything they gainsayed them, they were ready to hold a knife at their breasts He said that to give them content they had hanged one[6] of the company who had stolen their corn, and yet they regarded it not; that another of them had turned savage; that their people had mostly forsaken the town, and made their rendezvous where they got their victuals, because they would not take pains to bring

5 " His name was Phineas Pratt; an Indian followed him to kill him, but by missing his way, he escaped and got into Plymouth. This man was living in 1677, when Mr. Hubbard wrote his history. The Indian that followed him went to Manomet, and on his return visited Ply-mouth, where he was put in irons."—Hubbard's *Ms.*

6 Mr. Hubbard's account of this matter is as follows: "The company, as some report, pre-tended, in way of satisfaction, to punish him that did the theft; but in his stead, hanged a poor, decrepid old man that was unserviceable to the company, and burdensome to keep alive. This was the ground of the story, with which the merry gentleman that wrote the poem called *Hudibras*, did in his poetical fancy, make so much sport. The inhabitants of Plymouth tell the story much otherwise, as if the person hanged, was really guilty of stealing, as were many of the rest. Yet it is possible that justice may be executed, not on him that most deserved it, but on him that could best be spared, or was not likely to live long, if he had been let alone "

The lines referred to in *Hudibras*, are in Part II, Canto II, commencing with line 403:

> Though nice and dark the point appear
> (Quoth Ralph), it may hold up and clear,
> That Sinners may supply the place
> Of suff'ring Saints, is a plain case.
> Justice gives sentence many times
> On one man for another's crimes.
> Our brethren of New England use
> Choice malefactors to excuse,
> And hang the guiltless in their stead,
> Of whom the churches have less need;
> As lately 't happened: In a town
> There lived a Cobbler, and but one,
> That out of Doctrine could cut use,
> And mend men's lives as well as shoes.
> This precious Brother having slain
> In time of peace an Indian,
> Not out of malice, but mere zeal
> (Because he was an Infidel),
> The mighty Tottipottymoy
> Sent to our Elders an Envoy,
> Complaining sorely of the breach
> Of league, held forth by Brother Patch,
> Against the articles in force
> Between both churches, his and ours;
> For which he crav'd the Saints to render
> Into his hands, or hang th' offender.
> But they maturely having weigh'd
> They had no more but him o' th' trade
> (A man that serv'd them in a double
> Capacity, to teach and cobble),
> Resolv'd to spare him; yet, to do
> The Indian Hoghan Moghan, too,
> Impartial justice, in his stead did
> Hang an old Weaver that was bed-rid.
> Then wherefore may not you be skipp'd,
> And in your room another whipp'd?
> For all philosophers but the Skeptic,
> Hold whipping may be sympathetic.

This story is (says *History N. E.*, chap. iii, p. 102) here most ridiculously caricatured as a slur upon the churches of New England. We do not find that the people of Weston's plantation had any church . they were a set of needy adventurers. intent only on getting a subsistence. Mr. Neal says, that "he obtained a patent under *pretence* of propagating the discipline of the church of England in America."

it home; that they had sold their clothes for corn, and were ready
to perish with hunger and cold, and that they were dispersed into
three companies, having scarcely any powder and shot. As this
relation was grievous to us, so it gave us good encouragement to
proceed, and the wind coming fair next day, March 25, Captain
Standish being now fitted set forth for Massachusetts.

"The captain being come to Massachusetts, went first to the ship,
but found neither man or dog therein. On the discharge of a musket, the masters and some others showed themselves, who were on
shore gathering ground nuts and other food. After salutation, Captain Standish asked, how they durst so leave the ship, and live in
such security? They answered, like men senseless of their own
misery, that they feared not the Indians, but lived and suffered them
to lodge with them, not having sword or gun, or needing the same.
To which the captain replied, that if there was no cause, he was
glad. But upon further inquiry, understanding that those in whom
John Sanders had reposed most confidence, were at the plantation,
thither he went, and made known the Indians' purpose, and the
end of his own coming; and told them that if they durst not stay
there, it was the intention of the governor and people of Plymouth
to receive them, till they could be better provided for. These men
answered that they could expect no better, and it was God's mercy
that they were not killed before his coming, desiring that he would
neglect no opportunity to proceed; hereupon he advised them to
secrecy, and to order one-third of their company that were farthest
off to come home, and on pain of death to keep there, himself allowing them a pint of corn to a man, for a day, though that was spared
out of our feed   The weather proving very wet and stormy, it was
the longer before he could do anything.

" In the meantime, an Indian came to him and brought some furs,
but rather to get what he could from the captain, than to trade, and
though the captain carried things as smoothly as he could, yet, as
his return, the Indian reported that he saw by his eyes that he was
angry in his heart, and therefore began to suspect themselves discovered. This caused one Pecksuot, who was a Pinese (chief),
being a man of notable spirit to come to Hobamock (Standish's
Indian guide and interpreter), and tell him that he understood the
captain had come to kill himself and the rest of the savages there.
' Tell him,' said he, 'we know it, but fear him not, neither will we
shun him, but let him begin when he dare, he shall not take us un-
awares.'

"Many times after, divers of them, severally or a few together,
came to the plantation, where they would whet and sharpen the
point of their knives before his face, and use many other insulting
gestures and speeches. Among the rest Wittuwamat bragged of the
excellency of his knife, on the handle of which was pictured a woman's face. ' But,' said he, 'I have another at home, wherewith
I have killed both French and English, and that hath a man's face

on it, and by and by, these two must be married.' Further he said of that knife which he there had, ' *Hinnaim namen, binnaim michen, matta cuts,*' that is to say, ' *by and by it should see, by and by, it should eat, but not speak.*' Also, Pecksuot being a man of greater stature than the captain, told him : ' Though you are a great captain, yet you are but a little man ; though I be no sachem, yet I am a man of great strength and courage.' These things the captain observed, but bore them with great patience.

"On the next day, seeing he could not get many of them together at once, but Pecksuot and Wittuwamat being together, with another man and the brother of Wittuwamat, a youth of eighteen, putting many tricks on the weaker sort of men, and having about as many of his own men in the same room, the captain gave the word to his men, and the door being fast shut, he began himself with Pecksuot, and snatching his knife from his neck, after much struggling, killed him therewith ; the rest killed Wittuwamat and the other man ; the youth they took and hanged. It is incredible, how many wounds these men received before they died, not making any fearful noise, but catching at their weapons, and striving to the last. Hobomock stood by as a spectator, observing how our men demeaned themselves in the action ; which being ended, he smiling, broke forth and said : ' Yesterday Pecksuot bragged of his strength and stature, and told you that though you were a great captain, yet you were but a little man ; but to-day, I see you are big enough to lay him on the ground."[7]

" There being some women at the same time there, Captain Standish left them in the custody of Weston's people, at the town, and sent word to another company to kill those Indian men that were among them. These killed two more. Himself with some of his own men went to another place and killed another, but through the negligence of one man an Indian escaped, who discovered and crossed their proceedings.

" Captain Standish took one-half of his men, with one or two of Weston's and Hobamock, still seeking them. At length they espied a file of Indians making towards them, and there being a small advantage in the ground by reason of a hill, both companies strove for it. Captain Standish got it, whereupon the Indians

---

7 *Hobomok.* This friend of the English early adopted the Christian religion, and became an inmate of Capt. Standish's family, whom he was accustomed to accompany on his expeditions, as a guide and interpreter, and was often of great service to the English, with whom he continued till his death in perfect friendship. It is said that he was a notable *pinese* or chief counsellor of Massasoit ; yet he prefered to remain true to the interests of the English, rather than live in perfect enjoyment of those honors which his rank in the councils of his nation would secure to him. His attachment to the English was ever manifested, and in all the secret plots of the Indians, he was their steadfast friend and adviser. It is said of him, during the severe drought in 1623 (which lasted from early in May, to the middle of July, whereby the English were in great danger of famine, on account of the destruction of their crops), when visited by Mr. Alden, he broke out in language like this : " I am much troubled for the English, for I am afraid they will lose all their corn by the drought, and so they will be all starved ; as for the Indians, they can shift better for themselves." But when afterwards he met him, after their supplications for rain had been answered by Divine Providence, he said : " Now I see Englishman's God is a good God, for he hath heard you and sent you rain, and that without storms, tempests and thunders, which usually we have with our rain, which breaks down our corn, but yours stand whole and good still ; surely your God is a good God." He died in 1642, having served the colonists for nearly twenty years faithfully and cheerfully.—*Note to Hist. of Dux.*, p. 33.

retreated and took each man his tree, letting fly their arrows amain, especially at himself and Hobamock, whereupon Hobamock cast off his coat and chased them so fast that our people were not able to hold way with him. They could have but one certain mark, the arm and half the face of a notable villian as he drew (his bow) at Captain Standish, and break his arm, whereupon they fled into a swamp. When they were in a thicket they parlied, but got nothing but foul language, so our Captain dared the Sachem to come out and fight like a man, showing how base and womanlike he was in tongueing it as he did, but he refused and fled, so the Captain returned to the plantation where he released the women, and took not their beaver coats from them, nor suffered the least discourtesy to be offered them.

" Now were Weston's people resolved to leave the plantation and go to Monhegan, hoping to get passage and return [to England] with the fishing ships. The Captain told them he durst live there with fewer men than they were, yet since they were otherwise minded, according to his orders from the Governor and people of Plymouth, he would help them with corn, which he did, scarce leaving himself with more·than brought them home. Some of them disliked going to Monhegan, and desiring to go with him to Plymouth, bringing the head of Wittuwamet, which was set up on a fort.[8]

" This sudden and unexpected execution, hath so terrified and amazed the other people who intended to join with the Massachusencks against us, that they forsook their houses, running to and fro like men distracted ; living in swamps, and other desert places, and so brought diseases upon themselves, whereof many are dead ; a Canacum, Sachem of Manomet ; Aspinet of Nanset ; and Ianough of Matachiest. This Sachem (Ianough) in the midst of these distractions, said, ' the God of the English was offended with them, and would destroy them in his anger.' From one of these places, a boat was sent with presents to the governor, hoping thereby to work their peace ; but the boat was lost, and three of the people drowned, only one escaped, who returned ; so that none of them durst come among us."

The Indian (says Dr. Belknap) who had been confined at Plymouth on his examination, confessed the plot ; in which five persons were principally concerned, of whom two were killed. He protested his own innocence, and his life was spared, on condition he would carry a message to his Sachem, Obtakiest, demanding three of Weston's men, whom he held in custody. A woman returned with his answer, that the men were killed before the message arrived, for which he was very sorry.

8 This may excite in some minds an objection to the humanity of our forefathers. The reason assigned for it is, that it might prove a terror to others. In matters of war and public justice, they observed the customs and laws of the English nation. As late as the year 1747, the heads of the lords, who were concerned in the Scots rebellion, were set up over Temple Bar, the most frequented passage between London and Westminster.—*Dr. Belknap.*

Thus ended Weston's plantation within one year after it began. He had been one of the adventurers to Plymouth; but quitted them and took a separate patent; and his plantation was intended to rival that of Plymouth. He did not come in person to America, till after the dispersion of his people, some of whom he found among the eastern fishermen, and from whom he first heard of the ruin of his enterprise. In a storm he was cast away between the rivers Pascataqua and Merrimack, and was robbed by the natives of all which he saved from the wreck. Having borrowed a suit of clothes from some of the people at Pascataqua, he went to Plymouth, where in consideration of necessity, the government lent him two hundred weight of beaver, with which he sailed to the eastward, and such of his own people as were disposed to accompany him. He never repaid the debt (says Prince) but with enmity and reproach.

When the intelligence of the affair between Standish and Pecksuot reached the Rev. Mr. Robinson at Leyden, he wrote to the church at Plymouth "to consider the disposition of their captain, who was a warm temper. He hoped that the Lord had sent him among them for good, if they used him right; but he doubted whether there was not wanting that tenderness of the life of man, made after God's image, which was meet; and he thought it would have been happy if they had converted some before they had killed any." "Truly are these words (says Winsor, in his *His. of Dux.*) a monument to the character of Robinson, alike honorable and Chrsitianlike. But consider the situation of Standish; upon his decisive action at this moment, we cannot but feel that depended much, not merely the preservation of the company to whose succor he had come, but the existence, perhaps, of the whole colony. Had they been successful in their designs here, elated by their recent victory, they would have made the settlement of Plymouth the next object for their depredations, and the lives of the whole colony would have fallen victims to their cruel barbarity. This was not distant from the foresight of the captain. He struck a mighty blow and by determined action in time of doubt dispelled the fears of his followers and sent terror upon the enemy. His action needs no apology. He acted but the part of a brave defender of his country, who feels that upon his own vigorous exertions the defence of the people depends. And, says his biographer, men of his profession will admire his courage, his promptitude and decision in the execution of his orders. No one has ever charged him either with failures in point of obedience, or of wantonly exceeding the limits of his commission. He is called by Prince, one of those heroes of antiquity who choose to suffer affliction with the people of God; who through faith subdued kingdoms, wrought righteousness, obtained promises, stopped the mouths of lions, waxed valiant in fight, and turned to flight the armies of the aliens." *　　*　　*　　*　　*　　*

The next scene in which we see Captain Standish, was where the fishermen of Plymouth had erected a stage at Cape Ann, which was taken possession of in 1625 by a company from the west of England. Standish was ordered to retake it, and met with a refusal. The dispute grew warm, and came near resulting in open hostilities, which was only avoided by prudential means being taken by Roger Conant, the agent for the opposing party, and captain of the ship that brought the west countrymen over. The affair was compromised by the ship's crew building another stage for the Plymouth fishermen. Standish's conduct on this occasion was severely criticised by the friends of the west country adventurers. Mr. Hubbard, in his *Ms.*, p. 84, noticing the affair, says : " He had been bred a soldier in the low countries, and never entered into the school of Christ, or of John the Baptist; or if he ever was there, he had forgot his first lessons, to offer violence to no man, and to part with the cloak, rather than needlessly contend for the coat, though taken away without order. A little chimney is soon fired, so was the Plymouth captain, a man of very small stature, yet of a very hot and angry temper. The fire of his passion soon kindled, and, blown into a flame by hot words, might easily have consumed all, had it not been seasonably quenched."

The same writer, on another occasion, showed a better state of mind when he spoke of him as a " gentleman very expert in military service, by whom the people were all willing to be ordered in those concerns. He was likewise improved (employed) to good acceptance and success in affairs of the greatest moment in that colony, to whose interest he continued firm and steadfast to the last, and always managed his trust with great integrity and faithfulness."

In the autumn of 1625 he was sent over to England as agent of the colonists, to settle some matters of difference between them and merchants of London, their correspondents; at the same time to further their interests with the Council of New England.[9] Though there was a pestilence or plague existing in London at the time, he accomplished the objects of his mission and returned again to the colony in 1626, bringing with him the sad news of the death of Mr. Robinson, their pastor.

About this time, attempts were being made to form colonies within Massachusetts bay, at Cape Ann and Pascataqua (*Morton Memorial*). One of these colonies was under the direction of a Captain Wollaston, a man of some weight and influence. " He (says Dr. Belknap) pitched on the southern side of the bay, at the head of the creek, and called an adjoining hill Mount Wollaston (Quincy). One of his company was Thomas Morton, ' a pettifogger of Furnival's Inn,' who had some property of his own, or of other men committed to him. After a short trial, Wollaston not

9 "1625 * * * Merchant adventurers of London sent two ships on a trading voyage to New England; on their return they were laden with dry fish and furs; the smaller ship was towed by the larger till they reached the English channel, when, being cast off, she was captured by a Turkish man-of-war, and carried into Sallee, where the master and his men were made slaves."—Thacher's *Hist of P.*
Capt. Standish was a passenger in the larger vessel, and providentially escaped

finding his expectations realized, went to Virginia, with a great part of the servants; and being better pleased with that country, sent for the rest to come to him. Morton thought this a proper opportunity to make himself head of the company; and in a drunken frolic, persuaded them to depose Filcher, the Lieutenant, and set up for liberty and equality.

· Under this influence they soon became licentious and debauched. They sold their goods to the natives for furs, taught them the use of arms, and employed them in hunting. They invited and received fugitives from all the neighboring settlements, and thus endangered their safety, and obliged them to unite their strength in opposition to them. ·Captain Endicott, from Naumkeag, made them a visit, and gave them a small check by cutting down a Maypole which they had erected as a central point of dissipation and extravagance, but it was reserved for Captain Standish to break up their infamous combination. After repeated friendly admonitions, which were disregarded, at the request and joint expense[10] of the scattered planters, and by order of the government of Plymouth, he went to Mount Wollaston and summoned Morton to surrender. Morton prepared for his defence, armed his adherents, heated them with liquor, and answered Standish with abusive language; but when he stepped out of his house to take aim at his antagonist, the captain seized his musket with one hand, and his collar with the other, and made him prisoner. The others quietly submitted. No blood was shed, nor a gun fired. They were all conducted to Plymouth, from thence sent to England, where Morton was treated with less severity than he deserved, and was permitted to return and disturb the settlement, till the establishment of the Massachusetts Colony, when he retired to Pascataqua, and there ended his days."

Capt. Standish removed with his family to the north-west side of Plymouth harbor,[11] in 1631, but returned to Plymouth to spend the

---

10 From the bill of expense, sent to the Council of New England, may be seen the number and ability of the plantations in 1628; .

Plymouth contributed......	£2.10
Naumkeag (Salem),.	1.10
Pascataquack (Mason's company),....... ..	2.10
Mr. Jeffery and Mr. Burslem,.....	2.00
Nantascot......	1.10
Mr. Thompson (Squantum neck),...........	15·
Mr. Blackston (Boston),...........	12
Mr. Edward-Hitton (Dover),.......	1.00

See Gov. Bradford's Letter Book, in *His. Soc. Coll.*, III, 68 (Belknap).   £12.07

11 Brewster was also a settler on this neck, and in the neighborhood of the captain, whose house was situated to the south-east of the Mill, on a knoll near the shore. The sea, it is said traditionally, once flowed between this and Captain's hill, thus forming a neck, at the extremity of which was situated his house which stood probably about thirty rods from the bank, although it is not now more than as many yards. The bank here has been continually washing away, and since the beginning of the present century, thirty feet are known to have gone. And within the same period, there have been seen, about sixty feet from the present bank, two stumps of trees, each larger than a barrel. To the south of the house, where there is now a salt flat, not many years ago were to be seen four acres of good corn, and was originally covered with a growth of hickory. This is the fact as given me by Mr. Kent, who received it from Ezekiel Soule, Esq., who was informed of it by Mr. Ebenezer Bartlett, who died in 1781, aged 87 years, and who related it from his own experience.
There is but little doubt, that at the time of the settlement of Standish, this whole peninsula, or nearly the whole of it, was one thick forest. Until a few years ago, there were standing in another part of the neck, five large sized and aged whitewood trees, which bore the appellation

winter, to be the better enabled to attend public worship. In the following spring he was joined by his friends John Alden, Jonathan Brewster, Thomas Prence (Prince), and their families. The place received the name of Duxbury, or burrough, or burrow, in compliment to him, from Duxbury Hall, the seat of his family in England. The place at which he settled is in the south-eastern part of the town, on the peninsula from which arises the hill known as "Captain's Hill."

At a meeting of the General Court, January first, 1632, he was elected a member of the same, which office he held, with the exception of a few terms, till his death.

He was appointed, March 2, 1635-6, to drill the men of Plymouth and Duxbury in the use of arms, agreeable to the following order of the General Court :

Alfo, it was ordered and agreed upon that Captaine Myles Standifh and Lieutent Will. Holmes be employed in teaching the ufe of armes at the towne of Plymouth and Duxburrow, according to fuch order as fhall be taken thereabout; and the faid lieutenant have likewife the charge of the guarde of the towne, to fee their duty faithfully pformed; each of them having for their paines the fum of twenty pounds for this prefent yeare, to be paid in the beginning of Novembr next enfuing, either in money, corne, or beaver, as it fhall then paffe.

In 1637 the troubles with the Pequots commenced, when the General Court, consisting of William Bradford, gent., Gournor; Captain Myles Standish, Thomas Prence, Tymothy Hatherley, and John Jenney, gentlemen, met and made the following order :

of the "Brewster trees," and situated near the Nook point. Primeval forest trees were also standing at other places until of late years. The point called "Eagle's Nest," without doubt took its name from circumstances which the name indicates, as the trees, a few years ago standing here, continued to be a favorite place of these birds. The surface of the land in this vicinity, is probably now two or more feet higher than it was two centuries ago, owing to the vast drifts of sand which have been here formed.

Standish probably built his house about the time of his first coming to Duxbury, or about the year 1632. It was occupied by him until his death in 1656. His son Alexander then succeeded to the estate, who, it is said, built addition to it, in which he kept a store; and in corroboration of this tradition, it may not be known, that leaden weights have been found in the remains of this part of the building. A few years ago, when discoveries were first made here by Mr. Kent, the foundation stones were nearly in their original positions. The cement employed was evidently ground clam shells, and the roof was thatched The outline of the house is now hardly distinguishable. We have a tradition that it was burned down, and this is substantiated by the evident traces of fire still to be seen—but at what time is not perfectly known, though it has been supposed about the year 1665. About twenty or more years ago, Mr. Kent, then pastor of the church in the town, first opened the ground about the site. The first substance discovered was a quantity of barley, perfectly charred, and apparently inwrapped in a blanket. This was found in the east corner of the site, which was thought to be a small cellar. At the chimney in the new part were found the ashes, as perfectly fresh as though the fire had but just been extinguished ; and here also was found a portion of an andiron, an iron pot, and other articles. In other parts of the ground there was discovered a buccaneer gun-lock, a sickle, a hammer, a whetstone, a large hinge, a scythe wedge, portions of stone jugs and other pieces of earthenware ; large quantities of glass, and some beads, some of which show the action of great heat; several buckles, and among others a sword buckle; a brass kettle, a pair of scissors, a small glass phial, chisels and files, parts of pipes, and other articles of household use. There were also found a deer's horn, and a tomahawk of fine workmanship, possibly the veritable instrument of Hobomok. Here I may obferve, that numerous instruments of Indian manufacture have been ploughed up in various parts of the town, such as stone axes, tomahawks, arrowheads and gouges, generally all of perfect form. Many of these curiosities are in the cabinet of the Rev. Benjamin Kent, whose museum, at the close of his labors at Duxbury, contained upwards of four thousand specimens, collected by many years' assiduous attention to the subject.

Some few rods to the southward of the house, in a hollow towards the shore, is situated Standish's Spring. It has probably never been disturbed since the hero himself, more than two hundred years ago, first laid the stones around. Its water is clear, and is with a white sandy bottom, and it has never been known to have been dry.—Hist of Duxbury.

It is concluded and enacted by the Court, that the Colony of New Plymouth ſhall ſend forth ayd to aſſiſt them of Maſſachuſetts Bay and Connectacutt in their warre againſt the Pequin Indians, in revenge of the inocent blood of the Engliſh wᶜʰ the ſᵈ Pequins have barbarouſly ſhed, and refuſe to give ſatiſfaction for.

It is alſo enacted by the Court that there ſhall be thirty pſons ſent for land ſervice, and as many others as ſhall be ſufficient to manage the barge. Lieutenant William Holmes is elected to goe leader of the ſaid company. *Plymouth Rec. Court Orders*, 1, p. 6o.

This war ended in the entire subjugation of the Pequots, and the almost total annihilation of the tribe.

The colonists were permitted to enjoy a season of peace till 1642, when they were again disturbed by a conspiracy among the Indians. The General Court met the 27th of September of that year, to take into consideration the disturbed state of affairs, when Capt. Standish was appointed one of the council of war, as well as commander of the forces. He, together with Edward Winslow and Timothy Hatherley, were chosen commissioners to Massachusetts, whose duty it was to agree upon a plan of operations for conducting the war against the conspirators.

In October, 1643, he was again elected by the court as one of the five ·members of the council of war, and again in June, 1646, and again in 1653. In 1644 he was elected Treasurer of the colony, which office he enjoyed till his decease. In May, 1653, he acted as Deputy-Governor in the absence of Governor Bradford. At the same sitting of the court he was appointed to command the troops mustered into service on account of the war of England with the Dutch. Two vessels were pressed into service for an expedition against the Dutch at *Manhatoes* (New York). In June, 1654, he was ordered to be at Plymouth preparatory to marching to Manomet, to embark from thence on board the bark Adventer, and there form a junction with other troops under Major Sedgwick " on an intended expedition against the Dutch att the Manhatoes." The following is a copy of the order and the commission given him by the court.

1654, " Theſe[12] being well prouided for, were to goe forth vnder the
20 June— comund of Captaine Myles Standiſh, whoe was ordered to bee
[Bradford theire Comander in Chiefe; Leiftenant Mathew Fuller was
Governor] ordered to goe forth with him as leiftenant on this expedition; and Hezekiah Hoare was appointed enſigne bearer.

" The comiſſion given to Captaine Standiſh is as followeth:

" Whereas wee are required by his highneſs the Lord Protector of England, Ireland and Scotland, to afford aſſiſtance vnto the ſtate of England, in ordere thereunto, wee, hauing raiſed ſom forces ouer which wee doe conſtitute ouer wellbeloued frind, Capt Myles Standiſh, theire leader and comander in chiefe, of whoſe approued fidelitie and abilitie wee haue

---

12 Alluding to the men that had been drafted from the ſeveral towns.

long experience, vnto whofe wifdome and difcretion wee doe committ the leading and ordering of thefe our men, and vnto whom wee doe require our men to yield all due obedience as vnto theire comaunder; and that he be reddy, on the 28th of this pfent June att Plymouth, to receiue fuch men as fhall there be comitted to him, and vpon the 29th day march them vnto Sandwich, and theire further to receiue thofe that fhall bee b'e brought from thofe foar plantations vnto him; and from thence to march his men to Manomett, and there to fhip them aboard the barkque called the Aduenter, and foe taking the firft opportunitie of wind & weathers of fayling to the Monhatoes, or fuch place of randeuoos as *fhall* fhallbee appointed there to meet with Major Robert Sedgwicke and Capt John Leurett, the comiffioners in chiefe appointed by his highnefs the Lord Protector for the defigne and there to joyne with them for the carrying on of the faid defigne according to fuch direction as fhall be giuen him from time to time by the Comiffions in chiefe and counfell of Warr.

Plymouth, June 20, 1654.

Giuen under our hands and common feale of our goument,

WILLAM BRADFORD, Prefedent,

JOHN ALDEN,	THOMAS PRENCE,
THOMAS WILLETT,	WILLIAM COLLYARE,
JAMES CUDWORTH,	TIMOTHY HATHERLEY.
JOHN WINSLOW,	*Plymouth Court Rec.*, III, p. 55.

This was undoubtedly the last military expedition in which he was engaged, as he died October 3d, 1656, æ. 72, " a man full of years and honored by his generation." Secretary Morton in recording his departure says : " He growing very ancient, became sick of the Stone or Strangullion, whereof after his suffering of much dolorous pain, he fell asleep in the Lord, and was honorably buried at Duxbury."

" No stone (says Winsor) marks the resting place of his ashes, and we must seek in vain the place where reposes what was mortal of the immortal Standish. He was probably buried on his farm, or perhaps in the old burying ground in that vicinity at Harden Hill."

He requested, it will be perceived by reference to a copy of his will, p. 604, that he might be buried near his daughter Lora, and daughter-in-law Mary Standish. " There are (says Winsor) a short distance easterly from the site (alluded to above) two stones of considerable size which are about six feet apart and were thought perchance to mark the grave of some one of the family. A few years ago investigations were made, but without affording any foundation for the supposition. Their peculiar shape though evidently in their rough state, and the fact that their position to each other was exactly east and west, induced some persons to dig between them in hopes of making a discovery. Excavations were accordingly made to the depth of eight feet, without, however, any success. In a biographical sketch of the author, appended to Capt. Samuel Delano's

MILES STANDISH.

Voyages, and written in 1817, it is stated in speaking of Capt. Standish, 'here he died ; and some aged people in the close of the last century pointed out the spot where he was buried.'

· "An antiquarian friend, whose researches in Duxbury commenced about ten years after writing the above sketch, and who, as he has informed me, in his conversations with the octogenarians of that day, always especially inquired relative to the burial places of the first Pilgrims, tell me that he could neither find the slightest confirmation of the statement above, in the language of those who were, at the time specified in the account living in their prime ; nor moreover in the testimonies of such aged persons as also had manifested in their early days a desire to be informed by their elders on the same point, was there anything in its nature that could in the least degree substitute the belief.

"As to the credit which that sketch is entitled to in this respect we cannot of course judge, as it is indefinitely chargeable to ' a friend of Capt. Delano.' "—*Hist. Dux.*, p. 54, note.

His landed possessions were quite extensive, and his estate was considered large at the time. The following is a copy of his will, for which we are indebted to the *New England Register*.

The LAST WILL and TESTAMENT of captaine MYLES STANDISH, Exhibited before the Court held att Plymouth, the 4th of May, 1657, on the oath of captaine James Cudworth, and ordered to be recorded as followeth :
Given under my hand this March the 7th, 1655.
Witnesseth these present, that I, Myles Standish, Seni'r, of Duxburrow, being in p'rfect memory, yett deceased in my body, and knowing the fraile estate of man in his best estate, I doe make this to bee my last will and testament in manor and form following :
1. my will is that out of my whole estate my funeral charges be taken out and my body to bee buried in decent manor, and if I die att Duxburrow, my body to bee layed neare as conviently may bee to my two dear daughters, Lora Standish my daughter, and Mary Standish my daughter-in-law.
2. My will is that out of the remaining pte of my whole Estate that all my just and lawful debts, which I now owe or at the day of my death may owe, be paied.
3. Out of what remains according to the order of this government my will is that my dear loving wife Barbara Standish shall have third pte.
4. I have given to my son Josiah Standish upon his marriage one young horse,[13] five sheep and two heiffers, which I must upon that contract of marriage make forty pounds, yett not knowing whether the estate will bear it at present ; my will is that the residue remaine in the whole stocke and that any one of my four sons, viz. Allexander Standish, Myles Standish, Josias Standish, and Charles Standish may have forty pounds apeec ; if not that they may have proportionably to ye remaining pte bee it more or lesse.
5. My will that my eldest son Allexander shall have a double share in land.

13 In 1629, horses and mares were brought into Massachusetts Bay by Francis Higginson, formerly of Leicestershire, from which county many of the animals were imported. New York received its first horses in 1625, imported from Holland by the Dutch West India Company, probably of the Flanders breed.—Henry Wm. Herbert's *Horse and Horsemanship.* I, 109.
Horses were considered so valuable in 1657. the General Court of New Plymouth passed an ordinance, that every freeholder who kept three mares and would keep one horse for military service, should be exempt from watching and military duty.

6. My will is that soe long as they live single that the whole bee in ptnership betwix them.

7. I doe ordaine and make my dearly beloved wife Babara Standish, Allexander Standish, Myles Standish and Josias Standish joynt exequitors of this my last will and testament.

8. I doe by this my will make and appoint my loving friends Mr Timothy Hatherly and Capt. James Cudworth supervisors of this my last will, and that will bee pleascd to doe the office of Christian Love to bee healpfull to my poor wife and children by their Christian counsell and advisse, and if any difference should arise which I hope will not, my will is that my said supervissors shall determine the same, and that they see that my poor wife shall have as comfortable maintainence as my poor estate will beare the whole time of her life, which you my loveing frinds pleasse to doe though neither they nor I shall be able to recompenc, I do not doubt but the Lord will.   By me   MYLES STANDISH.

further my will is that Marrye Robenson, whom I tenderly love for her grandfathers sacke shall have three pounds in som thing to goe forward for her two years after my decease, which my will is my overseers shall see pformed.

ffurther my will is that my servant John Irish Junir have forty shillings more than his covenant which will upon the towne booke alwaies. provided he continew till the time hee covenanted bee expired in the service of my exequitors or of them with theire joynt consent.

March 7th 1655   By me   MYLES STANDISH.

9. I give unto my son and heir aparent Allexander Standish all my lands as heire apparrent by lawful decent in Ormistick Bousconge Wrightington Maudsby Newburrow Cranston and in the Isle of man, and given to mee as right heire by lawful decent, but surreptitiously detained from me my great grandfather being a 2ond or younger brother from the house of Standish of Standish.[14]   by mee   MYLES STANDISH.

March 7th 1655.

Witnessed by mee *James* Cudworth.

NOTE.—The word " surreptitiously," in the last clause was inserted [in

14 " In the fall of 1846, an association was formed among the descendants of Capt. Standish for the purpose of making investigations. and upwards of $3,000 were furnished to their agent, J. W. R. Bromley. Esq., who started on his mission in November of that year, and returned in October of the following year, without however, accomplishing the object of his search. I have been favored with the perusal of some of his correspondence with the Corresponding Secretary of the Association, and some brief minutes which I have gleaned from them may not be uninteresting. The property to which it was his object to prove the right of Capt. Standish, comprises large tracts of rich farming lands, including several valuable coal mines, and produces yearly income of £100,000 or more. From a commission, which was found. appointing Standish to a Lieutenancy in Her Majesty's forces on the continent, the date of his birth was found, as also from incidents of his life in New England, which have now become a portion of her history, and from other data in possession of his descendants, which all led to the conclusion that the year 1584 must have been that of his birth. The family seats are situated near the village of Chorley in Lancashire, and the records of this parish were thoroughly investigated from the year 1549 to 1552. And here in connection comes in an incident in the researches of Mr. Bromley, which deserves particular attention. and causes the fair conclusion, that Standish was the true and rightful heir to the estates, and that were truly " surreptitiously detained " from him, and are now enjoyed by those to whom they do not justly belong The records were all readily deciphered. with the exception of the years 1584, and 1555, the very dates, about which time Standish is supposed to have been born; and the parchment leaf which contained the registers of the births of these years was wholly illegible. and their appearance was such, that the conclusion was at once established, that it had been done purposely with pumice stone or otherwise. to destroy the legal evidence of the parentage of Standish, and his consequent title to the estates thereabout. The mutilation of these pages is supposed to have been accomplished, when about twenty years before, similar inquiries were made by the family in America. The rector of the parish, when afterwards requested by the investigator to certify that the pages were gone, at once suspected his design of discovering the title of the property, and taking advantage of the rigor of the law (as he had entered as an antiquarian researcher merely), compelled him to pay the sum of about £15, or suffer imprisonment.
As it was said that the Captain married his first wife in the Isle of Man, this island was visited with hopes of discovering there his marriage registered, but without success. as no records of a date early enough were to be found. And thus it will be seen that on account of the destruction of all legal proof, the property must forever remain hopelessly irrecoverable."—*Hist. Dux.* p. 97.

a blank left between the preceding and following word], apparently at a subsequent time, yet appears to be the hand of Sec. Morton.

An inventory of the goods and chatteles that Captaine Myles Standish, gent. was possessed of att his decease as they were shewed to us whose names are underwritten this 2ond of december, 1657, and exhibited to the Court held att Plymouth the 4 May 1657, on the oath of Mi⁹ Barbara Standish.

	£	s.	d.
It. one dwelling house and out houses with the land thereunto belonging, - - - - - - -	140	0	0
It. 4 oxen, - - - - - - - -	24	0	0
It. 2 mares, two coults, one young horse, - - -	43	0	0
It. 6 cows, 3 heifers and one calf, - - - -	29	0	0
It. 8 ewe sheep, two rames and one weather, - -	15	0	0
It. 14 swine, great and small, - - - - -	3	15	0
It. Wilson's dixonary, homer's Illiad, a comentary on James Ball cátterkesmer, - - - - -	0	12	0
It. another pcell in octavo, - - - - -	0	4	0
It. halfe a young heifer, - - - - -	1	0	0
It. one feather bed, bolster and 2 pillowes, - -	4	0	0
It. 1 blankett, a coverled and a rugg, - - -	1	5	0
It. 1 feather bed and bolster, - - - - -	4	0	0
It. 1 blankett and 2 ruggs, - - - - -	1	15	0
It. 1 feather bolster and old rugg, - - -	0	14	0
It. 4 paire sheets, - - - - - - -	3	0	0
It. 1 pr fine sheets, - - - - - -	1	4	0
It. 1 table cloth, 4 napkins, - - - - -	0	10	0
It. his wearing clothes, - - - - - -	10	0	0
It. 16 peeces of pewter, - - - - -	1	8	0
It. Eathen ware, - - - - - -	0	5	0
It. 3 brasse Kettles, one skillett, - - -	2	0	0
It. 4 iron potts, - - - - - -	1	8	0
It. a warming pan, a frying pan and cullender, - -	0	9	0
It. one paire stillyards, - - - - - -	0	10	0
It. 2 bedsteads, one table, 1 forme chaires, 1 chest and 2 boxes,	2	13	0
It. 1 bedstead, one settle bed, one box, 3 casks, - -	1	7	0
It. 1 bedstead, 3 chists, 3 vasses with sence bottles, 1 box, 4 casks, - - - - - - -	2	6	6
It. 1 still, - - - - - - -	0	12	0
It. 1 old setter, 1 chaise, one kneeding trough, 2 pailes, 2 traies,	0	16	0
It. one fowling peece 3 muskets, 4 carbines 2 small guns, and one old barrel, - - - - -	8	1	0
It. one sword ¹⁵ one cutles 3 belts, - - -	2	7	0
It. the history of the world and the Turkish history, - -	1	10	0
It. A chronicle of England and the country ffarmer, -	0	8	0
It. ye history of Queen Elizabeth, the star of Europe, -	1	10	0
It. Doctor Hales workes, Calvin's institutions, -	1	4	0
It. Wilcock's workes and mayor's, - - -	1	0	0
It. Roger's Seaven treatises and the ffrench akadamey, -	0	12	0
It. 3 old bibles, - - - - - - -	0	14	0
It. Ceser's comentaryes, Bariff's artillery, - - -	0	20	0

15 " His identical sword is said to be in the cabinet of the Pilgrim Society. His coat of mail has been seen by a descendant now living, but at that time was in such a state of decomposition as to crumble into pieces at the touch.   *   *   *   *   *   *   * There is in the possession of the Massachusetts Historical Society, another sword, which is also said to have belonged to Standish; but the history of the one at Plymouth is said to be established without a doubt. It was in possession of his son Capt. Josiah Standish. See Miss Caulkins' *Hist. of Norwich*, p. 118 ; *Hist. Dux*.

It. Preston's Sermons, Burroughes Christ in contentment, gospel conversation, passions of the mind, the phisisions practice, Burroughes Earthly mindedness, Burroughes discovery, - - - - - - - 1 4 0
It. Ball on faith, Brinsley's watch, Dod on The Lord's Supper, Sparke against herisey, Davenporte apollogye, - 0 15 0
It. A reply to Doctor Cotton on baptisme, The Garman History, The Sweden Intelligencer, reasons discussed, - - 0 10 0
It. 1 Testament, one psalme booke, Nature and grace in Conflict, a law booke, The mean in mourning allegation against B. P. of Durham, Johnson against hearing, - 0 6 0
It. pcell of old bookes of divers subjects—in quarto, - - 0 14 0
It. 2 beer casks, 1 chern, 2 spinning wheels, one powdering tubb, 2 old casks, one old flaskett, - - - 0 15 0
It. 1 mault mill, - - - - - - - 2 0 0
It. 2 sawes with divers carpenters tooles, - - - 1 19 0
It. a timber chaire with plow chaires, - - - - 1 6 0
It. 2 saddles, a pillion, one bridle. - - - - 1 0 0
It. old Iron, - - - - - - - 0 11 0
It. 1 chist and husking table, - - - - 0 8 0
It. 1 hatchett, 2 trammells, 2 iron doggs, 1 spitt, 1 fine forke, 1 lamp, 2 gars (?) one lanthorn, with old lumber, - - 2 1 0
It. in woole, - - - - - - - 0 15 0
It. in hemp and flax, - - - - - - 0 6 0
It. eleven bushels of wheat, - - - - - 2 5 0
It. 14 bushels of rye, - - - - - - 2 2 0
It. 30 bushels of pease, - - - - - 5 5 0
It. 25 bushels of indian corn, - - - - - 3 15 0
It. cast, and peakes, and plowirons and 1 brake, - - 2 5 0
It. axes, sickles, hookes, and other tooles, - - - 1 0 0.
It. eight iron hookes, 1 Spinning wheel, with other lumber, 0 14 0

JOHN ALDEN,   358 7 0
JAMES CUDWORTH.

DESCENDANTS OF MILES STANDISH.

Captain Standish's wife Barbara survived him. He had children, Alexander, Miles, Josiah, Charles, d. young; Lora died before her father, and John died young.

ALEXANDER was the oldest; he was admitted a freeman June 7, 1648; was town clerk from 1695 to 1700, and was often the town's deputy (grand jurors or supervisor); he inherited the homestead, and possessed other lands in the vicinity of Plymouth and Duxbury; he was a trader, and had considerable dealings with the Indians. His will is dated July 5, 1702, and proved Aug. 10, 1702; his estate inventoried the use of £600; he m. 1 Sarah, dau. of his father's rival, John Alden; had Miles, m. Experience Sherman (Holmes?); had 1 *Sarah*, b. April 15, 1704; m. Abner Weston, March 2, 1730; 2 *Patience*, b. Aug. 16, 1707; m. April 6, 1738, Caleb Jenny of

Dartmouth ; 3 *Priscilla*, b. April 1, 1710 ; m. Elisha Bisbee (?) ;
4 *Miles*, March 11, 1714 ; m. Mehetable Robbins, of Plymouth,
Dec. 17, 1738 ; had Miles, m. Naomi, dau. of Daniel Keith;
removed to Pennsylvania, and had a son Miles ; Penelope, bap.
June 27, 1741 ; m. Nathaniel Cobb, jr., 1763 ; Lydia, bap.
May 1, 1743 ; Experience, bap. Sept. 24, 1744 ; m. Simeon
Ames, 1765 ; Hannah, b. April 27, 1746 ; m. Daniel Fobes,
1769 ; Sarah, b. May 22, 1748 ; Priscilla, bap. 1755 ; Miles
sr., inherited the homestead, and died there Sept. 15, 1739 ;
his son Miles inherited the same, sold July 3, 1763, to Samuel
and Sylvanus Drew, who sold it to Wait Wadsworth, who sold
it to John, the father of John Faunce, and removed to South
Bridgewater, 1765 ; bought a farm at Titicut.—*Guide to
Plymouth.*

EBENEZER, b. 1672 ; he d. 1734 ; had 1 Ebenezer ; m. 1739 a
Churchill, and d. 1748 ; 2 Zachariah (South Bridgewater), d.
1780 ; m.; had Ebenezer, Hannah, Sarah, m. Josiah Cushman,
jr., 1749 ; Abigail, m. Samuel Wright, 1752 ; Peleg ; Zachariah ; 3, Moses, 1689, Plympton, m. Rachel ; d. 1769, æ. 80;
had Moses (the father of Moses, whose son is Moses of Boston) ; Capt. John, d. at Plympton, 1787 ; Aaron, Rachel, Rebecca, m. Zachariah Weston, 1751 ; 4 Hannah, 5 Zeruiah, m.
Zebedee Thompson, of H.; 6 Sarah, m. Josiah Cushman,
1749 ; 7 Mercy, 1716 ; m. 1736, Ebenezer Lobdell ; m. 2d,
Benjamin Weston ; d. 1794.

SARAH, m. Abraham Sampson.

LYDIA, m. Isaac Sampson.

MERCY, m. Caleb Sampson.

SARAH, m. Benjamin Soule.

ELIZABETH, m. Samuel Delano ; he (Alexander, son of Capt.
Miles) m. 2d, Desire, widow of Israel Holmes (maiden sur-name,
Doten).

THOMAS ; removed to Pembroke ; m. Mary ; had 1 David, m. Jan.
24, 1746, Hannah Magoun ; d. 1793, who had David Lemuel, b.
1746 ; d. 1824, æ. 74 ; m. Rachel Jackson, of Bath, where he
settled, and had David and Lemuel, Arno, Thomas, Jan. 23,
1825 ; m. Martha Bisbee, Feb. 10, 1748 ; d. June 18, 1759,
at Fort Miller ; had Thomas, who d. 1780 ; Mary, Jan. 21,
1733 ; William, June 24, 1737 ; Betty, Sept. 1739.

ICAHBOD, m. 1719, Phebe Pring ; d. 1772 ; " he was the man, probably a cooper, who d. at Halifax, 1772, leaving Mary, Phebe
and Desire, who m. David Hatch."—*His. of Bridgewater.*
" Desire m. a Weston, and probably David, who was killed in
Duxbury by the fall of a tree in 1689.—*His. of Dux.*

MILES, second son of Captain Miles Standish, removed to Boston
and m. Sarah, dau. John Winslow, July 19, 1660 ; he d. s. p.
about 1666 ; his widow m. 2d, Tobias Paine, 1669 ; 3d, Richard Middlecott; she d. 1726.

Capt. JOSIAH, third son of Captain Miles Standish, was appointed
Oct. 3, 1654, by the General Court, " Ensigne bearer of the
milletary companie of Duxburrow ;" and June 8, 1655, was
" admitted Freeman " by the same Court. May, 1657, he, together with his mother and brother Alexander, was accepted
by the Court as an executor of his father's estate. October 2,
1658, was made one of the Council of War. He removed to
East Bridgewater and was elected Lieutenant, which was
confirmed by the General Court, June 6, 1660. The same year
the Court granted him lands at Manomet. He returned to
Duxburrow about 1663 ; was member of the Grand Inquest
1664 ; Deputy to the General Court, 1665 ; Selectman, 1666 ;
member of the " Counsell of War," and " Grand Enquest "
and Board of Selectmen, 1667 ; Deputy to the General Court
from 1671 to 1682. Was appointed Captain about 1680.
He removed to Norwich, Conn., about 1686, bought land at
Preston, Ct., of John Parks, 1687. He m. 1st, Mary, dau. of
John Dingley of Marshfield, 1654, who d. the same year ; he
m. 2d, Sarah, dau. of Samuel Allen[16] of Braintree ; had I *Miles*,
who m. Dec. 5, 1700, Mehetable Adams. II *Josiah*, who was
admitted to the church at Preston, Dec. 25, 1700; married
—— ; had Mercy (prob. others) ; she m. —— Wheelock, and
had Mary (prob. others), who m. —— Bingham of Windham,
Ct.; and had Jerusha, who m. Sept. 19, 1769, Rev. Samuel
Kirkland;[17] and had Jerusha (for other descdts. of this marriage
see notice of the Rev. Samuel Kirkland), who married John H.
Lothrop, Esq., and had Mary Ann (and others); who m. Edmund
A. Wetmore (for her descdts. see under head of Edmund Ar-
nold, son of Rev. Oliver). III *Samuel*, b. in Dux.; m. in
Preston, Ct., June 1, 1710, Deborah Gates ; had 1 Deborah, b.
Dec. 27, 1711 ; d. 1805. unm. ; 2 Samuel, b. Dec. 1, 1713 ; had
Samuel; 3 Lois, b. Jan. 9, 1715 ; 4 Abigail, b. Feb. 9, 1717 ;
m. Rufus Rood ; 5 Sarah, b. Feb., 1719 ; d. 1745, unm. ; 6
Thomas, b. May 19, 1724 ; m. Content Ellis; m. 2d Dorcas
Bellows ; 7 Thomas, b. May 19, 1724; Williamstown, Mass. ;
m. widow Sarah Williams.—Hubbard's *Ms.* IV *Israel*, b.

16 " SAMUEL (Allen) Braintree, perhaps as early as 1622, freeman, 6 May, 1635, by W. Ann,
wh. d. 29 Sept., 1641, had Samuel, b. ab. 1633 ; Mary ; Sarah, 30 Mar. 1639 ; and W. Margaret,
whose family is unknown, but who had been widow of Edward Lamb, had James, Abigail ;
Joseph, 15 May, 1650 ; and perhaps one or two preceeding. His will of 2 Aug , 1669 was proved
16 Sept. foll. ; Mary. m. 24 Jan., 1656, Nathaniel Greenwood ; Sarah, m. Josiah Standish of Duxbury, as his sec. wife and Abigail, m. 1670, the sec. John Cary of the same."—Dr. Savage's *Gen.
Dict.*

17 Dr. Young's *Discourse on the Life and Character of the late John Thornton Kirkland, LL. D.*
Mr. Weaver who is engaged upon the genealogy of Windham families, we are informed expresses
a doubt of the correctness of Dr. Young's tracing of the genealogy of the Rev. Mr. Kirkland.
That he was a descendant of Standish there is no doubt.

———; m. Feb. 8, 1704, Elizabeth Richards. V *Mary.* VI *Lois.* VII *Mehitable,* and VIII *Mercy.*

NOTE.

"Col. Standish of Plattsburg, N. Y., son of a Doctor Standish, formerly of Plymton, was a descendant of Zechariah; Abigail Standish married Samuel Wright, 1752; Mrs. Bisbee, living in 1809, at Plymton, very aged, was a Standish, born at Captain's Hill in Duxbury; Betsey Bisbee Standish, died in East Bridgewater, 1792, aged 41; Isaiah Standish was in Rochester, 1805; Sarah Standish married Daniel French of East Bridgeport, 1817; Samuel Standish of Lebanon, Conn., had a son Israel, and a dau. Hannah, Israel had Elisha, Jonas, Amasa and Nathan, Elisha had a son Lodowick, Nathan had two sons, one of them Thomas, living in Lebanon; another in Bozrah; Ezra, a respectable man, and cousin of Lodowick, lived in Bozrah."

In making up our history of Capt. Standish, we have had occasion to refer to the following works: *Plymouth Colony Records; Mass. His. Soc. Coll.; His. Duxbury; His. of Bridgewater, Mass.; His. of Town of Plymouth; N. E. Register; Chronicles of the Pilgrims; etc.*

INDEX.

Thomas Whitmore (Wetmore) and his immediate Descendants:

Whitmore (Wetmore)

Thomas, 1, 2, 3, 4, 5, 6, 7, 11, 12, 13, 15, 16, 17, 18, 19, 22, 25, 26, 27, 30, 112.
Abigail, 12, 23, 25, 36.   [51.
Benjamin, 12, 23, 24, 25, 31, 36,
Beriah, 11, 23, 24, 25, 31, 32.
Elizabeth, 11, 25, 28, 49.
Hannah, 11, 23, 25, 30.
Hannah 2d, 12, 23, 25, 36.
Izrahiah, 6, 11, 23, 25, 27, 29, 32, 33, 112, 145, 282, 440, 447, 484, 498.

Whitmore (Wetmore)

John, 7, 11, 23, 24, 25, 27, 37.
Joseph, 11, 24, 25, 31, 35, 51.
Josiah, 11, 24, 25, 35.
Mahitable, 11, 24, 25, 35.
Mary, 11, 25, 28, 29.
Nathaniel, 11, 24, 25, 35, 505.
Samuel, 11, 23, 25, 30, 31, 32, 484.
Sarah, 11, 26, 30.
Sarah 2d, 11, 24, 25, 35.
Thomas, 11, 23, 24, 25, 30, 31, 49.

Descendants of John, Son of Thomas.

Wetmore

Abigail, 27, 37, 39, 40, 41, 45.
Ann Elizabeth, 42, 46.
Benjamin, 38, 40, 44, 45.
Caroline Marion, 43, 47.
Charles Morris, 44, 47.
Charles Whitman, 42, 46.
Christian, 37, 38, 39.
Clarinda, 40, 43.
Cynthia, 40, 43.
Ebenezer, 27, 37, 38, 39, 40, 41, 45.
Elisha, 38, 40, 41, 42, 44.
Eliza, 40, 45.
Elizabeth, 27, 37, 38, 40.
Elnathan, 40, 44.
Emily Jane, 43, 47.
Frances Cordelia, 43, 47.
George Sanford, 44, 47.

Wetmore

Hannah, 40, 45.
Harriet Euphrania, 43, 47.
Harriet Maria, 42, 46.
Henry Augustus, 43, 47.
Henry Elisha, 42, 46.
Henry Elnathan, 45, 47.
Ida Jane, 48.
Ida Thankful, 45, 47.
James A., 47.
James Howard, 42, 46.
John, 27, 37, 38, 39, 40, 41, 44, 45.
John E., 44, 47.
John Wallace, 42, 46.
Lois, 37, 38, 39.
Louisa, 40, 44.
Lovice, 42, 46.
Lucretia, 40, 45.

DESCENDANTS OF THOMAS, SON OF THOMAS.

DESCENDANTS OF SAMUEL, SON OF THOMAS.

Descendants of Samuel, son of Thomas.

Descendants of Samuel, son of Thomas.

616 INDEX.

DESCENDANTS OF REV. JAMES, SON OF IZRAHIAH, SON OF THOMAS.

Descendants of Rev. James, son of Izrahiah, son of Thomas.

Descendants of Rev. James, son of Izrahiah, son of Thomas.

DESCENDANTS OF JUDGE SETH, SON OF IZRAHIAH, SON OF THOMAS.

Descendants of Judge Seth, son of Izrahiah, son of Thomas.

Descendants of Judge Seth, son of Izrahiah, son of Thomas.

DESCENDANTS OF JEREMIAH, SON OF IZRAHIAH, SON OF THOMAS.

JOSIAH, SON OF IZRAHIAH, SON OF THOMAS AND HIS CHILDREN.

WETMORE
Esther, 498, 501.
Martha, 498, 499

WETMORE
Josiah, 31, 32, 34, 51, 444, 498, 499.

BERIAH, SON OF THOMAS AND HIS DESCENDANTS.

WETMORE
Andrew, 502, 503.
Anna, 503, 504.
Asahel, 503, 504.
Asher, 503, 504.
Beriah, 11, 34, 503, 508.
Bethiah, 34, 502.
Hannah, 34, 502, 503, 504.
Lament Stow, 503.
Lemuel, 503, 504.
Margeret, 34, 502, 503.

WETMORE
Mary, 503.
Nathan, 503, 504.
Nathaniel, 503, 504.
Philip, 503, 504.
Rachel, 503.
Rapelyea, 503, 504.
Samuel Bowman, 502, 503, 504.
Sarah, 34, 502.
Susannah, 502, 503.
Thomas, 34, 502, 503, 504.

NATHANIEL, SON OF THOMAS AND HIS DESCENDANTS.

WETMORE
Almira, 507, 508.
Almira Orvilla, 508, 511.
Aretas, 507, 509.
Barron Eugene, 509, 511.
Byron L., 510, 511.
Chloe, 506, 507.
Comfort, 505, 506.
Content, 505, 506.
Cornelia, 507, 510.
Cynthia, 507, 508, 509,
Cynthia Ann, 507, 510.
Deborah, 505.
Elisha Howard, 507, 509.
Elizabeth, 505, 506.
Esther, 35, 505.
George Warren, 510, 511.
Hannah, 506.
Harriet, 507, 509.
Harry, 507, 509.
Isaac, 505, 506, 507, 509.
Ira, 507, 509.
Jehiel R., 507, 509, 511.
John I., 508, 510, 511.
Lois, 506, 507.
Lovina, 507, 510.
Louisa, 507, 509.

WETMORE
Lucinda, 507, 510.
Lydia Louisa, 507, 508.
Marcy, 505.
Margaret, 506.
Martin B., 507, 509.
Martha, 507, 510.
Mary, 506, 507, 510, 511.
Mary Clarinda, 510, 511.
Mary M., 510, 511.
Mary Helen, 509, 511.
Mehitable, 506.
Minerva P., 507, 510.
Moses, 35, 505, 506, 507, 508.
Patience, 506, 507.
Polly Ann, 508, 511.
Reuben, 505, 506, 507, 508, 511.
Reuben B., 506.
Reuben C., 507.
Reuben D., 507
Reuben E., 507, 510, 511.
Stephen B., 505, 506, 507, 509, 510.
Stephen R., 507, 509, 511.
Sylvester J., 509, 511.
Thomas, 35, 505.
Zephora, 506.

80

JOSEPH, SON OF THOMAS, AND HIS DESCENDANTS.

Descendants of Wetmores, not Wetmore by Name.

Descendants of Wetmores, not Wetmore by Name.

Descendants of Wetmores, not Wetmore by Name.

WILLIAMSON
Lavinia Jane, 220.
Markus, 220.
Samuel, 220.
Susannah, 220.
William, 220
VAN ARSDALE
Henry, 482.

VAN ARSDALE
William Waldo, 482.
VANTINE
Ada, 520.
ZEILLY
Anna, 100.
Isabella, 100.
Mary Louisa, 100.

PERSONS WHO MARRIED WETMORES, OR THEIR DESCENDANTS.

ABRAHAMS, Elizabeth, 206, 207.
ADAMS, Isaac, 80.
John Q., 99.
Mary Elizabeth, 343.
ADKINS, Ephraim, 49.
Josiah, 28.
ALLEN, Mary, 34.
Mary Smith (widow), 57.
Samuel, 502.
ALLYN, Ruth, 512.
ALSOP, Joseph W., 303.
ALVORD, David, 57
ANDERSON, Mary, 265.
ARMSTRONG, Mary E., 304.
ASPINWALL, Emily, 304.
ATCONSON, Luke, 11.
Mary (widow), 11.
ATWATER, Mirah, 65.
William, 88.
AUBERRY, J. Russell, 510.
AUSTIN, Fanny C, 88.
AYLSARD, Eliza Laura, 266.
BACON, Abigail, 503.
Alvina, 509.
Andrew, 35.
George T., 99.
James, 54.
John, 35.
Joseph 51.
Marcy, 38.
Mary, 30, 32.
Mary, 340.
Nathaniel, 36.
BADGER, Elizabeth Ann, 452.
BAILEY, Deborah, 221.
Rhoda, 100.
BALDWIN, Elisha, 88.
BARBER, Sophronia, 525.
BARBOUR, Mary E., 106.
BARCLAY, Benjamin Spilsbury (Prof.), 344, 351.
BARNES, Charles G., 527.
BARRON, William, 510.

BARSTOW, Samuel, 501.
BEACH, Daniel, 73.
Sally, 72.
BEARDSLEY, Chauncey Gunn, 491.
BEATTEAY, Isaac O., 264
James, 264.
BEATTY, Achsa Richardson (widow), 72.
BEDELL, William J., 260.
BEEBE, Eleanor, 137.
BEECHER, Stephen Grenville, 107.
BELDEN, Jane, 65.
Samuel, 213.
BELL, Polly, 361.
BENHAM, Adna, 90.
BENNET, Daniel, 45.
BENTON, Chloe, 334, 337, 339.
BINNEY, Horace, Jr., 485.
BIRD, Mary Jane, 102.
BIRDSALL, Timothy, 220.
BISHOP, Samuel, 36.
BISSEL, Augustus E., 65.
Joel, 36.
BIXBY, Caroline, 102.
BLACK, John (Rev.), 263.
BLACKBURN, Erelina, 490.
BLACKLEY, Mary Josephine, 479.
BLAIR, John, 506.
BLAKE, Mr 513.
Rebecca, 512.
BLISS, George I., 259.
George Pidgeon, 257.
BLODGETT, Hannah, 340.
BOAM, John, 512.
BODDY, John, 42.
William, 42.
BOERUM, Sarah Taylor, 365, 366.
BOGARDUS, Sarah, 121.
BONNELL, Mary Ann Sophia, 258.
BOOTH, Sarah, 112.
BOSLEY, Eleazer R. V., 523.
BOSTWICK, Lorain L., 492.
BOUCK, Margeretta, 46.

Persons who married Wetmores, or their Descendants.

Persons who married Wetmores, or their Descendants.

COLLATERAL BRANCHES.

Collateral Branches.

Collateral Branches.

83

Collateral Branches.

Collateral Branches.

Collateral Branches.

Collateral Branches.

Collateral Branches.

Collateral Branches.

Collateral Branches.

NAMES INCIDENTALLY MENTIONED.

Names Incidental.

Names Incidental.

Names Incidental.

Names Incidental.

Names Incidental.

TITLES OF WORKS QUOTED.

Titles of Works Quoted.

Lightning Source UK Ltd.
Milton Keynes UK
UKHW010754110119
335238UK00008B/863/P